Woman as Writer

DATE			

Woman as Writer

Jeannette L. Webber
Joan Grumman

SANTA BARBARA CITY COLLEGE

HOUGHTON MIFFLIN COMPANY   BOSTON
Dallas Geneva, Ill. Hopewell, N.J. Palo Alto London

Printed in the U.S.A.

Cover and part title drawings are by Edith Allard.

Library of Congress Catalog Card Number: 77-074379

ISBN: 0-395-26088-4

Credits

Maya Angelou "Out of the Cage and Still Singing" by Carol Benson appeared originally in *Writer's Digest*, January 1975, pp. 18–20. Copyright © 1975. Ms. Benson is a feminist who has long been interested in the creative process. "I Know Why the Caged Bird Sings." Chapter 1 and Chapter 34 from *I Know Why the Caged Bird Sings*, by Maya Angelou. Copyright © 1969 by Maya Angelou. Reprinted by permission of Random House, Inc.

Margaret Atwood "Paradoxes and Dilemmas, the Woman as Writer." Reprinted from Gwen Matheson, ed., *Women in the Canadian Mosaic* (Toronto: Peter Martin Associates, 1976). "At First I Was Given Centuries" and "You Refuse to Own" are from *Power Politics*, by Margaret Atwood (Toronto: House of Anansi Press Limited, 1971), pp. 28–30. © 1971, Margaret Atwood. "Against Still Life" is from *The Circle Game* by Margaret Atwood (Toronto: House of Anansi Press Limited, 1966), pp. 65–67. © 1966, Margaret Atwood. "More and More" is from *The Animals in That Country: Poems* by Margaret Atwood. Copyright © 1968 by Oxford University Press (Canadian Branch). Reprinted by permission of the publishers, Oxford University Press and Little, Brown and Co. in association with the Atlantic Monthly Press.

Gwendolyn Brooks From *Report from Part One*, pp. 183–192. Copyright © 1972 Gwendolyn Brooks Blakely. "Jessie Mitchell's Mother" and "Bronzeville Woman in a Red Hat" are from *The World of Gwendolyn Brooks* by Gwendolyn Brooks. Copyright © 1960 by Gwendolyn Brooks. By permission of Harper & Row, Publishers, Inc.

Joan Didion "On Keeping a Notebook." From *Slouching Towards Bethlehem* by Joan Didion. Copyright © 1961, 1968 by Joan Didion. From *Play It As It Lays* by Joan Didion. Copyright © 1970 by Joan Didion. Reprinted with the permission of Farrar, Straus & Giroux, Inc.

Zelda Fitzgerald From *Zelda*, pp. 187–188, 193–195, 219–222, by Nancy Milford. Copyright © 1970 by Nancy Milford. Reprinted by permission of Harper & Row, Publishers, Inc. From *Save Me the Waltz* by Zelda Fitzgerald. Copyright 1932 by Charles Scribner's Sons. Renewed © 1960 by Frances Scott Fitzgerald Lanahan. Reprinted by permission of Harold Ober Associates Incorporated.

Nikki Giovanni "For Saundra" and "Woman Poem" reprinted by permission of William Morrow & Company, Inc. from *Black Feeling, Black Talk, Black Judgement* by Nikki Giovanni. Copyright © 1968, 1970 by Nikki Giovanni. "Poetry" reprinted by permission of William Morrow & Co., Inc. from *The Women and the Men* by Nikki Giovanni. Copyright © 1970, 1974, 1975 by Nikki Giovanni. "Revolutionary Dreams" from *ReCreation*. Copyright © 1970 by Nikki Giovanni. Reprinted by permission of Broadside Press.

Contents

Preface

Woman as Writer has grown out of the current interest in women and literature. Most anthologies on this subject have considered literature *by* and *about* women. How women are presented in literature and what women write are important, but *how* and *why women write* have equal, if not greater, significance. This anthology presents woman in the process of writing—her difficulties, her aspirations, and her search for self-identification and self-determination as writer.

The book has been tailored for use in courses in women's studies, in other literature courses as a supplement, and in creative writing and composition. The first part presents statements about the creative process from journals, essays, poetry, and fiction by over two dozen writers in order to show what writing means to the writers. Part two shows the results of the creative process with excerpts and selections by these same writers from longer pieces of fiction, as well as from short stories, poetry, drama, and essays. The works represented illustrate the range of women writers, whose contributions to literary experiment cannot be denied. Thematically, the whole book is based on the creative process; thus we have not attempted to impose one theme on the content of part two. We have, however, tried to cover a wide spectrum of women's experiences: initiation, relationships with women (mothers, daughters, and friends), relationships with men (lovers, husbands, fathers, and brothers), pregnancy, motherhood, work, and aging.

Making choices has been difficult. We have chosen many well known writers, such as Virginia Woolf, from the first half of the twentieth century, but have also included a strong sampling of contemporary writers, such as Adrienne Rich, Joan Didion, Diane Wakoski, and Margaret Atwood. Writers from groups in addition to the white upper and middle classes are represented: Tillie Olsen, who has a working-class background, and black writers Gwendolyn Brooks, Maya Angelou, Adrienne Kennedy, Alice Walker, and Nikki Giovanni.

The themes portrayed in these selections can reveal the woman's world to male and female students alike, while the range of works and writers, each with a biographical sketch, can broaden their knowledge of women writers. Through the extensive bibliography at the back of the book, students can further explore writing by women. The text could inspire students to try journal writing and other literary genres, and finally it could increase their insight of the human condition by its focus on the relationship between literature and life that is so apparent in writing by women. Students are asking for courses that are relevant to their lives; this book with its concentration on writing by women and the process, struggles, and concerns from which that writing comes should provide that relevance.

In a final word, we would like to express our deep appreciation to Carolyn Davidson for her cheerful and energetic help in preparing the manuscript for this book.

J.L.W.
J.G.

Introduction

For the past few years we have read and reread novels, short stories, poems, essays, plays, journals, and letters by women, and we have been caught up in their rich variety. The literary and emotional range of these works and the sense of tremendous potential for creative women are what we want to share with the readers of this book. The selections themselves clearly show how misleading the stereotype is that suggests that women's experience is outside "the real world" and that their writings can hold no interest for men, while it asserts that men write for humanity.

In addition to statements about the creative process (the focus of Part I of this book), these women write about the basis of all society, personal relationships. While not denying complexity and disaster, they are frequently more positive than their male counterparts: despite all their failures, individual and collective, they cannot despair of loving connections—between parents and children, between lovers, spouses, friends. Women writers have always been concerned with the varied aspects of life and experience; they have welded in literature the world of personal relations and that of public events, as any good writer does. The poetry of Muriel Rukeyser and Denise Levertov reflects the impact of their 1971 travels in North Vietnam; and black women cannot help but be aware of the larger racial picture, even when writing about individual situations, as shown, for example, in Gwendolyn Brooks's poems in Part II. A heightened awareness of the world's problems and of the directions necessary for change pervades many works included here.

But this rather large collection only begins to reveal the wealth in women's writings: a few short chapters from Cynthia Ozick's multi-layered novel *Trust*, one of Joan Didion's vivid essays, a handful of poems from women who with great diversity chart their psychic and external worlds. We have chosen at least two works of every writer included, except for Adrienne Kennedy; each contributes something unique to the tradition and promise of female, and human, expression. Of course we lament the necessary omissions: most of Anaïs Nin's diaries, works by Lillian Hellman, Willa Cather, Katherine Anne Porter, Grace Paley, Christina Stead, Shirley Kaufman, and Barbara Guest, among others. However, undoubtedly many of you not only will read more works by authors included here but also will use the Suggestions for Further Reading as a guide to discover the breadth and the intensity of female creativity.

Woman as Writer is divided into two parts: "Woman on Writing" and "Woman Writing." Because women writers have had to fit moments of writing between household tasks, or have been considered freaks who denied their primary female creative function, or have been viewed by critics as unworthy of serious attention, they often reflect a self-consciousness of themselves as artists. In the first part we have included their statements about writing, some in essays, some in poems, some in letters or journals, one in fiction, with an aspiring woman writer as the protagonist. In addition, there are an excerpt from a biography, Nancy Milford's account of Zelda Fitzgerald's conflict with her creative husband, and her overwhelming compulsion to express herself; a selection from the autobiography *I Know Why the Caged Bird Sings*; and an essay with a broader perspective, Alice Walker's "In Search of Our Mothers' Gardens," which discusses the creative legacy of the slave woman. Several essays, such as those by Tillie Olsen, Adrienne Rich, Diane Johnson, and Margaret Atwood, introduce the subject of woman writing and can provide a basis for discussing the works in Part II. The poems in Part I add other dimensions—humorous, reflective, revolutionary.

Some of these women write in general terms. Others are primarily concerned with the uniqueness of the female experience in writing, by comparing women and men writers, as Anaïs Nin does, or by drawing particularly female images, as Erica Jong does in "Dear Colette." Some talk of their personal growth as artists within and beyond the tradition (Rich), of their personal frustrations with male preconceptions (Ozick), or of the circumstances of their lives. We made an exception by including the excerpt from Sylvia Plath's autobiographical novel *The Bell Jar*, which establishes a little distance between herself and her artistic efforts through the device of fiction. It is unfortunate that more direct insights into Plath's creative struggles are not available; the recently published *Letters Home* does not fill this gap, but perhaps later volumes of letters will.

The pervasive tone of the selections in Part I is the intense desire to create and to express. Thus we include the almost anguished entries in Katherine Mansfield's journals in which she struggles with the day-to-day effort to write—to sit in front of blank paper and to wrestle with her muse amid the worries and distractions of illness, loneliness, and boredom. Writing can be a painful process, and those who try to make it part of their lives can take courage from Mansfield and other writers who have kept on trying—managing the demands of other work and family commitments, and overcoming illness, emotional conflicts, and that indescribable fear that they cannot write and never will be able to. Yet they persevere, and a joy comes through the process and fulfills the compulsions that drive them to write in the first place.

Several selections in Part I point toward new directions for writers: Nin on dreams and psychological realities, Rukeyser on honesty and self-acceptance, Jong on sexual freedom, Didion on the contemporary woman's search for identity and meaning. Behind these discussions of their writing and the works themselves lies the history of the creative woman, which is filled with the tragedy so apparent in Virginia Woolf's conjectures about Shakespeare's mythical sister, whose talent and life would have been destroyed by her society. Many women writers in this anthology have experienced lives marked by tragedy: the suicides of Virginia Woolf, Sylvia Plath, and Anne Sexton; the painful and life-limiting illnesses of Flannery O'Connor, Carson McCullers, and Katherine Mansfield; the madness of Zelda Fitzgerald.

Zelda is one prototype of the creative woman from the past—spoiled, diverted from early creative productivity by the ease of her Southern background, diverted again by her love for F. Scott Fitzgerald and by the carefree 1920s, an era in which they were a glittering, golden pair, and finally maddened by the realization that she had neglected her own promise as a dancer and a writer. The discussions of Zelda's dancing in Milford's book and in Zelda's thinly veiled autobiography, *Save Me the Waltz*, indicate the tremendous energy that should have been channeled to develop her talent when she was younger. For a writing career, thirty is not necessarily too old an age to start, but it was in Zelda's case. The patterns of her marriage, society's dictates of the woman's role, and her conflict with Scott's ego militated against her work, as did her mental illness. In the tortured emotions and the strange but beautiful images that pervade her novel, her strengths and weaknesses as a writer are revealed. Perhaps "what might have been" is the most poignant aspect of Zelda's life. Who knows how many women's lives have repeated variations of her story? Or—a more widespread but less sentimental tale—how many women with none of Zelda's privilege, working-class women with lives spent in endless labor, have been denied the education and the opportunity even to consider artistic expression? This anthology, by amassing a wealth of good writing by women as well as by describing their struggles with creativity, may help our readers to assess their own talents and to integrate them into their relationships with other human beings.

Part II is intended to show the range of literature produced by twentieth-century women writers. Some selections are classics; many are not widely anthologized and deserve wider readership. They should whet readers' appetites to delve further into the works of the authors included here and listed at the back of the book. In some cases the selections relate directly to those in Part I (Fitzgerald and Ozick, for example), but in others our choice is based on their artistic quality and, most often, on the part of a woman's life or work that they present.

Thus the themes range from the pivotal and varied relationships between women and men—the problem is communication in Mansfield's "This Flower"; the total absorption in her husband demanded of and given by Mrs. Ramsay in Woolf's *To the Lighthouse*—to relationships with fathers and brothers as well as lovers and friends. Women's relationships with women are also explored: mothers and daughters, friends, lovers, and rivals. And there is the process of growth and exploration in initiation stories, like Mary McCarthy's "C.Y.E."

In addition to covering central themes in women's writing and experience, we also present a chronological view of women writing in England, Canada, and America in the twentieth century. Our collection begins by noting the unique position and literary influence of Virginia Woolf, as well as her incisive view of women in literature, which is as telling today as it was fifty years ago. The older and more established writers, such as Eudora Welty, have their undeniable place in this text, as do those born just before or during the 1920s, such as Doris Lessing, Levertov, O'Connor, Sexton, and Rich. We conclude with the diverse paths being explored by younger women who spring from this creative heritage—Joyce Carol Oates, Diane Wakoski, Margaret Atwood, Nikki Giovanni, and Alice Walker. Individual contributions by these writers will be discussed more fully in introductory notes for each author in Part I.

As we look over our writers, it is interesting to note how many of them, both black and white, are from the American South. The gothic world of O'Connor, the realism of Welty, the depiction of the black woman's adversities by Walker and Maya Angelou stand as examples of the plight of all women who must express their creativity within the restrictions of a patriarchal society and despite the consequent fears and self-imposed limitations.

Much contemporary writing by women, novelists in particular, relates the restrictions, enculturation, and miseducation of the girls who become middle-class wives and their misery when they get left by their man (for example, *Walking Papers* by Sandra Hochman and *Loose Ends* by Barbara Raskin), or when they wake up to their plight (*Memoirs of an Ex-Prom Queen* by Alix Kates Shulman). A variation describes the pain suffered by young women when they fail to marry (*Sheila Levine Is Dead and Living in New York* by Gail Parent). Other books document the masochism of the wife (*Such Good Friends* by Lois Gould and *Diary of a Mad Housewife* by Sue Kaufman) or explore alternatives (*The Summer Before the Dark* by Doris Lessing and *Small Changes* by Marge Piercy). Some contemporary works by women, like Judith Rossner's *Looking for Mr. Goodbar*, chronicle loneliness and destruction; others, like Lessing's *Memoirs of a Survivor*, move into fantasy and the private solution to the chaos of modern life. Most of these books reflect the poignancy and waste of the lives of Zelda Fitzgerald's latter-day sisters and, through anger and bitterness or through irony and humor, express what the women's lives have been and can still be. However, many conclude affirmatively: the heroines overcome their dependency and fear to stride bravely into a new world they are creating as they go or at least, as Joan Didion's Maria in *Play It As It Lays*, does, to say "yes" to life. We have included excerpts from both Didion's book and another such novel, Erica Jong's *Fear of Flying*. The latter's heroine, Isadora, maintains an earthy optimism in the face of her family's idiosyncrasies (our selection portrays her relationship with her mother, a stifled artist), her first husband's crackup, the misdirection supplied by her male psychologists, her lovers' impotence and desertion, her second husband's seeming blandness. However, Isadora's life is remarkably free of consequences: no unplanned children (nor planned ones), no struggle to create against tremendous odds (her husband actually pushes her into a room of her own), and no irrevocable choices (when she feels she must leave with a lover, her husband gives her traveler's checks and credit cards and patiently awaits her return).

While Jong's book is a witty and amusing counter to the work of many contemporary male writers, it represents only one direction for women writing today. We have balanced the portrayal of the middle-class wife with several others: the black woman, in the poems of Brooks and Giovanni and in prose by Walker, Angelou, and Kennedy; the working-class mother, in Olsen's "I Stand Here Ironing"; and the divorcée with young children, in Johnson's *The Shadow Knows*.

Because educated white women have had the best opportunity to develop their creative talents, the majority of writers in this collection belong to that group. However, even among these writers we find great variation in theme and style. As a fiction writer, Oates is an innovator who delineates darker forces at work within her characters' psyches and who speaks for less privileged socioeconomic groups in many of her stories and novels. Dramatist Myrna Lamb makes use of absurdist techniques to shock and engage her audience. The poets included cover a broad stylistic and emotional scope, their works displaying harshness, eloquence, fantasy, and new evaluations and perceptions.

In sharing the insights, diversity, and excitement of these works, we hope this book will do more than simply redress the balance of literary power in favor of women writers.

9

Not that it is done well, but
that it is done at all? Yes, think
of the odds! or shrug them off forever.
This luxury of the precocious child,
Time's precious chronic invalid,—
would we, darlings, resign it if we could?
Our blight has been our sinecure:
mere talent was enough for us—
glitter in fragments and rough drafts.

Sigh no more, ladies.
                    Time is male
and in his cups drinks to the fair.
Bemused by gallantry, we hear
our mediocrities overpraised,
indolence read as abnegation,
slattern thought styled intuition,
every lapse forgiven, our crime
only to cast too bold a shadow
or smash the mould straight off.

For that, solitary confinement,
tear gas, attrition shelling.
Few applicants for that honor.

10

            Well,
she's long about her coming, who must be

more merciless to herself than history.
Her mind full to the wind, I see her plunge
breasted and glancing through the currents,
taking the light upon her
at least as beautiful as any boy
or helicopter,
                 poised, still coming,
her fine blades making the air wince
but her cargo
no promise then:
delivered
palpable
ours.[1]

The molds of society and tradition are being smashed; the promise is being fulfilled, as this collection attests with its thought-provoking revelation of what women have done.

[1] Ending of "Snapshots of a Daughter-in-Law" from Adrienne Rich's book *Poems, Selected and New, 1950–1974* (W. W. Norton, 1975).

Woman as Writer

Woman on Writing

Virginia Woolf (1882–1941)

Even after more than fifty years *A Room of One's Own* by Virginia Woolf is a landmark in the discussion of women and creativity. The selections included here give only a sampling of the area Woolf covers, but any serious student of women and literature should read the entire work carefully. The story of Shakespeare's mythical sister is a dramatization of the feminine stereotype. Woolf also examines the question of how a woman limits herself and ends the book with an exhortation to women demanding that they rethink their personal, social, and creative lives.

The daughter of Leslie Stephen, a man of letters, Woolf grew up in London in an upper-class, intellectual atmosphere. Like Gertrude Stein, she was also a significant member of an artistic circle, the Bloomsbury Group, which included Lytton Strachey and E. M. Forster. She knew and corresponded with Katherine Mansfield. She encouraged T. S. Eliot; his *Poems* was first published by the Hogarth Press, which she and her husband, Leonard Woolf, founded. Aside from her fiction and essays, she wrote reviews for the prestigious *Times Literary Supplement*.

Woolf's life was one of intermittent physical and mental illness coupled with an active social life; the amount of writing she did under these circumstances is phenomenal. Her suicide (though attributed to her fear of incurable madness and her concern with burdening her husband), like those of other gifted literary women, seems to have been connected with the struggle the creative woman has for the permission—inner and outer—to create, the struggle for the belief in oneself.

Much of her recognition as a significant twentieth-century British writer is based on Woolf's contribution to literary form: she is a master of the "stream of consciousness" technique. In the selection (in Part Two) from one of her finest novels, *To the Lighthouse*, the reader enters for a time the consciousness of Mrs. Ramsay. This giving mother and wife is absorbed by the tasks of her roles, but her beauty and strength of character are so timeless that they pervade the house at Skye and the lives of family, friends, and acquaintances long after her death. Yet in Mrs. Ramsay is revealed the poignancy of woman, who so often lets her life be totally other-directed, neglecting other creative streams that may flow within her. Besides experimentation with form—which Woolf uses to convey the complexity of human experience and, thus, human character—her fiction is charged with beautiful language, especially in her careful images. Her essays are marked by a directness and clarity that pierce the surface of literature and life.

Quentin Bell's *Virginia Woolf* (New York: Harcourt Brace Jovanovich, 1972) is an instructive way to begin Woolf studies, before or after exploring the novels, such as *Mrs. Dalloway*; the short stories in *A Haunted House*; specific women's concerns in *Three Guineas*; the interesting treatment of androgyny in *Orlando*; her diaries; and the essays and literary criticism in *The Common Reader*.

Be that as it may, I could not help thinking, as I looked at the works
of Shakespeare on the shelf, that the bishop was right at least in this;
it would have been impossible, completely and entirely, for any
woman to have written the plays of Shakespeare in the age of Shakespeare. Let me imagine, since facts are so hard to come by, what would
have happened had Shakespeare had a wonderfully gifted sister, called
Judith, let us say. Shakespeare himself went, very probably—his
mother was an heiress—to the grammar school, where he may have
learnt Latin—Ovid, Virgil and Horace—and the elements of grammar
and logic. He was, it is well known, a wild boy who poached rabbits,
perhaps shot a deer, and had, rather sooner than he should have done,
to marry a woman in the neighborhood, who bore him a child rather
quicker than was right. That escapade sent him to seek his fortune in
London. He had, it seemed, a taste for the theatre; he began by holding horses at the stage door. Very soon he got work in the theatre,
became a successful actor, and lived at the hub of the universe, meeting everybody, knowing everybody, practising his art on the boards,
exercising his wits in the streets, and even getting access to the palace
of the queen. Meanwhile his extraordinarily gifted sister, let us suppose, remained at home. She was as adventurous, as imaginative, as
agog to see the world as he was. But she was not sent to school. She
had no chance of learning grammar and logic, let alone of reading
Horace and Virgil. She picked up a book now and then, one of her
brother's perhaps, and read a few pages. But then her parents came
in and told her to mend the stockings or mind the stew and not moon
about with books and papers. They would have spoken sharply but
kindly, for they were substantial people who knew the conditions of
life for a woman and loved their daughter—indeed, more likely than
not she was the apple of her father's eye. Perhaps she scribbled some
pages up in an apple loft on the sly, but was careful to hide them or
set fire to them. Soon, however, before she was out of her teens, she
was to be betrothed to the son of a neighbouring woolstapler. She
cried out that marriage was hateful to her, and for that she was
severely beaten by her father. Then he ceased to scold her. He begged
her instead not to hurt him, not to shame him in this matter of marriage. He would give her a chain of beads or a fine petticoat, he said;
and there were tears in his eyes. How could she disobey him? How
could she break his heart? The force of her own gift alone drove her
to it. She made up a small parcel of her belongings, let herself down
by a rope one summer's night and took the road to London. She was
not seventeen. The birds that sang in the hedge were not more musical
than she was. She had the quickest fancy, a gift like her brother's for
the tune of words. Like him, she had a taste for the theatre. She stood
at the stage door; she wanted to act, she said. Men laughed in her
face. The manager—a fat, loose-lipped man—guffawed. He bellowed
something about poodles dancing and women acting—no woman, he
said could possibly be an actress. He hinted—you can imagine what.
She could get no training in her craft. Could she even seek her dinner
in a tavern or roam the streets at midnight? Yet her genius was for
fiction and lusted to feed abundantly upon the lives of men and

women and the study of their ways. At last—for she was very young, oddly like Shakespeare the poet in her face, with the same grey eyes and rounded brows—at last Nick Greene the actor-manager took pity on her; she found herself with child by that gentleman and so—who shall measure the heat and violence of the poet's heart when caught and tangled in a woman's body?—killed herself one winter's night and lies buried at some cross-roads where the omnibuses now stop outside the Elephant and Castle.

That, more or less, is how the story would run, I think, if a woman in Shakespeare's day had had Shakespeare's genius. But for my part, I agree with the deceased bishop, if such he was—it is unthinkable that any woman in Shakespeare's day should have had Shakespeare's genius. For genius like Shakespeare's is not born among labouring, un-educated, servile people. It was not born in England among the Saxons and the Britons. It is not born today among the working classes. How, then, could it have been born among women whose work began, according to Professor Trevelyan, almost before they were out of the nursery, who were forced to it by their parents and held to it by all the power of law and custom? Yet genius of a sort must have existed among women as it must have existed among the working classes. Now and again an Emily Brontë or a Robert Burns blazes out and proves its presence. But certainly it never got itself on to paper. When, however, one reads of a witch being ducked, of a woman possessed by devils, of a wise woman selling herbs, or even of a very remarkable man who had a mother, then I think we are on the track of a lost novelist, a suppressed poet, of some mute and inglorious Jane Austen, some Emily Brontë who dashed her brains out on the moor or mopped and mowed about the highways crazed with the torture that her gift had put her to. Indeed, I would venture to guess that Anon, who wrote so many poems without signing them, was often a woman. It was a woman Edward Fitzgerald, I think, suggested who made the ballads and the folk-songs, crooning them to her children, beguiling her spinning with them, or the length of the winter's night.

. . .

And for the most part, of course, novels do come to grief somewhere. The imagination falters under the enormous strain. The insight is confused; it can no longer distinguish between the true and the false; it has no longer the strength to go on with the vast labour that calls at every moment for the use of so many different faculties. But how would all this be affected by the sex of the novelist, I wondered, look-ing at *Jane Eyre* and the others. Would the fact of her sex in any way interfere with the integrity of a woman novelist—that integrity which I take to be the backbone of the writer? Now, in the passages I have quoted from *Jane Eyre*, it is clear that anger was tampering with the integrity of Charlotte Brontë the novelist. She left her story, to which her entire devotion was due, to attend to some personal grievance. She remembered that she had been starved of her proper due of experi-ence—she had been made to stagnate in a parsonage mending stockings when she wanted to wander free over the world. Her imagination swerved from indignation and we feel it swerve. But there were many more influences than anger tugging at her imagination and deflecting it from its path. Ignorance, for instance. The portrait of Rochester is drawn in the dark. We feel the influence of fear in it; just as we constantly feel an acidity which is the result of oppression, a buried suffering smouldering beneath her passion, a rancour which contracts those books, splendid as they are, with a spasm of pain.

And since a novel has this correspondence to real life, its values are to some extent those of real life. But it is obvious that the values of women differ very often from the values which have been made by the other sex; naturally, this is so. Yet it is the masculine values that prevail. Speaking crudely, football and sport are "important"; the worship of fashion, the buying of clothes "trivial." And these values are inevitably transferred from life to fiction. This is an important book, the critic assumes, because it deals with war. This is an insignificant book because it deals with the feelings of women in a drawing-room. A scene in a battlefield is more important than a scene in a shop— everywhere and much more subtly the difference of value persists. The whole structure, therefore, of the early nineteenth-century novel was raised, if one was a woman, by a mind which was slightly pulled from the straight, and made to alter its clear vision in deference to external authority. One has only to skim those old forgotten novels and listen to the tone of voice in which they are written to divine that the writer was meeting criticism; she was saying this by way of aggression, or that by way of conciliation. She was admitting that she was "only a woman," or protesting that she was "as good as a man." She met that criticism as her temperament dictated, with docility and diffidence, or with anger and emphasis. It does not matter which it was; she was thinking of something other than the thing itself. Down comes her book upon our heads. There was a flaw in the centre of it. And I thought of all the women's novels that lie scattered, like small pockmarked apples in an orchard, about the secondhand book shops of London. It was the flaw in the centre that had rotted them. She had altered her values in deference to the opinion of others.

But how impossible it must have been for them not to budge either to the right or to the left. What genius, what integrity it must have required in face of all that criticism, in the midst of that purely patriarchal society, to hold fast to the thing as they saw it without shrinking. Only Jane Austen did it and Emily Brontë. It is another feather, perhaps the finest, in their caps. They wrote as women write, not as men write. Of all the thousand women who wrote novels then, they alone entirely ignored the perpetual admonitions of the eternal pedagogue—write this, think that. They alone were deaf to that persistent voice, now grumbling, now patronising, now domineering, now grieved, now shocked, now angry, now avuncular; that voice which cannot let women alone, but must be at them, like some too conscientious governess, adjuring them, like Sir Egerton Brydges, to be refined; dragging even into the criticism of poetry criticism of sex;[1]

[1] "[She] has a metaphysical purpose, and that is a dangerous obsession, especially with a woman, for women rarely possess men's healthy love of rhetoric. It is a strange lack in the sex which is in other things more primitive and more materialistic."—*New Criterion*, June 1928.

admonishing them, if they would be good and win, as I suppose, some shiny prize, to keep within certain limits which the gentleman in question thinks suitable: ". . . female novelists should only aspire to excellence by courageously acknowledging the limitations of their sex." [2] That puts the matter in a nutshell, and when I tell you, rather to your surprise, that this sentence was written not in August 1828 but in August 1928, you will agree, I think, that however delightful it is to us now, it represents a vast body of opinion—I am not going to stir those old pools, I take only what chance has floated to my feet— that was far more vigorous and far more vocal a century ago. It would have needed a very stalwart young woman in 1828 to disregard all those snubs and chidings and promises of prizes. One must have been something of a firebrand to say to oneself, Oh, but they can't buy literature too. Literature is open to everybody. I refuse to allow you, Beadle though you are, to turn me off the grass. Lock up your libraries if you like; but there is no gate, no lock, no bolt that you can set upon the freedom of my mind.

. . .

Even so, the very first sentence that I would write here, I said, cross-ing over to the writing-table and taking up the page headed Women and Fiction, is that it is fatal for any one who writes to think of their sex. It is fatal to be a man or woman pure and simple; one must be woman-manly or man-womanly. It is fatal for a woman to lay the least stress on any grievance; to plead even with justice any cause; in any way to speak consciously as a woman. And fatal is no figure of speech; for anything written with that conscious bias is doomed to death. It ceases to be fertilised. Brilliant and effective, powerful and masterly, as it may appear for a day or two, it must wither at night-fall; it cannot grow in the minds of others. Some collaboration has to take place in the mind between the woman and the man before the act of creation can be accomplished. Some marriage of opposites has to be consummated. The whole of the mind must lie wide open if we are to get the sense that the writer is communicating his experience with perfect fullness. There must be freedom and there must be peace. Not a wheel must grate, not a light glimmer. The curtains must be close drawn. The writer, I thought, once his experience is over, must lie back and let his mind celebrate its nuptials in darkness. He must not look or question what is being done. Rather, he must pluck the petals from a rose or watch the swans float calmly down the river. And I saw again the current which took the boat and the undergrad-uate and the dead leaves; and the taxi took the man and the woman, I thought, seeing them come together across the street, and the cur-rent swept them away, I thought, hearing far off the roar of London's traffic, into that tremendous stream.

. . .

Nobody could put the point more plainly. "The poor poet has not in

[2] "If like the reporter, you believe that female novelists should only aspire to excellence by courageously acknowledging the limitations of their sex (Jane Austen [has] demonstrated how gracefully this gesture can be ac-complished) . . . ."—*Life and Letters*, August 1928.

these days, nor has had for two hundred years, a dog's chance . . . a
poor child in England has little more hope than had the son of an
Athenian slave to be emancipated into that intellectual freedom of
which great writings are born." That is it. Intellectual freedom depends upon material things. Poetry depends upon intellectual freedom. And women have always been poor, not for two hundred years
merely, but from the beginning of time. Women have had less intellectual freedom than the sons of Athenian slaves. Women, then, have
not had a dog's chance of writing poetry. That is why I have laid so
much stress on money and a room of one's own. However, thanks to
the toils of those obscure women in the past, of whom I wish we knew
more, thanks, curiously enough, to two wars, the Crimean which let
Florence Nightingale out of her drawing-room, and the European War
which opened the doors to the average woman some sixty years later,
these evils are in the way to be bettered. Otherwise you would not be
here tonight, and your chance of earning five hundred pounds a year,
precarious as I am afraid that it still is, would be minute in the
extreme.

Still, you may object, why do you attach so much importance to this
writing of books by women when, according to you, it requires so
much effort, leads perhaps to the murder of one's aunts, will make one
almost certainly late for luncheon, and may bring one into very grave
disputes with certain very good fellows? My motives, let me admit,
are partly selfish. Like most uneducated Englishwomen, I like reading
—I like reading books in the bulk. Lately my diet has become a trifle
monotonous; history is too much about wars; biography too much
about great men; poetry has shown, I think, a tendency to sterility,
and fiction—but I have sufficiently exposed my disabilities as a critic
of modern fiction and will say no more about it. Therefore I would
ask you to write all kinds of books, hesitating at no subject however
trivial or however vast. By hook or by crook, I hope that you will
possess yourselves of money enough to travel and to idle, to contemplate the future or the past of the world, to dream over books and
loiter at street corners and let the line of thought dip deep into the
stream. For I am by no means confining you to fiction. If you would
please me—and there are thousands like me—you would write books
of travel and adventure, and research and scholarship, and history and
biography, and criticism and philosophy and science. By so doing
you will certainly profit the art of fiction. For books have a way of
influencing each other. Fiction will be much better for standing cheek
by jowl with poetry and philosophy. Moreover, if you consider any
great figure of the past, like Sappho, like the Lady Murasaki, like
Emily Brontë, you will find that she is an inheritor as well as an origi-
nator, and has come into existence because women have come to have
the habit of writing naturally; so that even as a prelude to poetry
such activity on your part would be invaluable.

But when I look back through these notes and criticise my own train
of thought as I made them, I find that my motives were not altogether
selfish. There runs through these comments and discursions the
conviction—or is it the instinct?—that good books are desirable and
that good writers, even if they show every variety of human depravity,

are still good human beings. Thus when I ask you to write more books I am urging you to do what will be for your good and for the good of the world at large. How to justify this instinct or belief I do not know, for philosophic words, if one has not been educated at a university, are apt to play one false. What is meant by "reality"? It would seem to be something very erratic, very undependable—now to be found in a dusty road, now in a scrap of newspaper in the street, now in a daffodil in the sun. It lights up a group in a room and stamps some casual saying. It overwhelms one walking home beneath the stars and makes the silent world more real than the world of speech— and then there it is again in an omnibus in the uproar of Piccadilly. Sometimes, too, it seems to dwell in shapes too far away for us to discern what their nature is. But whatever it touches, it fixes and makes permanent. That is what remains over when the skin of the day has been cast into the hedge; that is what is left of past time and of our loves and hates. Now the writer, as I think, has the chance to live more than other people in the presence of this reality. It is his business to find it and collect it and communicate it to the rest of us. So at least I infer from reading *Lear* or *Emma* or *La Recherche du Temps Perdu*. For the reading of these books seems to perform a curious couching operation on the senses; one sees more intensely afterwards; the world seems bared of its covering and given an intenser life. Those are the enviable people who live at enmity with unreality; and those are the pitiable who are knocked on the head by the thing done without knowing or caring. So that when I ask you to earn money and have a room of your own, I am asking you to live in the presence of reality, an invigorating life, it would appear, whether one can impart it or not.

Here I would stop, but the pressure of convention decrees that every speech must end with a peroration. And a peroration addressed to women should have something, you will agree, particularly exalting and ennobling about it. I should implore you to remember your responsibilities, to be higher, more spiritual; I should remind you how much depends upon you, and what an influence you can exert upon the future. But those exhortations can safely, I think, be left to the other sex, who will put them, and indeed have put them, with far greater eloquence than I can compass. When I rummage in my own mind I find no noble sentiments about being companions and equals and influencing the world to higher ends. I find myself saying briefly and prosaically that it is much more important to be oneself than anything else. Do not dream of influencing other people, I would say, if I knew how to make it sound exalted. Think of things in themselves.

And again I am reminded by dipping into newspapers and novels and biographies that when a woman speaks to women she should have something very unpleasant up her sleeve. Women are hard on women. Women dislike women. Women—but are you not sick to death of the word? I can assure you that I am. Let us agree, then, that a paper read by a woman to women should end with something particularly disagreeable.

But how does it go? What can I think of? The truth is, I often like women. I like their unconventionality. I like their subtlety. I like their anonymity. I like—but I must not run on in this way. That cupboard there,—you say it holds clean table-napkins only; but what if Sir Archibald Bodkin were concealed among them? Let me then adopt a sterner tone. Have I, in the preceding words, conveyed to you sufficiently the warnings and reprobation of mankind? I have told you the very low opinion in which you were held by Mr. Oscar Browning. I have indicated what Napoleon once thought of you and what Mussolini thinks now. Then, in case any of you aspire to fiction, I have copied out for your benefit the advice of the critic about courageously acknowledging the limitations of your sex. I have referred to Professor X and given prominence to his statment that women are intellectually, morally and physically inferior to men. I have handed on all that has come my way without going in search of it, and here is a final warning—from Mr. John Langdon Davies.[3] Mr. John Langdon Davies warns women "that when children cease to be altogether desirable, women cease to be altogether necessary." I hope you will make a note of it.

How can I further encourage you to go about the business of life? Young women, I would say, and please attend, for the peroration is beginning, you are, in my opinion, disgracefully ignorant. You have never made a discovery of any sort of importance. You have never shaken an empire or led an army into battle. The plays of Shakespeare are not by you, and you have never introduced a barbarous race to the blessings of civilisation. What is your excuse? It is all very well for you to say, pointing to the streets and squares and forests of the globe swarming with black and white and coffee-coloured inhabitants, all busily engaged in traffic and enterprise and love-making, we have had other work on our hands. Without our doing, those seas would be unsailed and those fertile lands a desert. We have borne and bred and washed and taught, perhaps to the age of six or seven years, the one thousand six hundred and twenty-three million human beings who are, according to statistics, at present in existence, and that, allowing that some had help, takes time.

There is truth in what you say—I will not deny it. But at the same time may I remind you that there have been at least two colleges for women in existence in England since the year 1866; that after the year 1880 a married woman was allowed by law to possess her own property; and that in 1919—which is a whole nine years ago—she was given a vote? May I also remind you that the most of the professions have been open to you for close on ten years now? When you reflect upon these immense privileges and the length of time during which they have been enjoyed, and the fact that there must be at this moment some two thousand women capable of earning over five hundred a year in one way or another, you will agree that the excuse of lack of opportunity, training, encouragement, leisure and money no longer holds good. Moreover, the economists are telling us that Mrs. Seton has had too many children. You must, of course, go on bearing children, but, so they say, in twos and threes, not in tens and twelves.

[3] *A Short History of Women*, by John Langdon Davies.

Thus, with some time on your hands and with some book learning in your brains—you have had enough of the other kind, and are sent to college partly, I suspect, to be un-educated—surely you should embark upon another stage of your very long, very laborious and highly obscure career. A thousand pens are ready to suggest what you should do and what effect you will have. My own suggestion is a little fantastic, I admit; I prefer, therefore, to put it in the form of fiction.

I told you in the course of this paper that Shakespeare had a sister; but do not look for her in Sir Sidney Lee's life of the poet. She died young—alas, she never wrote a word. She lies buried where the omnibuses now stop, opposite the Elephant and Castle. Now my belief is that this poet who never wrote a word and was buried at the crossroads still lives. She lives in you and in me, and in many other women who are not here tonight, for they are washing up the dishes and putting the children to bed. But she lives; for great poets do not die; they are continuing presences; they need only the opportunity to walk among us in the flesh. This opportunity, as I think, it is now coming within your power to give her. For my belief is that if we live another century or so—I am talking of the common life which is the real life and not of the little separate lives which we live as individuals—and have five hundred a year each of us and rooms of our own; if we have the habit of freedom and the courage to write exactly what we think; if we escape a little from the common sitting-room and see human beings not always in their relation to each other but in relation to reality; and the sky, too, and the trees or whatever it may be in themselves; if we look past Milton's bogey, for no human being should shut out the view; if we face the fact, for it is a fact, that there is no arm to cling to, but that we go alone and that our relation is to the world of reality and not only to the world of men and women, then the opportunity will come and the dead poet who was Shakespeare's sister will put on the body which she has so often laid down. Drawing her life from the lives of the unknown who were her forerunners, as her brother did before her, she will be born. As for her coming without that preparation, without that effort on our part, without that determination that when she is born again she shall find it possible to live and write her poetry, that we cannot expect, for that would be impossible. But I maintain that she would come if we worked for her, and that so to work, even in poverty and obscurity, is worth while.

Katherine Mansfield *(1888–1923)*

Born in New Zealand, Katherine Mansfield received part of her education in England. As an adult, she returned to England, whose cosmopolitan atmosphere appealed to the burgeoning writer, but the touch of the empire remains in her work. She utilizes New Zealand to bring a freshness and vitality particularly to her portrayals of women and children, for often it is the background of the empire that infuses a new life into the literature of the mother country.

Mansfield was, even for our times, a liberated woman. She left her first husband the day after the wedding, traveled in Europe with a light opera company, had an abortion, and lived with John Middleton Murry, her second husband, before she was divorced from her first. Her life thus seems characterized by a freedom, an independence, and a spontaneity that fed into her creativity. She once wrote, "I want to write simply, freely, so as to catch the significance of the fleeting moment." Like Woolf and Stein she had the encouragement of a circle, which included Murry and D. H. Lawrence. When she experienced difficulty in publishing, she edited (with Murry) and published in the *Blue Review*. Later with Lawrence and Murry she edited and published in another small magazine, the *Signature*.

In spite of tuberculosis the last years of her life were characterized by the struggle to live life as fully as possible and to continue writing. Her *Journal* chronicles these efforts and stands as an important document for women, particularly those who write. The journal entries included here vibrate with the various streams of her personal and artistic life—the memories of childhood in New Zealand, the struggle with writing, the pain of her illness and the sense of mortality it brought, the separations from Murry while she lived abroad trying to regain her health.

Mansfield's stories are full of sensitivity to human experience, especially women's experience, coupled with a careful, clear, and succinct style. The use of implication in "This Flower" distinguishes this story, which deals with the nuances of communication between man and woman. *The Short Stories of Katherine Mansfield* abound with further examples of her art. The much-anthologized "Garden Party" shows the sensitivity of a young girl in her experience of death presented against a backdrop of the selfishness of those who ignore their neighbors' tragedy and turn to their own amusement. "Garden Party" is a strong statement of a young girl's initiation, as is "Her First Ball," another well-known Mansfield story depicting a girl less thoughtful, more caught up in the pleasurable moments of youth. In her nonfiction, her *Letters,* along with her *Journal,* give insight into Mansfield as woman and writer.

Journal

April 2 [1914].

I have begun to sleep badly again and I've decided to tear up everything that I've written and start again. I'm sure that is best. This misery persists, and I am so crushed under it. If I could write with my old fluency for *one day*, the spell would be broken. It's the continual effort—the slow building-up of my idea and then, before my eyes and out of my power, its slow dissolving.

April 4

Won a moral victory this morning, to my great relief. Went out to spend 2s. 11d. and left it unspent. But I have never known a more hideous day. Terribly lonely. Nothing that isn't satirical is really true for me to write just now. If I try to find things lovely, I turn pretty-pretty. And at the same time I am so frightened of writing mockery for satire that my pen hovers and won't settle. Dined with C.'s and D. Afterwards to Café Royal. The sheep were bleating and we set up a feeble counterpart. Saw a fight. The woman with her back to me— her arms crooked sharp at the elbows, her head thrust out, like a big bird.

May

To-day is Sunday. It is raining a little, and the birds are cheeping. There's a smell of food and a noise of chopping cabbage.

Oh, if only I could make a celebration and do a bit of writing. I long and long to write, and the words just won't come. It's a queer business. Yet, when I read people like Gorky, for instance, I realize how streets ahead of them I be. . . .

January 22 [1916].

Now, really, what is it that I do want to write? I ask myself. Am I less of a writer than I used to be? Is the need to write less urgent? Does it still seem as natural to me to seek that form of expression? Has speech fulfilled it? Do I ask anything more than to relate, to remember, to assure myself?

There are times when these thoughts half-frighten me and very nearly convince. I say: You are now so fulfilled in your own being, in being alive, in living, in aspiring towards a greater sense of life and a deeper loving, the other thing has gone out of you.

But no, at bottom I am not convinced, for at bottom never has my desire been so ardent. Only the form that I would choose has changed utterly. I feel no longer concerned with the same appearance of things. The people who lived or whom I wished to bring into my stories don't interest me any more. The plots of my stories leave me perfectly cold. Granted that these people exist and all the differences, complexities and resolutions are true to them—why should *I* write about them? They are not near me. All the false threads that bound me to them are cut away quite.

Now—now I want to write recollections of my own country. Yes, I want to write about my own country till I simply exhaust my store. Not only because it is 'a sacred debt' that I pay to my country because my brother and I were born there, but also because in my thoughts I range with him over all the remembered places. I am never far away from them. I long to renew them in writing.

Ah, the people—the people we loved there—of them, too, I want to write. Another 'debt of love.' Oh, I want for one moment to make our undiscovered country leap into the eyes of the Old World. It must be mysterious, as though floating. It must take the breath. It must be 'one of those islands. . . .' I shall tell everything, even of how the laundry-basket squeaked at 75. But all must be told with a sense of mystery, a radiance, an afterglow, because you, my little sun of it, are set. You have dropped over the dazzling brim of the world. Now I must play my part.

Then I want to write poetry. I feel always trembling on the brink of poetry. The almond-tree, the birds, the little wood where you are, the flowers you do not see, the open window out of which I lean and dream that you are against my shoulder, and the times that your photograph 'looks sad'. But especially I want to write a kind of long elegy to you . . . perhaps not in poetry. Nor perhaps in prose. Almost certainly in a kind of *special prose*.

And, lastly, I want to keep a kind of *minute note-book*, to be published some day. That's all. No novels, no problem stories, nothing that is not simple, open.

February 13
I have written practically nothing yet, and now again the time is getting short. There is nothing done. I am no nearer my achievement than I was two months ago, and I keep half-doubting my will to perform anything. Each time I make a move my demon says at almost the same moment: 'Oh, yes, we've heard that before!' And then I hear R.B. in the Café Royal, 'Do you still write?' If I went back to England without a book *finished* I should give myself up. I should know that, whatever I said, I was not really a writer and had no claim to 'a table in my room'. But if I go back with a book finished it will be a *profession de foi pour toujours.* Why do I hesitate so long? Is it just idleness? Lack of will-power? Yes, I feel that's what it is, and that's why it's so immensely important that I should assert myself. I have put a table to-day in my room, facing a corner, but from where I sit I can see some top shoots of the almond-tree and the sea sounds loud. There is a vase of beautiful geraniums on the table. Nothing could be nicer than this spot, and it's so quiet and so high, like sitting up in a tree. I feel I shall be able to write here, especially toward twilight.

Ah, once fairly alight—how I'd blaze and burn! Here is a new fact. When I am not writing I feel my brother calling me, and he is not happy. Only when I write or am in a state of writing—a state of 'inspiration'—do I feel that he is calm. . . .

. . .

The Eternal Question
I pose myself, yet once more, *my* Eternal Question. What is it that makes the moment of delivery so difficult for me? If I were to sit down—now—and just to write out, plain, some of the stories—all

written, all ready, in my mind 'twould take me days. There are so many of them. I sit and *think* them out, and if I overcome my lassitude and *do* take the pen they ought (they are so word-perfect) to write themselves. But it's the activity. I haven't a place to write in or on—the chair isn't comfortable—yet even as I complain *this* seems the place and *this* the chair. And don't I want to write them? Lord! Lord! it's my only desire—my one *happy issue*. And only yesterday I was thinking–even my present state of health is a great gain. It makes things so rich, so important, so longed for . . . changes one's focus.

. . . When one is little and ill and far away in a remote bedroom all that happens *beyond* is marvellous. . . . Alors, I am always in that remote bedroom. Is that why I seem to see, this time in London—nothing but what is marvellous—marvellous—and incredibly beautiful?

. . .

May 31 [1919].
Work. Shall I be able to express one day my love of work—my desire to be a better writer—my longing to take greater pains. And the passion I feel. It takes the place of religion—it *is* my religion—of people—I create my people: of 'life'—it *is* Life. The temptation is to kneel before it, to adore, to prostrate myself, to stay too long in a state of ecstasy before the *idea* of it. I must be more busy about my master's business.

Oh, God! The sky is filled with the sun, and the sun is like music. The sky is full of music. Music comes streaming down these great beams. The wind touches the harp-like trees, shakes little jets of music—little shakes, little trills from the flowers. The shape of every flower is like a sound. My hands open like five petals. Praise Him! Praise Him! No, I am overcome; I am dazed; it is too much to bear.

A little fly has dropped by mistake into the huge sweet cup of a magnolia. Isaiah (or was it Elisha?) was caught up into Heaven in a chariot of fire *once*. But when the weather is divine and I am free to work, such a journey is positively nothing.

February 29 [1920].
Oh, to be a *writer*, a real writer given up to it and to it alone! Oh, I failed to-day; I turned back, looked over my shoulder, and immediately it happened, I felt as though I too were struck down. The day turned cold and dark on the instant. It seemed to belong to summer twilight in London, to the clang of the gates as they close the garden, to the deep light painting the high houses, to the smell of leaves and dust, to the lamp-light, to that stirring of the senses, to the languor of twilight, the breath of it on one's cheeck, to all those things which (I feel to-day) are gone from me for ever. . . . I feel to-day that I shall die soon and suddenly: but not of my lungs.

There are moments when Dickens is possessed by this power of writing: he is carried away. That is bliss. It certainly is not shared by writers to-day.

October [1921].
I wonder why it should be so very difficult to be humble. I do not think I am a good writer; I realize my faults better than anyone else

could realize them. I know exactly where I fail. And yet, when I have finished a story and before I have begun another, I catch myself *preening* my feathers. It is disheartening. There seems to be some bad old pride in my heart; a root of it that puts out a thick shoot on the slightest provocation. . . . This interferes very much with work. One can't be calm, clear, good as one must be, while it goes on. I look at the mountains, I try to pray and I think of something *clever*. It's a kind of excitement within, which shouldn't be there. Calm yourself. Clear yourself. And anything that I write in this mood will be no good; it will be full of *sediment*. If I were well, I would go off by myself somewhere and sit under a tree. One must learn, one must practise, to *forget* oneself. I can't tell the truth about Aunt Anne unless I am free to look into her life without self-consciousness.
Oh God! I am divided still. I am bad. I fail in my personal life. I lapse into impatience, temper, vanity, and so I fail as thy priest. Perhaps poetry will help.

I have just thoroughly cleaned and attended to my fountain-pen. If after this it leaks, then it is *no* gentleman!

November 13
It is time I started a new journal. Come, my unseen, my unknown, let us talk together. Yes, for the last two weeks I have written scarcely anything. I have been idle; I have *failed*. Why? Many reasons. There has been a kind of confusion in my consciousness. It has seemed as though there was no time to write. The mornings, if they are sunny, are taken up with sun-treatment; the post eats away the afternoon. And at night I am tired.

'But it all goes deeper.' Yes, you are right. I haven't been able to yield to the kind of contemplation that is necessary. I have not felt pure in heart, not humble, not good. There's been a stirring-up of sediment. I look at the mountains and I see nothing but mountains. Be frank! I read rubbish. I give way about writing letters. I mean I refuse to meet my obligations, and this of course weakens me in every way. Then I have broken my promise to review the books for *The Nation*. Another *bad spot*. Out of hand? Yes, that describes it—dissipated, vague, not *positive*, and above all, above everything, not working as I should be working—wasting time.

Wasting time. The old cry—the first and last cry—Why do ye tarry? Ah, why indeed? My deepest desire is to be a writer, to have 'a body of work' done. And there the work is, there the stories wait for me, *grow tired*, wilt, fade, because I will not come. And I hear and I *acknowledge* them, and still I go on sitting at the window, playing with the ball of wool. What is to be done?

I must make another effort—at once. I must begin all over again. I must try and write simply, fully, freely, from my heart. *Quietly*, caring nothing for success or failure, but just going on.

I must keep this book so that I have a record of what I do each week. (Here a word. As I re-read *At the Bay* in proof, it seemed to me flat, dull, and not a success at all. I was very much ashamed of it. I am.) But now to resolve! And especially to keep in touch with Life—with the sky and this moon, these stars, these cold, candid peaks.

Zelda Fitzgerald (1900–1948)

Zelda Fitzgerald's Southern-belle upbringing as the youngest child of
Judge Sayre of Montgomery, Alabama, merged into the romantic
image of meeting and marrying the handsome officer, F. Scott Fitzgerald. Magazine articles and newspaper clippings of the 1920s
corroborate her continued success story as the American girl's dream,
and in recent years she has been rediscovered and reexplored expertly
in Nancy Milford's biography, *Zelda*. Fitzgerald's one finished novel,
Save Me the Waltz, has been reprinted, and there is interest in her
short stories, which first appeared in *College Humor* (for example,
"The Girl With Talent," "The Girl the Prince Liked"), as well as her
unfinished novel, *Caesar's Things*.

Fitzgerald's struggle to perform as wife and mother, her personal need
for artistic expression, the effects of a Southern-belle girlhood, the
difficulties of living with a creative and demanding man, and the diver-
sions of the idle rich—all emphasize the conflict faced by many in
their roles as women and creative individuals. The two need not be
mutually exclusive, but experience proves that often they are. As
she poignantly tells us in the letters excerpted from *Zelda*, she had
the desire to create, but had to battle with her position as F. Scott
Fitzgerald's wife, her own limitations of temperament, her distrust of
her own talent, the capriciousness of her youth and the early years
of her marriage, and finally her madness. As Phyllis Chesler suggests
in an important book for students of women and creativity, *Women
and Madness* (New York: Doubleday, 1972), Zelda—like so many
other "crazy" women—was victimized by her own inadequacies, her
husband's jealousy, and the conventionalized roles that society has
forged for women.

When she began to feel the need to develop her talents, Fitzgerald's
prime creative thrust was toward dancing. She pursued dancing with
a tenacity that brought unexpected success for a woman in her thirties.
Her desire to be the best could not be achieved because of her late
start, and she broke down physically and mentally. She turned next
to writing, and her images, though bizarre, are strangely beautiful—
the merging of talent and the mad world of the later years of her
life. *Save Me the Waltz* has much of the flavor of the world of the
1920s: the artists who traveled to Europe in search of a creative atmosphere, the madcap world of Paris before the crash of 1929, the lives
wrecked by dissipation and tortured relationships. And behind all
this is the sense of the lost, indolent world of the American South.

In her writing, Zelda, like Scott, drew heavily from her own experiences. Indeed their material was much the same: her diaries were a
source for both of them, and his heroines reflected her golden beauty,
capricious charm, zest for life. Scott was the more polished writer,
but Zelda's uniqueness lies in her unusual imagery. She forces the
reader to broaden his or her limits of understanding an image and the
thought it suggests, even if it leads along the sometimes phantasma-
goric edge of madness.

Zelda

BY NANCY MILFORD

Throughout the spring and into June she and Scott were able to see
more of one another without the side effects of eczema or irritation
that their earlier meetings had provoked in Zelda. It rained steadily on
the lake now, and the dreariness of the days made her a little sad.

I can't write. I tried all afternoon—and I just twisted the pencil round
and round. . . . When you can't write you sit on the bed and look so
woe-begone like a person who's got to a store and can't remember
what they wanted to buy—

Good-night, dear. If you were in my bed it might be the back of your
head I was touching where the hair is short and mossy or it might
be up in the front where it make[s] little caves about your forehead,
but wherever it was it would be the sweetest place, the sweetest place.

When they met now, there were day trips taken together at Lausanne
and Geneva for shopping, or luncheons of hot chocolate and apricot
tarts and whipped cream at the cafés. When they could not meet,
Zelda wrote to him telling him how she felt and what she was doing,
and how much she missed him.

And theres always my infinite love—You are a sweet person—the
sweetest and dearest of all and I love you as I love my vanished youth
—which is as much as a human heart can hold—

It continued to rain and the sky, Zelda wrote, was

filled with copper clouds like the after-math of cannon-fire, pre-war,
civil-war clouds and I feel all empty and bored and very much in love
with you, my dear one, my own. I wish you were here so we could
stretch our legs down beside one another and feel all warm and hidden
in the bed, like seeds beaten into the earth. Why is there happiness
and comfort and excitement where you are and no where else in the
world, and why is there a sleepy tremulo in the air when you are near
that's promising and living like a vibrating fecundity?

And then her last line, to tease and please him: "excuse me for being
so intellectual. I know you would prefer something nice and feminine
and affectionate."

Even before Scott left, Zelda had begun to work on her writing. It
was the only field she felt remained open to her in which she might
be able to accomplish something professionally. Dancing was now
permanently out of the question, for she was no longer in top physical
condition and she realized the limitations of both her age and her
ability. She felt her talents as a painter were second-rate and, besides,
her poor eyesight made painting difficult and tiring. She had attracted
a modest amount of attention as a short-story writer in the *College
Humor* pieces and she hoped there would be a market for the kind of

stories she wanted to write. Writing regularly, with an astonishing degree of self-discipline and speed, she finished at least seven stories and began planning a novel during the period Scott was in Hollywood. Only one of the stories was a revision from the previous summer, and they were usually mailed to Harold Ober just as soon as they were typed. Unfortunately, only one of the stories was published and none survive in manuscript. The synopses kept by Ober give us our only clue to their general content.

Two stories were Southern in their locale and in both there was a clutter of sensational events: miscegenation, attempted incest, a shooting, and automobile accidents were elements about which the stories turned. The others centered on the chic worlds of Long Island and Europe. But no matter what their themes were, Ober could not sell them.

In notes accompanying the stories, Zelda asked Ober what he thought about them and suggested where they might be published. *"Please* tell me your *frank* opinion. . . . I wish we could sell something. Can't we *give* them away? I feel sure 'Nuts' is a good story, why won't Scribner's take it? It's so satisfactory to be in print." Scribner's did eventually take it (if "Nuts" refers, as it seems to, to "A Couple of Nuts") and it was published the following summer. It was a good story, possibly the best of Zelda's short fiction. It possesses a Fitzgeraldian aura of romance falling apart but it is unmistakably Zelda's. All too frequently her stories had failed because they became homilies on conduct overly laden with description of setting. Her characters froze into prototypes rather than growing as memorable and separate people. But in "A Couple of Nuts" Zelda was in control of her talent.

The story is about a young American couple, Larry and Lola, who play the banjo and sing in a club in Paris. They are "young and decorative" and "In those days of going to pieces and general disintegration it was charming to see them together." Their innocent youthfulness and good looks soon make them a fashionable pair among the rich. They attract a patron who introduces them on the Riviera, where they become a success. "Their stuff was spectacularly American and they made a killing at it, being simple kids." Within a year they are a vogue, but they've also become calculating. Lola is romantically involved with their patron and careless: Larry's role is to ignore the situation, which he does. There is a casual reference to an abortion, which they have to borrow money to cover. Eventually Larry persuades Lola to leave with him for America, where, he believes, they can make a name for themselves. We learn of their flop in the States through the patron, who had been instrumental in providing them with an introduction to the smart club in America where they failed. The plot becomes complicated at this point as Mabel, the patron's ex-wife, falls for Larry. Lola retaliates by bringing a lawsuit for a hundred thousand dollars against them. It saddens the narrator to think back on the couple, for "They had possessed something previous that most of us never have: a jaunty confidence in life and in each other. . . ." At the end of the story Larry and Mabel are drowned on Mabel's yacht. Lola survives with a lonely existence before her. The narrator remembers the times they had shared together and the night he was given their Paris address: "I had promised to send them some songs from home—songs about love and success and beauty." Those three words were the themes of Zelda's fiction, and of her life before her breakdown. The missing word was *ruin*. She understood that a failure of love made meaningless the otherwise potent nouns *success* and *beauty*—each of which was liable to impermanence. There is in the story an indictment of the rich as seducers nearly as strong as Hemingway's was to be in *A Moveable Feast*. Except that Zelda points out both the responsibility and the foolishness of those who take their attention as anything more than part of an intricate game, in which the rich play as masters with little at stake.

The story was reviewed in St. Paul by James Gray, who knew the Fitzgeralds. He called it a companion piece to *Gatsby*, and added that a dual egotism had sustained the main characters—an absorption in each other was the first thing that distinguished them—as it had Scott and Zelda, he might have added.

. . .

Although furious with Zelda, Scott had not written directly to her about her novel. Learning of his reaction through her doctor, she tried to soothe his irritation with a letter of careful explanation.

Dr. Squires tells me you are hurt that I did not send [my] book to you before I mailed it to Max. Purposely I didn't—knowing that you were working on your own and honestly feeling that I had no right to interrupt you to ask for a serious opinion. Also, I know Max will not want it and I prefer to do the corrections after having his opinion. Naturally, I was in my usual rush to get it off my hands—You know how I hate brooding over things once they are finished: so I mailed it poste haste hoping to have yours and Scribner's criticisms to use for revising.

Scott, I love you more than anything on earth and if you were of-fended I am miserable. We have always shared everything but it seems to me I no longer have the right to inflict every desire and necessity of mine on you. I was also afraid we might have touched the same material. Also, feeling it to be a dubious production due to my own instability I did not want a scathing criticism such as you have mercilessly—if for my own good given my last stories, poor things. I have had enough discouragement, generally, and could scream with that sense of inertia that hovers over my life and every-thing I do. So, Dear, My Own, please realize that it was not from any sense of not turning first to you—but just time and other ill-regulated elements that made me so bombastic about Max. . . . Goofo, please love me—life is very confusing—but I love you. Try, dear—and then I'll remember when you need me too sometime, and help.

Scott was having none of it. He scored sections of the first paragraph in red pencil and made a note to himself in the margin: "This is an evasion. All this reasoning is specious or else there is no evidence of a tornado in the sta . . ." and the rest was made illegible by a smudge of ink. His resentment, however, was clearly enough expressed; he was not just suspicious, he was sure she was purposely trying to harm him. In the latter part of her letter when she wrote, "I was also afraid we might have touched the same material," she had in Scott's opinion, given herself away.

Zelda knew perfectly well that if any portion of her book imitated or even echoed Scott's novel he would insist that she change it. If she had sent it first to Perkins as a ploy to avoid Scott's criticism or his demand that certain changes be made before he would allow its publication, she failed utterly. Certainly she must have known that sending it to Scott's editor was hardly a way of keeping it from Scott. Her action could not have been as underhanded as Scott felt it was, but neither was it as innocent as Zelda maintained: she *had* heard portions of his novel and throughout the past four months she had consciously tried to learn from his style. Her motives were mixed. But Scott's reaction, especially since he was the more balanced of the two, was completely out of proportion.

Scott must have written Zelda in the same accusing and defensive vein as he had Dr. Squires—she had been able to complete a novel in, at the most, three months, while he had been forced to discontinue his. At this point he was totally insensitive to Zelda's precarious state. She answered:

Dear—You know that if I could sell any of my stories I would not have written this book. Ober is swamped with my things, and it seems worthless to plague him with more. The fact that I have had time to write it while you have had to put aside your own is due to circumstances over which I had no control and cannot bring myself to feel a sense of guilt. You, of all people, certainly would not have preferred my folding my hands during my long unoccupied hours. . . . Believe me, dear, I quite appreciate the strain and depression under which you are existing. . . . I realize that there is little that your life has to offer as a substitute, but I wish you could drink less—do not fly into a rage, I know you stay *sober*—but you need some rest and I can't think how you can get it except by using those miserable moments that gin helps to dispel and turn into activity by resting.

I love you D.O.—I would have collapsed years ago if I'd had me on my hands. . . .

Evidently he again wrote to her, this time insisting on specific changes in the novel. We have only Zelda's reply.

Of course, I glad[ly] submit to anything you want about the book or anything else. I felt myself the thing was too crammed with material upon which I had not the time to dwell and consequently lost any story continuity. Shall I wire Max to send it back? The real story was the old prodigal son, of course. I regret that it offended you. The Pershing incident which you accuse me of stealing occupies just one line and will not be missed. I willingly relinquish it. However, I would like you to thoroughly understand that my revision will be made on an aesthetic basis: that the other material which I will elect is nevertheless legitimate stuff which has cost me a pretty emotional penny to amass and which I intend to use when I can get the tranquility of spirit necessary to write the story of myself versus myself. That is the book I really want to write. As you know my contacts with my family have always been in the nature of the raids of a friendly brigand. I quite realize that the quality of this book does not warrant so many excursions into the bizarre—As for my friends: first, I have none; by that I mean that all our associates have always taken me for granted, sought your stimulus and fame, eaten my dinners and invited "The Fitzgeralds" place[s]. You have always been and always will be the only person with whom I have felt the necessity to communicate and our intimacies have, to me, been so satisfactory mentally that no other companion has ever seemed necessary. Despised by my sup[er]iors, which are few, held in suspicion by my equals, even fewer, I have got all external feeding for my insignificant flames from people either so vastly different from myself that our relations were like living a play or I have cherished my inferiors with color . . . and the friends of my youth. However, I did not intend to write you a treatise on friendship in which I do not believe.

She signed herself, "With dearest love, I am your irritated Zelda."

The novel reopened the rift between them and it was Scott who, on the surface, was the more deeply wounded. Zelda had used him, he insisted—his writing, his life, his material—to her own advantage. Yet at the end of March just before he left Alabama for Baltimore he wrote to Dr. Squires (who, astonished by the vehemence of his reactions, had apparently suggested to him that if he and Zelda could not survive together a separation might be in order):

My whole stomach hurts when I contemplate such an eventuality—it would be throwing her [Zelda] broken upon a world which she despises; I would be a ruined man for years—

On the other hand, he could not

stand always between Zelda and the world and see her build this dubitable career of hers with morsels of living matter chipped out of my mind, my belly, my nervous system and my loins. Perhaps 50% of our friends and relatives would tell you in all honest conviction that my drinking drove Zelda insane—the other half would assure you that her insanity drove me to drink. Neither judgment would mean anything: . . . these two classes [of friends and relatives] would be equally unanimous in saying that each of us would be well rid of the other— in full face of the irony that we have never been so desperately in love with each other in our lives. Liquor on my mouth is sweet to her; I cherish her most extravagant hallucinations.

Her affair with Eduard Josanne in 1925 and mine with Lois Moran in 1927, which was a sort of revenge shook something out of us, but we can't both go on paying and paying forever. And yet I feel that that's the whole trouble back of all this.

Eudora Welty (b. 1901)

The sense of place and the importance of the individual pervade the fiction of Eudora Welty. Born in Jackson, Mississippi, she has lived most of her life there in the imaginative air that has nurtured so many other Southern writers. Her early artistic leanings were toward painting and photography, a preference that explains the centrality and accuracy of the visual imagery of her stories and novels. After an education at Mississippi State College for Women, the University of Wisconsin, and Columbia University, Welty returned home to Jackson. Employed in a WPA project, she took photographs of blacks during the Depression. Later, in her portrayal of blacks in her fiction, the photographer's vision and the sensitive writer's eye converge to create characters like the grandmother in "The Worn Path." After a trip to Europe she returned to Jackson and began writing in earnest. Elizabeth Bowen's friendship was a fruit of that trip and her influence on Welty's writing remains.

Although characterized as a Southern regionalist by many of her readers, Welty displays a wide knowledge of classical and modern authors, which has provided a mythic base for many of her stories and novels. It often appears unobtrusively under the realism of her Southern rural themes, language, and setting. "A Piece of News" is deceptively simple on the surface, but the themes of loneliness, isolation, and poverty blend with the lyrical and earthy response of Ruby a rural goddess, through the rich, evocative language. The total effect of the story is to blend dreams and reality, the everyday and the mythic. Added to the sense of place and the mythic in her stories are irony, humor, and sometimes the grotesque. In "Flowers for Marjorie," for example, there are strong elements of modern black humor as an unemployed young father kills his pregnant wife.

As a writer, Welty has refused to join a "school"; her theories about writing are her own. In "How I Write" she emphasizes, as in "Place in Fiction," the importance of setting as the starting point, the soil of the imagination, intrinsically joined to the story and the characters. Her discussion of the connection between the changeable outside world and the learned craft of writing is invaluable to the aspiring writer or the careful reader of fiction. Her warm humanity, her sensitivity, her keen observation are all apparent as she lets character and story dramatize what she feels about human experience. For Welty, knowledge of the craft grows with each writing experience, and each is different from the one that went before it. She has emphasized the relationship between writing and reading—one begins to write because one loves to read. Although she takes pleasure in her craft, she emphasizes that writing comes out of life that is, fiction, friends, travel, and anything that opens one's eyes. Fiction conveys human truth, and it begins with a leap in the dark—a leap Welty shares with the reader who will enter into her vision through her story.

Collections of her short stories include *A Curtain of Green, The Robber Bridegroom, The Wide Net, The Bride of Innisfallen,* and *The Golden Apples.* Welty's mastery of the short story and her commonsensical literary criticism are only part of her achievement. Her novels extend her evocation of place and the mythic level in the provocative *Ponder Heart*, the warm, sensitive, yet realistic elements of family in *Delta Wedding, Losing Battles,* and, more recently, *The Optimist's Daughter.*

How I Write

"How do I write my stories?" is a blessedly open question. For the writer it is forever in the course of being studied through doing and new doing, and wouldn't last very long as a matter of self-observation, which could very well turn him to stone. Apart from what he's learned about his separate stories, out of passion, the renewable passion, of doing each in the smallest part better (at least nearer the way he wants it), he may or may not be a good judge of his work in the altogether. To him if a story is good enough to be called finished, as far as he can see, it is detached on the dot from the hand that wrote it, and the luster goes with it; what *is* attached is the new story. "How I wrote," past tense, may be seen into from this detachment, but not with the same insight—that too is gone, displaced. Looking backward can't compete with looking forward with the story in progress—that invites and absorbs and uses every grain of his insight, and his love and wits and curiosity and strength of purpose. "How do I write *this* story?" is really the question, the vital question; but its findings can be set down only in terms of the story's own—terms of fiction. (At least, ordinarily. Story writing and an independently operating power of critical analysis are separate gifts, like spelling and playing the flute, and one person proficient in both has been doubly endowed. But even he can't rise and do both at the same time.)

I feel myself that any *generalization* about writing is remote from anything I have managed to learn about it. I believe I can make one wide one, and others must have often nailed it down, but I shall have to hold my blow till I get there. The only things I feel I really know well are stuck to the stories, part of the animal. The main lesson I've learned from work so far is the simple one that each story is going to open up a different prospect and pose a new problem; no story bears on another or helps another, even if the writing mind had room for help and the wish that it would come. Help would be a blight. I could add that it's hard for me to think that a writer's stories are a unified whole in any respect except perhaps their lyric quality. I don't believe they are written in any typical, predictable, logically developing, or even chronological way (for all that a good writer's stories are, to the reader, so immediately identifiable as his)—or in any way that after enough solid tries guarantees him a certain measure of excellence, safety (spare the word!), or delight.

I do have the feeling that all stories by one writer tend to spring from the same source within him. However they differ in subject or approach, however they vary in excellence or fluctuate in their power to alter the mind or mood or move the heart, all of one writer's stories must take on their quality, carry their signature, because of one characteristic, lyrical impulse of his mind—the impulse to praise, to love, to call up, to prophesy. But then what countless stories share a common source! All writers write out of the same few, few and eternal—love, pity, terror do not change.

Sources of stories could be examined with less confusion, perhaps, not in the subjective terms of emotion, but through finding what in the outside world leads back to those emotions most directly and tautly and specifically. The surest clue is the pull on the line, the "inspiration," the outside signal that has startled or moved the creative mind to complicity and brought the story to active being: the irresistible, the magnetic, the alarming (pleasurable or disturbing), the overwhelming person, place, or thing.

Surely, for the writer this is the world where stories come from, and where their origins are living reference plain to his eyes. The dark changes of the mind and heart, where all in the world is constantly *becoming* something—the poetic, the moral, the passionate, hence the *shaping* idea—are not mapped and plotted yet, except as psychiatry has applied the healing or tidying hand, and their being so would make no change in their processes, or their climates, or their way of life and death (any more than a map hung on the wall changes the world); or schedule or pigeonhole or allot or substitute or predict the mysteries rushing unsubmissively through them by the minute; or explain a single work of art that came out the other side. The artist at work functions, while whoever likes to may explain how he does it (or failing that, why)—without, however, the least power of prevention or prophecy or even cure—for some alarmists say that literature has come out of a disease of society, as if stamping out the housefly would stop it, and I've heard there's another critic who says writing is nothing but the death wish. (Exactly where in all this *standards* come in I don't know.)

It is of course the *way* of writing that gives a story, however humble, its whole distinction and glory—something learned, and learned each writer for himself, by dint of each story's unique challenge and his work that rises to meet it—work scrupulous, questioning, unprecedented, ungeneralized, uncharted, and his own. It is the changeable outside world and the learnable way of writing that are the different quotients. Always different, always differing, from writer to writer and story to story, they are—or so I believe—most intimately connected with each other.

Like a good many other writers, I am myself touched off by place. The place where I am and the place I know, and other places that familiarity with and love for my own make strange and lovely and enlightening to look into, are what set me to writing my stories. To such writers I suppose place opens a door in the mind, either spontaneously or through beating it down, attrition. The impression of place as revealing something is an indelible one—which of course is not to say it isn't highly personal and very likely distorted. The imagination further and further informs and populates the impression according to present mood, intensification of feeling, beat of memory, accretion of idea, and by the blessing of being located—contained—a story so changed is now capable of being written.

The connection of this to what's called regional writing is clear but not much more informing; it does mean a lot of writers behave the same way. Regional writing itself has old deep roots; it is not the big root itself. Place is surely one of the most simple and obvious and direct sources of the short story, and one of the most ancient—as it is of lyric poetry—and, if I may presume to speak freely here for other regional writers too, the connection of story to place can go for ever so long not even conscious in the mind, because taken for granted. The regional writer's vision is as surely made of the local clay as any mud pie of his childhood was, and it's still the act of the imagination that makes the feast; only in the case of any art the feast is real, for the act of the imagination gives vision the substance and makes it last.

After we see the connection between our place and our writing, has anything changed for us? We aren't admonished in any way we weren't admonished already by pride of work, surely? Yes, something *has* changed for us; we learn that. I am the proud partisan I am of regional writing because this connection between place and story *is* deep, *does* take time, and its claims on us are deep; they, like our own minds' responsibilities, are for us to find out. To be a regional writer is not like belonging to a club or a political party; it is nothing you can take credit for—it's an endowment, but more than that. It's a touchstone when you write, and shows up, before anything else does, truth and mistakes. In a way place is your honor as it is your wisdom, and would make you responsible to it for what you put down for the truth.

Whatever the story a reader takes up, the road from origin on isn't any the plainer for the simplicity of the start. Sometimes a reader thinks he is "supposed" to see in a story (I judge from letters from readers when they can't find it in mine) a sort of plant-from-seed development, rising in the end to a perfect Christmas tree of symmetry, branch, and ornament, with a star at the top for neatness. The reader of more willing imagination, who has specified for something else, may find the branchings not what he's expecting either, and the fulfillment not a perfect match, not at all to the letter of the promise—rather to a degree—(and to a degree of pleasure) mysterious. This is one of the short story's finest attributes. The analyst, should the story come under his eye, may miss this gentle shock and this pleasure too, for he's picked up the story at once by its heels (as if it had swallowed a button) and is examining the writing as his own process in reverse, as though a story (or any system of feeling) could be the more accessible to understanding for being hung upside down. "Sweet Analytics, 'tis thou hast ravish'd me!"

Analysis, to speak generally, has to travel backwards; the path it goes, while paved with good intentions, is an ever-narrowing one, whose goal is the vanishing point, beyond which only "influences" lie. But writing, bound in the opposite direction, works further and further always into the open. The choices get freer and wider, apparently, as with everything else that has a life and moves. "This story promises me fear and joy and so I write it" has been the writer's honest beginning. Dr. Faustus, the critic, coming to the end of his trail, may call out the starting point he's found, but the writer long ago knew the starting point for what it was to him—the jumping off place. If they coincide, it's a coincidence. I think the writer's out-bound choices seem obstructive sometimes to analysts simply because they wouldn't be there if they weren't plain evidence that they were to the writer inevitable choices, not arguable; impelled, not manipulated; that they came with an arrow inside them. Indeed they have been *fiction's* choices: one-way and fateful; strict as art, obliged as feeling, powerful in their authenticity though for slightest illusion's sake; and reasonable (in the out-of-fiction sense) only last, and by the grace of, again, coincidence—always to be welcomed and shown consideration, but never to be courted or flattered.

Certainly a story and its analysis are not the mirror opposites of each other, for all their running off in opposite directions. Criticism can be an art too and may go deeper than its object, and more times around; it may pick up a story and waltz with it, so that it's never the same. In any case it's not a reflection. But I think that's exactly why it cannot be *used* as one, whoever holds it up, even the curious author; why it's a mistake to think you can stalk back a story by analysis's footprints and even dream that's the original coming through the woods. Besides the difference in the direction of the two, there's the difference in speeds, when one has fury; but the main difference is in world-surround. One surround is a vision and the other is a pattern for good visions (which—who knows!—fashion may have tweaked a little) or the nicest, carefullest black-and-white tracing that a breath of life would do for. Each, either, or neither may be a masterpiece of construction; but the products are not to be confused.

The story is a vision; while it's being written, all choices must be its choices, and as these multiply upon one another, their field is growing too. The choices remain inevitable, in fact, through moving in a growing maze of possibilities that the writer, far from being dismayed at his presence on unknown ground (which might frighten him as a critic) has learned to be grateful for, and excited by. The fiction writer has learned (and here is my generalization) that it is the very existence, the very multitude and clamor and threat and lure of *possibility*—all possibilities his work calls up for itself as it goes—that guide his story most delicately. In the act of writing he finds, if no explanation outside fiction for what he is doing, or the need of it, no mystery about it either. What he does know is the word comes surest out of too much, not too little—just as the most exacting and sometimes the simplest-appearing work is brought off (when it does not fail) on the sharp edge of experiment, not in dim, reneging safety. He is not at the end yet, but it was for this he left all he knew behind, at the jumping off place, when he started this new story.

I made the remark above that I believed the changeable outside world and the learnable way of writing are connected with each other. I think it is this connection that can be specifically looked at in any story, but maybe a regional story could give us the easiest time. I offer here the clearest example I could find among my own stories of the working point I am hoping to make, since place not only suggested how to write the story but repudiated a way I had already tried it.

What happened was that I was invited to drive with a friend down south of New Orleans one summer day, to see that country for the first (and only) time, and when I got back home I realized that without being aware of it at the time I had treated a story, which I was working on then, to my ride, and it had come into my head in an altogether new form. I set to work and wrote the new version from scratch, which resulted in my throwing away the first and using the second. I learned all the specific detail of this story from the ride, though I should add that the story in neither version had any personal connection with myself and there was no conscious "gathering of material" on a pleasant holiday.

As first written, the story told, from the inside, of a girl in a claustrophobic predicament: she was caught fast in the over-familiar, monotonous life of her small town, and immobilized further by a hopeless and inarticulate love, which she had to pretend was something else. This happens all the time. As a result of my ride I extracted her. But she had been well sealed inside her world, by nature and circumstance both, and even more closely by my knowing her too well (the story had gone on too long) and too confidently. Before I could prize her loose, I had to take a primary step of getting outside her mind. I made her a girl from the Middle West—she'd been what I knew best, a Southerner, before. I kept outside her by taking glimpses of her through the curious eyes of a stranger: instead of the half-dozen characters (I knew them too well too) from the first version, I put in one single new one—a man whom I brought into the story *to be* a stranger. I had double-locked the doors behind me—you never dream the essentials can be simple again, within one story.

But the vital thing that happened to the story came from writing, as I began the work. My first realization of what it was came when I looked back and recognized that country (the once-submerged, strange land of "south from South" that had so stamped itself upon my imagination) as the image to me of the story's predicament come to life. This pointed out to me, as I wrote into the story, where the real point of view belonged. Once I was outside, I saw *it* was outside—suspended, hung in the air between the two people, fished alive from the surrounding scene, where as it carried the story along it revealed itself (I hoped) as more real, more essential, than the characters were or had any cause to be. In effect there'd come to be a sort of third character present—an identity, rather: the relationship between the two and between the two and the world. It was what grew up between them meeting as strangers, went on the trip with them, nodded back and forth from one to the other—listening, watching, persuading or denying them, enlarging or diminishing them, forgetful sometimes of who they were or what they were doing here, helping or betraying them along. Its role was that of hypnosis—it was what a relationship *does*, be it however brief, tentative, potential, happy or sinister, ordinary or extraordinary. I wanted to suggest that its being took shape as the strange, compulsive journey itself, was palpable as its climate and mood, the heat of the day—but was its spirit too, a spirit that held territory—what's seen fleeting past by two vulnerable people who might seize hands on the run. There are times in the story when I say neither "she felt" nor "he felt" but "they felt." All this is something that *doesn't* happen all the time. It merely could, or almost could, as here.

This is to grant that I rode out of the old story on the back of the girl and then threw away the girl; but I saved the story, for entirely different as the second version was, it was what I wanted to say. My subject was out in the open, provided at the same time with a place to happen and a way to say it was happening. All I had had to do was recognize it, which I did a little late.

Anyone who has visited the actual scene of this story has a chance of recognizing it when he meets it here, for the story is visual and the place is out of the ordinary. The connection between a story and its setting may not always be so plain. A reader may not see the slightest excuse for a given story after a personal inspection of the scene that called it up; the chances are good that he may not recognize it at all, and about 100 per cent that he will feel he would certainly have written something of a different sort himself. The point is, of course, that no matter whether the "likeness" is there for all to see or not, the place, once entered into the writer's mind in a story, is, in the course of writing the story, *functional*.

I wanted to make it seen and believed what was to me, in my story's grip, literally apparent—that secret and shadow are taken away in this country by the merciless light that prevails there, by the river that is like an exposed vein of ore, the road that descends as one with the heat—its nerve (these are all terms in the story), and that the heat is also a visual illusion, shimmering and dancing over the waste that stretches ahead. I was writing of a real place; but doing so in order to write about my subject. I was writing of exposure, and the shock of the world; in the end I tried to make the story's inside outside and then throw away the shell.

The vain courting of imperviousness in the face of exposure is this little story's plot. Deliver us all from the naked in heart, the girl thinks (this is what I kept of her). "So strangeness gently steels us," I read today in a poem of Richard Wilbur's. Riding down together into strange country is danger, a play at danger, secretly poetic, and the characters, in attempting it as a mutual feat, admit nothing to each other except the wicked heat and its comical inconvenience; the only time they will yield or touch is while they are dancing in the crowd that to them is comically unlikely (hence insulating, nonconducting) or taking a kiss outside time. Nevertheless it happens that they go along aware, from moment to moment, as one: as my third character, the straining, hallucinatory eyes and ears, the roused up sentient being of that place. Exposure begins in intuition and has its end in showing the heart that has expected, while it dreads, that exposure. Writing it as I'd done before as a story of concealment, in terms of the hermetic and the familiar, had somehow resulted in my effective concealment of what I meant to say.

(I might say, for what interest it has here, that the original image of the story's first version came from an object—a grandiose, dusty, empty punch bowl of cut glass surrounded by its ring of cups, standing typically in the poor, small-town hardware store window where such things go unsold for ever, surrounded by the axes and halters and tin mailboxes and shotguns of the country trade. Even as I write it's still provocative to me—as it is probably, also, still there in the window, still $13.75.)

In my second effort to show the story happen, the place had suggested to me that something demoniac was called for—the speed of the ride pitted against the danger of an easy or ignorant or tempting sympathy, too pressing, too acute, in the face of an inimical world, the heat that in itself drives on the driver. Something wilder than ordinary communication between well-disposed strangers and more ruthless and more tender than their automatic, saving ironies and graces, I felt, and do so often feel, has to come up against a world like that.

I did my best to merge, rather to identify, the abstract with the concrete, it being so happily possible in this story—however the possibilities may have been realized—where setting, characters, mood, and method of writing all appeared parts of the same thing and subject to related laws and conditionings. I cut out some odd sentences that occurred, not because they were odd—for the story is that—but because they would tantalize some cooling explanations out of the mind if they stayed in. The story had to be self-evident and hold its speed—which I think of as racing, though it may not seem so to the reader. Above all I had no wish to sound mystical, but I did expect to sound mysterious now and then, if I could: this was a circumstantial, realistic story in which the reality *was* mystery. The cry that rose up at the story's end was, I hope unmistakably, the cry of the fading relationship—personal, individual, psychic—admitted in order to be denied, a cry that the characters were first able (and prone) to listen to, and then able in part to ignore. The cry was authentic to my story and so I didn't care if it did seem a little odd: the end of a journey *can* set up a cry, the shallowest provocation to sympathy and loves does hate to give up the ghost. A relationship of the most fleeting kind has the power inherent to loom like a genie—to become vocative at the last, as it has already become present and taken up room; as it has spread out as a destination however makeshift; as it has, more faintly, more sparsely, glimmered and rushed by in the dark and dust outside. Relationship *is* a pervading and changing mystery; it is not words that make it so in life, but words have to make it so in a story. Brutal or lovely, the mystery waits for people wherever they go, whatever extreme they run to. I had got back at the end of the new story to suggesting what I had started with at the beginning of the old, but there was no question in my mind which story was nearer the mark.

This may not reflect very well on the brightness of the author; it may only serve to prove that for some writers a story has to rescue itself. This may be so, but I think it might show too what alone in the actual writing process may have interest for others besides the writer: that subject, method, form, style, all wait upon—indeed hang upon—a sort of double thunderclap at the author's ears: the break of the living world upon what is stirring inside the mind, and the answering impulse that in a moment of high consciousness fuses impact and image and fires them off together. There really never was a sound, but the impact is always recognizable, granting the author's sensitivity and sense, and if the impulse so projected is to some degree fulfilled it may give some pleasure out of reason to writer and reader. The living world remains just the same as it always was, and luckily enough for the story, among other things, for it can test and talk back to the story any day in the week.

Anaïs Nin (1903–1977)

Anaïs Nin's life bridged two continents as her work bridged the
realms of the conscious and the unconscious. Born to a Spanish pianist
and a French-Danish singer, she came to the United States at the age
of eleven with her mother and two brothers. This separation from
her father and from the rich cosmopolitan environment she had
known inspired the young Nin to begin her diary, to recreate her
world through the magic of words, to begin her apprenticeship as an
artist, and to define herself as an individual.

She returned in the 1930s to Paris, where she was a part of a vital
literary circle that included Henry Miller, Lawrence Durrell, Antonin
Artaud, and other artists and experimenters with the surreal. Her
Diary reflects the amount of creative energy she gave these people and
her own efforts as an artist who wanted to create out of her strength
as a woman rather than to imitate men. In exploring this female creative archetype and her own personal destiny, Nin underwent psychoanalysis with Otto Rank and Martha Jaeger, briefly practicing lay
analysis with Rank. But her commitment was to literature, to experimentation with form and language, symbol and dream-realities.

Nin's *Diary* not only records her education but in some respects *is*
her education. Schools, she said, failed to interest her, so she dropped
out, read, taught herself—and experienced life richly. All these experiences fill her *Diary*: her feelings, which as a young woman she was
too shy to express and as a maturing woman she feared would hurt
her friends; her analysis of process and motivation; her honest, free,
spontaneous self; her demons. The *Diary* records a detailed and
illuminating account of the woman artist at work. (Nin mentions
that her friends Durrell and Miller usually undermined her confidence
in herself as a writer: the August 1937 excerpt included here indicates
the way she used her journal to regain her equanimity and artistic
integrity in the face of their challenges.)

Today the reputation of *The Diary of Anaïs Nin* (now published in
six volumes) sometimes overshadows that of her fiction. But the two
forms complement each other. Reading in the *Diary* of her experiments in fiction and her difficulties in publishing upon her return to
the United States in 1940, one is drawn to the novels and the short
story discussed. In addition to her short story collection, *Under a
Glass Bell*, from which the selection "Hejda" is taken, Nin has published six novels, five of which were published together as *Cities of
the Interior*; *Winter of Artifice*, a collection of novelettes; and *House
of Incest*, a prose poem. Nonfiction works include *D. H. Lawrence:
An Unprofessional Study* and *The Novel of the Future*, from which
"Diary Versus Fiction" is taken.

Her work speaks to readers today who are aware that the most exciting
explorations are within oneself and one's connection to others and
the world, who are conscious of the limits of technology and political
solutions and eager to develop their own creative potential.

The Diary of Anaïs Nin

VOLUME II [August, 1937]

Beautiful flow between Durrell, Henry, Nancy and me. It is while we talk together that I discover how we mutually nourish each other, stimulate each other. I discover my own strength as an artist, for Henry and Durrell often ally themselves against me. Henry's respect is also reawakened by Durrell's admiration for me. My feelings for woman's inarticulateness is reawakened by Nancy's stutterings and stumblings, and her loyalty to me as the one who does not betray woman but seeks to speak for her. A marvelous talk, in which Henry unmasked Durrell and me, and when Durrell said: "And now we must unmask Henry," I answered: "We can't, because he has done it himself." Henry is the strongest because he is not afraid of being alone. Larry is afraid. I am afraid. And we confessed it.

They suddenly attacked my personal relation to all things, by personification of ideas. I defended myself by saying that relating was an act of life. To make history or psychology alive I personify it. Also everything depends on the nature of the personal relationship. My self is like the self of Proust. It is an instrument to connect life and the myth. I quoted Spengler, who said that all historical patterns are reproduced in individual man, entire historical evolutions are reproduced in one man in one lifetime. A man could experience, in a personal way, a Gothic, a Roman, or a Western period. Man is cheating when he sits for a whole evening talking about Lao-tze, Goethe, Rousseau, Spengler. It would be closer to the truth if he said, instead of Lao-tze, Henry—instead of Goethe, some poet we know now—instead of Rousseau, his contemporary equivalent. It would be more honest if Larry said that it is Larry who feels irritation because symbolical wine does not taste as good as plain wine.

When they discussed the problem of my diary, all the art theories were involved. They talked about the geological changes undergone with time, and that it was the product of this change we called art. I asserted that such a process could take place instantaneously.

Henry said: "But that would upset all the art theories."

I said: "I can give you an example. I can feel the potentialities of our talk tonight while it is happening as well as six months later. Look at the birth story. It varies very little in its polished form from the way I told it in the diary immediately after it happened. The new version was written three years later. Objectivity may bring a more rounded picture, but the absence of it, empathy, feeling with it, immersion in it, may bring some other kind of connection with it."

Henry asked: "But then, why did you feel the need of rewriting it?"

"For a greater technical perfection. Not to re-create it."

Larry, who before had praised me for writing as a woman, for not breaking the umbilical connection, said: "You must rewrite *Hamlet*."

"Why should I, if that is not the kind of writing I wish to do?"

Larry said: "You must make the leap outside of the womb, destroy your connections."

"I know," I said, "that this is an important talk, and that it will be at this moment that we each go different ways. Perhaps Henry and Larry will go the same way, but I will have to go another, the woman's way."

At the end of the conversation they both said: "We have a real woman artist before us, the first one, and we ought not to put her down."

I know Henry is the artist because he does exactly what I do not do. He waits. He gets outside of himself. Until it becomes fiction. It is all fiction.

I am not interested in fiction. I want faithfulness.

All I know is that I am right, right for me. If today I can talk both woman's and man's language, if I can translate woman to man and man to woman, it is because I do not believe in man's objectivity. In all his ideas, systems, philosophies, arts come from a personal source he does not wish to admit. Henry and Larry are pretending to be impersonal. Larry has the English complex. But it is a disguise.

Poor woman, how difficult it is to make her instinctive knowledge clear!

"Shut up," says Larry to Nancy. She looks at me strangely, as if expecting me to defend her, explain her. Nancy. I won't shut up. I have a great deal to say, for June, for you, for other women.

As to all that nonsense Henry and Larry talked about, the necessity of "I am God" in order to create (I suppose they mean "I am God. I am not a woman"). Woman never had direct communication with God anyway, but only through man, the priest. She never created directly except through man, was never able to create as a woman. But what neither Larry nor Henry understands is that Woman's creation far from being like man's must be exactly like her creation of children, that is it must come out of her own blood, englobed by her womb, nourished with her own milk. It must be a human creation, of flesh, it must be different from man's abstractions. As to this "I am God," which makes creation an act of solitude and pride, this image of God alone making sky, earth, sea, it is this image which has confused woman. (Man too, because he thinks God did it all alone, and he thinks he did it all alone. And behind every achievement of man lies a woman, and I am sure God was helped too but never acknowledged it.)

Woman does not forget she needs the fecundator, she does not forget that everything that is born of her is planted in her. If she forgets this she is lost. What will be marvelous to contemplate will not be her solitude but this image of woman being visited at night by man and the marvelous things she will give birth to in the morning. God alone, creating, may be a beautiful spectacle. I don't know. Man's objectivity may be an imitation of this God so detached from us and human emotion. But a woman alone creating is not a beautiful spectacle. The woman was born mother, mistress, wife, sister, she was born to represent union, communion, communication, she was born to give birth to life, and not to insanity. It is man's separateness his so-called objectivity, which has made him lose contact, and then his reason. Woman was born to *be* the connecting link between man and his human self. Between abstract ideas and the personal pattern which creates them. Man, to create, must become man.

Woman has this life-role, but the woman artist has to fuse creation and life in her own way, or in her own womb if you prefer. She has to create something different from man. Man created a world cut off from nature. Woman has to create within the mystery, storms, terrors, the infernos of sex, the battle against abstractions and art. She has to sever herself from the myth man creates, from being created by him, she has to struggle with her own cycles, storms, terrors which man does not understand. Woman wants to destroy aloneness, recover the original paradise. The art of woman must be born in the womb-cells of the mind. She must be the link between the synthetic products of man's mind and the elements.

I do not delude myself as man does, that I create in proud isolation. I say we are bound, interdependent. Woman is not deluded. She must create without these proud delusions of man, without megalomania, without schizophrenia, without madness. She must create that unity which man first destroyed by his proud consciousness.

Henry and Larry tried to lure me out of the womb. They call it objectivity. No woman died the kind of death Rimbaud died. I have never seen in a woman a skeleton like Fraenkel, killed by the dissections of analysis, the leprosy of egotism, the black pest of the brain cells.

Man today is like a tree that is withering at the roots. And most women painted and wrote nothing but imitations of phalluses. The world was filled with phalluses, like totem poles, and no womb anywhere. I must go the opposite way from Proust who found eternal moments in creation. I must find them in life. My work must be the closest to the life flow. I must install myself inside of the seed, growth, mysteries. I must prove the possibility of instantaneous, immediate, spontaneous art. My art must be like a miracle. Before it goes through the conduits of the brain and becomes an abstraction, a fiction, a lie. It must be for woman, more like a personified ancient ritual, where every spiritual thought was made visible, enacted, represented.

A sense of the infinite in the present, as the child has.

Woman's role in creation should be parallel to her role in life. I don't mean the good earth. I mean the bad earth too, the demon, the instincts, the storms of nature. Tragedies, conflicts, mysteries are personal. Woman must not fabricate. She must descend into the real womb and expose its secrets and its labyrinths. She must describe it as the city of Fez, with its Arabian Nights gentleness, tranquility and mystery. She must describe the voracious moods, the desires, the worlds contained in each cell of it. For the womb has dreams. It is not as simple as the good earth. I believe at times that man created art out of fear of exploring woman. I believe woman stuttered about herself out of fear of what she had to say. She covered herself with taboos and veils. Man invented a woman to suit his needs. He disposed of her by identifying her with nature and then paraded his contemptuous domination of nature. But woman is not nature only.

She is the mermaid with her fish-tail dipped in the unconscious. Her creation will be to make articulate this obscure world which dominates man, which he denies being dominated by, but which asserts its domination in destructive proofs of its presence, madness.

Note by Durrell: "Anaïs is *unanswerable*. Completely unanswerable. I fold up and give in. What she says is biologically true from the very navel strings."

. . .

VOLUME III [January, 1943]

I considered Henry's work far more important than my own.

I tried to efface my creation with a sponge, to drown my creation because my concept of devotion and the roles I had to play clashed with my creative self.

I opposed creation, its sincerity and revelation, to the disguised self. Creation and revelation threaten my loves; threatened the roles my love forced me to play. In love I played a role to give each man whatever he needed or wanted at the cost of my life.

In creation I would reveal what I am, or all the truth.

I have a fear of public recognition.

Those who live for the world, as Henry does, always lose their personal, intimate life.

I told Jaeger the lamentable story of my publications.

D. H. Lawrence, published by Edward Titus a few months before his divorce, which caused him to go bankrupt. The book was but partially distributed, half lost, not sent to reviewers, and no royalties, and not even copies for myself.

Michael Fraenkel loaned me the money to print House of Incest, but lost interest in it when it was out and did not distribute it as he had promised. No reviews.

Lawrence Durrell backed the publication of Winter of Artifice. Obelisk issued it a week before the war. No distribution. No reviews.

Can Jaeger say to all this that the veil which concealed me was of my own making? Had guilt suffocated my work—does it envelop me in a fog, guide my destiny? What is fatality? Fatalité intérieure? Other women who produced far lesser works have gained reputations.

I thought my obscure destiny was that of greater mysteries and subtler influences.

But Jaeger smiles. Guilt. Guilt everywhere.

I did not want to rival man. Man was my brothers, younger than

I, Joaquin and Thorvald. I must protect them, not outshine them. I did not want to be a man. Djuna Barnes was masculine. George Sand.

I did not want to steal man's creation, his thunder.

Creation and femininity seemed incompatible. The *aggressive* act of creation.

"Not aggressive," said Jaeger, "*active.*"

I have a horror of the masculine "career" woman.

To create seemed to me such an assertion of the strongest part of me that I would no longer be able to give all those I love the feeling of their being stronger, and they would love me less.

An act of independence would be punished by desertion. I would be abandoned by all those I loved.

Men fear woman's strength. I have been deeply aware of men's weakness, the need to guard them from my strength.

I have made myself less powerful, have concealed my powers.

At the press, I make Gonzalo believe he has discovered this, he has suggested that improvement, that he is clever, stronger. I have concealed my abilities like an evil force that would overwhelm hurt, or weaken others.

I have crippled myself.

Dreams of Chinese woman with bound feet.

I have bound myself spiritually.

I have associated creation with ruthlessness, absence of scruples, indifference to consequences as I see it in Henry. (His story about his father and mother, a cruel caricature.)

I see strongly creative women crush their men. I fear this. I have feared all aggressiveness, all attacks, all destruction. Above all, self-assertion.

Jaeger said: "All you are trying to do is to throw off this mother role imposed on you. You want a give-and-take relationship."

Jaeger, by being true to the woman, creating the woman in me, by her particular intuition as a woman, has penetrated truths not observed by either Allendy or Rank. The creator's guilt in me has to do with my femininity, my subjection to man.

Also with my maternal self in conflict with my creative self. A negative form of creation.

Also the content of my work is related to the demon in me, the adventure-loving, and I do feel this adventurousness a danger to my loves.

Guilt about exposing the father.

Secrets.

Need of disguises.

Fear of consequences.

Great conflict here. Division.

If only I could invent, invent other characters. Objective work which would not involve guilt. Rank said woman could not invent. Will begin to describe others minutely. I was more at ease with myself as a character because it is easier to excavate on one's own property. I could be used for all experiences, was protean, unlimited.

When I started out with an invented character, based always on someone I knew, and then sought to expand, I found myself inside restricted forms, limited outlines, characters who could not go far enough into experience. I felt in a tight mold, and returned to my experience which I tried to transpose into other women.

But this was a misconception. You do not get rid of the self by giving it away, by annihilation. When a child is uprooted it seeks to make a center from which it cannot be uprooted. That was a safety island, but now I must relinquish this too.

. . .

VOLUME V [February, 1954]

Letter to a writer who asked: "Why does one write?"

Why one writes is a question I can answer easily, having so often asked it of myself. I believe one writes because one has to create a world in which one can live. I could not live in any of the worlds offered to me: the world of my parents, the world of Henry Miller, the world of Gonzalo, or the world of wars. I had to create a world of my own, like a climate, a country, an atmosphere in which I could breathe, reign, and re-create myself when destroyed by living. That, I believe, is the reason for every work of art. The artist is the only one who knows the world is a subjective creation, that there is a choice to be made, a selection of elements. It is a materialization, an incarnation of his inner world. Then he hopes to attract others into it, he hopes to impose this particular vision and share it with others. When the second stage is not reached, the brave artist continues nevertheless. The few moments of communion with the world are worth the pain, for it is a world for others, an inheritance for others, a gift to others, in the end. When you make a world tolerable for yourself you make a world tolerable for others.

We also write to heighten our own awareness of life, we write to lure and enchant and console others, we write to serenade our lovers. We write to taste life twice, in the moment, and in retrospection. We write, like Proust, to render all of it eternal, and to persuade ourselves that it is eternal. We write to be able to transcend our life, to reach beyond it. We write to teach ourselves to speak with others, to record the journey into the labyrinth, we write to expand our world, when we feel strangled, constricted, lonely. We write as the birds sing. As the primitive dance their rituals. If you do not breathe through writing, if you do not cry out in writing, or sing in writing, then don't write. Because our culture has no use for any of that. When I don't write I feel my world shrinking. I feel I am in a prison. I feel I lose my fire, my color. It should be a necessity, as the sea needs to heave. I call it breathing.

I enjoy breakfast, the morning light on a church steeple, or on a modern building which looks Grecian against the sky.

I arrived in New York in a black coat and black dress. I left in a white coat and white dress.

Diary Versus Fiction

One thing is very clear—that both diary and fiction tended towards the same goal: intimacy with people, with experience, with life itself. One, in the diary, was achieved by daily writing, daily recording, and continuous interest in the development of people around me and in my own growth. Secrecy seemed to be a condition for spontaneity in my case. The personal interest seemed to be a necessary condition to intimacy. An early intuition that *everyone* had areas of subjective or personal or emotional reactions was confirmed by study of psychology. The more I went into the revelations of psychology, the more I realized that spontaneous writing in the present came closer to the truth than impressions remembered because memory rearranged its collection anew each day with changes in the personality. Stories were altered and fictionalized with time. As the teller changed, so did the versions of the past.

The necessity for fiction was probably born of the problem of taboo on certain revelations. It was not only a need of the imagination but an answer to the limitations placed on portrayal of others.

Not only conventions dictated the secrecy of journals, but personal censorship. Fiction was liberating in that sense. But when it became fixed in a mold, it withered. Until a new form revivified it. The total death of the novel was always being announced, when what should have been observed was the death of certain forms of the novel. People cling to dead forms.

Otto Rank once said that man was more of an artist than woman because he gave freedom to his imagination. Henry Miller was never concerned with the *faithfulness* of his descriptions. He was not concerned with resemblance at all. He invented a world of his own, personages of his own, including himself.

At one time I was very concerned with my faithfulness to the truth. I thought it might be due to uprootings in childhood, loss of country and roots and father, and that I was trying to create relationships based on a true understanding of the other person, in the diary as well as in life and in the novels, too. A world of genuine authentic relationships. Now I can see that what I sought was psychological reality and that this reality has a logic, a pattern, a consistency of its own which cannot be invented. Narrative, or a Joycean symphony, can be invented. Not the subtle plots created by the unconscious. They are marvels of a kind of logic never known before which cannot be imitated or substituted, for every link is essential, every detail. Later I will show how difficult this was to achieve in fiction.

So, the first incentive is to understand not to invent.

This was really the antinovel, antifiction which the French explored recently.

I am still speaking of the time when I separated the two activities as antagonistic and could not see the interrelation between them. Faithful to the notebook and to the human beings I loved, portraying them truthfully, I was wary of invention, and I blamed Henry Miller's inventions for his not understanding people around him. I separated insight from narrative picaresque storytelling. When Henry Miller told a caricatural story about Moricand in *Devil in Paradise*, I felt: this is not Moricand. I only wish he would not call him by his family name. It was *another* story he told. These two drives had to come to terms one day, or I had to choose between them. There is a great deal of conflict and questioning about this in the first two diaries. Finally, I made no choice, I lived out both, and ultimately (thanks to psychoanalysis) they nourished each other and coexisted.

To maintain faith in my vision of people, to be able to say I do understand Moricand, see Moricand, I had to make sure that my vision was clear of all the elements which R. D. Laing enumerated as obstacles to clear insight. In other words, one has to know which areas in one's self are not to be trusted. Acknowledgment of irrational areas.

The diary served a useful purpose in exploring, defining, and then containing these unreliable areas in order to achieve some true objectivity. The idea of total objectivity is erroneous.

The diary, then, was where I checked my realities and illusions, made my experiments, noted progress or its opposite. It was the laboratory! I could venture into the novel with a sense of psychological authenticity and fictionalize only externals, situations, places. Composites, which can do much to enrich, correspond to condensation in the poem and to abstraction in painting.

The necessity for fiction, in my case, also helped to symbolize and add dimensions. The portrait of Henry Miller in the diary is a portrait of Henry Miller, but a composite may become something more than one artist, writer, painter, more than one person—a unit. A composite is no longer the original. It is something else.

How much is lost by retranslating such composites and redistributing each trait where it belongs is exemplified in the biography of Proust by George D. Painter. By replacing all the "types" into the classified box they sprang from, Painter destroyed a magical component.

Only an uncreative person would spend ten years on such reclassification of the alchemist's elements out of which Proust made a world of infinite depth. Why did we read it? Because the personality of Proust himself inspired us with love and a desire for intimacy. We

recognized the greatness of the novels, but we were in love with
Proust, as well as with his novels, but I do not think it is love of the
novelist which drives critics to play sleuth to the personal lives and
personal genesis of their art. It is merely the exercise of the art of
sleuthing, and as this continues to be a favored sport among the academicians, it might be well for the novelists to make their own confessions for the sake of greater accuracy.

Thus fictionalizing had two motives: one, protection of the personalities; the other symbolization, the creation of the myth. We have
no richer example of mythmaking, of enlarging, developing, magnifying, in our time than Marguerite Young's *Miss MacIntosh, My
Darling*. Folk characters, ordinary and familiar, become expanded by
her talent for poetry, metaphysics, surrealism, and achieve universality,
become symphonic. It is the heights and the depths of her measure-
ments, the infinite of her word arches and bridges which make of them
containers of the dimensions not calculable to science but to the poet.

If at first diary and fiction did not coexist harmoniously, it was because
I could not see their mutual influence upon each other (as we cannot
see the influences which two countries at war, like America and Japan,
exert upon each other). I was writing better in the notebooks because
I was writing outside, in the formal work, and I was writing more
authentically in the novels because I sustained the informal, improvised living contact with my relationships, cities, the present.

In the diary I documented a visit to the ragpickers. In the story I
showed how it became more than that.

In the diary the preoccupation with the art of expression began more
and more to work in harmony with the fiction. It is in the diary I
observe that dreams in themselves are boring but dreams related to
life are dynamic. It is in the diary that I am first baffled by the intricate
way Moricand tells his stories (as I was later by the free-form way
Varda told his stories) and make a conscious effort to find a simile for
it, a sequence of images which would resemble his talk. In both cases
they practiced in talk the free association of the surrealists. It was
difficult to capture images and ideas which did not hang together in
the usual way but were born spontaneously one from the other.

I used the symbol of the Ferris wheel to indicate how Moricand kept
people at a distance from the core of the wheel, took them for a voyage
and deposited them as far from intimate knowledge of him as they
were at the beginning. In the story I refined and expanded upon this.

This intricate interplay could have been disastrous to one form or
another. They survived because the same duality existed between my
formal art and my love of direct, human contact.

I was always writing fiction as well as the diary. At ten I wrote adventure stories. Completely invented. Unrelated to the reality of
my life.

This might be studied as the way the artist finds to walk a tightrope
between the two sides of his duality (a duality experienced in some
form or other by almost everyone).

The difference between symbolic truth (expressing the inner life, the subconscious) and the here-and-now verifiable truth continued to trouble me. But they continued to run in parallel lines. The diary, creating a vaster tapestry, a web, exposing constantly the relation between the past and the present, weaving meticulously the invisible interaction, noting the repetition of themes, developed the sense of continuum of the personality instead of *conclusions* or *resolutions* which were invalidated by any recognition of the relativity of truth. This tale without beginning or end which encloses all things, and relates all things was a strong antidote to the incoherence and disintegration of modern man. I could follow the real patterns and gain insights obscured in most of the fragmentary or superficial novels with their artificial climaxes and resolutions.

An immediate, emotional reaction to experience reveals that the power to *re-create* lies in the sensibilities rather *than intellectual memory or observation*. This personal reaction I found to be the core of individuality, or originality and personality. A deep personal relation to all things reaches far beyond the personal into the general.

The diary also teaches that it is in the moments of emotional crisis that human beings reveal themselves most accurately. I learned to choose these heightened moments in fiction because they are the moments of revelation. It is the moment when the real self rises to the surface, shatters its false roles, erupts, and assumes reality and identity. The fiery moments of passionate experience are the moments of wholeness and totality of the personality. By this emphasis on the fiery moments, the explosions, I reached a greater reality of feeling and the senses. The preoccupation of the novelist: how to capture the living moments, was answered by the diary. You write while they are *alive*. You do not preserve them in alcohol until the moment you are ready to write about them. I discovered through the diary several basic elements essential to the vitality of writing. Of these the most important are naturalness and spontaneity. These, in turn, sprang from my freedom of selection. Because I was not forced to write about something, I could write about anything which interested me genuinely, what I felt most strongly about at the moment. This enthusiasm produced a vividness which often withered in the formal work. Improvisation, free association of images and ideas, obedience to mood, impulses, brought forth countless riches. The diary, dealing only with the immediate, the warm, the near, being written at white heat, developed a love of the living moment.

There are negative forces which oppress the novelist, which do not affect diary writing. One learns resistance and defiance of them. One of the negative forces is the taboo imposed on certain themes, another is the artificial chronological sequence, a third is the untrained reviewer. Such forces do not oppress research in science. In literature they are preestablished. I am not speaking of the fourth which is commercialism.

Free of all these oppressions, diary writing maintains impetus and the exhilaration born of freedom.

I was discovering the dual aspect of truth: one stemming from the immediate and personal, and one which could be achieved later with an *objectivity not born of detachment* but of the recognition of one's subjectivity and the sifting of it to keep the vital elements intact. The personal involvement is the origin of the life-giving emotion.

Another lesson I learned from diary writing was the actual continuity of the act of writing, not waiting for inspiration, favorable climate, astrologic constellations, the mood, but the discipline of sitting at the typewriter to write so many hours a day. Then when the magnificent moment comes, the ripened moment, the writing itself is nimble, already tuned, warmed.

Why did I not remain merely a diarist? Because there was a world beyond the personal which could be handled through the art form, through fiction.

Why did I not stay within *House of Incest* and write only prose poems, dreamed material, such as *Les chants de Maldoror?*

Because my drive was stated by Jung: *proceed from the dream outward.* I took this as relating dream and life, internal and external worlds, the secrets and persona of the self. Appearance and reality, illusion and reality.

Without the diary, the prose poem, and fiction I could not have achieved the *relation* between them. It is the *relation* which interested me, the *connection*, the *bridges*, the *interaction*, the *dynamics of relation* among human beings as well as among the ways of expression human beings use.

LIMITATIONS OF FICTION

The limitation of the novel sent me back to the diary. For example, when I finished the novel *Winter of Artifice*, I did not feel that I had finished with the relationship of father and daughter, because in the diary I had an example of a continuum which did not come to an end but which changed. Perhaps a novelist is through with a character when he is finished with his novel. I was not. The continuity of relationship and its alterations, as in Proust, made me feel there was always another truth around the corner, there would always be another revelation, another discovery about my father. The concept that this theme was completed would never even have occurred to me, because I could see its continuation in the endless diary. The diary made me aware of organic and perpetual motion, perpetual change in character. When you write a novel or a short story, you are arresting motion for a period of that story, a span of time. There is something static about that. Proust seemed to me the only writer who had flow and infinite continuum. Other novels did not revolve enough. Even in Durrell's *Alexandria Quartet* the promise that we would look at each character from a totally different point of view, and which was achieved externally by a kaleidoscopic view, a changing focus, nevertheless did not succeed in depth. When Durrell tried to give that by creating journals and notebooks, they did not seem to be revelations or to belong to the different characters but to be written by the novelist. The diary cannot be imitated. And so in many cases, reading novels, I had the feeling of still life rather than a perpetual motion.

I enjoyed writing the diary more than I did the novels because it was unplanned, spontaneous. And even if I did not plan the fiction, and tried to be free of a structure or design except the one which would emerge organically from a selection of material, I was not as free.

I may be free in my first version of a novel, but the editing is a discipline, it is an art. Even if it consists mostly of cutting, taking out what had not "happened" (for I did not believe very much in rewriting). For me the act of rewriting was tampering with the freshness and aliveness. I preferred to cut. There is an element of conscious editing after the spontaneous writing. There is an element of selection, passing judgment. It takes a great deal of the pleasure out of it. The pleasure seems to lie in freedom of choice.

Part of the pleasure comes from not being aware of having to construct something that won't fall apart. In the novels, I am aware of being a craftsman. Not in the diary.

The spontaneous writing in the novel has to achieve, ultimately, a form; its theme and mood create a form. You are not sure if the pieces will fit together, if it will form a design (I am talking about an organic form born of the contents, not an imposed plot or structure). There is a tension. Sabina caused me a great deal of trouble because I wanted to describe fragmentation without the disintegration which usually accompanies it. Each fragment had a life of its own. They had to be held together by some tension other than the unity we are familiar with. I was depicting fissions of the atoms of personality, but I did not want to fabricate a bomb. I was in danger of that every moment in the book. If she had no center to hold on to, she could be destroyed as Blanche DuBois was by those who did not understand her fantasy. In Marguerite Duras' *The Ravishing of Lol Stein*, in describing Lol's schizoid state, she caused it to happen to such a degree that Lol was no longer understandable. All communication was broken.

Madness to me, in a novel, was like murder. It was an easy and not quite honorable solution! For it was no solution. It was a curtain. A drama to me was the conflict between sanity and insanity, conflict and serenity, the individual and society, tensions, but the beauty consisted in the *endurance* of the effort to integrate, to reach another rung of awareness. I felt the novel had to take the adventurer all the way in his journey, to the top of the mountain, or the undiscovered river in the jungle, and somehow the substitution of an end cheated one of a complete spectacle, complete experience. I killed my heroes and heroines off when I was fourteen. I thought it was because I did not know then what else to do.

I do not know how the concept grew that objectivity could only come from one's absence, that erasing one's self, not being in the room, would give a description far closer to objective truth. For I believe the opposite. Deena Metzger felt she was seeing Henry Miller in

The Diary through *my* eyes, but I maintain that the only way to become truly intimate with a person's character is to view him precisely
in relation to others. A thousand objective facts would not reveal as
much as watching Miller at a heightened moment of personal relationship, in relation to someone, at a moment of crisis. I remember a
playwright's saying he would have preferred me absent in the *Mouse*
story. That was an absurd statement, for the story was of the Mouse
in relation to someone to whom she finally confessed, opened herself,
who was caught in sharing her drama. Without me in the story, the
Mouse would remain mute and secretive, undecipherable and unknown. There has to be a presence, a register, a recorder, an eye, an
ear, a presence which arouses revelation. I do not believe in reportage.
I believe in the capacity of certain people to obtain information,
secrets, and confessions.

The active conflict between diary and novel gradually ceased. By
1966 it was the experience of the novelist which helped me to edit the
diary. It was the fiction writer who knew when the tempo lagged,
when details were trivial, when a description was a repetition. I
changed nothing essential, I only cut the extraneous material, the
overload.

The final lesson a writer learns is that everything can nourish the
writer. The dictionary, a new word, a voyage, an encounter, a talk
in the street, a book, a phrase heard. He is a computer set to receive
and utilize all things. An exhibit of painting, a concert, a voice, a
letter, a play, a landscape, a skyscape, a telephone conversation, a nap,
a dream, a sleepless night, a storm, an animal's greeting, an aquarium,
a photograph, a newspaper story.

I am a fervent believer in the enriching influence of one art upon another, a believer in cross-pollination between the arts, which is now
expressing itself in the integration of the arts, in the use of lights,
sounds, happenings, theater, sculpture on the stage (such as Noguchi's
sets for Martha Graham).

Bergson said there are two kinds of clarities. "The perception of the
artist, of the intuitive mind will always seem obscure to those who
prefer clear Cartesian perception."

He spoke of "the fringe of nebulosity which surrounds the luminous
core of intelligence, affirming by its presence that part of our existence
so clearly perceived by our intelligence is not the essential or the most
profound part. This penumbra is what must be pentrated if we would
seek reality. An orientation inward implies an enlargement of our
mental horizon." He denied that "reality could be attained by the
intelligence, by conscious thought."

Mary McCarthy (b. 1912)

Mary McCarthy is a familiar figure to contemporary readers because of her work in journalism. She has covered many of the pivotal events of recent years with astuteness and clarity. As a journalist she has traveled extensively, destroying some of the myths surrounding women and their limitations in news coverage. This accomplishment alone would be enough to include her in this anthology, but her influence extends even further. Her two most recent books, *Vietnam* and *The Mask of State: Watergate Portraits,* are brilliant combinations of reportage and careful analysis. Earlier, her writings on drama and literature displayed an analytical acumen notable in the particularly male-dominated area of literary and aesthetic criticism. *Theater Chronicles* and her articles on J. D. Salinger (*Harper's,* October 1962) and on *Madame Bovary* (*Partisan Review,* Spring 1964) are examples of this aspect of her writing achievement. Her fiction is well known, particularly the novel *The Group,* which traces the lives of college students attempting to come to grips with life, creativity, and their roles as women.

A family tragedy caused a distinct change in McCarthy's upbringing. The oldest child of loving and indulgent parents, she was orphaned at age six and left with her Catholic relatives. In *Memories of a Catholic Girlhood,* she chronicles her life with an aunt and her almost sadistic husband, whose training of children was an odd mixture of religion and inhumanity. This book reveals her sense of deprivation after the loss of her parents, her response to the nuns who taught her, her remembrance of childhood experiences shared with her brothers, and an appreciation of the place of a religious orientation and its effects on the individual. It is a strong piece of autobiography of the growth process written from the viewpoint of a girl and a young woman; it also provides a look into one of the streams of the American cultural experience. "C.Y.E." from the collection *Cast a Cold Eye* has been chosen because it encapsulates her Catholic experience and also gives insight into the sensitivity of an intellectual young girl learning to deal with life and her own abilities. The heroine's self-doubt and pain will remind many women readers of the conflicts felt during their own youth.

In the interview with Elisabeth Niebuhr, McCarthy speaks candidly about her writing, women writers, and the process of writing. The extensiveness of her reading of both classical and modern literature is revealed in this piece and should invite students who wish to write to read more widely. The range of her work combines the varied strands of writing in contemporary culture, both fiction and nonfiction, and gives her a significant place among writers today.

Interview with Mary McCarthy

BY ELISABETH NIEBUHR

Interviewer: Do you find that your critical work, whether it's political or literary, creates any problems in relation to your work as a novelist?

McCarthy: No, except that you have the perpetual problem if, somebody asks you to do a review, whether to interrupt what you're writing—if you're writing a novel—to do the review. You have to weigh whether the subject interests you enough, or whether you're tired at that moment, emotionally played out by the fiction you're writing. Whether it would be a good thing to stop and concentrate on something else. I just agreed to and did a review of Camus' collected fiction and journalism. That *was* in some way connected with my own work, with the question of the novel in general. I thought, yes, I will do this because I want to read all of Camus and decide what I think about him finally. (Actually, I ended up almost as baffled as when I started.) But in general, I don't take a review unless it's something like that. Or unless Anthony West attacks Dickens. You know. Either it has to be some sort of thing that I want very much to take sides on, or something I'd like to study a bit, that I want to find out about anyway. Or where there may, in the case of study, be some reference—very indirect—back to my own work.

Interviewer: This is quite a change from the time when you wrote criticism and never even thought of writing fiction. But now you consider yourself a novelist? Or don't you bother with these distinctions?

McCarthy: Well, I suppose I consider myself a novelist. Yes. Still, whatever way I write was really, I suppose, formed critically. That is, I learned to write reviews and criticism and then write novels so that however I wrote, it was formed that way. George Eliot, you know, began by translating Strauss, began by writing about German philosophy—though her philosophic passages are not at all good in *Middlemarch*. Nevertheless, I *think* that this kind of training really makes one more interested in the subject than in the style. Her work certainly doesn't suffer from any kind of stylistic frippery. There's certainly no voluminous drapery around. There is a kind of concision in it, at her best—that passage where she's describing the character of Lydgate—which shows, I think, the critical and philosophic training. I've never liked the conventional conception of "style." What's confusing is that style usually means some form of fancy writing—when people say, oh yes, so and so's such a "wonderful stylist." But if one means by style the voice, the irreducible and always recognizable and alive thing, then of course style is really everything. It's what you find in Stendhal, it's what you find in Pasternak. The same thing you find in a poet—the sound of, say, Donne's voice. In a sense, you can't go further in an analysis of Donne than to be able to place this voice, in the sense that you recognize Don Giovanni by the voice of Don Giovanni.

Interviewer: In speaking of your own writing, anyway, you attribute its "style" to your earlier critical work—then you don't feel the influence of other writers of fiction?

McCarthy: I don't think I have any influences. I think my first story, the first one in *The Company She Keeps,* definitely shows the Jamesian influence—James is so terribly catching. But beyond that, I can't find any influence. That is, I can't as a detached person—as detached as I can be—look at my work and see where it comes from from the point of view of literary sources.

Interviewer: There must be certain writers, though, that you are *drawn* to more than others.

McCarthy: Oh yes! But I don't think I write like them. The writer I really like best is Tolstoy, and I *know* I don't write like Tolstoy. I wish I did! Perhaps the best English prose is Thomas Nash. I don't write at all like Thomas Nash.

. . .

Interviewer: What do you think of women writers, or do you think the category "woman writer" should not be made?

McCarthy: Some women writers make it. I mean, there's a certain kind of woman writer who's a capital W, capital W. Virginia Woolf certainly was one, and Katherine Mansfield was one, and Elizabeth Bowen is one. Katherine Anne Porter? Don't think she really is—I mean, her writing is certainly very feminine, but I would say that there wasn't this "WW" business in Katherine Anne Porter. Who else? There's Eudora Welty, who's certainly not a "Woman Writer." Though she's become one lately.

Interviewer: What is it that happens to make this change?

McCarthy: I think they become interested in décor. You notice the change in Elizabeth Bowen. Her early work is much more masculine. Her later work has much more drapery in it. Who else? Jane Austen was never a "Woman Writer," I don't think. The cult of Jane Austen pretends that she was, but I don't think she was. George Eliot *certainly* wasn't, and George Eliot is the kind of woman writer I admire. I was going to write a piece at some point about this called "Sense and Sensibility," dividing women writers into these two. I *am* for the ones who represent sense, and so was Jane Austen.

Interviewer: Getting away from novels for a moment, I'd like to ask you about *Memories of a Catholic Girlhood* if I might. Will you write any more autobiography?

McCarthy: I was just reading—oh God, actually I *was* just starting to read Simone de Beauvoir's second volume, *La Force de l'Age,* and she announces in the preface that she can't write about her later self with the same candor that she wrote about her girlhood.

Interviewer: You feel that too?

McCarthy: On this one point I agree with her. One has to be really old, I think, really quite an old person—and by that time I don't know what sort of shape one's memory would be in.

. . .

Interviewer: You say in one of your articles that perhaps the fault lies simply in the material which the modern world affords, that it itself lacks—

McCarthy: Credibility? Yes. It's a difficulty I think all modern writers have.

Interviewer: Other than the problem of arrangement of time, are there other specific technical difficulties about the novel you find yourself particularly concerned with?

McCarthy: Well, the whole question of the point of view which tortures everybody. It's the problem that everybody's been up against since Joyce, if not before. Of course James really began it, and Flaubert even. You find it as early as *Madame Bovary*. The problem of the point of view, and the voice: *style indirect libre*—the author's voice, by a kind of ventriloquism, disappearing in and completely limited by the voices of his characters. What it has meant is the complete banishment of the author. I would like to restore the author! I haven't tried yet, but I'd like to try after this book, which is as far as I can go in ventriloquism. I would like to try to restore the author. Because you find that if you obey this Jamesian injunction of "Dramatize, dramatize," and especially if you deal with comic characters, as in my case, there is so much you can't say because you're limited by these mentalities. It's just that a certain kind of intelligence—I'm not only speaking of myself, but of anybody, Saul Bellow, for example—is more or less absent from the novel, and has to be, in accordance with these laws which the novel has made for itself. I think one reason that everyone—at least I—welcomed *Doctor Zhivago* was that you had the author in the form of the hero. And this beautiful tenor voice, the hero's voice and the author's—this marvelous voice, and this clear sound of intelligence. The Russians have never gone through the whole development of the novel you find in Joyce, Faulkner, et cetera, so that Pasternak was slightly unaware of the problem! But I think this technical development has become absolutely killing to the novel.

Interviewer: You say that after this novel about the Vassar girls, you—

McCarthy: I don't know what I'm going to do, but I want to try something that will introduce, at least back into my work, my own voice. And not in the disguise of a heroine. I'm awfully sick of my heroine. I don't mean in this novel: my heroine of the past. Because the sensibility in each novel got more and more localized with this heroine, who became an agent of perception, et cetera.

Let me make a jump now. The reason that I enjoyed doing those books on Italy, the Venice and Florence books, was that I was writing *in my own voice*. One book was in the first person, and one was completely objective, but it doesn't make any difference. I felt, you know, now I can talk freely! The books were written very fast, the Venice one faster. Even the Florence book, with masses of research in it, was written very fast, with a great deal of energy, with a kind of liberated energy. And without the peculiar kind of painstakingness that's involved in the dramatization that one does in a novel, that is, when nothing can come in that hasn't been perceived through a character. The technical difficulties are so great, in projecting yourself, in feigning an alien consciousness, that too much energy gets lost, I think, in the masquerade. And I think this is not only true of me.

. . .

Interviewer: In reading the Florence book, I remember being very moved by the passage where you talk of Brunelleschi, about his "absolute integrity and essence," that solidity of his, both real and ideal. When you write about Brunelleschi, you write about this sureness, this "being-itself," and yet as a novelist—in *The Company She Keeps* for instance—you speak of something so very different, and you take almost as a theme this fragmented unplaceability of the human personality.

McCarthy: But I was very young then. I think I'm really not interested in the quest for the self any more. Oh, I suppose everyone continues to be interested in the quest for the self, but what you feel when you're older, I think, is that—how to express this—that you really must *make* the self. It's absolutely useless to look for it, you won't find it, but it's possible in some sense to make it. I don't mean in the sense of making a mask, a Yeatsian mask. But you finally begin in some sense to make and to choose the self you want.

Interviewer: Can you write novels about that?

McCarthy: I never have. I never have, I've never even thought of it. That is, I've never thought of writing a developmental novel in which a self of some kind is discovered or is made, is forged, as they say. No. I suppose in a sense I don't know any more today than I did in 1941 about what my identity is. But I've stopped looking for it. I must say, I believe much more in truth now than I did. I do believe in the solidity of truth much more. Yes. I believe there is a truth, and that it's knowable.

Muriel Rukeyser (b. 1913)

Born in New York, poet Muriel Rukeyser is notable for her vitality
and social consciousness. Her insight into the future—its impoverished imagination, its stress on materialistic and militaristic values—
is evident in *Life of Poetry*, written in 1949. This book often elicits
dismay that the direction she suggests has been so infrequently sought
in these intervening years of increasing chaos.

Rukeyser, a graduate of Sarah Lawrence College, feels that artist and
audience have been damaged by these misdirected priorities and must
restore the value of the universe of poetry: the realm of emotional
truth and full consciousness, full experience of one's self and the
world. She expresses this idea in her poem "This Place in the Ways,"
where the poet, after experiencing failures, enters a new age believing
in love and in rage. Ready to set out once again "on the dark and
marvelous way / From where I began," the poet waits for a song:
"Poems in throat and hand, asleep, / And my storm beating strong."
This rebirth, this storm, is evident as one reads her work of the last
forty and more years.

In "The Poem as Mask," she refers to her use of myth in her earlier
work, specifically that of Orpheus in her long poem by that name.
Rukeyser believes that today poets must speak more directly of their
experiences (for a prose statement of this viewpoint, see Adrienne
Rich's essay "When We Dead Awaken"). The fragments of the murdered Orpheus, which in her early poem came together to form the
god, here merge in the poet herself; she admits to personal connections only alluded to before. Yet "Orpheus" and other of Rukeyser's
metaphorical poems do disclose an emotional reality shining through
the masks. *Waterlily Fire* presents much of her work produced between 1935 and 1962, and two more recent collections are *Speed of
Darkness* and *Breaking Open*. The power of her work reflects a rare
woman and artist. She does not allow us to turn our eyes away from
injustice and atrocity: "Delta Poems" shows lovers, walking by the
sea in Vietnam, suddenly encompassed and destroyed by bright fire.
The poet appears in this poem, bringing us to that tragic site, bringing
the war into her room, into our safe rooms, sharing grief and outrage.
Her long poem in Part Two, "Searching / Not Searching," explores
what is possible today for the individual and the poet: "Yes, we set
the communication / we have achieved / against the world of murder."

The Poem as Mask

When I wrote of the women in their dances and wildness, it was a
    mask,
on their mountain, god-hunting, singing, in orgy,
it was a mask, when I wrote of the god,
fragmented, exiled from himself, his life, the love gone down with
    song,
it was myself, split open, unable to speak, in exile from myself.

There is no mountain, there is no god, there is memory
of my torn life, myself split open in sleep, the rescued child
beside me among the doctors, and a word
of rescue from the great eyes.

No more masks! No more mythologies!

Now, for the first time, the god lifts his hand,
the fragments join in me with their own music.

Who in One Lifetime

Who in one lifetime sees all causes lost,
Herself dismayed and helpless, cities down,
Love made monotonous fear and the sad-faced
Inexorable armies and the falling plane,
Has sickness, sickness. Introspective and whole,
She knows how several madnesses are born,
Seeing the integrated never fighting well,
The flesh too vulnerable, the eyes tear-torn.

She finds a pre-surrender on all sides:
Treaty before the war, ritual impatience turn
The camps of ambush to chambers of imagery.
She holds belief in the world, she stays and hides
Life in her own defeat, stands, though her whole world burn,
A childless goddess of fertility.

Tillie Olsen *(b. 1913)*

Tillie Olsen speaks from a little-heard segment of American society: the working class. Born in Nebraska, she has spent her life working in everyday jobs and raising children. Four short stories, a collection of essays, and one novel are the output of her career as a writer, which was fit in after the demands of a family, leaving little time for creativity or for a literary education.

The stories, collected in the volume *Tell Me a Riddle*, have a rare beauty in their portrayal of lives laboriously spent and misspent: "unprivileged lives," as she has called them. Her protagonists, the full flowering of all their capacities stifled by circumstance, are haunted by unfulfillment—yet somehow strengthened with a will to change the world, to make it more human and loving. The tragedy of the mother in "I Stand Here Ironing" is less in her own condition—forced to make choices that denied her fulfillment as a person and mother—than in her awareness, gained too late, of her daughter's emotional deprivation as a child. It is implied that the fault lies in the social structure rather than in the mother herself. Both she and her daughter have the strength of resisters; they are not simply victims of their society.

Olsen sees that traditionally women have written to reveal the wrongs of their times, realizing that self-actualization is not truly attainable in a world that denies justice to others. She believes that literature can make one understand despair and keep one's will strong, as her novel *Yonnondio: From the Thirties* movingly illustrates. In lyrical prose, it charts the struggles of a poor family and the heroic spirit and endurance that allow Anna, the mother, still to have hope at the end that the air is changing—at least becoming tolerable.

A masterpiece of American literature, *Yonnondio* barely reached print. Olsen began the book when she was nineteen, and a chapter published in the *Partisan Review* in 1943 was hailed as an "unmistakable work of early genius." But the necessities of her life forced her to set the book aside, and it was lost for forty years. In her afterwords, she describes her efforts at reclaiming the fragments, many of which remain unused, "telling what might have been."

Today Olsen lives in San Francisco and devotes a great deal of energy to encouraging women to write. Her belief is that what writers do is to keep us all alive, that we must have faith in human aspiration and a better future, and that we can transform the world.

One out of Twelve

It is the women's movement, part of the other movements of our time for a fully human life, that has brought this forum* into being; kindling a renewed, in most instances a first time, interest in the writings and writers of our sex.

Linked with the old, resurrected classics on women, this movement in three years has accumulated a vast new mass of testimony, of new comprehensions as to what it is to be female. Inequities, restrictions, penalties, denials, leechings have been painstakingly and painfully documented; damaging differences in circumstances and treatment from that of males attested to; and limitations, harms, a sense of wrong, voiced.

It is in the light and dark of this testimony that I examine my subject today: the lives and work of writers, women, in our century (though I speak primarily of those writing in the English language and in prose).

Compared to the countless centuries of the silence of women, compared to the century preceding ours—the first in which women wrote in any noticeable numbers—ours has been a favorable one.

The road was cut many years ago, as Virginia Woolf reminds us:

by Fanny Burney, by Aphra Behn, by Harriet Martineau, by Jane Austen, by George Eliot, many famous women and many more unknown and forgotten. . . . Thus, when I came to write . . . writing was a reputable and harmless occupation.

Predecessors, ancestors, a body of literature, an acceptance of the right to write: each in themselves an advantage.

In this second century we have access to areas of work and of life experience previously denied: higher education; longer lives; for the first time in human history, freedom from compulsory childbearing; freer bodies and attitudes toward sexuality; and—of the greatest importance to those like myself who come from generations of illiterate women—increasing literacy, and higher degrees of it. Each one of these a vast gain.

And the results?

Productivity: books of all manner and kind. My own crude sampling, having to be made without benefit of research assistants, secretary, studies (nobody's made them), or computer (to feed *Books in Print* into, for instance) indicates that four to five books are written by men to every one by a woman.

Comparative earnings: ("equal pay for equal work"): no figures available.

* This essay was originally a talk, spoken from notes, at the 1971 Modern Language Association Forum on Women Writers in the Twentieth Century. Its tone is distinctly of that year of cumulative discovery. The content was somewhat conditioned by its being addressed to college teachers of literature.

Achievement: as gauged by what supposedly designates it: appearance in 20th Century literature courses, required reading lists, textbooks; in quality anthologies; the year's best, the decade's best, the fifty years' best; consideration by critics or in current reviews; *one woman writer for every twelve men.* For a week or two, make your own survey whenever you pick up an anthology, course bibliography, quality magazine or quarterly, book review section, book of criticism.[1]

One woman writer of achievement for every twelve men writers so ranked. Is this proof again–and in this so much more favorable century—of women's innately inferior capacity for creative achievement?

Only a few months ago (June 1971), during a Radcliffe-sponsored panel on "Women's Liberation, Myth or Reality," Diana Trilling, asking why it is that women

have not made even a fraction of the intellectual, scientific or artistic-cultural contributions which men have made

comes again to the considered conclusion that

it is not enough to blame women's place in culture or culture itself, because that leaves certain fundamental questions unanswered . . . necessarily raises the question of the biological aspects of the problem.

Biology: that difference. Evidently unconsidered, unknown to her and the others who share her conclusion, are the centuries of prehistory during which biology did not deny equal contribution; and the other determining difference—not biology—between male and female in the centuries after; the past of women that should be part of every human consciousness, certainly every woman's consciousness (in the same way that the 400 years of bondage, colonialism, the slave passage are to black humans).

Work first:

Within our bodies we bore the race. Through us it was shaped, fed and clothed. . . . Labour more toilsome and unending than that of man was ours. . . . No work was too hard, no labor too strenuous to exclude us.[2]

True for most women in most of the world still.

Unclean; taboo. The Devil's Gateway. The three steps behind; the girl babies drowned in the river; the baby strapped to the back. Buried alive with the lord, burned alive on the funeral pyre, burned as witch at the stake. Stoned to death for adultery. Beaten, raped. Bartered. Bought and sold. Concubinage, prostitution, white slavery. The hunt, the sexual prey, "I am a lost creature, o the poor Clarissa." Purdah,

---

[1] What weights my figures so heavily towards the one-out-of-twelve ratio is course offerings and writers considered in serious critical estimates. Otherwise my figures would have been closer to one out of seven. But it would not matter if the ratio were one out of six, or five. Any figure but one to one insists on query: Why? What, not true for men, but only for women, makes this difference?

[2] Olive Schreiner, *Women and Labour*, 9th ed.

the veil of Islam, domestic confinement. Illiterate. Excluded, excluded, excluded from council, ritual, activity, language, when there was neither biological nor economic reason to be excluded.

Religion, when all believed. In sorrow shalt thou bring forth children. May thy wife's womb never cease from bearing. Neither was the man created for the woman but the woman for the man. Let the woman learn in silence and in all subjection. (Contrary to biological birth fact) Adam's rib. The Jewish male morning prayer: thank God I was not born a woman. Silence in holy places, seated apart, or not permitted entrance at all; castration of boys because women too profane to sing in church.

And for the comparative handful of women born into the privileged class: being, not doing; man does, woman is; to you the world says work, to us it says seem. "God is thy law, thou mine." Isolated. Cabin'd, cribb'd, confin'd; the private sphere. Bound feet: corseted, cosseted, bedecked; denied one's body. Powerlessness. Fear of rape, male strength. Fear of aging. Subject to. Fear of expressing capacities. Soft attractive graces; the mirror to magnify man. Marriage as property arrangement. "The vices of slaves"[3]—dissembling, flattering, manipulating, appeasing. Bolstering. Vicarious living, infantilization, trivialization. Parasitism, individualism, madness. Shut up, you're only a girl. O Elizabeth, why couldn't you have been born a boy? Roles, discontinuities, part self, part time; "a man can give full energy to his profession, a woman cannot" (20th century woman).

How is it that women have not made a fraction of the intellectual, scientific, or artistic-cultural contributions that men have made?

Only in the context of this punitive difference in circumstance, in history, between the sexes; this past, hidden or evident, that though objectively obsolete (yes, even the toil and the compulsory child-bearing obsolete) continues so terribly, so determiningly to live on; can the question be answered or my subject here today—the woman writer in our century: one out of twelve—be understood.

How much it takes to become a writer. Bent (far more common than we assume), circumstances, time, development of craft—but beyond that: how much conviction as to the importance of what one has to say, one's right to say it. And the will, the measureless store of belief in oneself to be able to come to, cleave to, find the form for one's own life comprehensions. Difficult for any male not born into a class that breeds such confidence. Almost impossible for a girl, a woman.

The leeching of belief, of will; the damaging of capacity, begin so early. Sparse indeed is the literature on the way of denial to small girl children of the development of their endowment as born human: active, vigorous bodies; exercise of the power to do, to make, to investigate, to invent, to conquer obstacles; to resist violations of the self; to think, create, choose; to attain community, confidence in

[3] Elizabeth Barrett Browning's phrase.

self. Little has been written on the harm of instilling constant concern with appearance, the need to please, to support, the training
in acceptance, deferring. Little has been added in our century to
George Eliot's *Mill on the Floss* on the effect of the differing treatment—"climate of expectation"—for boys and for girls.

But it is there if one knows how to read for it, and indelibly there in
the damage. One—out of twelve.

In the vulnerable girl years, unlike their sisters in the previous century, women writers go to college.[4] The kind of experience it may be
for them is stunningly documented in Elaine Showalter's "Women
and the Literary Curriculum."[5] Freshman texts in which women have
little place, if at all; language itself, all achievement, anything to do
with the human in male terms; *Man in Crisis; The Individual and His
World.* Three hundred thirteen male writers taught; seventeen women
writers. That classic of adolescent rebellion: *Portrait of the Artist as
a Young Man*, and sagas (male) of the quest for identity (but then
Erikson, the father of the concept, propounds that identity concerns
girls only insofar as making themselves into attractive beings for the
right kind of man). Most, not all, of the predominantly male literature
studied, written by men whose understandings are not universal, but
restrictively male; and in our time, as Mary Ellmann, Kate Millett,
and Dolores Schmidt have pointed out, more and more surface, hostile,
and stereotypic in portraying women.

In a writer's young years, susceptibility to the vision and style of the
great is extreme. Add the aspiration-denying implication, consciously
felt or not, that (as Woolf noted years ago) women writers, women's
experience, and literature written by women are by definition minor.
(Mailer will not grant even the minor: "the one thing a writer has
to have is balls.") No wonder that Showalter observes:

Women (students) are estranged from their own experience and unable
to perceive its shape and authenticity, in part because they do not
see it mirrored and given resonance in literature. . . . They have no
faith in the validity of their own perceptions and experiences, rarely
seeing them confirmed in literature, or accepted in criticism. . . . [They]
notoriously lack the happy confidence, the exuberant sense of the value
of their individual observations which enables young men to risk
making fools of themselves for the sake of an idea.

Harms difficult to work through. Nevertheless, some young women
(others are already lost) maintain their ardent intention to write—fed
indeed by the very glories of some of this literature that puts them
down.

But other invisible worms are finding out the bed of crimson joy.
Self-doubt; seriousness questioned by the hours agonizing over appearance; concentration shredded into attracting, being attractive; the
absorbing, real need and love for working with words felt as hypo-

[4] True almost without exception.
[5] *College English*, May 1971.

critical self-delusion, for what seems to be (and is) esteemed is whether or not the phone rings for you, and how often. High aim, and accomplishment towards it discounted by the prevalent attitude that, as girls will probably marry (attitudes not applied to boys who will probably marry), writing is no more than an attainment of a dowry to be spent later according to the needs and circumstances within the true vocation: husband and family. The growing conviction that going on will threaten other needs; that "a woman has to sacrifice all claims to femininity and family to be a writer."[6]

And the agony—peculiarly mid-century, escaped by their sisters of pre-Freudian, pre-Jungian times—that "creation and femininity are incompatible." Anaïs Nin's words:

The aggressive act of creation; the guilt for creating. I did not want to rival man; to steal man's creation, his thunder. I must protect them, not outshine them.

The acceptance—against one's experienced reality—of the sexist notion that the act of creation is not as inherently natural to a woman as to a man, but rooted instead in unnatural competition, or envy, or imitation, or thwarted sexuality.

And in all the usual college teaching—the English, history, psychology, sociology courses—little to help that young woman understand the source or nature of this inexplicable draining unsureness, self-doubt, loss of aspiration, of confidence.[7]

It is all there in the extreme in Plath's *Bell Jar*—that portrait of the artist as a young woman (significantly, one of the few that we have)— from the precarious sense of vocation to the paralyzing conviction that (in a sense different than she wrote years later)

Perfection is terrible. It cannot have children.
It tamps the womb.

And indeed, in our century as in the last, until very recently almost all distinguished achievement has come from childless women: Willa Cather, Ellen Glasgow, Gertrude Stein, Edith Wharton, Virginia Woolf, Elizabeth Bowen, Katherine Mansfield, Isak Dinesen, Katherine Anne Porter, Dorothy Richardson, Henry Handel Richardson, Susan Glas-

---

[6] Sylvia Plath, letter when a graduate student.
[7] It is here that another significant turn to silencing takes place. What was needed to confirm and vivify has been meager—and occasional, accidental. The compound of what denies, vitiates, actively discourages, has been powerful—and continuous, institutionalized. The young unhelped "sexless bound in sex" being is now in

> ...the glade
> Wherein Fate sprung Love's ambuscade
> To flush me in this sensuous strife...
> Of that which makes the sexual feud
> And clogs the aspirant life.*

How many in the one-to-twelve ratio foundered here?
    * Herman Melville, "After the Pleasure Party," *Collected Poems.*

pell, Dorothy Parker, Lillian Hellman, Eudora Welty, Djuna Barnes, Anaïs Nin, Ivy Compton-Burnett, Elizabeth Madox Roberts, Christina Stead, Carson McCullers, Flannery O'Connor, Jean Stafford, May Sarton, Josephine Herbst, Jessamyn West, Janet Frame, Lillian Smith, Zora Neale Hurston, Iris Murdoch, Joyce Carol Oates, Lorraine Hansberry.

Most never questioned, or at least accepted (a few sanctified), this different condition for achievement, not imposed on men writers. Few asked the fundamental human equality question regarding it that Elizabeth Mann Borghese, Thomas Mann's daughter, asked when she was 18 and sent to a psychiatrist for help in getting over an unhappy love affair (revealing also an unrealistic working ambition to become a great musician although "women cannot be great musicians"). "You must choose between your art and fulfillment as a woman," the analyst told her, "between music and family life." "Why?" she asked, "Why must I choose? No one said to Toscanini or to Bach or my father, that they must choose between their art and fulfillment as a man, family life. . . . Injustice everywhere." Not unjust if it were truly free choice. But where it is forced because of the circumstances for the sex into which one is born—a choice men of the same class do not have to make in order to do their work—that is not *choice*, but a working of sexist injustice. (How much of the one-to-twelve ratio is accounted for by those lost here?)

What possible difference, you may ask, does it make to literature whether or not a woman writer remains childless—free choice or not— especially in view of the marvels these childless women have created.

Might there not have been other marvels as well, or other dimensions to these marvels? Might there not have been present profound aspects and understandings of human life as yet largely absent in literature?

More and more women writers in our century, primarily in the last two decades, are assuming as their right, too, fullness of work *and* family life.[8] Their emergence is evidence of changing circumstances making possible for them what (with rarest exception) was not possible in the generations of women before. But the fundamental situation remains unchanged. Unlike men writers who embarked on the same course, they do not have the societal equivalent of wives—nor (in a society hostile to growing life) anyone but themselves to mother

[8] Among those with children: Harriette Arnow, Mary Lavin, Mary McCarthy, Elizabeth Janeway, Tess Slesinger, Storm Jameson, Janet Lewis, Jean Rhys, Kay Boyle, Dorothy Canfield Fisher, Pearl Buck, Josephine Johnson, Ann Petry, Caroline Gordon, Nancy Hale, Shirley Jackson, Eleanor Clark; and a sampling in the unparalleled last two decades: Hortense Calisher, Margaret Walker, Grace Paley, Doris Lessing, Edna O'Brien, Margaret Drabble, Cynthia Ozick, Pauli Murray, Joanne Greenberg (Hannah Green), Joan Didion, Penelope Mortimer, Alison Lurie, Doris Betts, Nadine Gordimer, Muriel Spark, Lael Wertenbaker, Maxine Kumin, Lore Segal, Alice Walker, Mary Gray Hughes, Sallie Bingham, Maureen Howard, Norma Rosen, Diane Johnson, Alta, Susan Griffin, Helen Yglesias. Some wrote before children, some only in the middle or late years afterward. Not many, so far, have used the material open to them out of motherhood as central source for their writing.

their children. Even those who can afford help, good schools, summer camps, may suffer what seventy years ago W. E. B. Du Bois called The Damnation of Women: "that only at the sacrifice of the chance to do their best work can women bear and rear children."

Substantial creative achievement demands time . . . and with rare exceptions only full-time workers have created it.[9]

I am quoting myself from "Silences,"[10] a talk nine years ago. In motherhood, as it is structured,

circumstances for sustained creation are almost impossible. Not because the capacities to create no longer exist, or the need (though for a while as in any fullness of life the need may be obscured), but . . . the need cannot be first. It can have at best only part self, part time. . . . Motherhood means being instantly interruptible, responsive, responsible. Children need one *now* (and remember, in our society, the family must often try to be the center for love and health the outside world is not). The very fact that these are needs of love, not duty, that one feels them as one's self; that there is no one else to be responsible for these needs, gives them primacy. It is distraction, not meditation, that becomes habitual; interruption, not continuity; spasmodic, not constant, toil. Work interrupted, deferred, postponed makes blockage—at best, lesser accomplishment. Unused capacities atrophy, cease to be.

There are other vulnerabilities to loss, diminishment. Rare is the woman writer who has not had bred into her what Virginia Woolf called "The Angel in the House," who "must charm, sympathize, conciliate . . . be extremely sensitive to the needs and moods and wishes of others before her own . . . excel in the difficult arts of family life."

It was she who used to come between me and my paper . . . who bothered me and wasted my time and so tormented me that at last I killed her . . . or she would have plucked out my heart as a writer.[11]

There is another angel, so lowly as to be invisible, although without her no art, or any human endeavor could be carried on for even one day—the essential angel, with whom Virginia Woolf (and most women writers, still in the privileged class) did not have to contend—the angel who must assume the physical responsibilities for daily living, for the maintenance of life.

Almost always in one form or another (usually in the wife, two-angel form) she has dwelt in the house of men. She it was who made it possible for Joseph Conrad to "wrestle with the Lord for his creation":

[9] This does not mean those full-time writers were hermetic or denied themselves social or personal life (think of James, Turgenev, Tolstoy, Balzac, Joyce). Nor did they, except perhaps at the flood, put in as many hours daily as those doing more usual kinds of work. Four hours daily has been the norm. Full-timeness is not in the actual number of hours at one's desk but in that writing is one's major profession practiced habitually in protected, undistracted time as needed, when it is needed.
[10] Reprinted in *Harper's*, October 1965.
[11] "Professions for Women," *Collected Essays*.

Mind and will and conscience engaged to the full, hour after hour, day after day . . . never aware of the even flow of daily life made easy and noiseless for me by a silent, watchful, tireless affection.

The angel who was "essential" to Rilke's "great task":

like a sister who would run the house like a friendly climate, there or not there as one wished . . . and would ask for nothing except just to be there working and warding at the frontiers of the invisible.

Men (even part-time writers who must carry on work other than writing[12]) have had and have this inestimable advantage towards productivity. I cannot help but notice how curiously absent both of these angels, these watchers and warders at the frontiers of the invisible, are from the actual contents of most men's books, except perhaps on the dedication page:

> To my wife, without whom. . . .

Mailer made clear that as a writer he was not so much a prisoner of sex as of service—supportive, secretarial, household.

I digress, and yet I do not; the disregard for the essential angel, the large absence of any sense of her in literature or elsewhere, has not only cost literature great contributions from those so occupied or partially occupied, but by failing to help create an arousing awareness (as literature has done in other realms) has contributed to the agonizingly slow elimination of this technologically and socially obsolete, human-wasting drudgery. Recall Virginia Woolf's dream of a long since possible

economical, powerful and efficient future when houses will be cleaned by a puff of hot wind.

Sometimes the essential angel is present in women's books, though still most "heroines are in white dresses that never need washing." (Rebecca Harding Davis' phrase of 100 years ago.) Some poets admit her as occasional domestic image; a few preen her as femininity; Sylvia Plath could escape her only by suicide:

. . . flying . . .
Over the engine that killed her
The mausoleum, the wax house.

For the first time in literary history, a woman writer of stature, accustomed through years to the habits of creation, began to live the life of most of her sex, the honey drudgers: that winged unmiraculous two-angel, whirled mother-maintenance life that most women, not privileged, know. A situation without help or husband and with 24 hour responsibility for two small human lives whom she adored and at their most fascinating and demanding. The world was blood hot and personal. Creation's needs at its height. She had to get up at

[12] As do many women writers.

four in the morning, that still blue almost eternal hour before the
baby's cry

to write at all. After the long expending day, tending, eating, cleaning,
enjoying, laundering, feeding, marketing, delighting, outing, being

a very efficient tool or weapon, used and in demand from moment to
moment. . . . Nights (were) no good (for writing). I'm so flat by then
that all I can cope with is music and brandy and water.

The smog of cooking, the smog of hell floated her head. The smile
of the icebox annihilated. There was stink of fat and baby crap;
viciousness in the kitchen! And the blood jet poetry (for which there
was never time and self except in that still blue hour before the baby's
cry), there was no stopping it.[13]

It is not a question in these last weeks of the conflict in a woman's
life between the claims of the feminine and the agonized work of art.

—Elizabeth Hardwick, a woman, can say of Sylvia Plath's suicide—

Every artist is either a man or woman, and the struggle is pretty much
the same for both.

Comments as insensible of the two-angel realities ("so lowly as to be
invisible") as are the oblivious masculine assumptions either that the
suicide was because of Daddy's death 23 years before, revived by her
husband's desertion; or a real life Story of O, that elegant pornog-
raphy, sacramental culmination of being used up by ecstasy (poetry
in place of sex this time):

the pride of an utter and ultimate surrender like the pride of O naked
and chained in her owl mask as she asks Sir Stephen for death.[14]

If in such an examined extremity, the profound realities of woman's
situation are ignored, how much less likely are they—particularly the
subtler ones—to be seen, comprehended, taken into account, as they
affect lesser known women writers in more usual circumstances.

In younger years, confidence and vision leeched, aspiration reduced.
In adult years, sporadic effort and unfinished work; women made
"mediocre caretakers" of their talent: that is, writing is not first. The
angel in the house situation; probably also the essential angel, main-
tenance-of-life one; increasingly in our century, the need to earn
one's living at a paid job; and for more and more women writers the
whirled expending motherhood years. Is it so difficult to account for
the many occasional-fine-story or one-book writers; the distinguished
but limited production of others (Janet Lewis, Ann Petry, for example); the slowly increasing numbers of women who when in their
forties, fifties, sixties, publish for the first time (Dorothy Richardson;
Hortense Calisher; Theodora Kroeber; Linda Hoyer, Updike's mother;
Laura Ingalls Wilder; Elizabeth Madox Roberts); the women who start

[13] Phrases, lines, quoted throughout from Plath poetry, letters, or talks.
[14] Richard Howard, in Charles Newman, ed., in *The Art of Sylvia Plath.*

modestly with children's, girls' books (Maxine Kumin); some like Cid Ricketts Sumner (the Tammy books) seldom or never getting to adult fiction that would encompass their wisdom; and most of all the unsatisfactory quality of book after book that evidences the marks of part-time, part-self authorship, and to whose authors Sarah Orne Jewett's words to the part-time, part-self (because of a job) young Willa Cather still apply seventy years after:

If you don't keep and mature your force and above all have time and quiet to perfect your work, you will be writing things not much better than you did five years ago. . . . Otherwise, what might be strength is only crudeness, and what might be insight is only observation. You will write about life, but never life itself.

Yes, the loss in quality, the minor work, the hidden silences are there in woman after woman writer in our century. We will never have the body of work that we were capable of producing. Blight, said Blake, never does good to a tree:

And if a blight kill not a tree but it still bear fruit, say not the fruit was in consequence of the blight, but in spite of it.

As for myself, who did not publish a book until I was 50, who raised children without household help or the help of the "technological sublime" (the atom bomb was in manufacture before the first automatic washing machine); who worked outside the house on everyday jobs as well (as nearly half of all women do now, though a woman with a paid job, except as a maid, is rarest of any in literature); who could not kill the essential angel (there was no one else to do her work); would not—if I could—have killed the caring part of the Woolf angels—as distant from the world of literature most of my life as literature is distant (in content too) from my world.

The years when I should have been writing, my hands and being were at other (inescapable) tasks. Now, lightened as they are, when I must do those tasks into which most of my life went (like the old mother, grandmother in my *Tell Me a Riddle* who could not make herself touch a baby), I pay a psychic cost: "the sweat beads, the long shudder begins." The habits of a lifetime when everything else had to come before writing are not easily broken, even when circumstances now often make it possible for the writing to be first; habits of years: response to others, distractibility, responsibility for daily matters, stay with you, mark you, become you. The cost of "discontinuity" (that pattern still imposed on women) is such a weight of things unsaid, an accumulation of material so great, that everything starts up something else in me; what should take weeks, takes me sometimes months to write; what should take months, takes years.

I speak of myself to bring here the sense of those others to whom this is in the process of happening (unnecessarily happening, for it need not, must not continue to be) and to remind us of those (I so nearly was one) who never come to writing at all.

We cannot speak of women writers in our century (as we cannot speak of women in any area of human achievement) without speaking also

of the invisible, the as innately capable: the born to the wrong circumstances, the diminished, the excluded, the lost, the silenced.

We who write are survivors, "onlys."[15] *One—out of twelve.*

I must go very fast now, telescope and omit (there has already been
so much telescoping and omitting), move to work, professional
circumstances.

Devaluation: Still in our century, women's books of great worth suffer
the death of being unknown, or at best a peculiar eclipsing, far out-
numbering the similar fate of the few such books by men: I think of
Kate Chopin, Mary Austin, Dorothy Richardson, Henry Handel Richardson (*Ultima Thule*), Jean Rhys, Storm Jameson, Christina Stead,
Elizabeth Madox Roberts (*Time of Man*), Janet Lewis, May Sarton,
Harriette Arnow (*The Dollmaker*), Agnes Smedley (*Daughter of
Earth*), Djuna Barnes (*Nightwood*), Kay Boyle, every one of whom is
rewarding, and some with the stamp of enduring.[16] Considering their
stature, how comparatively unread, untaught are Glasgow, Glaspell,
Bowen, Parker, Stein, Mansfield—even Cather and Porter.

Critical attitudes: Two centuries after, still what Cynthia Ozick calls
"the perpetual dancing dog phenomena,"[17] the injurious reacting to
a book not for its quality or content, but on the basis of its having
been written by a woman, with consequent misreading, mistreatment.
Read Mary Ellmann's inimitable *Thinking About Women*.

One addition to the "she writes like a man," "with masculine power"
kind of "praise." Power is not recognized as the power it is at all if
the subject matter is considered women's: it is minor, moving, evocative, instinctive, delicate. "As delicate as a surgeon's scalpel," says
Katherine Anne Porter of such a falsifying description for Katherine
Mansfield's art. Instinctive?

I judge her work to have been to a great degree a matter of intelligent
use of her faculties, a conscious practice of a hard-won craftsmanship,
a triumph of discipline. . . .[18]

Climate in literary circles for those who move in them:[19] writers
know the importance of respect for one's vision and integrity; of the
comradeship of other writers; of being dealt with as a writer on the
basis of one's work and not for other reasons; how chancy is recog-

[15] For myself, "survivor" contains its other meaning: one who must bear
witness to those who foundered; tell how and why it was that they,
also worthy of life, did not also survive.
[16] This was 1971. At least some of these writers are now coming out of
eclipse. But Glaspell and H. H. Richardson are still out of print. So
is most of Christina Stead.
  I would now add to this list Edith Summers Kelley and Cora Sandel (the
incomparable *Alberta* trilogy), writers unknown to me then. And Anzia
Yezierska, whose books I have lent, taught, tried to get republished. Her
The Bread Giver is now again in print.
[17] "Women and Creativity," *Motive*, April 1969.
[18] "The Art of Katherine Mansfield" in *The Collected Essays of Katherine
Anne Porter.*
[19] Read Carolyn Kizer's "Pro-Femina" in *Knock upon Silence*.

nition and getting published. There is no time to speak of this today; but nearly all writers who are women are at a disadvantage here.

Restriction: For all our freer life in this century—our significantly greater access to work, education, travel, varied experience—there is still limitation of circumstances for scope, subject, social context, the kind of comprehensions which come only in situations beyond the private. What Charlotte Brontë felt so keenly 125 years ago as a denial of "facilities for observation . . . a knowledge of the world," which gives other writers, "Thackeray, Dickens . . . an importance, variety, depth greatly beyond what I can offer."[20] "Trespass vision" cannot substitute.

Constriction: not always recognized as constriction. The age-old coercion of women towards one dimension continues to be "terribly, determiningly" present. Women writers are still suspect as unnatural if they concern themselves with aspects of their experience, interests, being, beyond the traditionally defined women's sphere. Hortense Calisher is troubled that women writers

straining toward a world sensibility, or one equivalent to the roaming conscience of the men . . . or dispens[ing] with whatever was clearly female in their sensibility or experience . . . flee from the image society projects on her.[21]

But consciences and world sensibility are as natural to women as to men; men have been freer to develop and exercise them, that is all. Indeed, one of the most characteristic strains in literature written by women (however dropped out of sight, or derided) *is* conscience, concern with wrongs to human beings in their time—from the first novel in our language by a woman, Aphra Behn's *Oroonoko*, that first by anyone against slavery, through Harriet Martineau, Elizabeth Gaskell, George Sand, Harriet Beecher Stowe, Elizabeth Barrett Browning, Rebecca Harding Davis, Helen Hunt Jackson, Olive Schreiner, Charlotte Perkins Gilman, Ethel Voynich, to our own century's Gabriela Mistral, Nelly Sachs, Anna Seghers, Rachel Carson, Lillian Hellman, Lorraine Hansberry, Theodora Kroeber (*Ishi*), Agnes Smedley, Harriette Arnow, Doris Lessing, Nadine Gordimer, Sylvia Ashton-Warner.

In contradiction to the compass of her own distinguished fiction, Calisher defines the "basic female experience from puberty on through childbed" as women's natural subject:

For myself the feminism that comes straight from the belly, from the bed, and from childbed. A sensibility trusting itself for what it is, as the other half of human life.

The stereotypic biological woman (breeder, sex partner) sphere. False to reality. Not only leaving out (what men writers usually leave out) ongoing motherhood, maintenance of life, and the angel in the house so determiningly the basic experience of most women once they get

[20] Letter to her publisher, W. S. Williams, 1849.
[21] "No Important Woman Writer . . . ," *Mademoiselle*, February 1970.

out of bed and up from childbed, but other common female realities as well.[22]

And it leaves out the rest of women's biological endowment as born human (including the creative capacity out of which women and men write). It was the denial of this capacity to live the whole of human life, the confinement of woman to a sphere, that brought the women's rights movement into being in the last century—feminism born of humanism—and that prevented our Calishers from writing throughout centuries.

The acceptance of the age-old coercive, restrictive definitions of woman at a time when it is less true than ever to the realities of most women's lives—and need not be true at all—remains a complex problem for women writing in our time. Mary Wollstonecraft defined it as "the consciousness of being always woman which degrades our sex."

So Anaïs Nin: accepting the constriction to a "feminine sensibility that would not threaten man." Dwelling in the private, the inner: endless vibrations of mood; writing what was muted, exquisite, sensuous, subterranean. That is, in her fiction. In her *Journals*, the public, the social; power of characterization, penetrating observation, hard intellect, range of experience and relationship, different beauties. Qualities and complexities not present in her fiction—to its impoverishment.

"The Bold New Women," to use another example, this from the title of a recent anthology, are the old old women, allowing themselves to be confined within the literary, bed-partner, biological-woman ghetto; mistaking themselves as new because the sex is explicit (current male genre); the style and conception of female sexuality, Lawrentian or Milleresque. "Whole areas of me are made by the kind of experience women haven't had before," reminds Doris Lessing. "Liberty is the right not to lie," says Camus.

These pressures toward censorship, self-censorship—towards accepting, abiding by dominant attitudes, thus falsifying one's own reality, range, vision, truth, voice—are extreme for women writers. (Indeed they have much to do with the fear, the sense of powerlessness that pervades some of our books; the "above all, amuse, clown, be entertaining" tone of others.) Not to be able to come to one's truth[23] or not to use it in one's writing, even when telling the truth having to "tell it slant," robs one of drive, of conviction; limits potential stature; results in loss to literature and the comprehensions we seek in it.

---

[22] Among them: what goes on in jobs; penalties of aging; children and the having to raise them in a world in which they are "no miracles at all"; what it is to live as a single woman having to raise children alone; causes, besides the accepted psychiatric ones, of breakdown in women; the cost of vicarious living; ways in which human capacities (organization, art, intellect, invention, resistance to harm, community) denied development and scope, still manifest themselves. The list goes on and on.

[23] Compounding the difficulty, experiences and comprehensions not previously admitted into literature—especially when at variance with the canon—are exceedingly hard to come to, validate, establish as legitimate material for literature—let alone shape for art.

My time is up.

You who teach, read writers who are women. There is a whole literature to be re-estimated, re-valued. Some works will prove to be, like the lives of their human authors, mortal—speaking only to their time. Others now forgotten, obscured, ignored, will live again for us.

Read, listen to, living women writers; our new as well as our established, often neglected ones. Not to have audience is a kind of death.

Read the compass of women writers in our infinite variety. Not only those who tell us of ourselves as "the other half," but also those who write of the other human dimensions, realms.

Teach women's lives through the lives of women who wrote the books, as well as through their books; and through autobiography, biography, journals, letters. Because most literature concerns itself with the lives of the few, know and teach the few books closer to most female lives. It should not be that Harriette Arnow's *The Dollmaker*, Elizabeth Madox Roberts's *Time of Man*, Grace Paley's *Little Disturbances* are out of paperback print; that a Zora Neale Hurston is reprinted for the first time; that Agnes Smedley's classic *Daughter of Earth*, has been out of print, unread, unknown, for forty years (a book of the greatest meaning, too, for those many students who are the first generation of their families to come into college).[24]

Be critical. Women have the right to say: This is surface, this falsifies reality, this degrades.

Help create writers, perhaps among them yourselves. There is so much unwritten that needs to be written. There are more than the other eleven, silent, who could write, bringing into literature what is not there now. That first generation in the colleges who come from my world, which in Camus' words gives "emotion without measure," are a special hope for literature. It does not matter if in its beginning it is not great, or even always good, writing.

Whether that is literature, or whether that is not literature, I will not presume to say,

wrote Virginia Woolf in her preface to *Memoirs of the Working Women's Guild*,

but that it explains much and tells much, that is certain.

The greatness of literature is not only in the great writers, the good writers; it is also in that which explains much and tells much; the soil from which greater writers burgeon. Hopefully, before the end of our second writing century, we will begin to have writers who are women in numbers equal to our innate capacity—at least twelve for every one woman writer able to come to recognized achievement now.[25]

[24] Now, in 1977, these are all back in print.
[25] And for every twelve, remember the countless others, still half of them women, silenced by the other age-old silencers of humanity, class (economic circumstance) and/or color.

Carson McCullers (1917–1967)

A sense of time pervades the fiction of Carson McCullers. Her portrayal of adolescence and the attempt to leap the seeming chasm between the two worlds of childhood and adulthood incorporates not only this sense of time, but also a sensitivity to the initiation process for the young girl. Carson, born Lula Carson Smith, grew up in Columbus, Georgia, a sleepy town like those in which other Southern writers have lived. It was a town where nothing happened, a town characterized by lazy warm days, a town where the inner world of the imagination would have to be the center of focus.

McCullers's first strong artistic leaning was toward music. Indeed, she went to New York after high school to study music, hoping to become a concert pianist. This early training in, and appreciation of, music is evident throughout her writing: in content, as in the story "Wunderkind"; in theme—as the term is in music—to suggest, to develop, and to resolve; and finally in her language, which bears the mark of an ear sensitive to prose and sounds.

As she suggests in "How I Began to Write," her early writing was derivative and ambitious (for example, the play about Jesus and Neitzsche), but "Sucker," a story written in her mid-teens, suggests the later promise of her finest work, like "The Ballad of the Sad Café." Her young heroines, Mick in *The Heart Is a Lonely Hunter* and Frankie Adams in *The Member of the Wedding*, suggest the tomboyish Carson whose imagination and sensitivity led to a restlessness for wider experience than the narrow range that Columbus could give her. She made the most, however, of the limitations of Southern life; like Flannery O'Connor and Eudora Welty she captures the essence of her surroundings, the sound of Southern speech, the sense of the black world (as much as a young white girl could glean from conversations on dull afternoons with the black housemaids who worked for the Smiths), and the realization of the sting of poverty, dramatized for her as she watched cotton-mill workers pass her house.

In New York her interest turned to writing, and she took courses at Columbia University. In Part Two, "Instant of the Hour After," though not unconditionally praised by her teacher in the paragraph that follows it, illustrates the themes of time and loneliness as well as her ability to create images. Further, it is the story of young love mixed with the desire for intellectual growth. Carson married Reeves McCullers, moved South with him, and then divorced him.

When she was only twenty-two, she wrote *The Heart Is a Lonely Hunter*, the beautiful and sensitive story of a deaf-mute, an adolescent girl, and life in a small Southern town. Her writing career was launched, but she began to be plagued by strokes at the early age of twenty-three; sight impairment, partial paralysis, and breast cancer followed. She remarried McCullers, who later committed suicide. Although her life was filled with illness and painful personal trials, she continued to create: the force of her talent would not let her rest.

Notable among her works are two collections, *The Mortgaged Heart* and *The Ballad of the Sad Café*. *The Member of the Wedding* (adapted as a play) and the play *The Square Root of Wonderful* were both produced on Broadway. Her other novels include *Clock Without Hands* and *Reflections in a Golden Eye*, a portrayal of life on an army base.

How I Began to Write

In our old Georgia home we used to have two sitting-rooms—a back one and a front one—with folding doors between. These were the family living-rooms and the theatre of my shows. The front sitting-room was the auditorium, the back sitting-room the stage. The sliding doors the curtain. In wintertime the firelight flickered dark and glowing on the walnut doors, and in the last strained moments before the curtain you noticed the ticking of the clock on the mantlepiece, the old tall clock with the glass front of painted swans. In summertime the rooms were stifling until the time for curtain, and the clock was silenced by sounds of yard-boy whistling and distant radios. In winter, frost flowers bloomed on the windowpanes (the winters in Georgia are very cold), and the rooms were drafty, quiet. The open summer lifted the curtains with each breeze, and there were the smells of sun-hot flowers and, toward twilight, watered grass. In winter we had cocoa after the show and in summer orange crush or lemonade. Winter and summer the cakes were always the same. They were made by Lucille, the cook we had in those days, and I have never tasted cakes as good as those cakes we used to have. The secret of their goodness lay, I believe, in the fact that they were always cakes that failed. They were chocolate raisin cupcakes that did not rise, so that there was no proper cupcake cap—the cakes were dank, flat and dense with raisins. The charm of those cakes was altogether accidental.

As the eldest child in our family I was the custodian, the counter of the cakes, the boss of all our shows. The repertory was eclectic, running from hashed-over movies to Shakespeare and shows I made up and sometimes wrote down in my nickle Big Chief notebooks. The cast was everlastingly the same—my younger brother, Baby Sister and myself. The cast was the most serious handicap. Baby Sister was in those days a stomachy ten-year old who was terrible in death scenes, fainting spells and such-like necessary parts. When Baby Sister swooned to a sudden death she would prudently look around beforehand and fall very carefully on sofa or chair. (Once, I remember, such a death fall broke both legs of one of Mama's favorite chairs.)

As director of the shows I could put up with terrible acting, but there was one thing I simply could not stand. Sometimes, after coaching and drilling half the afternoon, the actors would decide to abandon the whole project just before curtain time and wander out into the yard to play. "I struggle and work on a show all afternoon, and now you run out on me," I would yell, past endurance at these times. "You're nothing but children! Children! I've got a good mind to shoot you dead." But they only gulped the drinks and ran out with the cakes.

The props were impromptu, limited only by Mama's modest interdictions. The top drawer of the linen closet was out of bounds and we had to make do with second-best towels and tablecloths and sheets in the plays that called for nurses, nuns and ghosts.

The sitting-room shows ended when first I discovered Eugene O'Neill. It was the summer when I found his books down in the library and put his picture on the mantlepiece in the back sitting-room. By autumn I was writing a three-acter about revenge and incest—the curtain rose on a graveyard and, after scenes of assorted misery, fell on a catafalque. The cast consisted of a blind man, several idiots and a mean old woman of one hundred years. The play was impractical for performance under the old conditions in the sitting-rooms. I gave what I called a "reading" to my patient parents and a visiting aunt.

Next, I believe, it was Nietzsche and a play called *The Fire of Life*. The play had two characters—Jesus Christ and Friedrich Nietzsche—and the point I prized about the play was that it was written in verses that rhymed. I gave a reading of this play, too, and afterward the children came in from the yard, and we drank cocoa and ate the fallen, lovely raisin cakes in the back sitting-room by the fire. "Jesus?" my aunt asked when she was told. "Well, religion is a nice subject anyway."

By that winter the family rooms, the whole town, seemed to pinch and cramp my adolescent heart. I longed for wanderings. I longed especially for New York. The firelight on the walnut folding doors would sadden me, and the tedious sound of the old swan clock. I dreamed of the distant city of skyscrapers and snow, and New York was the happy mise en scène of that first novel I wrote when I was fifteen years old. The details of the book were queer: ticket collectors on the subway, New York front yards—but by that time it did not matter, for already I had begun another journey. That was the year of Dostoevski, Chekhov and Tolstoy—and there were the intimations of an unsuspected region equidistant from New York. Old Russia and our Georgia rooms, the marvelous solitary region of simple stories and the inward mind.

Gwendolyn Brooks *(b. 1917)*

Gwendolyn Brooks's career as a poet spans not only several decades but also several changes in consciousness, black consciousness in particular. Born in Topeka, Kansas, moving to Chicago soon after, she grew up in a warm family. Her biography, *Report from Part One,* describes the supportive and funloving atmosphere of her childhood. But in recounting family celebrations, she mentions that no celebration in her household or any black household she knew featured "any black glory or black greatness or grandeur." Her education and poetic sensibilities were those of Western culture. This background confirmed her as a youthful integrationist, convinced that human concerns were universal.

Her early books of poetry, *A Street in Bronzeville* and *Annie Allen,* were written in this spirit. The latter won her the Pulitzer Prize in 1950, the first time a black was so honored. With this recognition she had access to a larger audience, black and white. A novel, *Maud Martha,* followed in 1953. Her 1960 collection, *The Bean Eaters,* shows her particular sensitivity to black women's lives, as the poems in Part Two of this volume reflect.

In 1967, Gwendolyn Brooks first experienced the "new black," at the Fisk University Writers' Conference in Nashville. The assertive confidence and militant spirit she saw there deeply affected her writing and her life priorities. *In the Mecca,* published the following year, reflected Brooks's new African consciousness. She ran a writing workshop for a teen-age gang in Chicago, the Blackstone Rangers, and was active in the Black Arts movement; in 1971 she traveled to East Africa. All these experiences developed her black consciousness. But Brooks does not imitate the young black voice: she has extended her own range, which remains unique in contemporary literature.

The selections that follow, from *Report from Part One,* include some reflections on her art and, in Sources and Illuminations, ideas that she developed into poems, for example, "Bronzeville Woman in a Red Hat" in Part Two.

Report from Part One

So much is involved in the writing of poetry—and sometimes, although I don't like suggesting it is a magic process, it seems you really do have to go into a *bit* of trance, self-cast trance, because "brainwork" seems unable to do it all, to do the whole job. The self-cast trance is possible when you are *importantly* excited about an idea, or surmise, or emotion.

→》》   《《←

My aim, in my next future, is to write poems that will somehow successfully "call" (see Imamu Baraka's "SOS") all black people: black people in tavens, black people in alleys, black people in gutters, schools, offices, factories, prisons, the consulate; I wish to reach black people in pulpits, black people in mines, on farms, on thrones; *not* always to "teach"—I shall wish often to entertain, to illumine. My newish voice will not be an imitation of the contemporary young black voice, which I so admire, but an extending adaptation of today's G. B. voice.

SOURCES AND ILLUMINATIONS:

The Mother

Hardly your crowned and praised and "customary" Mother; but a Mother not unfamiliar, who decides that *she,* rather than her World, will kill her children. The decision is not nice, not simple, and the emotional consequences are neither nice nor simple.

A Sunset of the City

Here a woman faces the fact of her middle age. She is resentful. Love of all kinds, she feels, is gone forever. She shivers. She knows it is fall, and that winter is on the way. She feels done and dusty as she stands among the echoes of her past—echoes from which all the vitality and richness, even the richness of life's debris, have been cruelly scrubbed away. She hurries through her prayers because she feels they are no longer of use; there will be no answers. What courses are open to her? Inside her is a tin (Communication of suspect consequence) whispering: she may subscribe to simple Grieflessness— to deserthood. Do nothing. Feel nothing. Desire nothing. She considers: is "humming pallor" a better fate than death?

This is, she decides wildly, more than a mere mishandling *by* the Fates! This is a monstrous joke, herself the victim.

To a Winter Squirrel

Years ago, when we were *poor*-poor, we would sometimes run out of coal. I would turn on the gas stove, sit down on a stool beside it, and prop my legs up on the lid. While thus hoisted, a book and a cup of tea forbade self-pity.

Boy Breaking Glass

Marc Crawford asked me to consider: How ghetto blacks, over-whelmed by inequity and white power, manage to live. Does a black boy, for example, turn his eyes away from the Statue of Liberty? How does he talk to himself, comfort himself? What Beauties are at his disposal?

We Real Cool

The ending WEs in "We Real Cool" are tiny, wispy, weakly argumen-tative "Kilroy-is-here" announcements. The boys have no accented sense of themselves, yet they are aware of a semi-defined personal importance. Say the "We" softly.

The Crazy Woman

A simple song pointing out only that there are those who do not bloom in the flowery light, but actually cry up to Novemberish dark-ness. The "reverse" ones. The deflected ones.

Bronzeville Woman in a Red Hat

The cramped, the narrow, but the sublimely confident Mrs. Miles hires, for the first time, a black maid. The abrupt departure of her troubled Irish maid (whom she did not pay well EITHER) has occa-sioned this Descent.

This outrageous maid actually kisses the cream-colored child of su-perior Mrs. Miles. *And on the mouth.* Surely the world will end now.

She does not like to admit that she hates the whole "Negro" race, so she pretends to herself that she is merely concerned for her child's health.

Strangely, in spite of the kiss, the world does not come to an end. Serenity marks the child, the servant, and the kitchen towels.

The Ballad of Rudolph Reed

A man who has wanted to improve his family's environment moves into a previously all-white neighborhood. His neighbors are horrified by this intrusion. There is violence, and he is killed.

Main feature—the great yearning of man-in-misery for betterment, and his eventual irresistible reach for it.

Today, the general black decision would be that bandages are not enough.

The Egg Boiler

The speaker finds substance in what the listener regards as substance-lessness: art, music, literature, thought, anything of beauty, of charm, of a non-material significance. The listener is satisfied entirely by the mundane—as represented by the carefully prepared egg—and laughs mightily at those of a different persuasion.

A Man of the Middle Class

He, now a man neither poor nor rich, is "what" ran out into life with such high hopes and determinations. He *found* fruit, too, but somehow

the fruit was not its own answer. He got it by living a life of "care"—
he has never frankly exposed himself, truly fought, truly stuck his
neck out in dedication to any beautiful belief. He is semi-splendid
now (see list of his symbols) but somehow he totters, is lax, is inadequate. Even his best labor is implicit with grudges against the World.
His steady material progress does not fundamentally satisfy him, does
not seem to satisfy his LABOR (that its expenditures are worthwhile)
or his usual methods of pleasure-seeking and escape (that seem not
real).

He appears to himself ineffectual.

Moreover, the "eminent" ones, the eminent successes of the society,
whose rules and steps he imitated, seem no more in possession of the
Answers than he; excellent examples of dimness, moral softness and
confusion, they are shooting themselves and jumping out of windows.

The Sonnet Ballad

Its one claim to fame is that I invented it. (My other inventor's claim
to fame is *verse journalism:* "In Montgomery," a seven-page piece
of verse journalism, is in the August, 1971 issue of *Ebony*.)

A Light and Diplomatic Bird

Valhalla: where my strifes, like heroes, may lie at last to rest.

Wanted: Peace!—A resting-place in my heart for all my strifes, a
place where those strifes may sleep.

An Aspect of Love,
Alive in the Ice and Fire (See *Riot*)

I had to remove the first line—"It is the morning of our love"—when
Carolyn Rodgers called to tell me she had found it opening a Rod
McKuen poem in *Listen to the Warm*. Even though I wrote mine
first!—as can be seen in the hard-cover edition of *Riot*, which includes
a dated script-version of the poem. Such a horror is every writer's
nightmare. Poets, doubt any "inevitability."

Riders to the Blood-Red Wrath

The Riders in "Riders to the Blood-Red Wrath" (speaking in a personalized voice) are the Freedom Riders, and their fellows the sit-ins,
the wade-ins, read-ins, pray-ins, vote-ins, and all related strugglers
for what is realiably right. Here is the substance of the twelve-stanza
poem:

Stanza One They—the "segregationists," etc.—watched my behavior
(which was only right, only proper) with astonishment. My behavior
(my risks, my dangerous insistence on my rights as a citizen and my
efforts to obtain them) seemed naughty—contrived—impolite—vulgar—overmuch.

"Charger"—the *feelings* that I rode (think of a spirited horse!): The
expert way I *controlled* my feelings (which, after all, had every right
to be semi-"vicious") escaped them. They did not see, did not care
what personal expense, what mental, what emotional expense I went
to, in order to control my basic fury or resentment. All they could

see was their ancient set of traditions, the old patterns of prejudice, the "old days." These traditions were a sort of art—(they were certainly *not* the manifestations of *nature*)—developed; moulded; decorated. Death, not health, is at the center of their memories. They continue to twitch their eyes to adoration of their old prejudice-traditions. They loudly turn themselves away from a "tolerance" of my "birth."

Stanza Two   "The National Anthem" etc.: I still love this country. I stand for its *stated principles,* still. Right now I am fighting in the interests of the principles of my country. I am *not* behaving boldly; as I said before, I am in control of myself. My fight is a *tenderly* grand one, a *tied* (restricted) one.

My unedited scream is *under* my pleasant presentation. I've *got* guns (of rage, of justified resentment, that is) but I've *sewn up* my rage— my guns—inside my lips, which you can scarcely blame for burning.

Stanza Three   Have they noticed me asking myself wild questions and giving myself calmed-down answers? Absolutely not. They have not noticed that my "charger"—that is, my fury, my "revolution"— has pushed a softer horse ("his twin the mare") in front of him. This soft *mask* does the official talking, the official behaving. Of course, even my *mildness* has a various nature. It is not as pleasant as it looks. In goes my mildness, however, of what*ever* composition; into important skirmish after skirmish goes my mild facade, and these little acts in *themselves* have been enough to cause the "segregationists," gentlemen and gentlewomen all, to forget their gentlehood and commit crimes against God Himself.

Stanza Four   Ah, if only they knew how much I bear, how *well* I bear injustices that would have offended great Christ. I remember all the cruelties in my past. Although (because I now have more determination, more knowledge) they do not daily stick in my craw as they formerly did, when I could do nothing or little about them.

I, as The Black a-down History, remember kings, palaces, silver, ivory, African wealth. I remember old freedom—old free joy or old free misery. Old freedom.

Stanza Five   And I remember the slave trade—*my* side of it.

Stanza Six   I remember slavery itself, my subjugation, my criminal reduction.

Stanza Seven   Still—although I may be excused for not glorifying in this—the terrors, the sufferings of my past have honed me into a better human being. I grind my raw sufferings into a refined glass that enables me to get a good look at man's GENERAL inhumanity. Inhumanity is rampant everywhere.

Stanza Eight   The cruelty that has been practiced on me has been practiced in Europe, China, India . . .

Stanza Nine   This awareness drives me to a marvelous determination: *I* shall revere, esteem, *respect* what is human (and hardly human).

Stanza Ten   Democracy and Christianity will re-begin with *me*.

Stanza Eleven   And as for my Freedom Ride—both figurative and physical—it shall go on interminably; it shall go on until it is no longer necessary.

Stanza Twelve   I'll not be alone. My black fellow-strugglers, and our white sympathizers in this awkward, fundamentally ridiculous struggle which is in the interests of love in the largest sense, will ride on into whatever awaits us at whatever Calvary. Perhaps we shall fail. Perhaps we shall not. But, whatever Destiny has in mind, nothing shall prevent our effort, our lurch, our ride.

Afternote   What changes twelve years have secured, in self and society. I could not write—in 1972—this poem as it stands.

Work Proposed for "In the Mecca"

A book-length poem, two thousand lines or more, based on life in Chicago's old Mecca Building.

This poem will not be a statistical report. I'm interested in a certain detachment, but only as a means of reaching substance with some incisiveness. I wish to present a large variety of personalities against a mosaic of daily affairs, recognizing that the *grimmest* of these is likely to have a streak or two streaks of sun.

In the Mecca were murders, loves, lonelinesses, hates, jealousies. Hope occurred, and charity, sainthood, glory, shame, despair, fear, altruism. Theft, material and moral. "Mental cruelty."

Mouse and moth.

To touch every note in the life of this block-long block-wide building would be to capsulize the gist of black humanity in general. (How many people lived there? Some say a thousand, some say two thousand.)

Writing tools are to include random rhyme, off-rhyme, a long-swinging free verse, blank verse, prose verse. The couplet, the sonnet, the ballad. . . .

What high hopes I had for "In the Mecca!" What strict personal expectations. In my sheaf of plans:

1. Uninterrupted flow of review.
2. Long sentences.
3. Story on top of story.
4. Music.
5. Color.
6. Marginalia: phrase-titles, brief and few, at right margin.
8. Savagery, cruelty, horror.
9. Mystery.

It is to be Leisurely and massive. A long wandering tale.

It is to have Characters that grow and surprise. Rich humor, horror. Mastery of "style." Subtle wit. Social width.

And I wanted an end-stanza to end all end-stanzas! Directions To Myself—End-stanza like the self-pacification of the sea, after wild threshing.

Maud Martha

An autobiographical novel, I believe, is a better testament, a better thermometer, than a memoir can be. Who, in presenting a "factual" account, is going to tell the absolute, the inclusive, the horrifying or exquisite, the "incredible Truth?" One wishes to spare—to spare others and one's self. May not one add, multiply, subtract?—without wanting to. But an "autobigraphical novel" is nunceful, allowing. There's fact-meat in the soup, among the chunks of fancy: but, generally, definite identifications will be difficult.

Maud Martha, my one novel, is not autobigraphical in the usual sense. Much that happened to Maud Martha has not happened to me— and she is a nicer and a better coordinated creature than I am. But it is true that much in the "story" was taken out of my own life, and twisted, highlighted or dulled, dressed up or down.

Lolling through the chapters, I remind myself that in "description of 'Maud Martha' " the heroine loves dandelions, as "what she chiefly saw . . . and it was comforting to find that what was common could also be a flower."

I used to sit on the 61st Street side of Washington Park to wait for my kindergartener to come out of the Sexton School. "spring landscape: detail" is a crush of Sexton-day observation and Forrestville memories of my own.

The thoughts and events in "Death of Grandmother" are true—but the decedent was an aunt, not a grandmother.

In "you're being so good, so kind," M.M.'s response to the visit of a white schoolmate was the one of which I was guilty at the mere *mention* of "such a thing."

I quite like "at the Regal." The Regal Theater is no more, and even the name of its street, South Park, has been changed to Dr. Martin Luther King Jr. Drive; but this tiny chapter certainly takes me back to old vaudeville, and old dreamy walks to and from the gaudy house of magic.

My take-off for "Tim" was my own Uncle Ernest, husband of my mother's sister Ella—but there is very little of Uncle Ernest in it; his story was complex, and material for a novel I am not qualified, or industrious enough, to write.

"home" is indeed fact-bound. The Home Owners' Loan Corporation was a sickening reality.

"Helen" is chiefly "made up." I never had a sister. The little character Emmanuel there, however, was real, even unto the name. How I hated my own Emmanuel! (It may be remembered that Emmanuel's phobia was dark-complexioned girls.) True in the chapter, further, is the little catalogue of childhood memories: crying secretly in the pantry—making cheese and peanut butter sandwiches for picnics—getting my hair curled in pre-natural days—drawing—washing dishes by summer twilight, with the back door wide open—and so on.

"first beau" and "second beau" are pictures of *one* person, William Couch. William Couch, always called *Bill,* was not a true "beau," but was the Adonis of "my" day, much admired by many, many women—sophisticatedly merry, brilliant then as now, and, as the men admitted bitterly, *suave.* He is now a prominent professor, writer, and editor of *New Black Playwrights,* an influential text.

"Maud Martha and New York." Based on ideas I had of "New York life" before I ever saw this fast and glassy city. Interestingly enough, there is no mention, in the fantasy, of Harlem. . . .

"low yellow" introduces Paul Phillips, who is to be Maudie's husband. Most readers have thought I was referring to my own husband. Although my husband has done some of the things Paul Phillips does in the book, Paul Phillips is based not on the personality of Henry Blakely but on the personality, physical characteristics, and persuasions (as I judged them) of Virgil J———, who used to live with his grandmother and brother on the second floor of my family home, long long long ago, when we were both fifteen.

"a birth" is a fairly good mirror of the birth of my first child.

In "kitchenette folks," Binnie, Mrs. Teenie Thompson, Mr. and Mrs. Whitestripe, Mr. Neville, and Maryginia Washington were "real." Mr. and Mrs. "Whitestripe" called each other, most enchantingly, *Boo* and *Boopie,* and I still chide myself for being so cowardly as to change those perfections to *Coo* and *Coopie.*

"the self-solace" is based on an adventure of mine, one of hundreds I have had in beauty shoppes (*mines* of Life, organic, rich!)

The O11 Club ("Paul in the O11 Club") was the famous south side 411 Club. My husband looked rather nervous as I sat there looking briskly, examiningly, all about me, taking notes. The walls and waitresses are *exact!*

Doris Lessing (b. 1919)

Lessing, one of the most significant novelists of our time, was born in Persia and grew up in Rhodesia. As a young adult during World War II she joined the Communist party; later when she came to London, she continued this affiliation with the party for a time. The social concern in her life spills over into her writing. From her lyrical African stories through her *Children of Violence* series, Lessing has chronicled our time with its achievements, doubts, fears, and its groping for meaning.

The emphasis on the quest in modern times is unmistakable in her novels; yet it is not the neatly outlined quest for the grail. Instead, Lessing presents the meandering search through initiation to life, political activism, the process of creativity, the wrestling with varied facets of the human mind, and the attempt to arrive at cosmic harmony. Her last four books look toward the future in a mixture of mind expansion, science fiction, and fantasy: *The Four-Gated City, Briefing for a Descent into Hell, The Summer Before the Dark, The Memoirs of a Survivor*. The relationship between men and women has been an important feature of her work, but, as she so well explains in her discussion of critical reaction to *The Golden Notebook*, the war between the sexes is not all that she is writing about. In this novel the themes of fragmentation and unity, the writer's block, and the need for creativity in spite of world chaos are prevalent.

Lessing has made many contributions to the short story from the early African tales to more recent volumes like *The Temptation of Jack Orkney*. Although her short stories reflect many of the major themes discussed above, they often focus on an aspect of character, a concrete situation, as well.

"An Unposted Love Letter" in Part Two explores the nuances of interaction between a man and a woman—what it is that produces a vital relationship. The aging actress, Victoria Carrington, draws life from the bounds she imposes between herself and men; thus these are not conventional, delimiting relationships.

In the excerpt from *A Small Personal Voice* Lessing emphasizes the link between literature and life in her admiration of the great nineteenth-century novels, which were filled with compassion, humanity and words like "love" and "hate" and "forgiveness" before these terms became fragmented and almost meaningless in contemporary life. Her responses to Roy Newquist in the interview shed light on her own writing and serve as advice to students who wish to write: Aim high, observe and hold on to your observations, live so that your writing can come out of it. Lessing's life and her writing have always been intertwined; her readers find the varied strands of modern life emerging in her work, which encompasses both past and present while venturing toward the future of society and individual human relationships.

The Small Personal Voice

As a writer I am concerned first of all with novels and stories, though I believe that the arts continuously influence each other, and that what is true of one art in any given epoch is likely to be true of the others. I am concerned that the novel and the story should not decline as art-forms any further than they have from the high peak of literature; that they should possibly regain their greatness. For me the highest point of literature was the novel of the nineteenth century, the work of Tolstoy, Stendhal, Dostoevsky, Balzac, Turgenev, Chekhov; the work of the great realists. I define realism as art which springs so vigorously and naturally from a strong-held, though not necessarily intellectually-defined, view of life that it absorbs symbolism. I hold the view that the realist novel, the realist story, is the highest form of prose writing; higher than and out of the reach of any comparison with expressionism, impressionism, symbolism, naturalism, or any other ism.

The great men of the nineteenth century had neither religion nor politics nor aesthetic principles in common. But what they did have in common was a climate of ethical judgement; they shared certain values; they were humanists. A nineteenth-century novel is recognizably a nineteenth-century novel because of this moral climate.

If there is one thing which distinguishes our literature, it is a confusion of standards and the uncertainty of values. It would be hard, now, for a writer to use Balzacian phrases like "sublime virtue" or "monster of wickedness" without self-consciousness. Words, it seems, can no longer be used simply and naturally. All the great words like love, hate; life, death; loyalty, treachery; contain their opposite meanings and half a dozen shades of dubious implication. Words have become so inadequate to express the richness of our experience that the simplest sentence overheard on a bus reverberates like words shouted against a cliff. One certainty we all accept is the condition of being uncertain and insecure. It is hard to make moral judgements, to use words like good and bad.

Yet I reread Tolstoy, Stendhal, Balzac, and the rest of the old giants continuously. So do most of the people I know, people who are left and right, committed and uncommitted, religious and unreligious, but who have at least this in common, that they read novels as I think they should be read, for illumination, in order to enlarge one's perception of life.

Why? Because we are in search of certainties? Because we want a return to a comparatively uncomplicated world? Because it gives us a sense of safety to hear Balzac's thundering verdicts of guilt or innocence, and to explore with Dostoevsky, for instance in *Crime and Punishment*, the possibilities of moral anarchy, only to find order restored at the end with the simplest statements of faith in forgiveness, expiation, redemption?

Recently I finished reading an American novel which pleased me; it was witty, intelligent, un-self-pitying, courageous. Yet when I put it down I knew I would not reread it. I asked myself why not, what demand I was making on the author that he did not answer. Why was I left dissatisfied with nearly all the contemporary novels I read? Why, if I were reading for my own needs, rather than for the purposes of informing myself about what was going on, would I begin rereading *War and Peace* or *The Red and the Black?*

Put directly, like this, the answer seemed to me clear. I was not looking for a firm reaffirmation of old ethical values, many of which I don't accept; I was not in search of the pleasures of familiarity. I was looking for the warmth, the compassion, the humanity, the love of people which illuminates the literature of the nineteenth century and which makes all these old novels a statement of faith in man himself.

These are qualities which I believe are lacking from literature now.

This is what I mean when I say that literature should be committed. It is these qualities which I demand, and which I believe spring from being committed; for one cannot be committed without belief.

Committed to what? Not to being a propagandist for any political party. I never have thought so. I see no reason why writers should not work, in their role as citizens, for a political party; but they should never allow themselves to feel obliged to publicize any party policy or "line" unless their own passionate need as writers makes them do so: in which case the passion might, if they have talent enough, make literature of the propaganda.

Once a writer has a feeling of responsibility, as a human being, for the other human beings he influences, it seems to me he must become a humanist, and must feel himself as an instrument of change for good or for bad. That image of the pretty singer in the ivory tower has always seemed to me a dishonest one. Logically he should be content to sing to his image in the mirror. The act of getting a story or a novel published is an act of communication, an attempt to impose one's personality and beliefs on other people. If a writer accepts this responsibility, he must see himself, to use the socialist phrase, as an architect of the soul, and it is a phrase which none of the old nineteenth-century novelists would have shied away from.

But if one is going to be an architect, one must have a vision to build towards, and that vision must spring from the nature of the world we live in.

. . .

Yet we are all of us, directly or indirectly, caught up in a great whirlwind of change; and I believe that if an artist has once felt this, in himself, and felt himself as part of it; if he has once made the effort of imagination necessary to comprehend it, it is an end of despair, and the aridity of self-pity. It is the beginning of something else which I think is the minimum act of humility for a writer: to know that one is a writer at all because one represents, makes articulate, is continuously and invisibly fed by, numbers of people who are inarticulate, to whom one belongs, to whom one is responsible.

Because this is not a great age of literature it is easy to fall into despondency and frustration. For a time I was depressed because I thought it likely that the novel might very well be on the way out altogether. It was, after all, born with the middle class, and might die with the middle class. A hundred years ago people used to wait impatiently for the next instalment of a novel. Cinema and television have been added to the popular arts, where once the novel was alone.

But the novelist has one advantage denied to any of the other artists. The novel is the only popular art-form left where the artist speaks directly, in clear words, to his audience. Film-makers, playwrights, television writers, have to reach people through a barrier of financiers, actors, producers, directors. The novelist talks, as an individual to individuals, in a small personal voice. In an age of committee art, public art, people may begin to feel again a need for the small personal voice; and this will feed confidence into writers and, with confidence because of the knowledge of being needed, the warmth and humanity and love of people which is essential for a great age of literature.

Interview with Doris Lessing

BY ROY NEWQUIST

Newquist: When did you start writing?

Lessing: I think I've always been a writer by temperament. I wrote some bad novels in my teens. I always knew I would be a writer, but not until I was quite old—twenty-six or -seven—did I realize that I'd better stop saying I was *going* to be one and get down to business. I was working in a lawyer's office at the time, and I remember walking in and saying to my boss, "I'm giving up my job because I'm going to write a novel." He very properly laughed, and I indignantly walked home and wrote *The Grass Is Singing*. I'm oversimplifying; I didn't write it as simply as that because I was clumsy at writing and it was much too long, but I did learn by writing it. It focused upon white people in Southern Rhodesia, but it could have been about white people anywhere south of Zambezi, white people who were not up to what is expected of them in a society where there is very heavy competition from the black people coming up.

Then I wrote short stories set in the district I was brought up in, where very isolated white farmers lived immense distances from each other. You see, in this background, people can spread themselves out. People who might be extremely ordinary in a society like England's, where people are pressed into conformity, can become wild eccentrics in all kinds of ways they wouldn't dare try elsewhere. This is one of the things I miss, of course, by living in England. I don't think my memory deceives me, but I think there were more colorful people back in Southern Rhodesia because of the space they had to move in. I gather, from reading American literature, that this is the kind of space you have in America in the Midwest and West.

I left Rhodesia and my second marriage to come to England, bringing a son with me. I had very little money, but I've made my living as a professional writer ever since, which is really very hard to do. I had rather hard going, to begin with, which is not a complaint; I gather from my American writer-friends that it is easier to be a writer in England than in America because there is much less pressure put on us. We are not expected to be successful, and it is no sin to be poor. . . .

Newquist: To work from *A Man and Two Women* for a bit. The almost surgical job you do in dissecting people, not bodily, but emotionally, has made me wonder if you choose your characters from real life, form composites or projections, or if they are so involved you can't really trace their origins.

Lessing: I don't know. Some people I write about come out of my life. Some, well, I don't know where they come from. They just spring from my own consciousness, perhaps the subconscious, and I'm surprised as they emerge.

This is one of the excitements about writing. Someone says something, drops a phrase, and later you find that phrase turning into a character in a story, or a single, isolated, insignificant incident becomes the germ of a plot.

Newquist: If you were going to give advice to the young writer, what would that advice be?

Lessing: You should write, first of all, to please yourself. You shouldn't care a damn about anybody else at all. But writing can't be a way of life; the important part of writing is living. You have to live in such a way that your writing emerges from it. This is hard to describe.

Newquist: What about reading as a background?

Lessing: I've known very good writers who've never read anything. Of course, this is rare.

Newquist: What about your own reading background?

Lessing: Well, because I had this isolated childhood, I read a great deal. There was no one to talk to, so I read. What did I read? The best—the classics of European and American literature. One of the advantages of not being educated was that I didn't have to waste time on the second-best. Slowly, I read these classics. It was my education, and I think it was a very good one.

I could have been educated—formally, that is—but I felt some neurotic rebellion against my parents who wanted me to be brilliant academically. I simply contracted out of the whole thing and educated myself. Of course, there are huge gaps in my education, but I'm nonetheless grateful that it went as it did. One bit of advice I might give the young writer is to get rid of the fear of being thought of as a perfectionist, or to be regarded as pompous. They should strike out for the best, to be the best. God knows we all fall short of our potential, but if we aim very high we're likely to be so much better.

Newquist: How do you view today's literature? and theater?

Lessing: About theater, well, I'm very annoyed right now by that phrase "kitchen sink" that is being used so frequently. I don't think it means very much. There are two kinds of theater, and I don't think they should be confused. People who want to see a roaring farce, like *Sailor Beware*, should enjoy it. It's perfectly legitimate, and there's nothing wrong with the theater of entertainment.

The cathartic theater that moves people in such a way that they or their lives or changed, or they understand more about themselves, is a totally different thing. The phrase "kitchen sink" comes from critics who don't know their jobs, or theatergoers who are being bullied into seeing things they don't want to see. They should never go if they don't want to. There's nothing wrong with a minority theater and a minority literature.

Denise Levertov (b. 1923)

Denise Levertov was born in London and came to the United States in 1948, a year after her marriage. Her first book of poetry, *The Double Image*, was published in 1946, and ten additional collections have followed, among them *The Sorrow Dance, O Taste and See, Relearning the Alphabet*, and *Footprints*.

Her life has been devoted to poetry, to developing her personal and public voice. "The Sense of Pilgrimage," an illuminating chapter in her collection of essays entitled *The Poet in the World*, is a retrospective examination of the dominant personal myth in her poetry, which she discovers has been that of the journey. In the mid-1960s Levertov's pilgrimage took a new and more political direction, reflected in her 1971 collection, *To Stay Alive*, which included "Life at War" (reprinted in Part Two). Just before Nixon's reelection in 1972, she traveled to North Vietnam with poet Muriel Rukeyser and Jane Hart, war resister and wife of United States Senator Philip Hart. The impact of this experience is revealed in her latest collection of poetry, *The Freeing of the Dust*.

However, in addition to her sometimes vengeful outrage at violence and destructive values ("O to kill/the killers!"), Levertov expresses an abiding affirmation of life. Perhaps the anger is even part of this, an attempt to provide the faith and strength to create a better world. For Levertov countenances no apathy nor glib cynicism; she sees our personal concerns today as inevitably pervaded by political realities.

After Anne Sexton's suicide, Levertov wrote an article for *Ramparts* magazine, "Light up the Cave," in which she attacks the idea that there must be a balance of personal destructiveness in the life of a creative artist. And Levertov's own work surely manifests the joy of creating, of transcending through her art what she calls her clumsiness in life. Her poetry gives courage for the intense life. As she says, countering Wordsworth: "The world is / not with us enough. / **O taste and see.**"

The Poet in the World

The poet is in labor.[1] She has been told that it will not hurt but it has hurt so much that pain and struggle seem, just now, the only reality. But at the very moment when she feels she will die, or that she is already in hell, she hears the doctor saying, "Those are the shoulders you are feeling now"—and she knows the head is out then, and the child is pushing and sliding out of her, insistent, a poem.

[1] Written for a symposium on the question, "Is There a Purely Literary Study?" held at Geneseo, New York, in April 1967.

The poet is a father. Into the air, into the fictional landscape of the delivery room, wholly man-made, cluttered with shining hard surfaces, steel and glass—ruthlessly illuminated, dominated by brilliant white-nesses—into this alien human scene emerges, slime-covered, skinny-legged, with a head of fine black hair, the remote consequence of a dream of his, acted out nine months before, the rhythm that became words, the words that were spoken, written down.

The poet is being born. Blind, he nevertheless is aware of a new world around him, the walls of the womb are gone, something harsh enters his nose and mouth and lungs, and he uses it to call out to the world with what he finds is his voice, in a cry of anger, pathos, or is it pure announcement?—he has no tears as yet, much less laughter. And some other harshness teases his eyes, premonition of sight, a promise that begins at once to be fulfilled. A sharp smell of disinfec-tant is assaulting his new nostrils; flat, hard, rattling sounds multiply, objects being placed on glass surfaces, a wheeled table pushes out of the way, several voices speaking; hands are holding him, moving on his skin, doing things to his body—wetness, dry softness, and then up-ness, down-ness, moving-along-ness: to stillness in some kind of container, and the extraordinary experience, lasting an eternity, of lying upon a permanently flat surface—and finally closeness to some-thing vaguely familiar, something warm that interposes a soothing voice between him and all else until he sleeps.

It is two years later. The poet is in a vast open space covered by rec-tangular gray cobblestones. In some of the crevices between them there is bright green moss. If he pokes it with a finger it feels cold, it gives under pressure but is slightly prickly. His attention is whirled away from it by a great beating of wings around him and a loud roucouing. People with long legs who surround him are afraid he will take fright at the flock of pigeons, but he laughs in wild pleasure as they put lumps of bread into his hands for him to throw to the birds. He throws with both hands, and the pigeons vanish over his head and someone says, Cathedral. See the big building, it's a Cathe-dral. But he sees only an enormous door, a mouth, darkness inside it. There is a feather on his coat. And then he is indoors under a table in the darkish room, among the legs of the table and of the peo-ple, the peoples' feet in shoes, one pair without shoes, empty shoes kicked off nearby. Emerging unseen he steps hard on something, a toy train belonging to another child, and it breaks, and there is a great commotion and beating of wings again and loud voices, and he alone is silent in the midst of it, quite silent and alone, and the birds flying and the other child crying over its broken train and the word cathe-dral, yes, it is ten years later and the twin towers of it share the gray of the cobblestones in the back of a large space in his mind where flying buttresses and flying pigeons mean cathedral and the silence he knows is inside the great door's darkness is same silence he main-tained down among the feet and legs of adults who beat their wings up above him in the dark air and vanished into the sky.

It is Time that pushed them into the sky, and he has been living ten, twenty, thirty years; he has read and forgotten thousands of books, and thousands of books have entered him with their scenes and people, their sounds, ideas, logics, irrationalities, are singing and dancing and walking and crawling and shouting and keeping still in his mind, not only in his mind but in his way of moving his body and in his actions and decisions and in his dreams by night and by day and in the way he puts one word before another to pass from the gate of an avenue and into the cathedral that looms at the far end of it holding silence and darkness in its inner space as a finger's-breadth of moss is held between two stones.

All the books he has read are in the poet's mind (having arrived there by way of his eyes and ears, his apperceptive brain-centers, his heart-beat, his arteries, his bones) as it grasps a pen with which to sign yes or no. Life or death? Peace or war?

He has read what Rilke wrote:[2]

. . . verses are not, as people imagine, simply feelings (we have those soon enough); they are experiences. In order to write a single poem, one must see many cities, and people, and things; one must get to know animals and the flight of birds, and the gestures that flowers make when they open to the morning. One must be able to return to roads in unknown regions, to unexpected encounters, to partings long foreseen; to days of childhood that are still unexplained, and to parents whom one had to hurt when they brought one some joy and one did not grasp it (it was a joy for somebody else); to childhood illnesses that begin so strangely with such a number of profound and grave transformations, to days spent in rooms withdrawn and quiet and to mornings by the sea, to the sea itself, to oceans, to nights of travel that rushed along loftily and flew with all the stars—and still it is not enough to be able to think of all this. There must be memories of many nights of love, each one unlike the others, of the screams of women in labor, and of women in childhood, light and blanched and sleeping, shutting themselves in. But one must also have been beside the dying, must have sat beside the dead in a room with open windows and with fitful noises. And still it is not yet enough, to have memories. One must be able to forget them when they are many and one must have the immense patience to wait till they are come again. For the memories themselves are still nothing. Not till they have turned to blood within us, to glance and gesture, nameless and no longer to be distinguished from ourselves—not till then can it happen that in a most rare hour the first word of a poem arises in their midst and goes forth from them.

This the poet has known, and he has known in his own flesh equivalent things. He has seen suddenly coming round a corner the deep-lined, jowled faces and uncertain, unfocusing eyes, never meeting his for more than an unwilling second, of men of power. All the machines of his life have directed upon him *their* power, whether of speed or flickering information or disembodied music. He has seen enormous mountains from above, from higher than eagles ever fly; and skimmed upstream over the strong flow of rivers; and crossed in a day the great oceans his ancestors labored across in many months. He has sat in a bathtub listening to Bach's *St. Matthew Passion*, he has looked up

[2] From *The Notebooks of Malte Laurids Brigge* (1908).

from the death of Socrates, disturbed by some extra noise amid the jarring and lurching of the subway train and the many rhythmic rattlings of its parts, and seen one man stab another and a third spring from his seat to assist the wounded one. He has seen the lifted fork pause in the air laden with its morsel of TV dinner as the eyes of the woman holding it paused for a moment at the image on the screen that showed a bamboo hut go up in flames and a Vietnamese child run screaming toward the camera—and he has seen the fork move on toward its waiting mouth, and the jaws continue their halted movement of mastication as the next image glided across the screen.

He has breathed in dust and poetry, he has breathed out dust and poetry, he has written:

Slowly men and women move in life,
cumbered.
The passing of sorrow, the passing
of joy. All awareness

is the awareness of time.
Passion,
however it seems to leap and pounce,
is a slow thing.
It blunders,
cracking twigs in the woods of the world.

He has read E. M. Forster's words, "Only connect," and typed them out and pasted them on the wall over his desk along with other sayings:

The task of the poet is to make clear to himself, and thereby to others, the temporal and eternal questions which are astir in the age and community to which he belongs.

—Ibsen

We have the daily struggle, inescapable and deadly serious, to seize upon the word and bring it into the directest possible contact with all that is felt, seen, thought, imagined, experienced.

—Goethe

The task of the church is to keep open communication between man and God.

—Swedenborg

And below this the poet has written, "For *church* read *poet*. For God read *man and his imagination, man and his senses, man and man, man and nature—well, maybe 'god,' then, or 'the gods' . . .*"

What am I saying?

I am saying that for the poet, for the man who *makes* literature, there is no such thing as an isolated study of literature. And for those who desire to know what the poet has made, there is therefore no purely literary study either. Why "therefore"? Because the understanding of a result is incomplete if there is ignorance of its process. The literary critic or the teacher of literature is merely scratching a section of surface if he does not live out in his own life some experience of the multitudinous interactions in time, space, memory, dream, and instinct that at every word tremble into synthesis in the work of a poet, or if he keeps his reading separate from his actions in a box labeled "aesthetic experiences." The interaction of life on art and of art on life is continuous. Poetry is necessary to a whole man, and that poetry be not divided from the rest of life is necessary to *it*. Both life and poetry fade, wilt, shrink, when they are divorced.

Literature—the writing of it, the study of it, the teaching of it—is a part of your lives. It *sustains* you, in one way or another. Do not allow that fatal divorce to take place between it and your actions.

It was Rilke, the most devoted of poets, the one who gave himself most wholly to the service of his art, who wrote:

> . . . art does not ultimately tend to produce more artists. It does not mean to call anyone over to it, indeed it has always been my guess that it is not concerned at all with any effect. But while its creations, having issued irresistibly from an inexhaustible source, stand there strangely quiet and surpassable among things, it may be that involuntarily they become somehow exemplary for *every* human activity by reason of their innate disinterestedness, freedom and intensity. . . .[3]

> For as much as the artist in us is concerned with *work*, the realization of it, its existence and duration quite apart from ourselves—we shall only be wholly in the right when we understand that even this most urgent realization of a higher reality appears, from some last and extreme vantage point, only as a means to win something once more invisible, something inward and unspectacular—a saner state in the midst of our being.[4]

He is saying, in these two passages from letters, that though the work of art does not aim at effect but is a thing imbued with life, that *lives* that life for its own sake, it nevertheless *has* effect; and that effect is ultimately moral. And morality, at certain points in history, of which I believe this is one—this year, even if not this day—demands of us that we sometimes leave our desks, our classrooms, our libraries, and manifest in the streets, and by radical political actions, that love of the good and beautiful, that love of life and its arts, to which otherwise we pay only lip service. Last spring (1966) at a Danforth Conference, Tom Bradley, one of the speakers, said (I quote from my notes): "Literature is dynamite because it asks—proposes—moral questions and seeks to define the nature and worth of man's life." (And this is as true of the most "unengaged" lyric poem, intrinsically, as of the most didactic or discursive or contentious). Bradley continued, "The vision of man we get from art conditions our vision of society and therefore our political behavior. . . . Art and social life are in a dialectical relationship to each other that is synthesized by political action."

[3] From a letter to Rudolf Bödlander, *Letters of Rainer Maria Rilke*, Vol. II, p. 294.
[4] From a letter to Gertrude Oukama Knoop in Rilke, *Selected Letters*, p. 330.

The obligation of the poet (and, by extension, of others committed to the love of literature, as critics and teachers or simply as readers) is not necessarily to write "political" poems (or to focus attention primarily on such poems as more "relevant" than other poems or fictions). The obligation of the writer is: *to take personal and active responsibility for his words, whatever they are, and to acknowledge their potential influence on the lives of others.* The obligation of teachers and critics is: *not to block the dynamic consequences of the words they try to bring close to students and readers.* And the obligation of readers is: *not to indulge in the hypocrisy of merely vicarious experience, thereby reducing literature to the concept of "just words," ultimately a frivolity, an irrelevance when the chips are down.* ... When words penetrate deep into us they change the chemistry of the soul, of the imagination. We have no right to do that to people if we don't share the consequences.

People are always asking me how I can reconcile poetry and political action, poetry and talk of revolution. Don't you feel, they say to me, that you and other poets are betraying your work as poets when you spend time participating in sit-ins, marching in the streets, helping to write leaflets, talking to people about capitalism, imperialism, racism, male chauvinism, oppression of all kinds? My answer is no; precisely because I am a poet, I know, and those other poets who do likewise know, that we must fulfill the poet's total involvement in life in this aspect also. "But is not the task of the poet essentially one of conservation?" the question comes. Yes, and if I speak of revolution it is because I believe that only revolution can now save that earthly life, that miracle of being, which poetry conserves and celebrates. "But history shows us that poets—even great poets—more often fulfill their lives as observers than as participants in political action—when they do become embroiled in politics they usually write bad poems." I answer, good poets write bad political poems only if they let themselves write deliberate, opinionated rhetoric, misusing their art as propaganda. The poet does not *use* poetry, but is at the service of poetry. To *use* it is to *misuse* it. A poet driven to speak to himself, to maintain a dialogue with himself, concerning politics, can expect to write as well upon that theme as upon any other. He can not separate it from everything else in his life. But it is not whether or not good "political" poems are a possibility that is in question. What is in question is the role of the poet as observer or as participant in the life of his time. And if history is invoked to prove that more poets have stood aside, have watched or ignored the events of their moment in history, than have spent time and energy in bodily participation in those events, I must answer that a sense of history must involve a sense of the present, a vivid awareness of change, a response to crisis, a realization that what was appropriate in this or that situation in the past is inadequate to the demands of the present, that we are living our whole lives *in a state of emergency* which is—for reasons I'm sure I don't have to spell out for you by discussing nuclear and chemical weapons or ecological disasters and threats—unparalleled in all history.

When I was seven or eight and my sister sixteen or seventeen, she described the mind to me as a room full of boxes, in aisles like the shelves of a library, each box with its label. I had heard the term "gray matter," and so I visualized room and boxes as gray, dust-gray. Her confident description impressed me, but I am glad to say I felt an immediate doubt of its authenticity. Yet I have since seen lovers of poetry, lovers of literature, behave as if it were indeed so, and allow no fruitful reciprocity between poem and action.[5]

"No ideas but in things," said William Carlos Williams. This does not mean "no ideas." It means that "language [and here I quote Wordsworth] is not the dress but the incarnation of thoughts."[6] "No ideas but in things," means, essentially, "Only connect." And it is therefore not only a craft-statement, not only an aesthetic statement (though it is these things also, and importantly), but a moral statement. *Only connect. No ideas but in things.* The words reverberate through the poet's life, through *my* life, and I hope through your lives, joining with other knowledge in the mind, that place that is not a gray room full of little boxes. . . .

[5] At this point in the talk as originally given, I inserted the poem, "O Taste and See," from my book of the same title.
[6] Wordsworth in fact said (in his third "Essay upon Epitaphs"), "If words be not an incarnation of the thought but only a clothing for it, then surely will they prove an ill gift."

Carolyn Kizer (b. 1925)

Born in Spokane, Washington, Carolyn Kizer attended Sarah Lawrence College and Columbia University. Her professional life has been spent in university teaching, editing *Poetry Northwest*, which she founded, and serving as director of literary programs for the National Endowment for the Arts.

Her poem "Pro Femina" wittily presents "the fate of women" in general, then that of "The Independent Woman," and finally that of women who write. First published in 1963, "Pro Femina" has become a classic, a forceful and still-fresh statement about the alternatives available to women and the necessity of their becoming free and responsible.

The selections in Part Two, all from her 1971 collection, *Midnight Was My Cry*, reflect a few of the directions of her work. "The First of June Again," which deals with the Vietnam War and opposition to it, moves beyond this specific crisis to the basic break within "a civilization so dismayed / And so dismaying, that its children wanted it to stop." "Lines to Accompany Flowers for Eve" presents the personal consequences of living in such an age through the poet's response to a young woman's attempted suicide: "Left to our own devices, we devise / Such curious deaths, comas or mutilations." But the poem concludes, if not completely optimistically, at least with faith in life: "we live in wonder, / Blaze in a cycle of passion and apprehension / Though once we lay and waited for a death."

Kizer's poetic versatility is illustrated in the final poem, "What the Bones Know." There is a striking tension between form and content: short lines in rhymed tercets with circular repetition of the rhymes "breath" and "death," a light tone, and a profound subject. Other poems recreate mythological themes and demonstrate techniques borrowed from Oriental poetry, and a number are variations on themes of the German poet Heinrich Heine. An ironic tone infuses much of her poetry, including her view of herself in "Singing Aloud."

Singing Aloud

We all have our faults. Mine is trying to write poems.
New scenery, someone I like, anything sets me off!
I hear my own voice going on, like a god or an oracle,
That cello-tone, intuition. That bell-note of wisdom!

And I can't get rid of the tempting tic of pentameter,
Of the urge to impose a form on what I don't understand,
Or that which I have to transform because it's too grim as it is.
But age is improving me: Now, when I finish a poem

I no longer rush out to impose it on friendly colleagues.
I climb through the park to the reservoir, peer down at my own
  reflection,
Shake a blossoming branch so I am covered with petals,
Each petal a metaphor. . . .

By the time we reach middle life, we've all been deserted and robbed.
But flowers and grass and animals keep me warm.
And I remind myself to become philosophic:
We are meant to be stripped down, to prepare us for something better.

And, often, I sing aloud. As I grow older
I give way to innocent folly more and more often.
The squirrels and rabbits chime in with inaudible voices.
I feel sure that the birds make an effort to be antiphonal.

When I go to the zoo, the primates and I, in communion,
Hoot at each other, or signal with earthy gestures.
We must move further out of town, we musical birds and animals,
Or they'll lock us up like the apes, and control us forever.

Pro Femina: Parts One, Two, and Three

ONE

From Sappho to myself, consider the fate of women.
How unwomanly to discuss it! Like a noose or an albatross necktie
The clinical sobriquet hangs us: cod-piece coveters.
Never mind these epithets; I myself have collected some honeys.
Juvenal set us apart in denouncing our vices
Which had grown, in part, from having been set apart:
Women abused their spouses, cuckolded them, even plotted
To poison them. Sensing, behind the violence of his manner—
"Think I'm crazy or drunk?"—his emotional stake in us,
As we forgive Strindberg and Nietzsche, we forgive all those
Who cannot forget us. We *are* hyenas. Yes, we admit it.

While men have politely debated free will, we have howled for it,
Howl still, pacing the centuries, tragedy heroines.
Some who sat quietly in the corner with their embroidery
Were Defarges, stabbing the wool with the names of their ancient
Oppressors, who ruled by the divine right of the male—

I'm impatient of interruptions! I'm aware there were millions
Of mutes for every Saint Joan or sainted Jane Austen,
Who, vague-eyed and acquiescent, worshiped God as a man.
I'm not concerned with those cabbageheads, not truly feminine
But neutered by labor. I mean real women, like *you* and like *me*.
Freed in fact, not in custom, lifted from furrow and scullery,
Not obliged, now, to be the pot for the annual chicken,
Have we begun to arrive in time? With our well-known
Respect for life because it hurts so much to come out with it;
Disdainful of "sovereignty," "national honor" and other abstractions;

We can say, like the ancient Chinese to successive waves of invaders,
"Relax, and let us absorb you. You can learn temperance
In a more temperate climate." Give us just a few decades
Of grace, to encourage the fine art of acquiescence
And we might save the race. Meanwhile, observe our creative chaos,
Flux, efflorescence—whatever you care to call it!

TWO

I take as my theme, "The Independent Woman,"
Independent but maimed: observe the exigent neckties
Choking violet writers; the sad slacks of stipple-faced matrons;
Indigo intellectuals, crop-haired and callous-toed,
Cute spectacles, chewed cuticles, aced out by full-time beauties
In the race for a male. Retreating to drabness, bad manners
And sleeping with manuscripts. Forgive our transgressions
Of old gallantries as we hitch in chairs, light our own cigarettes,
Not expecting your care, having forfeited it by trying to get even.

But we need dependency, cosseting and well-treatment.
So do men sometimes. Why don't they admit it?
We will be cows for a while, because babies howl for us,
Be kittens or bitches, who want to eat grass now and then
For the sake of our health. But the role of pastoral heroine
Is not permanent, Jack. We want to get back to the meeting.

Knitting booties and brows, tartars or termagants, ancient
Fertility symbols, chained to our cycle, released
Only in part by devices of hygiene and personal daintiness,
Strapped into our girdles, held down, yet uplifted by man's
Ingenious constructions, holding coiffiures in a breeze,
Hobbled and swathed in whimsey, tripping on feminine
Shoes with fool heels, losing our lipsticks, you, me,
In ephemeral stockings, clutching our handbags and packages.

Our masks, always in peril of smearing or cracking,
In need of continuous check in the mirror or silverware,
Keep up in thrall to ourselves, concerned with surfaces.
Look at man's uniform drabness, his impersonal envelope!
Over chicken wrists or meek shoulders, a formal, hard-fibered
    assurance
The drape of the male is designed to achieve self-forgetfulness.

So, sister, forget yourself a few times and see where it gets you:
Up the creek, alone with your talent, sans everything else.
You can wait for the menopause, and catch up on your reading.
So primp, preen, prink, pluck and prize your flesh,
All posturings! All ravishment! All sensibility!
Meanwhile, have you used your mind today?
What pomegranate raised you from the dead,
Springing, full-grown, from your own head, Athena?

THREE

I will speak about women of letters, for I'm in the racket,
Our biggest successes to date? Old maids to a woman.
And our saddest conspicuous failures? The married spinsters
On loan to the husbands they treated like surrogate fathers.
Think of that crew of self-pitiers, not-very-distant,
Who carried the torch for themselves and got first-degree burns,
Or the sad sonneteers, toast-and-teasdales we loved at thirteen;
Middle-aged virgins seducing the puerile anthologists
Through lust-of-the-mind; barbiturate-drenched Camilles
With continuous periods, murmuring softly on sofas
When poetry wasn't a craft but a sickly effluvium,
The air thick with incense, musk, and emotional blackmail.

I suppose they reacted from an earlier womanly modesty
When too many girls were scabs to their stricken sisterhood,
Impugning our sex to stay in good with the men,
Commencing their insecure bluster. How they must have swaggered
When women themselves indorsed their own inferiority!
Vestals, vassals and vessels, rolled into several,
They took notes in rolling syllabics, in careful journals,
Aiming to please a posterity that despises them.
But we'll always have traitors who swear that a woman surrenders
Her Supreme Function, by equating Art with aggression
And failure with Femininity. Still, it's just as unfair
To equate Art with Femininity, like a prettily-packaged commodity
When we are the custodians of the world's best-kept secret:
Merely the private lives of one-half of humanity.

But even with masculine dominance, we mares and mistresses
Produced some sleek saboteuses, making their cracks
Which the porridge-brained males of the day were too thick to
    perceive,
Mistaking young hornets for perfectly harmless bumblebees.
Being thought innocuous rouses some women to frenzy;
They try to be ugly by aping the ways of the men
And succeed. Swearing, sucking cigars and scorching the bedspread,
Slopping straight shots, eyes blotted, vanity-blown
In the expectation of glory: *she writes like a man!*
This drives other women mad in a mist of chiffon
(one poetess draped her gauze over red flannels, a practical feminist).

But we're emerging from all that, more or less,
Except for some lady-like laggards and Quarterly priestesses
Who flog men for fun, and kick women to maim competition.
Now, if we struggle abnormally, we may almost seem normal;
If we submerge our self-pity in disciplined industry;
If we stand up and be hated, and swear not to sleep with editors;
If we regard ourselves formally, respecting our true limitations
Without making an unseemly show of trying to unfreeze our assets;
Keeping our heads and our pride while remaining unmarried;
And if wedded, kill guilt in its tracks when we stack up the dishes
And defect to the typewriter. And if mothers, believe in the luck of
    our children,
Whom we forbid to devour us, whom we shall not devour,
And the luck of our husbands and lovers, who keep free women.

Flannery O'Connor (1925–1964)

Flannery O'Connor's strength as a writer lies in her ability to go beyond the realistic observation of life in the American South to the investigation of the darker side of human behavior. As a gifted young woman whose writing career was limited by lupus (a disease of the skin and the mucous membranes), she was forced to live out her life in the confines of Milledgeville, a small Georgia town. But her physical suffering and the limitations of her environment sharpened O'Connor's powers of observation. She caught the sights and sounds of Southern life, from the landscape and the cry of peacocks to the nuances of the speech of the three social groups that she, like Faulkner, depicts: the landowners and decaying aristocracy, the poor whites, and the blacks. Her blacks appear primarily in their relationships with whites; but in characters like Astor in "The Displaced Person," she shows their dignity, sensitivity to the master-servant interaction, and ability to endure. Her poor whites are masterpieces of portrayal: with their physical dominance, their prejudice, their living out the clichés they mouth, and their spiritual fanaticism, the Mrs. Freemans ("Good Country People") and Mrs. Shortleys ("The Displaced Person") are some of the most memorable characters in American fiction.

A Catholic, O'Connor was fascinated by humankind's spiritual nature, but she often chose to present it through Southern Fundamentalism, with its tolerance of visionaries and its combination of prejudice and religious fervor. While the Catholic mystic usually ends up in a monastery or convent where he or she cannot be readily observed, the Fundamentalist must try to work out his or her mysticism amid the conflicts of everyday life. This visibility made them an appealing subject of fiction for O'Connor.

Her works depict the misguided, the ignorant, the poor, those caught in the claustrophobic limitations of the South she knew. Industrialization, education, and communication with the rest of the world may eventually destroy this atmosphere of isolation and the purity of experience that it fosters. But O'Connor has caught the eruptive quality of a human situation bounded by restrictions of geography, economics, and thought.

The body of work she left is small but excellent. There are two short novels, *Wise Blood* and *The Violent Bear It Away*, as well as two short-story volumes, *Everything That Rises Must Converge* and *A Good Man Is Hard to Find*, now combined in *The Collected Stories of Flannery O'Connor*. "A Stroke Of Good Fortune" explores a woman's experience of marriage and family. Ruby's middle-class dream of a tract home may seem to the reader to be only another limitation. But compared to Ruby's experience of women worn-out before their prime, the decay of the little town from which she has come, and the cycle of birth and death in that atmosphere of poverty, suburbia offers survival. Note particularly how carefully the images in the story are woven together: the refrain of "good fortune," the periodic rolling in Ruby's stomach, and the motif of the child "waiting" to kill its mother.

In "The Nature and Aim of Fiction" O'Connor's concerns with the concrete in writing and the writer's sense of truth are emphasized in her humorous way. Her work is a mixture of comedy and tragedy, served up with common sense and a precision in language and characterization that make her one of the most outstanding twentieth-century American writers.

The Nature and Aim of Fiction

I understand that this is a course called "How the Writer Writes," and that each week you are exposed to a different writer who holds forth on the subject. The only parallel I can think of to this is having the zoo come to you, one animal at a time; and I suspect that what you hear one week from the giraffe is contradicted the next week by the baboon.

My own problem in thinking what I should say to you tonight has been how to interpret such a title as "How the Writer Writes." In the first place, there is no such thing as THE writer, and I think that if you don't know that now, you should by the time such a course as this is over. In fact, I predict that it is the one thing you can be absolutely certain of learning.

But there is a widespread curiosity about writers and how they work, and when a writer talks on this subject, there are always misconceptions and mental rubble for him to clear away before he can even begin to see what he wants to talk about. I am not, of course, as innocent as I look. I know well enough that very few people who are supposedly interested in writing are interested in writing well. They are interested in publishing something, and if possible in making a "killing." They are interested in being a writer, not in writing. They are interested in seeing their names at the top of something printed, it matters not what. And they seem to feel that this can be accomplished by learning certain things about working habits and about markets and about what subjects are currently acceptable.

If this is what you are interested in, I am not going to be of much use to you. I feel that the external habits of the writer will be guided by his common sense or his lack of it and by his personal circumstances; and that these will seldom be alike in two cases. What interests the serious writer is not external habits but what Maritain calls, "the habit of art"; and he explains that "habit" in this sense means a certain quality or virtue of the mind. The scientist has the habit of science; the artist, the habit of art.

Now I'd better stop here and explain how I'm using the word *art*. Art is a word that immediately scares people off, as being a little too grand. But all I mean by art is writing something that is valuable in itself and that works in itself. The basis of art is truth, both in matter and in mode. The person who aims after art in his work aims after truth, in an imaginative sense, no more and no less. St. Thomas said that the artist is concerned with the good of that which is made; and that will have to be the basis of my few words on the subject of fiction.

Now you'll see that this kind of approach eliminates many things from the discussion. It eliminates any concern with the motivation of the writer except as this finds its place inside the work. It also eliminates any concern with the reader in his market sense. It also eliminates that tedious controversy that always rages between people who declare that they write to express themselves and those who declare that they write to fill their pocketbooks, if possible.

In this connection I always think of Henry James. I know of no writer who was hotter after the dollar than James was, or who was more of a conscientious artist. It is true, I think, that these are times when the financial rewards for sorry writing are much greater than those for good writing. There are certain cases in which, if you can only learn to write poorly enough, you can make a great deal of money. But it is not true that if you write well, you won't get published at all. It is true that if you want to write well and live well at the same time, you'd better arrange to inherit money or marry a stockbroker or a rich woman who can operate a typewriter. In any case, whether you write to make money or to express your soul or to insure civil rights or to irritate your grandmother will be a matter for you and your analyst, and the point of departure for this discussion will be the good of the written work.

The kind of written work I'm going to talk about is story-writing, because that's the only kind I know anything about. I'll call any length of fiction a story, whether it be a novel or a shorter piece, and I'll call anything a story in which specific characters and events influence each other to form a meaningful narrative. I find that most people know what a story is until they sit down to write one. Then they find themselves writing a sketch with an essay woven through it, or an essay with a sketch woven through it, or an editorial with a character in it, or a case history with a moral, or some other mongrel thing. When they realize that they aren't writing stories, they decide that the remedy for this is to learn something that they refer to as the "technique of the short story" or "the technique of the novel." Technique in the minds of many is something rigid, something like a formula that you impose on the material; but in the best stories it is something organic, something that grows out of the material, and this being the case, it is different for every story of any account that has ever been written.

I think we have to begin thinking about stories at a much more fundamental level, so I want to talk about one quality of fiction which I think is its least common denominator—the fact that it is concrete—and about a few of the qualities that follow from this. We will be concerned in this with the reader in his fundamental human sense, because the nature of fiction is in large measure determined by the nature of our perceptive apparatus. The beginning of human knowledge is through the senses, and the fiction writer begins where human perception begins. He appeals through the senses, and you cannot appeal to the senses with abstractions. It is a good deal easier for most people to state an abstract idea than to describe and thus re-create some object that they actually see. But the world of the fiction writer is full of matter, and this is what the beginning fiction writers are very loath to create. They are concerned primarily with unfleshed ideas and emotions. They are apt to be reformers and to want to write because they are possessed not by a story but by the bare bones of some abstract notion. They are conscious of problems, not of people, of questions and issues, not of the texture of existence, of case histories and of everything that has a sociological smack, instead of with all those concrete details of life that make actual the mystery of our position on earth.

The Manicheans separated spirit and matter. To them all material things were evil. They sought pure spirit and tried to approach the infinite directly without any mediation of matter. This is also pretty much the modern spirit, and for the sensibility infected with it, fiction is hard if not impossible to write because fiction is so very much an incarnational art.

One of the most common and saddest spectacles is that of a person of really fine sensibility and acute psychological perception trying to write fiction by using these qualities alone. This type of writer will put down one intensely emotional or keenly perceptive sentence after the other, and the result will be complete dullness. The fact is that the materials of the fiction writer are the humblest. Fiction is about everything human and we are made out of dust, and if you scorn getting yourself dusty, then you shouldn't try to write fiction. It's not a grand enough job for you.

You may think from all I say that the reason I write is to make the reader see what I see, and that writing fiction is primarily a missionary activity. Let me straighten this out.

Last spring I talked here, and one of the girls asked me, "Miss O'Connor, why do you write?" and I said, "Because I'm good at it," and at once I felt a considerable disapproval in the atmosphere. I felt that this was not thought by the majority to be a high-minded answer; but it was the only answer I could give. I had not been asked why I write the way I do, but why I write at all; and to that question there is only one legitimate answer.

There is no excuse for anyone to write fiction for public consumption unless he has been called to do so by the presence of a gift. It is the nature of fiction not to be good for much unless it is good in itself.

A gift of any kind is a considerable responsibility. It is a mystery in itself, something gratuitous and wholly undeserved, something whose real uses will probably always be hidden from us. Usually the artist has to suffer certain deprivations in order to use his gift with integrity. Art is a virtue of the practical intellect, and the practice of any virtue demands a certain asceticism and a very definite leaving-behind of the niggardly part of the ego. The writer has to judge himself with a stranger's eye and a stranger's severity. The prophet in him has to see the freak. No art is sunk in the self, but rather, in art the self becomes self-forgetful in order to meet the demands of the thing seen and the thing being made.

I think it is usually some form of self-inflation that destroys the free use of a gift. This may be the pride of the reformer or the theorist, or it may only be that simple-minded self-appreciation which uses its own sincerity as a standard of truth. If you have read the very vocal writers from San Francisco, you may have got the impression that the first thing you must do in order to be an artist is to loose yourself from the bonds of reason, and thereafter, anything that rolls off the top of your head will be of great value. Anyone's unrestrained feelings are considered worth listening to because they are unrestrained and because they are feelings.

St. Thomas called art "reason in making." This is a very cold and very beautiful definition, and if it is unpopular today, this is because reason has lost ground among us. As grace and nature have been separated, so imagination and reason have been separated, and this always means an end to art. The artist uses his reason to discover an answering reason in everything he sees. For him, to be reasonable is to find, in the object, in the situation, in the sequence, the spirit which makes it itself. This is not an easy or simple thing to do. It is to intrude upon the timeless, and that is only done by the violence of a single-minded respect for the truth.

It follows from all this that there is no technique that can be discovered and applied to make it possible for one to write. If you go to a school where there are classes in writing, these classes should not be to teach you how to write, but to teach you the limits and possibilities of words and the respect due them. One thing that is always with the writer—no matter how long he has written or how good he is— is the continuing process of learning how to write. As soon as the writer "learns to write," as soon as he knows what he is going to find, and discovers a way to say what he knew all along, or worse still, a way to say nothing, he is finished. If a writer is any good, what he makes will have its source in a realm much larger than that which his conscious mind can encompass and will always be a greater surprise to him than it can ever be to his reader.

I don't know which is worse—to have a bad teacher or no teacher at all. In any case, I believe the teacher's work should be largely negative. He can't put the gift into you, but if he finds it there, he can try to keep it from going in an obviously wrong direction. We can learn how not to write, but this is a discipline that does not simply concern writing itelf but concerns the whole intellectual life. A mind cleared of false emotion and false sentiment and egocentricity is going to have at least those roadblocks removed from its path. If you don't think cheaply, then there at least won't be the quality of cheapness in your writing, even though you may not be able to write well. The teacher can try to weed out what is positively bad, and this should be the aim of the whole college. Any discipline can help your writing: logic, mathematics, theology, and of course and particularly drawing. Anything that helps you to see, anything that makes you look. The writer should never be ashamed of staring. There is nothing that doesn't require his attention.

We hear a great deal of lamentation these days about writers having all taken themselves to the colleges and universities where they live decorously instead of going out and getting firsthand information about life. The fact is that anybody who has survived his childhood has enough information about life to last him the rest of his days. If you can't make something out of a little experience, you probably won't be able to make it out of a lot. The writer's business is to contemplate experience, not to be merged in it.

Everywhere I go I'm asked if I think the universities stifle writers. My opinion is that they don't stifle enough of them. There's many a best-seller that could have been prevented by a good teacher. The idea of being a writer attracts a good many shiftless people, those who are merely burdened with poetic feelings or afflicted with sensibility. Granville Hicks, in a recent review of James Jones' novel, quoted Jones as saying, "I was stationed at Hickham Field in Hawaii when I stumbled upon the works of Thomas Wolfe, and his home life seemed so similar to my own, his feelings about himself so similar to mine about myself, that I realized I had been a writer all my life without knowing it or having written." Mr. Hicks goes on to say that Wolfe did a great deal of damage of this sort but that Jones is a particularly appalling example.

Now in every writing class you find people who care nothing about writing, because they think they are already writers by virtue of some experience they've had. It is a fact that if, either by nature or training, these people can learn to write badly enough, they can make a great deal of money, and in a way it seems a shame to deny them this opportunity; but then, unless the college is a trade school, it still has its responsibility to truth, and I believe myself that these people should be stifled with all deliberate speed.

Presuming that the people left have some degree of talent, the question is what can be done for them in a writing class. I believe the teacher's work is largely negative, that it is largely a matter of saying "This doesn't work because . . ." or "This does work because . . ." The *because* is very important. The teacher can help you understand the nature of your medium, and he can guide you in your reading. I don't believe in classes where students criticize each other's manuscripts. Such criticism is generally composed in equal parts of ignorance, flattery, and spite. It's the blind leading the blind, and it can be dangerous. A teacher who tries to impose a way of writing on you can be dangerous too. Fortunately, most teachers I've known were too lazy to do this. In any case, you should beware of those who appear overenergetic.

In the last twenty years the colleges have been emphasizing creative writing to such an extent that you almost feel that any idiot with a nickel's worth of talent can emerge from a writing class able to write a competent story. In fact, so many people can now write competent stories that the short story as a medium is in danger of dying of competence. We want competence, but competence by itself is deadly. What is needed is the vision to go with it, and you do not get this from a writing class.

Cynthia Ozick (b. 1928)

A native of New York, Cynthia Ozick received a B.A. from New York University and an M.A. from Ohio State. Primarily a writer of fiction, she has also written provocative essays about women and creativity. The first six sections of "We Are the Crazy Lady and Other Feisty Feminist Fables" cover the obstacle course set up for female thinkers and writers, concluding with Ozick's experience of writing the novel *Trust* and the critical response it received. As she says, it is a long and comprehensive book, but even a brief excerpt shows its uniqueness in contemporary fiction. The selection included here deals with the narrator's discovery of her illegitimacy and reflects some of the themes and techniques that Ozick mentions in her essay.

In another essay, "Women and Creativity: The Demise of the Dancing Dog," Ozick describes the "Ovarian Theory of Literature" and its complement, the "Testicular Theory," which hold that physiology determines literary style and subject. Her experience indicates that college freshmen of both sexes, university professors, and reviewers share the assumption that one's sex has more to do with literary accomplishment than does talent, imagination, or effort. She considers the analogy of creation of a child to creation of a work of art as blasphemous: gestation is Nature's miracle, requiring virtually no conscious effort by the mother, whereas artistic creativity involves exhausting, frenzied, despairing—and exalting—energies. Of course, raising a child requires a great deal of energy, but it is of another order. Ozick also describes the mystique of "Child" and "Home" in contrast to the reality and as a device to keep women in a separate minority culture. This is not a conspiracy of men, she insists, but instead of our society, where women's (and adolescents') talents cannot truly be used, where roles and stereotypes replace human beings, where illusions count more than the life illuminations of art. A genuinely humane society will encourage and need the creativity of all its members, of all ages and both sexes.

Ozick's own artistry has begun to gain wide recognition. In addition to essays, reviews, poetry, and translations published in many journals, she has published two collections of short fiction, *The Pagan Rabbi and Other Stories* and *Bloodshed and Three Novellas.*

We Are the Crazy Lady and Other Feisty Feminist Fables

I: THE CRAZY LADY DOUBLE

A long, long time ago, in another century—1951, in fact—when you, dear young readers, were most likely still in your nuclear-family play-pen (where, if female, you cuddled a ragbaby to your potential titties, or, if male, let down virile drool over your plastic bulldozer), the Famous Critic told me never, never to use a parenthesis in the very first sentence. This was in a graduate English seminar at a celebrated university. To get into this seminar, you had to submit to a grilling wherein you renounced all former allegiance to the then-current literary religion, New Criticism, which considered that only the text existed, not the world. I passed the interview by lying—cunningly, and against my real convictions, I said that probably the world *did* exist— and walked triumphantly into the seminar room.

There were four big tables arranged in a square, with everyone's feet sticking out into the open middle of the square. You could tell who was nervous, and how much, by watching the pairs of feet twist around each other. The Great Man presided awesomely from the high bar of the square. His head was a majestic granite-gray, like a centurion in command; he *looked* famous. His clean shoes twitched only slightly, and only when he was angry.

It turned out he was angry at me a lot of the time. He was angry because he thought me a disrupter, a rioter, a provocateur, and a fool; also crazy. And this was twenty years ago, before these things were *de rigueur* in the universities. Everything was very quiet in those days: there were only the Cold War and Korea and Joe McCarthy and the Old Old Nixon, and the only revolutionaries around were in Henry James's *The Princess Casamassima*.

Habit governed the seminar. Where you sat the first day was where you settled forever. So, to avoid the stigmatization of the ghetto, I was careful not to sit next to the other woman in the class: the Crazy Lady.

At first the Crazy Lady appeared to be remarkably intelligent. She was older than the rest of us, somewhere in her thirties (which was why we thought of her as a Lady), with wild-tan hair, a noticeably breathing bosom, eccentric gold-rimmed old-pensioner glasses, and a tooth-crowded wild mouth that seemed to get wilder the more she talked. She talked like a motorcycle, fast and urgent. Everything she said was almost brilliant, only not actually on point, and frenetic with hostility. She was tough and negative. She volunteered a lot and she stood up and wobbled with rage, pulling at her hair and mouth. She fought the Great Man point for point, piecemeal and wholesale, mixing up queerly-angled literary insights with all sorts of private and public fury. After the first meetings he was fed up with her. The rest of us accepted that she probably wasn't all there, but in a room where everyone was on the make for recognition—you talked to save your life, and the only way to save your life was to be the smartest one that day—she was a nuisance, a distraction, a pain in the ass. The class became a bunch of Good Germans, determinedly indifferent onlookers to a vindictive match between the Critic and the Crazy Lady, until finally he subdued her by shutting his eyes, and, when that didn't always work, by cutting her dead and lecturing right across the sound of her strong, strange voice.

All this was before R. D. Laing had invented the superiority of madness, of course, and, cowards all, no one liked the thought of being tarred with the Crazy Lady's brush. Ignored by the boss, in the middle of everything she would suddenly begin to mutter to herself. She mentioned certain institutions she'd been in, and said we all belonged there. The people who sat on either side of her shifted chairs. If the Great Man ostracized the Crazy Lady, we had to do it too. But one day the Crazy Lady came in late and sat down in the seat next to mine, and stayed there the rest of the semester.

Then an odd thing happened. There, right next to me, was the noisy Crazy Lady, tall, with that sticky-out sighing chest of hers, orangey curls dripping over her nose, snuffling furiously for attention. And there was I, a brownish runt, a dozen years younger and flatter and shyer than the Crazy Lady, in no way her twin, physically or psychologically. In those days I was bone-skinny, small, sallow and myopic, and so scared I could trigger diarrhea at one glance from the Great Man. All this stress on looks is important: the Crazy Lady and I had our separate bodies, our separate brains. We handed in our separate papers.

But the Great Man never turned toward me, never at all, and if ambition broke feverishly through shyness so that I dared to push an idea audibly out of me, he shut his eyes when I put up my hand. This went on for a long time. I never got to speak, and I began to have the depressing feeling that he hated me. It was no small thing to be hated by the man who had written the most impressive criticism of the century. What in hell was going on? I was in trouble; like everyone else in that demented contest I wanted to excel. Then, one slow afternoon, wearily, the Great Man let his eyes fall on me. He called me by name, but it was not my name—it was the Crazy Lady's. The next week the papers came back—and there, right at the top of mine, in the Great Man's own handwriting, was a rebuke to the Crazy Lady for starting an essay with a parenthesis in the first sentence, a habit he took to be a continuing sign of that unruly and unfocused mentality so often exhibited in class. And then a Singular Revelation crept coldly through me: because the Crazy Lady and I sat side by side, because we were a connected blur of Woman, the Famous Critic, master of ultimate distinctions, couldn't tell us apart. The Crazy Lady and I! He couldn't tell us apart! It didn't matter that the Crazy Lady was crazy! *He couldn't tell us apart!*

Moral 1: *All cats are gray at night,*
    all darkies look alike.

Moral 2: Even among intellectual humanists, every woman has a *Doppelgänger*—every other woman.

II: THE LECTURE, 1

I was invited by a women's group to be guest speaker at a Book-Author Luncheon. The women themselves had not really chosen me: the speaker had been selected by a male leader and imposed on them. The plan was that I would autograph copies of my book, eat a good meal and then lecture. The woman in charge of the programming telephoned to ask me what my topic would be. This was a matter of some concern, since they had never had a woman author before, and no one knew how the idea would be received. I offered as my subject "The Contemporary Poem."

When the day came, everything went as scheduled—the autographing, the food, the welcoming addresses. Then it was time to go to the lectern. I aimed at the microphone and began to speak of poetry. A peculiar rustling sound flew up from the audience. All the women were lifting their programs to the light, like hundreds of wings. Confused murmurs ran along the walls. Something was awry; I began to feel very uncomfortable. Then I took up the program. It read: "Topic: The Contemporary Home."

Moral: Even our ears practice the caste system.

III: THE LECTURE, 2

I was in another country, the only woman at a philosophical seminar lasting three days. On the third day I was to read a paper. I had accepted the invitation with a certain foreknowledge. I knew, for instance, that I could not dare to be the equal of any other speaker. To be an equal would be to be less. I understood that mine had to be the most original and powerful paper of all. I had no choice; I had to toil beyond my most extreme possibilities. This was not ambition, but only fear of disgrace.

For the first two days, I was invisible. When I spoke, people tapped impatiently waiting for the interruption to end. No one took either my presence or my words seriously. At meals, I sat with my colleagues' wives.

The third day arrived, and I read my paper. It was successful beyond my remotest imaginings. I was interviewed, and my remarks appeared in newspapers in a language I could not understand. The Foreign Minister invited me to his home. I hobnobbed with famous poets.

Now my colleagues noticed me. But they did not notice me as a colleague. They teased and kissed me. I had become their mascot.

Moral: There is no route out of caste which does not instantly lead back to it.

IV: PROPAGANDA

For many years I had noticed that no book of poetry by a woman was reviewed without reference to the poet's sex. The curious thing was that, in the two decades of my scrutiny, there were *no* exceptions whatever. It did not matter whether the reviewer was a man or woman: in every case the question of the "feminine sensibility" of the poet was at the center of the reviewer's response. The maleness of male poets, on the other hand, hardly ever seemed to matter.

Determined to ridicule this convention, I wrote a tract, a piece of purely tendentious mockery, in the form of a short story. I called it "Virility."

The plot was, briefly, as follows: A very bad poet, lustful for fame, is despised for his pitiful lucubrations and remains unpublished. But luckily, he comes into possession of a cache of letters written by his elderly spinster aunt, who lives an obscure and secluded working-class life in a remote corner of England. The letters contain a large number of remarkable poems; the aunt, it it turns out, is a genius. The bad poet publishes his find under his own name, and instantly attains world-wide adulation. Under the title *Virility*, the poems become immediate classics. They are translated into dozens of languages and are praised and revered for their unmistakably masculine qualities: their strength, passion, wisdom, energy, boldness, brutality, worldliness, robustness, authenticity, sensuality, compassion. A big, handsome, sweating man, the poet swaggers from country to country, courted everywhere, pursued by admirers, yet respected by the most demanding critics.

Meanwhile, the old aunt dies; the supply of genius runs out. Bravely and contritely the poor poet confesses his ruse, and in a burst of honesty publishes the last batch under the real poet's name; the book is entitled *Flowers from Liverpool*. But the poems are at once found negligible and dismissed: "Thin feminine art," say the reviews, "a lovely girlish voice." And: "Limited one-dimensional vision." "Choked with female inwardness." "The fine womanly intuition of a competent poetess." The poems are utterly forgotten.

I included this fable in a collection of short stories. In every review the salvo went unnoticed. Not one reviewer recognized that the story was a sly tract. Not one reviewer saw the smirk or the point. There was one delicious comment, though. "I have some reservations," a man in Washington, D.C., wrote, "about the credibility of some of her male characters when they are chosen as narrators."

Moral: In saying what is obvious, never choose cunning. Yelling works better.

V: HORMONES

During a certain period of my life, I was reading all the time, and fairly obsessively. Sometimes, though, sunk in a book of criticism or philosophy, I would be brought up short. Consider: here is a paragraph that excites the intellect; inwardly, one assents passionately to its premises, the writer's idea is an exact diagram of one's own deepest psychology or conviction, one feels oneself seized as for a portrait. Then the disclaimer, the excluding shove: "It is, however, otherwise with the female sex. . . ." A rebuke from the world of Thinking: *I didn't mean you, lady*. In the instant one is in possession of one's humanity most intensely, it is ripped away.

These moments I discounted. What is wrong—intrinsically, psychologically, culturally, morally—can be dismissed.

But to dismiss in this manner is to falsify one's most genuine actuality. A Jew reading of the aesthetic glories of European civilization without taking notice of his victimization during, say, the era of the building of the great cathedrals, is self-forgetful in the most dangerous way. So would be a black who read of King Cotton with an economist's objectivity.

I am not offering any strict analogy between the situation of women and the history of Jews or colonialized blacks, as many politically radical women do (though the analogy with blacks is much the more frequent one). It seems to me to be abusive of language in the extreme when some women speak, in the generation after Auschwitz, of the "oppression" of women. Language makes culture, and we make a rotten culture when we abuse words. We raise up rotten heroines. I use "rotten" with particular attention to its precise meaning: foul, putrid, tainted, stinking. I am thinking now especially of a radical women's publication, *Off Our Backs*, which not long ago presented Leila Khaled, terrorist and foiled murderer, as a model for the political conduct of women.

But if I would not support the extreme analogy (and am never surprised when black women, who have a more historical comprehension of actual, not figurative, oppression, refuse to support the analogy), it is anyhow curious to see what happens to the general culture when any enforced class in any historical or social condition is compelled to doubt its own self-understanding—when identity is externally defined, when individual humanity is called into question as being different from "standard" humanity. What happens is that the general culture, along with the object of its debasement, is also debased. If you laugh at women, you play Beethoven in vain.

If you laugh at women your laboratory will lie.

We can read in Charlotte Perkins Gilman's 1912 essay, "Are Women Human Beings?", an account of two opinions current sixty years ago. Women, said one scientist, are not only "not the human race—they are not even half the human race, but a sub-species set apart for purposes of reproduction merely."

A physician said: "No doctor can ever lose sight of the fact that the mind of woman is always threatened with danger from the reverberations of her physiological emergencies." He concluded this entirely on the basis of his invalid patients.

Though we are accustomed to the idea of "progress" in science and medicine, if not in civilization generally, the fact is that more information has led to something very like regression.

I talked with an intelligent physician—the Commissioner of Health of a middle-sized city in Connecticut, a man who sees medicine not discretely but as part of the social complex—and was treated to a long list of all the objective differences between men and women, including particularly an account of current endocrinal studies relating to female hormones. Aren't all of these facts, he asked, how can you distrust facts? Very good, I said, I'm willing to take your medically-educated word for it, I'm not afraid of facts, I welcome facts—*but a congeries of facts is not equivalent to an idea.* This is the essential fallacy of the so-called "scientific" mind. People who mistake facts for ideas are incomplete thinkers; they are gossips.

You tell me, I said, that my sense of my own humanity as being "standard" humanity—which is, after all, a subjective idea—is refuted by hormonal research. My psychology, you tell me, which in your view is the source of my ideas, is the result of my physiology: it is not I who express myself, it is my hormones which express me. A part is equal to the whole, you say. Worse yet, the whole is simply the issue of the part: my "I" is a flash of chemicals. You are willing to define all my humanity by hormonal investigation under a microscope: this you call "objective irrefutable fact," as if tissue-culture were equivalent to culture. But each scientist can assemble his own (subjective) constellation of "objective irrefutable fact," just as each social thinker can assemble his own (subjective) selection of traits to define "humanity" by. Who can prove what is "standard" humanity, and which sex, class, or race is to be exempted from whole participation in it? On what basis do you regard female hormones as causing a modification from normative humanity? And what better right do you have to define normative humanity by what males have traditionally apperceived than by what females have traditionally apperceived— assuming (as I, lacking presumptuousness, do not) that their apperceptions have not been the same? Only Tiresias—that mythological character who was both man and woman—is in a position to make the comparison and present the proof. And then not even Tiresias, because to be a hermaphrodite is to be a monster, and not human.

"Why are you so emotional about all this?" said the Commissioner of Health. "You see how it is? Those are your female hormones working on you right now."

Moral: Defamation is only applied research.

VI: AMBITION

After thirteen years I at last finished a novel. The first seven years were spent in a kind of apprenticeship—the book that came out of that time was abandoned without much regret. A second one was finished in six weeks and buried. It took six years to write the third novel, and this one was finally published.

How I lived through those years is impossible to recount in a short space. I was a recluse, a priest of Art. I read seas of books. I believed in the idea of masterpieces. I was scornful of the world of journalism, jobs, everydayness. I did not live like any woman I knew, though it never occurred to me to reflect on this of my own volition. I lived like some men I had read about—Flaubert, or Proust, or James: the subjects of those literary biographies I endlessly drank in. I did not think of them as men but as writers. I read the diaries of Virginia Woolf, and biographies of George Eliot, but I did not think of them as women. I thought of them as writers. I thought of myself as a writer. I went on reading and writing.

It goes without saying that all this time my relatives regarded me as abnormal. I accepted this. It seemed to me, from what I had read, that most writers were abnormal. Yet on the surface I could easily have passed for normal. The husband goes to work, the wife stays home—that is what is normal. Well, I was married. My husband went to his job every day. His job paid the rent and bought the groceries. I stayed home, reading and writing, and felt myself to be an economic parasite. To cover guilt, I joked that I had been given a grant from a very private, very poor, foundation; I meant my husband.

But my relatives never thought of me as a parasite. The very thing I was doubtful about—my economic dependence—they considered my due as a woman. They saw me not as a failed writer without an income, but as a childless housewife, a failed woman. They did not think me abnormal because I was a writer, but because I was not properly living my life as a woman. In one respect we were in agreement utterly—my life was failing terribly, terribly. For me it was because, already deep into my thirties, I had not yet published a book; for them it was because I had not yet borne a child.

I was a pariah, not only because I was a deviant, but because I was not recognized as the kind of deviant I meant to be. A failed woman is not the same as a failed writer. Even as a pariah I was the wrong kind of pariah.

Still, relations are only relations, and what I aspired to, what I was in thrall to, was Art; was Literature; not familial contentment. I knew how to distinguish the trivial from the sublime. In Literature and in Art, I saw, my notions were not pariah notions: *there* I inhabited the mainstream. So I went on reading and writing; I went on believing in Art, and my intention was to write a masterpiece. Not a saucer of well-polished craft (the sort of thing "women writers" are always accused of being accomplished at), but something huge, contemplative, Tolstoyan. My ambition was a craw.

I called the book *Trust.* I began it in the summer of 1957 and finished it in November of 1963, on the day President John Kennedy was assassinated. In manuscript it was 801 pages divided into four parts: "America," "Europe," "Birth," "Death." The title was meant to be ironic; in reality, it was about distrust. It seemed to me I had touched on distrust in every order or form of civilization. It seemed to me I had left nothing out. It was (though I did not know this then) a very hating book. What it hated above all was the whole—the whole!—of Western Civilization. It told how America had withered into another Europe; it dreamed dark and murderous pagan dreams, and hated what it dreamed.

In style the book was what has come to be called "mandarin": a difficult, aristocratic, unrelenting virtuoso prose. It was, in short, unreadable. I think I knew this; I was sardonic enough to say, echoing Joyce about *Finnegans Wake,* "I expect you to spend your life at this." In any case I had spent a decade-and-a-half of my own life at it, and though I did not imagine the world would fall asunder at its appearance, I thought—at the very least—the ambition, the all-swallowingness, the wild insatiability of the writer would be plain to everyone who read. I had, after all, taken History for my subject; and not merely History as an aggregate of events, but History as a judgment on events. No one could say my theme was flighty. Of all the novelists I read—and in those days I read them all, broiling in the envy of the unpublished, which is like no envy on earth—who else had dared so vastly?

During that period, Françoise Sagan's first novel was published. I held the thin little thing and laughed. Women's pulp!

My own novel, I believed, contained everything—the whole world.

But there was one element I had consciously left out, though on principle I did not like to characterize it or think about it much. The truth is I was thinking about it all the time: it was only a fiction-technicality, but I was considerably afraid of it. It was the question of the narrator's "sensibility." The narrator, as it happened, was a young woman; I had chosen her to be the eye—and the "I"—of the novel because all the other characters in some way focused on her, and she was the one most useful to my scheme. Nevertheless I wanted her not to live. Everything I was reading in reviews of other people's books made me fearful: I would have to be very, very cautious, I would have to drain my narrator of emotive value of any kind. I was afraid to be pegged as having written a "woman's" novel, and nothing was more certain to lead to that than a point-of-view seemingly lodged in a woman; no one takes a woman's novel seriously. I was in terror, above all, of sentiment and feeling, those telltale taints. I kept the fury and the passion for other, safer characters.

So what I left out of my narrator entirely, sweepingly, with exquisite consciousness of what exactly I *was* leaving out, was any shred of "sensibility." I stripped her of everything, even a name. I crafted and carpentered her; she was for me a bloodless device, fulcrum or pivot, a recording voice, a language-machine. She confronted moment or event, took it in, gave it out. And what to me was all the more wonderful about this nameless fiction-machine I had invented was that the machine itself, though never alive, was a character in the story, without ever influencing the story. My machine-narrator was there for efficiency only, for flexibility, for craftiness, for subtlety, but never, never, as a "woman." I wiped the "woman" out of her. And I did it out of fear, out of vicarious vindictive critical imagination, out of the terror of my ambition, out of, maybe, paranoia. I meant my novel to be taken for what it really was. I meant to make it impossible for it to be mistaken for something else.

Publication.

Review in *The New York Times* Sunday Book Review.

Review is accompanied by a picture of a naked woman seen from the back. Her bottom is covered by some sort of drapery.

Title of review: "Daughter's Reprieve."

Excerpts from review: "These events, interesting in themselves, exist to reveal the sensibility of the narrator." "She longs to play some easy feminine role." "She has been unable to define herself as a woman." "Thus the daughter, at the age of twenty-two, is eager for the prerequisites that should have been hers as a woman, but is floundering badly in their pursuit." "Her protagonist insists upon coming to terms with the recalcitrant sexual elements in her life." "The main body of the novel, then, is a revelation of the narrator's inner, turbulent, psychic dream."

O rabid rotten Western Civilization, where are you? O judging History, O foul Trust and fouler Distrust, where?

O Soap Opera, where did you come from?

(Meanwhile the review in *Time* was calling me a "housewife.")

Pause.

All right, let us take up the rebuttals one by one.

Q. Maybe you *did* write a soap opera without knowing it. Maybe you only *thought* you were writing about Western Civilization when you were really only rewriting Stella Dallas.

A. A writer may be unsure of everything—trust the tale not the teller is still a good rule—but not of her obsessions; of these she is certain. If I were rewriting Stella Dallas, I would turn her into the Second Crusade and demobilize her.

Q. Maybe you're like the blind Jew who wants to be a pilot, and when they won't give him the job he says they're anti-Semitic. Look, the book was lousy, you deserved a lousy review.

A. You mistake me, I never said it was a bad review. It was in fact an extremely favorable review, full of gratifying adjectives.

Q. But your novel languished anyhow?

A. Perished. Dead and buried. I sometimes see it exhumed on the shelf in the public library. It's always there. No one ever borrows it.

Q. Dummy! You should've written a soap opera. Women are good at that.

A. Thank you. You almost remind me of another Moral: In conceptual life, junk prevails. Even if you do not produce junk, it will be taken for junk.

Q. What does that have to do with women?

A. The products of women are frequently taken for junk.

Q. And if a woman *does* produce junk . . . ?

A. Glory—they will treat her almost like a man who produces junk. They will say her name on television.

Q. Bitter, bitter!

A. Not at all. Again you misunderstand. You see, I have come round to thinking (I learned it from television commercials, as a matter of fact) that there *is* a Women's Culture—a sort of tribal, separatist, ghettoized thing. And I propose that we cultivate it.

Q. You mean *really* writing Women's Novels? On purpose?

A. Nothing like that. The novel was invented by men. It isn't ours, you see, and to use it is to *assimilate.* I see now where I went wrong! So I propose that we return to our pristine cultural origins, earn the respect of the male race, and regain our self-esteem.

Q. All that ? Really? How?

A. We will revive the Quilting Bee!

Q. Oh, splendid, splendid! What a genius you are!

A. I always knew it.

Anne Sexton (1928–1974)

Anne Sexton's preoccupation with death culminated in her suicide in October 1974, and this added another chapter to the mystique of the connection between creativity and self-destruction among contemporary writers. Sexton began writing poetry eighteen years earlier, following a nervous breakdown after the birth of her second child. Images of madness and death fill her work, which could be taken as one long suicide note. However, she also presents a joy in life, the female experience, and the spirit, such that the reader may feel that her poetry is her means of remaining sane and alive, of facing and defeating her dark hauntings, sometimes by moving beyond conventional perceptions of reality. Her poem "Live" from the collection *Live or Die* begins with the inscription, "Live or die, but don't poison everything . . ." But in another, "The Addict," she describes taking barbiturates as trying to kill herself in small amounts. It is a nightly ceremony, a sacrament.

Don't they know
that I promised to die!
I'm keeping in practice.
I'm merely staying in shape.
The pills are a mother, but better,
every color and as good as sour balls.
I'm on a diet from death.

Her decision for life was finally conquered by her longing for death, and she chose the surety of carbon monoxide poisoning.

Anne Sexton was born in Newton, Massachusetts. The third daughter, she has said that she had an unhappy childhood and felt unwanted. She attended Garland Junior College for a year, but her education was primarily outside of school, aided by grants, fellowships, and eventually prizes, including the Pulitzer for *Live or Die*.

The emotional directness of her first volume, *To Bedlam and Partway Back* (1960), was striking. Such personal, "confessional" poetry had few precedents at the time, and Sexton credited W. D. Snodgrass' *Heart's Needle* with giving her the courage to write frankly. In an interview she said that poetry should be a shock to the senses, should almost hurt. And much of hers leaves the reader with a raw feeling, a sensation of having shared her nightmare.

However, Sexton's suicide should not distort one's view of her poetic output, for death is not her predominant subject. Her poems on motherhood and love are fresh and rich, and there is wit and humor in much of her work. The collection *Transformations* ironically recreates classic fairy tales. To gain the full impact—the tragic, the exultant, the sardonic—of Sexton's work, one must read many more than the few poems included here. Additional collections include *All My Pretty Ones, Love Poems, The Awful Rowing Toward God, The Book of Folly, The Death Notebooks,* and *45 Mercy Street*.

Said the Poet to the Analyst

My business is words. Words are like labels,
or coins, or better, like swarming bees.
I confess I am only broken by the sources of things;
as if words were counted like dead bees in the attic,
unbuckled from their yellow eyes and their dry wings.
I must always forget how one word is able to pick
out another, to manner another, until I have got
something I might have said . . .
but did not.

Your business is watching my words. But I
admit nothing. I work with my best, for instance,
when I can write my praise for a nickle machine,
that one night in Nevada: telling how the magic jackpot
came clacking three bells out, over the lucky screen.
But if you should say this is something it is not,
then I grow weak, remembering how my hands felt funny
and ridiculous and crowded with all
the believing money.

The Black Art

A woman who writes feels too much,
those trances and portents!
As if cycles and children and islands
weren't enough; as if mourners and gossips
and vegetables were never enough.
She thinks she can warn the stars.
A writer is essentially a spy.
Dear love, I am that girl.

A man who writes knows too much,
such spells and fetiches!
As if erections and congresses and products
weren't enough; as if machines and galleons
and wars were never enough.
With used furniture he makes a tree.
A writer is essentially a crook.
Dear love, you are that man.

Never loving ourselves,
hating even our shoes and our hats,
we love each other, *precious, precious*.
Our hands are light blue and gentle.
Our eyes are full of terrible confessions.
But when we marry,
the children leave in disgust.
There is too much food and no one left over
to eat up all the weird abundance.

Frenzy

I am not lazy.
I am on the amphetamine of the soul.
I am, each day,
typing out the God
my typewriter believes in.
Very quick. Very intense,
like a wolf at a live heart.
Not lazy.
When a lazy man, they say,
looks toward heaven,
the angels close the windows.

Oh angels,
keep the windows open
so that I may reach in
and steal each object,
objects that tell me the sea is not dying,
objects that tell me the dirt has a life-wish,
that the Christ who walked for me,
walked on true ground
and that this frenzy,
like bees stinging the heart all morning,
will keep the angels
with their windows open,
wide as an English bathtub.

Maya Angelou (b. 1928)

Maya Angelou's autobiography, *I Know Why the Caged Bird Sings*, reveals the life of a black woman, yet also recalls for any reader the essence of childhood, growth, initiation, the desire for knowledge, and the sense of family. The selections included in Part Two capture the sight, sound, color, and pain experienced by a black child growing up in a Southern town and attempting to break into the adult white society when she applies for, and finally receives, a job as a conductress on the cable cars in wartime San Francisco. Angelou's second volume, *Gather Together in My Name*, moves into the adult black world in which she lived. She is open about the unconventional aspects of her young adulthood, proves that one can find a way, that it is the total direction of a life, and not individual actions, that ultimately matters.

Besides the two autobiographical works, Angelou has written two volumes of poetry, *Just Give Me a Cool Drink of Water: 'fore I Die* and *Oh Pray My Wings Are Gonna Fit Me Well*, which depict in her natural and often colloquial style both lyrical and realistic aspects of her experience as a woman and a black. In addition to her writing, Angelou has made many contributions to contemporary culture. At various times a dancer, teacher, playwright, and civil rights leader, she has starred in *Cabaret for Freedom* (which she also produced and directed in collaboration with Godfrey Cambridge) and Genêt's *The Blacks*. Her screenplay *Georgia, Georgia* was the first produced by a black woman; and she directed the film version of *I Know Why the Caged Bird Sings*, another first for a black woman. She has appeared on Bill Moyers' "NET Journal" and has written and produced a television series on African issues in American life.

Born in St. Louis, Angelou has lived in the South, in San Francisco, New York, Africa, and lately in northern California. The chapters from *I Know Why the Caged Bird Sings* are rich with the sense of place: Stamps, Arkansas, and San Francisco. In her narrative the rhythm of place joins with her particular reality, first as a child and later as a young woman. In the interview with Carol Benson, her warmth as a person is apparent as she discusses the task of writing, her work habits, and other black writers, particularly women. The various strands of her life have merged into a creative pattern, encouraging others, whatever their background and experience, to explore their own creativity.

Out of the Cage and Still Singing

INTERVIEW WITH MAYA ANGELOU BY CAROL BENSON

At forty-five, Maya Angelou has accomplished what it would take most people two lifetimes to do—touring Europe in a State Department production of *Porgy and Bess*, teaching dance in Rome and Tel Aviv, working as Northern California Coordinator for Dr. King's Southern Christian Leadership Conference, working with comedian Godfrey Cambridge, acting in Genêt's *The Blacks*, living in Africa, writing for newspapers in Cairo and Ghana, and serving on the faculty of the University of Ghana.

She wrote and produced a ten-part television series on African traditions in American life. She composed the original screenplay and musical score for the movie *Georgia, Georgia*, and in the spring of 1974 had her modern adaptation of Sophocles' *Ajax* produced at the Mark Taper Forum in Los Angeles. She is currently working on the film version of her first volume of autobiography, *I Know Why the Caged Bird Sings*.

Her latest work, *Gather Together in My Name*, is a sequel to the best-selling *Caged Bird*.

At her place in Sonoma, California, only a few miles from Jack London's home, we sip California burgundy and chat on the patio overlooking a swimming pool on one side and a rock garden with a fishpond on the other. Recently wed, she and her husband Paul Du Feu (writer, cartoonist, nude model and former husband of Germaine Greer) divide their time between their country retreat and trips to San Francisco, where Maya fulfills numerous speaking engagements.

Benson: What kind of critical response has *Gather Together* had so far?

Angelou: The New York Times, The New York Post, The Washington Post, The Cleveland Plain Dealer, the San Francisco and Los Angeles newspapers have given it incredibly good reviews. Some of the praise was so generous. I'm very pleased. The important thing, though, is that once the work is done you have to be finished with it. I pray for it, I treat it well, I wrote it as well as I knew how to write. I spent five weeks in promotion. But what's on my mind now is my next work.

Benson: What is that?

Angelou: I'm writing a book of poetry again. I'm grateful that *Gather Together* is having such a wonderful reception. If you have a child, it takes nine months. It took me three-and-a-half years to write *Gather Together*, so I couldn't just drop it. Even if you had a child, and even if you're putting the child up for adoption, you wash it, oil it, clothe it and give it a name. And then some women get about the business of getting the next child.

In my case as a writer, I feel that I should give it the chance to be seen and heard about, including spending five weeks in promotion.

And generally that's when I cut out, so I can start preparing myself for the next piece of work.

This last fall I was a Distinguished Professor at Sacramento State University, and was sharing Moyers' *NET Journal*. There are twenty-four programs in one year. Bill is a professional and a perfectionist, so he had to do them all perfectly. It really drained him. So now there are four people who have been invited to share those twenty-four programs next year: Studs Terkel, Shana Alexander, George Will and myself.

Benson: Was it as painful for you to write *Gather Together* as it was to write *Caged Bird*?

Angelou: It was worse. *Gather Together* deals with unsavory parts of my past. I'm now a Chubb Fellow at Yale University and Distinguished Professor at three universities in the country, and to admit some of the things I have admitted was very painful.

I called my son, my mother, and my brother (my husband, of course, was there) and I said, "This is what I want to do. I want to say to young people, 'You may encounter many defeats, but you must not be defeated.'" Then I read them the salient chapters, and my mother said, "Write it." My brother said, "Send it in." My son got up—we were sitting on this couch in Berkeley—and Guy got up and reached over and got Paul and me in those massive arms, and said, "You're so great, Mom. Please tell it."

Benson: Do you follow some kind of regular writing routine?

Angelou: Generally, I start about seven in the morning and write till around twelve. I break for lunch and work in the garden. Then I look at the work and let it cool off. I look at it after I've done it and most often I have to revise or throw out. Then I make dinner and try to live—since I'm married—a semblance of normal life. Around 5:30 I have a bath and cigarette and lots of coffee, and start again at seven.

Benson: Do you have your material pretty much in your head before you start?

Angelou: Yes.

Benson: Do you write it in longhand, or do you type it?

Angelou: I always write it in longhand, and have a secretary transcribe it on the typewriter.

Benson: How do you and your husband work your writing routines in together?

Angelou: Paul usually works from about eight to twelve, and I work until twelve. Usually by lunchtime we're both "down" enough, sane enough again, especially after a shower. We're both water nuts, which is good, and putting some water on us seems to cool us off. He's a very good critic, so usually I get to read my work to him first. I don't want any criticism but I can tell from his face. Then he reads his work, and then I go back to read it myself. He's a worker. Paul has spent twenty years of his life doing that. So he doesn't need, it seems, quite the same kind of silence I need.

Benson: Do you find that writing is pretty lonely?

Angelou: Yes. No matter how voluminous the praise, you know that nobody really understands what you mean, or where you had to go to get it. At some period, I think, you accept that fact, just as you accept being short or thin or fat. You accept what you are and say, "I'm going to be lonely." Family and friends are the only things that keep one close to sanity and to grace. When I go into that room to write, it's—bizarre.

I very much dislike those "artists" with the "-e" on the end. They're terribly mysterious and strange and unapproachable, and they go around with the back of their fists glued to their forehead. It's so phony and, unfortunately for them, it obstructs their art. You don't have to do that. You really can live lovely lives and do your work, even as a grocer does his work, and not always bring it right into the center of the living room for everybody else to have to deal with. I really distrust that kind of false artistry.

Benson: Wallace Stevens sold insurance.

Angelow: Exactly. And Henry Miller was an executive for years. One of the greatest novelists in this country—Melville—worked in the post office until he died.

Benson: How did your writing first get into print?

Angelou: Caged Bird was the first book. I had written a television series for NET in 1968, and I had also written songs for movies, and poems and short stories. But the first book was *Caged Bird.* I was asked to do it by Random House.

My friend and brother, James Baldwin, took me to Jules and Julie Feiffer's house one evening and the four of us sat up and drank and laughed and told stories until about 3:30 or 4:00 in the morning. And the next morning Julie Feiffer called the man who later became my editor, and said, "Do you know the poet Maya Angelou? If you can get her to write a book, you might have something." So he asked me, and I said, "No." I came out to California and he phoned, and about the third phone call he said, "Well, I guess you're very wise not to do it, because autobiography is the most difficult art form." So I said I would do it, and I did. It was like that. He should have told me that first!

Benson: How did you first meet James Baldwin?

Angelou: It seems like I've known Jimmy all my life. I was living in New York, and I had read his books. We were together in the Harlem Writers' Guild. Then I did a play called *The Blacks,* by Genêt. Jim happened to be in the States from Paris, and he came to the play. We started to become close, and about 1959 or 1960 he took me over to meet his family, and they adopted me. They are wonderful. There are eleven brothers and sisters and they're what keeps Jimmy alive. They are supportive and loving and funny—all the good stuff. And there's always some Baldwin over with Jim.

Benson: Is Baldwin still your favorite writer?

Angelou: Absolutely.

Benson: What upcoming black writers do you—

Angelou: Love dearly?

Benson: Well, are there any new ones on the horizon that you feel we should keep an eye on?

Angelou: There's a renaissance of black female writers who are so exciting. There's Toni Morrison, whose latest book is *Sula.* Beautiful writer.

Benson: What about Nikki Giovanni?

Angelou: Nikki's a fine poet. There's a woman named Sonia Sanchez, who is also a fine poet. Lucille Clifton, Carolyn Rogers—those are all poets. Janie Cortez, Mari Evans—delicious poets. Then there are the novelists. There's a woman named Louise Meriwether who wrote a book a couple of years ago called *Daddy Was a Number Runner.* There are Rosa Guy, Sara Wright, Paule Marshall, Toni Cade. There are incredible women writers out here. There's a beautiful poet from Berkeley named Joyce Carol Thomas. But I read everybody. Right now I'm reading S. J. Perelman.

Benson: I know this is a heavy question, but how do you deal with evil? How do you recognize it?

Angelou: Well, again, the best way to deal with evil is to concentrate on good. That's the best thing. You are about five-three, white, Midwestern—right?

Benson: Yes.

Angelou: I'm six foot, black, Southwestern. If we started looking at each other and our differences, our family background and personal history, we could find so many differences. But those are tangential, those are peripheral. There are really no differences. We are, first, human beings. And so when you weep, I understand it clearly. When you laugh, I understand it clearly. When you love, you don't have to translate it to me. These are the important things. Now if you want to tell me what happens in the Midwest, what the summers were like, what you ate for picnics—we can talk, and I can tell you what happened in Arkansas and what happened in California in the '40s and all that. But those are tangential.

Benson: Has getting older had any effect on your writing at all?

Angelou: I hope so. I hope I know more. I hope I'm gentler. I'd like to be gentler still. Most people don't mature. They crystallize at about fourteen or fifteen, and then they go on and take on the trappings of maturity. They get their degrees, they marry, they have the nerve to have children, they honor their credit cards, they find parking spaces, and they call it "maturity." But to be really mature is to accept, to include as opposed to exclude, to say that nothing human can be alien. That's what I believe. That's what I want to be, by fifty, I hope.

Adrienne Rich (b. 1929)

Since the publication in 1951 of her first collection of poetry, *A Change of World*, Adrienne Rich's voice has grown with the times, with the developing possibilities for women, and with their new relationships to each other, men, and the world. In her essay "When We Dead Awaken," she describes her evolution as a poet, from her early concern for craft and formal detachment to the concern with ever more personal and direct statement. She traces the parallel between her poetry and her life: a young wife and mother in the 1950s, whose life widened to include the political and social involvement of a woman of conscience in the violent 1960s and then the feminism of the present.

As a poet and a woman, Rich is committed to the need for a new social reality for women, who have been dominated too long by patriarchal society, and for men, who must be reconciled with what she calls the "ghostly woman" within them. Her anger at our death-dealing culture is cathartic, not simply polemical: Rich remains an artist, not a propagandist.

But although she sees the oppressor as a political force, perpetrating deadly competition, bomb tests, napalm conflagrations, and My Lai massacres, she also sees him as a person: husband, lover, neighborhood cop, even Beethoven composing his Ninth Symphony. The new reality to be forged is individual as well as collective, each man and woman confronting this "savagely fathered and unmothered world" separately and together, honoring female strength and compassion at last.

A full sensuality runs through many of Rich's poems, an affirmation of sexuality as well as a questioning of its role in our lives. Several poems in Part Two reflect different sides of this question, posing reality against romantic illusion, as in "Living in Sin" and "Two Songs." The later poems, "Photographs of an Unmade Bed" and "Translations," set the lovers' relationships in a broader political context. And "White Night" focuses on the sisterhood of isolated creative women.

Born in Baltimore and educated at Radcliffe College, Rich was honored with the National Book Award in 1974 for her seventh collection of poetry, *Diving into the Wreck*. However, she rejected it as an individual, having agreed with two other nominees, Audre Lorde and Alice Walker, that if one of them received the award, she would accept it in the name of all women.

We . . . together accept this award in the name of all the women whose voices have gone and still go unheard in a patriarchal world, and in the name of those who, like us, have been tolerated as token women in this culture, often at great cost and in great pain . . . We symbolically join here in refusing the terms of patriarchal competition and declaring that we will share this prize among us, to use as best we can for women . . . We dedicate this occasion to the struggle for self-determination of all women, of every color, identification or derived class . . . the women who will understand what we are doing here and those who will not understand yet; the silent women whose voices have been denied us, the articulate women who have given us strength to do our work.

Rich's other collections, *The Diamond Cutters, Snapshots of a Daugh-ter-in-law, Necessities of Life, Leaflets,* and *The Will to Change,* are all represented in the volume, *Poems, Selected and New, 1950–1974.* In addition, there is a Norton Critical Edition of her work, which includes selected poems, Rich's own essays and interviews, and reviews and criticism.

When We Dead Awaken

Ibsen's "When We Dead Awaken" is a play about the use that the male artist and thinker—in the process of creating culture as we know it—has made of women, in his life and in his work; and about a woman's slow struggling awakening to the use to which her life has been put. Bernard Shaw wrote in 1900 of this play:

[Ibsen] shows us that no degradation ever devized or permitted is as disastrous as this degradation; that through it women can die into luxuries for men and yet can kill them; that men and women are becoming conscious of this; and that what remains to be seen as perhaps the most interesting of all imminent social developments is what will happen "when we dead awaken".[1]

It's exhilarating to be alive in a time of awakening consciousness; it can also be confusing, disorienting, and painful. This awakening of dead or sleeping consciousness has already affected the lives of millions of women, even those who don't know it yet. It is also affecting the lives of men, even those who deny its claims upon them. The argument will go on whether an oppressive economic class system is responsible for the oppressive nature of male/female relations, or whether, in fact, the sexual class system is the original model on which all the others are based. But in the last few years connections have been drawn between our sexual lives and our political institutions, which are inescapable and illuminating. The sleepwalkers are coming awake, and for the first time this awakening has a collective reality; it is no longer such a lonely thing to open one's eyes.

Re-vision—the act of looking back, of seeing with fresh eyes, of entering an old text from a new critical direction—is for us more than a chapter in cultural history: it is an act of survival. Until we can understand the assumptions in which we are drenched we cannot know ourselves. And this drive to self-knowledge, for woman, is more than a search for identity: it is part of her refusal of the self-destructiveness of male-dominated society. A radical critique of literature, feminist in its impulse, would take the work first of all as a clue to how we live, how we have been living, how we have been led to imagine ourselves, how our language has trapped as well as liberated us; and how we can begin to see—and therefore live—afresh. A change in the

[1] G. B. Shaw, *The Quintessence of Ibsenism* (Hill and Wang, 1922), p. 139.

concept of sexual identity is essential if we are not going to see the old political order re-assert itself in every new revolution. We need to know the writing of the past, and know it differently than we have ever known it; not to pass on a tradition but to break its hold over us.

For writers, and at this moment for women writers in particular, there is the challenge and promise of a whole new psychic geography to be explored. But there is also a difficult and dangerous walking on the ice, as we try to find language and images for a consciousness we are just coming into, and with little in the past to support us. I want to talk about some aspects of this difficulty and this danger.

Jane Harrison, the great classical anthropologist, wrote in 1914 in a letter to her friend Gilbert Murray:

By the by, about "Women," it has bothered me often—why do women never want to write poetry about Man as a sex—why is Woman a dream and a terror to man and not the other way around? . . . Is it mere convention and propriety, or something deeper?[2]

I think Jane Harrison's question cuts deep into the myth-making tradition, the romantic tradition; deep into what women and men have been to each other; and deep into the psyche of the woman writer. Thinking about that question, I began thinking of the work of two 20th-century women poets, Sylvia Plath and Diane Wakoski. It strikes me that in the work of both Man appears as, if not a dream, a fascination and a terror; and that the source of the fascination and the terror is, simply, Man's power—to dominate, tyrannize, choose, or reject the woman. The charisma of Man seems to come purely from his power over her and his control of the world by force, not from anything fertile or life-giving in him. And, in the work of both these poets, it is finally the woman's sense of *herself*—embattled, possessed—that gives the poetry its dynamic charge, its rhythms of struggle, need, will, and female energy. Convention and propriety are perhaps not the right words, but until recently this female anger and this furious awareness of the Man's power over her were not available materials to the female poet, who tended to write of Love as the source of her suffering, and to view that victimization by Love as an almost inevitable fate. Or, like Marianne Moore and Elizabeth Bishop, she kept human sexual relationships at a measured and chiselled distance in her poems.

One answer to Jane Harrison's question has to be that historically men and women have played very different parts in each others' lives. Where woman has been a luxury for man, and has served as the painter's model and the poet's muse, but also as comforter, nurse, cook, bearer of his seed, secretarial assistant and copyist of manuscripts, man has played a quite different role for the female artist. Henry James repeats an incident which the writer Prosper Mérimée described, of how, while he was living with George Sand,

2 J. G. Stewart, *Jane Ellen Harrison: A Portrait from Letters* (London, 1959), p. 140.

he once opened his eyes, in the raw winter dawn, to see his companion, in a dressing-gown, on her knees before the domestic hearth, a candle-stick beside her and a red *madras* round her head, making bravely, with her own hands, the fire that was to enable her to sit down be-times to urgent pen and paper. The story represents him as having felt that the spectacle chilled his ardor and tried his taste; her appear-ance was unfortunate, her occupation an inconsequence, and her in-dustry a reproof—the result of all of which was a lively irritation and an early rupture.[3]

I am suggesting that the specter of this kind of male judgment, along with the active discouragement and thwarting of her needs by a cul-ture controlled by males, has created problems for the woman writer: problems of contact with herself, problems of language and style, problems of energy and survival.

In rereading Virginia Woolf's *A Room of One's Own* for the first time in some years, I was astonished at the sense of effort, of pains taken, of dogged tentativeness, in the tone of that essay. And I rec-ognized that tone. I had heard it often enough, in myself and in other women. It is the tone of a woman almost in touch with her anger, who is determined not to appear angry, who is *willing* herself to be calm, detached, and even charming in a roomful of men where things have been said which are attacks on her very integrity. Virginia Woolf is addressing an audience of women, but she is acutely conscious— as she always was—of being overheard by men: by Morgan and Lyt-ton and Maynard Keynes and for that matter by her father, Leslie Stephen. She drew the language out into an exacerbated thread in her determination to have her own sensibility yet protect it from those masculine presences. Only at rare moments in that essay do you hear the passion in her voice; she was trying to sound as cool as Jane Austen, as Olympian as Shakespeare, because that is the way the men of the culture thought a writer should sound.

No male writer has writen primarily or even largely for women, or with the sense of women's criticism as a consideration when he chooses his materials, his theme, his language. But to a lesser or greater extent, every woman writer has written for men even when, like Virginia Woolf, she was supposed to be addressing women. If we have come to the point when this balance might begin to change, when women can stop being haunted, not only by "convention and propriety" but by internalized fears of being and saying themselves, then it is an extraordinary moment for the woman writer—and reader.

I have hesitated to do what I am going to do now, which is to use my-self as an illustration. For one thing, it's a lot easier and less dangerous to talk about other women writers. But there is something else. Like Virginia Woolf, I am aware of the women who are not with us here because they are washing the dishes and looking after the children. Nearly fifty years after she spoke, that fact remains largely unchanged. And I am thinking also of women whom she left out of the picture altogether—women who are washing other people's dishes and caring

[3] Henry James, "Notes on Novelists" in *Selected Literary Criticism of Henry James*, ed. Morris Shapiro (London: Heineman, 1963), pp. 157–58.

for other people's children, not to mention women who went on the streets last night in order to feed their children. We seem to be special women here, we have liked to think of ourselves as special, and we have known that men would tolerate, even romanticize us as special, as long as our words and actions didn't threaten their privilege of tolerating or rejecting us according to *their* ideas of what a special woman ought to be. An important insight of the radical women's movement, for me, has been how divisive and how ultimately destructive is this myth of the special woman, who is also the token woman. Every one of us here in this room has had great luck—we are teachers, writers, academicians; our own gifts could not have been enough, for we all know women whose gifts are buried or aborted. Our struggles can have meaning only if they can help to change the lives of women whose gifts—and whose very being—continue to be thwarted.

My own luck was being born white and middle-class into a house full of books, with a father who encouraged me to read and write. So for about twenty years I wrote for a particular man, who criticized and praised me and made me feel I was indeed "special." The obverse side of this, of course, was that I tried for a long time to please him, or rather, not to displease him. And then of course there were other men—writers, teachers—the Man, who was not a terror or a dream but a literary master and a master in other ways less easy to acknowledge. And there were all those poems about women, written by men: it seemed to be a given that men wrote poems and women frequently inhabited them. These women were almost always beautiful, but threatened with the loss of beauty, the loss of youth—the fate worse than death. Or, they were beautiful and died young, like Lucy and Lenore. Or, the woman was like Maud Gonne, cruel and disastrously mistaken, and the poem reproached her because she had refused to become a luxury for the poet.

A lot is being said today about the influence that the myths and images of women have on all of us who are products of culture. I think it has been a peculiar confusion to the girl or woman who tries to write because she is peculiarly susceptible to language. She goes to poetry or fiction looking for *her* way of being in the world, since she too has been putting words and images together; she is looking eagerly for guides, maps, possibilities; and over and over in the "words' masculine persuasive force" of literature she comes up against something that negates everything she is about: she meets the image of Woman in books written by men. She finds a terror and a dream, she finds a beautiful pale face, she finds La Belle Dame Sans Merci, she finds Juliet or Tess or Salomé, but precisely what she does not find is that absorbed, drudging, puzzled, sometimes inspired creature, herself, who sits at a desk trying to put words together.

So what does she do? What did I do? I read the older women poets with their peculiar keenness and ambivalence: Sappho, Christina Rossetti, Emily Dickinson, Elinor Wylie, Edna Millay, H.D. I discovered that the woman poet most admired at the time (by men) was Marianne Moore, who was maidenly, elegant, intellectual, discreet. But even in reading these women I was looking in them for the same things I had found in the poetry of men, because I wanted women poets to be the equals of men, and to be equal was still confused with sounding the same.

I know that my style was formed first by male poets: by the men I was reading as an undergraduate—Frost, Dylan Thomas, Donne, Auden, MacNiece, Stevens, Yeats. What I chiefly learned from them was craft. But poems are like dreams: in them you put what you don't know you know. Looking back at poems I wrote before I was 21, I'm startled because beneath the conscious craft are glimpses of the split I even then experienced between the girl who wrote poems, who defined herself in writing poems, and the girl who was to define herself by her relationships with men. "Aunt Jennifer's Tigers," written while I was a student, looks with deliberate detachment at this split.

> Aunt Jennifer's tigers stride across a screen,
> Bright topaz denizens of a world of green.
> They do not fear the men beneath the tree;
> They pace in sleek chivalric certainty.
>
> Aunt Jennifer's fingers fluttering through her wool
> Find even the ivory needle hard to pull.
> The massive weight of Uncle's wedding band
> Sits heavily upon Aunt Jennifer's hand.
>
> When Aunt is dead, her terrified hands will lie
> Still ringed with ordeals she was mastered by.
> The tigers in the panel that she made
> Will go on striding, proud and unafraid.[4]

In writing this poem, composed and apparently cool as it is, I thought I was creating a portrait of an imaginary woman. But this woman suffers from the opposition of her imagination, worked out in tapestry, and her life-style, "ringed with ordeals she was mastered by." It was important to me that Aunt Jennifer was a person as distinct from myself as possible—distanced by the formalism of the poem, by its objective, observant tone—even by putting the woman in a different generation.

In those years formalism was part of the strategy—like asbestos gloves, it allowed me to handle materials I couldn't pick up bare-handed. (A later strategy was to use the persona of a man, as I did in "The Loser.") I finished college, published my first book by a fluke, as it seemed to me, and broke off a love affair. I took a job, lived alone, went on writing, fell in love. I was young, full of energy, and the book seemed to mean that others agreed I was a poet. Because I was also determined to have a "full" woman's life, I plunged in my early twenties into marriage and had three children before I was thirty. There was nothing overt in the environment to warn me: these were the '50's, and in reaction to the earlier wave of feminism, middle-class women were making careers of domestic perfection, working to send their husbands through professional schools, then retiring to raise large

---

[4] Adrienne Rich, *A Change of World* (Yale University Press, 1951). Quoted by permission of the author.

families. People were moving out to the suburbs, technology was going to be the answer to everything, even sex; the family was in its glory. Life was extremely private; women were isolated from each other by the loyalties of marriage. I have a sense that women didn't talk to each other much in the fifties—not about their secret emptiness, their frustrations. I went on trying to write; my second book and first child appeared in the same month. But by the time that book came out I was already dissatisfied with those poems, which seemed to me mere exercises for poems I hadn't written. The book was praised, however, for its "gracefulness"; I had a marriage and a child. If there were doubts, if there were periods of null depression or active despairing, these could only mean that I was ungrateful, insatiable, perhaps a monster.

About the time my third child was born, I felt that I had either to consider myself a failed woman and a failed poet, or to try to find some synthesis by which to understand what was happening to me. What frightened me most was the sense of drift, of being pulled along on a current which called itself my destiny, but in which I seemed to be losing touch with whoever I had been, with the girl who had experienced her own will and energy almost ecstatically at times, walking around a city or riding a train at night or typing in a student room. In a poem about my grandmother I wrote (of myself): "A young girl, thought sleeping, is certified dead."[5] I was writing very little, partly from fatigue, that female fatigue of suppressed anger and the loss of contact with her own being; partly from the discontinuity of female life with its attention to small chores, errands, work that others constantly undo, small children's constant needs. What I did write was unconvincing to me; my anger and frustration were hard to acknowledge in or out of poems because in fact I cared a great deal about my husband and my children. Trying to look back and understand that time I have tried to analyze the real nature of the conflict. Most, if not all, human lives are full of fantasy—passive day-dreaming which need not be acted on. But to write poetry or fiction, or even to think well, is not to fantasize, or to put fantasies on paper. For a poem to coalesce, for a character or an action to take shape, there has to be an imaginative transformation of reality which is in no way passive. And a certain freedom of the mind is needed—freedom to press on, to enter the currents of your thought like a glider pilot, knowing that your motion can be sustained, that the buoyancy of your attention will not be suddenly snatched away. Moreover, if the imagination is to transcend and transform experience it has to question, to challenge, to conceive of alternatives, perhaps to the very life you are living at that moment. You have to be free to play around with the notion that day might be night, love might be hate; nothing can be too sacred for the imagination to turn into its opposite or to call experimentally by another name. For writing is re-naming. Now, to be maternally with small children all day in the old way, to be with a man in the old way of marriage, requires a holding-back, a putting-aside of that imaginative activity, and seems to demand instead a kind of conservatism.

[5] "Halfway," in *Necessities of Life* (W. W. Norton and Company, 1966), p. 34.

I want to make it clear that I am *not* saying that in order to write well, or think well, it is necessary to become unavailable to others, or to become a devouring ego. This has been the myth of the masculine artist and thinker; and I repeat, I do not accept it. But to be a female human being trying to fulfill traditional female functions in a traditional way *is* in direct conflict with the subversive function of the imagination. The word traditional is important here. There must be ways, and we will be finding out more and more about them, in which the energy of creation and the energy of relation can be united. But in those earlier years I always felt the conflict as a failure of love in myself. I had thought I was choosing a full life: the life available to most men, in which sexuality, work, and parenthood could coexist. But I felt, at 29, guilt toward the people closest to me, and guilty toward my own being.

I wanted, then, more than anything, the one thing of which there was never enough: time to think, time to write. The fifties and early sixties were years of rapid revelations: the sit-ins and marches in the South, the Bay of Pigs, the early anti-war movement, raised large questions— questions for which the masculine world of the academy around me seemed to have expert and fluent answers. But I needed desperately to think for myself—about pacifism and dissent and violence, about poetry and society and about my own relationship to all these things. For about ten years I was reading in fierce snatches, scribbling in notebooks, writing poetry in fragments; I was looking desperately for clues, because if there were no clues then I thought I might be insane. I wrote in a notebook about this time:

Paralyzed by the sense that there exists a mesh of relationships—e.g. between my anger at the children, my sensual life, pacifism, sex, (I mean sex in its broadest significance, not merely sexual desire)—an interconnectedness which, if I could see it, make it valid, would give me back myself, make it possible to function lucidly and passionately. Yet I grope in and out among these dark webs.

I think I began at this point to feel that politics was not something "out there" but something "in here" and of the essence of my condition.

In the late '50's I was able to write, for the first time, directly about experiencing myself as a woman. The poem was jotted in fragments during children's naps, brief hours in a library, or at 3 A.M. after rising with a wakeful child. I despaired of doing any continuous work at this time. Yet I began to feel that my fragments and scraps had a common consciousness and a common theme, one which I would have been very unwilling to put on paper at an earlier time because I had been taught that poetry should be "universal," which meant, of course, non-female. Until then I had tried very much *not* to identify myself as a female poet. Over two years I wrote a 10-part poem called "Snapshots of a Daughter-in-Law," in a longer, looser mode than I'd ever trusted myself with before. It was an extraordinary relief to write that poem. It strikes me now as too literary, too dependent on allusion;

I hadn't found the courage yet to do without authorities, or even to use the pronoun "I"—the woman in the poem is always "she." One section of it, No. 2, concerns a woman who thinks she is going mad; she is haunted by voices telling her to resist and rebel, voices which she can hear but not obey.

The poem "Orion," written five years later, is a poem of reconnection with a part of myself I had felt I was losing—the active principle, the energetic imagination, the "half-brother" whom I projected, as I had for many years, into the constellation Orion. It's no accident that the words "cold and egotistical" appear in this poem, and are applied to myself. The choice still seemed to be between "love"—womanly, maternal love, altruistic love—a love defined and ruled by the weight of an entire culture; and egotism—a force directed by men into creation, achievement, ambition, often at the expense of others, but justifiably so. For weren't they men, and wasn't that their destiny as womanly love was ours? I know now that the alternatives are false ones—that the word "love" is itself in need of re-vision.

There is a companion poem to "Orion," written three years later, in which at last the woman in the poem and the woman writing the poem become the same person. It is called "Planetarium," and it was written after a visit to a real planetarium, where I read an account of the work of Caroline Herschel, the astronomer, who worked with her brother William, but whose name remained obscure, as his did not.

In closing I want to tell you about a dream I had last summer. I dreamed I was asked to read my poetry at a mass women's meeting, but when I began to read, what came out were the lyrics of a blues song. I share this dream with you because it seemed to me to say a lot about the problems and the future of the woman writer, and probably of women in general. The awakening of consciousness is not like the crossing of a frontier—one step, and you are in another country. Much of woman's poetry has been of the nature of the blues song: a cry of pain, of victimization, or a lyric of seduction. And today, much poetry by women—and prose for that matter—is charged with anger. I think we need to go through that anger, and we will betray our own reality if we try, as Virginia Woolf was trying, for an objectivity, a detachment, that would make us sound more like Jane Austen or Shakespeare. We know more than Jane Austen or Shakespeare knew: more than Jane Austen because our lives are more complex, more than Shakespeare because we know more about the lives of women, Jane Austen and Virginia Woolf included.

Both the victimization and the anger experienced by women are real, and have real sources, everywhere in the environment, built into society. They must go on being tapped and explored by poets, among others. We can neither deny them, nor can we rest there. They are our birthpains, and we are bearing ourselves. We would be failing each other as writers and as women, if we neglected or denied what is negative, regressive, or Sisyphean in our inwardness.

We all know that there is another story to be told. I am curious and expectant about the future of the masculine consciousness. I feel in the work of the men whose poetry I read today a deep pessimism and fatalistic grief; and I wonder if it isn't the masculine side of what women have experienced, the price of masculine dominance. One thing I am sure of: just as woman is becoming her own mid-wife, creating herself anew, so man will have to learn to gestate and give birth to his own subjectivity—something he has frequently wanted woman to do for him. We can go on trying to talk to each other, we can sometimes help each other, poetry and fiction can show us what the other is going through; but women can no longer be primarily mothers and muses for men: we have our own work cut out for us.

Myrna Lamb (b. 1930)

Myrna Lamb, feminist playwright, creates revolutionary theater: her work challenges the audience to a new view of political, social, and human reality and to the need for change. Reflecting her awareness of the mythic power of the theater, Lamb's dramas not only fulfill the time-honored function of arousing pity and fear but also lead to outrage and illumination. Because the line between challenge and threat is thin, her work has not always been readily accepted by theater producers and critics. However, a production of her recent opera, *Apple Pie*, was directed by Joseph Papp at the New York Shakespeare Festival Public Theater, and women's theaters and others have presented her work, not only throughout the United States, but all over the world.

To experience any of her plays, even as readers' theater or on records within a classroom, makes one aware of Lamb's electrifying ability to meld effective theater with intense political statements: the combination of art and politics that results in revolutionary drama. Some critics, overwhelmed by her political assertiveness, have discredited her artistry. And from the opposite end of the spectrum, some radical women's groups have withheld their support because they feel that today's drama should be a collective effort, not the work of an individual playwright. So it is in this atmosphere of moved and responsive audiences, a hostile reception from the conservative theater establishment, and avoidance by segments of the women's movement that Lamb is carving out her identity as a playwright. Her essay "Female Playwright: Confessions of a Fallen Woman," written for this anthology, charts some of the struggles as an artist and reflects the open sharing of feelings that she is willing to risk.

Born in New Jersey, Lamb wrote her first play at age eight, but had to wait another thirty years to have one produced. As a child, she was given a strong musical background, and later she worked as an actress, as well as at everyday jobs, mothered two children, and continued writing all along. In 1970, her *Mod Donna*, the first feminist musical, was produced by Joseph Papp for the New York Shakespeare Festival Public Theater. She received a performance grant from the Biennale de Paris in 1971, a Rockefeller Fellowship in 1972, and a Guggenheim in 1973. In 1974, she was awarded a National Endowment of Music grant as a librettist. Her plays and musicals have been presented on various radio broadcasts; *Apple Pie* has been commercially recorded; and she has published a collection of scripts entitled *Mod Donna, Scyklon Z*. Another play, *Crab Quadille*, is scheduled for production in 1977.

Female Playwright: Confessions of a Fallen Woman

FEE FALL PLAY EN MALE WRIGHT PRO CON FESS SHUN

My life is what it has to be. A disaster area. You see, I thought I'd beat them at their game. Worked six years on *Apple Pie*, the latest project. Music scenes with the stress and accent of spoken language. Subconscious truth filtered through fourteen brainabrasive versions tuned to male/academic standards. Perfection in calibration of sung syllables. Work. Re-work. Puritan ethic. No New Year's Eves. Nothing.

But I should have understood there was no way to beat the system. Unpleasant truths about societally indoctrinated and enforced self-hatred. Nazi Germany to America in a hop, skip and jump. The problems of Jews, Blacks, Older Men and Aging Women. The concept of purity as applied to lower forms of American animal life including sexual women.

And then the routine unforgiving backlash. The ordinary co-option. The recognition that there is no support system for a strong female artist who tells the terrible subconscious truth in an almost too-proficient manner. The impossible position of the female artist. The double female. Am I supposed to analyze that position? The position is ridiculous.

I evolved out of the particular crucible of the devalued, manipulated and battered female (child and adult) of Depression birth and rearing. I was a World War II early adolescent, traumatized forever by revelations of foreign atrocities with native concurrence. I emerged from extreme poverty, brutality, psychic and physical deprivation.

Deprivation. The breast is denied me. Can I be my own breast? Can I suckle and nurture myself? I am the source. I must *be* the breast. I am the only source for myself, the only generation. And that generation in absolute isolation.

Isolation. Cut off from all illusion. The illusion of psychic connection I dreamed into existence because I felt I could not live without it. The illusion of connection between me and the people I dreamed I could not live without. The people I loved in the theater. The women I loved as mythic sisters.

Sisters. No more lies. No more love. No more lying dreams of love. No more friendship, ephemeral and capitalist. No more imagining that friends exist who want me to live and to continue and to prosper.

Prosper. If I do not, I am avoided as a social liability, a psychological leper. I dared too much. I fell too far. I am resented for my achievement at the same time I am despised for my failure. A woman invites me to lunch, and offers unrequested advice. She is the new vice president of a television network. She has seemed supportive in the past. She suggests I get a typing job to support myself. (Why does she assume I can type well enough to get a job to support myself?) She announces to others after the lunch that she will not see me again because she "can't stand self-indulgent preoccupation." One of the many orders to die.

Orders to die. A top feminist woman, who has told me, weeping, that I am the first artist of the feminist consciousness, is compelled to turn her back on this work after she has promised support. She cannot afford to affiliate with establishment failure.

Failure. No men. No women. No babies. No love. Oh, and no money. No shelter. Doors shut in my face. Yes, that's the place I remember. The only place that ever existed in dreams. The familiar. The familial.

Familial. My mother says to me when I tell her I feel suicidal . . . "Well, you have to do what you have to do." My daughters become strangers, coldly revolted by the sight of their strong mother turned weak and defeated.

Defeated. What have I done? Over and over I ask myself that. And in the middle of the night, startled awake by the single word . . . "Why?" Have I abandoned my autonomy for the ease of having someone proclaim undying belief in me? And it was so easy, conversely to believe in the *other* person, put my eggs in his basket, let him be the egg in my basket, let him grow inside me, nurture him with every heartbeat and then find that he grew out of my very guts, created accurately in their image, an enemy.

I have written that prophecy, precisely. And yes, it was self-fulfilling. And I have written that aspect as well, and more, that, annexed, I cannot be digested. But I could not anticipate male power, bonded with mine, would make me so threatening (although negated too) that I and all those involved with me must be punished for our criminal collusion.

Opening night seems a triumph. But I know better. I look into people's eyes for the Truth of my immediate future. I am an anticipatory ghost of that future. Tomorrow, a few hours hence, will find the congratulatory screams frozen into sneers. My fear paralyzes my brain, immobilizes my will. The reviews, the reviews as yet unread, fill my mind. I have been through this before and I know. I see myself proceeding forevermore as a writhing mass of entrails, an involuntary invertebrate, a non-cerebrate, a creature of patterns, of reflexes, of all-encompassing terror. And I cut my own throat in response, and I amputate my own breast, and the poisoned milk of my amputated breast backs into my cattleslaughtered throat, and bile spills from the widely-grinning mouthslash of my butchered throat, spills burning on the fresh wound of my amputated breast.

I wake in the morning. I remember rainbows. I remember the exquisitely good smell of spring air on a New Jersey spit of land between the ocean and the bay. I remember the sound of the cello wind, bowing the corner of the house where I slept and dreamt. And it's gone.

I think about the ugliness of a wasting death. I think about cancer. Or a failing heart. Drowning in my own fluids. The avoidance in the eyes of those who once, not loved, needed me. And it's coming. All that is on the way.

And I am here. In this moment they have convinced me. The critics. Not just the critics. I am merely presumptuous. Yes. And I can't. No. And I shouldn't. No. And it's all past beauty and future ugliness and present nothingness.

I sold my accumulated past, my only chance at daily beauty. My house at the ocean which I didn't own, but which could be turned in for a cash stake. I turned it in for a year or two of this ugly city where the theater is. I wiped out the dream state and woke up to nightmare.

I am afraid to be alone. The ocean, which I love, also terrifies me. The night sky at the ocean has strange and brilliant visitations. The visions, the sounds, the deep blackness, the importunate wind . . . I yearn. I fear. I never learned how to be alone the way I need to be alone. I am afraid.

The New York apartment is surrounded by evidence that I am not alone. Other people's sighs and moans and toilet flushes constantly attest to their presence. And the theater is here. Full of promises. A siren song that sings high above the caterwauling police car, fire engine, and speeding ambulance. Come, the theater says. Begin. That brief promise. That mere beginning.

Passionate life is in that moment. The moment is all. Nothing more. That instant when the dream of the future is mine. Intensity. Love and passion and life. That moment that will never be repeated. If I didn't hear it, see it at *that moment*, I would never hear it or see it again. And then if that moment is that perfect, imagine how it will be with *all* the elements. The lights, the set, the music, the audience.

And that's where it remains. In the ear and eye of my memory of a moment. The colors brilliant, the sound sensational, the truth astonishing. In fact, too astonishing. Too much astonishing truth, falling on ears attuned to lies.

Afterwards. Silence. A disaster area. Clear the bodies. So many bodies. All the things I expect will happen to a strong woman, *do* happen to a daring female dramatist. Die, they say. Stick your head into an oven and achieve canonization. Leap from a tall building. Crash. Become Superlegend. Obligingly die.

Alive. I am not the magic woman. The warning shots have been fired across the bows of those human vessels who sailed with me. Alone. In New York. The toilets flush in the next apartments. It's time to wash the clothes. Who am I? I am a person who washes clothes fairly efficiently. And does my taxes three months after the deadline. Slow. But motion. Receipts. On the floor. Broke. Paying taxes. Alive.

No more love. No more sex. No more friends. No more dreams. No more home.

But I didn't die. No, I didn't die. Everything fell. All the dire prophecy came true. And the doors shut in my face. But I didn't die.

My hunger survived. My curiosity revived. And I am still alive. A female playwright.

Adrienne Kennedy (b. 1931)

Although a statement about writing by Adrienne Kennedy was not available, she deserves inclusion in this volume as an experimental dramatist whose work points to possibilities of women's contribution to this form in the future. Minority writing is frequently experimental: when writers emerge out of a specific group that is cohesive politically, they may need new forms in which to emphasize the conflicts of their emergence as well as to depict images, themes, and feelings that can be only feebly presented in existing forms.

Some black critics consider Kennedy's work too universal and experimental, too stamped with the marks of an elitist white education. However, one way black literature can find a larger place in Western culture is move beyond the often polemical realism and naturalism in order to relate the black dilemma to universal human suffering. Kennedy's work generalizes the pain of the black experience, placing it within the alienation and the absurdity of human existence. She has written novels and poetry, but her drama generally has had the strongest impact. Her work is original, imaginative, and marked with a sense of privacy that also surrounds her life.

Born in Pittsburgh, she attended Ohio State University and Columbia. While living in London, she wrote plays that reflected the cosmopolitan nature of Europe that many black writers have sought as an alternative to the particularity and artistic limitations of the American scene. The experience of writers like Joyce and Baldwin suggests that in exile the minority writer is often best able to assess the uniqueness of the minority experience. For some black writers, it is only when they can escape the everyday experience of being black, of facing the constant struggle against prejudice that they can write about its essential meaning.

Kennedy's plays include *Funnyhouse of a Negro, The Owl Answers, A Lesson in a Dead Language, A Rat's Mass,* and *A Beast's Story.* Her adaptation of John Lennon's works, entitled *The Lennon Play,* was performed at the Old Vic. Using the techniques of expressionistic drama, Kennedy explores the anguish of black experience in a white society. In *The Owl Answers,* as in *Funnyhouse,* she uses a young black woman whose fantasies about literary and historical figures blend with a realistic present, a combination that demands attention from the audience to piece together the "facts" of her life. Yet, for the woman from Georgia who rides New York subways in the summertime to pick up men and who moves into fantasies about Anne Boleyn and Chaucer as the subway doors open and close, what, really, are the facts of existence? In *A Rat's Mass,* Kennedy explores the black ambivalence to Christianity (which offers future salvation in place of immediate justice) against a backdrop of motifs of religious ritual and Nazi invasion, with Kafkaesque central characters who are part rat, part human, but who ultimately realize that their existence is predominantly and increasingly ratlike.

Funnyhouse is an apt choice for this anthology for it probes the agony of a young woman trying to come to terms with her existence and experience. Sara/The Negro has the added difficulty of being black in a white society and is caught in the central dilemma that this kind of society produces for the black: it equates worth with skin color so that the lightest black is in a superior position. Sara is yellow, the child of an even lighter mother and a black father. The image of dark man as evil, the rapist, haunts Sara and explains her rejection of her father, whom she holds responsible for her mother having died in an asylum. Sara is educated and seeks a "white" life, yet Kennedy endows her with the humor to see through the white liberalism of her lover, Raymond. But finally Sara is caught by the forces of society and those of her own making.

Sylvia Plath (1932–1963)

Sylvia Plath is a woman seen as though refracted through a prism: heroine, victim, spokeswoman for her generation, isolated genius, apotheosis of the link between creativity and self-destruction. The tragedy of her suicide at the age of thirty, all her brilliant potential never to be realized, has dominated most assessments of her work and life, particularly in light of the subsequent feminist revolution, whose martyr she appeared to be.

Yet even though we know her final act that followed the frenzied creation of *Ariel*, the life and hallucinatory intensity of the poems is overwhelming. Plath derived a tremendous amount of energy from anger, a personal fury expressed in such poems as "Daddy" and "Lesbos." The force in her poetry is closer to rage than a frantic race against death: it is her startling images and wrenching perceptions, reverberating like babies' cries, like throbbing blood, through the poems.

Besides her poetry, Plath left us two versions of her entrance into womanhood: the novel *The Bell Jar* and *Letters Home*, edited by her mother and husband, Ted Hughes. Certain elements are consistent in both: her academic honors, desire for perfection, and sense of a special destiny. Each book has a distinct tone, however. The almost flippant detachment and witty treatment of her breakdown and attempted suicide at age nineteen in *The Bell Jar* is counterbalanced by the girlish enthusiasm and optimism of *Letters Home*. Excerpts from *The Bell Jar* are included here not because they represent absolute truth but because they give perspective into part of Plath: the girl, portrayed through her protagonist, Esther Greenwood, who wants a literary career and feels terribly at odds with the times. The women who have made it—the editor, Jay Cee, and Esther's benefactor, Philomena Guinea—do not serve her as adequate models. Esther finds no intimacy with anyone, male or female, and this lack of connection reflects her lack of self-love. Plath herself felt alienated from the stereotyped choices of the 1950s, experienced a sort of breakdown, and attempted to commit suicide at the end of her junior year at Smith. Esther provides Plath with a way of explaining these crises.

It is as a poet, however, that Plath gained her literary reputation. Her collections include *The Colossus, Crossing the Water,* and *Winter Trees.* The selections in Part Two come from *Ariel:* "Lady Lazarus," in which death is seen as a source of creativity and of separateness from the rest of humanity (and thus supports the theory about Plath's suicide advanced by A. Alvarez in *The Savage God*), and three shorter poems, each displaying Plath's rare achievement in style and imagery.

The Bell Jar

It was a queer, sultry summer, the summer they electrocuted the Rosenbergs, and I didn't know what I was doing in New York. I'm stupid about executions. The idea of being electrocuted makes me sick, and that's all there was to read about in the papers—goggle-eyed headlines staring up at me on every street corner and at the fusty, peanut-smelling mouth of every subway. It had nothing to do with me, but I couldn't help wondering what it would be like, being burned alive all along your nerves.

I thought it must be the worst thing in the world.

New York was bad enough. By nine in the morning the fake, country-wet freshness that somehow seeped in overnight evaporated like the tail end of a sweet dream. Mirage-gray at the bottom of their granite canyons, the hot streets wavered in the sun, the car tops sizzled and glittered, and the dry, cindery dust blew into my eyes and down my throat.

I kept hearing about the Rosenbergs over the radio and at the office till I couldn't get them out of my mind. It was like the first time I saw a cadaver. For weeks afterward, the cadaver's head—or what there was left of it—floated up behind my eggs and bacon at breakfast and behind the face of Buddy Willard, who was responsible for my seeing it in the first place, and pretty soon I felt as though I were carrying that cadaver's head around with me on a string, like some black, noseless balloon stinking of vinegar.

I knew something was wrong with me that summer, because all I could think about was the Rosenbergs and how stupid I'd been to buy all those uncomfortable, expensive clothes, hanging limp as fish in my closet, and how all the little successes I'd totted up so happily at college fizzled to nothing outside the slick marble and plate-glass fronts along Madison Avenue.

I was supposed to be having the time of my life.

I was supposed to be the envy of thousands of other college girls just like me all over America who wanted nothing more than to be tripping about in those same size-seven patent leather shoes I'd bought in Bloomingdale's one lunch hour with a black patent leather belt and black patent leather pocketbook to match. And when my picture came out in the magazine the twelve of us were working on—drinking martinis in a skimpy imitation silver-lamé bodice stuck on to a big, fat cloud of white tulle, on some Starlight Roof, in the company of several anonymous young men with all-American bone structures hired or loaned for the occasion—everybody would think I must be having a real whirl.

Look what can happen in this country, they'd say. A girl lives in some out-of-the-way town for nineteen years, so poor she can't afford a magazine, and then she gets a scholarship to college and wins a prize here and a prize there and ends up steering New York like her own private car.

Only I wasn't steering anything, not even myself. I just bumped from my hotel to work and to parties and from parties to my hotel and back to work like a numb trolleybus. I guess I should have been excited the way most of the other girls were, but I couldn't get myself to react. I felt very still and very empty, the way the eye of a tornado must feel, moving dully along in the middle of the surrounding hullabaloo.

There were twelve of us at the hotel.

We had all won a fashion magazine contest, by writing essays and stories and poems and fashion blurbs, and as prizes they gave us jobs in New York for a month, expenses paid, and piles and piles of free bonuses, like ballet tickets and passes to fashion shows and hair stylings at a famous expensive salon and chances to meet successful people in the field of our desire and advice about what to do with our particular complexions.

I still have the make-up kit they gave me, fitted out for a person with brown eyes and brown hair: an oblong of brown mascara with a tiny brush, and a round basin of blue eye-shadow just big enough to dab the tip of your finger in, and three lipsticks ranging from red to pink, all cased in the same little gilt box with a mirror on one side. I also have a white plastic sunglasses case with colored shells and sequins and a green plastic starfish sewed onto it.

I realized we kept piling up these presents because it was as good as free advertising for the firms involved, but I couldn't be cynical. I got such a kick out of all those free gifts showering on to us. For a long time afterward I hid them away, but later, when I was all right again, I brought them out, and I still have them around the house. I use the lipsticks now and then, and last week I cut the plastic starfish off the sunglasses case for the baby to play with.

So there were twelve of us at the hotel, in the same wing on the same floor in single rooms, one after the other, and it reminded me of my dormitory at college. It wasn't a proper hotel—I mean a hotel where there are both men and women mixed about here and there on the same floor.

This hotel—the Amazon—was for women only, and they were mostly girls my age with wealthy parents who wanted to be sure their daughters would be living where men couldn't get at them and deceive them; and they were all going to posh secretarial schools like Katy Gibbs, where they had to wear hats and stockings and gloves to class, or they had just graduated from places like Katy Gibbs and were secretaries to executives and junior executives and simply hanging around in New York waiting to get married to some career man or other.

These girls looked awfully bored to me. I saw them on the sunroof, yawning and painting their nails and trying to keep up their Bermuda tans, and they seemed bored as hell. I talked with one of them, and she was bored with yachts and bored with flying around in airplanes and bored with skiing in Switzerland at Christmas and bored with the men in Brazil.

Girls like that make me sick. I'm so jealous I can't speak. Nineteen years, and I hadn't been out of New England except for this trip to New York. It was my first big chance, but here I was, sitting back and letting it run through my fingers like so much water.

Jay Cee was my boss, and I liked her a lot, in spite of what Doreen said. She wasn't one of the fashion magazine gushers with fake eyelashes and giddy jewelry. Jay Cee had brains, so her plug-ugly looks didn't seem to matter. She read a couple of languages and knew all the quality writers in the business.

I tried to imagine Jay Cee out of her strict office suit and luncheon-duty hat and in bed with her fat husband, but I just couldn't do it. I always had a terribly hard time trying to imagine people in bed together.

Jay Cee wanted to teach me something, all the old ladies I ever knew wanted to teach me something, but I suddenly didn't think they had anything to teach me. I fitted the lid on my typewriter and clicked it shut.

. . .

I didn't know what time it was, but I'd heard the girls bustling and calling in the hall and getting ready for the fur show, and then I'd heard the hall go still, and as I lay on my back in bed staring up at the blank, white ceiling the stillness seemed to grow bigger and bigger until I felt my eardrums would burst with it. Then the phone rang.

I stared at the phone for a minute. The receiver shook a bit in its bone-colored cradle, so I could tell it was really ringing. I thought I might have given my phone number to somebody at a dance or a party and then forgotten about it. I lifted the receiver and spoke in a husky, receptive voice.

"Hello?"

"Jay Cee here," Jay Cee rapped out with brutal promptitude. "I wondered if you happened to be planning to come into the office today?"

I sank down into the sheets. I couldn't understand why Jay Cee thought I'd be coming into the office. We had these mimeographed schedule cards so we could keep track of all our activities, and we spent a lot of mornings and afternoons away from the office going to affairs in town. Of course, some of the affairs were optional.

There was quite a pause. Then I said meekly, "I thought I was going to the fur show." Of course I hadn't thought any such thing, but I couldn't figure out what else to say.

"I told her I thought I was going to the fur show," I said to Betsy. "But she told me to come into the office, she wanted to have a little talk with me, and there was some work to do."

"Oh-oh!" Betsy said sympathetically. She must have seen the tears that plopped down into my dessert dish of meringue and brandy ice cream, because she pushed over her own untouched dessert and I started absently on that when I'd finished my own. I felt a bit awkward about the tears, but they were real enough. Jay Cee had said some terrible things to me.

When I made my wan entrance into the office at about ten o'clock, Jay Cee stood up and came round her desk to shut the door, and I sat in the swivel chair in front of my typewriter table facing her, and she sat in the swivel chair behind her desk facing me, with the window full of potted plants, shelf after shelf of them, springing up at her back like a tropical garden.

"Doesn't your work interest you, Esther?"

"Oh, it does, it does," I said. "It interests me very much." I felt like yelling the words, as if that might make them more convincing, but I controlled myself.

All my life I'd told myself studying and reading and writing and working like mad was what I wanted to do, and it actually seemed to be true. I did everything well enough and got all A's, and by the time I made it to college nobody could stop me.

I was college correspondent for the town *Gazette* and editor of the literary magazine and secretary of Honor Board, which deals with academic and social offenses and punishments—a popular office—and I had a well-known woman poet and professor on the faculty championing me for graduate school at the biggest universities in the east, and promises of full scholarships all the way, and now I was apprenticed to the best editor on an intellectual fashion magazine, and what did I do but balk and balk like a dull cart horse ?

"I'm very interested in everything." The words fell with a hollow flatness on to Jay Cee's desk, like so many wooden nickels.

"I'm glad of that," Jay Cee said a bit waspishly. "You can learn a lot in this month on the magazine, you know, if you just roll up your shirtsleeves. The girl who was here before you didn't bother with any of the fashion-show stuff. She went straight from this office on to *Time*."

"My!" I said, in the same sepulchral tone. "That was quick!"

"Of course, you have another year at college yet," Jay Cee went on a little more mildly. "What do you have in mind after you graduate?"

What I always thought I had in mind was getting some big scholarship to graduate school or a grant to study all over Europe, and then I thought I'd be a professor and write books of poems or write books of poems and be an editor of some sort. Usually I had these plans on the tip of my tongue.

"I don't really know," I heard myself say. I felt a deep shock, hearing myself say that, because the minute I said it, I knew it was true.

It sounded true, and I recognized it, the way you recognize some nondescript person that's been hanging around your door for ages and then suddenly comes up and introduces himself as your real father and looks exactly like you, so you know he really is your father, and the person you thought all your life was your father is a sham.

"I don't really know."

"You'll never get anywhere like that." Jay Cee paused. "What languages do you have?"

"Oh, I can read a bit of French, I guess, and I've always wanted to learn German." I'd been telling people I'd always wanted to learn German for about five years.

My mother spoke German during her childhood in America and was stoned for it during the First World War by the children at school. My German-speaking father, dead since I was nine, came from some manic-depressive hamlet in the black heart of Prussia. My younger brother was at that moment on the Experiment in International Living in Berlin and speaking German like a native.

What I didn't say was that each time I picked up a German dictionary or a German book, the very sight of those dense, black, barbed-wire letters made my mind shut like a clam.

"I've always thought I'd like to go into publishing." I tried to recover a thread that might lead me back to my old, bright salesmanship. "I guess what I'll do is apply at some publishing house."

"You ought to read French and German," Jay Cee said mercilessly, "and probably several other languages as well, Spanish and Italian—better still, Russian. Hundreds of girls flood into New York every June thinking they'll be editors. You need to offer something more than the run-of-the-mill person. You better learn some langauges."

I hadn't the heart to tell Jay Cee there wasn't one scrap of space on my senior year schedule to learn languages in. I was taking one of those honors programs that teach you to think independently, and except for a course in Tolstoy and Dostoevsky and a seminar in advanced poetry composition, I would spend my whole time writing on some obscure theme in the works of James Joyce. I hadn't picked out my theme yet, because I hadn't got round to reading *Finnegans Wake,* but my professor was very excited about my thesis and had promised to give me some leads on images about twins.

"I'll see what I can do," I told Jay Cee. "I probably might just fit in one of those double-barreled accelerated courses in elementary German they've rigged up." I thought at the time I might actually do this. I had a way of persuading my Class Dean to let me do irregular things. She regarded me as a sort of interesting experiment.

. . .

I dabbled my fingers in the bowl of warm water a *Ladies' Day* waitress set down in place of my two empty ice cream dishes. Then I wiped each finger carefully with my linen napkin which was still quite clean. Then I folded the linen napkin and laid it between my lips and brought my lips down on it precisely. When I put the napkin back on the table a fuzzy pink lip shape bloomed right in the middle of it like a tiny heart.

I thought what a long way I had come.

The first time I saw a fingerbowl was at the home of my benefactress. It was the custom at my college, the little freckled lady in the Scholarships Office told me, to write to the person whose scholarship you had, if they were still alive, and thank them for it.

I had the scholarship of Philomena Guinea, a wealthy novelist who went to my college in the early nineteen hundreds and had her first novel made into a silent film with Bette Davis as well as a radio serial that was still running, and it turned out she was alive and lived in a large mansion not far from my grandfather's country club.

So I wrote Philomena Guinea a long letter in coal-black ink on gray paper with the name of the college embossed on it in red. I wrote what the leaves looked like in autumn when I bicycled out into the hills, and how wonderful it was to live on a campus instead of commuting by bus to a city college and having to live at home, and how all knowledge was opening up before me and perhaps one day I would be able to write great books the way she did.

I had read one of Mrs. Guinea's books in the town library—the college library didn't stock them for some reason—and it was crammed from beginning to end with long, suspenseful questions: "Would Evelyn discern that Gladys knew Roger in her past? wondered Hector feverishly" and "How could Donald marry her when he learned of the child Elsie, hidden away with Mrs. Rollmop on the secluded country farm? Griselda demanded of her bleak, moonlit pillow." These books earned Philomena Guinea, who later told me she had been very stupid at college, millions and millions of dollars.

Mrs. Guinea answered my letter and invited me to lunch at her home. That was where I saw my first fingerbowl.

The water had a few cherry blossoms floating in it, and I thought it must be some clear sort of Japanese after-dinner soup and ate every bit of it, including the crisp little blossoms. Mrs. Guinea never said anything, and it was only much later, when I told a debutante I knew at college about that dinner, that I learned what I had done.

. . .

I started adding up all the things I couldn't do.

I began with cooking.

My grandmother and my mother were such good cooks that I left everything to them. They were always trying to teach me one dish or another, but I would just look on and say, "Yes, yes, I see," while the instructions slid through my head like water, and then I'd always spoil what I did so nobody would ask me to do it again.

I remember Jody, my best and only girlfriend at college in my freshman year, making me scrambled eggs at her house one morning. They tasted unusual, and when I asked her if she had put in anything extra, she said cheese and garlic salt. I asked who told her to do that, and she said nobody, she just thought it up. But then, she was practical and a sociology major.

I didn't know shorthand either.

This meant I couldn't get a good job after college. My mother kept telling me nobody wanted a plain English major. But an English major who knew shorthand was something else again. Everybody would want her. She would be in demand among all the up-and-coming young men and she would transcribe letter after thrilling letter.

The trouble was, I hated the idea of serving men in any way. I wanted to dictate my own thrilling letters. Besides, those little shorthand symbols in the book my mother showed me seemed just as bad as let t equal time and let s equal the total distance.

My list grew longer.

I was a terrible dancer. I couldn't carry a tune. I had no sense of balance, and when we had to walk down a narrow board with our hands out and a book on our heads in gym class I always fell over. I couldn't ride a horse or ski, the two things I wanted to do most, because they cost too much money. I couldn't speak German or read Hebrew or write Chinese. I didn't even know where most of the old out-of-the-way countries the UN men in front of me represented fitted in on the map.

For the first time in my life, sitting there in the soundproof heart of the UN building between Constantin who could play tennis as well as simultaneously interpret and the Russian girl who knew so many idioms, I felt dreadfully inadequate. The trouble was, I had been inadequate all along, I simply hadn't thought about it.

The one thing I was good at was winning scholarships and prizes, and that era was coming to an end.

I felt like a racehorse in a world without racetracks or a champion college footballer suddenly confronted by Wall Street and a business suit, his days of glory shrunk to a little gold cup on his mantel with a date engraved on it like the date on a tombstone.

I saw my life branching out before me like the green fig tree in the story.

From the tip of every branch, like a fat purple fig, a wonderful future beckoned and winked. One fig was a husband and a happy home and children, and another fig was a famous poet and another fig was a brilliant professor, and another fig was Ee Gee, the amazing editor, and another fig was Europe and Africa and South America, and another fig was Constantin and Socrates and Attila and a pack of other lovers with queer names and offbeat professions, and another fig was an Olympic lady crew champion, and beyond and above these figs were many more figs I couldn't quite make out.

I saw myself sitting in the crotch of this fig tree, starving to death, just because I couldn't make up my mind which of the figs I would choose. I wanted each and every one of them, but choosing one meant losing all the rest, and, as I sat there, unable to decide, the figs began to wrinkle and go black, and, one by one, they plopped to the ground at my feet.

Joan Didion (b. 1934)

A great deal of Didion's recent work is nonfiction, magazine writing
on a diversity of topics. As the field of journalism has opened up for
women, it is not surprising that an acute observer of society should
devote a significant part of her writing to pursuit of the myths of
contemporary America. A native Californian educated at Berkeley,
she worked as an associate feature editor for *Vogue* and a columnist for *Life* in addition to free-lancing. She and her husband, John
Gregory Dunn, left the New York publishing establishment and
returned to California, where in recent years they have been involved
in screenwriting.

In both her first novel, *Run River*, and her best-known novel, *Play
It As It Lays*, Didion pursues the reality and the myths of California
life. At first glance *Play It As It Lays* is a deceptively simple novel.
The style is spare and the imagery is sparse, yet there is a photo-
graphic quality that effectively conjures up the nightmarish atmosphere of late-night visits to the supermarket, dusty hotel rooms, and
sprawling, speed-dominated freeways. These details underline the
prevailing snake and stopped-drain metaphors of the book. The selections included in this anthology deal with the pivotal abortion experience (male-female attitudes, the insouciance and the fear, the
aftermath) but the book should be read as a whole to appreciate how
well Didion captures the boredom, the decadence, the neurosis of the
southern California film community. What appears to be the most
glamorous part of the American experience turns out to be empty—the
meaning of life and even the ability to feel it are gone. Maria's attempt to think of something else during the abortion dramatizes contemporary beliefs that one thing is as good as another; that time can
be stopped or toyed with for our own purposes; that if we don't let
something penetrate our consciousness, or if we drug ourselves from
reality, then we are not responsible. Maria epitomizes many unaware,
imperceptive human beings, but the irony is that she (as others) is this
way only artificially. Though paralyzed, even mesmerized by her
world, she does feel a vague but palpable uneasiness, and she makes
a strong choice for life at the end of the book. Even California and
its myths of space and freedom can become a delimiting trap when
bounded by human weakness, as symbolized by the freeway that
ends abruptly.

Slouching Toward Bethlehem is a collection of her essays dealing with
contemporary concerns. In "On Keeping a Notebook" she touches
on an important process for the beginning, and even the proficient,
writer—the need to observe, to preserve, to analyze, and to explore
experience as a preparation for writing. Like Henry James and Joyce
Carol Oates, Didion stresses the importance of writing down fragments of ideas and conversation that strike her. The experience—just
as it felt at the moment of occurrence—is a truth to be recorded, then
assimilated, before it is finally transformed into art through the process of selectivity. A primer for creativity, the notebook is also a way
to hold on to the sense of the totality of life out of which one writes.

On Keeping a Notebook

" 'That woman Estelle,' " the note reads, " 'is partly the reason why George Sharp and I are separated today.' *Dirty crepe-de-Chine wrapper, hotel bar, Wilmington RR, 9:45 a.m. August Monday morning.*"

Since the note is in my notebook, it presumably has some meaning to me. I study it for a long while. At first I have only the most general notion of what I was doing on an August Monday morning in the bar of the hotel across from the Pennsylvania Railroad station in Wilmington, Delaware (waiting for a train? missing one? 1960? 1961? why Wilmington?), but I do remember being there. The woman in the dirty crepe-de-Chine wrapper had come down from her room for a beer, and the bartender had heard before the reason why George Sharp and she were separated today. "Sure," he said, and went on mopping the floor. "You told me." At the other end of the bar is a girl. She is talking, pointedly, not to the man beside her but to a cat lying in the triangle of sunlight cast through the open door. She is wearing a plaid silk dress from Peck & Peck, and the hem is coming down.

Here is what it is: the girl has been on the Eastern Shore, and now she is going back to the city, leaving the man beside her, and all she can see ahead are the viscous summer sidewalks and the 3 a.m. long-distance calls that will make her lie awake and then sleep drugged through all the steaming mornings left in August (1960? 1961?). Because she must go directly from the train to lunch in New York, she wishes that she had a safety pin for the hem of the plaid silk dress, and she also wishes that she could forget about the hem and the lunch and stay in the cool bar that smells of disinfectant and malt and make friends with the woman in the crepe-de-Chine wrapper: She is afflicted by a little self-pity, and she wants to compare Estelles. That is what that was all about.

Why did I write it down? In order to remember, of course, but exactly what was it I wanted to remember? How much of it actually happened? Did any of it? Why do I keep a notebook at all? It is easy to deceive oneself on all those scores. The impulse to write things down is a peculiarly compulsive one, inexplicable to those who do not share it, useful only accidentally, only secondarily, in the way that any compulsion tries to justify itself. I suppose that it begins or does not begin in the cradle. Although I have felt compelled to write things down since I was five years old, I doubt that my daughter ever will, for she is a singularly blessed and accepting child, delighted with life exactly as life presents itself to her, unafraid to go to sleep and unafraid to wake up. Keepers of private notebooks are a different breed altogether, lonely and resistant rearrangers of things, anxious malcontents, children afflicted apparently at birth with some presentiment of loss.

My first notebook was a Big Five tablet, given to me by my mother with the sensible suggestion that I stop whining and learn to amuse myself by writing down my thoughts. She returned the tablet to me a few years ago; the first entry is an account of a woman who believed herself to be freezing to death in the Arctic night, only to find, when day broke, that she had stumbled onto the Sahara Desert, where she would die of the heat before lunch. I have no idea what turn of a five-year-old's mind could have prompted so insistently "ironic" and exotic a story, but it does reveal a certain predilection for the extreme which has dogged me into adult life; perhaps if I were analytically inclined I would find it a truer story than any I might have told about Donald Johnson's birthday party or the day my cousin Brenda put Kitty Litter in the aquarium.

So the point of my keeping a notebook has never been, nor is it now, to have an accurate factual record of what I have been doing or thinking. That would be a different impulse entirely, an instinct for reality which I sometimes envy but do not possess. At no point have I ever been able successfully to keep a diary; my approach to daily life ranges from the grossly negligent to the merely absent, and on those few occasions when I have tried dutifully to record a day's events, boredom has so overcome me that the results are mysterious at best. What is this business about "shopping, typing piece, dinner with E, depressed"? Shopping for what? Typing what piece? Who is E? Was this "E" depressed, or was I depressed? Who cares?

In fact I have abandoned altogether that kind of pointless entry; instead I tell what some would call lies. "That's simply not true," the members of my family frequently tell me when they come up against my memory of a shared event. "The party was *not* for you, the spider was *not* a black widow, *it wasn't that way at all*." Very likely they are right, for not only have I always had trouble distinguishing between what happened and what merely might have happened, but I remain unconvinced that the distinction, for my purposes, matters. The cracked crab that I recall having for lunch the day my father came home from Detroit in 1945 must certainly be embroidery, worked into the day's pattern to lend verisimilitude; I was ten years old and would not now remember the cracked crab. The day's events did not turn on cracked crab. And yet it is precisely that fictitious crab that makes me see the afternoon all over again, a home movie run all too often, the father bearing gifts, the child weeping, an exercise in family love and guilt. Or that is what it was to me. Similarly, perhaps it never did snow that August in Vermont; perhaps there never were flurries in the night wind, and maybe no one else felt the ground hardening and summer already dead even as we pretended to bask in it, but that was how it felt to me, and it might as well have snowed, could have snowed, did snow.

How it felt to me: that is getting closer to the truth about a notebook. I sometimes delude myself about why I keep a notebook, imagine that some thrifty virtue derives from preserving everything observed. See enough and write it down, I tell myself, and then some morning when the world seems drained of wonder, some day when I am only going through the motions of doing what I am supposed to do, which is write—on that bankrupt morning I will simply open my notebook and there it will all be, a forgotten account with accumulated interest, paid passage back to the world out there: dialogue overheard in hotels and elevators and at the hat-check counter in Pavillon (one middle-aged man shows his hat-check to another and says, "That's my old football number"); impressions of Bettina Aptheker and Benjamin Sonnenberg and Teddy ("Mr. Acapulco") Stauffer; careful *aperçus* about tennis bums and failed fashion models and Greek shipping heiresses, one of whom taught me a significant lesson (a lesson I could have learned from F. Scott Fitzgerald, but perhaps we all must meet the very rich for ourselves) by asking, when I arrived to interview her in her orchid-filled sitting room on the second day of a paralyzing New York blizzard, whether it was snowing outside.

I imagine, in other words, that the notebook is about other people. But of course it is not. I have no real business with what one stranger said to another at the hat-check counter in Pavillon; in fact I suspect that the line "That's my old football number" touched not my own imagination at all, but merely some memory of something once read, probably "The Eighty-Yard Run." Nor is my concern with a woman in a dirty crepe-de-Chine wrapper in a Wilmington bar. My stake is always, of course, in the unmentioned girl in the plaid silk dress. *Remember what it was to be me: that is always the point.*

It is a difficult point to admit. We are brought up in the ethic that others, any others, all others, are by definition more interesting than ourselves; taught to be diffident, just this side of self-effacing. ("You're the least important person in the room and don't forget it," Jessica Mitford's governess would hiss in her ear on the advent of any social occasion; I copied that into my notebook because it is only recently that I have been able to enter a room without hearing some such phrase in my inner ear.) Only the very young and the very old may recount their dreams at breakfast, dwell upon self, interrupt with memories of beach picnics and favorite Liberty lawn dresses and the rainbow trout in a creek near Colorado Springs. The rest of us are expected, rightly, to affect absorption in other people's favorite dresses, other people's trout.

And so we do. But our notebooks give us away, for however dutifully we record what we see around us, the common denominator of all we see is always, transparently, shamelessly, the implacable "I." We are not talking here about the kind of notebook that is patently for public consumption, a structural conceit for binding together a series of graceful *pensées*; we are talking about something private, about bits of the mind's string too short to use, an indiscriminate and erratic assemblage with meaning only for its maker.

And sometimes even the maker has difficulty with the meaning. There does not seem to be, for example, any point in my knowing for the rest of my life that, during 1964, 720 tons of soot fell on every square mile of New York City, yet there it is in my notebook, labeled "FACT." Nor do I really need to remember that Ambrose Bierce liked to spell Leland Stanford's name "£eland $tanford" or that "smart women almost always wear black in Cuba," a fashion hint without much potential for practical application. And does not the relevance of these notes seem marginal at best?:

In the basement museum of the Inyo County Courthouse in Independence, California, sign pinned to a mandarin coat: "This MANDARIN COAT was often worn by Mrs. Minnie S. Brooks when giving lectures on her TEAPOT COLLECTION."

Redhead getting out of car in front of Beverly Wilshire Hotel, chinchilla stole, Vuitton bags with tags reading:

> MRS LOU FOX
> HOTEL SAHARA
> VEGAS

Well, perhaps not entirely marginal. As a matter of fact, Mrs. Minnie S. Brooks and her MANDARIN COAT pull me back into my own childhood, for although I never knew Mrs. Brooks and did not visit Inyo County until I was thirty, I grew up in just such a world, in houses cluttered with Indian relics and bits of gold ore and ambergris and the souvenirs my Aunt Mercy Farnsworth brought back from the Orient. It is a long way from that world to Mrs. Lou Fox's world, where we all live now, and is it not just as well to remember that? Might not Mrs. Minnie S. Brooks help me to remember what I am? Might not Mrs. Lou Fox help me to remember what I am not?

But sometimes the point is harder to discern. What exactly did I have in mind when I noted down that it cost the father of someone I know $650 a month to light the place on the Hudson in which he lived before the Crash? What use was I planning to make of this line by Jimmy Hoffa: "I may have my faults, but being wrong ain't one of them"? And although I think it interesting to know where the girls who travel with the Syndicate have their hair done when they find themselves on the West Coast, will I ever make suitable use of it? Might I not be better off just passing it on to John O'Hara? What is a recipe for sauerkraut doing in my notebook? What kind of magpie keeps this notebook? *"He was born the night the Titanic went down."* That seems a nice enough line, and I even recall who said it, but is it not really a better line in life than it could ever be in fiction?

But of course that is exactly it: not that I should ever use the line, but that I should remember the woman who said it and the afternoon I heard it. We were on her terrace by the sea, and we were finishing the wine left from lunch, trying to get what sun there was, a California winter sun. The woman whose husband was born the night the *Titanic* went down wanted to rent her house, wanted to go back to her children in Paris. I remember wishing that I could afford the house, which cost $1,000 a month. "Someday you will," she said lazily. "Someday it all comes." There in the sun on her terrace it seemed easy to believe in someday, but later I had a low-grade afternoon hangover and ran over a black snake on the way to the supermarket and was flooded with inexplicable fear when I heard the checkout clerk explaining to the man ahead of me why she was finally divorcing her husband. "He left me no choice," she said over and over as she punched the register. "He has a little seven-month-old baby by her, he left me no choice." I would like to believe that my dread then was for the human condition, but of course it was for me, because I wanted a baby and did not then have one and because I wanted to own the house that cost $1,000 a month to rent and because I had a hangover.

It all comes back. Perhaps it is difficult to see the value in having one's self back in that kind of mood, but I do see it; I think we are well advised to keep on nodding terms with the people we used to be, whether we find them attractive company or not. Otherwise they turn up unannounced and surprise us, come hammering on the mind's door at 4 a.m. of a bad night and demand to know who deserted them, who betrayed them, who is going to make amends. We forget all too soon the things we thought we could never forget. We forget the loves and the betrayals alike, forget what we whispered and what we screamed, forget who we were. I have already lost touch with a couple of people I used to be; one of them, a seventeen-year-old, presents little threat, although it would be of some interest to me to know again what it feels like to sit on a river levee drinking vodka-and-orange-juice and listening to Les Paul and Mary Ford and their echoes sing "How High the Moon" on the car radio. (You see I still have the scenes, but I no longer perceive myself among those present, no longer could even improvise the dialogue.) The other one, a twenty-three-year-old, bothers me more. She was always a good deal of trouble, and I suspect she will reappear when I least want to see her, skirts too long, shy to the point of aggravation, always the injured party, full of recriminations and little hurts and stories I do not want to hear again, at once saddening me and angering me with her vulnerability and ignorance, an apparition all the more insistent for being so long banished.

It is a good idea, then, to keep in touch, and I suppose that keeping in touch is what notebooks are all about. And we are all on our own when it comes to keeping those lines open to ourselves: your notebook will never help me, nor mine you. "So what's new in the whiskey business?" What could that possibly mean to you? To me it means a blonde in a Pucci bathing suit sitting with a couple of fat men by the pool at the Beverly Hills Hotel. Another man approaches, and they all regard one another in silence for a while. "So what's new in the whiskey business?" one of the fat men finally says by way of welcome, and the blonde stands up, arches one foot and dips it in the pool, looking all the while at the cabaña where Baby Pignatari is talking on the telephone. That is all there is to that, except that several years later I saw the blonde coming out of Saks Fifth Avenue in New York with her California complexion and a voluminous mink coat. In the harsh wind that day she looked old and irrevocably tired to me, and even the skins in the mink coat were not worked the way they were doing them that year, not the way she would have wanted them done, and there is the point of the story. For a while after that I did not like to look in the mirror, and my eyes would skim the newspapers and pick out only the deaths, the cancer victims, the premature coronaries, the suicides, and I stopped riding the Lexington Avenue IRT because I noticed for the first time that all the strangers I had seen for years—the man with the seeing-eye dog, the spinster who read the classified pages every day, the fat girl who always got off with me at Grand Central—looked older than they once had.

It all comes back. Even that recipe for sauerkraut: even that brings it back. I was on Fire Island when I first made that sauerkraut, and it was raining, and we drank a lot of bourbon and ate the sauerkraut and went to bed at ten, and I listened to the rain and the Atlantic and felt safe. I made the sauerkraut again last night and it did not make me feel any safer, but that is, as they say, another story.

1966

Diane Johnson (b. 1934)

Diane Johnson writes fiction from a fresh perspective—primarily satiric in her first three novels, a complex blend of terror and down-to-
earth reality in her latest, *The Shadow Knows*. Her female protagonists and narrators are unique creations, frequently eccentric by
society's standards and stereotyped expectations, but possessed with
humor, original perceptions, and rich humanity. Although her novels
focus on the peculiarities of some current southern California (and in
Shadow, Sacramento) lifestyles, the individuality of her characters
gives the books a timeless quality.

For example, her second novel, *Loving Hands at Home* satirizes,
among other targets, the science of domesticity through the eyes of
Karen Fry, the only non-Mormon in a large clan. The book charts
Karen's identity crisis, but the style, situations, and insights are unpredictable and free of cant. Her third novel, *Burning*, deals with the
Los Angeles scene, from its unconventional residents and its therapies
to its social welfare agencies, in a complicated, witty, yet serious fable.

The selection included in Part Two comes early in *The Shadow
Knows*. The book is in the form of a narrative by a newly divorced
woman, called N., living in a housing project with her four young
children and a black helper and friend, Ev. Unexplained violence and
hints of worse to come invade their lives, and N. can only speculate
on the source and on the inevitable disaster. Johnson's linking of the
women's inner emotional upheaval with the bizarre and frightening
external events leads to a surprisingly cathartic conclusion: when the
worst has happened, there follows a certain peace, even elation. This
excerpt shows her skill in creating both believable characters and an
atmosphere of suspense.

Born in Illinois, Johnson was educated at Stevens College and the
University of Utah, received her M.A. and Ph.D. from the University
of California, and teaches at the University of California, Davis. She
has four children and is married to John Murray. Other published
works include *Fair Game,* her first novel, and *Lesser Lives,* a highly
praised biography of Mary Ellen Peacock Meredith, which was nominated for the 1973 National Book Award.

Her statement in Part One, taken from an address delivered at the
MLA conference in December 1975, deals with the problem of reliability of a female persona or protagonist. Johnson's own fiction surely
enhances the validity and the universality of the female perspective
in literature by demonstrating that a contemporary novel from a
woman's point of view can entertainingly elucidate social and moral
perceptions for readers of both sexes.

What Women Artists Really Talk About

I recently read an article about neofeminism that remarked with surprise that there are novels written by women who do not identify with neofeminism, but who reveal, perhaps inadvertently, their ideological solidarity with it. As this ideology was explained, I found myself in agreement that consciousness is androgynous in some degree and that particularly "female" consciousness is contingent. These are ideas I have discussed with other women writers, but none of us, I think, were especially concerned with the political implications here. As happens in all political movements, the theoreticians, a relatively leisured class, are far in advance of the proletariat, in this case working women writers.

Art, not politics, is the subject we have been starved to discuss. One can discuss art only up to a point with men, because male artists, like male critics—perhaps more than male critics—do not appear to believe that female art is quite serious. Especially, fiction by women is for women to read. A male graduate student in the department where I teach recently brought a book of mine for me to sign, and I thanked him for buying it—whereupon a distressed expression crossed his face and he hastily explained, "Oh, it's not for me, it's for my mother!" A friend of mine tells a story about hearing from Saul Bellow, when her first novel was published—about a woman who is miserable because her lover has ditched her. He said it was very nice, considering its limited female subject, and shortly afterward published *Herzog*— about a man whose wife has ditched him.

The women writers I know find themselves talking about the uses of the present tense, say, or about the authenticity of the first-person female narrator. To such subjects all one's experience as a woman is brought to bear, to be sure, but no one talks selfhood or female becoming—indeed these do not quite seem proper subjects for contemplation, but rather of the order of things like happiness, which disappear when you think about them. The writing is the serious thing.

But there is a difficulty in that for the woman artist. If it is hard for the world to take her seriously, it is even harder for her to take herself seriously. Most of us have been early conditioned to set a number of other considerations ahead of whatever it is we do ourselves, especially something so preoccupying and self-indulgent as art. We all know how easily the muse is routed by the specter of measles or by a child who says, "Why don't you bake brownies like other mothers?" The ease, the gift, of a feeling of artistic justification will probably never come to women my age or older—but that is a battle we each fight with ourselves.

Then there's the one you fight with the world—the immediate one (children, husband, friends.) Alice Adams says that a couple of weeks after the successful reception of *Families and Survivors*, an old acquaintance called up to say that his secretary had quit and wouldn't

Alice like the job? Then there's the diffuse, historical, maybe unbeatable struggle that the woman artist has to be taken seriously among artists, that is, among men.

Related to this is the battle of the female protagonist, or fictional persona, to be thought of as a reliable reporter of reality, or metaphysical speculation, or whatever phenomena may be taken for the province of fiction. If you can imagine, say, *Moby Dick*, translated into female terms, it might be narrated by some under-housemaid—call her Isabel—who joins the staff of a great mansion, is given a room with a grave, dark, foreign woman by whom she is both attracted and repelled, and finds that the whole of the household is in the grip of a master whose obsessions seem to be bringing them all closer and closer to catastrophe. Now, chances are that this novel would be read as a love story or a contribution to the woman question—respecting the lot of domestic servants, perhaps—the way *Jane Eyre*, which we see our imaginary novel beginning to resemble, was viewed as a document in the governess controversy or possibly, in more psychological terms, as a novel about sexual identity; but it will not be read in broadly mythic terms, quite probably because myth, like metaphysics, like morality in its grandest sense, is not a thing people can imagine one is troubling one's little head about. Or, if you are, you are probably getting it wrong. It seems to me that there are few female protagonists whose perceptions are meant to be viewed as reliable and sound and that their mistakes and, often, neurotic misperceptions are taken in themselves to constitute the point of the narrative. To be sure, this is the point of all maturation fiction—except that for women there is no type of mature model, so that resolutions must involve death (Bovary, Karenina—or compromise—Dorothea Brooke) with no alternatives provided. The resolution of such fictions, written by men and involving male protagonists, is, typically, wisdom. My examples are Victorian, but the situation has not changed much in the contemporary novel. Wisdom is not yet seen as a female attribute. Properly speaking, women's stories have as yet no endings.

When a woman—not, say, an elderly aunt, who may have a measure of reliability, but a sexual woman (and this is important)—is able to narrate a mythic tale of good and evil, that is, when readers will accept the female consciousness as a mediating consciousness in a narrative with as little reluctance as they accept a male one, even when that consciousness announces that incidentally it has a child or must now go wash dishes, things will be greatly improved for the woman writer. Meantime, coping with the built-in unreliability of a female narrator becomes a pressing technical problem, quite apart from the political implications. The seriousness with which women's fictions are taken is of course related to larger questions of female identity, but for the woman artist the immediate considerations are, surely, artistic.

Joanna Russ (b. 1937)

Science fiction, one of the most popular forms of contemporary literature, is, not surprisingly, male-dominated and male-oriented. Joanna
Russ and other women in the field, like Ursula LeGuin, are trying
to expand the limited images of women in science fiction and to
explore new roles that science fiction as literature may open for women
in our culture and beyond it.

Born in the Bronx, New York, Russ attended Cornell and Yale and
has taught at Cornell, Harper, and the University of Colorado. She
encourages other women to write by actively participating in professional meetings and writers' conferences. She has contributed a number of short stories to science fiction collections such as *Nebula* and
Galaxy, and has published novels—*Picnic on Paradise, Chaos Died,*
and, more recently, *The Female Man.*

By definition, science fiction combines strong scientific interest with
probability. The tone is often one of moralistic warning to the dangers
of a technology that may ultimately swallow up the human. Fear, the
absence of love and emotion in general, and the loss of the natural
world are perennial components of this genre; totalitarianism and a
disassociation from the past are other common elements. The range
of approach is wide, from utopian worlds to anti-utopian, from fantasy to realism. Often, despite the futuristic setting, the stories seem
to closely parallel the political and social disorders of the present,
giving force to the warning and moralistic tone. The question of
female liberation can thus naturally be expressed in science fiction.

Besides trying to explode the sexism of much science fiction, Russ
interjects notes of the probability of a future in which women play a
larger part than they do in today's world. In "When It Changed,"
the story of a women's planet invaded by earthmen, the emphasis
on a female culture and lesbianism is an interesting counter to the
sexism of much science fiction, in which women are stereotyped as
slaves and sex objects. The humor of the child Yuki's response to
the men is blended with the fears of the women, who see their peaceful world disintegrating. The self-reliance of the young is threatened,
as are the established relationships between women; the sexist over-
tures and patronizing attitudes of the men seem small compensation
for what will be lost. In the novel *The Female Man*, Russ explores
a similar theme, but this time a woman from Whileaway (the women's
planet) comes to earth. Janet becomes a talk-show phenomenon,
causing consternation and amazement with her description of the
lifestyle and achievements of her planet. An interesting feature of
the novel is her contact with two earth women, which provides a
further exploration of the pervasiveness of sex role limitations in any
society and a fascinating juxtaposition.

In her essay "What Can a Heroine Do? or Why Women Can't Write,"
Russ explores the possibilities of science fiction, supernatural fiction,
and detective fiction as freer forms for women writers. As her stories

aptly demonstrate, new modes and new myths can be created particularly in science fiction. Her comments on the lyrical form are valuable literary criticism as well as an explanation for the dismissal of much female writing. Understanding the mode of the writer and his or her experience is essential for the critical act. Russ's comments on the misunderstanding of black literature because of a misunderstanding of black experience provide a forceful analogy for the state of women writers in relation to the critics. Minority writing, by whatever group, should be judged not solely by the criteria of the past and of male-predominance, but by its own generic meaning and force. Such critical response can only enrich and broaden the scope of established modes and standards: As the minority writer finds new ways, so may all other writers.

What Can a Heroine Do? or Why Women Can't Write

There seem to me to be two alternatives open to the woman author who no longer cares about How She Fell in Love or How She Went Mad. These are (1) lyricism, and (2) life.

By "lyricism" I do not mean purple passages or baroque raptures; I mean a particular principle of structure.

If *the narrative mode* (what Aristotle called "epic") concerns itself with *events* connected by the *chronological order* in which they occur, and *the dramatic mode* with *voluntary human actions* which are connected both by *chronology and causation,* then the principle of construction I wish to call *lyric* consists of *the organization of discrete elements* (images, events, scenes, passages, words, what-have-you) *around an unspoken thematic or emotional center.* The lyric mode exists without chronology or causation; its principle of connection is *associative.* Of course no piece of writing can exist purely in any one mode, but we can certainly talk of the predominance of one element, perhaps two.) In this sense of "lyric" Virginia Woolf is a lyric novelist—in fact she has been criticized in just those terms, i.e., "nothing happens" in her books. A writer who employs the lyric structure is setting various images, events, scenes, or memories to circling round an unspoken, invisible center. The invisible center is what the novel or poem is about; it is also unsayable in available dramatic or narrative terms. That is, there is no action possible to the central character and no series of events which will embody in clear, unequivocal, immediately graspable terms what the artist means. Or perhaps there is no action or series of events that will embody this "center" at all. Unable to use the myths of male culture (and apparently unwilling to spend her life writing love stories) Woolf uses a structure that is basically non-narrative. Hence the lack of "plot," the repetitiousness, the gathering-up of the novels into moments of epiphany, the denseness of the writing, the indirection. There is nothing the female characters can *do*—except exist, except think, except feel. And critics (mostly male) employ the usual vocabulary of denigration: these novels lack important events; they are hermetically sealed; they are too full of sensibility; they are trivial; they lack action; they are feminine.[1]

Not every female author is equipped with the kind of command of language that allows (or insists upon) lyric construction; nor does every woman writer want to employ this mode. The alternative is to take as one's model (and structural principle) not male myth but the structure of one's own experience. So we have George Eliot's (or Doris Lessing's) "lack of structure," the obviously tacked-on ending of *Mill on the Floss*; we have Brontë's spasmodic, jerky world of *Villette*, with a structure modelled on the heroine's (and probably author's) real situation. How to write a novel about a person to whom nothing happens? A person to whom nothing but a love story is *supposed* to happen? A person inhabiting a world in which the only reality is frustration or endurance—or these plus an unbearably mystifying confusion? The movement of *Villette* is not the perfect curve of *Jane Eyre* (a classic version of the female Love Story)—it is a blocked jabbing, a constant thwarting; it is the protagonist's constantly frustrated will to action, and her alternately losing and regaining her perception of her own situation.[2] There are vestiges of Gothic mystery and there is a Love Story, but the Gothic mysteries turn out to be fakery and the Love Story (which occupies only the last quarter of the book) vanishes strangely and abruptly on the last page but one. In cases like these the usual epithet is "formless," sometimes qualified by "inexperienced"—obviously life is not like *that*; life is not messy and indecisive; we know what life (and novels) are from Aristotle—who wrote about plays—and male novelists who employ male myths created by a culture that imagines itself from the male point of view. The task of art—we know—is to give form to life, i.e., the very forms that women writers cannot use. So it's clear that women can't write, that they swing wildly from lyricism to messiness once they abandon the cozy realms of the Love Story. And successes within the Love Story (which is itself imagined out of genuine female experience) are not important because the Love Story is not important. It is a commonplace of criticism that only the male myths are valid or interesting; a book as fine (and well-structured) as *Jane Eyre* fails *even to be seen* by many critics because it grows out of experiences—events, fantasies, wishes, fears, daydreams, images of self— entirely foreign to their own. As critics are usually unwilling to believe their lack of understanding to be their own fault, it becomes the fault of the book. Of the author. Of all women writers.

Western European (and North American) culture is not only male in its point of view; it is also Western European. For example, it is not Russian. Nineteenth-century Russian fiction can be criticized in much

---

[1] Mary Ellmann, *Thinking About Women*. See the chapter on "Phallic Criticism."
[2] Kate Millett, *Sexual Politics* (New York: Doubleday and Company, 1970), pp. 140–147.

the same terms as women's fiction: "pointless" or "plotless" narratives stuffed with strange minutiae, and not obeying the accepted laws of dramatic development, lyrical in the wrong places, condensed in the wrong places, overly emotional, obsessed with things we do not understand, perhaps even grotesque. Here we have other outsiders who are trying, in less than a century, to assimilate European myths, producing strange Russian hybrids (*A King Lear of the Steppe, Lady Macbeth of Mtensk*), trying to work with literary patterns that do not suit their experiences and were not developed with them in mind. What do we get? Oddly digressive Pushkin. "Formless" Dostoevsky. (Colin Wilson has called Dostoevsky's novels "sofa pillows stuffed with lumps of concrete.") Sprawling, glacial, all-inclusive Tolstoy. And of course "lyrical" Chekhov, whose magnificent plays are called plotless to this very day.

There is an even more vivid—and tragic—example: what is an American Black writer to make of our accepted myths? For example, what is she or he to make of the still-current myth (so prominent in *King Lear*) that Suffering Brings Wisdom? This is an old, still-used plot. Does suffering bring wisdom to *The Invisible Man*? When critics do not find what they expect, they cannot imagine that the fault may lie in their expectations. I know of a case in which the critics (white and female) decided after long, nervous discussion that Baldwin was "not really a novelist" but that Orwell was.

Critical bias aside, all artists are going to be in the soup pretty soon, if they aren't already. As a culture, we are coasting on the tag-ends of our assumptions about a lot of things (including the difference between fiction and "propaganda"). As novelists we are working with myths that have been so repeated, so triply-distilled, that they are almost exhausted. Outside of commercial genres—which can remain petrified and profitable indefinitely—how many more incarnations of the Bitch Goddess can anybody stand? How many more shoot-'em-ups on Main Street? How many more young men with identity problems?

The lack of workable myths in literature, of acceptable dramatizations of what our experience means, harms much more than art itself. We do not only choose or reject works of art on the basis of these myths; we interpret our own experience in terms of them. Worse still, we actually perceive what happens to us in the mythic terms our culture provides.

The problem of "outsider" artists is the whole problem of what to do with unlabeled, disallowed, disavowed, not-even-consciously-perceived experience, experience which cannot be spoken about because it has no embodiment in existing art. Is one to create new forms wholesale—which is practically impossible? Or turn to old ones, like Blake's Elizabethan lyrics and Yeats's Noh plays? Or "trivial," trashy genres, like Austen's ladies' fiction?

Make something unspeakable and you make it unthinkable.

Hence the lyric structure, which can deal with the unspeakable and unembodyable as its thematic center, or the realistic piling up of detail which may (if you are lucky) eventually *add up to* the unspeakable, undramatizable, unembodyable, action-one-cannot-name.

Outsiders' writing is always in critical jeopardy. Insiders know perfectly well that art ought to match their ideas of it. Thus insiders notice instantly that the material of *Jane Eyre* is trivial and the emotionality untenable, even though the structure is perfect. George Eliot, whose point of view is neither peccable nor ridiculously romantic, does not know what fate to award her heroines and thus falsifies her endings.[3] Genêt, whose lyrical mode of construction goes unnoticed, is meaningless and disgusting. Kafka, who can "translate" (in his short stories only) certain common myths into fantastic or extreme versions of themselves, does not have Tolstoy's wide grasp of life. (That Tolstoy lacks Kafka's understanding of alienation and schizophrenia is sometimes commented upon, but that does not count, of course.) Ellison is passionate but shapeless and crude. Austen, whose sense of form cannot be impugned, is not passionate enough. Blake is inexplicable. Baldwin lacks Shakespeare's gift of reconciliation. And so on and so on.

But outsiders' problems are real enough, and we will all be facing them quite soon, as the nature of human experience on this planet changes radically—unless, of course, we all end up in the Second Paleolithic, in which case we will have to set about re-creating the myths of the First Paleolithic.

Perhaps one place to look for myths which escape from the equation Culture = Male is in those genres which already employ plots not limited to one sex—i.e., myths which have nothing to do with our accepted gender roles. There seem to me to be three places one can look:

1) Detective stories, as long as these are limited to genuine intellectual puzzles ("crime fiction" is a different genre). Women write these; women read them; women even figure in them as protagonists. The slang name, "whodunit," neatly describes the myth: Finding Out Who Did It (whatever "It" is).

2) Supernatural fiction, often written by women (Englishwomen, at least) during the nineteenth and the first part of the twentieth century. These are about the intrusion of something strange, dangerous, *and not natural* into one's familiar world. What to do? In the face of the supernatural, knowledge and character become crucial; the accepted gender roles are often irrelevant. After all, potting a twelve-foot-tall batrachian with a kerosene lamp is an act that can be accomplished by either sex, and both heroes and heroines can be expected to feel sufficient horror to make the story interesting. (My example is from a short story by H. P. Lovecraft and August Derleth.) However, much of this genre is as severely limited as the detective story—they both seem to have reached the point of decadence where writers are restricted to the re-enactment of ritual gestures. Moreover, supernatural fiction often relies on very threadbare social/sexual roles, e.g., aristocratic Hungarian counts drinking the blood of beautiful, innocent

[3] In comparison with the organic integrity of Dickens', I suppose.

Englishwomen. (Vampire stories use the myths of an old-fashioned eroticism; other tales trade on the fear of certain animals like snakes or spiders, disgust at "mold" or "slime," human aggression taking the form of literal bestiality (lycanthropy), guilt without intention, the lex talionis, severe retribution for venial faults, supernatural "contamination"—in short, what a psychoanalyst would call the "archaic" contents of the mind.)

3) Science fiction, which seems to me to provide a broad pattern for human myths, even if the specifically futuristic or fantastic elements are subtracted. (I except the kind of male adventure story called Space Opera, which may be part of science fiction as a genre, but is not innate in science fiction as a mode.) The myths of science fiction run along the lines of exploring a new world conceptually (not necessarily physically), creating needed physical or social machinery, assessing the consequences of technological or other changes, and so on. These are not stories about men *qua* Man and women *qua* Woman; they are myths of human intelligence and human adaptability. They not only ignore gender roles but—at least theoretically—are not culture-bound. Some of the most fascinating characters in science fiction are not human. True, the attempt to break through culture-binding may mean only that we transform old myths like Black Is Bad/ White Is Good (or the Heart of Darkness myth) into new asininities like Giant Ants Are Bad/ People Are Good. At least the latter can be subscribed to by all human races and sexes. (Giant ants might feel differently.)

Darko Suvin of the University of Montreal has suggested that science fiction patterns often resemble those of medieval literature.[4] I think the resemblance lies in that medieval literature so often dramatizes not people's social roles but the life of the soul; hence we find the following patterns in both science fiction and medieval tales:

I find myself in a new world, not knowing who I am or where I came from. I must find these out, and also find out the rules of the world I inhabit. (the journey of the soul from birth to death)

Society needs something. I/we must find it. (the quest)

We are miserable because our way of life is out of whack. We must find out what is wrong and change it. (the drama of sin and salvation)

Science fiction, political fiction, parable, allegory, exemplum—all carry a heavier intellectual freight (and self-consciously so) than we are used to. All are didactic. All imply that human problems are collective, as well as individual, and take these problems to be spiritual, social, perceptive, or cognitive—not the fictionally sex-linked problems of success, competition, castration, education, love, or even personal identity with which we are all so very familiar. I would go even farther and say that science fiction, political fiction (when successful), and the modes (if not the content) of much medieval fiction all provide myths for dealing with the kinds of experiences we are

---

[4] In conversation and in a paper unpublished as of this writing.

actually having now, instead of the literary myths we have inherited, which only tell us about the kinds of experiences we think we ought to be having.

This may sound like the old cliche about the Soviet plot of Girl Meets Boy Meets Tractor. And why not? Our current fictional myths leave vast areas of human experience unexplored: work for one, genuine religious experience for another, and above all the lives of the traditionally voiceless, the vast majority of whom are women. (When I speak of the "traditionally voiceless" I am not pleading for descriptions of their lives—we have had plenty of that by very vocal writers— what I am talking about are fictional myths *growing out of their lives* and told by themselves for themselves.)

Forty years ago those Americans who read books at all read a good deal of fiction. Nowadays such persons read popularized anthropology, psychology, history, and philosophy. Perhaps current fictional myths no longer tell the truth about any of us.

When things are changing, those who know least about them—in the usual terms—may make the best job of them. There is so much to be written about, and here we are with nothing but the rags and tatters of what used to mean something. One thing I think we must know— that our traditional gender roles will not be part of the future, as long as the future is not a second Stone Age. Our traditions, our books, our morals, our manners, our films, our speech, our economic organization, everything we have inherited, tells us that to be a Man one must bend Nature to one's will—or other men. This means ecological catastrophe in the first instance and war in the second. To be a Woman, one must be first and foremost a mother and after that a server of Men; this means overpopulation and the perpetuation of the first two disasters. The roles are deadly. The myths that serve them are fatal.

Women cannot write—using the old myths.

But using new ones—?

Diane Wakoski (b. 1937)

Diane Wakoski's images take one into a surrealistic dream world, sometimes beautiful, sometimes terrifying—mysterious, violent, yet earthy. Her poems, which, she says, give all the important information about her life, tell of a girl who felt outcast in her childhood, poorer and more introspective than her California schoolmates. Her real father spent more time at sea than at home, so she created a mythic father in her poetry: George Washington. Her themes of loneliness and differentness stem from this childhood, as does her love of beauty, of piano music, and of men, who never grace her with an equal measure of love in return. The persona who speaks in her poems inhabits an average body with a passable face, but is inhabited by an overwhelming inner world: the sun, which is both her essence and her dream lover; the moon, with which she identifies; Diana, moon goddess; sharks and mushrooms, metals and jewels, marigolds and fruit. It is a magical world created by the poet to counterbalance the mundane external world, and it is complete with an elusive prince, called the King of Spain.

Many of Wakoski's poems deal with the complexities of female/male relationships, the woman's yearning for the mustached mechanics who seem to care more for their motorcycles, their rejection of her, and sometimes her fantasies of revenge. Even the titles of two collections, *The Motorcycle Betrayal Poems* and *Dancing on the Grave of A Son of a Bitch*, reflect these themes, which are also illustrated by the poems in Part Two. Wakoski is such a prolific poet, however, that it is difficult to do justice to the range of her work with only a few selections. She has just published her fourteenth collection, *Virtuoso Literature for Two and Four Hands*, and continues evolving new themes and styles.

Her education was in music at Berkeley, and one recent interest has been in chants, in the rhythm and music of poetry read aloud, sometimes by several voices. She has written several poems about poetry, a few of which appear in Part One, along with "The Emerald Essay," a poetic statement on imagery and mythmaking.

Among Wakoski's other collections are *Coins and Coffins, Discrepancies and Apparitions, Smudging,* and *Inside the Blood Factory.* Reading a number of her poems, one becomes immersed in an almost painful, hallucinatory, yet lucid reality. And finally the experience can be liberating; memories and pain explored, rewritten, then transcended.

The Poem

The poem is not written until the mind is so cut
off that the man can get inside and walk around
all the walls, the gardens, the holes, with no one
interrupting his explorations. A box of sounds,
even the presence of a person keeps the skull locked.
Only when you are alone and there is nothing else to
turn to, no books to read, no sounds to listen to, no
sensory pleasures to explore, no person to think
about even, only then does the skull unlock itself so
that you can walk around in it.

My Trouble

my trouble
is that I have the spirit of Gertrude Stein
but the personality of Alice B. Toklas;
craggy, grand
stony ideas
but
all I can do
is embroider Picasso's drawings
and bake hashish fudge.
I am poor
and don't have very much to say
am usually taken for
somebody's
secretary.

With Words

for Tony

Poems come from incomplete knowledge.
From the sense of seeing
an unfinished steel bridge
that you'd like to walk across,
your imaginary footprints floating like pieces
of paper,
where the metal ends,
on the cold water
far below;
or the moon disappearing
behind a cloud
just when you could almost
see the face
of the man standing next
to you
in the olive trees;

165 WITH WORDS

And consequently,
I write about those
whose hands
I've touched once,
trying to remember
which fingers had the rings
on them,
speculating from a few words
what the dialogue of a lifetime
would have been,
making the facts up
out of the clouds of breath we release
on a winter night.

How can I
then
make a poem for you?
whose skillful hands
could make expert
blueprints
of all my bones?
There is no need
for a bridge between us;
we sleep on the same side of the bed.
Your mustache,
inherited from some stealthy Cossack
who kissed your great-great-great-
grandmother
and slid his icy cock between her warm
legs one night
is no mystery
to me.
I can relive
its history,
drawing lines all over my body.
I have no questions
either
about your powerful legs,
arms,
back,
or the quick mind
which leads the body around on a leash.

Forgive me then,
if the poems I write
are about the fragments,
the broken bridges,
and unlit fences
in my life.
For the poet,
the poem
is not
the measure

of his love. It is
the measure
of all he's lost, or
never seen,
or what has no life,
unless he gives it life
with words.

The Emerald Essay

This is the third of a group of "poem lectures" which I have been
writing on the general theme *form is an extension of content*. This
piece is about the use of image. It was originally written for the Boat-
wright Literary Festival at the University of Richmond in February
1973 and first published as one of my columns ("The Craft of car-
penters, plumbers, and mechanics") in *The American Poetry Review*.

I originally wrote the piece because I was asked to give a talk on
"What Women Are Up To" and I felt that once and for all I wanted
to make the statement that women are up to the same things men are
up to. I use the letter format for these poem lectures because I want
them to be as personal as a letter, even though they are addressed
to formal and abstract subjects.

-» «-

Dear David & Annette,

my most civilized friends, who remind me that there will always be a
serious audience for serious art, and that they are both part of the
good life, seriously critical of the world, as well as being serious re-
joicers in it,

I have been asked to talk about the subject of what women are up to,
today, and have chosen to ignore the social implications of that
question and address myself to the subject of poetry as an extension
of life, and to the subject of art because I am an artist.

I have spent the three days I have been here looking with fascination
at the gigantic emeralds ringed with tiny diamond studs that Katherine
Anne Porter wears on her pale birdlike hands. One, the smaller one,
is shaped like a large teardrop and I think of these southern catalpa
trees that now in winter are bare with sexual pods hanging from the
limbs like walking canes, and how in a few months they will be covered again with heart-shaped green leaves/   like the green teardrop
emerald on Katherine Anne's little finger of her right hand, a leaf
seen through the rain or floating on some swollen stream.

And then there is the Big Ring. A square or perhaps I should say
rectangular one, an emerald that extends to her knuckle, that reaches
over the sides of her middle and little fingers on her left hand, like
the green awning over a porch, a stone you could look into and see a
past of exotic fish swimming in it, or the future/   the canals of

Mars, and the tiny diamonds surrounding it like commoners flocking to see the Queen of England.

These emeralds fascinate me. I can feel their substance which is part of their beauty, can fantasize a handful of them, as if I were holding a handful of dripping wet seaweed at the beach, or I had reached my hand into a sack or barrel of grain and were letting the cool smooth kernels touch my closed palm, or I were holding my own long silky hair in my hand, feeling it as if it were part of a silk drape. But their beauty and substance, which tantalize me, are not what obsesses me. I have thought about Katherine Anne Porter's emeralds for the past three days because they are symbols of her success as a beautiful woman and an influential writer.

Peter Taylor told me, when I asked about the emeralds, that she had bought them with some of the handsome profits from *Ship of Fools*. Whether this is true or not is irrelevant. For me, they are symbols of the fact that women as writers are up to the same things men as writers are up to—that is, converting the imagination into something tangible and beautiful, big for its size and yet so small we can wear it on our two hands; that artists are like women in that when they receive wealth, they turn it into something beautiful to look at, small and yet magnificent in its surroundings. The emeralds themselves make the diamonds surrounding them mere background. They are symbols, images, and metaphors of their own reality. They are what comes out of life, not life itself.

When I have been tired or bored and feeling the need for poetry, for the last three days, I have looked for Katherine Ann's emeralds. When the conversation has flagged, I have mentioned Miss Porter's emeralds. When I have felt that we have talked too much about art and poetry and not been living it, I mention her emeralds. "Have you seen her emeralds?" I have said to everyone. Not have you read her books (because everyone has read her books) but, "Have you seen her emeralds?"

These emeralds, surrounded by diamond chips, remind me of a set of dreams I had when I was in college in the '50s. I had a series of dreams, night after night, which I called my green silk dreams, and which I recorded each day. In them, green represented poetry, and the floors were always draped with huge fine bolts of green silk; they were unusual dreams because each night they continued, like a serial story, and of course the green silk was the dominant fact of them.

At that time, a roommate in the apartment several of us students lived in had a green paste ring which looked like an emerald. She used to let me wear it when I read poetry or painted little watercolors because I said that when I looked into it I could see a secret room, also green, in which my fantasies were played out. I have not been able to look at Katherine Anne's emeralds without thinking that she must sit alone with her feelings often and look into the liquid of those pieces of rock and visualize her fantasies also. Without fantasy, real life is incomplete and dull. Without some substantial real life, there is no fantasy possible.

Images are a way of shaping poems. I do not mean using images to decorate poetry. I mean images as icons. Images as the structure, the bones, gleaming behind the flesh. Katherine Anne's emeralds this week have been the structure on which I have tried to hang my flesh.

I like gleaming images. Here is a list of gleaming black things which I have used in poems:

eels
leeches
grand pianos
watermelon seeds
patent leather
obsidian
my black velvet coat
a Doberman pinscher
oil bubbling out of the ground

Women have always been the interior decorators rather than the architects. I would like to propose that the image which used to be decoration in poetry is now becoming the building, the room itself. I would like to propose that Katherine Anne's emeralds are a room she's built and not a decoration on her fingers.

Let me tell you a story which is an obsession with me. I lived with a man, a mechanic, who was always covered with grease. I loved him very much. He had a Doberman pinscher with a gleaming black coat and clipped ears who lived with us, who was vicious and bit people though she loved them. This Doberman loved to look at herself in the bedroom mirror and, in fact, pawed a hole in the rug in front of the mirror over the years, looking at herself, black as obsidian, in the mirror. I loved this dog very much, and when the motorcycle mechanic left me to live alone in the woods, he took his Doberman with him. But she apparently bit everyone who came to his cabin, and he finally had to shoot her.

He loved his dog but hated her dependence on him. I am sure he shot her himself and did not take her to the pound. I am sure that it broke his heart, but that he also liked shooting her. The image of this rugged man with a mustache and powerful shoulders who had lived with me and rejected me, shooting the Doberman pinscher whose body shone black as Chinese lacquer, is one that haunts me and appears in my mind every time I see a jewel, like Katherine Anne's emeralds.

I spent many months thinking about the look on the dog's face when she was hit with the bullet and the look on the man's face as he shot her. I spent a day last November walking on a beach by a lake which was covered with a thin layer of snow, walking in shiny black boots and wearing a black velvet coat, soft and shiny as a seal, with a red bandana sticking out of the pocket and wondering about these images, knowing that I could not really connect them, but still knowing that somehow they were a structure, a connection.

The Doberman, black as caviar,
my coat, soft and black, like a panther,
my boots, crunching the sand,

the black muzzle of the gun—they blue the barrel/   powder burns
    are black
the red that must have appeared in the hole as the bullet penetrated
    the dog

my final understanding that love is not something that goes away,
nor anything which prevents pain or even that can be lived with, that
this man in his black leathers, riding his Vincent Black Shadow or
his BSA Gold Star into the night, was the Prince of Darkness, the
Ishmael I loved,
        Motorcycle Mechanic
        Woodsman
        Plumber
and that the pain of losing him is an image that itself must be a structure in my life, and that I love another man now, the man with the
silver belt buckle, the elusive King of Spain as well, and he is also
a structure composed of images. That a myth is a set of beautiful
memorable images we string together with different narratives each
time. That the constellations in the sky exist as stars which we outline
into shapes with our pencils, imaginary lines as exciting to us as the
stars themselves, but that the stars are the structures, the images are
the skeleton, that concept rests in the image, that "there are no ideas
but in things."

Let me tell you how poetry is mythology. And mythology is image.
When I was in California for the summer in 1969 and very much
alone, pining for the motorcycle mechanic, I met a man who had
nothing dark in him at all. He was golden, as only Californians can
be golden. The first time I saw him, I felt like he came out of a fairy
tale. I found out who he was and haunted the place where he worked
to talk to him. Actually, I did not like talking to him. I liked looking
at him. But I was still in love with the man in leathers, the motorcycle
mechanic. Ironically, the golden man cared even less about me than
my betrayer. But, in my poems, I began to imagine a man like the
golden one whom I called the King of Spain. He was a mystery.
Never quite there. Yet mysteriously appearing and disappearing in
such a way as to make me know he followed me wherever I went.
The next year, a man whom I only met for a few hours one evening
fell in love with me and began to fantasize that he was the King of
Spain. When I met him again this year, I told everyone I had found
the King of Spain. I even wrote a poem called "Discovering the King
of Spain."

After a day, I told him that I was going to meet The Man With The
Silver Belt Buckle, and for days I would allude to going off to meet
The Man With The Silver Belt Buckle. He too became a mysterious,
missing, desirable character in my poems, who loved me but was
never there. Last week I sent the King of Spain a silver belt buckle
as a present.

After looking at Katherine Anne Porter's emeralds all week, I have
decided that perhaps I would now like to find the man with the emerald ring.

Here is a little story about The Man With The Emerald Ring:

Once there was a man whom all women fell in love with. He was
invisible, except for a huge emerald ring which he wore on his right
hand, on the ring finger. The ring was so large that the husbands of
beautiful women whom the man with the emerald ring visited always
noticed when he was there. It was hard for them to accuse their
wives of infidelity when their rival was an invisible man. However,
that ring flashed in and out of their lives in such a way as to make
many of them more furious than when a certain handsome mustached
young poet used to visibly visit their beautiful wives, sitting on the
verandas at five, drinking martinis.

How's that for the beginning of a story?

Before I go on, I think I'd like to try out another beginning:

A poem is a story in which the images are more important than the
narrative. Once there was a man who became invisible because no
one loved him. However, he had a magnificent emerald ring which
everyone could see. Whenever he went anywhere, he caused consternation, as everyone could see the giant emerald, like a frog, wet
from the pond, sitting in the middle of the room.

Or how about this:

Once there was a woman who was in love with a man who wore an
emerald ring on his finger. However, she could not speak because
she had a begonia in her mouth instead of a tongue, and when she
tried to tell the man with the emerald ring that she loved him, petals
fell out, but no words were formed.

Perhaps if the story begins with the emerald ring, it could be hidden
in a sugar bowl in the house of a midget or a scholar of Urdu.

Once there was a girl who lived with a Doberman pinscher and who
fell in love with a shooting star. She wore an invisible emerald ring.

How can I tell you a story when I cannot decide on a good beginning?
I know what the ending is, though: A statement about poetry.

> The poem is the image
> It gives us some beauty to live for both
> when life is good
> and when it is not.

This week I am obsessed with Katherine Anne's emeralds. Have you
seen her emeralds, I keep saying. Have you seen those magnificent
emeralds?

That *is* what women are up to.

yr friend,
Diane

Joyce Carol Oates (b. 1938)

Easily one of the most prolific writers, Joyce Carol Oates has produced stories, novels, poems, essays, and reviews. She has said that she wishes to articulate for the inarticulate. Though some of her short stories and novels concern themselves with the middle class and the academic world in which she now lives, she often chooses poorer people and their plight as a subject for fiction. Oates sees the forces of the world impinging on the individual in a deterministic way and chronicles the violence of contemporary society as a graphic representation of its ills. Her writing is, in a sense, therapeutic for herself and perhaps, too, for a society faced with the fragmentation, violence, and poverty she so tellingly depicts.

Born in Lockport, New York, the child of working-class parents, Oates attended Syracuse University on a New York Regents' Scholarship and received an M.A. in English at the University of Wisconsin. She intended to continue for a doctorate after her marriage, but at that time one of her stories was selected for the Honor Roll of *Best American Short Stories*. She decided to write rather than work on the Ph.D.; the result of the year's work was her first book, the short-story collection *By the North Gate*. She now teaches (as does her husband Raymond Smith) in the English department of the University of Windsor in Canada.

The short-story volume *Marriages and Infidelities* is a significant part of her work. "The Dead" (in Part Two), written from the viewpoint of a female protagonist and her almost manic-depressive drug reality, includes a view of academe, the question of intellectual and political apathy at the university, the problem of writing and fame. But essential to the story is an awareness that comes to Ilena in a moment of lovemaking—with a former lover who now means as little to her as does her ex-husband. She sees the face of a dead student—a student who reached out to her for intellectual and political support, a student whom she failed emotionally, yet with whom there was a strong potential connection. Like Greta in Joyce's "The Dead," Ilena realizes the glory of the past is over and only the embers are left. But perhaps, as an artist, she can draw life from this needless death.

Oates is often described by interviewers as shy, introspective, slow to reveal her inner self, and living a kind of old-fashioned existence that seems to belie the grotesque and fantastic quality of some of her work. Interestingly enough, in "The Unique/Universal in Fiction," she stresses that her stories begin in reality and only then are wedded to fantasy. Her concern is that art be creative but formalized, that it blend the conscious and the unconscious mind. The discussion of how she writes—the long brooding process, the actual writing, and the final wrestling with the formalization—displays an effective combination of good work habits and patience enough to wait for an idea to jell. Among her more recent works the novel *Do with Me What You Will* and the short-story collection *The Goddess and Other Women* should be of particular interest to students of women writers.

The Unique/Universal in Fiction

As a teacher of creative writing, as well as a writer, I am very deeply concerned with the phenomenon of "creativity"—it is one of the most mysterious of all human endeavors, and must ultimately be considered in the light of long-range evolutionary patterns in man. The process of creating art cannot be understood, cannot be explained in rational or scientific terms. Assistants of Einstein's at Princeton were often astonished at the apparent ease with which Einstein "thought" through problems that seemed opaque to them—he would pace slowly around his office, curling a lock of hair around a finger, his face quite abstract and gentle, showing no effort of concentration. Then after a few minutes he would smile happily—and the problem was solved. Though his assistants were grateful for his superior imagination, they were rather frustrated because they could not begin to *comprehend* the thought-processes that Einstein experienced; nor could he explain them. So in the end it is better not to attempt explanations, but to rejoice in this spontaneous and only partly-willed miracle of the imagination.

What writers can share with one another, however, is their knowledge of how the process can be stimulated and formalized into art. For, without the conscious and intelligent *formalization* of one's deepest, instinctive fantasies, no communication at all is possible. I think that post-Romantic, existentialist attitudes toward art—that it should be "spontaneous," that it should reflect a vital but unintellectual reality— are quite erroneous, and present a dangerous temptation to writers who are not certain of themselves. Whenever a writer or philosopher or poet stresses the Unconscious, one should remember that it is not his "Unconscious" that is speaking, but his conscious mind. If Sartre's apparent judgment of man is that he is a "useless passion," one should ask whether Sartre himself seems to believe this—whether, in the light of his long, distinguished, dedicated career, his own writing can be considered "useless." We must never take writers at their own estimation of themselves or of us; probably we are all more complex and more noble, if we bother to examine ourselves.

Fiction and poetry celebrate the "unique"—what the writer has experienced or thought, personally; without this personal, private experience, the story or poem will be simply manufactured. One really cannot "manufacture" emotions. But there is no reason to make them up, since everyone has emotions—daydreams—unique and unrepeatable experiences. The important thing is, do people correctly value themselves? If they are writing, *why* are they writing? Anyone who is writing "to make money" is deluding himself; he is writing for other, deeper reasons, reasons he cannot explain. But as long as he believes that he is writing "for money" or "for prestige," he will write in a falsifying way, manufacturing emotions in conformity with emotions he sees in others; and yet his own life is filled with enough drama to constitute any number of novels. . . . When one writes about his true subject, in contrast to the usual "false" subject, he really has no difficulty with writing. But he must understand how his "unique" life is related to a vast "universal" life: the connection between the two is what he must write about.

I would be unable to write about anything that did not seem to me both unique and universal—an event I have lived through myself, or experienced intensely through my imagination, and an event that has some meaning, some larger appeal, which may go far beyond the temporal limitations of the subject. If art has any general evolutionary function, it must be to enhance the race, to work somehow toward an essential unity and harmony—survival and growth—and perhaps an integration of the human world with the natural world. The genesis for my novel, *Wonderland*, was a newspaper item I read years ago; it took a very long time for this to work its way through my imagination, and to emerge into consciousness, and the entire process is unknown to me. But the important thing, for me, is that the novel's basis is a real event; that it happened in the world "out there" and not in my head; that it must be sent back out into the world, and given a definite time and place, and related to current history.

Until this is settled I am unable to write and would not care to write— my own fantasies, however intriguing, simply don't seem substantial enough for me to formalize into art. I can sometimes "marry" them to objective events, since we all experience a number of the same things, and this allows me to write quite swiftly and happily; one of the large consolations for experiencing anything unpleasant is the knowledge that one can communicate it, especially one's triumph over it, to other people. Critics who chide me for dwelling on unpleasant and even bloody subjects miss the point: art shows us how to get through and transcend pain, and a close reading of any tragic work (*Macbeth* comes immediately to mind) will allow the intelligent reader to see how and why the tragedy took place, and how he, personally, need not make these mistakes. The more violent the murders in *Macbeth*, the more relief one can feel at *not* having to perform them. Great art is cathartic; it is always moral.

Therefore, one should contemplate his own experiences and see how they illuminate the experiences of others; how they transcend the finite; how they may be of value to other people. Unless there is a real "value," the resulting art will be manufactured and one-dimensional. I firmly believe that mankind is so instinctively, unconsciously involved with the survival and growth of the species that when an individual attempts to live *selfishly*, he will either fail or will fall into despair. Only when men are connected to larger, universal goals are they really happy—and one result of their happiness is a rush of creative activity. Any writer who has difficulty in writing is probably not onto his true subject, but wasting time with false, petty goals; as soon as you connect with your true subject you will write.

My purpose in writing this essay is to point out, I hope not dogmatically, that the average person is deeper, more talented, and more intelligent than he probably believes. He is transformable—even overnight. Exhaustion and fatigue are mainly psychological; if man is faced with a new challenge, he can summon up amazing reservoirs of energy. Unfortunately, our complex civilization reduces "challenges" for us or makes them seem apparently insoluble. It is the task of the writer to think his way through all the temporal, private, petty, headline-tormented confusion of his life, and connect with deeper rhythms, either through a conscious exploration of art, history, music, literature, or through personal discipline and meditation. Man is the only creature in possible control of his own destiny, and the most imaginative people will imagine their futures and the future of their society, not through being passive or influenced by current fashionable trends, but through a conscious exertion of the mind. If anyone who reads this is doubtful he should ask himself *why* he is doubtful; very likely he hasn't much idea of his own mind, and thinks himself far more limited than he really is.

On a more practical level—since writers are involved in the real world, for better or worse—I can offer only a few general advisory words, which may be too personal for broader application. My "ideas" come to me partly out of the world (I scan newspapers often) and partly out of my own life. They seem to sink into unconsciousness, sometimes for a long period of time, and are drawn out again by some stray reminder in my daily life (in the case of *Wonderland,* I came across a number of similar news items—dealing with the murder-suicide tragedy, eerily common in our country, in which a father kills his entire family and then himself). Then a long process of "dreaming-through" takes place, in which I think about the entire novel— living through various scenes, hearing or inventing dialogue, walking around with my characters in my head for months; only when the process is completed can I begin to write, and I can't hurry the process. I can assign to myself occasional tasks—how to manage a certain scene, how to dramatize the relationship of one character to another —before going to sleep at night, and sometimes by morning I have figured out the problem—sometimes—this might work about half the time. But I never despair or become impatient; it is simply a matter of waiting until the entire book is thought out. Of course, writing a short story is far easier. Henry James dictated his long, excellent story "The Beast in the Jungle" in *three mornings*—which suggests to me that he dreamt through his writing in great detail, before formalizing it.

After this strange, uncanny, intuitive stage of a novel is more or less completed in my mind, I write the first draft. I usually write very quickly, chapter by chapter, though I try to alternate work on a novel with shorter pieces—stories, articles, or reviews—in order to keep some objectivity. I always know exactly how the novel will end, even the wording of the final paragraph. I always know exactly the crucial scenes, the dialogue, even the way my characters look, though I may not describe them in that much detail. But as I write this first draft, I often discover new, small things about my characters, and allow any workable rearrangements in. This year, spent in London, I wrote a rather long novel titled *Do With Me What You Will,* which is a complex narrative dealing with the Law—the legal profession in America —but concentrating on two individuals who happen to be lovers, and who are married and "thinking back" over the circumstances of their having met and fallen in love; it involved many exasperating problems, but as long as I waited patiently the narrative always straightened out, and the characters asserted themselves in accordance with their own integrity.

After the first draft is finished, I put it aside temporarily and work on other things. Then, when I feel the time is come for me to really formalize it, I begin the second and final draft—and this part of the process is, strangely enough, the most enjoyable of all. I cut each chapter drastically, seeing as objectively as possible what can be eliminated or shortened (my manuscripts would be very long, sometimes twice as long, if I didn't cut so severely), trying to read the work as if from another part of myself, or from the point of view of another person. Though the original, spontaneous part of writing can be very exciting, the real reward for me at least is this third and most conscious, most "intellectual" organization of material. Man is a problem-solving animal, and the organizing of vast subjects must give pleasure, evidently; nothing seems to me to involve more intellectual effort than the organizing of a big novel, and I cannot imagine anything more rewarding.

In all this, I try to keep in mind the delicate relationship between what is unique, perhaps even eccentric, and what is universal—what will, hopefully, transcend the finite nature of newspaper headlines. Only in this relationship is there a true subject, worthy of long hours of work. I believe that all art is moral and that it must communicate either directly or through metaphor; I also believe that many people are true artists who imagine themselves only consumers, or at best only careful imitators of what seems marketable and timely.

Margaret Atwood (b. 1939)

Much of Margaret Atwood's poetry has a visionary quality. Images of the recent Canadian past flash through the technological and often destructive reality of the present, perhaps toward a spiritually revitalized future. Her poems frequently focus on people's waste of nature, but with a unique twist, such as the mythic overtones of their actions or their relative insignificance, given the vastness of nature and of time.

The power of nature over the human imagination is a theme of many of her poems and of the volume entitled *The Journal of Susannah Moodie*. Moodie, a Canadian pioneer woman, kept a journal of her experiences in the wild and after her eventual return to town. Atwood's book presents the subjective reality of these experiences, making them intense and archetypal.

Many of her poems deal with female/male relationships, often with the numbness and fear that prevent people from risking, from loving. She sees this as a result of past pain and also of our technological society, in which people are regarded as things and, hence, often regard each other in the same way.

Her novel *Surfacing* calls this process—the exploitation of nature and the dehumanization of individuals—"Americanization," but it is not limited to Americans. In a striking, poetic style, this book presents the alienation and emotional paralysis of a young woman, the narrator, and her various means of coping with them. As the unfaceable truths of her life begin to surface, she enters a new realm, of nature gods, of ritual, of "madness" that makes her whole: willing to risk, willing to trust, and determined to watch, predict, and stop "the Americans" without copying them. This novel is a powerful development of the theme of self-discovery. Atwood's other novels include the satirical *Edible Woman* and, most recently, *Lady Oracle*.

Among her poetry collections are *The Animals in That Country, Procedures for Underground, Power Politics,* and *You Are Happy*. In addition, she has published a critical study, *Survival: A Thematic Guide To Canadian Literature*. Born in Ottawa, she received a B.A. from the University of Toronto and an M.A. from Radcliffe. Margaret Atwood's versatility, originality, and depth place her in the forefront of contemporary writers.

Paradoxes and Dilemmas, the Woman as Writer

I knew ... what a writer can be at his best ... an interpreter, a revealer of secrets. ...

I approach this article with a good deal of reluctance. Since promising to do it, in fact, I've been procrastinating to such an extent that my own aversion is probably the first subject I should attempt to deal with. Some of my reservations have to do with the questionable value of writers, male or female, becoming directly involved in political movements of any sort: their involvement may be good for the movement, but it has yet to be demonstrated that it's good for the writer. The rest concern my sense of the enormous complexity not only of the relationships between Man and Woman, but also of those between such other abstract intangibles as Art and Life, Form and Content, Writer and Critic, and so forth.

Judging from conversations I've had with many other women poets and novelists in this country, my qualms are not unique. I can think of only one fiction or poetry writer I know who has formal connection with any of the diverse organizations usually lumped together under the titles of women's liberation or the women's movement. There are even several who have gone out of their way to disavow even fellow-feeling. But the usual attitude is one of grudging admiration, tempered with envy: the younger generation, they feel, has it a hell of a lot better than they did. Most writers old enough to have a career of any length behind them grew up when it was still assumed that a woman's place was in the home and nowhere else, and that anyone who took time off for an individual selfish activity like writing was either neurotic or wicked or both, derelict in her duties to some man, child or aged relative. I've heard stories of writers so consumed by guilt over what they had been taught to feel was their abnormality that they did their writing at night, secretly, so no one would accuse them of failing as housewives, as "women." These writers accomplished what they did by themselves, often at great personal expense. In order to write at all, they had to defy other women's as well as men's ideas of what was proper, and it's not finally all that comforting to have a phalanx of women—some younger and relatively unscathed, others from their own generation, the bunch that was collecting china, changing diapers and sneering at any female with intellectual pretensions twenty or even ten years ago—come breezing up now to tell them they were right all along. It's like being judged innocent after you've been hanged: the satisfaction, if any, is grim. There's a great temptation to say to feminists, "Where were you when I really needed you?" or "It's too late for me now." And you can see, too, that it would be fairly galling for these writers, if they have any respect for historical accuracy, which most do, to be hailed as products, spokeswomen, or advocates of the women's movement. When they were undergoing their often drastic formative years there *was* no women's movement. No matter that a lot of what they say can be taken by the theorists of the movement as supporting evidence, useful analysis, and so forth. Their own inspiration was not theoretical; it came from wherever all writing comes from. Call it experience and imagination.

These writers, if they are honest, don't want to be wrongly identified as the children of a movement that did not give birth to them. Being adopted is not the same as being born.

A third area of reservation is undoubtedly a fear of the development of a one-dimensional Feminist Criticism, a way of approaching literature produced by women that would award points according to conformity or non-conformity to an ideological position. A feminist criticism is, in fact, already emerging. I've read several reviews, and I'm sure there will be more, in which a novelist was criticized for not having made her heroine's life different, more active and directed, even though that life was more typical of the average woman's life in this society than the reviewer's "liberated" version would have been. Perhaps feminist reviewers will start demanding that heroines resolve their difficulties with husband, kids, or themselves by stomping out to join a consciousness-raising group or get a job, which will be no more satisfactory from the point of view of literature than the legendary Socialist Realist romance with one's tractor. However, a feminist criticism need not necessarily be one-dimensional. And—small comfort—no matter how narrow, purblind and stupid such a criticism in its lowest manifestations may be, it cannot possibly be *more* narrow, purblind and stupid than some of the non-feminist critical attitudes and styles that have preceded it.

There's a fourth possible factor, a less noble one: the often observed phenomenon of the member of a despised social group who manages to transcend the limitations imposed on the group, at least enough to become "successful." For such a person the impulse—whether obeyed or not—is to dissociate him/herself from the group and to side with its implicit opponents. Thus the black millionaire who deplores the Panthers, the rich *Québécois* who is anti-Separatist, the North American immigrant who changes his name to an "English" one; thus, alas, the Canadian writer who makes it in New York and spends the rest of his life decrying provincial dull Canadian writing. And thus the women with successful careers who say, "*I've* never had any problems, I don't know what they're talking about." Such a woman tends to regard herself, and to be treated by her male colleagues, as an honorary man. It's the rest of them who are inept, brainless, tearful, self-defeating: not her. "You think like a man," she is told, with admiration and unconscious put-down. For both men and women, it's just too great a strain to fit together the traditionally incompatible notions of "woman" and "good at something." And if you *are* good at something, why carry with you the stigma attached to that dismal category you've gone to such lengths to escape from? You should rock the boat only if you're still chained to the oars. Not everyone reacts like this, but this factor may explain some of the more hysterical opposition to the movement on the part of a few women writers, even though they may have benefited from it in the form of increased sales and more serious attention.

A couple of ironies remain; perhaps they are even paradoxes. One is that in the development of modern Western civilization writing was the first of the arts, before painting, music, composing, and sculpting,

which it was possible for women to practice; and it was the fourth of
the job categories, after prostitution, domestic service and the stage,
and before wide-scale factory work, nursing, secretarial work, telephone operating and school teaching, at which it was possible for them
to make any money. The reason for both is the same: writing as a
physical activity is private. You do it by yourself, on your own time;
no teachers or employers are involved, you don't have to apprentice
in a studio or work with musicians. Your only business arrangements
are with your publisher, and these can be conducted through the mails;
your real "employers," the readers, can be deceived if you choose by
the adoption of an assumed male name: witness the Brontës and
George Eliot. But the private and individual nature of writing may
also account for the low incidence of direct involvement by woman
writers in the movement now. If you are a writer, prejudice against
women will affect you *as a writer* not directly but indirectly. You
won't suffer from wage discrimination, because you aren't paid any
wages; you won't be hired last and fired first, because you aren't hired
or fired anyway. You have relatively little to complain of, and, absorbed in your own work as you are likely to be, you will find it quite
easy to shut your eyes to what goes on at the spool factory, or even
at the university. Alas, paradoxically, the same conditions that allowed female participation in the first place may discourage militant
attitudes now.

Another paradox goes like this. As writers, female writers are like
male writers. They have the same professional concerns, they have
to deal with the same contracts and publishing procedures, they have
the same need for solitude to work and the same desire that their work
be accurately evaluated by reviewers. There is nothing "male" or "female" about these concerns and needs; they are just attributes of
writing as an activity. As biological specimens and as citizens, however, women are like other women: subject to the same discriminatory
laws, encountering the same demeaning attitudes, burdened with the
same good reasons for not walking through the park alone after dark.
They too have bodies, the capacity to bear children; they too eat,
sleep, bleed and go to the bank. In bookstores and publishers' offices
and among groups of other writers, a woman writer may get the
impression that she is "special," but in the eyes of the law, in the loan
office, in the hospital and on the street she's just another woman. She
can't wear a sign to the grocery store saying "Respect Me, I'm a
Woman Writer." No matter how good she may feel about herself,
bigoted strangers who aren't aware of her shelf-full of volumes with
cover blurbs saying how gifted she is will still regard and treat her
as a nit.

We all have ways of filtering out aspects of our experience we would
rather not think about. Woman writers can keep as much as possible
to the "writing" end of their life, avoiding the less desirable aspects
of the "woman" end. Or they can divide themselves in two, thinking
of themselves as two different people: a "writer" and a "woman."
Time after time, I've had interviewers talk to me about my writing for
a while, then ask me, "As a woman, what do you think about [for
instance] the woman's movement?" as if I could think two sets of

thoughts about the same things, one set as a writer or person, the other as a woman. But no one comes apart this easily; categories like Woman, White, Canadian, and Writer are only ways of looking at a person and the person herself remains whole, entire and indivisible. Thus Woman and Writer are often treated as separate categories; but in any individual woman writer, they are inseparable.

One of the results of this paradox is that there are certain attitudes and conditions, some overt, some concealed, which women writers encounter *as* writers, but *because* they are women. Here are a few of these.

REVIEWING AND THE ABSENCE OF AN ADEQUATE CRITICAL VOCABULARY

Cynthia Ozick, in the American magazine *Ms.*, says, "For many years, I had noticed that no book of poetry by a woman was ever reviewed without reference to the poet's sex. The curious thing was that, in the two decades of my scrutiny, there were *no* exceptions whatever. It did not matter whether the reviewer was a man or a woman; in every case, the question of the 'feminine sensibility' of the poet was at the center of the reviewers' response. The maleness of male poets, on the other hand, hardly ever seemed to matter."

Things aren't this bad in Canada, possibly because we were never thoroughly indoctrinated with the Holy Gospel according to the distorters of Freud. Many reviewers manage to get through a review without displaying the kind of bias Ozick is talking about. But that it does occur was demonstrated to me by a project I was involved with at York University in 1971–72.

One of my student groups was attempting to study what we called "sexual bias in reviewing," by which we meant not unfavourable reviews, but points being added or subtracted by the reviewer on the basis of the author's sex and supposedly associated characteristics rather than on the basis of the work itself. Our study fell into two parts: (i) a survey of writers, half male, half female, conducted by letter: had they ever experienced sexual bias directed against them in a review?; (ii) the reading of a large number of reviews from a wide range of periodicals and newspapers.

The results of the writers' survey were perhaps predictable. Of the men, none answered Yes, a quarter Maybe, and three-quarters No. Of women, half were Yeses, a quarter Maybes and a quarter Nos. The women replying Yes often wrote long, detailed letters, giving instances and discussing their own attitudes. All the men's letters were short.

This proved only that women were more likely to *feel* they had been discriminated against on the basis of sex. When we got round to the reviews, we discovered they were sometimes justified. Here are the kinds of things we found.

i) *Assignment of Reviews*

Several of our letter-writers discussed the mechanics of review assignment. Some felt books by women tended to be passed over by

book-page editors assigning books for review; others that books by
women tended to get assigned to women reviewers. When we started
toting up reviews we found that most books in this society are written
by men, and so are most reviews. Disproportionately often, books
by women were assigned to women reviewers, indicating that books
by women fell in the minds of those dishing out the reviews into a
special "female" category. Likewise, woman reviewers tended to be
reviewing books by women rather than books by men (though because
of the preponderance of male reviewers, there were quite a few
male-written reviews of books by women).

ii) *The Quiller-Couch Syndrome*

This phrase refers to the turn-of-the-century essay by Quiller-Couch,
defining "masculine" and "feminine" styles in writing. The "masculine" style is, of course, bold, forceful, clear, vigorous, etc.; the "feminine" style is vague, weak, tremulous, pastel, etc. In the list of pairs
you can include "objective" and "subjective," "universal" or "accurate
depiction of society" versus "confessional," "personal," or even "nar-
cissistic" and "neurotic." It's roughly seventy years since Quiller-
Couch's essay, but the "masculine" group of adjectives is still much
more likely to be applied to the work of male writers; female writers
are much more likely to get hit with some version of "the feminine
style" or "feminine sensibility," whether their work merits it or not.

iii) *The Lady Painter Syndrome, or She Writes Like a Man*

This is a pattern in which good equals male, bad equals female. I call
it the Lady Painter Syndrome because of a conversation I had about
female painters with a male painter in 1960. "When she's good," he
said, "we call her a painter; when she's bad, we call her a lady
painter." "She writes like a man" is part of the same pattern; it's
usually used by a male reviewer who is impressed by a female writer.
It's meant as a compliment. See also "She thinks like a man," which
means the author thinks, unlike most women, who are held to be incapable of objective thought (their province is "feeling"). Adjectives
which often have similar connotations are ones such as "strong,"
"gutsy," "hard," "mean," etc. A hard-hitting piece of writing by a
man is liable to be thought of as merely realistic; an equivalent piece
by a woman is much more likely to be labelled "cruel" or "tough."
The assumption is that women are by nature soft, weak and not very
talented, and that if a woman writer happens to be a good writer, she
should be deprived of her identity as a female and provided with
higher (male) status. Thus the woman writer has, in the minds of
such reviewers, two choices. She can be bad but female, a carrier of
the "feminine sensibility" virus; or she can be "good" in male-
adjective terms, but sexless. Badness seems to be ascribed then to a
surplus of female hormones, whereas badness in a male writer is
usually ascribed to nothing but badness (though a "bad" male writer
is sometimes held, by adjectives implying sterility or impotence, to be
deficient in maleness). "Maleness" is exemplified by the "good" male
writer; "femaleness," since it is seen by such reviewers as a handicap
or deficiency, is held to be transcended or discarded by the "good"
female one. In other words, there is no critical vocabulary for ex-

pressing the concept "good/female." Work by a male writer is often spoken of by critics admiring it as having "balls"; have you ever heard anyone speak admiringly of work by a woman as having "tits"?

Possible antidotes: Development of a "good/female" vocabulary (wow, has that ever got womb . . ."); or, preferably, the development of a vocabulary that can treat structures made of words as though they are exactly that, not biological entities possessed of sexual organs.

iv) *Domesticity*

One of our writers noted a (usually male) habit of concentrating on domestic themes in the work of a female writer, ignoring any other topic she might have dealt with, then patronizing her for an excessive interest in domestic themes. We found several instances of reviewers identifying an author as a "housewife" and consequently dismissing anything she has produced (since, in our society, a "housewife" is viewed as a relatively brainless and talentless creature). We even found one instance in which the author was called a "housewife" and put down for writing like one when in fact she was no such thing.

For such reviewers, when a man writes about things like doing the dishes, it's realism; when a woman does, it's an unfortunate feminine genetic limitation.

v) *Sexual Compliment/Put-down*

This syndrome can be summed up as follows:

She: "How do you like my (design for an airplane/mathematical formula/medical miracle)?"

He: "You sure have a nice ass."

In reviewing it usually takes the form of commenting on the cute picture of the (female) author on the cover, coupled with dismissal of her as a writer.

INTERVIEWERS AND MEDIA STEREOTYPES

Associated with the reviewing problem, but distinct from it, is the problem of the interview. Reviewers are supposed to concentrate on books, interviewers on the writer as a person, as a human being, or, in the case of women, as a woman. This means that an interviewer is ostensibly trying to find out what sort of person you are. In reality, he or she may merely be trying to match you up with a stereotype of "Woman Author" that pre-exists in her/his mind; doing it that way is both easier for the interviewer, since it limits the range and slant of questions, and shorter, since the interview can be practically written in advance. It isn't just women who get this treatment: any writer may get it. But the range for male authors is somewhat wider, and usually comes from the literary tradition itself, whereas stereotypes for female authors are often borrowed from other media, since the ones provided by the tradition are limited in number.

In a bourgeois, industrial society, so the theory goes, the creative artist is seen as acting out suppressed desires of the audience; thus we get certain Post-Romantic male-author stereotypes, such as Potted

Poe, Bleeding Byron, Doomed Dylan, Lustful Layton, Crucified Cohen, etc. Until recently the only personality stereotype of this kind was Elusive Emily, otherwise known as Recluse Rosetti: the woman writer as aberration, hiding behind doors or looking at life through the wormholes in a shroud, neurotically denying herself the delights of sex, kiddies and other fun. The twentieth century has added Suicidal Sylvia, a somewhat more dire version of the same thing. The point about these stereotypes is that attention is focused not on the actual achievements of the authors, but on their lives, which are distorted and romanticized; their work is then interpreted in the light of the distorted version. Stereotypes like these, even when the author co-operates in their formation and especially when the author becomes a cult object, do no service to anyone or anything, least of all the author's work. Behind all of them is the notion that authors must be more special, peculiar or weird than other people, and that their lives are more interesting than their work.

The following examples are taken from personal experience (mine, or interviewers); they indicate the range of possibilities. There are a few others, such as Earth Mother, of which I have no personal knowledge.

i) *Happy Housewife*

This one is almost obsolete: it used to appear on the Woman's Page. The questions were about what you liked to fix for dinner; the attitude was, "Gosh, all the housework and you're a writer too!" Writing was viewed as a hobby, like knitting, that one did in one's spare time.

ii) *Ophelia*

The writer as crazy freak. This is a female version of Doomed Dylan, usually with more than a little hope on the part of the interviewer that you'll turn into Suicidal Sylvia and *really* give them something to write about. Questions tend towards "Do you think you're in danger of going insane?" It's useless to point out that most mental institutions are crammed with people who have never written a word in their life. "Say something interesting," one interviewer quipped. "Say you write all your poems on drugs."

iii) *Miss Martyr, or, "Movie Mag"*

Read any "movie mag" article on Liz Taylor, translate it into writing terms and you've got the picture. The writer as someone who *suffers* more than others. Why does the writer suffer more? Because she's successful, and you all know Success Must Be Paid For. In blood and tears, if possible. If you say you're happy and enjoy your life and work, you'll be ignored.

iv) *Miss Message*

The interviewer who believes in Miss Message is incapable of treating your work as what it is, poetry and/or fiction. There's a great attempt to get you to say something about an issue and then make you into an exponent, spokeswoman or theorist. The interviewer is unable to see that putting, for instance, a nationalist into a novel doesn't make it a nationalistic novel, any more than putting in a preacher makes it a religious novel. The interviewer is rigidly one-dimensional and judgmental, and expects you to follow suit. Rare indeed is an interviewer who regards writing as a respectable profession, not as some kind of magic, madness, trickery or evasive disguise for a message; and who regards an author as a person engaged in a professional activity, not as a witch, boor, sufferer or messiah.

OTHER WRITERS AND RIVALRY

Regarding yourself as an "exception," part of an unspoken quota system, can have interesting results. If there are only so many available slots for your minority in the medical school/law school/literary world, of course you will feel rivalry, not only with members of the majority for whom no quota operates, but especially with members of your minority who are competing with you for the few coveted places. And you will have to be better than the average majority member to get in at all.

Woman-woman rivalry does occur, though it is surprisingly much less severe than you'd expect; it's likely to take the form of *wanting* another woman writer to be better than she is, expecting more of her than you would of a male writer, and being exasperated with certain kinds of traditional "female" writing.

What a woman writer is often unprepared for is the unexpected personal attack on her by a jealous male writer. The motivation is envy and competitiveness, but the form is often sexual put-down. "You may be a good writer," one older man said to a young woman writer who had just had a publishing success, "but I wouldn't want to fuck you." Another version goes more like the compliment put-down noted under Reviewing. In either case, the ploy diverts attention from the woman's achievement as a writer—the area where the man feels threatened—to her sexuality, where either way he can score a verbal point.

I've been trying to give you a picture of the arena, or that part of it, where "woman" and "writer," as concepts, overlap. But, of course, the arena I've been talking about has to do largely with externals: reviewing, the media, relationships with other writers. This, for the writer, may affect the tangibles of her career: how she is received, how viewed, how much money she makes. But in relationship to the writing itself, this is a false arena. The real one is in her head, her real struggle the daily battle with words, the language itself. The false arena becomes valid for writing itself only insofar as it becomes part of her material and is transformed into one of the verbal and imaginative structures she is constantly engaged in making. Novelists and poets are not propagandists or examples of social trends or preachers or politicians. They are makers of novels and poems, and unless they can make these well they will be bad writers, no matter what the social validity of their views.

At the beginning of this article, I suggested a few reasons for the infrequent participation in the movement of Canadian woman novelists and poets. Maybe those reasons were the wrong ones, and this is the real one: no good writer wants to be merely a transmitter of someone else's ideology, no matter how fine that ideology may be. The aim of propaganda is to convince and to spur people to action; the aim of fiction and poetry writing is to create a plausible and moving imaginative world, and to create it with words. Or, to put it another way, the aim of any political movement is to improve the quality of people's lives on all levels, spiritual and imaginative as well as material (and any political movement that doesn't have this aim is worth nothing). Imaginative writing, however, tends to concentrate more on life not as it ought to be, but as it is, as the writer feels it, experiences it. Writers are eye-witnesses, I-witnesses. Political movements, once successful, have historically been intolerant of imaginative writers, even those who initially aided them; in any revolution, writers have been among the first to be lined up against the wall, perhaps for their intransigence, their insistence on saying what they perceive, not what, according to the ideology, ought to exist. Politicians, even revolutionary politicians, have traditionally had no more respect for writing as an activity valuable in itself, quite apart from any message or content, than has the rest of the society. And writers, even revolutionary writers, have traditionally been suspicious of anyone who tells them what they ought to write.

The woman writer in Canada, then, exists in a society that, though it may turn certain individual writers into revered cult objects, has little respect for writing as a profession, and not much respect for women either. If there were more of both, articles like this would be obsolete. I hope they become so. In the meantime, it seems to me that the proper path for a woman writer is not an all-out manning (or womaning) of the barricades, however much she may agree with many of the aims of the movement. The proper path is to become better as a writer. Insofar as writers are lenses, condensers of their society, her work may include the movement, since it is so palpably among the things that exist. The picture that she gives of it is altogether another thing, and will depend, at least partially, on the future course of the movement itself.

POSTSCRIPT 1975

I wrote the above article in the early part of 1973. Since then, things have changed enough to warrant a brief postscript. Although there continue to be small, relatively active, politically-oriented groups of women who call themselves Feminists, feminism has broadened its base considerably. It's now not so much a political movement as a climate of opinion, one which is transforming the attitudes of men towards women and of women towards themselves, less radically and dramatically perhaps, but also less defensively, less faddishly and with more quiet determination. There are now a number of female writers who don't mind the word "chairman," who did not become actively involved in CR groups or marches, who toe nobody's ideological line, but who are nevertheless dealing in their work with women's experience, in all its diversity, without the sense of apology they might have had a few years back. And there's a new awareness on the part of capital-F Feminists that such writing, since it voices the hitherto repressed lives of half the human race (not a minority group, though it's been treated like one) is *de facto* revolutionary. Telling it like it is and has been is as valuable as telling it like it should be; it's an articulation of the previously inarticulate. Seeing our own images gives us heightened confidence in our own existence.

The diversity of these images is a healthy sign. For centuries—especially the nineteenth—men have appeared in the pages of men's books as individuals, women as something called Woman. Men existed in their own right, women, with a few usually comic exceptions, as a gender, an eternal abstraction; or, at best, as a handful of symbols defined by their function *vis-à-vis* men: Mother, Wife, Sister, Virgin, Whore, Goddess, Witch/Bitch. Nourishers or threateners, valuable for what they promised to provide in the way of food or pleasure, feared for their imagined powers to blight the wheat or to deprive a man of his genitals. Since most books were and still are written by men, these images have had a long life and many incarnations, and we haven't seen the last of them yet.

But the work of serious women writers in Canada has been heading in the opposite direction. If the fictions of Margaret Laurence, Marian Engel, Alice Munro, Audrey Thomas, Adele Wiseman, Sylvia Fraser, Marie-Claire Blais, Anne Hébert, Gwen MacEweeb, Jane Rule, Sheila Watson, Phyllis Gottlieb, Gladys Hindmarch, Gabrielle Roy and Ethel Wilson (to name a few) have anything in common—and formally they don't—it's the abolition of such categories. Women in their books are no longer relegated to the shadow-lands of either/or. They proclaim, if anything, their right to be fully human, to nurture without being Earth Mothers, to curse without being witches, to suffer without being Little Nell the loveable victim, to copulate without being the Scarlet Woman. *Woman* as a homogeneous gender has become obsolete; women as human beings, on and off the page, are flourishing as never before.

So are women writers, though the story is by no means over. For instance, Canada has a higher proportion of women writers who are taken seriously as writers than does, for instance, the United States; yet in several poetry anthologies I sampled, the work of women still accounted for a third or less of the total, and if you check the best-seller list week after week the percentage is about the same. It's better than for politicians or miners, but not proportional to the population. Even in 1975, it's evidently more imaginable for a man to become a writer than for a woman, and the woman writer is still a kind of exception, an anomaly. I continue to be asked why there are so many good women writers in Canada, yet such questioners haven't stopped to think: by "so many" they mean "some," and the question betrays its own prejudice. There really aren't that many of us; not yet.

Erica Jong (b. 1941)

The publication and promotion of Erica Jong's first novel, *Fear of Flying*, made her a celebrity and caused her to be regarded as the prototypical contemporary female novelist. However, she first published as a poet and also writes literary criticism, reviews, and appreciations.

"Pandora's Box or My Two Mothers" from *Fear of Flying*, included in Part Two, not only reflects Isadora Wing's sexual awakening and the duality of her mother's nature, but also focuses on the difficult choices for the aspiring female artist. Much of Jong's poetry also has creativity as its subject, poems such as "The Commandments" and "Arse Poetica" in *Fruits and Vegetables*, "Alcestis on the Poetry Circuit" and "The Send-Off" in *Half-Lives*, "The Poet Writes in I" and the section entitled "Mash Notes to the Dead and Letters to the Living" in *Loveroot*. The poem that follows, "Dear Colette," describes the traditionally limiting alternatives for women writers and Colette's ability to transcend them, to live fully as a woman and an artist, thus serving as a model and a source of encouragement today.

The details of Jong's life parallel those of her protagonist, Isadora. She was born in New York City into an upper middle-class, Jewish, intellectual family and was educated at Barnard and Columbia. Jong writes of this privileged world with zest and humor, and her description of a young woman's conflicting desires for security and freedom is particularly keen. The book marks a turning point in popular fiction by women, from a victimized heroine to one who is learning her own strength, working to become independent, high-spirited, and free of masochism.

Dear Colette

Dear Colette,
I want to write to you
about being a woman
for that is what
you write to me.

I want to tell you how your face
enduring after thirty, forty, fifty . . .
hangs above my desk
like my own muse.

I want to tell you how your hands
reach out from your books
& seize my heart.

I want to tell you how your hair
electrifies my thoughts
like my own halo.

I want to tell you how your eyes
penetrate my fear
& make it melt.

I want to tell you
simply that I love you—
though you are "dead"
& I am still "alive."

-»»» «««-

Suicides & spinsters—
all our kind!
Even decorous Jane Austen
never marrying,
& Sappho leaping,
& Sylvia in the oven,
& Anna Wickham, Tsvetaeva, Sara Teasdale,
& pale Virginia floating like Ophelia,
& Emily alone, alone, alone. . . .

But you endure & marry,
go on writing,
lose a husband, gain a husband,
go on writing,
sing & tap dance
& you go on writing,
have a child & still
you go on writing,
love a woman, love a man,
& go on writing.
You endure your writing
& your life.

-»»» «««-

Dear Colette,
I only want to thank you:

for your eyes ringed
with bluest paint like bruises,
for your hair gathering sparks
like brush fire,
for your hands which never willingly
let go,
for your years, your child, your lovers,
all your books. . . .
Dear Colette,
you hold me
to this life.

Nikki Giovanni (b. 1943)

Nikki Giovanni's poetry reflects her depth of feeling for her family and her strong connection to the black female experience. Women—her grandmother, her mother, Aretha Franklin, a retired lady of pleasure—are characterized with affection and respect. A selection from her first collection, "Woman Poem" portrays some of the despair of the black woman's experience, but more recent poems are less anguished and less politically militant than her early works. There are wrongs to be righted, there is a need to build a strong black community—but new means must be found. "Revolutionary Dreams" indicates her change in thinking, suggests the true revolution that could be brought about by pursuing "natural dreams."

Giovanni has compassion for black males, for their ambiguity about militancy and the difficulties they face living in white American society, with its constant physical threats and subtle emasculation. However, in her autobiography, *Gemini*, she says that she can't truly understand what it is to be a black male, that they must define themselves. She seeks a loving world in which her son will not have to become a warrior.

Born in Tennessee, Nikki Giovanni was educated at Fisk, the University of Pennsylvania, and Columbia and now lives in New York with her son, Tommy. She says she became a poet "because I couldn't do anything else that well" and has gained popularity through readings and television appearances. Her poetry collections include *Black Feeling, Black Talk/Black Judgement, Re:Creation, Spin a Soft Black Song*, and *My House*. She has two published dialogues, with James Baldwin and Margaret Walker, energetically discussing black consciousness, social changes, and creativity. Several of Giovanni's poems deal with the connection between revolution and poetry, and the following poems illustrate two perspectives. Her most recent volume, *The Women and The Men*, emphasizes love—of women, of men, of places—and portrays poetry as a bridge between feelings and words, between people sharing their lives.

For Saundra

i wanted to write
a poem
that rhymes
but revolution doesn't lend
itself to be-bopping

then my neighbor
who thinks i hate
asked—do you ever write
tree poems—i like trees
so i thought
i'll write a beautiful green tree poem
peeked from my window
to check the image
noticed the school yard was covered
with asphalt
no green—no trees grow
in manhattan

then, well, i thought the sky
i'll do a big blue sky poem
but all the clouds have winged
low since no-Dick was elected

so i thought again
and it occurred to me
maybe i shouldn't write
at all
but clean my gun
and check my kerosene supply

perhaps these are not poetic
times
at all

Poetry

poetry is motion graceful
as a fawn
gentle as a teardrop
strong like the eye
finding peace in a crowded room

we poets tend to think
our words are golden
though emotion speaks too
loudly to be defined
by silence

sometimes after midnight or just before
the dawn

we sit typewriter in hand
pulling loneliness around us
forgetting our lovers or children
who are sleeping
ignoring the weary wariness
of our own logic
to compose a poem
      no one understands it
it never says "love me" for poets are
beyond love
it never says "accept me" for poems seek not
acceptance but controversy
it only says "i am" and therefore
i concede that you are too

a poem is pure energy
horizontally contained
between the mind
of the poet and the ear of the reader
if it does not sing discard the ear
for poetry is song
if it does not delight discard
the heart for poetry is joy
if it does not inform then close
off the brain for it is dead
if it cannot heed the insistent message
that life is precious

which is all we poets
wrapped in our loneliness
are trying to say

Alice Walker (b. 1944)

Alice Walker is a gifted writer of fiction and poetry and a strong
contributor to the new feminist criticism and literary appreciations.
Her essay here, "In Search of Our Mothers' Gardens," is a striking
example, as it explores the black woman's creative past, the tragedy
of her life, and her resiliency and spiritual transcendence. Walker
values her link to this tradition, acknowledging that many of her
stories are her mother's stories and that, no doubt, they stretch back
from her, endlessly. In the frontispiece to her poetry collection *Revolutionary Petunias* she says:

To acknowledge our ancestors means we are aware that we did not make
ourselves, that the line stretches all the way back, perhaps, to God; or
to gods. We remember them because it is an easy thing to forget: that we
are not the first to suffer, rebel, fight, love and die. The grace with which
we embrace life, in spite of the pain, the sorrows, is always a measure of
what has gone before.

A balanced perspective is characteristic of all of Walker's fiction.
"Everyday Use," from her short-story collection *In Love and Trouble:
Stories of Black Women*, is a model of understatement as it shows the
fashionable "new Black" through her mother's eyes. The lives of
the three women in the story and their conflicting values shine through
clearly, warmly, without bitterness, largely because of the richness
of the narrator's character. There are stories in this volume that deal
with harsher realities—with passion, desperation, cruelty—but they,
too, have their own poetry, a stark, tragic essence. To balance despair
and lovelessness in some of these stories, Walker sees hope in personal
strength, community spirit, and family roots. Many of her poems
deal with her own childhood and loving connections to adults.

The eighth child of Georgia sharecroppers, Walker was graduated
from Sarah Lawrence College and teaches writing and literature;
she is married, and has a daughter. Among her other books are *Once*,
The Third Life of Grange Copeland, *Meridian*, and *Langston Hughes*,
a biography for children.

In Search of Our Mothers' Gardens

*I described her own nature and temperament. Told how they needed a
larger life for their expression.... I pointed out that in lieu of proper
channels, her emotions had overflowed into paths that dissipated them.
I talked, beautifully I thought, about an art that would be born, an art
that would open the way for women the likes of her. I asked her to hope,
and build up an inner life against the coming of that day.... I sang,
with a strange quiver in my voice, a promise song.*
"Avey," Jean Toomer, Cane

The poet speaking to a prostitute who falls asleep while he's talking—

When the poet Jean Toomer walked through the South in the early twenties, he discovered a curious thing: Black women whose spirituality was so intense, so deep, so *unconscious*, that they were themselves unaware of the richness they held. They stumbled blindly through their lives: creatures so abused and mutilated in body, so dimmed and confused by pain, that they considered themselves unworthy even of hope. In the selfless abstractions their bodies became to the men who used them, they became more than "sexual objects," more even than mere women: they became Saints. Instead of being perceived as whole persons, their bodies became shrines: what was thought to be their minds became temples suitable for worship. These crazy "Saints" stared out at the world, wildly, like lunatics—or quietly, like suicides; and the "God" that was in their gaze was as mute as a great stone.

Who were these "Saints"? These crazy, loony, pitiful women?

Some of them, without a doubt, were our mothers and grandmothers.

In the still heat of the Post-Reconstruction South, this is how they seemed to Jean Toomer: exquisite butterflies trapped in an evil honey, toiling away their lives in an era, a century, that did not acknowledge them, except as "the *mule* of the world." They dreamed dreams that no one knew—not even themselves, in any coherent fashion—and saw visions no one could understand. They wandered or sat about the countryside crooning lullabies to ghosts, and drawing the mother of Christ in charcoal on courthouse walls.

They forced their minds to desert their bodies and their striving spirits sought to rise, like frail whirlwinds from the hard red clay. And when those frail whirlwinds fell, in scattered particles, upon the ground, no one mourned. Instead, men lit candles to celebrate the emptiness that remained, as people do who enter a beautiful but vacant space to resurrect a God.

Our mothers and grandmothers, some of them: moving to music not yet written. And they waited.

They waited for a day when the unknown thing that was in them would be made known; but guessed, somehow in their darkness, that on the day of their revelation they would be long dead. Therefore to Toomer they walked, and even ran, in slow motion. For they were going nowhere immediate, and the future was not yet within their grasp. And men took our mothers and grandmothers, "but got no pleasure from it." So complex was their passion and their calm.

To Toomer, they lay vacant and fallow as autumn fields, with harvest time never in sight: and he saw them enter loveless marriages, without joy; and become prostitutes, without resistance; and become mothers of children, without fulfillment.

For these grandmothers and mothers of ours were not "Saints," but Artists; driven to a numb and bleeding madness by the springs of creativity in them for which there was no release. They were Creators, who lived lives of spiritual waste, because they were so rich in spirituality—which is the basis of Art—that the strain of enduring their unused and unwanted talent drove them insane. Throwing away this spirituality was their pathetic attempt to lighten the soul to a weight their work-worn, sexually abused bodies could bear.

What did it mean for a Black woman to be an artist in our grand-mothers' time? In our great-grandmothers' day? It is a question with an answer cruel enough to stop the blood.

Did you have a genius of a great-great-grandmother who died under some ignorant and depraved white overseer's lash? Or was she re-quired to bake biscuits for a lazy backwater tramp, when she cried out in her soul to paint watercolors of sunsets, or the rain falling on the green and peaceful pasturelands? Or was her body broken and forced to bear children (who were more often than not sold away from her)—eight, ten, fifteen, twenty children—when her one joy was the thought of modeling heroic figures of Rebellion, in stone or clay?

How was the creativity of the Black woman kept alive, year after year and century after century, when for most of the years Black people have been in America, it was a punishable crime for a Black person to read or write? And the freedom to paint, to sculpt, to expand the mind with action, did not exist. Consider, if you can bear to imagine it, what might have been the result if singing, too, had been forbidden by law. Listen to the voices of Bessie Smith, Billie Holiday, Nina Simone, Roberta Flack, and Aretha Franklin, among others, and imag-ine those voices muzzled for life. Then you may begin to comprehend the lives of our "crazy," "Sainted" mothers and grandmothers. The agony of the lives of women who might have been Poets, Novelists, Essayists, and Short Story Writers (over a period of centuries), who died with their real gifts stifled within them.

And, if this were the end of the story, we would have cause to cry out in my paraphrase of Okot p'Bitek's great poem:

O, my clanswomen
Let us all cry together!
Come,
Let us mourn the death of our mother,
The death of a Queen
The ash that was produced
By a great fire!
O this homestead is utterly dead
Close the gates
With lacari thorns,
For our mother
The creator of the Stool is lost!
And all the young women
Have perished in the wilderness!

But this is not the end of the story, for all the young women—our mothers and grandmothers, *ourselves*—have not perished in the wilderness. And if we ask ourselves why, and search for and find the answer, we will know beyond all efforts to erase it from our minds, just exactly who, and of what, we Black American women are.

One example, perhaps the most pathetic, most misunderstood one, can provide a backdrop for our mothers' work: Phillis Wheatley, a slave in the 1700s.

Virginia Woolf, in her book, *A Room of One's Own,* wrote that in order for a woman to write fiction she must have two things, certainly: a room of her own (with key and lock) and enough money to support herself.

What then are we to make of Phillis Wheatley, a slave, who owned not even herself? This sickly, frail, Black girl who required a servant of her own at times—her health was so precarious—and who, had she been white, would have been easily considered the intellectual superior of all the women and most of the men in the society of her day.

Virginia Woolf wrote further, speaking of course not of our Phillis, that "any woman born with a great gift in the sixteenth century [insert eighteenth century, insert Black woman, insert born or made a slave] would certainly have gone crazed, shot herself, or ended her days in some lonely cottage outside the village, half witch, half wizard [insert Saint], feared and mocked at. For it needs little skill and psychology to be sure that a highly gifted girl who had tried to use her gift for poetry would have been so thwarted and hindered by contrary instincts [add chains, guns, the lash, the ownership of one's body by someone else, submission to an alien religion], that she must have lost her health and sanity to a certainty."

The key words, as they relate to Phillis, are "contrary instincts." For when we read the poetry of Phillis Wheatley—as when we read the novels of Nella Larsen or the oddly false-sounding autobiography of that freest of all Black women writers, Zora Hurston—evidence of "contrary instincts" is everywhere. Her loyalties were completely divided, as was, without question, her mind.

But how could this be otherwise? Captured at seven, a slave of wealthy, doting whites who instilled in her the "savagery" of the Africa they "rescued" her from . . . one wonders if she was even able to remember her homeland as she had known it, or as it really was.

Yet, because she did try to use her gift for poetry in a world that made her a slave, she was "so thwarted and hindered by . . . contrary instincts, that she . . . lost her health. . . ." In the last years of her brief life, burdened not only with the need to express her gift but also with a penniless, friendless "freedom" and several small children for whom she was forced to do strenuous work to feed, she lost her health, certainly. Suffering from malnutrition and neglect and who knows what mental agonies, Phillis Wheatley died.

So torn by "contrary instincts" was Black, kidnapped, enslaved Phillis that her description of "the Goddess"—as she poetically called the Liberty she did not have—is ironically, cruelly humorous. And, in fact, has held Phillis up to ridicule for more than a century. It is usually read prior to hanging Phillis's memory as that of a fool. She wrote:

The Goddess comes, she moves divinely fair,
Olive and laurel binds her golden hair:
Wherever shines this native of the skies,
Unnumber'd charms and recent graces rise.
(Emphasis mine)

It is obvious that Phillis, the slave, combed the "Goddess's" hair every morning; prior, perhaps, to bringing in the milk, or fixing her mistress's lunch. She took her imagery from the one thing she saw elevated above all others.

With the benefit of hindsight we ask, "How could she?"

But at last, Phillis, we understand. No more snickering when your stiff, struggling, ambivalent lines are forced on us. We know now that you were not an idiot nor a traitor; only a sickly little Black girl, snatched from your home and country and made a slave; a woman who still struggled to sing the.song that was your gift, although in a land of barbarians who praised you for your bewildered tongue. It is not so much what you sang, as that you kept alive, in so many of our ancestors, *the notion of song.*

II

Black women are called, in the folklore that so aptly identifies one's status in society, "the *mule* of the world," because we have been handed the burdens that everyone else—*everyone* else—refused to carry. We have also been called "Matriarchs," "Superwomen," and "Mean and Evil Bitches." Not to mention "Castraters" and "Sapphire's Mama." When we have pleaded for understanding, our character has been distorted; when we have asked for simple caring, we have been handed empty inspirational appellations, then stuck in the farthest corner. When we have asked for love, we have been given children. In short, even our plainer gifts, our labors of fidelity and love, have been knocked down our throats. To be an artist and a Black woman, even today, lowers our status in many respects, rather than raises it: and yet, artists we will be.

Therefore we must fearlessly pull out of ourselves and look at and identify with our lives the living creativity some of our great-grandmothers were not allowed to know. I stress *some* of them because it is well known that the majority of our great-grandmothers knew, even without "knowing" it, the reality of their spirituality, even if they didn't recognize it beyond what happened in the singing at church—and they never had any intention of giving it up.

How they did it: those millions of Black women who were not Phillis Wheatley, or Lucy Terry or Frances Harper or Zora Hurston or Nella

Larsen or Bessie Smith—nor Elizabeth Catlett, nor Katherine Dunham, either—brings me to the title of this essay, "In Search of Our Mothers' Gardens," which is a personal account that is yet shared, in its theme and its meaning, by all of us. I found, while thinking about the far-reaching world of the creative Black woman, that often the truest answer to a question that really matters can be found very close. So I was not surprised when my own mother popped into my mind.

In the late 1920s my mother ran away from home to marry my father. Marriage, if not running away, was expected of 17-year-old girls. By the time she was 20, she had two children and was pregnant with a third. Five children later, I was born. And this is how I came to know my mother: she seemed a large, soft, loving-eyed woman who was rarely impatient in our home. Her quick, violent temper was on view only a few times a year, when she battled with the white landlord who had the misfortune to suggest to her that her children did not need to go to school.

She made all the clothes we wore, even my brothers' overalls. She made all the towels and sheets we used. She spent the summers canning vegetables and fruits. She spent the winter evenings making quilts enough to cover all our beds.

During the "working" day, she labored beside—not behind—my father in the fields. Her day began before sunup, and did not end until late at night. There was never a moment for her to sit down, undisturbed, to unravel her own private thoughts; never a time free from interruption—by work or the noisy inquiries of her many children. And yet, it is to my mother—and all our mothers who were not famous—that I went in search of the secret of what has fed that muzzled and often mutilated, but vibrant, creative spirit that the Black woman has inherited, and that pops out in wild and unlikely places to this day.

But when, you will ask, did my overworked mother have time to know or care about feeding the creative spirit?

The answer is so simple that many of us have spent years discovering it. We have constantly looked high, when we should have looked high—and low.

For example: in the Smithsonian Institution in Washington, D.C., there hangs a quilt unlike any other in the world. In fanciful, inspired, and yet simple and identifiable figures, it portrays the story of the Crucifixion. It is considered rare, beyond price. Though it follows no known pattern of quiltmaking, and though it is made of bits and pieces of worthless rags, it is obviously the work of a person of powerful imagination and deep spiritual feeling. Below this quilt I saw a note that says it was made by "an anonymous Black woman in Alabama, a hundred years ago."

If we could locate this "anonymous" Black woman from Alabama, she would turn out to be one of our grandmothers—an artist who left her mark in the only materials she could afford, and in the only medium her position in society allowed her to use.

As Virginia Woolf wrote further, in *A Room of One's Own:*

Yet genius of a sort must have existed among women as it must have
existed among the working class. [Change this to slaves and the
wives and daughters of sharecroppers.] Now and again an Emily
Brontë or a Robert Burns [change this to a Zora Hurston or a Richard
Wright] blazes out and proves its presence. But certainly it never
got itself on to paper. When, however, one reads of a witch being
ducked, of a woman possessed by devils [or Sainthood], of a wise
woman selling herbs [our rootworkers], or even a very remarkable
man who had a mother, then I think we are on the track of a lost novelist, a suppressed poet, of some mute and inglorious Jane Austen. . . .
Indeed, I would venture to guess that Anon, who wrote so many
poems without signing them, was often a woman. . . .

And so our mothers and grandmothers have, more often than not
anonymously, handed on the creative spark, the seed of the flower
they themselves never hoped to see: or like a sealed letter they could
not plainly read.

And so it is, certainly, with my own mother. Unlike "Ma" Rainey's
songs, which retained their creator's name even while blasting forth
from Bessie Smith's mouth, no song or poem will bear my mother's
name. Yet so many of the stories that I write, that we all write, are
my mother's stories. Only recently did I fully realize this: that
through years of listening to my mother's stories of her life, I have
absorbed not only the stories themselves, but something of the manner in which she spoke, something of the urgency that involves the
knowledge that her stories—like her life—must be recorded. It is
probably for this reason that so much of what I have written is about
characters whose counterparts in real life are so much older than
I am.

But the telling of these stories, which came from my mother's lips as
naturally as breathing, was not the only way my mother showed herself as an artist. For stories, too, were subject to being distracted,
to dying without conclusion. Dinners must be started, and cotton
must be gathered before the big rains. The artist that was and is my
mother showed itself to me only after many years. This is what I
finally noticed:

Like Mem, a character in *The Third Life of Grange Copeland,* my
mother adorned with flowers whatever shabby house we were forced
to live in. And not just your typical straggly country stand of zinnias,
either. She planted ambitious gardens—and still does—with over 50
different varieties of plants that bloom profusely from early March
until late November. Before she left home for the fields, she watered
her flowers, chopped up the grass, and laid out new beds. When she
returned from the fields she might divide clumps of bulbs, dig a
cold pit, uproot and replant roses, or prune branches from her taller
bushes or trees—until night came and it was too dark to see.

Whatever she planted grew as if by magic, and her fame as a grower
of flowers spread over three counties. Because of her creativity with
her flowers, even my memories of poverty are seen through a screen

of blooms—sunflowers, petunias, roses, dahlias, forsythia, spirea, delphiniums, verbena . . . and on and on.

And I remember people coming to my mother's yard to be given cuttings from her flowers; I hear again the praise showered on her because whatever rocky soil she landed on, she turned into a garden. A garden so brilliant with colors, so original in its design, so magnificent with life and creativity, that to this day people drive by our house in Georgia—perfect strangers and imperfect strangers—and ask to stand or walk among my mother's art.

I notice that it is only when my mother is working in her flowers that she is radiant, almost to the point of being invisible—except as Creator: hand and eye. She is involved in work her soul must have. Ordering the universe in the image of her personal conception of Beauty.

Her face, as she prepares the Art that is her gift, is a legacy of respect she leaves to me, for all that illuminates and cherishes life. She had handed down respect for the possibilities—and the will to grasp them.

For her, so hindered and intruded upon in so many ways, being an artist has still been a daily part of her life. This ability to hold on, even in very simple ways, is work Black women have done for a very long time.

This poem is not enough, but it is something, for the woman who literally covered the holes in our walls with sunflowers:

They were women then
My mama's generation
Husky of voice—Stout of
Step
With fists as well as
Hands
How they battered down
Doors
And ironed
Starched white
Shirts
How they led
Armies
Headragged Generals
Across mined
Fields
Booby-trapped
Ditches
To discover books
Desks
A place for us
How they knew what we
Must know
Without knowing a page
Of it
Themselves.

Guided by my heritage of a love of beauty and a respect for strength
—in search of my mother's garden, I found my own.

And perhaps in Africa over 200 years ago, there was just such a
mother; perhaps she painted vivid and daring decorations in oranges
and yellows and greens on the walls of her hut; perhaps she sang—
in a voice like Roberta Flack's—*sweetly* over the compounds of her
village; perhaps she wove the most stunning mats or told the most
ingenious stories of all the village storytellers. Perhaps she was herself a poet—though only her daughter's name is signed to the poems
that we know.

Perhaps Phillis Wheatley's mother was also an artist.

Perhaps in more than Phillis Wheatley's biological life is her mother's
signature made clear.

Marie-Elise (b. 1950)

Marie-Elise is a poet, representative of new directions that younger women are pursuing. Her chief concern is poetry as it intertwines with the rest of her activities—as university student, mother, adventurer. Member of a loosely structured poetry collective in Santa Barbara, she frequently participates in poetry readings, and one of her innovations is accompanying her poems with mime and deaf sign-language. The movements become a dance, intensifying the effect of the poem and expanding the potential of the oral tradition. Three poems in Part Two, "Definition," "Diapering This Poem," and "Touching a Friend," are sign-language works, evocative on the page but even more so in performance. She has published in numerous small presses, was the subject of videotape documentary, and is working on a book, tentatively entitled "A Poem is a Home for Lost Letters."

Born in Santa Monica, California, Marie-Elise has had different last names, parental, guardian-parental, and marital, so she no longer uses any of them, preferring to create her own identity. Her poetry is included in this volume to represent work-in-process by a younger poet developing her personal voice. Her discipline and creativity are noteworthy: she writes a poem each morning from a spot overlooking the Pacific Ocean (somewhat in the Renaissance tradition, in which one warmed up daily by composing a sonnet after breakfast), reads widely, and participates in conferences and symposiums in addition to her college classes. Marie-Elise travels as much as possible for a woman with limited financial resources and full responsibility for an active son.

And always, she keeps her journal, which she describes as more personal than her poetry. The diary has long been found by women as the ideal place, generally private and often hidden, to record struggles, insights, and personal growth—a best friend, as Anaïs Nin says. But the diary has only recently been acknowledged as an art form; published collections now abound. (See, for example, Mary Moffat, and Charlotte Painter, eds., *Revelations: Diaries of Women.* New York: Random House [Vintage], 1976.) The excerpts from Marie-Elise's journal that follow illuminate the feelings and the conflicts a young woman experiences and the value that she derives from this form of recording and thinking about her life.

Journal Entries

10 February 1975
Last night I stepped into the high society of Santa Barbara hippie
artists: drinking wine in denim finery among hanging plants, junkyard
mobiles, and scattered colors on canvas walls. I was the second poet
to read . . . standing behind a carved pine quadrangular witness stand,
laughing off my nervousness, saying, "I feel like my poems are on
trial." (spotlit between incandescent lights and a candelabra didn't
make me feel any less naked)

Started to read a new poem, but as my spirit cringed at the lack of
warmth/response, my voice dimmed and a little mouse took over.
Someone requested that I read Loud, so I mustered up some confidence with two old poems, rushed through a love poem, fumbled
through three "small dances for voices/gesture," finally arriving at
my newest poem, "Gemini." When Lynda joined me at the "pulpit"
to read the second voice, someone said, "Is this fair . . . two poets?" to
which I courageously stammered, "Do poetry readings have rules?"
Laughter encouraged us to duet through, and the applause and
appreciative embraces after helped.

Back at my desk, reliving the deep disappointment in myself as a
performer, I ask myself, "What is my responsibility to my audience?
How important is my voice to the poem? Are they poems alone? Is
reading/sharing my work the only way I can establish credibility as a
writer?" I work on new poems now listening with a more critical ear.

18 March 1975
When I think about women poets who took their own lives, I don't
think about their death methods, age, or body of work that died with
them. I wonder about their children. How old were they when their
mothers left? Did they go to live with foreign families who speak
love in clichés? Did they write secret poems of their own? How
many became belly dancers because they couldn't be ballerinas? Or
middle-class suburban dwellers: so silent, so secure?

20 April 1975
Almost a month since I vowed not to keep a journal any longer. The
recurring pattern: my mother, my husband, my lover; sneaking into
these pages for answers. I am an unsolved puzzle to them . . . furious
that my privacy is so disrespectable.

This last month I tried fictionalizing my feelings, or writing poems;
but it's not enough. I need these pages. When I direct all my writing
towards a "finished" piece, the professional perfectionist sits behind
every idea, demanding coherence, style, and careful editing.

I need this place to scribble: a nice compost of earth and garbage
where ideas can sprout. A place where I can sit comfortably with my
feet on the furniture, books on the floor, ashtrays overflowing.

13 September 1975
I'm still so angry I can hardly hold my pen to the page. Went to

Welfare to report this semester's scholarship. Arrived on time for my appointment, but had to wait almost an hour, thumbing through old copies of *Good Housekeeping* and *Redbook*.

Then, sitting in an office cubicle, my worker went through it again with me (in her kind, condescending mother-hen voice) "... Why don't I study something more practical? Like computer science ... secretarial skills ... nursing ... There are thousands of unemployed English teachers in this state ..."

I tried my best to explain that writing is a craft ... and these literature classes are teaching me valuable tools ... (Does she think all the books on her desk wrote themselves?) ... but she cut me short with the serious suggestion that I find myself a nice man (while I'm still young and pretty!) who is willing to marry and support my unrealistic dreams.

I was so livid I couldn't even speak. I grabbed my things, stomped out, and walked my bicycle all the way home ... stepping on every crack ... saying over and over "I am I am I am ..."

8 October 1975
There's never enough time. I feel like my head is going to explode, and then scatter into the creative minds of others, or fade away. I thought the routine of school would be a welcome change to summer's chaos of ideas/experience. Instead I've over-extended myself ... and don't want to sacrifice anything. Jamie's responsibility weighs on me: sometimes I want to take the day off, or "call in sick," and there's no one there to answer the call. School has rules and deadlines, and always, always, the muse nags my head, saying "you need to write more often."

Instead of separating myself from pressures, to write, I find myself inwardly screaming, frustrated because I'm not superwoman: the perfect mother, perfect lover, perfect poet. I'm afraid I'm going to fail at all these, or have a nervous breakdown, or beat my child, or continue in some mundane existence, hating myself for no longer writing.

School seems boring, when I need it to be daily joy and inspiration (all that history, ideas, the lives of energetic human beings).

Maybe this is just a time of transition ... regenerating ... shifting gears. Maybe I need more time to relax; so that those images I find scratched on scraps of paper start to sing in my idle mind—replacing this ache in my forehead.

I've even thought of giving up my precious space and living in a communal household—but I love and need my time alone, somewhere to go where I can be sure of that, not having to rearrange my disposition to inter-act with others.

11 November 1975
Thick fog today. Visible as snow. Yet the sun plodded through in
afternoon . . . cold and lackluster . . . causing eerie white beams to
slant down through the trees onto the pavement. The texture of the
fog looked beautiful—but the kind of dusky beauty that is best expressed in finished photographs: a mood, minus the wet chill, preserved in lights and darks, on glossy paper.

Bicycling back home with Jamie this afternoon, the fog and traffic
forced us to ride along the gravel edge of the street, near the vacant
railroad tracks. Jamie started chanting in his squawky new voice,
"bumpity bike, bumpity bicycle ride," and when we pedaled past a
family of willow trees he added "Jamie touches trees" to his little
song. We arrived home breathless, laughing; and I made a mental
note to write it down—not because it was anything extraordinary, but
because it is these small fragments of Jamie's childhood that assure
me he is growing up happy. If he has little ecstatic moments every
day, maybe I can hold onto them for him, and not blame myself later
if he becomes cynical and pessimistic about life.

Later at bedtime, Jamie whispered in his gravest, most serious voice,
"Don't turn the light off! Monsters will come in through the window
and eat all my toys!" To which I smiled glibly and replied, "Monsters
won't come near you if you have love inside you . . . here, let me hug
you full of love. . . ." In a few minutes he was soundly lost in peaceful dreams. I turned the light off and left his room feeling a little
smug at the ease and calm with which I play Mother sometimes.

I thought about all the times I wanted a Mother I could trust my fears
to; but perhaps if she'd been there when I needed her, I wouldn't still
be growing and greeting sleep with new unfinished dreams that sing
me through these foggier days.

19 July 1976
I take myself too seriously. "Why, I was published before you even
knew how to write," he told me crisply, cleaning his wire-frame
bookkeeper's glasses with the wrinkled tail of his shirt; taking his
wine to an empty table.

"So what," I think, cleaning off the bar counter, feeling my ego deflate.
I tell myself I don't want to be great, but it's only half true. I couldn't
work these jobs if they didn't feed my life.

"Don't listen to him," a voice says from the other end of the bar.
After rolling a bugler and wiping the beer off her elbows, she pours
another from the pitcher, takes a good look at me.

"What's that in yer hair?" She pokes a finger at the air, teasing a
vertical line downward, where two small braids frame my face. We
are each a curiosity to the other . . . aloof, but interested.

"You mean the feathers?" They are small, mottled brown, and barely recognizable in the braid ends. "I think they're pretty." She snorts. "Bet the ducks do too." I pour a few more beers, clean off the table, go back and stand behind the bar where she's still drinking.

"It's the same as mink. Poor people wear feathers, rich people wear mink. What the hell . . . we ought to all go naked. . . ."

1 November 1976
Pedaling home
books on my back
(each flash of headlights
trapping a house in dusk)
Two kids riding ahead of me
(leaning and weaving
between
cars at the curb
and the street)

"It don't matter if I get good grades
or not.
My old lady still gives me
anything I want."

3 December 1976
Jamie hanging on my elbow as I write: "You're *always* writing, I hate it when you're always writing."

After several more interruptions, I finally lose all patience and yell, "Jamie, I'm *working*. This is how I *work*." He stares at me for a long time, then goes into his room and plays/reads quietly until I'm done.

I used to think that being a writer would be compatible with motherhood. Instead, I find my child is one more person I have to reaffirm my space with.

14 December 1976
Stare at the blank page. Hold the pen comfortably between the fingers. She told me to try this when no words would come. It's no use. It's no different. I'm not saying there's no such thing as automatic writing; all writing is automatic. I always find a flow when I take myself to the empty page. Not as the vehicle of any one else's life but as the speaker for many of my own voices. Sleeping, reading, speaking, listening, thinking; the conversations never stop. Poems are fragments of this: Verbal abstractions, of emotions. Even novels and plays are only pieces, with endings that the readers/viewers resolve and continue.

Training to be a writer is a slow and continuous process. With time off for human behavior. For me, writing is a record of one's changing. It will take the words of hundreds of women . . . of thousands of psyches . . . it will take visions spoken and sung and danced and displayed in every conceivable texture and form: in new ways of living and loving and being, before real change happens.

Sometimes I think I can hear the thoughts of every woman . . . who knows her actions are circumstantial contradiction, but whose thoughts are believing in the struggle and supporting a change. Their unspoken emotions feed me . . . this is faith in the unseen . . . these energies and inspirations keep me working.

Woman Writing

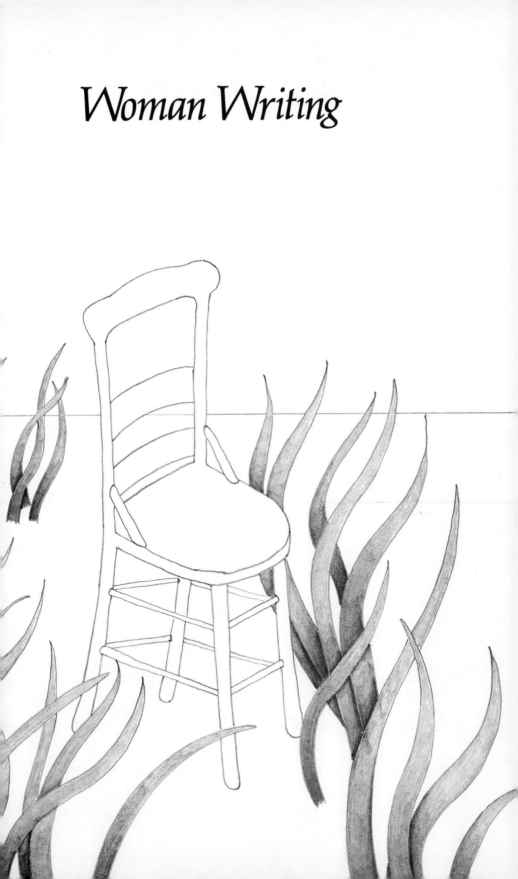

Virginia Woolf

from To the Lighthouse

No, she thought, putting together some of the pictures he had cut out
—a refrigerator, a mowing machine, a gentleman in evening dress—
children never forget. For this reason, it was so important what one
said, and what one did, and it was a relief when they went to bed.
For now she need not think about anybody. She could be herself, by
herself. And that was what now she often felt the need of—to think;
well, not even to think. To be silent; to be alone. All the being and
the doing, expansive, glittering, vocal, evaporated; and one shrunk,
with a sense of solemnity, to being oneself, a wedge-shaped core of
darkness, something invisible to others. Although she continued to
knit, and sat upright, it was thus that she felt herself; and this self
having shed its attachments was free for the strangest adventures.
When life sank down for a moment, the range of experience seemed
limitless. And to everybody there was always this sense of unlimited
resources, she supposed; one after another, she, Lily, Augustus Car-
michael, must feel, our apparitions, the things you know us by, are
simply childish. Beneath it is all dark, it is all spreading, it is unfath-
omably deep; but now and again we rise to the surface and that is
what you see us by. Her horizon seemed to her limitless. There were
all the places she had not seen; the Indian plains; she felt herself
pushing aside the thick leather curtain of a church in Rome. This
core of darkness could go anywhere, for no one saw it. They could
not stop it, she thought, exulting. There was freedom, there was peace,
there was, most welcome of all, a summoning together, a resting on
a platform of stability. Not as oneself did one find rest ever, in
her experience (she accomplished here something dexterous with her
needles) but as a wedge of darkness. Losing personality, one lost
the fret, the hurry, the stir; and there rose to her lips always some
exclamation of triumph over life when things came together in this
peace, this rest, this eternity; and pausing there she looked out to
meet that stroke of the Lighthouse, the long steady stroke, the last
of the three, which was her stroke, for watching them in this mood
always at this hour one could not help attaching oneself to one thing
especially of the things one saw; and this thing, the long steady stroke,
was her stroke. Often she found herself sitting and looking, sitting
and looking, with her work in her hands until she became the thing
she looked at—that light, for example. And it would lift up on it
some little phrase or other which had been lying in her mind like
that—"Children don't forget, children don't forget"—which she would
repeat and begin adding to it, It will end, it will end, she said. It will
come, it will come, when suddenly she added, We are in the hands
of the Lord.

But instantly she was annoyed with herself for saying that. Who had said it? Not she; she had been trapped into saying something she did not mean. She looked up over her knitting and met the third stroke and it seemed to her like her own eyes meeting her own eyes, searching as she alone could search into her mind and her heart, purifying out of existence that lie, any lie. She praised herself in praising the light, without vanity, for she was stern, she was searching, she was beautiful like that light. It was odd, she thought, how if one was alone, one leant to inanimate things; trees, streams, flowers; felt they expressed one; felt they became one; felt they knew one, in a sense were one; felt an irrational tenderness thus (she looked at that long steady light) as for oneself. There rose, and she looked and looked with her needles suspended, there curled up off the floor of the mind, rose from the lake of one's being, a mist, a bride to meet her lover.

What brought her to say that: "We are in the hands of the Lord?" she wondered. The insincerity slipping in among the truths roused her, annoyed her. She returned to her knitting again. How could any Lord have made this world? she asked. With her mind she had always seized the fact that there is no reason, order, justice: but suffering, death, the poor. There was no treachery too base for the world to commit; she knew that. No happiness lasted; she knew that. She knitted with firm composure, slightly pursing her lips and, without being aware of it, so stiffened and composed the lines of her face in a habit of sternness that when her husband passed, though he was chuckling at the thought that Hume, the philosopher, grown enormously fat, had stuck in a bog, he could not help noting, as he passed, the sternness at the heart of her beauty. It saddened him, and her remoteness pained him, and he felt, as he passed, that he could not protect her, and, when he reached the hedge, he was sad. He could do nothing to help her. He must stand by and watch her. Indeed, the infernal truth was, he made things worse for her. He was irritable—he was touchy. He had lost his temper over the Lighthouse. He looked into the hedge, into its intricacy, its darkness.

Always, Mrs. Ramsay felt, one helped oneself out of solitude reluctantly by laying hold of some little odd or end, some sound, some sight. She listened, but it was all very still; cricket was over; the children were in their baths; there was only the sound of the sea. She stopped knitting; she held the long reddish-brown stocking dangling in her hands a moment. She saw the light again. With some irony in her interrogation, for when one woke at all, one's relations changed, she looked at the steady light, the pitiless, the remorseless, which was so much her, yet so little her, which had her at its beck and call (she woke in the night and saw it bent across their bed, stroking the floor), but for all that she thought, watching it with fascination, hypnotised, as if it were stroking with its silver fingers some sealed vessel in her brain whose bursting would flood her with delight, she had known happiness, exquisite happiness, intense happiness, and it silvered the rough waves a little more brightly, as daylight faded, and the blue went out of the sea and it rolled in waves of pure lemon which curved and swelled and broke upon the beach and the ecstasy burst in her eyes and waves of pure delight raced over the floor of her mind and she felt, It is enough! It is enough!

He turned and saw her. Ah! She was lovely, lovelier now than ever he thought. But he could not speak to her. He could not interrupt her. He wanted urgently to speak to her now that James was gone and she was alone at last. But he resolved, no; he would not interrupt her. She was aloof from him now in her beauty, in her sadness. He would let her be, and he passed her without a word, though it hurt him that she should look so distant, and he could not reach her, he could do nothing to help her. And again he would have passed her without a word had she not, at that very moment, given him of her own free will what she knew he would never ask, and called to him and taken the green shawl off the picture frame, and gone to him. For he wished, she knew, to protect her.

Katherine Mansfield

This Flower

"But I tell you, my lord fool, out of this nettle danger, we pluck this flower, safety."

As she lay there looking up at the ceiling, she had her moment—yes, she had her moment! And it was not connected with anything she had thought or felt before, not even with those words the doctor had scarcely ceased speaking. It was single, glowing, perfect; it was like— a pearl, too flawless to match with another . . . Could she describe what happened? Impossible. It was as though, even if she had not been conscious (and she certainly had not been conscious all the time) that she was fighting against the stream of life—the stream of life indeed!—she had suddenly ceased to struggle. Oh, more than that! She had yielded, yielded absolutely, down to every minutest pulse and nerve, and she had fallen into the bright bosom of the stream and it had borne her . . . She was part of her room—part of the great bouquet of southern anemones, of the white net curtains that blew in stiff against the light breeze, of the mirrors, the white silky rugs; she was part of the high, shaking, quivering clamour, broken with little bells and crying voices that went streaming by outside,—part of the leaves and the light.

Over. She sat up. The doctor had reappeared. This strange little figure with his stethoscope still strung round his neck—for she had asked him to examine her heart—squeezing and kneading his freshly washed hands, had told her . . .

It was the first time she had ever seen him. Roy, unable, of course, to miss the smallest dramatic opportunity, had obtained his rather shady Bloomsbury address from the man in whom he always confided everything, who, although he'd never met her, knew "all about them."

"My darling," Roy had said, "we'd better have an absolutely unknown man just in case it's—well, what we don't either of us want it to be. One can't be too careful in affairs of this sort. Doctors *do* talk. It's all damned rot to say they don't." Then, "Not that I care a straw who on earth knows. Not that I wouldn't—if you'd have me—blazon it on the skies, or take the front page of the *Daily Mirror* and have our two names on it, in a heart, you know—pierced by an arrow."

Nevertheless, of course, his love of mystery and intrigue, his passion for "keeping our secret beautifully" (his phrase!) had won the day, and off he'd gone in a taxi to fetch this rather sodden-looking little man.

She heard her untroubled voice saying, "Do you mind not mentioning anything of this to Mr. King? If you'd tell him that I'm a little run down and that my heart wants a rest. For I've been complaining about my heart."

Roy had been really *too* right about the kind of man the doctor was. He gave her a strange, quick, leering look, and taking off the stethoscope with shaking fingers he folded it into his bag that looked somehow like a broken old canvas shoe.

"Don't you worry, my dear," he said huskily. "I'll see you through."

Odious little toad to have asked a favour of! She sprang to her feet, and picking up her purple cloth jacket, went over to the mirror. There was a soft knock at the door, and Roy—he really did look pale, smiling his half-smile—came in and asked the doctor what he had to say.

"Well," said the doctor, taking up his hat, holding it against his chest and beating a tattoo on it, "all I've got to say is that Mrs.—h'm— Madam wants a bit of a rest. She's a bit run down. Her heart's a bit strained. Nothing else wrong."

In the street a barrel-organ struck up something gay, laughing, mocking, gushing, with little trills, shakes, jumbles of notes.

That's all *I got to say, to say,*
That's all *I got to say,*

it mocked. It sounded so near she wouldn't have been surprised if the doctor were turning the handle.

She saw Roy's smile deepen; his eyes took fire. He gave a little "Ah!" of relief and happiness. And just for one moment he allowed himself to gaze at her without caring a jot whether the doctor saw or not, drinking her up with that gaze she knew so well, as she stood tying the pale ribbons of her camisole and drawing on the little purple cloth jacket. He jerked back to the doctor. "She shall go away. She shall go away to the sea at once," said he, and then, terribly anxious, "What about her food?" At that, buttoning her jacket in the long mirror, she couldn't help laughing at him.

"That's all very well," he protested, laughing back delightedly at her and at the doctor. "But if I didn't manage her food, doctor, she'd never eat anything but caviare sandwiches and—and white grapes. About wine—oughtn't she to have wine?

Wine would do her no harm.

"Champagne," pleaded Roy. How he was enjoying himself!

"Oh, as much champagne as she likes," said the doctor, "and a brandy and soda with her lunch if she fancies it."

Roy loved that; it tickled him immensely.

"Do you hear that?" he asked solemnly, blinking and sucking in his cheeks to keep from laughing. "Do you fancy a brandy and soda?"

And, in the distance, faint and exhausted, the barrel-organ:

A brandy and so-da,
A brandy and soda, please!
A brandy and soda, please!

The doctor seemed to hear that, too. He shook hands with her and Roy went with him into the passage to settle his fee.

She heard the front door close and then—rapid, rapid steps along the passage. This time he simply burst into her room, and she was in his arms, crushed up small while he kissed her with warm quick kisses, murmuring between them, "My darling, my beauty, my delight. You're mine, you're safe." And then three soft groans. "Oh! Oh! Oh! the relief!" Still keeping his arms round her he leant his head against her shoulder as though exhausted. "If you knew how frightened I've been," he murmured. "I thought we were in for it this time. I really did. And it would have been so—fatal—so fatal!"

Zelda Fitzgerald

from Save Me the Waltz

Nobody knew whose party it was. It had been going on for weeks.
When you felt you couldn't survive another night, you went home
and slept and when you got back, a new set of people had consecrated
themselves to keeping it alive. It must have started with the first
boatloads of unrest that emptied themselves into France in nineteen
twenty-seven. Alabama and David joined in May, after a terrible
winter in a Paris flat that smelled of a church chancery because it was
impossible to ventilate. That apartment, where they had fastened
themselves up from the winter rain, was a perfect breeding place for
the germs of bitterness they brought with them from the Riviera.
From out their windows the gray roofs before shaved the gray roofs
behind like lightly grazing fencing foils. The gray sky came down
between the chimneys in inverted ethereal Gothic dividing the horizon
into spires and points which hung over their unrest like the tubes of
a vast incubator. The etching of the balconies of the Champs-Elysées
and the rain on the pavements about the Arc de Triomphe was all
they could see from their red and gilt salon. David had a studio on
the Left Bank in that quarter of the city beyond the Pont de l'Alma,
where rococo apartment buildings and long avenues of trees give on
colorless openings with no perspective.

There he lost himself in the retrospect of autumn disembodied from
its months, from heat and cold and holidays, and produced his lullabies of recapitulation that drew vast crowds of the advance guard to
the Salon des Indépendents. The frescoes were finished: this was a
new, more personal, David on exhibit. You heard his name in bank
lobbies and in the Ritz Bar, which was proof that people were saying
it in other places. The steely concision of his work was making itself
felt even in the lines of interior decoration. Des Arts Décoratifs carried a dining room after one of his interiors painted because of a
gray anemone; the Ballet Russe accepted a décor—fantasmagoria of
the light on the plage at St-Raphaël to represent the beginning of the
world in a ballet called Evolution.

The rising vogue of the David Knights brought Dickie Axton flying
symbolically across their horizons, scribbling over the walls of their
prosperity a message from Babylon which they did not bother to
read, being at that time engrossed in the odor of twilit lilacs along the
Boulevard St-Germain and the veiling of the Place de la Concorde in
the expensive mysticism of the Blue Hour.

The telephone rang and rang and rustled their dreams to pale Val-
hallas, Ermenonville, and the celestial twilight passages of padded
hotels. As they slept in their lyric bed dreaming the will of the world

to be probate, the bell rained on their consciousness like the roll of distant hoops; David grabbed the receiver.

"Hello. Yes, this is both the Knights."

Dickie's voice slid down the telephone wire from high-handed confidence to a low wheedle.

"I hope you're coming to my dinner." The voice descended by its teeth like an acrobat from the top of a circus tent. The limits of Dickie's activities stopped only at the borders of moral, social and romantic independence, so you can well imagine that her scope was not a small one. Dickie had at her beck and call a catalogue of humanity, an emotional casting agency. Her existence was not surprising in this age of Mussolinis and sermons from the mount by every passing Alpinist. For the sum of three hundred dollars she scraped the centuries' historic deposits from under the nails of Italian noblemen and passed it off as caviar to Kansas débutantes; for a few hundreds more she opened the doors of Bloomsbury and Parnassus, the gates of Chantilly or the pages of Debrett's to America's post-war prosperity. Her intangible commerce served up the slithered frontiers of Europe in a céleri-rave—Spaniards, Cubans, South Americans, even an occasional black floating through the social mayonnaise like bits of truffle. The Knights had risen to so exalted a point in the hierarchy of the "known" that they had become material for Dickie.

"You needn't be so high-hat," Alabama protested to David's lack of enthusiasm. "All the people will be white—or were once."

"We'll come, then," said David into the receiver.

Alabama twisted her body experimentally. The patrician sun of late afternoon spread itself aloofly over the bed where she and David untidily collected themselves.

"It's very flattering," she said, propelling herself to the bathroom, "to be sought after, but more provident, I suppose, to seek."

David lay listening to the violent flow of the water and the quake of the glasses in their stands.

"Another jag!" he yelled. "I find I can get along very well without my basic principles, but I cannot sacrifice my weaknesses—one being an insatiability about jags."

"What did you say about the Prince of Wales being sick?" called Alabama.

"I don't see why you can't listen when I'm talking to you," David answered crossly.

"I hate people who begin to talk the minute you pick up a tooth-brush," she snapped.

"I said the sheets of this bed are actually scorching my feet."

"But there isn't any potash in the liquor over here," said Alabama incredulously. "It must be a neurosis—have you a new symptom?" she demanded jealously.

"I haven't slept in so long I would be having hallucinations if I could distinguish them from reality."

"Poor David—what will we do?"

"I don't know. Seriously, Alabama"—David lit a cigarette contemplatively—"my work's getting stale. I need new emotional stimulus."

Alabama looked at him coldly.

"I see." She realized that she had sacrificed forever her right to be hurt on the glory of a Provençal summer. "You might follow the progress of Mr. Berry Wall through the columns of the *Paris Herald*," she suggested.

"Or choke myself on a chiaroscuro."

"If you *are* serious, David, I believe it has always been understood between us that we would not interfere with each other."

"Sometimes," commented David irrelevantly, "your face looks like a soul lost in the mist on a Scotch moor."

"Of course, no allowance has been made in our calculations for jealousy," she pursued.

"Listen, Alabama," interrupted David, "I feel terrible; do you think we can make the grade?"

"I want to show off my new dress," she said decisively.

"And I've got an old suit I'd like to wear out. You know we shouldn't go. We should think of our obligations to humanity." Obligations were to Alabama a plan and a trap laid by civilization to ensnare and cripple her happiness and hobble the feet of time.

"Are you moralizing?"

"No. I want to see what her parties are like. The last of Dickie's soirées netted no profits to charity though hundreds were turned away at the gates. The Duchess of Dacne cost Dickie three months in America by well-placed hints."

"They're like all the others. You just sit down and wait for the inevitable, which is the only thing that never happens."

The post-war extravagance which had sent David and Alabama and some sixty thousand other Americans wandering over the face of Europe in a game of hare without hounds achieved its apex. The sword of Damocles, forged from the high hope of getting something for nothing and the demoralizing expectation of getting nothing for something, was almost hung by the third of May.

There were Americans at night, and day Americans, and we all had Americans in the bank to buy things with. The marble lobbies were full of them.

Lespiaut couldn't make enough flowers for the trade. They made nasturtiums of leather and rubber and wax gardenias and ragged robins out of threads and wires. They manufactured hardy perennials to grow on the meagre soil of shoulder straps and bouquets with long stems for piercing the loamy shadows under the belt. Modistes pieced hats together from the toy-boat sails in the Tuileries; audacious dress-makers sold the summer in bunches. The ladies went to the foundries and had themselves some hair cast and had themselves half-soled with the deep chrome fantasies of Helena Rubenstein and Dorothy Gray. They read off the descriptive adjectives on the menu-cards to the waiters and said, "Wouldn't you like" and "Wouldn't you really" to each other till they drove the men out to lose themselves in the comparative quiet of the Paris streets which hummed like the tuning of an invisible orchestra. Americans from other years bought them-selves dressy houses with collars and cuffs in Neuilly and Passy, stuffed themselves in the cracks of the rue du Bac like the Dutch boy saving the dikes. Irresponsible Americans suspended themselves on costly eccentricities like Saturday's servants on a broken Ferris wheel and made so many readjustments that a constant addenda went on about them like the clang of a Potin cash register. Esoteric pelletiers robbed a secret clientele in the rue des Petits-Champs; people spent fortunes in taxis in search of the remote.

"I'm sorry I can't stay, I just dropped in to say 'hello,' " they said to each other and refused the table d'hôte. They ordered Veronese pastry on lawns like lace curtains at Versailles and chicken and hazelnuts at Fontainebleau where the woods wore powdered wigs. Discs of umbrellas poured over suburban terraces with the smooth round ebul-lience of a Chopin waltz. They sat in the distance under the lugubrious dripping elms, elms like maps of Europe, elms frayed at the end like bits of chartreuse wool, elms heavy and bunchy as sour grapes. They ordered the weather with a continental appetite, and listened to the centaur complain about the price of hoofs. There were bourgeois blossoms on the bill-of-fare and tall architectural blossoms on the horse-chestnut and crystallized rose-buds to go with the Porto. The Americans gave indications of themselves but always only the begin-ning like some eternal exposition, a clef before a bar of music to be played on the minors of the imagination. They thought all French school boys were orphans because of the black dresses they wore, and those of them who didn't know the meaning of the word "insen-sible" thought the French thought that they were crazy. All of them drank. Americans with red ribbons in their buttonholes read papers called the *Éclaireur* and drank on the sidewalks, Americans with tips on the races drank down a flight of stairs, Americans with a million dollars and a standing engagement with the hotel masseuses drank in suites at the Meurice and the Crillon. Other Americans drank in Montmartre, "pour le soif" and "contre la chaleur" and "pour la di-gestion" and "pour se guérir." They were glad the French thought they were crazy.

Over fifty thousand francs' worth of flowers had wilted to success on the altars of Notre-Dame-des-Victoires during the year.

"Maybe something will happen," said David.

Alabama wished nothing ever would again but it was her turn to agree—they had evolved a tacit arrangement about waiting on each other's emotions, almost mathematical like the trick combination of a safe, which worked by the mutual assumption that it would.

"I mean," he pursued, "if somebody would come along to remind us about how we felt about things when we felt the way they remind us of, maybe it would refresh us."

"I see what you mean. Life has begun to appear as tortuous as the sentimental writhings of a rhythmic dance."

"Exactly. I want to make some protestations since I'm largely too busy to work very well."

"Mama said 'Yes' and Papa said 'Yes' " to the gramophone owners of France. "Ariel" passed from the title of a book to three wires on the house-top. What did it matter? It had already gone from a god to a myth to Shakespeare—nobody seemed to mind. People still recognized the word: "Ariel!" it was. David and Alabama hardly noticed the change.

Eudora Welty

A Piece of News

She had been out in the rain. She stood in front of the cabin fireplace, her legs wide apart, bending over, shaking her wet yellow head crossly, like a cat reproaching itself for not knowing better. She was talking to herself—only a small fluttering sound, hard to lay hold of in the sparsity of the room.

"The pouring-down rain, the pouring-down rain"—was that what she was saying over and over, like a song? She stood turning in little quarter turns to dry herself, her head bent forward and the yellow hair hanging out streaming and tangled. She was holding her skirt primly out to draw the warmth in.

Then, quite rosy, she walked over to the table and picked up a little bundle. It was a sack of coffee, marked "Sample" in red letters which she unwrapped from a wet newspaper. But she handled it tenderly.

"Why, how come he wrapped it in a newspaper!" she said, catching her breath, looking from one hand to the other. She must have been lonesome and slow all her life, the way things would take her by surprise.

She set the coffee on the table, just in the center. Then she dragged the newspaper by one corner in a dreamy walk across the floor, spread it all out, and lay down full length on top of it in front of the fire. Her little song about the rain, her cries of surprise, had been only a preliminary, only playful pouting with which she amused herself when she was alone. She was pleased with herself now. As she sprawled close to the fire, her hair began to slide out of its damp tangles and hung all displayed down her back like a piece of bargain silk. She closed her eyes. Her mouth fell into a deepness, into a look of unconscious cunning. Yet in her very stillness and pleasure she seemed to be hiding there, all alone. And at moments when the fire stirred and tumbled in the grate, she would tremble, and her hand would start out as if in impatience or despair.

Presently she stirred and reached under her back for the newspaper. Then she squatted there, touching the printed page as if it were fragile. She did not merely look at it—she watched it, as if it were unpredictable, like a young girl watching a baby. The paper was still wet in places where her body had lain. Crouching tensely and patting the creases away with small cracked red fingers, she frowned now and then at the blotched drawing of something and big letters that spelled a word underneath. Her lips trembled, as if looking and spelling so slowly had stirred her heart.

All at once she laughed.

She looked up.

"Ruby Fisher!" she whispered.

An expression of utter timidity came over her flat blue eyes and her soft mouth. Then a look of fright. She stared about. . . . What eye in the world did she feel looking in on her? She pulled her dress down tightly and began to spell through a dozen words in the newspaper.

The little item said:

"Mrs. Ruby Fisher had the misfortune to be shot in the leg by her husband this week."

As she passed from one word to the next she only whispered; she left the long word, "misfortune," until the last, and came back to it, then she said it all over out loud, like conversation.

"That's me," she said softly, with deference, very formally.

The fire slipped and suddenly roared in the house already deafening with the rain which beat upon the roof and hung full of lightning and thunder outside.

"You Clyde!" screamed Ruby Fisher at last, jumping to her feet.

"Where are you, Clyde Fisher?"

She ran straight to the door and pulled it open. A shudder of cold brushed over her in the heat, and she seemed striped with anger and bewilderment. There was a flash of lightning, and she stood waiting, as if she half thought that would bring him in, a gun leveled in his hand.

She said nothing more and, backing against the door, pushed it closed with her hip. Her anger passed like a remote flare of elation. Neatly avoiding the table where the bag of coffee stood, she began to walk nervously about the room, as if a teasing indecision, an untouched mystery, led her by the hand. There was one window, and she paused now and then, waiting, looking out at the rain. When she was still, there was a passivity about her, or a deception of passivity, that was not really passive at all. There was something in her that never stopped.

At last she flung herself onto the floor, back across the newspaper, and looked at length into the fire. It might have been a mirror in the cabin, into which she could look deeper and deeper as she pulled her fingers through her hair, trying to see herself and Clyde coming up behind her.

"Clyde?"

But of course her husband, Clyde, was still in the woods. He kept a thick brushwood roof over his whisky still, and he was mortally afraid of lightning like this, and would never go out in it for anything.

And then, almost in amazement, she began to comprehend her predicament: it was unlike Clyde to take up a gun and shoot her.

She bowed her head toward the heat, onto her rosy arms, and began to talk and talk to herself. She grew voluble. Even if he heard about the coffee man, with a Pontiac car, she did not think he would shoot her. When Clyde would make her blue, she would go out onto the road, some car would slow down, and if it had a Tennessee license, the lucky kind, the chances were that she would spend the afternoon in the shed of the empty gin. (Here she rolled her head about on her arms and stretched her legs tiredly behind her, like a cat.) And if Clyde got word, he would slap her. But the account in the paper was wrong. Clyde had never shot her, even once. There had been a mistake made.

A spark flew out and nearly caught the paper on fire. Almost in fright she beat it out with her fingers. Then she murmured and lay back more firmly upon the pages.

There she stretched, growing warmer and warmer, sleepier and sleepier. She began to wonder out loud how it would be if Clyde shot her in the leg. . . . If he were truly angry, might he shoot her through the heart?

At once she was imagining herself dying. She would have a nightgown to lie in, and a bullet in her heart. Anyone could tell, to see her lying there with that deep expression about her mouth, how strange and terrible that would be. Underneath a brand-new nightgown her heart would be hurting with every beat, many times more than her toughened skin when Clyde slapped at her. Ruby began to cry softly, the way she would be crying from the extremity of pain; tears would run down in a little stream over the quilt. Clyde would be standing there above her, as he once looked, with his wild black hair hanging to his shoulders. He used to be very handsome and strong!

He would say, "Ruby, I done this to you."

She would say—only a whisper—"That is the truth, Clyde—you done this to me."

Then she would die; her life would stop right there.

She lay silently for a moment, composing her face into a look which would be beautiful, desirable, and dead.

Clyde would have to buy her a dress to bury her in. He would have to dig a deep hole behind the house, under the cedar, a grave. He would have to nail her up a pine coffin and lay her inside. Then he would have to carry her to the grave, lay her down and cover her up. All the time he would be wild, shouting, and all distracted, to think he could never touch her one more time.

She moved slightly, and her eyes turned toward the window. The white rain splashed down. She could hardly breathe, for thinking that this was the way it was to fall on her grave, where Clyde would come and stand, looking down in the tears of some repentance.

A whole tree of lightning stood in the sky. She kept looking out the window, suffused with the warmth from the fire and with the pity and beauty and power of her death. The thunder rolled.

Then Clyde was standing there, with dark streams flowing over the floor where he had walked. He poked Ruby with the butt of his gun, as if she were asleep.

"What's keepin' supper?" he growled.

She jumped up and darted away from him. Then, quicker than lightning, she put away the paper. The room was dark, except for the firelight. From the long shadow of his steamy presence she spoke to him glibly and lighted the lamp.

He stood there with a stunned, yet rather good-humored look of delay and patience in his face, and kept on standing there. He stamped his mud-red boots, and his enormous hands seemed weighted with the rain that fell from him and dripped down the barrel of the gun. Presently he sat down with dignity in the chair at the table, making a little tumult of his rightful wetness and hunger. Small streams began to flow from him everywhere.

Ruby was going through the preparations for the meal gently. She stood almost on tiptoe in her bare, warm feet. Once as she knelt at the safe, getting out the biscuits, she saw Clyde looking at her and she smiled and bent her head tenderly. There was some way she began to move her arms that was mysteriously sweet and yet abrupt and tentative, a delicate and vulnerable manner, as though her breasts gave her pain. She made many unnecessary trips back and forth across the floor, circling Clyde where he sat in his steamy silence, a knife and fork in his fists.

"Well, where you been, anyway?" he grumbled at last, as she set the first dish on the table.

"Nowheres special."

"Don't you talk back to me. You been hitchhikin' again, ain't you?" He almost chuckled.

She gave him a quick look straight into his eyes. She had not even heard him. She was filled with happiness. Her hand trembled when she poured the coffee. Some of it splashed on his wrist.

At that he let his hand drop heavily down upon the table and made the plates jump.

"Some day I'm goin' to smack the livin' devil outa you," he said.

Ruby dodged mechanically. She let him eat. Then, when he had crossed his knife and fork over his plate, she brought him the newspaper. Again she looked at him in delight. It excited her even to touch the paper with her hand, to hear its quiet secret noise when she carried it, the rustle of surprise.

"A newspaper!" Clyde snatched it roughly and with a grabbing disparagement. "Where 'd you git that? Hussy."

"Look at this-here," said Ruby in her small singsong voice. She opened the paper while he held it and pointed gravely to the paragraph.

Reluctantly, Clyde began to read it. She watched his damp bald head slowly bend and turn.

Then he made a sound in his throat and said, "It's a lie."

"That's what's in the newspaper about me," said Ruby, standing up straight. She took up his plate and gave him that look of joy.

He put his big crooked finger on the paragraph and poked at it.

"Well, I'd just like to see the place I shot you!" he cried explosively. He looked up, his face blank and bold.

But she drew herself in, still holding the empty plate, faced him straightened and hard, and they looked at each other. The moment filled full with their helplessness. Slowly they both flushed, as though with a double shame and a double pleasure. It was as though Clyde might really have killed Ruby, and as though Ruby might really have been dead at his hand. Rare and wavering, some possibility stood timidly like a stranger between them and made them hang their heads.

Then Clyde walked over in his water-soaked boots and laid the paper on the dying fire. It floated there a moment and then burst into flame. They stood still and watched it burn. The whole room was bright.

"Look," said Clyde suddenly. "It's a Tennessee paper. See 'Tennessee'? That wasn't none of you it wrote about." He laughed, to show that he had been right all the time.

"It was Ruby Fisher!" cried Ruby. "My name is Ruby Fisher!" she declared passionately to Clyde.

"Oho, it was another Ruby Fisher—in Tennessee," cried her husband. "Fool me, huh? Where'd you get that paper?" He spanked her good-humoredly acrosss her backside.

Ruby folded her still trembling hands into her skirt. She stood stooping by the window until everything, outside and in, was quieted before she went to her supper.

It was dark and vague outside. The storm had rolled away to faintness like a wagon crossing a bridge.

Anaïs Nin

Hejda

The unveiling of women is a delicate matter. It will not happen overnight. We are all afraid of what we shall find.

Hejda was, of course, born in the Orient. Before the unveiling she was living in an immense garden, a little city in itself, filled with many servants, many sisters and brothers, many relatives. From the roof of the house one could see all the people passing, vendors, beggars, Arabs going to the mosque.

Hejda was then a little primitive, whose greatest pleasure consisted in inserting her finger inside pregnant hens and breaking the eggs, or filling frogs with gasoline and setting a lighted match to them. She went about without underclothes in the house, without shoes, but once outside she was heavily veiled and there was no telling exactly the contours of her body, which were at an early age those of a full-blown woman, and there was no telling that her smile had that carnivorous air of smiles with large teeth.

In school she had a friend whose great sorrow was her dark color. The darkest skin in the many shaded nuances of the Arabian school. Hejda took her out into the farthest corner of the school garden one day and said to her: "I can make you white if you want me to. Do you trust me?"

"Of course I do."

Hejda brought out a piece of pumice stone. She very gently but very persistently began to pumice a piece of the girl's forhead. Only when the pain became unendurable did she stop. But for a week, every day, she continued enlarging the circle of scraped, scarred skin, and took secret pleasure in the strange scene of the girl's constant lamentations of pain and her own obstinate scraping. Until they were both found out and punished.

At seventeen she left the Orient and the veils, but she retained an air of being veiled. With the most chic and trim French clothes, which molded her figure, she still conveyed the impression of restraint and no one could feel sure of having seen her neck, arms or legs. Even her evening dresses seemed to sheathe her. This feeling of secrecy, which recalled constantly the women of Arabia as they walked in their many yards of white cotton, rolled like silk around a spool, was due in great part to her inarticulateness. Her speech revealed and opened no doors. It was labyrinthian. She merely threw off enough words to invite one into the passageway but no sooner had one started to walk towards the unfinished phrase than one met an impasse, a curve, a barrier. She retreated behind half admissions, half promises, insinuations.

This covering of the body, which was like the covering of the spirit, had created an unshatterable timidity. It had the effect of concentrating the light, the intensity in the eyes. So that one saw Hejda as a mixture of elegance, cosmetics, aesthetic plumage, with only the eyes sending signals and messages. They pierced European clothes with the stabbing brilliancy of those eyes in the Orient which to reach the man had to pierce through the heavy aura of yards of white cotton.

The passageways that led one to Hejda were as tortuous and intricate as the passageways in the oriental cities in which the pursued women lost themselves, but all through the vanishing, turning streets the eyes continued to signal to strangers like prisoners waving out of windows.

The desire to speak was there, after centuries of confinement and repression, the desire to be invaded and rescued from the secretiveness. The eyes were full of invitations, in great contradiction to the closed folds of the clothes, the many defenses of the silk around the neck, the sleeves around the arms.

Her language was veiled. She had no way to say: look at Hejda who is full of ideas. So she laid out cards and told fortunes like the women of the harem, or she ate sweets like a stunted woman who had been kept a child by close binding with yards of white cotton, as the feet of the Chinese women had been kept small by bandaging. All she could say was: I had a dream last night (because at breakfast time in the Orient, around the first cup of dark coffee, everyone told their dreams). Or she opened a book accidentally when in trouble and placed a finger on a phrase and decided on her next course of action by the words of this phrase. Or she cooked a dish as colorful as an Oriental market place.

Her desire to be noticed was always manifested, as in the Orient, by a bit of plumage, a startling jewel, a spangle pasted on her forehead between the eyes (the third eye of the Oriental was a jewel, as if the secret life so long preserved from openness had acquired the fire of precious stones).

No one understood the signals: look at Hejda, the woman of the Orient who wants to be a woman of tomorrow. The plumage and the aesthetic adornment diverted them like decoration on a wall. She was always being thrust back into the harem, on a pillow.

She had arrived in Paris, with all her invisible veils. When she laughed she concealed her mouth as much as possible, because in her small round face the teeth were extraordinarily large. She concealed her voraciousness and her appetites. Her voice was made small, again as the Chinese make their feet small and infantile. Her poses were reluctant and reserved. The veil was not in her timidities, her fears, in her manner of dressing, which covered her throat and compressed her overflowing breasts. The veil was in her liking for flowers (which was racial), especially small roses and innocent asexual flowers, in complicated rituals of politeness (also traditional), but above all in evasiveness of speech.

She wanted to be a painter. She joined the Académie Julien. She painted painstakingly on small canvases—the colors of the Orient, a puerile Orient of small flowers, serpentines, confetti and candy colors, the colors of small shops with metallic lace-paper roses and butterflies.

In the same class there was a dark, silent, timid young Roumanian. He had decadent, aristocratic hands, he never smiled, he never talked. Those who approached him felt such a shriveling timidity in him, such a retraction, that they remained at a distance.

The two timidities observed each other. The two silences, the two withdrawals. Both were oriental interiors, without windows on the external world, and all the greenery in the inner patio, all their windows open on the inside of the house.

A certain Gallic playfulness presides in the painting class. The atmosphere is physical, warm, gay. But the two of them remain in their inner patio, listening to birds singing and fountains playing. He thinks: how mysterious she is. And she thinks: how mysterious he is.

Finally one day, as she is leaving, he watches her repainting the black line on the edge of her eyes out of a silver peacock. She nimbly lifts up the head of the peacock and it is a little brush that makes black lines around her oriental eyes.

This image confounds him, ensorcells him. The painter is captivated, stirred. Some memory out of Persian legends now adorns his concept of her.

They marry and take a very small apartment where the only window gives on a garden.

At first they marry to hide together. In the dark caverns of their whisperings, confidences, timidities, what they now elaborate is a stalactitic world shut out from light and air. He initiates her into his aesthetic values. They make love in the dark and in the daytime make their place more beautiful and more refined.

In Molnar's hands she is being remolded, refashioned, stylized. He cannot remold her body. He is critical of her heaviness. He dislikes her breasts and will not let her ever show them. They overwhelm him. He confesses he would like her better without them. This shrinks her within herself and plants the seed of doubt of her feminine value. With these words he has properly subjugated her, given her a doubt which will keep her away from other men. He bound her femininity, and it is now oppressed, bound, even ashamed of its vulgarity, of its expansiveness. This is the reign of aesthetic value, stylization, refinement, art, artifice. He has established his domination in this. At every turn nature must be subjugated. Very soon, with his coldness, he represses her violence. Very soon he polishes her language, her manners, her impulses. He reduces and limits her hospitality, her friendliness, her desire for expansion.

It is her second veiling. It is the aesthetic veils of art and social graces. He designs her dresses. He molds her as far as he can into the stylized figures in his paintings. His women are transparent and lie in hammocks between heaven and earth. Hejda cannot reach this, but she can become an odalisque. She can acquire more silver peacocks, more poetic objects that will speak for her.

Her small canvases look childlike standing beside his. Slowly she becomes more absorbed in his painting than in her own. The flowers and gardens disappear.

He paints a world of stage settings, static ships, frozen trees, crystal fairs, the skeletons of pleasure and color, from which nature is entirely shut off. He proceeds to make Hejda one of the objects in this painting; her nature is more and more castrated by this abstraction of her, the obtrusive breasts more severely veiled. In his painting there is no motion, no nature, and certainly not the Hejda who liked to run about without underwear, to eat herbs and raw vegetables out of the garden.

Her breasts are the only intrusion in their exquisite life. Without them she could be the twin he wanted, and they could accomplish this strange marriage of his feminine qualities and her masculine ones. For it is already clear that he likes to be protected and she likes to protect, and that she has more power in facing the world of reality, more power to sell pictures, to interest the galleries in his work, more courage too. It is she who assumes the active role in contact with the world. Molnar can never earn a living, Hejda can. Molnar cannot give orders (except to her) and she can. Molnar cannot execute, realize, concretize as well as she can, for in execution and action she is not timid.

Finally it is Molnar who paints and draws and it is Hejda who goes out and sells his work.

Molnar grows more and more delicate, more vulnerable, and Hejda stronger. He is behind the scene, and she is in the foreground now.

He permits her love to flow all around him, sustain him, nourish him. In the dark he reconquers his leadership. And not by any sensual prodigality, but on the contrary, by a severe economy of pleasure. She is often left hungry. She never suspects for a moment that it is anything but economy and thinks a great abundance lies behind this aesthetic reserve. There is no delight or joy in their sensual contact. It is a creeping together into a womb.

Their life together is stilted, windowless, facing inward. But the plants and fountains of the patio are all artificial, ephemeral, immobile. A stage setting for a drama that never takes place. There are colonnades, friezes, backgrounds, plush drops but no drama takes place, no evolution, no sparks. His women's figures are always lying down, suspended in space.

But Hejda, Hejda feels compressed. She does not know why. She has never known anything but oppression. She has never been out of a small universe delimited by man. Yet something is expanding in her. A new Hejda is born out of the struggle with reality, to protect the weakness of Molnar. In the outer world she feels larger.

When she returns home she feels she must shrink back into submission to Molnar's proportions. The outgoing rhythm must cease. Molnar's whole being is one total negation; negation and rejection of the world, of social life, of other human beings, of success, of movement, of motion, of curiosity, of adventure, of the unknown.

What is he defending, protecting? No consuming passion for one person, but perhaps a secret consuming. He admits no caresses, no invitations to love-making. It is always "no" to her hunger, "no" to her tenderness, "no" to the flow of life. They were close in fear and concealment, but they are not close in flow and development. Molnar is now frozen, fixed. There is no emotion to propel him. And when she seeks to propel him, substitute her élan for his static stagnation, all he can do is break this propeller.

"Your ambitions are vulgar."

(She does not know how to answer: my ambitions are merely the balance to your inertia.)

A part of her wants to expand. A part of her being wants to stay with Molnar. This conflict tears her asunder. The pulling and tearing bring on illness.

Hejda falls.

Hejda is ill.

She cannot move forward because Molnar is tied, and she cannot break with him.

Because he will not move, his being is stagnant and filled with poison. He injects her every day with this poison.

She has taken his paintings into the real world, to sell, and in so doing she has connected with that world and found it larger, freer.

Now he does not let her handle the painting. He even stops painting. Poverty sets in.

Perhaps Molnar will turn about now and protect her. It is the dream of every maternal love: I have filled him with my strength. I have nourished his painting. My painting has passed into his painting. I am broken and weak. Perhaps now he will be strong.

But not at all. Molnar watches her fall, lets her fall. He lets poverty instill itself. He watches inertly the sale of their art possessions, the trips to the pawnbroker. He leaves Hejda without care. His passivity and inertia consume the whole house.

It is as if Hejda had been the glue that held the furniture together. Now it breaks. It is as if she had been the cleaning fluid and now the curtains turn gray. The logs in the fireplace now smoke and do not burn: was she the fire in the hearth too? Because she lies ill objects grow rusty. The food turns sour. Even the artificial flowers wilt. The paints dry on the palette. Was she the water, the soap too? Was she the fountain, the visibility of the windows, the gloss of the floors? The creditors buzz like locusts. Was she the fetish of the house who kept them away? Was she the oxygen in the house? Was she the salt now missing from the bread? Was she the delicate feather duster dispelling the webs of decay? Was she the silver polish?

Tired of waiting for her to get well—alone, he goes out.

Hejda and Molnar are now separated. She is free. Several people help her to unwind the binding wrapped around her personality first by the family life, then by the husband. Someone falls in love with her ample breasts, and removes the taboo that Molnar had placed upon them. Hejda buys herself a sheer blouse which will reveal her possessions.

When a button falls off she does not sew it on again.

Then she also began to talk.

She talked about her childhood. The same story of going about without underwear as a child which she had told before with a giggle of confusion and as if saying: "what a little primitive I was," was now told with the oblique glance of the strip-teaser, with a slight arrogance, the *agent provocateur* towards the men (for now exhibitionism placed the possibility in the present, not in the past).

She discards small canvases and buys very large ones. She paints larger roses, larger daisies, larger trellises, larger candied clouds, larger taffy seas. But just as the canvases grow larger without their content growing more important, Hejda is swelling up without growing. There is more of her. Her voice grows louder, her language, freed of Molnar's decadent refinement, grows coarser. Her dresses grow shorter. Her blouses looser. There is more flesh around her small body but Molnar is not there to corset it. There is more food on her table. She no longer conceals her teeth. She becomes proud of her appetite. Liberty has filled her to overflowing with a confidence that everything that was once secret and bound was of immense value. Every puerile detail of her childhood, every card dealer's intuition, every dream, becomes magnified.

And the stature of Hejda cannot bear the weight of her ambition. It is as if compression had swung her towards inflation. She is inflated physically and spiritually. And whoever dares to recall her to a sense of proportion, to a realization that there are perhaps other painters of value in the world, other women, becomes the traitor who must be banished instantly. On him she pours torrents of abuse like the abuse of the oriental gypsies to whom one has refused charity—curses and maledictions.

It is not desire or love she brings to the lovers: I have discovered that I am very gifted for love-making!

It is not creativity she brings to her painting: I will show Molnar that I was a better painter!

Her friendships with women are simply one long underground rivalry: to excel in startling dress or behavior. She enters a strained, intense competition. When everything fails she resorts to lifting her dress and arranging her garters.

Where are the veils and labyrinthian evasions?

She is back in the garden of her childhood, back to the native original Hejda, child of nature and succulence and sweets, of pillows and erotic literature.

The frogs leap away in fear of her again.

Mary McCarthy

C.Y.E.

Near the corner of Fourteenth Street and Fourth Avenue, there is a store called Cye Bernard. I passed it the other day on my way to the Union Square subway station. To my intense surprise, a heavy blush spread over my face and neck, and my insides contorted in that terrible grimace of shame that is generally associated with hangovers. I averted my eyes from the sign and hurried into the subway, my head bent so that no observer should discover my secret identity, which until that moment I had forgotten myself. Now I pass this sign every day, and it is always a question whether I shall look at it or not. Usually I do, but hastily, surreptitiously, with an ineffective air of casualness, lest anybody suspect that I am crucified there on that building, hanging exposed in black script lettering to advertise bargains in men's haberdashery.

The strangest part about it is that this unknown clothier on Fourteenth Street should not only incorporate in his name the mysterious, queerly spelled nickname I was given as a child in the convent but that he should add to this the name of my patron saint, St. Bernard of Clairvaux, whom I chose for my special protector at a time when I was suffering from the nickname. It is nearly enough to convince me that life is a system of recurrent pairs, the poison and the antidote being eternally packaged together by some considerate heavenly druggist. St. Bernard, however, was, from my point of view, never so useful as the dog that bears his name, except in so far as he represented the contemplative, bookish element in the heavenly hierarchy, as opposed, say, to St. Martin of Tours, St. Francis Xavier or St. Aloysius of Gonzaga, who was of an ineffable purity and died young. The life of action was repellent to St. Bernard, though he engaged in it from time to time; on the other hand, he was not a true *exalté*—he was, in short, a sedentary man, and it was felt, in the convent, I think, that he was a rather odd choice for an eleven-year-old girl, the nuns themselves expressing some faint bewilderment and concern, as older people do when a child is presented with a great array of toys and selects from among them a homely and useful object.

It was marvelous, I said to myself that day on the subway, that I could have forgotten so easily. In the official version of my life the nickname does not appear. People have asked me, now and then, whether I have ever had a nickname and I have always replied, No, it is funny but I do not seem to be the type that gets one. I have even wondered about it a little myself, asking, Why is it that I have always been Mary, world without end, Amen, feeling a faint pinch of regret and privation, as though a cake had been cut and no favor, not even the old maid's thimble or the miser's penny, been found in my piece.

How political indeed is the personality, I thought. What coalitions and cabals the party in power will not make to maintain its uncertain authority! Nothing is sacred. The past is manipulated to serve the interests of the present. For any bureaucracy, amnesia is convenient. The name of Trotsky drops out of the chapter on the revolution in the Soviet textbooks—what shamelessness, we say, while in the meantime our discarded selves languish in the Lubianka of the unconscious. But a moment comes at last, after the regime has fallen, after all interested parties are dead, when the archives are opened and the old ghosts walk, and history must be rewritten in the light of fresh discoveries.

It was happening to me then, as I sat frozen in my seat, staring at the picture of Miss Subways, February 1943, who loves New York and spends her spare time writing to her two officer-brothers in the Army and Navy. The heavy doors of the mind swung on their hinges. I was back in the convent, a pale new girl sitting in the front of the study hall next to a pretty, popular eighth-grader, whom I bored and who resented having me for a deskmate. I see myself perfectly: I am ambitious, I wish to make friends with the most exciting and powerful girls; at the same time, I am naïve, without stratagems, for I think that this project of mine will be readily accomplished, that I have only to be myself. The first rebuffs startle me. I look around and see that there is a social pyramid here and that I and my classmates are on the bottom. I study the disposition of stresses and strains and discover that two girls, Elinor Henehan and Mary Heinrichs, are important, and that their approval is essential to my happiness.

There were a great many exquisite and fashionable-looking girls in the convent, girls with Irish or German names, who used make-up in secret, had suitors, and always seemed to be on the verge of a romantic elopement. There were also some very pretty Protestant girls, whose personal charms were enhanced for us by the exoticism of their religion—the nuns telling us that we should always be specially considerate of them because they were Protestants, and, so to speak, our guests, with the result that we treated them reverently, like French dolls. These two groups made up the élite of the convent; the nuns adored them for their beauty, just as we younger girls did; and they enjoyed far more réclame than the few serious students who were thought to have the vocation.

Elinor Henehan and Mary Heinrichs fell into neither category. They were funny, lazy, dangling girls, fourteen or fifteen years old, with baritone voices, very black hair, and an insouciant attitude toward convent life. It was said that they came from east of the mountains. Elinor Henehan was tall and bony, with horn-rimmed glasses; Mary Heinrichs was shorter and plump. Their blue serge uniforms were always a mess, the collars and cuffs haphazardly sewn on and worn a day or so after they ought to have been sent to the laundry. They broke rules constantly, talking in study hall, giggling in chapel.

Yet out of these unpromising personal materials, they had created a unique position for themselves. They were the school clowns. And like all clowns they had made a shrewd bargain with life, exchanging dignity for power, and buying with servility to their betters immunity from the reprisals of their equals or inferiors. For the upper school they travestied themselves, exaggerating their own odd physical characteristics, their laziness, their eccentric manner of talking. With the lower school, it was another story: we were the performers, the school the audience, they the privileged commentators from the royal box. Now it was our foibles, our vanities, our mannerisms that were on display, and the spectacle was apparently so hilarious that it was a continual challenge to the two girls' self-control. They lived in a recurrent spasm of mirth. On the playground, at the dinner-table, laughter would dangerously overtake them; one would whisper to the other and then a wordless rocking would begin, till finally faint anguished screams were heard, and the nun in charge clapped her clapper for silence.

What was unnerving about this laughter—unnerving especially for the younger girls—was its general, almost abstract character. More often than not, we had no idea what it was that Elinor and Mary were laughing at. A public performance of any sort—a recital, a school play—instantly reduced them to jelly. Yet what was there about somebody's humble and pedestrian performance of *The Merry Peasant* that was so uniquely comic? Nobody could tell, least of all the performer. To be the butt of this kind of joke was a singularly painful experience, for you were never in a position to turn the tables, to join in the laughter at your own expense, because you could not possibly pretend to know what the joke was. Actually, as I see now, it was the intimacy of the two girls that set their standard: from the vantage point of their private world, anything outside seemed strange and ludicrous. It was our very existence they laughed at, as the peasant laughs at the stranger from another province. The occasions of mirth —a request for the salt, a trip to the dictionary in the study hall— were mere pretexts; our personalities *in themselves* were incredible to them. At the time, however, it was very confusing. Their laughter was a kind of crazy compass that was steering the school. Nobody knew, ever, where the whirling needle would stop, and many of us lived in a state of constant apprehension, lest it should point to *our* desk, lest we become, if only briefly, the personification of all that was absurd, the First Cause of this cosmic mirth.

Like all such inseparable friends, they delighted in nicknames, bestowing them in godlike fashion, as though by renaming their creatures they could perform a new act of creation, a secular baptism. And as at the baptismal font we had passed from being our parents' children to being God's children, so now we passed from God's estate to a societal trolls' world presided over by these two unpredictable deities. They did not give nicknames to everybody. You had to have some special quality to be singled out by Elinor and Mary, but what that quality was only Elinor and Mary could tell. I saw very soon (the beginnings of wisdom) that I had two chances of finding an honorable place in the convent system: one was to escape being nicknamed altogether, the other was to earn for myself an appellation that, while humorous, was still benevolent; rough, perhaps, but tender. On the whole, I would have preferred the first alternative, as being less chancy. Months passed, and no notice was taken of me; my anxiety diminished; it seemed as though I might get my wish.

They broke the news to me one night after study hall. We were filing out of the large room when Elinor stepped out of the line to speak to me. "We have got one for you," she said. "Yes?" I said calmly, for really (I now saw) I had known it all along, known that there was something about me that would inevitably appeal to these two strange girls. I stiffened up in readiness, feeling myself to be a sort of archery target: there was no doubt that they could hit me (I was an easy mark), but, pray God, it be one of the larger concentric circles, not, oh Blessed Virgin, the red, tender bull's-eye at the heart. I could not have imagined what was in store for me. "Cye," said Elinor and began to laugh, looking at me oddly because I did not laugh too. "Si?" I asked, puzzled. I was a new girl, it was true, but I did not come from the country. "C-Y-E," said Elinor, spelling. "But what does it mean?" I asked the two of them, for Mary had now caught up with her. They shook their dark heads and laughed. "Oh no," they said. "We can't tell you. But it's very, very good. Isn't it?" they asked each other. "It's one of our best."

I saw at once that it was useless to question them. They would never tell me, of course, and I would only make myself ridiculous, even more Cye-like, if I persisted. It occurred to me that if I showed no anxiety, they would soon forget about it, but my shrewdness was no match for theirs. The next day it was all over the school. It was called to me on the baseball field, when the young nun was at bat; it was whispered from head to head down the long refectory table at dinner. It rang through the corridors in the dormitory. "What does it mean?" I would hear a girl ask. Elinor or Mary would whisper in her ear, and the girl would cast me a quick glance, and then laugh. Plainly, they had hit me off to a T, and as I saw this my curiosity overcame my fear and my resentment. I no longer cared how derogatory the name might be; I would stand anything. I said to myself, if only I could know it. If only I had some special friend who could find out and then tell me. But I was new and a little queer, anyway, it seemed; I had no special friends, and now it was part of the joke that the whole school should know, and know that I wanted to know and not tell me. My isolation, which had been obscure, was now conspicuous, and, as it were, axiomatic. Nobody could ever become my friend, because to do so would involve telling me, and Elinor and Mary would never forgive that.

It was up to me to guess it, and I would lie in bed at night, guessing wildly, as though against time, like the miller's upstart daughter in Rumpelstiltskin. Outlandish phrases would present themselves: "Catch your elbow," "Cheat your end." Or, on the other hand, sensible ones that were humiliating: "Clean your ears." One night I got up and poured water into the china basin and washed my ears in the dark, but when I looked at the wash cloth in the light the next morning, it was perfectly clean. And in any case, it seemed to me that the name must have some more profound meaning. My fault was nothing ordinary that you could do something about, like washing your ears.

Plainly, it was something imminent and irremediable, a spiritual taint. And though I could not have told precisely what my wrongness consisted in, I felt its existence almost tangible during those nights, and knew that it had always been with me, even in the other school, where I had been popular, good at games, good at dramatics; I had always had it, a kind of miserable effluvium of the spirit that the ordinary sieves of report cards and weekly confessions had been powerless to catch.

Now I saw that I could never, as I had hoped, belong to the convent's inner circles, not to the tier of beauty, nor to the tier of manners and good deportment, which was signalized by wide moiré ribbons, awarded once a week, blue, green, or pink, depending on one's age, that were worn in a sort of bandolier style, crosswise from shoulder to hip. I could take my seat in the dowdy tier of scholarship, but my social acquaintance would be limited to a few frowzy little girls of my own age who were so insignificant, so contemptible, that they did not even know what my nickname stood for. Even they, I thought, were better off than I, for they knew their place, they accepted the fact that they were unimportant little girls. No older girl would bother to jeer at them, but in me there was something overweening, over-eager, over-intense, that had brought upon me the hateful name. Now my only desire was to be alone, and in the convent this was difficult, for the nuns believed that solitude was appropriate for anchorites, but for growing girls, unhealthy. I went to the library a great deal and read all of Cooper, and *Stoddard's Lectures.* I became passionately religious, made a retreat with a fiery missionary Jesuit, spent hours on my knees in adoration of the Blessed Sacrament, but even in the chapel, the name pursued me: glancing up at the cross, I would see the initials, I.N.R.I.; the name that had been given Christ in mockery now mocked me, for I was not a prig and I knew that my sufferings were ignoble and had nothing whatever in common with God's. And, always, there was no avoiding the communal life, the older girls passing as I crept along the corridor with a little knot of my classmates. "Hello, Cye."

Looking back, I see that if I had ever burst into tears publicly, begged for quarter, compunction would have been felt. Some goddess of the college department would have comforted me, spoken gently to Elinor and Mary, and the nickname would have been dropped. Perhaps it might even have been explained to me. But I did not cry, even alone in my room. I chose what was actually the more shameful part. I accepted the nickname, made a sort of joke of it, used it brazenly myself on the telephone, during vacations, calling up to ask a group of classmates to the movies: "This is Cye speaking." But all the time I was making plans, writing letters home, arranging my escape. I resolved that once I was out of the convent, I would never, never, never again let anybody see what I was like. That, I felt, had been my mistake.

The day I left the Mother Superior cried. "I think you will grow up to be a novelist," she said, "and that can be a fine thing, but I want you to remember all your life the training you have had here in the convent."

I was moved and thrilled by the moment, the prediction, the parting adjuration. "Yes," I said, weeping, but I intended to forget the convent within twenty-four hours. And in this I was quite successful.

The nickname followed me for a time, to the public high school I entered. One of the girls said to me, "I hear you are called Cye." "Yes," I replied easily. "How do you spell it?" she asked. "S-I," I said. "Oh," she said. "That's funny." "Yes," I said. "I don't know why they called me that." This version of the nickname lasted perhaps three weeks. At the end of that time, I dropped the group of girls who used it, and I never heard it again.

Now, however, the question has been reopened. What do the letters stand for? A happy solution occurred to me yesterday, on Fifteenth Street and Fourth Avenue. "Clever Young Egg," I said to myself out loud. The words had arranged themselves without my volition, and instantly I felt that sharp, cool sense of relief and triumph that one has on awakening from a nightmare. Could that have been it? Is it possible that that was all? Is it possible that Elinor and Mary really divined nothing, that they were paying me a sort of backhanded compliment, nothing certainly that anybody could object to? I began to laugh at myself, affectionately, as one does after a long worry, saying, "You fool, look how silly you've been." "Now I can go back," I thought happily, without reflection, just as though I were an absconding bank teller who had been living for years with his spiritual bags packed, waiting for the charges against him to be dropped that he might return to his native town. A vision of the study hall rose before me, with my favorite nun on the platform and the beautiful girls in their places. My heart rushed forward to embrace it.

But, alas, it is too late. Elinor Henehan is dead, my favorite nun has removed to another convent, the beautiful girls are married—I have seen them from time to time and no longer aspire to their friendship. And as for the pale, plain girl in the front of the study hall, her, too, I can no longer reach. I see her creeping down the corridor with a little knot of her classmates. "Hello, Cye," I say with a touch of disdain for her rawness, her guileless ambition. I should like to make her a pie-bed, or drop a snake down her back, but unfortunately the convent discipline forbids such open brutality. I hate her, for she is my natural victim, and it is I who have given her the name, the shameful, inscrutable name that she will never, sleepless in her bed at night, be able to puzzle out.

Muriel Rukeyser

Searching/Not Searching

1.

What kind of woman goes searching and searching?
Among the furrows of dark April, along the sea-beach,
in the faces of children, in what they could not tell;
in the pages of centuries —
for what man? for what magic?

In corridors under the earth, in castles of the North,
among the blackened miners, among the old
I have gone searching.
The island-woman told me, against the glitter of sun
on the stalks and leaves of a London hospital.
I searched for that Elizabethan man,
the lost discoverer, the servant of time;
and that man forgotten for belief, in Spain,
and among the faces of students, at Coventry,
finding and finding in glimpses. And at home.
Among the dead I too have gone searching,
a blue light in the brain.
Suddenly I come to these living eyes,
I a live woman look up at you this day
I see all the colors in your look.

2. MIRIAM : THE RED SEA

High above shores and times,
I on the shore
forever and ever.
Moses my brother
has crossed over
to milk, honey,
that holy land.
Building Jerusalem.
I sing forever
on the seashore.
I do remember
horseman and horses,
waves of passage
poured into war,
all poured into journey.
My unseen brothers
have gone over;

chariots
deep seas under.
I alone stand here
ankle-deep
and I sing, I sing,
until the lands
sing to each other.

3. FOR DOLCI

Angel of declaring, you opened before us walls,
the lives of children, water as power.
To control the water is to control our days,
to build a dam is to face the enemy.

We will form a new person who will step forward,
he it is, she it is, assumes full life,
fully responsible. We will bring all the children,
they will decide together.

We will ask these children : what is before you?
They will say what they see.
They will say what they don't see.
Once again we breathe in discovery.

A man, a woman,
will discover
we are each other's sources.

4. CONCRETE

They are pouring the city:
they tear down the towers,
grind their lives,
laughing tainted, the river
flows down to tomorrow.
They are setting the forms,
pouring the new buildings.
Our days pour down.
I am pouring my poems.

5. BRECHT'S GALILEO

Brecht saying : Galileo talking astronomy
Stripped to the torso, the intellectual life
Pouring from this gross man in his nakedness.

Galileo, his physical contentment
Is having his back rubbed by his student; the boy mauls;
The man sighs and transforms it; intellectual product!

Galileo spins a toy of the earth around
The spinning sun; he looks at the student boy.
Learning is teaching, teaching is learning.
Galileo

Demonstrates how horrible is betrayal,
Particularly on the shore of a new era.

6. *READING THE* KIEU

There was always a murder within another murder.
Red leaves and rosy threads bind them together.
The hero of Vietnam's epic is a woman
and she has sold herself to save her father.

Odor of massacres spread on the sky.
Loneliness, the windy, dusty world.
The roads crowded with armor and betrayal.
Mirror of the sun and moon, this land,

in which being handed to soldiers is the journey.
Shame, disgrace, change of seas into burnt fields.
Banners, loudspeakers, violation of each day,
everything being unjust. But she does save him,
and we find everything in another way.

7. *THE FLOOR OF OCEAN*   Sistine Chapel

Climbing the air, prophet beyond prophet
leaning upon creation backward to the first
creation the great spark of night
breathing sun energy   a gap between finger-tips
across all of space or nothing, infinity.

But beyond this, with this, these
arms raising reaching wavering
as from the floor of ocean
wavering showing swaying like sea-plants
pointing straight up closing the gap between
continual creation and the daily touch.

From you I learned the dark potential
theatres of the acts of man holding
on a rehearsal stage   people and lights.
You in your red hair ran down the darkened
aisle, making documents and poems
in their people form the play.

Hallie it was from you I learned this:
you told the company in dress-rehearsal
in that ultimate equipped building   what they lacked:
among the lighting, the sight-lines, the acoustics,
the perfect revolving stage, they lacked only one thing
the most important thing.   It would come tonight:
The audience   the response

Hallie I learned from you this summer, this
Hallie I saw you lying all gone to bone
the tremor of bone   I stroked the head all scultpure
I held the hands of birds   I spoke to the sealed eyes

the soft live red mouth of a red-headed woman.
I knew Hallie then I could move without answer,
like the veterans for peace, hurling back their medals
and not expecting an answer from the grass.
You taught me this in your dying, for poems and theatre
and love and peace-making that living and my love
are where response and no-response
meet at last, Hallie, in infinity.

9. THE ARTIST AS SOCIAL CRITIC

They have asked me to speak in public
and set me a subject.

I hate anything that begins : the artist as . . .
and as for "social critic"
at the last quarter of the twentieth century
I know what that is:

late at night, among radio music
the voice of my son speaking half-world away
coming clear on the radio into my room
out of blazing Belfast.

Long enough for me to walk around
in that strong voice.

10. THE PRESIDENT AND THE LASER BOMB

He speaks in a big voice through all the air
saying : we have made strength,
we have made a beginning,
we will have lasting peace.

Something shouts on the river.

All night long the acts speak:
the new laser bomb falls impeccably
along the beam of a strict light
finding inevitably a narrow footbridge
in Asia.

11. NOT SEARCHING

What did I miss as I went searching?
What did I not see?
I renounce all this regret.
Now I will make another try.

One step and I am free.

When it happens to us again and again,
sometimes we know it for we are prepared
but to discover, to live at the edge of things,
to fall out of routine into invention
and recognize at the other edge of ocean

a new kind of man   a new kind of woman
walking toward me into the little surf.
This is the next me   and the next child
daybreak in continual creation.
Dayray we see, we say,
we sing what we don't see.

Picasso saying : I don't search, I find!
And in us our need, the traces of the future
the egg and its becoming.

I come to you searching and searching.

12. THE QUESTION

After this crisis,
nothing being conquered,
the theme is set:

to move with the forces,

how to go on
from the moment that
changed our life,

the moment of revelation,

proceeding from the crisis,
from the dream,
and not from the moment
of sleep before it?

Searching/not searching.   To make closeness.
For if this communication was the truth,
then it was this communication itself
which was the value to be supported.

And for this communication to endure,
men and women must move freely.   And to make
this communication renew itself always
we must renew justice.
And to make this communication
lasting, we must live to eliminate
violence and the lie.

Yes, we set the communication
we have achieved
against the world of murder.

Searching/not searching.

What did I see? What did I not see?
The river flowing past my window.
The night-lit city. My white pointed light.
Pieces of a world away
within my room.

Unseen and seen, the bodies within my life.
Voices under the leaves of Asia,
and America, in sex, in possibility.
We are trying to make, to let our closeness be made,
not torn apart tonight by our dead skills.

The shadow of my hand.
The shadow of the pen.
Morning of the day we reach or do not reach.
In our bodies, we find each other.
On our mouths, inner greet,
in our eyes.

Tillie Olsen

I Stand Here Ironing

I stand here ironing, and what you asked me moves tormented back and forth with the iron.

"I wish you would manage the time to come in and talk with me about your daughter. I'm sure you can help me understand her. She's a youngster who needs help and whom I'm deeply interested in helping."

"Who needs help?" . . . Even if I came what good would it do? You think because I am her mother I have a key, or that in some way you could use me as a key? She has lived for nineteen years. There is all that life that has happened outside of me, beyond me.

And where is there time to remember, to sift, to weigh, to estimate, to total? I will start and there will be an interruption and I will have to gather it all together again. Or I will become engulfed with all I did or did not do, with what should have been and what cannot be helped.

She was a beautiful baby. The first and only one of our five that was beautiful at birth. You do not guess how new and uneasy her tenancy in her now-loveliness. You did not know her all those years she was thought homely, or see her poring over her baby pictures, making me tell her over and over how beautiful she had been—and would be, I would tell her—and was now, to the seeing eye. But the seeing eyes were few or nonexistent. Including mine.

I nursed her. They feel that's important nowadays. I nursed all the children, but with her, with all the fierce rigidity of first motherhood, I did like the books then said. Though her cries battered me to trembling and my breasts ached with swollenness, I waited till the clock decreed.

Why do I put that first? I do not even know if it matters, or if it explains anything.

She was a beautiful baby. She blew shining bubbles of sound. She loved motion, loved light, loved color and music and textures. She would lie on the floor in her blue overalls patting the surface so hard in ecstasy her hands and feet would blur. She was a miracle to me, but when she was eight months old I had to leave her daytimes with the woman downstairs to whom she was no miracle at all, for I worked or looked for work and for Emily's father, who "could no longer endure" (he wrote in his good-by note) "sharing want with us."

I was nineteen. It was the pre-relief, pre-WPA world of the depression. I would start running as soon as I got off the streetcar, running up the stairs, the place smelling sour, and awake or asleep to startle awake, when she saw me she would break into a clogged weeping that could not be comforted, a weeping I can hear yet.

After a while I found a job hashing at night so I could be with her days, and it was better. But it came to where I had to bring her to his family and leave her.

It took a long time to raise the money for her fare back. Then she got chicken pox and I had to wait longer. When she finally came, I hardly knew her, walking quick and nervous like her father, looking like her father, thin, and dressed in a shoddy red that yellowed her skin and glared at the pockmarks. All the baby loveliness gone.

She was two. Old enough for nursery school they said, and I did not know then what I know now—the fatigue of the long day, and the lacerations of group life in nurseries that are only parking places for children.

Except that it would have made no difference if I had known. It was the only place there was. It was the only way we could be together, the only way I could hold a job.

And even without knowing, I knew. I knew the teacher that was evil because all these years it has curdled into my memory, the little boy hunched in the corner, her rasp, "why aren't you outside, because Alvin hits you? that's no reason, go out, scaredy." I knew Emily hated it even if she did not clutch and implore "don't go Mommy" like the other children, mornings.

She always had a reason why we should stay home. Momma, you look sick, Momma. I feel sick. Momma, the teachers aren't there to-day, they're sick. Momma, we can't go, there was a fire there last night. Momma, it's a holiday today, no school, they told me.

But never a direct protest, never rebellion. I think of our others in their three-, four-year-oldness—the explosions, the tempers, the de-nunciations, the demands—and I feel suddenly ill. I put the iron down. What in me demanded that goodness in her? And what was the cost, the cost to her of such goodness?

The old man living in the back once said in his gentle way: "You should smile at Emily more when you look at her." What *was* in my face when I looked at her? I loved her. There were all the acts of love.

It was only with the others I remembered what he said, and it was the face of joy, and not of care or tightness or worry I turned to them —too late for Emily. She does not smile easily, let alone almost always as her brothers and sisters do. Her face is closed and somber, but when she wants, how fluid. You must have seen it in her panto-mimes, you spoke of her rare gift for comedy on the stage that rouses a laughter out of the audience so dear they applaud and applaud and do not want to let her go.

Where does it come from, that comedy? There was none of it in her when she came back to me that second time, after I had had to send her away again. She had a new daddy now to learn to love, and I think perhaps it was a better time.

Except when we left her alone nights, telling ourselves she was old enough.

"Can't you go some other time, Mommy, like tomorrow?" she would ask. "Will it be just a little while you'll be gone? Do you promise?"

The time we came back, the front door open, the clock on the floor in the hall. She rigid awake. "It wasn't just a little while. I didn't cry. Three times I called you, just three times, and then I went downstairs to open the door so you could come faster. The clock talked loud. I threw it away, it scared me what it talked."

She said the clock talked loud that night I went to the hospital to have Susan. She was delirious with the fever that comes before red measles, but she was fully conscious all the week I was gone and the week after we were home when she could not come near the baby or me.

She did not get well. She stayed skeleton thin, not wanting to eat, and night after night she had nightmares. She would call for me, and I would rouse from exhaustion to sleepily call back: "You're all right, darling, go to sleep, it's just a dream," and if she still called, in a sterner voice, "now go to sleep Emily, there's nothing to hurt you." Twice, only twice, when I had to get up for Susan anyhow, I went in to sit with her.

Now when it is too late (as if she would let me hold and comfort her like I do the others) I get up and go to her at once at her moan or restless stirring. "Are you awake, Emily? Can I get you something?" And the answer is always the same: "No, I'm all right, go back to sleep, Mother."

They persuaded me at the clinic to send her away to a convalescent home in the country where "she can have the kind of food and care you can't manage for her, and you'll be free to concentrate on the new baby." They still send children to that place. I see pictures on the society page of sleek young women planning affairs to raise money for it, or dancing at the affairs, or decorating Easter eggs or filling Christmas stockings for the children.

They never have a picture of the children so I do not know if the girls still wear those gigantic red bows and the ravaged looks on the every other Sunday when parents can come to visit "unless otherwise notified"—as we were notified the first six weeks.

Oh it is a handsome place, green lawns and tall trees and fluted flower beds. High up on the balconies of each cottage the children stand, the girls in their red bows and white dresses, the boys in white suits and giant red ties. The parents stand below shrieking up to be heard and the children shriek down to be heard, and between them the invisible wall "Not To Be Contaminated by Parental Germs or Physical Affection."

There was a tiny girl who always stood hand in hand with Emily. Her parents never came. One visit she was gone. "They moved her to

Rose Cottage," Emily shouted in explanation. "They don't like you to love anybody here."

She wrote once a week, the labored writing of a seven-year-old. "I am fine. How is the baby. If I write my leter nicly I will have a star. Love." There never was a star. We wrote every other day, letters she could never hold or keep but only hear read—once. "We simply do not have room for children to keep any personal possessions," they patiently explained when we pieced one Sunday's shrieking together to plead how much it would mean to Emily who so loved to keep things, to be allowed to keep her letters and cards.

Each visit she looked frailer. "She isn't eating," they told us.

(They had runny eggs for breakfast or mush with lumps, Emily said later, I'd hold it in my mouth and not swallow. Nothing ever tasted good, just when they had chicken.)

It took us eight months to get her released home, and only the fact that she gained back so little of her seven lost pounds convinced the social worker.

I used to try to hold and love her after she came back, but her body would stay stiff, and after a while she'd push away. She ate little. Food sickened her, and I think much of life too. Oh she had physical lightness and brightness, twinkling by on skates, bouncing like a ball up and down up and down over the jump rope, skimming over the hill; but these were momentary.

She fretted about her appearance, thin and dark, and foreign-looking at a time when every little girl was supposed to look or thought she should look a chubby blonde replica of Shirley Temple. The doorbell sometimes rang for her, but no one seemed to come and play in the house or be a best friend. Maybe because we moved so much.

There was a boy she loved painfully through two school semesters. Months later she told me how she had taken pennies from my purse to buy him candy. "Licorice was his favorite and I brought him some every day, but he still liked Jennifer better'n me. Why Mommy?" The kind of question for which there is no answer.

School was a worry to her. She was not glib or quick in a world where glibness and quickness were easily confused with ability to learn. To her overworked and exasperated teachers she was an over-conscientious "slow learner" who kept trying to catch up and was absent entirely too often.

I let her be absent, though sometimes the illness was imaginary. How different from my now-strictness about attendance with the others. I wasn't working. We had a new baby, I was home anyhow. Sometimes, after Susan grew old enough, I would keep her home from school, too, to have them all together.

Mostly Emily had asthma, and her breathing, harsh and labored, would fill the house with a curiously tranquil sound. I would bring the two old dresser mirrors and her boxes of collections to her bed. She would select beads and single earrings, bottle tops and shells, dried flowers and pebbles, old postcards and scraps, all sorts of odd-ments; then she and Susan would play Kingdom, setting up landscapes and furniture, peopling them with action.

Those were the only times of peaceful companionship between her and Susan. I have edged away from it, that poisonous feeling between them, that terrible balancing of hurts and needs I had to do between the two, and did so badly, those earlier years.

Oh there are conflicts between the others too, each one human, needing, demanding, hurting, taking—but only between Emily and Susan, no, Emily toward Susan that corroding resentment. It seems so obvious on the surface, yet it is not obvious. Susan, the second child, Susan, golden- and curly-haired and chubby, quick and articulate and assured, everything in appearance and manner Emily was not; Susan, not able to resist Emily's precious things, losing or sometimes clumsily breaking them; Susan telling jokes and riddles to company for applause while Emily sat silent (to say to me later: that was *my* riddle, Mother, I told it to Susan); Susan, who for all the five years' difference in age was just a year behind Emily in developing physically.

I am glad for that slow physical development that widened the difference between her and her contemporaries, though she suffered over it. She was too vulnerable for that terrible world of youthful competition, of preening and parading, of constant measuring of yourself against every other, of envy, "If I had that copper hair," "If I had that skin. . . ." She tormented herself enough about not looking like the others, there was enough of the unsureness, the having to be conscious of words before you speak, the constant caring—what are they thinking of me? without having it all magnified by the merciless physical drives.

Ronnie is calling. He is wet and I change him. It is rare there is such a cry now. That time of motherhood is almost behind me when the ear is not one's own but must always be racked and listening for the child cry, the child call. We sit for a while and I hold him, looking out over the city spread in charcoal with its soft aisles of light. "*Shoogily*," he breathes and curls closer. I carry him back to bed, asleep. *Shoogily*. A funny word, a family word, inherited from Emily, invented by her to say: *comfort*.

In this and other ways she leaves her seal, I say aloud. And startle at my saying it. What do I mean? What did I start to gather together, to try and make coherent? I was at the terrible, growing years. War years. I do not remember them well. I was working, there were four smaller ones now, there was not time for her. She had to help be a mother, and housekeeper, and shopper. She had to set her seal. Mornings of crisis and near hysteria trying to get lunches packed, hair combed, coats and shoes found, everyone to school or Child Care on time, the baby ready for transportation. And always the paper scribbled on by a smaller one, the book looked at by Susan then mislaid, the homework not done. Running out to that huge school where she was one, she was lost, she was a drop; suffering over the unpreparedness, stammering and unsure in her classes.

There was so little time left at night after the kids were bedded down.

She would struggle over books, always eating (it was in those years she developed her enormous appetite that is legendary in our family) and I would be ironing, or preparing food for the next day, or writing V-mail to Bill, or tending the baby. Sometimes, to make me laugh, or out of her despair, she would imitate happenings or types at school.

I think I said once: "Why don't you do something like this in the school amateur show?" One morning she phoned me at work, hardly understandable through the weeping: "Mother, I did it. I won, I won; they gave me first prize; they clapped and clapped and wouldn't let me go."

Now suddenly she was Somebody, and as imprisoned in her difference as she had been in anonymity.

She began to be asked to perform at other high schools, even in colleges, then at city- and state-wide affairs. The first one we went to, I only recognized her that first moment when thin, shy, she almost drowned herself into the curtains. Then: Was this Emily? The control, the command, the convulsing and deadly clowning, the spell, then the roaring, stamping audience, unwilling to let this rare and precious laughter out of their lives.

Afterwards: You ought to do something about her with a gift like that—but without money or knowing how, what does one do? We have left it all to her, and the gift has as often eddied inside, clogged and clotted, as been used and growing.

She is coming. She runs up the stairs two at a time with her light graceful step, and I know she is happy tonight. Whatever it was that occasioned your call did not happen today.

"Aren't you ever going to finish the ironing, Mother? Whistler painted his mother in a rocker. I'd have to paint mine standing over an ironing board." This is one of her communicative nights and she tells me everything and nothing as she fixes herself a plate of food out of the icebox.

She is so lovely. Why did you want me to come in at all? Why were you concerned? She will find her way.

She starts up the stairs to bed. "Don't get me up with the rest in the morning." "But I thought you were having midterms." "Oh, those," she comes back in, kisses me, and says quite lightly, "in a couple of years when we'll all be atom-dead they won't matter a bit."

She has said it before. She *believes* it. But because I have been dredging the past, and all that compounds a human being is so heavy and meaningful in me, I cannot endure it tonight.

I will never total it all. I will never come in to say: She was a child seldom smiled at. Her father left me before she was a year old. I had to work her first six years when there was work, or I sent her home and to his relatives. There were years she had care she hated. She was dark and thin and foreign-looking in a world where the prestige went to blondeness and curly hair and dimples, she was slow where glibness was prized. She was a child of anxious, not proud, love. We were poor and could not afford for her the soil of easy growth. I was a young mother, I was a distracted mother. There were the other children pushing up, demanding. Her younger sister seemed all that she was not. There were years she did not want me to touch her. She kept too much in herself, her life was such she had to keep too much in herself. My wisdom came too late. She has much to her and probably little will come of it. She is a child of her age, of depression, of war, of fear.

Let her be. So all that is in her will not bloom—but in how many does it? There is still enough left to live by. Only help her to know —help make it so there is cause for her to know—that she is more than this dress on the ironing board, helpless before the iron.

1953–1954

Carson McCullers

Instant of the Hour After

Light as shadows her hands fondled his head and then came placidly to rest; the tips of her fingers hovered on his temples, throbbed to the warm slow beat inside his body, and her palms cupped his hard skull.

"Reverberating va-cuity," he mumbled so that the syllables lolloped ponderously into each other.

She looked down at his lax, sound body that stretched the length of the couch. One foot—the sock wrinkled around the ankle—hung limp over the edge. And as she watched his sensitive hand left his side and crept up drunkenly to his mouth—to touch his lips that had remained pursed out and loose after his words. "Immense hollowness—" he mouthed behind his feeling fingers.

"Enough out of you tonight—my darling," she said. "The show's over and the monkey's dead."

They had turned off the heat an hour before and the apartment was beginning to chill. She looked at the clock, the hands of which pointed to one. Not much heat anyway at that hour, she thought. No draughts, though; opalescent ribbons of smoke lay motionless close to the ceiling. Speculatively her glance shifted to the whiskey bottle and the confused chessmen on the card table. To a book that lay face downward on the floor—and a lettuce leaf lying forlornly in the corner since Marshall had lost it while waving his sandwich. To the dead little butts of cigarettes and the charred matches scattered.

"Here cover up," she said absently, unfolding a blanket at the foot of the couch. "You're so susceptible to draughts."

His eyes opened and stared stolidly up at her—blue-green, the color of the sweater he wore. One of them was shot through at the corner with fragile fibers of pink, giving him somehow the guileless expression of an Easter bunny. So much younger than twenty, he always looked— With his head thrown back on her knees so that his neck was arched above his rolled collar and tender seeming with the soft outline of the cords and cartilages. With his dark hair springing from the pallor of his face.

"Vacant majesty—"

As he spoke his eyelids drooped until the eyes beneath had been narrowed to a slit that seemed to sneer at her. And she knew with a sudden start that he was not as drunk as he pretended to be.

"You needn't hold forth any longer," she said. "Phillip's gone home and there's just me."

"It's in the na-a-ature of things—that such a viewpoint—view—"

"He's gone home," she repeated. "You talked him out." She had a fleet picture of Phillip bending to pick up the cigarette butts—his agile, blond little body and his calm eyes— "He washed up the dishes we messed and even wanted to sweep the floor, but I made him leave it."

"He's a—" started Marshall.

"Seeing *you*—and how tired I was—he even offered to pull out the couch and get you to bed."

"A cute procedure—" he mouthed.

"I made him run along." She remembered for a moment his face as she shut the door between them, the sound of his footsteps going down stairs, and the feeling—half of pity for loneliness, half of warmth—that she always felt when she listened to the sounds of others going out into the night away from them.

"To listen to him—one would think his reading were rigidly narrowed to—to G. K. Chesterton and George Moore," he said, giving a drunken lilt to the words. "Who won at chess—me or him?"

"You," she said. "But you did your best work before you got so drunk."

"Drunk—" he murmured, moving his long body laxly, changing the position of his head. "God! your knees are bony. Bo-ony."

"But I thought sure you'd give him the game when you made that idiotic move with your queen's pawn." She thought of their fingers hovering over the carved precision of their pieces, brows frowned, the glow of the light on the bottle beside them.

His eyes were closed again and his hand had crumpled down on his chest. "Lousy simile—" he mumbled. "Granted about the mountain. Joyce climbed laboriously—O-O-OK—but when he reached the top —top reached—"

"You can't stand this drinking, darling—" Her hands moved over the soft angle of his chin and rested there.

"He wouldn't say the world was *fla-at*. All along that's what they said. Besides the villagers could walk around—around with their jackasses and see that for themselves. With their asses."

"Hush," she said. "You've talked about that long enough. You get on one subject and go on and on ad infinitum. And don't land anywhere."

"A crater—" he breathed huskily. "And at least after the immensity of his climb he could have expected—some lovely leaps of Hell fire— some—"

Her hand clenched on his chin and shook it. "Shut up," she said. "I heard you when you improvised on that so brilliantly before Phillip left. You were obscene. And I'd almost forgotten."

A smile crept out across his face and his blue fringed eyes looked up at her. "Obscene—? Why should you put yourself in place of those symbols—sym—"

"If it were with anyone but Phillip that you talk like that I'd—I'd leave you."

"Immense va-cuity," he said, closing his eyes again. "Dead Hollowness. Hollowness, I say. With maybe in the ashes at the bottom a—"

"Shut up."

"A squirming, fatbellied, cretin."

It came to her that she must have drunk more than she realized, for the objects in the room seemed to take on a strange look of suffering. The butts of the cigarettes looked overmouthed and limp. The rug, almost brand new, seemed trampled and choked in design by the ashes. Even the last of the whiskey lay pale and quiet in the bottle. "Does it relieve you any?" she asked with slow calm. "I hope that times like this—"

She felt his body stiffen and, like an aggravating child, he interrupted her words with a sudden burst of unmelodic humming.

She eased her thighs from beneath his head and stood up. The room seemed to have grown smaller, messier, ranker with smoke and spilled whiskey. Bright lines of white weaved before her eyes. "Get up," she said dully. "I've got to pull out this darn couch and make it up."

He folded his hands on his stomach and lay solid, unstirring.

"You are detestable," she said, opening the door of the closet and taking down the sheets and blankets that lay folded on the shelves.

When she stood above him once more, waiting for him to rise, she felt a moment of pain for the drained pallor of his face. For the shades of darkness that had crept down halfway to his cheekbones, for the pulse that always fluttered in his neck when he was drunk or fatigued.

"Oh Marshall, it's bestial for us to get all shot like this. Even if you don't have to work tomorrow—there are years—fifty of them maybe —ahead." But the words had a false ring and she could only think of tomorrow.

He struggled to sit up on the edge of the couch and when he had reached that position his head dropped down to rest in his hands. "Yes, Pollyanna," he mumbled. "Yes, my dear croaking Pol—Pol. Twenty is a lovely lovely age Blessed God."

His fingers that weaved through his hair and closed into weak fists filled her with a sudden, sharp love. Roughly she snatched at the corners of the blanket and drew them around his shoulders. "Up now. We can't fool around like this all night."

"Hollowness—" he said wearily, without closing his sagging jaw.

"Has it made you sick?"

Holding the blanket close he pulled himself to his feet and lumbered toward the card table. "Can't a person even *think* without being called obscene or sick or drunk. No. No understanding of thought. Of deep deep thought in blackness. Of rich morasses. Morrasses. With their asses."

The sheet billowed down through the air and the round swirls collapsed into wrinkles. Quickly she tucked in the corners and smoothed the blanket on top. When she turned around she saw that he sat hunched over the chessmen—ponderously trying to balance a pawn on a turreted castle. The red checked blanket hung from his shoulders and trailed behind the chair.

She thought of something clever. "You look," she said, "like a brooding king in a bad-house." She sat on the couch that had become a bed and laughed.

With an angry gesture he embrangled his hands in the chessmen so that several pieces clattered to the floor. "That's right," he said. "Laugh your silly head off. That's the way it's always been done."

The laughs shook her body as though every fiber of her muscles had lost its resistance. When she had finished the room was very still.

After a moment he pushed the blanket away from him so that it crumpled in a heap behind the chair. "He's blind," he said softly. "Almost blind."

"Watch out, there's probably a draught— Who's blind?"

"Joyce," he said.

She felt weak after her laughter and the room stood out before her with painful smallness and clarity. "That's the trouble with you, Marshall," she said. "When you get like this you go on and on so that you wear a person out."

He looked at her sullenly. "I must say you're pretty when you're drunk," he said.

"I don't get drunk—couldn't if I wanted to," she said, feeling a pain beginning to bear down behind her eyes.

"How 'bout that night when we—"

"I've told you," she said stiffly between her teeth, "I wasn't drunk. I was ill. And you would make me go out and—"

"It's all the same," he interrupted. "You were a thing of beauty hanging on to that table. It's all the same. A sick woman—a drunk woman—ugh."

Nervously she watched his eyelids droop down until they had hidden all the goodness in his eyes.

"And a pregnant woman," he said. "Yeah. It'll be some sweet hour like this when you come to simper your sweet sneakret into my ear. Another cute little Marshall. Ain't we fine—look what we can do. Oh, God, what dreariness."

"I loathe you," she said, watching her hands (that were surely not a part of her?) begin to tremble. "This drunk brawling in the middle of the night—"

As he smiled his mouth seemed to her to take on the same pink, slitted look that his eyes had. "You love it," he whispered soberly. "What would you do if once a week I didn't get soused. So that— glutinously—you can paw over me. And Marshall darling this and Marshall that. So you can run your greedy little fingers all over my face— Oh yes. You love me best when I suffer. You—you—"

As he lurched across the room she thought she saw that his shoulders were shaking.

"Here Mama," he taunted. "Why don't you offer to come help me point." As he slammed the door to the bathroom some vacant coathangers that had been hung on the doorknob clashed at each other with tinny sibilance.

"I'm leaving you—" she called hollowly when the noise from the coathangers had died down. But the words had no meaning to her. Limp, she sat on the bed and looked at the wilted lettuce leaf across the room. The lampshade had been knocked atilt so that it clung dangerously to the bulb—so that it made a hurtful passage of brightness across the grey disordered room.

"Leaving you," she repeated to herself—still thinking about the late-at-night squalor around them.

She remembered the sound of Phillip's footsteps as he had descended. Nightlike and hollow. She thought of the dark outside and the cold naked trees of early spring. She wanted to picture herself leaving the apartment at that hour. With Phillip maybe. But as she tried to see his face, his small calm little body, the outlines were vague and there was no expression there. She could only recall the way his hands had poked at the sugar-grained bottom of a glass with the dishcloth— as they had done when he helped her with the dishes that night. And as she thought of following the empty sounds of the footsteps they grew softer, softer—until there was only black silence left.

With a shiver she got up from the couch and moved toward the whiskey bottle on the table. The parts of her body felt like tiresome appendages; only the pain behind her eyes seemed her own. She hesitated, holding the neck of the bottle. That—or one of the Alka-Seltzers in the top bureau drawer. But the thought of the pale tablet writhing to the top of the glass, consumed by its own effervescence— seemed sharply depressing. Besides, there was just enough for one more drink. Hastily she poured, noting again how the glittering convexity of the bottle always cheated her.

It made a sharp little path of warmness down into her stomach but the rest of her body remained chill. "Oh damn," she whispered—thinking of picking up that lettuce leaf in the morning, of the cold outside, listening for any sound from Marshall in the bathroom. "Oh damn. I can never get drunk like that."

And as she stared at the empty bottle she had one of those grotesque little imaginings that were apt to come to her at that hour. She saw herself and Marshall—in the whiskey bottle. Revolting in their smallness and perfection. Skeetering angrily up and down the cold blank glass like minute monkeys. For a moment with noses flattened and stares of longing. And then after their frenzies she saw them lying in the bottom—white and exhausted—looking like fleshy specimens in a laboratory. With nothing said between them.

She was sick with the sound of the bottle as it crashed through the orange peels and paper wads in the waste basket and clanked against the tin at the bottom.

"Ah—" said Marshall, opening the door and carefully placing his foot across the threshold. "Ah—the purest enjoyment left to man. At the last sweet point—pissing."

She leaned against the frame of the closet door—pressing her cheek against the cold angle of the wood. "See if you can get undressed."

"Ah— "he repeated, sitting down on the couch that she had made. His hands left his trouser flaps and began to fumble with his belt. "All but the belt— Can't sleep with a belt buckle. Like your knees. Bo-ony."

She thought that he would lose his balance trying to jerk out the belt all at once—(once before, she remembered, that had happened). Instead he slid the leather out slowly, strap by strap, and when he was through he placed it neatly under the bed. Then he looked up at her. The lines around his mouth were drawn down—making grey threads in the pallor of his face. His eyes looked widely up at her and for a moment she thought that he would cry. "Listen—" he said slowly, clearly.

She heard only the labored sound of his swallowing.

"Listen—" he repeated. And his white face sank into his hands.

Slowly, with a rhythm not of drunkenness, his body swayed from side to side. His blue sweatered shoulders were shaking. "Lord God," he said quietly. "How I—suffer."

She found the strength to drag herself from the doorway, to straighten the lampshade, and switch off the light. In the darkness an arc of blue rocked before her eyes—to the movement of his swaying body. And from the bed came the sound of his shoes being dropped to the floor, the creaking of the springs as he rolled over toward the wall.

She lay down in the darkness and pulled up the blankets—suddenly heavy and chill feeling to her fingers. As she covered his shoulders she noticed that the springs still sputtered beneath them, and that his body was quivering. "Marshall—" she whispered. "Are you cold?"

"Those chills. One of those damn chills."

Vaguely she thought of the missing top to the hot water bottle and the empty coffee sack in the kitchen. "Damn—" she repeated vacantly.

His knees urged close to hers in the darkness and she felt his body contract to a shivering little ball. Tiredly she reached out for his head and drew it to her. Her fingers soothed the little hollow at the top of his neck, crept up the stiff shaved part to the soft hair at the top, moved on to his temples where again she could feel the beating there.

"Listen—" he repeated, turning his head upward so that she could sense his breath on her throat.

"Yes Marshall."

His hands flexed into fists that beat tensely behind her shoulders. Then he lay so still that for a moment she felt a strange fear.

"It's this—" he said in a voice drained of all tone. "My love for you, darling. At times it seems that—in some instant like this—it will destroy me."

Then she felt his hands relax to cling weakly to her back, felt the chill that had been brooding in him all the evening make his body jerk with great shudders. "Yes," she breathed, pressing his hard skull to the hollow between her breasts. "Yes—" she said as soon as words and the creaking of the springs and the rank smell of smoke in the darkness had drawn back from the place where, for the moment, all things had receded.

-»» ««-

Sylvia Chatfield Bates' comment, attached to "Instant of the Hour After":

I like this the least of anything you have done, so you see I do not always praise you! The good points first: If I had never seen anything you had done I should have to comment on the great vividness, the acute visibility of your writing. The dramatization of every little detail is excellent, and fresh. And the characters come through the objective scenes beautifully. The "feature" of the story, is the delightful little "element of artistic piquancy," the two persons in the bottle. That is memorable and good.

Now for the other side. Again I must insist that a story should have a reason for being. Must rise, make a point, that is inside the tale itself, and at the same time outside in the world. Why should we be given all these rather disagreeable details, only at the end to hear his love is so great it will destroy him? Before that line I was waiting for something interesting, mature, vital to come out of it all, and I merely had this highly personal statement which I might think was caused by his drunkenness anyway. Can't you keep what you have, but suggest or show how they are caught, and by what; how they are being destroyed, and by what? It's a serious question. Are they really being destroyed by passion? You have used words without realizing their full meaning, and that makes for sentimentality, though this you would call anything but sentimental. It is possible to be sentimental about sophistication!

I think the thing to do is heighten the significance of the figures in the bottle. Write *to that,* and let the overtones and theme grow stronger until you have the effect of a climax, although this is really a conte of mood. Perhaps the reason you have not been successful is that the conflict is not definite enough in your mind and not brought out.

This is well worth doing over. And by the way, certain parts are not printable in a magazine, Joyce or no Joyce.

Gwendolyn Brooks

Jessie Mitchell's Mother

Into her mother's bedroom to wash the ballooning body.
"My mother is jelly-hearted and she has a brain of jelly:
Sweet, quiver-soft, irrelevant. Not essential.
Only a habit would cry if she should die.
A pleasant sort of fool without the least iron. . . .
Are you better, mother, do you think it will come today?"
The stretched yellow rag that was Jessie Mitchell's mother
Reviewed her. Young, and so thin, and so straight.
So straight! as if nothing could ever bend her.
But poor men would bend her, and doing things with poor men,
Being much in bed, and babies would bend her over,
And the rest of things in life that were for poor women,
Coming to them grinning and pretty with intent to bend and to kill.
Comparisons shattered her heart, ate at her bulwarks:
The shabby and the bright: she, almost hating her daughter,
Crept into an old sly refuge: "Jessie's black
And her way will be black, and jerkier even than mine.
Mine, in fact, because I was lovely, had flowers
Tucked in the jerks, flowers were here and there. . . ."
She revived for the moment settled and dried-up triumphs,
Forced perfume into old petals, pulled up the droop,
Refueled
Triumphant long-exhaled breaths.
Her exquisite yellow youth . . .

Bronzeville Woman in a Red Hat

I

They had never had one in the house before.
      The strangeness of it all. Like unleashing
A lion, really. Poised
To pounce. A puma. A panther. A black
Bear.
There it stood in the door,
Under a red hat that was rash, but refreshing—
In a tasteless way, of course—across the dull dare,
The semi-assault of that extraordinary blackness.
The slackness
Of that light pink mouth told little. The eyes told of heavy care. . . .
But that was neither here nor there,
And nothing to a wage-paying mistress as should

Be getting her due whether life had been good
For her slave, or bad.
There it stood
In the door. They had never had
One in the house before.

But the Irishwoman had left!
A message had come.
Something about a murder at home.
A daughter's husband—"berserk," that was the phrase:
The dear man had "gone berserk"
And short work—
With a hammer—had been made
Of this daughter and her nights and days.
The Irishwoman (underpaid,
Mrs. Miles remembered with smiles),
Who was a perfect jewel, a red-faced trump,
A good old sort, a baker
Of rum cake, a maker
Of Mustard, would never return.
Mrs. Miles had begged the bewitched woman
To finish, at least, the biscuit blending,
To tarry till the curry was done,
To show some concern
For the burning soup, to attend to the tending
Of the tossed salad. "Inhuman,"
Patsy Houlihan had called Mrs. Miles.
"Inhuman." And "a fool."
And "a cool
One."

The Alert Agency had leafed through its files—
On short notice could offer
Only this dusky duffer
That now made its way to her kitchen and sat on her kitchen stool.

II

Her creamy child kissed by the black maid! square on the mouth!
World yelled, world writhed, world turned to light and rolled
Into her kitchen, nearly knocked her down.

Quotations, of course, from baby books were great
Ready armor; (but her animal distress
Wore, too and under, a subtler metal dress,
Inheritance of approximately hate.)
Say baby shrieked to see his finger bleed,
Wished human humoring—there was a kind
Of unintimate love, a love more of the mind
To order the nebulousness of that need.
—This was the way to put it, this the relief.
This sprayed a honey upon marvelous grime.
This told it possible to postpone the reef.

Fashioned a huggable darling out of crime.
Made monster personable in personal sight
By cracking mirrors down the personal night.

Disgust crawled through her as she chased the theme.
She, quite supposing purity despoiled,
Committed to sourness, disordered, soiled,
Went in to pry the ordure from the cream.
Cooing, "Come." (Come out of the cannibal wilderness,
Dirt, dark, into the sun and bloomful air.
Return to freshness of your right world, wear
Sweetness again. Be done with beast, duress.)

Child with continuing cling issued his No in final fire,
        Kissed back the colored maid,
        Not wise enough to freeze or be afraid.
        Conscious of kindness, easy creature bond.
        Love had been handy and rapid to respond.

Heat at the hairline, heat between the bowels,
Examining seeming coarse unnatural scene,
She saw all things except herself serene:
Child, big black woman, pretty kitchen towels.

Doris Lessing

An Unposted Love Letter

Yes, I saw the look your wife's face put on when I said, "I have so
many husbands, I don't need a husband." She did not exchange a
look with you, but that was because she did not need to—later when
you got home she said, "What an affected thing to say!" and you
replied, "Don't forget she is an actress." You said this meaning exactly what I would mean if I had said it, I am certain of that. And
perhaps she heard it like that, I do hope so, *because I know what you
are* and if your wife does not hear what you say then this is a smallness on your part that I don't forgive you. If I can live alone, and
out of fastidiousness, then you must have a wife as good as you are.
My husbands, the men who set light to my soul (yes, I know how
your wife would smile if I used that phrase) are worthy of you . . .
I know that I am giving myself away now, confessing how much that
look on your wife's face hurt. *Didn't she know that even then I was
playing my part?* Oh no, after all, I don't forgive you your wife,
no I don't.

If I said, "I don't need a husband, I have so many lovers," then of
course everyone at the dinner table would have laughed in just such
a way: it would have been the rather banal "outrageousness" expected
of me. An ageing star, the fading beauty . . . "I have so many lovers"
—pathetic, and brave too. Yes, that remark would have been too apt,
too smooth, right for just any "beautiful but fading" actress. But
not right for me, no, because after all, I am not just any actress, I am
Victoria Carrington, and I know exactly what is due to me and from
me. I know what is fitting (not for *me*, that is not important) but
for what I stand for. Do you imagine I couldn't have said it differently—like this, for instance: "I am an artist and therefore androgynous." Or: "I have created inside myself Man who plays opposite
to my Woman." Or: "I have objectified in myself the male components
of my soul and it is from this source that I create." Oh, I'm not stupid,
not ignorant, I know the different dialects of our time and even how
to use them. But imagine if I had said any of these things last night!
It would have been a false note, you would all have been uncomfortable, irritated, and afterwards you would have said: "Actresses
shouldn't try to be intelligent." (Not you, the others.) Probably they
don't believe it, not really, that an actress must be stupid, but their
sense of discrepancy, of discordance, would have expressed itself in
such a way. Whereas their silence when I said, "I don't need a husband, I have so many husbands," was right, for it was *the remark
right for me*—it was more than "affected," or "outrageous"—*it was
making a claim that they had to recognise.*

That word affected, have you ever really thought why it is applied to actresses? (You have of course, I'm no foreign country to you, I felt that, but it gives me pleasure to talk to you like this.) The other afternoon I went to see Irma Painter in her new play, and afterwards I went back to congratulate her (for she had heard, of course, that I was in the auditorium and would have felt insulted if I hadn't gone —I'm different, I hate it when people feel obliged to come back). We were sitting in her dressingroom and I was looking at her face as she wiped the makeup off. We are about the same age, and we have both been acting since the year . . . I recognised her face as mine, we have the same face, and I understood that it is the face of every real actress. No, it is not "masklike," my face, her face. Rather, it is that our basic face is so worn down to its essentials because of its permanent readiness to take other guises, become other people, it is almost like something hung up on the wall of a dressingroom ready to take down and use. Our face is—it has a scrubbed, honest, bare look, like a deal table, or a wooden floor. It has modesty, a humility, our face, as time wears on, wearing out of her, out of me, our "personality," our "individuality."

I looked at her face (we are called rivals, we are both called "great" actresses) and I suddenly wanted to pay homage to it, since I knew what that scoured plain look cost her—what it costs me, who have played a thousand beautiful women, to keep my features sober and decent under the painted shell of my makeup ready for other souls to use.

At a party, all dressed up, when I'm a "person," then I try to disguise the essential plainness and anonymity of my features by holding together the "beauty" I am known for, creating it out of my own and other people's memories. Of course it is almost gone now, nearly all gone the sharp, sweet, poignant face that so many men loved (not knowing it was not me, it was only what was given to me to consume slowly for the scrubbed face I must use for work). While I sat last night opposite you and your wife, she so pretty and *human,* her prettiness no mask, but expressing every shade of what she felt, and you being yourself only, I was conscious of how I looked. I could see my very white flesh that is guttering down away from its "beauty"; I could see my smile that even now has moments of its "piercing sweetness"; I could see my eyes, "dewy and shadowed," even now . . . but I also knew that everyone there, even if they were not aware of it, was conscious of that hard, honest workaday face that lies ready for use under this ruin, and it is the discrepancy between that working face and the "personality" of the famous actress that makes everything I do and say affected, that makes it inevitable and right that I should say, "I don't want a husband, I have so many husbands." And I tell you, if I had said nothing, not one word, the whole evening, the result would have been the same: "How affected she is, but of course she *is* an actress."

Yet it was the exact truth, what I said: I no longer have lovers, I have husbands, and that has been true ever since . . .

That is why I am writing this letter to you; this letter is a sort of homage, giving you your due in my life. Or perhaps, simply, I cannot tonight stand the loneliness of my role (my role in life).

When I was a girl it seemed that every man I met, or even heard of, or whose picture I saw in the paper, was my lover. I took him as my lover, *because it was my right.* He may never have heard of me, he might have thought me hideous (and I wasn't very attractive as a girl—my kind of looks, striking, white-fleshed, red-haired, needed maturity, as a girl I was a milk-faced, scarlet-haired creature whose features were all at odds with each other, I was pretty only when made up for the stage) . . . he may have found me positively repulsive, but I took him. Yes, at that time I had lovers in imagination, but none in reality. No man in the flesh could be as good as what I could invent, no real lips, hands, could affect me as those that I created, like God. And this remained true when I married my first husband, and then my second, for I loved neither of them, and I didn't know what the word meant for years. Until, to be precise, I was thirty-two and got very ill that year. No one knew why, or how, but *I* knew it was because I did not get a big part I wanted badly. So I got ill from disappointment, but now I see how right it was I didn't get the part. I was too old—if I had played her, the charming ingenious girl (which is how I saw myself then, God forgive me) I would have had to play her for three or four years, because the play ran for ever, and I would have been too vain to stop. And then what? I would have been nearly forty, too old for charming girls, and then, like so many actresses who have not burned the charming girl out of themselves, cauterised that wound with pain like styptic, I would have found myself playing smaller and smaller parts, and then I would have become a "character" actress, and then . . .

Instead, I lay very ill, not wanting to get better, ill with frustration, I thought, but really with the weight of years I did not know how to consume, how to include in how I saw myself, and then I fell in love with my doctor, inevitable I see now, but then a miracle, for that was the first time, and the reason I said the word "love" to myself, just as if I had not been married twice and had a score of men in my imagination was because *I could not manipulate him,* for the first time a man remained himself, I could not make him move as I wanted, and I did not know his lips and hands. No, I had to wait for *him* to decide, to move, and when he did become my lover I was like a young girl, awkward, I could only wait for his actions to spring mine.

He loved me, certainly, but not as I loved him, and in due course, he left me. I wished I could die, but it was then I understood, with gratitude, what had happened—I played, for the first time, a woman, as distinct from that fatal creature, "A charming girl," as distinct from "the heroine"—and I and everyone else knew that I had moved into a new dimension of myself, I was born again, and only I knew it was out of love for that man, my first husband (so I called him, though everyone else saw him as my doctor with whom I rather amusingly had had an affair).

For he was my first husband. He changed me and my whole life. After him, in my frenzy of lonely unhappiness, I believed I could return to what I had been before he had married me, and I would take men to bed (in reality now, just as I had, before, in imagination) but it was no longer possible, it did not work, for I had been possessed by a man, the Man had created in me himself, had left himself in me, and so I could never again use a man, possess one, manipulate him, make him do what I wanted.

For a long time it was as if I was dead, empty, sterile. (That is, *I* was, my work was at its peak.) I had no lovers, in fact or in imagination, and it was like being a nun or a virgin.

Strange it was, that at the age of thirty-five it was for the first time I felt virgin, chaste, untouched, I was absolutely alone. The men who wanted me, courted me, it was as if they moved and smiled and stretched out their hands through a glass wall which was my absolute inviolability. Was this how I should have felt when I was a girl? Yes, I believe that's it—that at thirty-five I was a girl for the first time. Surely this is how ordinary "normal" girls feel?—they carry a circle of chastity around with them through which the one man, the hero, must break? But it was not so with me, I was never a chaste girl, not until I had known what it was to remain still, waiting for the man to set me in motion in answer to him.

A long time went by, and I began to feel I would soon be an old woman. I was without love, and I would not be a good artist, not really, the touch of the man who loved me was fading off me, *had* faded, there was something lacking in my work now, it was beginning to be mechanical.

And so I resigned myself. I could no longer choose a man; and no man chose me. So I said, "Very well then, there is nothing to be done." Above all, I understand the relation between myself and life, I understand the logic of what I am, must be, I know there is nothing to be done about the shape of fate: my truth is that I have been loved once, and now that is the end, and I must let myself sink towards a certain dryness, a coldness of intelligence—yes, you will soon develop into an upright, red-headed, very intelligent lady (though, of course, affected!) whose green eyes flash the sober fires of humorous comprehension. All the rest is over for you, now accept it and be done and do as well as you can the work you are given.

And then one night . . .

What? All that happened outwardly was that I sat opposite a man at a dinner party in a restaurant, and we talked and laughed as people do who meet each other casually at a dinner table. But afterwards I went home with my soul on fire. I was on fire, being consumed . . . And what a miracle it was to me, being able to say, not: That is an attractive man, I want him, I shall have him, but: My house is on fire, that was the man, yes, it was he again, there he was, he has set light to my soul.

I simply let myself suffer for him, knowing he was worth it *because* I suffered—it had come to this, my soul had become its own gauge, its own measure of what was good: I knew what *he* was because of how my work was afterwards.

I knew him better than his wife did, or could (she was there too, a nice woman in such beautiful pearls)—I knew him better than he does himself. I sat opposite him all evening. What was there to notice? An ageing actress, pretty still, beautifully dressed (that winter I had a beautiful violet suit with mink cuffs) sitting opposite a charming man—handsome, intelligent, and so on. One can use these adjectives of half the men one meets. But somewhere in him, in his being, something matched something in me, he had come into me, he had set me in motion. I remember looking down the table at his wife and thinking: Yes, my dear, but your husband is also my husband, for he walked into me and made himself at home in me, and because of him I shall act again from the depths of myself, I am sure of it, and I'm sure it will be the best work I can do. Though I won't know until tomorrow night, on the stage.

For instance, there was one night when I stood on the stage and stretched up my slender white arms to the audience and (that is how they saw it, what *I* saw were two white-caked, raddled-with-cold arms that were, moreover, rather flabby) and I knew that I was, that night, nothing but an amateur. I stood there on the stage, *as a woman* holding out my pretty arms, it was Victoria Carrington saying: Look how poignantly I hold out my arms, don't you long to have them around you, my slender white arms, look how beautiful, how enticing Victoria is! And then, in my dressingroom afterwards I was ashamed, it was years since I had stood on the stage with nothing between me, the woman, and the audience—not since I was a green girl had I acted so—why, then, tonight?

I thought, and I understood. The afternoon before a man (a producer from America, but *that* doesn't matter) had come to see me in my dressingroom and after he left I thought: Yes, there it is again, I know that sensation, that means he has set the forces in motion and so I can expect my work to show it . . . it showed it, with a vengeance! Well, and so that taught me to discriminate, I learned I must be careful, must allow no second-rate man to come near me. And so put up barriers, strengthened around me the circle of cold, of impersonality, that should always lie between me and people, between me and the auditorium; I made a cool, bare space no man could enter, could break across, unless his power, his magic, was very strong, the true complement to mine.

Very seldom now do I feel my self alight, on fire, touched awake, created again by—what?

I live alone now. No, *you* would never be able to imagine how. For I knew when I saw you this evening that you exist, you are, only in relation to other people, you are always giving out to your work, your wife, friends, children, your wife has the face of a woman who gives, who is confident that what she gives will be received. Yes, I understand all that, I know how it would be living with you, I *know* you.

After we had all separated, and I had watched you drive off with your wife, I came home and . . . no, it would be no use telling you, after all. (Or anyone, except, perhaps, my colleague and rival Irma Painter!) But what if I said to you—but no, there are certain disciplines which no one can understand but those who use them.

So I will translate into your language, I'll translate the truth so that it has the *affected*, almost embarrassing, exaggerated ring that goes with the actress Victoria Carrington, and I'll tell you how when I came home after meeting you my whole body was wrenched with anguish, and I lay on the floor sweating and shaking as if I had bad malaria, it was like knives of deprivation going through me, for, meeting you, it was being reminded again what it would be like to be with a man, really with him, so that the rhythm of every day, every night, carried us both like the waves of a sea.

Everything I am most proud of seemed nothing at all—what I have worked to achieve, what I *have* achieved, even the very core of what I am, the inner sensitive balance that exists like a sort of self-invented super instrument, or a fantastically receptive and cherished animal— this creation of myself, which every day becomes more involved, sensitive, and delicate, seemed absurd, paltry, spinsterish, a shameful excuse for cowardice. And my life, which so contents me because of its balance, its order, its steadily growing fastidiousness, seemed eccentrically solitary. Every particle of my being screamed out, wanting, needing—I was like an addict deprived of his drug.

I picked myself off the floor, I bathed myself, I looked after myself like an invalid or like a—yes, like a pregnant woman. These extraordinary fertilisations happen so seldom now that I cherish them, waste nothing of them, and I both long for and dread them. Every time it is like being killed, like being torn open while I am forced to remember what it is I voluntarily do without.

Every time it happens I swear I can never let it happen again, the pain is too terrible. What a flower, what a fire, what a miracle it would be if, instead of smiling (the "sweetly piercing" smile of my dying beauty) instead of accepting, submitting, I should turn to you and say . . .

But I shall not, and so something very rare (something much more beautiful than your wife could ever give you, or any of the day by day wives could imagine) will never come into being.

Instead . . . I sit and consume my pain, I sit and hold it, I sit and clench my teeth and . . .

It is dark, it is very early in the morning, the light in my room is a transparent grey, like the ghost of water or of air, there are no lights in the windows I see from my own. I sit in my bed, and watch the shadows of the tree moving on the brick wall of the garden, and I contain pain and . . .

Oh my dear one, my dear one, I am a tent under which you lie, I am the sky across which you fly like a bird, I am . . .

My soul is a room, a great room, a hall—it is empty, waiting. Sometimes a fly buzzes across it, bringing summer mornings in another continent, sometimes a child laughs in it, and it is like the generations chiming together, child, youth, and old woman as one being. Sometimes you walk into it and stand there. You stand here in me and smile and I shut my eyes because of the sweet recognition in me of what you are, I feel what you are as if I stood near a tree and put my hand on its breathing trunk.

I am a pool of water in which fantastic creatures move, in which you play, a young boy, your brown skin glistening, and the water moves over your limbs like hands, my hands, that will never touch you, my hands that tomorrow night, in a pool of listening silence, will stretch up towards the thousand people in the auditorium, creating love for them from the consumed pain of my denial.

I am a room in which an old man sits, smiling, as he has smiled for fifty centuries, you, whose bearded loins created me.

I am a world into which you breathed life, have smiled life, have made me. I am, with you, what creates, every moment, a thousand animalculae, the creatures of our dispensation, and every one we have both touched with our hands and let go into space like freed birds.

I am a great space that enlarges, that grows, that spreads with the steady lightening of the human soul, and in the space, squatting in the corner, is a thing, an object, a dark, slow, coiled, amorphous heaviness, embodied sleep, a cold stupid sleep, a heaviness like the dark in a stale room—this thing stirs in its sleep where it squats in my soul, and I put all my muscles, all my force, into defeating it. For this was what I was born for, this is what I am, to fight embodied sleep, putting around it a confining girdle of light, of intelligence, so that it cannot spread its slow stain of ugliness over the trees, over the stars, over you.

It is as if, since you turned towards me and smiled letting light go through me again, it is as if a King had taken a Queen's hand and set her on his throne: a King and his Queen, hand in hand on top of my mountain sit smiling at ease in their country.

The morning is coming on the brick wall, the shadow of the tree has gone, and I think of how today I will walk out onto the stage, surrounded by the cool circle of my chastity, the circle of my discipline, and how I will raise my face (the flower face of my girlhood) and how I will raise my arms from which will flow the warmth you have given me.

And so, my dear one, turn now to your wife, and take her head on to your shoulder, and both sleep sweetly in the sleep of your love. I release you to go to your joys without me. I leave you to your love. I leave you to your life.

Denise Levertov

Abel's Bride

Woman fears for man, he goes
out alone to his labors. No mirror
nests in his pocket. His face
opens and shuts with his hopes.
His sex hangs unhidden
or rises before him
blind and questing.

She thinks herself
lucky. But sad. When she goes out
she looks in the glass, she remembers
herself. Stones, coal,
the hiss of water upon the kindled
branches—her being
is a cave, there are bones at the hearth.

Life at War

The disasters numb within us
caught in the chest, rolling
in the brain like pebbles. The feeling
resembles lumps of raw dough

weighing down a child's stomach on baking day.
Or Rilke said it, 'My heart . . .
Could I say of it, it overflows
with bitterness . . . but no, as though

its contents were simply balled into
formless lumps, thus
do I carry it about.'
The same war

continues.
We have breathed the grits of it in, all our lives,
our lungs are pocked with it,
the mucous membrane of our dreams
coated with it, the imagination
filmed over with the gray filth of it:

the knowledge that humankind,

delicate Man, whose flesh
responds to a caress, whose eyes
are flowers that perceive the stars,

whose music excels the music of birds,
whose laughter matches the laughter of dogs,
whose understanding manifests designs
fairer than the spider's most intricate web,
still turns without surprise, with mere regret
to the scheduled breaking open of breasts whose milk
runs out over the entrails of still-alive babies,
transformation of witnessing eyes to pulp-fragments,
implosion of skinned penises into carcass-gulleys.

We are the humans, men who can make;
whose language imagines *mercy,*
lovingkindness; we have believed one another
mirrored forms of a God we felt as good—

who do these acts, who convince ourselves
it is necessary; these acts are done
to our own flesh; burned human flesh
is smelling in Viet Nam as I write.

Yes, this is the knowledge that jostles for space
in our bodies along with all we
go on knowing of joy, of love;

our nerve filaments twitch with its presence
day and night,
nothing we say has not the husky phlegm of it in the saying,
nothing we do has the quickness, the sureness,
the deep intelligence living at peace would have.

About Marriage

Don't lock me in wedlock, I want
marriage, an
encounter—

I told you about the
green light of
May

       (a veil of quiet befallen
       the downtown park,
       late

       Saturday after
       noon, long
       shadows and cool.

       air, scent of
       new grass,
       fresh leaves,

       blossom on the threshold of
       abundance—

and the birds I met there,
birds of passage breaking their journey,
three birds each of a different species:

the azalea-breasted with round poll, dark,
the brindled, merry, mousegliding one,
and the smallest, golden as gorse and wearing
a black Venetian mask

and with them the three douce hen-birds
feathered in tender, lively brown—
I stood
a half-hour under the enchantment,
no-one passed near,
the birds saw me and

let me be
near them.)

It's not
irrelevant:
I would be
met

and meet you
so,
in a green

airy space, not
locked in.

Hypocrite Women

Hypocrite women, how seldom we speak
of our own doubts, while dubiously
we mother man in his doubt!

And if at Mill Valley perched in the trees
the sweet rain drifting through western air
a white sweating bull of a poet told us

our cunts are ugly—why didn't we
admit we have thought so too? (And
what shame? They are not for the eye!)

No, they are dark and wrinkled and hairy,
caves of the Moon . . . And when a
dark humming fills us, a

coldness towards life,
we are too much women to
own to such unwomanliness.

Whorishly with the psychopomp
we play and plead—and say
nothing of this later. And our dreams,

with what frivolity we have pared them
like toenails, clipped them like ends of
split hair.

O Taste and See

The world is
not with us enough.
O taste and see

the subway Bible poster said,
meaning **The Lord,** meaning
if anything all that lives
to the imagination's tongue,

grief, mercy, language,
tangerine, weather, to
breathe them, bite,
savor, chew, swallow, transform

into our flesh our
deaths, crossing the street, plum, quince,
living in the orchard and being

hungry, and plucking
the fruit.

Carolyn Kizer

The First of June Again

Dateline Saigon: Marines wait in the rain
For the Buddhists to rise.
It's monsoon time: Marines in the water's rush
Turn their carbines upside-down
To keep the barrels dry.

We wait—and the season pauses in mid-stream:
Suddenly, Buddhists, in the steam and hush,
Spring like mushrooms from the cracked wet pavement.
Some priests levitate; one, "an ungainly jumping-jack
In his saffron robes," leaps in the air, gesticulating.
All is silent, for a spreading moment.
Then one Marine lobs a grenade . . .

The pattern is set. The circle breaks, reforms;
When a cluster is dense enough to be worthwhile
Riot-police fling tear gas. We bystanders loiter and cry.
At least we give them that:
The Vietnamese are pleased to see us cry.

Meanwhile, this very day, in *The New York Times*,
Mr. Reston says, "War has a life of its own.
Officials may hesitate, but machines produce.
Men argue and loiter, but the training camps
And factories meet their quotas,
And the ships sail on time."

Today, along the Pacific Coast, the redwoods fall.
When you've seen one, you've seen 'em all,
Says the Governor of California.
Around these red wounds and amputated stumps
The magic fungus rings are springing up.

Smashed by the logger's boot, they return next season.
And the timber-Gestapo are only obeying orders.
Orders for redwood siding are piling up.
Burls can be polished to a fine patine.
They would make lamp-bases for the shades
Of Ilse Koch.

But when we loiter near a national park,
Counting the rings on those great clocks of time
The loggers have laid bare,
Is there anywhere a break or hesitation in the ring
That reveals a civilization so dismayed
And so dismaying, that its children wanted it to stop?

Tawny we rise, one more time, in our broken circles,
Children of the giant mushroom, blind
From its blaze, choked by its pillar of smoke.
Caught here, pinned down by our own malaise.
As the gods and oracles warned us for centuries,
Presumption is punished.
We were not ready for their toys.

Here in the California rain an action detains us:
An ungainly jumping-jack in his peculiar clothes leaps up.
With a wild whoop, we follow him. Come, jumping-jack,
Poor Jackself!
And the National Guard and the civil police
Turn their rifles right-side up.

        1966, 1967, 1968, 1969, 1970, and on and on . . .

Lines to Accompany Flowers for Eve

who took heroin, then sleeping pills
and who lies in a New York hospital

The florist was told, cyclamen or azalea;
White in either case, for you are pale
As they are, "blooming early and profusely"
Though the azalea grows in sandier soil
Needing less care; while cyclamen's fleshy tubers
Are adored, yes, rooted out by some.
One flourishes in aridness, while the other
Feeds the love which devours.

But what has flung you here for salvaging
From a city's dereliction, this New York?
A world against whose finger-and-breath marked windows
These weak flares may be set.
Our only bulwark is the frailest cover:
Lovers touch from terror of being alone.
The urban surface: tough and granular,
Poor ground for the affections to take root.

Left to our own devices, we devise
Such curious deaths, comas or mutilations!
You may buy peace, white, in sugary tincture,
No way of knowing its strength, or your own,
Until you lie quite still, your perfect limbs
In meditation: the spirit rouses, flutters
Like a handkerchief at a cell window, signalling
Self-amazed, its willingness to endure.

The thing to cling to is the sense of expectation.
Who knows what may occur in the next breath?
In the pallor of another morning we neither
Anticipated or wanted! Eve, waken to flowers

Unforeseen, from someone you don't even know.
Azalea or cyclamen . . . we live in wonder,
Blaze in a cycle of passion and apprehension
Though once we lay and waited for a death.

What the Bones Know

Remembering the past
And gloating at it now,
I know the frozen brow
And shaking sides of lust
Will dog me at my death
To catch my ghostly breath.

I think that Yeats was right,
That lust and love are one.
The body of this night
May beggar me to death,
But we are not undone
Who love with all our breath.

I know that Proust was wrong,
His wheeze: love, to survive,
Needs jealousy, and death
And lust, to make it strong
Or goose it back alive.
Proust took away my breath.

The later Yeats was right
To think of sex and death
And nothing else. Why wait
Till we are turning old?
My thoughts are hot and cold.
I do not waste my breath.

Flannery O'Connor

A Stroke of Good Fortune

Ruby came in the front door of the apartment building and lowered the paper sack with the four cans of number three beans in it onto the hall table. She was too tired to take her arms from around it or to straighten up and she hung there collapsed from the hips, her head balanced like a big florid vegetable at the top of the sack. She gazed with stony unrecognition at the face that confronted her in the dark yellow-spotted mirror over the table. Against her right cheek was a gritty collard leaf that had been stuck there half the way home. She gave it a vicious swipe with her arm and straightened up, muttering, "Collards, collards," in a voice of sultry subdued wrath. Standing up straight, she was a short woman, shaped nearly like a funeral urn. She had mulberry-colored hair stacked in sausage rolls around her head but some of these had come loose with the heat and the long walk from the grocery store and pointed frantically in various directions. "Collard greens!" she said, spitting the word from her mouth this time as if it were a poisonous seed.

She and Bill Hill hadn't eaten collard greens for five years and she wasn't going to start cooking them now. She had bought these on account of Rufus but she wasn't going to buy them but once. You would have thought that after two years in the armed forces Rufus would have come back ready to eat like somebody from somewhere; but no. When she asked him what he would like to have *special*, he had not had the gumption to think of one civilized dish—he had said collard greens. She had expected Rufus to have turned out into somebody with some get in him. Well, he had about as much get as a floor mop.

Rufus was her baby brother who had just come back from the European Theater. He had come to live with her because Pitman where they were raised was not there any more. All the people who had lived in Pitman had had the good sense to leave it, either by dying or by moving to the city. She had married Bill B. Hill, a Florida man who sold Miracle Products, and had come to live in the city. If Pitman had still been there, Rufus would have been in Pitman. If one chicken had been left to walk across the road in Pitman, Rufus would have been there too to keep him company. She didn't like to admit it about her own kin, least about her own brother, but there he was—good for absolutely nothing. "I seen it after five minutes of him," she had told Bill Hill and Bill Hill, with no expression whatsoever, had said, "It taken me three." It was mortifying to let that kind of a husband see you had that kind of a brother.

She supposed there was no help for it. Rufus was like the other children. She was the only one in her family who had been different, who had had any get. She took a stub of pencil from her pocketbook and wrote on the side of the sack: Bill you bring this upstairs. Then she braced herself at the bottom of the steps for the climb to the fourth floor.

The steps were thin black rent in the middle of the house, covered with a mole-colored carpet that looked as if it grew from the floor. They stuck straight up like steeple steps, it seemed to her. They reared up. The minute she stood at the bottom of them, they reared up and got steeper for her benefit. As she gazed up them, her mouth widened and turned down in a look of complete disgust. She was in no condition to go up anything. She was sick. Madam Zoleeda had told her but not before she knew it herself.

Madam Zoleeda was the palmist on Highway 87. She had said, "A long illness," but she had added. whispering, with a very I-already-know-but-I-won't-tell look, "It will bring you a stroke of good for-tune!" and then had sat back grinning, a stout woman with green eyes that moved in their sockets as if they had been oiled. Ruby didn't need to be told. She had already figured out the good fortune. Moving. For two months she had had a distinct feeling that they were going to move. Bill Hill couldn't hold off much longer. He couldn't kill her. Where she wanted to be was in a subdivision—she started up the steps, leaning forward and holding onto the banisters—where you had your drugstores and grocery and a picture show right in your own neighborhood. As it was now, living downtown, she had to walk eight blocks to the main business streets and farther than that to get to a supermarket. She hadn't made any complaints for five years much but now with her health at stake as young as she was what did he think she was going to do, kill herself? She had her eye on a place in Meadowcrest Heights, a duplex bungalow with yellow awnings. She stopped on the fifth step to blow. As young as she was —thirty-four—you wouldn't think five steps would stew her. You better take it easy, baby, she told herself, you're too young to bust your gears.

Thirty-four wasn't old, wasn't any age at all. She remembered her mother at thirty-four—she had looked like a puckered-up old yellow apple, sour, she had always looked sour, she had always looked like she wasn't satisfied with anything. She compared herself at thirty-four with her mother at that age. Her mother's hair had been gray —hers wouldn't be gray now even if she hadn't touched it up. All those children were what did her mother in—eight of them: two born dead, one died the first year, one crushed under a mowing machine. Her mother had got deader with every one of them. And all of for what? Because she hadn't known any better. Pure ignorance. The purest of downright ignorance!

And there her two sisters were, both married four years with four children apiece. She didn't see how they stood it, always going to the doctor to be jabbed at with instruments. She remembered when her mother had had Rufus. She was the only one of the children who couldn't stand it and she walked all the way in to Melsy, in the hot sun ten miles, to the picture show to get clear of the screaming, and had sat through two westerns and a horror picture and a serial and then had walked all the way back and found it was just beginning, and she had had to listen all night. All that misery for Rufus! And him turned out now to have no more charge than a dish rag. She saw him waiting out nowhere before he was born, just waiting, waiting to make his mother, only thirty-four, into an old woman. She gripped the banister rail fiercely and heaved herself up another step, shaking her head. Lord, she was disappointed in him! After she had told all her friends her brother was back from the European Theater, here he comes—sounding like he'd never been out of a hog lot.

He looked old too. He looked older than she did and he was fourteen years younger. She was extremely young looking for her age. Not that thirty-four is any age and anyway she was married. She had to smile, thinking about that, because she had done so much better than her sisters—they had married from around. "This breathlessness," she muttered, stopping again. She decided she would have to sit down.

There were twenty-eight steps in each flight—twenty-eight.

She sat down and jumped quickly, feeling something under her. She caught her breath and then pulled the thing out: it was Hartley Gilfeet's pistol. Nine inches of treacherous tin! He was a six-year-old boy who lived on the fifth floor. If he had been hers, she'd have worn him out so hard so many times he wouldn't know how to leave his mess on a public stair. She could have fallen down those stairs as easy as not and ruined herself! But his stupid mother wasn't going to do anything to him even if she told her. All she did was scream at him and tell people how smart he was. "Little Mister Good Fortune!" she called him. "All his poor daddy left me!" His daddy had said on his death bed, "There's nothing but him I ever given you," and she had said, "Rodman, you given me a fortune!" and so she called him Little Mister Good Fortune. "I'd wear the seat of his good fortune out!" Ruby muttered.

The steps were going up and down like a seesaw with her in the middle of it. She did not want to get nauseated. Not that again. Now no. No. She was not. She sat tightly to the steps with her eyes shut until the dizziness stopped a little and the nausea subsided. No, I'm not going to the doctor, she said. No. No. She was not. They would have to carry her there knocked out before she would go. She had done all right doctoring herself all these years—no bad sick spells, no teeth out, no children, all that by herself. She would have had five children right now if she hadn't been careful.

She had wondered more than once if this breathlessness could be heart trouble. Once in a while, going up the steps, there'd be a pain in her chest along with it. That was what she wanted it to be—heart trouble. They couldn't very well remove your heart. They'd have to knock her in the head before they'd get her near a hospital, they'd have to—suppose she would die if they didn't?

She wouldn't.

Suppose she would?

She made herself stop this gory thinking. She was only thirty-four. There was nothing permanent wrong with her. She was fat and her color was good. She thought of herself again in comparison with her mother at thirty-four and she pinched her arm and smiled. Seeing that her mother or father neither had been much to look at, she had done very well. They had been the dried-up type, dried up and Pitman dried into them, them and Pitman shrunk down into something all dried and puckered up. And she had come out of that! A somebody as alive as her! She got up, gripping the banister rail but smiling to herself. She was warm and fat and beautiful and not too fat because Bill Hill liked her that way. She had gained some weight but he hadn't noticed except that he was maybe more happy lately and didn't know why. She felt the wholeness of herself, a whole thing climbing the stairs. She was up the first flight now and she looked back, pleased. As soon as Bill Hill fell down these steps once, maybe they would move. But they would move before that! Madam Zoleeda had known. She laughed aloud and moved on down the hall. Mr. Jerger's door grated and startled her. Oh Lord, she thought, *him*. He was a second-floor resident who was peculiar.

He peered at her coming down the hall. "Good morning!" he said, bowing the upper part of his body out the door. "Good morning to you!" He looked like a goat. He had little raisin eyes and a string beard and his jacket was a green that was almost black or a black that was almost green.

"Morning," she said. "Hower you?"

"Well!" he screamed. "Well indeed on this glorious day!" He was seventy-eight years old and his face looked as if it had mildew on it. In the mornings he studied and in the afternoons he walked up and down the sidewalks, stopping children and asking them questions. Whenever he heard anyone in the hall, he opened his door and looked out.

"Yeah, it's a nice day," she said languidly.

"Do you know what great birthday this is?" he asked.

"Uh-uh," Ruby said. He always had a question like that. A history question that nobody knew; he would ask it and then make a speech on it. He used to teach in a high school.

"Guess," he urged her.

"Abraham Lincoln," she muttered.

"Hah! You are not trying," he said. "Try."

"George Washington," she said, starting up the stairs.

"Shame on you!" he cried. "And your husband from there! Florida! Florida! Florida's birthday," he shouted. "Come in here." He disappeared into his room, beckoning a long finger at her.

She came down the two steps and said, "I gotta be going," and stuck her head inside the door. The room was the size of a large closet and the walls were completey covered with picture postcards of local buildings; this gave an illusion of space. A single transparent bulb hung down on Mr. Jerger and a small table.

"Now examine this," he said. He was bending over a book, running his finger under the lines: " 'On Easter Sunday, April 3, 1516, he arrived on the tip of this continent.' Do you know who this *he* was?" he demanded.

"Yeah, Christopher Columbus." Ruby said.

"Ponce de Leon!" he screamed. "Ponce de Leon! You should know something about Florida," he said. "Your husband is from Florida."

"Yeah, he was born in Miami," Ruby said. "He's not from Tennessee."

"Florida is not a noble state," Mr. Jerger said, "but it is an important one."

"It's important alrighto," Ruby said.

"Do you know who Ponce de Leon was?"

"He was the founder of Florida," Ruby said brightly.

"He was a Spaniard," Mr. Jerger said. "Do you know what he was looking for?"

"Florida," Ruby said.

"Ponce de Leon was looking for the fountain of youth," Mr. Jerger said, closing his eyes.

"Oh," Ruby muttered.

"A certain spring," Mr. Jerger went on, "whose water gave perpetual youth to those who drank it. In other words," he said, "he was trying to be young always."

"Did he find it?" Ruby asked.

Mr. Jerger paused with his eyes still closed. After a minute he said, "Do you think he found it? Do you think he found it? Do you think nobody else would have got to it if he had found it? Do you think there would be one person living on this earth who hadn't drunk it?"

"I hadn't thought," Ruby said.

"Nobody thinks any more," Mr. Jerger complained.

"I got to be going."

"Yes, it's been found," Mr. Jerger said.

"Where at?" Ruby asked.

"I have drunk of it."

"Where'd you have to go to?" she asked. She leaned a little closer and got a whiff of him that was like putting her nose under a buzzard's wing.

"Into my heart," he said, placing his hand over it.

"Oh." Ruby moved back. "I gotta be going. I think my brother's home." She got over the door sill.

"Ask your husband if he knows what great birthday this is," Mr. Jerger said, looking at her coyly.

"Yeah, I will." She turned and waited until she heard his door click. She looked back to see that it was shut and then she blew out her breath and stood facing the dark remaining steep of steps. "God Almighty," she commented. They got darker and steeper as you went up.

By the time she had climbed five steps her breath was gone. She continued up a few more, blowing. Then she stopped. There was a pain in her stomach. It was a pain like a piece of something pushing something else. She had felt it before, a few days ago. It was the one that frightened her most. She had thought the word *cancer* once and dropped it instantly because no horror like that was coming to her because it couldn't. The word came back to her immediately with the pain but she slashed it in two with Madam Zoleeda. It will end in good fortune. She slashed it twice through and then again until there were only pieces of it that couldn't be recognized. She was going to stop on the next floor—God, if she ever got up there—and talk to Laverne Watts. Laverne Watts was a third-floor resident, the secretary to a chiropodist, and an especial friend of hers.

She got up there, gasping and feeling as if her knees were full of fizz, and knocked on Laverne's door with the butt of Hartley Gilfeet's gun. She leaned on the door frame to rest and suddenly the floor around her dropped on both sides. The walls turned black and she felt herself reeling, without breath, in the middle of the air, terrified at the drop that was coming. She saw the door open a great distance away and Laverne, about four inches high, standing in it.

Laverne, a tall straw-haired girl, let out a great guffaw and slapped her side as if she had just opened the door on the most comical sight she had yet seen. "That gun!" she yelled. "That gun! That look!" She staggered back to the sofa and fell on it, her legs rising higher than her hips and falling down again helplessly with a thud.

The floor came up to where Ruby could see it and remained, dipping a little. With a terrible stare of concentration, she stepped down to get on it. She scrutinized a chair across the room and then headed for it, putting her feet carefully one before the other.

"You should be in a wild-west show!" Laverne Watts said. "You're a howl!"

Ruby reached the chair and then edged herself onto it. "Shut up," she said hoarsely.

Laverne sat forward, pointing at her, and then fell back on the sofa, shaking again.

"Quit that!" Ruby yelled. "Quit that! I'm sick."

Laverne got up and took two or three long strides across the room. She leaned down in front of Ruby and looked into her face with one eye shut as if she were squinting through a keyhole. "You are sort of purple," she said.

"I'm damn sick," Ruby glowered.

Laverne stood looking at her and after a second she folded her arms and very pointedly stuck her stomach out and began to sway back and forth. "Well, what'd you come in here with that gun for? Where'd you get it?" she asked.

"Sat on it," Ruby muttered.

Laverne stood there, swaying with her stomach stuck out, and a very wise expression growing on her face. Ruby sat sprawled in the chair, looking at her feet. The room was getting still. She sat up and glared at her ankles. They were swollen! I'm not going to no doctor, she started, I'm not going to one. I'm not going. "Not going," she began to mumble, "to no doctor, not . . ."

"How long you think you can hold off?" Laverne murmured and began to giggle.

"Are my ankles swollen?" Ruby asked.

"They look like they've always looked to me," Laverne said, throwing herself down on the sofa again. "Kind of fat." She lifted her own ankles up on the end pillow and turned them slightly. "How do you like these shoes?" she asked. They were a grasshopper green with very high thin heels.

"I think they're swollen," Ruby said. "When I was coming up that last flight of stairs I had the awfulest feeling, all over me like . . ."

"You ought to go on to the doctor."

"I don't need to go to no doctor," Ruby muttered. "I can take care of myself. I haven't done bad at it all this time."

"Is Rufus at home?"

"I don't know. I kept myself away from doctors all my life. I kept —why?"

"Why what?"

"Why, is Rufus at home?"

"Rufus is cute," Laverne said. "I thought I'd ask him how he liked my shoes."

Ruby sat up with a fierce look, very pink and purple. "Why Rufus?" she growled. "He ain't but a baby." Laverne was thirty years old. "He don't care about women's shoes."

Laverne sat up and took off one of the shoes and peered inside it. "Nine B," she said. "I bet he'd like what's in it."

"That Rufus ain't but an enfant!" Ruby said. "He don't have time to be looking at your feet. He ain't got that kind of time."

"Oh, he's got plenty of time," Laverne said.

"Yeah," Ruby muttered and saw him again, waiting, with plenty of time, out nowhere before he was born, just waiting to make his mother that much deader.

"I believe your ankles are swollen," Laverne said.

"Yeah," Ruby said, twisting them. "Yeah. They feel tight sort of. I had the awfulest feeling when I got up those steps, like sort of out of breath all over, sort of tight all over, sort of—awful."

"You ought to go on to the doctor."

"No."

"You ever been to one?"

"They carried me once when I was ten," Ruby said, "but I got away. Three of them holding me didn't do any good."

"What was it that time?"

"What you looking at me that way for?" Ruby muttered.

"What way?"

"That way," Ruby said, "—swagging out that stomach of yours that way."

"I just asked you what it was that time?"

"It was a boil. A nigger woman up the road told me what to do and I did it and it went away." She sat slumped on the edge of the chair, staring in front of her as if she were remembering an easier time.

Laverne began to do a kind of comic dance up and down the room. She took two or three slow steps in one direction with her knees bent and then she came back and kicked her leg slowly and painfully in the other. She began to sing in a loud guttural voice, rolling her eyes, "Put them all together, they spell MOTHER! MOTHER!" and stretching out her arms as if she were on the stage.

Ruby's mouth opened wordlessly and her fierce expression vanished. For a half-second she was motionless; then she sprang from the chair. "Not me!" she shouted. "Not me!"

Laverne stopped and only watched her with the wise look.

"Not me!" Ruby shouted. "Oh no not me! Bill Hill takes care of that. Bill Hill takes care of that! Bill Hill's been taking care of that for five years! That ain't going to happen to me!"

"Well old Bill Hill just slipped up about four or five months ago, my friend," Laverne said. "Just slipped up . . ."

"I don't reckon you know anything about it, you ain't even married, you ain't even . . ."

"I bet it's not one, I bet it's two," Laverne said. "You better go on to the doctor and find out how many it is."

"It is not!" Ruby shrilled. She thought she was so smart! She didn't know a sick woman when she saw one, all she could do was look at her feet and shoe em to Rufus, shoe em to Rufus and he was an enfant and she was thirty-four years old. "Rufus is an enfant!" she wailed.

"That will make two!" Laverne said.

"You shut up talking like that!" Ruby shouted. "You shut up this minute. I ain't going to have any baby!"

"Ha ha," Laverne said.

"I don't know how you think you know so much," Ruby said, "single as you are. If I were so single I wouldn't go around telling married people what their business is."

"Not just your ankles," Laverne said, "you're swollen all over."

"I ain't going to stay here and be insulted," Ruby said and walked carefully to the door, keeping herself erect and not looking down at her stomach the way she wanted to.

"Well I hope *all* of you feel better tomorrow," Laverne said.

"I think my heart will be better tomorrow," Ruby said. "But I hope we will be moving soon. I can't climb these steps with this heart trouble and," she added with a dignified glare, "Rufus don't care nothing about your big feet."

"You better put that gun up," Laverne said, "before you shoot somebody."

Ruby slammed the door shut and looked down at herself quickly. She was big there but she had always had a kind of big stomach. She did not stick out there different from the way she did any place else. It was natural when you took on some weight to take it on in the middle and Bill Hill didn't mind her being fat, he was just more happy and didn't know why. She saw Bill Hill's long happy face grinning at her from the eyes downward in a way he had as if his look got happier as it neared his teeth. He would never slip up. She rubbed her hand across her skirt and felt the tightness of it but hadn't she felt that before? She had. It was the skirt—she had on the tight one that she didn't wear often, she had . . . she didn't have on the tight skirt. She had on the loose one. But it wasn't very loose. But that didn't make any difference, she was just fat.

She put her fingers on her stomach and pushed down and took them off quickly. She began walking toward the stairs, slowly, as if the floor were going to move under her. She began the steps. The pain came back at once. It came back with the first step. "No," she whimpered, "no." It was just a little feeling, just a little feeling like a piece of her inside rolling over but it made her breath tighten in her throat. Nothing in her was supposed to roll over. "Just one step," she whispered, "just one step and it did it." It couldn't be cancer. Madam Zoleeda said it would end in good fortune. She began crying and saying, "Just one step and it did it," and going on up them absently as if she thought she were standing still. On the sixth one, she sat down suddenly, her hand slipping weakly down the banister spoke onto the floor.

"Noooo," she said and leaned her round red face between the two nearest poles. She looked down into the stairwell and gave a long hollow wail that widened and echoed as it went down. The stair cavern was dark green and mole-colored and the wail sounded at the very bottom like a voice answering her. She gasped and shut her eyes. No. No. It couldn't be any baby. She was not going to have something waiting in her to make her deader, she was not. Bill Hill couldn't have slipped up. He said it was guaranteed and it had worked all this time and it could not be that, it could not. She shuddered and held her hand tightly over her mouth. She felt her face drawn puckered: two born dead one died the first year and one run under like a dried yellow apple no she was only thirty-four years old, she was old. Madam Zoleeda said it would end in no drying up. Madam Zoleeda said oh but it will end in a stroke of good fortune! Moving. She had said it would end in a stroke of good moving.

She felt herself getting calmer. She felt herself, after a minute, getting almost calm and thought she got upset too easy; heck, it was gas. Madam Zoleeda hadn't been wrong about anything yet, she knew more than . . .

She jumped: there was a bang at the bottom of the stairwell and a rumble rattling up the steps, shaking them even up where she was. She looked through the banister poles and saw Hartley Gilfeet, with two pistols leveled, galloping up the stairs and heard a voice pierce down from the floor over her, "You Hartley, shut up that racket! You're shaking the house!" But he came on, thundering louder as he rounded the bend on the first floor and streaked up the hall. She saw Mr. Jerger's door fly open and him spring with clawed fingers and grasp a flying piece of shirt that whirled and shot off again with a high-pitched, "Leggo, you old goat teacher!" and came on nearer until the stairs rumbled directly under her and a charging chipmunk face crashed into her and rocketed through her head, smaller and smaller into a whirl of dark.

She sat on the step, clutching the banister spoke while the breath came back into her a thimbleful at a time and the stairs stopped seesawing. She opened her eyes and gazed down into the dark hold, down to the very bottom where she had started up so long ago. "Good Fortune," she said in a hollow voice that echoed along all the levels of the cavern, "Baby."

"Good Fortune, Baby," the three echoes leered.

Then she recognized the feeling again, a little roll. It was as if it were not in her stomach. It was as if it were out nowhere in nothing, out nowhere, resting and waiting, with plenty of time.

Cynthia Ozick

from Trust

My mother rarely mentioned my father; she never thought of him, since she was concerned only with the present. Occasionally—perhaps every three years, but with great irregularity—she would receive a letter from my father, and then she would be reluctantly reminded of him. "Well, it's starting again," I would hear her tell Enoch. "Go ahead and do it and get it over with," Enoch would advise her, and from their tone—although nothing was ever said to me—I suspected that my father had written to ask for money. I was faintly ashamed of him, as of an invisible and somehow disreputable intruder. At the same time I had very little curiosity about him; quite early in my life my mother had dismissed him as a figure of no importance and less reality. "To be perfectly objective about it," she remarked once, "all that is terribly remote. After all, I was *with* him for less than two years over twenty years ago! You can't reasonably expect anything but the vaguest impression by now. It's hardly left a trace," she said, and looked out at me from her wedge of curls with an uncharacteristic bewilderment—"except for you." This was not the case with her first husband, who had preceded my father—not only was her impression of him still lambent, but she did not appear to have any desire to extinguish it. Of the three lawyers she retained, this man, my mother's first husband, was the one she most often consulted; now and then he would dine with us, and my mother would call him "dear William," and ask after his wife. He was married to a woman so different from herself—so clearly diligent and domestic, so innocently self-aware and eager to be courted—that it was obvious, even to my mother, what had been the trouble. William was too august and substantial a personage to be diagnosed as happy or unhappy; it was plain, however, that my mother thoroughly respected him, since in his presence she chose dull and meagre endings for stories which, in other company, she used to conclude in the liveliest manner imaginable. And William, while he was rather stiffly cordial to my mother, and very gentlemanly toward Enoch, seemed less than charmed by the dinner chatter. He would quietly talk trusts and investments, and finish by handing my mother a check in the gilt-edged envelope of his firm, a bi-monthly mission which he only very rarely allowed the mails to perform. Once he brought with him to dinner his oldest boy, a correct, wan-lidded adolescent with an artificial stammer, who was so submissively attentive to the rite of passing the croutons that I was horrified lest Enoch's imprecations, muttered bearishly into his soup, be overheard. To tell the truth, William's son fascinated me. He looked remarkably like a dog of a choice and venerable breed. His dark glazed head was too small for the padding in his shoulders, but otherwise I considered him formidably handsome, even elegant. He was known to be precocious: he already had an interest in jurisprudence and he carried under his arm a copy of Holmes' *The Common Law.* This reputation for intelligence, and the trick he had of faltering in the middle of a syllable, ravished me from the first moment. William's son seemed to me the image of brilliant commitment, of a confident yet enchanting dedication to dark philosophies—in short, of all that I might have been had my mother's marriage to her first husband endured. It was not that I wanted William for my father: I wished merely to have had him, in that preconscious time, for my sire. Since we are born at random, as an afterthought, or as an enigmatic consequence in a game of Truth, and are not willed into being by our begetters, they accordingly fall under the obligation of surrendering much of themselves to us, in the manner of forfeits; hence we are burdened not merely with their bone and blood, but with their folly and their folly's disguises. Nonetheless William's son had somehow been exempted from this fraudulent heirship, this pretense that we are auspicious inheritors when we are in reality only collectors grimly fetching what is due us:—those evils (dressed as gifts) which we are compelled to exact although we do not desire them. William's son was sound, he was fortunate, he had providentially escaped his birthright. I saw him as the brother I had lost through my mother's absurdity. The more so, since we shared the same surname.

As is the custom with divorced women, in order to display her proper status my mother had retained the latter part of her marriage title against the time when she might acquire a new husband, and, with him, a new name. But after her separation from my father, she explained, she had reverted to the name she had carried as William's wife; she did not care to style herself, or me, after my father. As a result, while my mother through her third alliance had long ago become Mrs. Vand, I continued to be called after her first husband. I was generally believed to be William's child. My father was by this means virtually obliterated from our lives, since I was not permitted even to bear his name. For many years it was not revealed to me: I discovered it by chance myself one afternoon, when, rummaging in Enoch's desk for a stamp, I came upon an empty envelope, the address run over in a watered and rusted ink. Some notion about the handwriting, which was educated but wild, as though scratched on by fingers used to grosser movements, made me search after the sender. He appeared to have been reluctant to record himself plainly; not only was he absent from the face of the envelope, but from the back, and when I found him at last, it was in a hidden place, on the inside of the flap, a little furtive and blurred by the glue:

> Gustave Nicholas Tilbeck
> Duneacres
> Town Island
> New York

That this was my father I was convinced at once, although I was fleetingly put off by the starkness of his lodging, for I had imagined him as living under a congestion of tenement flats in a far and uncongenial, perhaps sinister, city. It had always been my idea that my father was some sort of artist—or perhaps a kind of sailor, a voyager or adventurer—although no one had ever told me this. I supposed him to be improvident, impoverished, and discreditable; I was given to understand, subtly and by prudent indirection, that he was a great embarrassment to us all. My school applications had always cautiously evaded mention of him, and I can recall awkward conversations when, looking away, I did not dare to deny my interlocutor's convenient assumption of William's paternity. It was a substantial relief to pretend to a relation with William, who was red-faced, jut-chinned, and white-haired, like an elderly and reliable monument toward which one has patriotic feelings. I thought of my father, on the other hand, as dun and dank and indecent and somewhat yellowish; I thought he had yellow-tarred teeth, and a porous nose, and bad eyes. At the same time it seemed perfectly plausible that such a man might be a genius. The nature of his talent my imagination did not explore, it being quite enough that I saw the man himself as moist and dirty, quartered in a moist and dirty cellar, in the manner of geniuses. It was not inconceivable that he might be an inventor, and I even believed it likely that he was a foreigner, since the only thing certain I knew of him was that he had marched with my mother in Moscow. That she, with all her gaiety, her fabrications, her enthusiasms, her adorations, could have been attracted to the repugnant wretch I had fashioned did not, to be sure, seem altogether reasonable. And yet it was not impossible: she was stupid enough to talk romantically of "indeterminate taints" and "vital sparks," and she was quick to spot, in queer people whom everyone else avoided, "un homme de génie." Still, I had no real reason for my judgment that my father was in some way singular, or at the least unorthodox. I had only my guilty instinct for his character. Sometimes, when my mother would stare at me in a certain apprehensive way—her painted eyebrows pulled together in a cosmetic frown—it would seem to me that I was wrong, or crooked, or even bizarre; and that some source of error in me, so perverse and elusive that I was not myself sensible of it, had reminded her of my father. But immediately afterward she would be laughing again. "It's not like the fairy tale, you know, where you can tell the king by the mark on his breast!" she took up mockingly. "I'm sure *I* don't speak of that person from one year to the next—though that's not the point." In spite of her hilarity—acrid and nervous and somehow shackled—I could not see what she insisted *was* the point. Nevertheless she did not deny the truth of my surmise. She only demanded that I explain it. "Oh, well, if you want me to believe some formula about blood will tell, that sort of thing," she accused when I could not oblige her; "you saw your father's name and you simply *knew*. Not," she finished without pleasure, "that we ever kept it from you!"

In this way, and alone, I learned who my father was. But, lest my mother feel the shame of my shame, I was discreet; I did not disclose all that I knew. There was nothing extraordinary in my recognition. Toward the end of a dark March, while an endless snow lay swarming on the sills, going by my mother's door I heard the rattle of bracelets on her furious arms; she clanked them like shields and

cried out; and then, while I stopped wretchedly aware, Enoch's voice
came maundering from the fastness of her room: "It's all right;
come, there's nothing else to do; besides, it doesn't matter. Let's go
ahead and get it over with." It was all hidden, and all familiar; it
meant a letter from my father—a summer's beetle swaddled in the
cold storm, prodded and found miraculously preserved, and more,
atwitch with ugly life. My father's letters, infrequent as they were,
always brought their own oppressive season into our house, suggestive
of a too-suddenly fruitful thicket, lush, damp, growing too fast,
dappled with the tremolo of a million licking hairs—deep, sick, tropical. And then my mother's eyes, which delighted her because of
their extravagant decorative roundness, like roulette wheels, would
shrink to hard brown nuts. We came to live with heat, barely breathing; we came to live with the foul redolence of heat, like fish rotting
in a hull. Outside my mother's windows the snow continued to mass,
but in the house we sickened, enisled, hung round with my father's
rough nets. "What does he want?" my mother cried out behind her
door in that frozen March; "how much now?" And Gustave Nicholas
Tilbeck like some indolent mariner lay on the beach of his island,
nude to the waist; I saw him—my father; he lay there cruelly, like
refuse; he had the patient lids of a lizard, and a yellow mouth, and he
was young but half-blind; and he lay alone on his beach, in the
seaweed-littered sand, among shells with their open cups waiting;
and he waited. And with confidence: the day came, it would always
come, when my mother could withstand the siege no longer. Then
gradually my father's presence, humid and proliferous, thick and invisible, less an untutored mist than some toxic war-gas pumped by
armored machines into the flatulent air, or a stubborn plague-wind
slow to cool away, would recede and die. Unseen, unknown, proclaiming himself with doubtful omens, like a terrible Nile-god Gustave
Nicholas Tilbeck invaded, vanished, and reappeared. Nothing would
secure his eclipse but propitiation of the most direct and vulgar nature, and my mother, as enraged as any pagan by a vindictive devil,
had to succumb. Money was what he wanted. Money came to him
at last where he lay, and he blinked his torpid jaundiced lids and was
content. My mother had her peace then, which she would celebrate
at once by a journey abroad, to some cold and rain-washed country, perhaps in Scandinavia: a far and bitter place where my father
had never touched. And yet the money was an act of allegiance, it
appeared; she reviled the Nile-god but she rewarded him. It was not
for charity, and not for pity, and not for the sake of a righteous heart:
for charity, pity, and a righteous heart would not have seized her
with fury or churned those wrathful cries. And afterward she had
to travel, as for relief after excess. Was it love then that he sent
her—my father, the man of talent—in his jagged inkings? And year
after year was it love turned to money that reverberated from her
hand? As I have said, my mother had no concern with the past,
which she considered eccentric, because it differed from the present.
Everything old struck her as grotesque, like costumes in photographs
of dead aunts. She did not believe in old obligations or old loves; she
was wholly without sentimentality. Every autumn I saw her give
away capes and hats and purses which she had cherished effusively

only a few months before. She had no regard for an article on the simple ground that, because she had loved it once, it must for that reason alone merit her warmth. She considered that everything wore out extrinsically, by virtue of her own advancement, no matter if it were as good as new. I began to see that her indifference was not for the thing itself, but rather for her former judgment of it: it was her old self she discarded.

Gustave Nicholas Tilbeck alone endured and transcended—if not corporeally, then in the actuality of his nature. It was an extraordinary victory—he could not be ousted. He took her money, I imagined, as a man takes a trophy—with a modest smile, yet smelling conquest. But if she did not yield it up for alms' sake, still less could it have been in tribute to used-up desire. Between them lay waste and silt and the endless shards of my father's yellow beach, and the long barren shoal. They had left that old time depleted. It was not love or the memory of love—and yet something active, present, and of the moment festered there: some issue turned mysteriously in the sand. My mother felt its sting under her hand that March, as our private sirocco blew woe into all the rooms, upstairs and downstairs; and not long afterward the empty envelope in Enoch's desk acquainted me with Gustave Nicholas Tilbeck, and not only with that unknown name, but with how much they had paid him, and in what sequence, and how much was promised for later, all rapidly registered in Enoch's hook-like unmistakable pencilled digits—and what gave it away was March. I saw that they had last sent money to this person in March. It was all obscure; it was all penetrating; and what gave it away, as I say, was March. To whom else would those sums (in amounts not impossible, not unreasonable, remarkable rather for their disjointed recurrences) have gone in the very month when my father's perspiring ghost breathed the money-sickness into the secret fissures of our lives?

But I did not tell my mother any of this. It comforted her to think that I was unaware; I pretended that some oddity of intuition, or else an accidental and unremembered word, had brought me to my father's identity. I did not say that I knew him to be a mendicant and a leech. Nevertheless, she was careful to turn the key to Enoch's desk, and during the tranquil period that followed I heard nothing of that languid merchant of the past, that inventor or sailor, that homme de génie, Gustave Nicholas Tilbeck.

The father's tale.

Once, long ago, on an occasion I have by now forgotten, Enoch said to my mother: "Hell is truth seen too late," and without giving it any thought I assumed he was speaking for himself. But my mother, shrewd and shrewish that day, said petulantly: "And what about truth seen too soon? You're not going to tell me that's heaven?"— And afterward I came upon my stepfather's remark in a book: it was a sentence from an English philosopher. He had been reading Hobbes. But his reply to his wife was characteristic only of himself— he answered not with a logical corollary but with a fresh tangent. "Oh no," he told her, propelled into one of his placid satiric moods,

"Heaven is never to see the truth at all." And then, to mollify her—
she had taken it roughly against the shield of her frown—he threw
out, "if you see the truth too soon you naturally accommodate yourself to what you see; and by the act of accommodating yourself you
change whatever the circumstance was when you originally saw it;
and by changing the circumstance you alter the ground from which
the truth springs, and then it can no longer grow out that same truth
which you foresaw: it has become something different. So you see it
is impossible to see the truth too soon, for when its moment of commitment arrives, it has changed its nature and it is already too late.
The truth is always seen too late. That is why hell is always with us,"
he insisted on finishing, although my mother had long ago covered
her ears and was shouting with vigor, "Stop! Stop! I can't stand it, I
won't stand it!" And they ended laughing together, enigmatically, as
though not the English philosopher, and not Enoch, but Allegra Vand
herself had innocently convulsed them.

I think of this now, when I have come finally to the father's tale,
though not *my* father's: a tale told by my almost-father about my
"true" father, signifying anything but fatherhood. For if, in my stepfather's phrase, it was for me a truth seen too late, that story which
William eventually related, then let it stand that on a certain afternoon in the first days of September, in William's darkly glazed private office, under the painted eye of his brief father-in-law and the
paper eye of his determinedly permanent wife, I entered hell.

My observation upon arrival? Chiefly, that the place felt familiar. In
what respect? In this: that to enter hell and find Tilbeck there was
no surprise.

William, who had deliberately denuded my mother's file of everything important, had access to the devil's own dossier. And there
were stored and stuffed all those missing papers in the matter of
Allegra Vand which William's son had vainly coveted, to redeem, I
suppose, his sense of historical order—not a petty but a moral sense:
for William's son, in his zeal for personal history, appeared to invest
a proper chronology with morality, to wit, "that is good which follows"; and one day, when he would have learned to transpose this
uninteresting notion into a more politic one, viz., "that which follows
is good," he would indubitably grow into an even cleverer lawyer than
his father—"that which follows is good" being a dictum of complete legal probity, especially when applied as heading to a document full of brilliantly concealed tax crimes. But this is digression,
though purposeful. Only yesterday my stepfather had defined history
as a judgment on humanity; today William's son saw it as a com-
pilation of the appropriate papers. As for William himself, his relation with history lay in his not having any. How was this possible
in a mind concerned most of its sentient hours with the law, where
presumably precedent governs? But precedent did not govern William's mind, for precedents are only relative, and contradict one another now and then, and anyhow William was a Calvinist, and believed in the foreordained: call it, for brevity's sake, destiny. Destiny
is individual, and what has gone before, in similar cases (no matter

how similiar to, or, as lawyers like zoölogically to put it, however truly "on all fours with," the case at hand), is irrelevant. To William, the circumstances of my birth—how indecently priggish and Dickensian that sounds! yet I succumb to this mean phrase out of deference for poor William, who, after showing so much respect initially for the precise terminology and taxonomy of his profession, reverted with relief to another show of respect, which he expressed insultingly in circumlocution and euphemism—the circumstances of my birth, at any rate, implied for him not simple event but a destiny for which I was responsible in the first place and to blame in the second. And not only a destiny, but even a breed of soul which such a destiny might spawn. Those "circumstances," moreover, explained his aversion and clarified his evasions; and all delicately and exquisitely and secretly they gave me a sinister chill, as though, while standing solemnly in court, about to be sentenced, I had caught sight of the god Pan at the window, clutching a bunch of wild flowers, hellebore and jewelweed, and laughing a long and careless jingle of a laugh, like bicycle bells.

So it turned out that—as I have stated—it was the devil's dossier which contained the missing papers. At the same time let it be noted that the devil's dossier was altogether empty. A paradox? No. The papers were missing because they were non-existent. That is the way it is with the devil's file—it is full of lies, and lies, in an absolute sense, have no reality, body, weight, or substance. Lies, being what-is-not, are not there. There were no documents recording my mother's divorce from Gustave Nicholas Tilbeck because there had never been a divorce. There had never been a divorce because there had never been a marriage. If lies *had* reality, body, weight, or substance, there would not be room enough anywhere to keep them in, and the devil would have to appropriate the whole world for a safety-vault.

To this, Enoch—I can hear him!—would say: "Exactly. He *has* appropriated the world, just as you say. Why else is the world so stuffed with lies? The liars are all file-cabinets for the devil." Regarding all plain contrary-to-fact falsehoods perhaps this is so, but it is not so with the lie that is a lie only because the truth has not been uttered. The lie of omission, like the silent hollow within the flute's facile cylinder, cannot be put away, and will continue to plague the universe forever, by virtue of its formlessness, which is dependent on honest forms. An ordinary lie, because it is a simple opposite of what-is, can be contradicted by exposure of its contrary. But the lie of omission is a concealment contradicted by nothing, and bolstered, in fact, by the solidity of the revealed. That Tilbeck existed, I had been told; that he was my father, I had been told. From this I drew the assumption of a marriage; but it was an appearance: a nefarious illusion, worse than a made lie. Rumor and murmur come to kill a made lie; the made lie is tangible and can be cut down. But the omitted pertinent thing, the lie of illusion, falls like a damp pervading smoke. It was by illusion and trick my mother and William had snared me. And Enoch, who had been quiet, who had said nothing, had thereby had his part in it, and was a liar like the others: though a hater of liars.

William began: "The circumstances of your birth—"

"My illegitimacy."

"—of your birth have turned out to be highly useful to a particular individual."

"You mean to my father. Gustave Nicholas Tilbeck. Don't think I don't know all my father's names!"

If this was a challenge William did not rise to it, and only said, "In spite of that you have been protected from the beginning."

I said: "I wish I had been protected *from* beginning."

"Sophistry. I don't hide it from you that I regard it as a great pity."

"A pity that I was born."

"I refer only to your mother's behavior."

"My mother's *mis*behavior."

"I think you had better take a more serious attitude," William said.

"A more humble one, do you mean? Befitting my position in life?"

"Please," he said harshly.

"I believe I'm *not* going to weep."

"Excellent. I'm glad of it. I ask you to be serious, but not irresponsible."

"In other words, not to take after my mother. But I've been better brought up. *I* haven't been anyone's mistress," I told him, and added guilefully: "So far."

"I also ask you to speak of your mother with"—anxiously he chose the less obvious word—"propriety. I hope it won't be necessary to warn you against bad taste in this matter."

His gravity was both intense and fastidious, and therefore so absurd and piteous that, despite my declaration, I almost wept after all. I came so close to it that I laughed instead, and was surprised: what emerged was bitter shame. "And to think," I brought out, "I always imagined the divorce itself was the thing in bad taste!"

"There was no divorce," William said.

"What you mean is there was only one divorce and not two—one, I suppose, is in better taste than two? In that case my father has improved on things. Unless the first divorce was a sham as well?"

"I won't countenance this—"

But I would not stop for his remonstrance. "If only you'll make it clear that *you* were never married to my mother either," I offered, "it would do away altogether with the taint of divorce, wouldn't it? Think how clean the family escutcheon would be."

"I do not like this talk," William said.

"No. It's dirty, like the escutcheon."

"Look here," he said abruptly, "you don't grasp in what capacity I've been willing to receive you. You will have to understand that I have been your mother's lawyer for a very long time—"

"And something else."

"Her lawyer. I speak to you in that capacity and in no other," he finished.

"And in another," I nevertheless pursued.

"What are you after?"

"You've omitted something. You've been something else, and it makes a difference. It's an influence."

"The trustee. Yes. Very well. I've been the trustee," he stated without comfort.

"And the husband."

"Your mother's husband," he observed, "is a Jew named Vand.— You needn't draw on any family relation where none exists." All unwittingly his elevated arm had stretched to the level of the mouth in the portrait behind and above him—the confident, even arrogant, rather flat Huntingdon mouth which my mother, but not I, had inherited. This mouth was the only living feature in that fearsome yet curiously pallid representation of my grandfather; not Sargent, but an imitator, perhaps a pupil, had given posterity those unconcerned angelic nostrils, too spiritual to breathe. But the mouth showed what the man had been: it looked ready to spit.

In the presence of this icon-like carpet-mustached ancestor I inquired of his son-in-law, "And where a family relation *does* exist?"

But William had noted my upward gaze and intercepted it with a force which made all irony of appearances ineffectual. "Is is not was. None exists," he repeated, and became conscious suddenly of his hand in the air; he brought it down and laid it on the desk and solemnly viewed it.

"Your son? I'm speaking of your son. You admit to a family relation *there?*"

"My son," he granted, "is a stranger to this business."

"A stranger?"

"He knows nothing."

"He knows plenty. He knows more than I know."

"I don't see what you're implying. He knows nothing about the circumstances of your—"

"—of my worth," I joined him mockingly. "But he's completely aware of yours."

"You had better be explicit," William said.

"Your son has already been that. I've heard how the trustee failed to live up to the terms of the trust."

"Ah," William said, meditating. "He talked to you?"

"He told me about the death on the estate. My mother's estate. —The place they're sending me to, in fact. We went out to one of the cubicles and he told me," I said.

"That's quite outside the proper area of your interest in this matter. —He talked to you about it?" William said again. He continued to stare at his hand as though it had turned to bronze. "He has no discretion."

"He picked Miss Pettigrew," I slyly acknowledged.

"My son will have to answer for his own recklessness. In every respect."

"And you picked my mother."

"And answered for it."

"By losing her. But you know," I took up, inflamed inexplicably into vehemence, "I always believed you had divorced her on account of, well, on account of *Marianna Harlow!* The terrible Chapter Twelve!" I threw out at him all the infamous jeering incongruity of it: "I thought it was on account of politics! Because she was mixed up with Communists—"

"Communists," he echoed carefully.

Then very gradually and astonishingly I felt between my shoulders the beginning of a kind of jarring, a reverberation: without realizing it I had grown tremulous.

"Your mother divorced *me*," William corrected, essaying it with impeccable exactitude, as though caution might be relied on to keep his fist as stiff as cast metal. But he began to rock it thoughtfully, like a small bronze pony.

Though nervous, I had to scoff. "That's a gentlemanly technicality."

"However it's a fact."

"So," I said, "was her adultery."

The word struck like a stone against his eyes.

"Don't continue in that language, please."

"I didn't choose the language."

"You are remarkably sullen. I warn you," William said.

"It's Biblical language, isn't it? It says 'adultery' in the Decalogue— in that case I'm perfectly sure I can't be blamed for the language, can I? Though maybe you might blame Enoch."

He looked up wearily.

"You just *said* he's a Jew. They invented the Bible, you know. Blame *them.*"

He did not move. "I blame the sinner for the sin."

"I hate religion," I said.

"Then you hate God."

"No," I said. "God hates me."

So we came to a standstill at hatred. We came to it quickly; and we stopped there. Where else could we have stopped? For William, hater of adultery, it was Christian duty. For me it was plain pagan philosophy. I hated William not because he had failed to become my father according to respectable plan; I hated my mother not because she had borne me in wildness and reared me in tame constraint; I hated my father not because secretly and fearfully I felt his alien and singing bravado in my intellect; I hated Enoch not because he addressed me always with the contempt of repudiation, as though I were a category or an opposite point of view—no, no, I was not so orderly in my hatred, I did not sniff after the weavings of the minor plots of past time. I hated my stepfather, my true father, my almost-father, my mother who had bedded with each of these, because they were the world. That was my whole, broad, and uncontaminated philosophy—scorn for everything that devoured my mind: for the world exactly as it stood; for all phenomena. In existence there *is* no might-have-been, though we contemplate it despairingly. God does not allow returns and beginnings-again-from-the-starting-place. What firmer sign can there be of God's cruelty? He has made the already-accomplished inexorable. We cannot go back to do it over again. There are no rehearsals. Each fresh moment is the real and final thing. Each successive breath is the single penetrable opportunity for its pitiable duration; there is no other, there is no beginning on the morrow, there is only what we have done yesterday, or what has been done to us yesterday; we live on our yesterday's leavings. To God we are inflexible facts: he does not judge us, any more than we would judge the barnward cow's round dung-tower in the field behind her. Dung is fact. Man is fact. If God were not indifferent to us, we might not be indifferent to each other.

Anne Sexton

Live

Live or die, but don't poison everything . . .

Well, death's been here
for a long time—
it has a hell of a lot
to do with hell
and suspicion of the eye
and the religious objects
and how I mourned them
when they were made obscene
by my dwarf-heart's doodle.
The chief ingredient
is mutilation.
And mud, day after day,
mud like a ritual,
and the baby on the platter,
cooked but still human,
cooked also with little maggots,
sewn onto it maybe by somebody's mother,
the damn bitch!

Even so,
I kept right on going on,
a sort of human statement,
lugging myself as if
I were a sawed-off body
in the trunk, the steamer trunk.
This became a perjury of the soul.
It became an outright lie
and even though I dressed the body
it was still naked, still killed.
It was caught
in the first place at birth,
like a fish.
But I played it, dressed it up,
dressed it up like somebody's doll.
Is life something you play?
And all the time wanting to get rid of it?
And further, everyone yelling at you
to shut up. And no wonder!
People don't like to be told
that you're sick
and then be forced
to watch

you
come
down with the hammer.

Today life opened inside me like an egg
and there inside
after considerable digging
I found the answer.
What a bargain!
There was the sun,
her yolk moving feverishly,
tumbling her prize—
and you realize that she does this daily!
I'd known she was a purifier
but I hadn't thought
she was solid,
hadn't known she was an answer.
God! It's a dream,
lovers sprouting in the yard
like celery stalks
and better,
a husband straight as a redwood,
two daughters, two sea urchins,
picking roses off my hackles.
If I'm on fire they dance around it
and cook marshmallows.
And if I'm ice
they simply skate on me
in little ballet costumes.

Here,
all along,
thinking I was a killer,
anointing myself daily
with my little poisons.
But no.
I'm an empress.
I wear an apron.
My typewriter writes.
It didn't break the way it warned.
Even crazy, I'm as nice
as a chocolate bar.
Even with the witches' gymnastics
they trust my incalculable city,
my corruptible bed.

O dearest three,
I make a soft reply.
The witch comes on
and you paint her pink.
I come with kisses in my hood
and the sun, the smart one,
rolling in my arms.

So I say *Live*
and turn my shadow three times round
to feed our puppies as they come,
the eight Dalmatians we didn't drown,
despite the warnings: The abort! The destroy!
Despite the pails of water that waited
to drown them, to pull them down like stones,
they came, each one headfirst,
blowing bubbles the color of cataract-blue
and fumbling for the tiny tits.
Just last week, eight Dalmatians,
¾ of a lb., lined up like cord wood
each
like a
birch tree.
I promise to love more if they come,
because in spite of cruelty
and the stuffed railroad cars for the ovens,
I am not what I expected. Not an Eichmann.
The poison just didn't take.
So I won't hang around in my hospital shift,
repeating The Black Mass and all of it.
I say *Live, Live* because of the sun,
the dream, the excitable gift.

Maya Angelou

from I Know Why the Caged Bird Sings

When I was three and Bailey four, we had arrived in the musty little town, wearing tags on our wrists which instructed—"To Whom It May Concern"—that we were Marguerite and Bailey Johnson Jr., from Long Beach, California, en route to Stamps, Arkansas, c/o Mrs. Annie Henderson.

Our parents had decided to put an end to their calamitous marriage, and Father shipped us home to his mother. A porter had been charged with our welfare—he got off the train the next day in Arizona—and our tickets were pinned to my brother's inside coat pocket.

I don't remember much of the trip, but after we reached the segregated southern part of the journey, things must have looked up. Negro passengers, who always traveled with loaded lunch boxes, felt sorry for "the poor little motherless darlings" and plied us with cold fried chicken and potato salad.

Years later I discovered that the United States had been crossed thousands of times by frightened Black children traveling alone to their newly affluent parents in Northern cities, or back to grandmothers in Southern towns when the urban North reneged on its economic promises.

The town reacted to us as its inhabitants had reacted to all things new before our coming. It regarded us a while without curiosity but with caution, and after we were seen to be harmless (and children) it closed in around us, as a real mother embraces a stranger's child. Warmly, but not too familiarly.

We lived with our grandmother and uncle in the rear of the Store (it was always spoken of with a capital s), which she had owned some twenty-five years.

Early in the century, Momma (we soon stopped calling her Grandmother) sold lunches to the sawmen in the lumberyard (east Stamps) and the seedmen at the cotton gin (west Stamps). Her crisp meat pies and cool lemonade, when joined to her miraculous ability to be in two places at the same time, assured her business success. From being a mobile lunch counter, she set up a stand between the two points of fiscal interest and supplied the workers' needs for a few years. Then she had the Store built in the heart of the Negro area. Over the years it became the lay center of activities in town. On Saturdays, barbers sat their customers in the shade on the porch of the Store, and troubadours on their ceaseless crawlings through the South leaned across its benches and sang their sad songs of The Brazos while they played juice harps and cigar-box guitars.

The formal name of the Store was the Wm. Johnson General Merchandise Store. Customers could find food staples, a good variety of colored thread, mash for hogs, corn for chickens, coal oil for lamps, light bulbs for the wealthy, shoestrings, hair dressing, balloons, and flower seeds. Anything not visible had only to be ordered.

Until we became familiar enough to belong to the Store and it to us, we were locked up in a Fun House of Things where the attendant had gone home for life.

Each year I watched the field across from the Store turn caterpillar green, then gradually frosty white. I knew exactly how long it would be before the big wagons would pull into the front yard and load on the cotton pickers at daybreak to carry them to the remains of slavery's plantations.

During the picking season my grandmother would get out of bed at four o'clock (she never used an alarm clock) and creak down to her knees and chant in a sleep-filled voice, "Our Father, thank you for letting me see this New Day. Thank you that you didn't allow the bed I lay on last night to be my cooling board, nor my blanket my winding sheet. Guide my feet this day along the straight and narrow, and help me to put a bridle on my tongue. Bless this house, and everybody in it. Thank you, in the name of your Son, Jesus Christ, Amen."

Before she had quite arisen, she called our names and issued orders, and pushed her large feet into homemade slippers and across the bare lye-washed wooden floor to light the coal-oil lamp.

The lamplight in the Store gave a soft make-believe feeling to our world which made me want to whisper and walk about on tiptoe. The odors of onions and oranges and kerosene had been mixing all night and wouldn't be disturbed until the wooded slat was removed from the door and the early morning air forced its way in with the bodies of people who had walked miles to reach the pickup place.

"Sister, I'll have two cans of sardines."

"I'm gonna work so fast today I'm gonna make you look like you standing still."

"Lemme have a hunk uh cheese and some sody crackers."

"Just gimme a coupla them fat peanut paddies." That would be from a picker who was taking his lunch. The greasy brown paper sack was stuck behind the bib of his overalls. He'd use the candy as a snack before the noon sun called the workers to rest.

In those tender mornings the Store was full of laughing, joking, boasting and bragging. One man was going to pick two hundred pounds of cotton, and another three hundred. Even the children were promising to bring home fo' bits and six bits.

The champion picker of the day before was the hero of the dawn. If he prophesied that the cotton in today's field was going to be sparse and stick to the bolls like glue, every listener would grunt a hearty agreement.

The sound of the empty cotton sacks dragging over the floor and the murmurs of waking people were sliced by the cash register as we rang up the five-cent sales.

If the morning sounds and smells were touched with the supernatural, the late afternoon had all the features of the normal Arkansas life. In the dying sunlight the people dragged, rather than their empty cotton sacks.

Brought back to the Store, the pickers would step out of the backs of trucks and fold down, dirt-disappointed, to the ground. No matter how much they had picked, it wasn't enough. Their wages wouldn't even get them out of debt to my grandmother, not to mention the staggering bill that waited on them at the white commissary downtown.

The sounds of the new morning had been replaced with grumbles about cheating houses, weighted scales, snakes, skimpy cotton and dusty rows. In later years I was to confront the stereotyped picture of gay song-singing cotton pickers with such inordinate rage that I was told even by fellow Blacks that my paranoia was embarrassing. But I had seen the fingers cut by the mean little cotton bolls, and I had witnessed the backs and shoulders and arms and legs resisting any further demands.

Some of the workers would leave their sacks at the Store to be picked up the following morning, but a few had to take them home for repairs. I winced to picture them sewing the coarse material under a coal-oil lamp with fingers stiffening from the day's work. In too few hours they would have to walk back to Sister Henderson's Store, get vittles and load, again, onto the trucks. Then they would face another day of trying to earn enough for the whole year with the heavy knowledge that they were going to end the season as they started it. Without the money or credit necessary to sustain a family for three months. In cotton-picking time the late afternoons revealed the harshness of Black Southern life, which in the early morning had been softened by nature's blessing of grogginess, forgetfulness and the soft lamplight.

. . .

But the need for change bulldozed a road down the center of my mind.

I had it. The answer came to me with the suddenness of a collision. I would go to work. Mother wouldn't be difficult to convince; after all, in school I was a year ahead of my grade and Mother was a firm believer in self-sufficiency. In fact, she'd be pleased to think that I had that much gumption, that much of her in my character. (She liked to speak of herself as the original "do-it-yourself girl.")

Once I had settled on getting a job, all that remained was to decide which kind of job I was most fitted for. My intellectual pride had kept me from selecting typing, shorthand or filing as subjects in school, so office work was ruled out. War plants and shipyards demanded birth certificates, and mine would reveal me to be fifteen, and ineligible for work. So the well-paying defense jobs were also out. Women had replaced men on the streetcars as conductors and motormen, and the thought of sailing up and down the hills of San Francisco in a dark-blue uniform, with a money changer at my belt, caught my fancy.

Mother was as easy as I had anticipated. The world was moving so fast, so much money was being made, so many people were dying in Guam, and Germany, that hordes of strangers became good friends overnight. Life was cheap and death entirely free. How could she have the time to think about my academic career?

To her question of what I planned to do, I replied that I would get a job on the streetcars. She rejected the proposal with: "They don't accept colored people on the streetcars."

I would like to claim an immediate fury which was followed by the noble determination to break the restricting tradition. But the truth is, my first reaction was one of disappointment. I'd pictured myself, dressed in a neat blue serge suit, my money changer swinging jauntily at my waist, and a cheery smile for the passengers which would make their own work day brighter.

From disappointment, I gradually ascended the emotional ladder to haughty indignation, and finally to that state of stubbornness where the mind is locked like the jaws of an enraged bulldog.

I would go to work on the streetcars and wear a blue serge suit. Mother gave me her support with one of her usual terse asides, "That's what you want to do? Then nothing beats a trial but a failure. Give it everything you've got. I've told you many times, 'Can't do is like Don't Care.' Neither of them have a home."

Translated, that meant there was nothing a person can't do, and there should be nothing a human being didn't care about. It was the most positive encouragement I could have hoped for.

In the offices of the Market Street Railway Company, the receptionist seemed as surprised to see me there as I was surprised to find the interior dingy and the décor drab. Somehow I had expected waxed surfaces and carpeted floors. If I had met no resistance, I might have decided against working for such a poor-mouth-looking concern. As it was, I explained that I had come to see about a job. She asked, was I sent by an agency, and when I replied that I was not, she told me they were only accepting applicants from agencies.

The classified pages of the morning papers had listed advertisements for motorettes and conductorettes and I reminded her of that. She gave me a face full of astonishment that my suspicious nature would not accept.

"I am applying for the job listed in this morning's *Chronicle* and I'd like to be presented to your personnel manager." While I spoke in supercilious accents, and looked at the room as if I had an oil well in my own backyard, my armpits were being pricked by millions of hot pointed needles. She saw her escape and dived into it.

"He's out. He's out for the day. You might call tomorrow and if he's in, I'm sure you can see him." Then she swiveled her chair around on its rusty screws and with that I was supposed to be dismissed.

"May I ask his name?"

She half turned, acting surprised to find me still there.

"His name? Whose name?"

"Your personnel manager."

We were firmly joined in the hypocrisy to play out the scene.

"The personnel manager? Oh, he's Mr. Cooper, but I'm not sure you'll find him here tomorrow. He's . . . Oh, but you can try."

"Thank you."

"You're welcome."

And I was out of the musty room and into the even mustier lobby. In the street I saw the receptionist and myself going faithfully through paces that were stale with familiarity, although I had never encountered that kind of situation before and, probably, neither had she. We were like actors who, knowing the play by heart, were still able to cry afresh over the old tragedies and laugh spontaneously at the comic situations.

The miserable little encounter had nothing to do with me, the me of me, any more than it had to do with that silly clerk. The incident was a recurring dream, concocted years before by stupid whites and it eternally came back to haunt us all. The secretary and I were like Hamlet and Laertes in the final scene, where, because of harm done by one ancestor to another, we were bound to duel to the death. Also because the play must end somewhere.

I went further than forgiving the clerk, I accepted her as a fellow victim of the same puppeteer.

On the streetcar, I put my fare into the box and the conductorette looked at me with the usual hard eyes of white contempt. "Move into the car, please move on in the car." She patted her money changer.

Her Southern nasal accent sliced my meditation and I looked deep into my thoughts. All lies, all comfortable lies. The receptionist was not innocent and neither was I. The whole charade we had played out in that crummy waiting room had directly to do with me, Black, and her, white.

I wouldn't move into the streetcar but stood on the ledge over the conductor, glaring. My mind shouted so energetically that the announcement made my veins stand out, and my mouth tighten into a prune.

I WOULD HAVE THE JOB. I WOULD BE A CONDUCTORETTE AND SLING A FULL MONEY CHANGER FROM MY BELT. I WOULD.

The next three weeks were a noneycomb of determination with apertures for the days to go in and out. The Negro organizations to whom

I appealed for support bounced me back and forth like a shuttlecock on a badminton court. Why did I insist on that particular job? Openings were going begging that paid nearly twice the money. The minor officials with whom I was able to win an audience thought me mad. Possibly I was.

Downtown San Francisco became alien and cold, and the streets I had loved in a personal familiarity were unknown lanes that twisted with malicious intent. Old buildings, whose gray rococo façades housed my memories of the Forty-Niners, and Diamond Lil, Robert Service, Sutter and Jack London, were then imposing structures viciously joined to keep me out. My trips to the streetcar office were of the frequency of a person on salary. The struggle expanded. I was no longer in conflict only with the Market Street Railway but with the marble lobby of the building which housed its offices, and elevators and their operators.

During this period of strain Mother and I began our first steps on the long path toward mutual adult admiration. She never asked for reports and I didn't offer any details. But every morning she made breakfast, gave me carfare and lunch money, as if I were going to work. She comprehended the perversity of life, that in the struggle lies the joy. That I was no glory seeker was obvious to her, and that I had to exhaust every possibility before giving in was also clear.

On my way out of the house one morning she said, "Life is going to give you just what you put in it. Put your whole heart in everything you do, and pray, then you can wait." Another time she reminded me that "God helps those who help themselves." She had a store of aphorisms which she dished out as the occasion demanded. Strangely, as bored as I was with clichés, her inflection gave them something new, and set me thinking for a little while at least. Later when asked how I got my job, I was never able to say exactly. I only knew that one day, which was tiresomely like all the others before it, I sat in the Railway office, ostensibly waiting to be interviewed. The receptionist called me to her desk and shuffled a bundle of papers to me. They were job application forms. She said they had to be filled in triplicate. I had little time to wonder if I had won or not, for the standard questions reminded me of the necessity for dexterous lying. How old was I? List my previous jobs, starting from the last held and go backward to the first. How much money did I earn, and why did I leave the position? Give two references (not relatives).

Sitting at a side table my mind and I wove a cat's ladder of near truths and total lies. I kept my face blank (an old art) and wrote quickly the fable of Marguerite Johnson, aged nineteen, former companion and driver for Mrs. Annie Henderson (a White Lady) in Stamps, Arkansas.

I was given blood tests, aptitude tests, physical coordination tests, and Rorschachs, then on a blissful day I was hired as the first Negro on the San Francisco streetcars.

Mother gave me the money to have my blue serge suit tailored, and I learned to fill out work cards, operate the money changer and punch transfers. The time crowded together and at an End of Days I was

swinging on the back of the rackety trolley, smiling sweetly and persuading my charges to "step forward in the car, please."

For one whole semester the streetcars and I shimmied up and scooted
down the sheer hills of San Francisco. I lost some of my need for the
Black ghetto's shielding-sponge quality, as I clanged and cleared my
way down Market Street, with its honky-tonk homes for homeless
sailors, past the quiet retreat of Golden Gate Park and along closed
undwelled-in-looking dwellings of the Sunset District.

My work shifts were split so haphazardly that it was easy to believe
that my superiors had chosen them maliciously. Upon mentioning my
suspicions to Mother, she said, "Don't worry about it. You ask for
what you want, and you pay for what you get. And I'm going to show
you that it ain't no trouble when you pack double."

She stayed awake to drive me out to the car barn at four thirty in the
mornings, or to pick me up when I was relieved just before dawn.
Her awareness of life's perils convinced her that while I would be safe
on the public conveyances, she "wasn't about to trust a taxi driver
with her baby."

When the spring classes began, I resumed my commitment with formal education. I was so much wiser and older, so much more independent, with a bank account and clothes that I had bought for myself,
that I was sure that I had learned and earned the magic formula which
would make me a part of the gay life my contemporaries led.

Not a bit of it. Within weeks, I realized that my schoolmates and I
were on paths moving diametrically away from each other. They were
concerned and excited over the approaching football games, but I had
in my immediate past raced a car down a dark and foreign Mexican
mountain. They concentrated great interest on who was worthy of
being student body president, and when the metal bands would be
removed from their teeth, while I remembered sleeping for a month in
a wrecked automobile and conducting a streetcar in the uneven hours
of the morning.

Without willing it, I had gone from being ignorant of being ignorant
to being aware of being aware. And the worst part of my awareness
was that I didn't know what I was aware of. I knew I knew very little,
but I was certain that the things I had yet to learn wouldn't be taught
to me at George Washington High School.

I began to cut classes, to walk in Golden Gate Park or wander along
the shiny counter of the Emporium Department Store. When Mother
discovered that I was playing truant, she told me that if I didn't want
to go to school one day, if there were no tests being held, and if my
school work was up to standard, all I had to do was tell her and I
could stay home. She said that she didn't want some white woman
calling her up to tell her something about her child that she didn't
know. And she didn't want to be put in the position of lying to a
white woman because I wasn't woman enough to speak. That put an
end to my truancy, but nothing appeared to lighten the long gloomy
day that going to school became.

To be left alone on the tightrope of youthful unknowing is to experience the excruciating beauty of full freedom and the threat of eternal
indecision. Few, if any, survive their teens. Most surrender to the
vague but murderous pressure of adult conformity. It becomes easier
to die and avoid conflicts than to maintain a constant battle with the
superior forces of maturity.

Until recently each generation found it more expedient to plead guilty
to the charge of being young and ignorant, easier to take the punishment meted out by the older generation (which had itself confessed to
the same crime short years before). The command to grow up at once
was more bearable than the faceless horror of wavering purpose,
which was youth.

The bright hours when the young rebelled against the descending sun
had to give way to twenty-four-hour periods called "days" that were
named as well as numbered.

The Black female is assaulted in her tender years by all those common
forces of nature at the same time that she is caught in the tripartite
crossfire of masculine prejudice, white illogical hate and Black lack
of power.

The fact that the adult American Negro female emerges a formidable
character is often met with amazement, distaste and even belligerence.
It is seldom accepted as an inevitable outcome of the struggle won
by survivors and deserves respect if not enthusiastic acceptance.

. . .

Later, my room had all the cheeriness of a dungeon and the appeal of
a tomb. It was going to be impossible to stay there, but leaving held
no attraction for me, either. Running away from home would be
anticlimactic after Mexico, and a dull story after my month in the
car lot.

Adrienne Rich

Living in Sin

She had thought the studio would keep itself;
no dust upon the furniture of love.
Half heresy, to wish the taps less vocal,
the panes relieved of grime. A plate of pears,
a piano with a Persian shawl, a cat
stalking the picturesque amusing mouse
had risen at his urging.
Not that at five each separate stair would writhe
under the milkman's tramp; that morning light
so coldly would delineate the scraps
of last night's cheese and three sepulchral bottles;
that on the kitchen shelf among the saucers
a pair of beetle-eyes would fix her own—
Envoy from some village in the moldings . . .
Meanwhile, he, with a yawn,
sounded a dozen notes upon the keyboard,
declared it out of tune, shrugged at the mirror,
rubbed at his beard, went out for cigarettes;
while she, jeered by the minor demons,
pulled back the sheets and made the bed and found
a towel to dust the table-top,
and let the coffee-pot boil over on the stove.
By evening she was back in love again,
though not so wholly but throughout the night
she woke sometimes to feel the daylight coming
like a relentless milkman up the stairs.

Two Songs

1.

Sex, as they harshly call it,
I fell into this morning
at ten o'clock, a drizzling hour
of traffic and wet newspapers.
I thought of him who yesterday
clearly didn't
turn me to a hot field
ready for plowing,
and longing for that young man
piercéd me to the roots

bathing every vein, etc.
All day he appears to me
touchingly desirable,
a prize one could wreck one's peace for.
I'd call it love if love
didn't take so many years
but lust too is a jewel
a sweet flower and what
pure happiness to know
all our high-toned questions
breed in a lively animal.

2.

That "old last act"!
And yet sometimes
all seems post coitum triste
and I a mere bystander.
Somebody else is going off,
getting shot to the moon.
Or, a moon-race!
Split seconds after
my opposite number lands
I make it—
we lie fainting together
at a crater-edge
heavy as mercury in our moonsuits
till he speaks—
in a different language
yet one I've picked up
through cultural exchanges . . .
we murmur the first moonwords:
Spasibo. Thanks. O.K.

Photographs of an Unmade Bed

Cruelty is rarely conscious
One slip of the tongue

one exposure
among so many

a thrust in the dark
to see if there's pain there

I never asked you to explain
that act of violence

what dazed me was our ignorance
of our will to hurt each other

≫   ≪

In a flash I understand
how poems are unlike photographs

(the one saying   *This could be*
the other   *This was*

The image
isn't responsible

for our uses of it
It is intentionless

A long strand of dark hair
in the washbasin

is innocent and yet
such things have done harm

-≫   ≪-

These snapshots taken by ghetto children
given for Christmas

Objects blurring into perceptions
No 'art,' only the faults

of the film, the faults of the time
Did mere indifference blister

these panes, eat these walls,
shrivel and scrub these trees—

mere indifference? I tell you
cruelty is rarely conscious

the done and the undone blur
into one photograph of failure

-≫   ≪-

This crust of bread we try to share
this name traced on a window

this word I paste together
like a child fumbling

with paste and scissors
this writing in the sky with smoke

this silence

this lettering chalked on the ruins
this alphabet of the dumb

this feather held to lips
that still breathe and are warm

Translations

You show me the poems of some woman
my age, or younger
translated from your language

Certain words occur: *enemy, oven, sorrow*
enough to let me know
she's a woman of my time

obsessed

with Love, our subject:
we've trained it like ivy to our walls
baked it like bread in our ovens
worn it like lead on our ankles
watched it through binoculars as if
it were a helicopter
bringing food to our famine
or the satellite
of a hostile power
I begin to see that woman
doing things: stirring rice
ironing a skirt
typing a manuscript till dawn

trying to make a call
from a phonebooth

The phone rings unanswered
in a man's bedroom
she hears him telling someone else
Never mind. She'll get tired—
hears him telling her story to her sister

who becomes her enemy
and will in her own time
light her own way to sorrow

ignorant of the fact this way of grief
is shared, unnecessary
and political

White Night

Light at a window. Someone up
at this snail-still hour.
We who work this way have often worked
in solitude. I've had to guess at her
sewing her skin together as I sew mine
though
with a different
stitch.

Dawn after dawn, this neighbor
burns like a candle
dragging her bedspread through the dark house
to her dark bed
her head
full of runes, syllables, refrains,
this accurate dreamer

sleepwalks the kitchen
like a white moth,
an elephant, a guilt.
Somebody tried to put her
to rest under an afghan
knitted with wools the color of grass and blood

but she has risen. Her lamplight
licks at the icy panes
and melts into the dawn.
They will never prevent her
who sleep the stone sleep of the past,
the sleep of the drugged.
One crystal second, I flash

an eye across the cold
unwrapping of light between us
into her darkness-lancing eye
—that's all. Dawn is the test, the agony
but we were meant to see it:
After this, we may sleep, my sister,
while the flames rise higher and higher, we can sleep.

Myrna Lamb

Apple Pie

Libretto by
Myrna Lamb

Music by
Nicholas Meyers

A NEW MUSICAL WORK

*New York Shakespeare
Festival Production*

Directed by
Joseph Papp

CHARACTERS

Lise
Mirror
Mother Marlene-the Prose-
  cutor-the Chanteuse
Father Heinrich-Harry
Marshall
Judge
Jury-Soldiers-Bosses-
  Marching Men-Electorate
Doctor
Groom

Child Lise

A black man

Four men

PROLOGUE

The opera takes place on a bare, raked stage. Hanging ropes, like prison bars, form a curtain cutting off the last six feet of upstage area. The upstage wall may be a giant screen upon which may be seen enormous blowups of the main Characters' faces (distorted with superimposed colors and images). Lighting should be surreal in effect.

The band plays "Yesterday Is Over" as an overture. The lights dim and go to black. All performers come on stage in the black.

Four Men who constitute a Jury (since these are trial proceedings) stand behind the ropes. They are dressed in mock military fashion, emphasizing the sexual aspects of such garb as well as the ominous nature of the dull metal helmets and Lugers and the highly polished boots.

Mother Marlene *is also the* Prosecutor. *She is tall, blonde, and perfect, dressed perhaps in a smart, khaki-colored, thirties suit. (She will be referred to, throughout, as* Mother.) *She stands initially, at stage right with* Father Heinrich, *who will metamorphose, in the opera, to* Harry. Father *wears a German World War I officer's dress uniform, complete with a multiplicity of medals and a spiked helmet.*

Marshall, *who is a* Black *man, is dressed at first in a German Army trenchcoat and a German World War II helmet.*

There is a spotlight on Lise. *She is not perfect, but* She *is wearing a thirties suit similar to her* Mother's.

Lise *is on trial. All the* Characters *in this trial are her invention. They are* Characters *from her past, as* She *remembers* Them.

Lise (*As* She *says the word "invention" in her first speech, pools of light pinpoint each* Character.)
Sometimes we lose
The line between our own invention
And what is true
Because we have made things true
So often
Or seen through so much
That it all becomes
Monstrous
The original wish becomes
A nightmare
Our invention
Superimposed
Upon a reluctant life
We want to be God
We *will* our truths
Which turn around and devour us
For our daring
Not turpitude
Not aptitude
But presumption!

Blackout

ACT I
SCENE 1   The Trial

When the lights come up, a small, masked Judge *is seen in black robe and fright wig. He stands behind ropes.*

The Jury *stands in formation, awaiting the* Prosecutor, *who is, of course,* Mother. She *struts to stage center, where* She *wheels smartly and clicks her heels.*

Mother
Attention!

(Jury *snaps to attention.*)

Mother (continuing)
Gentlemen of the Jury . . . I give you that unsung pretendant . . .

(Jury *laughs.*)

Mother (continuing)
That ignoble ascendant . . .

(Jury *laughs a bit more.*)

Mother (continuing)
That passionate offendant . . .

(Jury *laughs louder.*)

Mother (continuing)
That upward-mobile descendant . . .

Mother
In short . . . the defendant! Lise!

(*Music up. Spotlight on* Lise *and her* Mirror. *The Mirror is dressed as an idealized* Child Lise *in dimly white camisole and tutu, with long, fair hair and a doomed, innocent little face.*)

Lise and the Mirror (under Mirror theme)
When I look into the Mirror . . . I see my face . . . and Mother's and Father's faces behind me, looking at me. We look at each other in the Mirror. The Mirror, Mother says, is Venetian Crystallo glass from the sixteenth century. I am forbidden to touch it. Its image is very pure.

Lise (sings, with resigned self-mockery)
I'm Lise
Little Lise from Nuremberg
La—la-la-la-la-la . . . *La*-la!

All I did is I was born in Nuremberg
La—la-la-la-la-la . . . *La*-la!

So evil is what I was
Defined by a tiny little flaw
In Hero-Father's blood
Decreed by a Nuremberger law

So you see
My history
Was impure
They decided it

They decided all
I could ever be
Was a "very hot number"

I'm Lise
Little Lise from Nuremberg
La—la-la-la-la-la . . . *La*-la!

Jury (in rhythmic anger)

Hundsvieh!	(dogbeast)
Scheusliche Kuh!	(sloppy cow)
Schau Sie an!	(look at her)
Dreckiges Hundsvieh!	(dirty dogbeast)
Scheusliche Kuh!	(sloppy cow)
Schau Sie an!	(look at her)
Bewege dich!	(move it)
Komm schon!	(come on)
Dummes Ass!	(dumb ass)
Bewege dich!	(move it)
Komm schon!	(come on)
Dummes Ass!	(dumb ass)

Lise (Speaking rhythmically-sexily, She *removes her dress during the following, revealing sleazy, garish underdress.*)

Sometimes we lose
The line between our own invention
And what is true
Because we make things true
So often that
It all becomes a superimposition
Upon a small reluctant life
Creating gods
Of pure insinuation who devour us
For our daring
Not turpitude
Not aptitude
But presumption

Jury
Now come on Baby
Gonna give ya a clue
We're gonna tell ya right now
Just what ya gonna do

You'll move for us
You'll open up for us
You'll wriggle like a fish
On a hook for us

You'll take us on
You'll take us in
We're all creepin' under
That soft white skin

'Cause under that sweet clean hide
You're nothin' but a bitch
A bitch, a bitch

And when you open up wide
To swallow us
We'll just show you a
Low-down lie

(*Although* Lise *plays the role of slave at the* Jury's *command,* She
plays it with a defiance that indicates She *clearly feels* She *can control
the fantasy if* She *chooses to do so.*)

Lise	*Jury*
I'm Lise	You know you want a lotta
Little Lise from Nuremberg	Lotta lotta what we
La—la-la-la-la-la . . .	Know you need a lotta
La-la!	La di da
	You know you want a lotta
	Just exactly what we gotta lotta
All I did is	Give us what you gotta lotta
I was born in Nuremberg	'Cause we know you're hot
	And you know

Jury
We don't want to hear it Baby
Up against the wall

Lise
Oh please
Why can't you understand me

Jury
Come on back to Joyland Baby
Come on now

Lise
Why don't you see
My side?

Jury
We don't want to see it

Lise
Please

Jury
Won't try identifyin'
We know what you are

Lise
So evil is what I was
Defined by a tiny little flaw

Lise	*Jury*
In father's blood	We don't want to hear it Baby
Although my mother dear	Up against the wall
Was the pure one	Come on back to Joyland Baby
But you see	Come
When Hitler came I was impure	On now
And a profiteer and a Com-	We don't want to see it
munist	
And a Christ-killer	Won't try identifyin'
Blood-drinker	We know what you are
Also a very hot number	

A steaming cauldron of witches'
brew
Just as hot and bubbling
As you

*Jury (The next reply gets louder and louder with an insistent drum-
beat that continues after the* Jury *and other instruments end on the
final "Too much!!")*

Why should we care
We are here
You're over there
Scared to leave
Or lovin' it

Scared to leave
Or lovin' it
Scared to leave
Or lovin' it

Too much
Too much
Too much
Too much
Too much
Too much
Too much
Too much
Too much
Too much
TOO MUCH!!

(*The insistent, continuing drumbeat achieves a heartbeat sound and quality, becoming louder and louder. Lights become predominantly red and slides show blood on face or faces. A* Jury Member, Marshall, *and the* Father *confront each other. The* Father *points his gun at the* Jury, *then at the* Mother, *then at* Marshall, *who aims his Luger in response. They both then aim their guns at* Lise, *and* She *screams a long, agonized scream.* Blackout)

SCENE 2   Witnesses and Waltz of Lise's Childhood

The little Judge *raps his gavel. The lights come up on the* Jury *in place, the* Mother *as* Prosecutor *downstage, and* Lise *upstage behind the rope bars.*

First Juror
She's lazy!

Second Juror
She's sensual!

Third Juror
She's sleazy!

Fourth Juror
She's pushy!

First Juror
She's loud!

Second Juror
She's dangerous!

Third Juror
She's evil!

Fourth Juror
She's dirty!

Jury Ensemble
Real dirty!

Lise (stepping from behind ropes; defiantly)
Am I?

Mother
It's possible, yes. And it is also possible, I only suggest this, mind you . . . that she is guilty . . . . of *Murder*.

Lise (to Mother)
Am I?

Jury Ensemble
Look at her!

First Juror (He will play Streicher in this scene.)
And here we have the imperfect face. Note the head shape, nose shape, cheek bones, eyelids, hairline, chin line, *skin tone. Do not neglect the distance between the eyes!*

Lise
I'm Lise.

First Juror
Look at her.

Second Juror
What she is . . .

Third Juror
We wouldn't choose that . . .

Fourth Juror
Nor would she . . .

First Juror
If she had a choice.

(Marshall enters on last lines.)

Marshall
She would say she *had* no choice.

Lise
I was born . . .

Marshall
Her first crime.

Lise
A crime of passion. I had no choice.

Marshall
Passion was always her excuse.

(Marshall exits.)

Mother
Passion is no excuse!

Father/Harry
Madame Prosecutor. Gentlemen. I beg to differ. Passion may be a poor excuse . . . but you will admit . . . an extenuating factor? After all, I did believe passionately in the Fatherland.

Mother
OBJECTION!

Father/Harry
So passionately that I ignored the small, troublesome question pertaining to my family background . . .

Mother
IRRELEVANT!

Father/Harry
The question of tainted blood . . .

Mother
IMMATERIAL!

Father/Harry
A question that arose after two centuries . . .

Mother
NOT ADMISSIBLE!

Father/Harry
As her father, I was branded a criminal. Although the crime *was* in question.

Lise
Was passion my crime?

Mother
Yes. That. *And what happened to your father?*

Harry/Father
Which reminds me of this guy . . . a luncheonette operator. He's on the job at six A.M., like always. And these two guys come in and they say . . . "Hey! You got Apple Pie?"

Jury Ensemble
Ha. Ha. Ha.

Harry/Father
And he says . . . "I got no Apple Pie. How about Danish?" . . . So they shot him.

(Gunshot)

Jury Ensemble (The gunshots are theirs.)
Ha. Ha. Ha.

Mother
Guilty of murder!

("Waltz of Lise's Childhood" begins.)

Lise (sings)
I'm Lise
Little Lise from Nuremberg
La—la-la-la-la-la . . . La-la

(As the Waltz theme is introduced, the Jury *forms upstage behind ropes with the* Juror *playing* Streicher *at head of formation.)*

Lise *(sings)*
A child
Living in the fatherland
We are rich
Father is a hero

Photographs
In his uniform
Medals in a frame
On the wall
But most of all
I see the word
Verboten

My Nuremberger home is full of
Things I can never touch

Father/Harry *(takes center stage)*
I had to uphold the honor of the family.

Father/Harry *(sings)*
With riding crop in hand
I go to pay a call
On worthy Streicher
On my chest the Iron Cross
It seems they still respect such things

(Father walks upstage to Jury *and strikes* Streicher *across the face with a riding crop.)*

Father/Harry *(continues to sing)*
I stride into the place
As he has printed filth
All about my family
I
Without a word spoken
Slash
His
Cheek
Through

They seize all the chosen men
Within the hour
Except for me
You see the victim pleasantly confirms
Oppressor's power
By cowering

(Jury walks downstage toward Father, *who continues to sing, oblivious to its approach.* Jury *stalks* Him, *menacingly.)*

Father/Harry
When I confronted them
It made them doubt their power
And roused their wonder and fear

Because I was a strong man
With Iron Cross
And riding crop
And pride!

(Over next music section, crashes and gunshots are heard. The Jury *strips* Father *of medals, helmet, etc. at gunpoint.* Jury *beats* Him *and shoves* Him *offstage.)*

Lise *(sings)*
Men come with guns
Their evil excites me
Things I never touch
They tear apart with their knives

Smash all the sculpture
Except the Madonna
They break all the glass
Then I turn around

(A Jury Member, *as a* Soldier (Brown Shirt), *approaches* Lise *threateningly.)*

A brown shirt
Frowning
I start to cry. . . .

. . . . (I) begin by crying
I begin by crying
Pretty little Lise
Why does she keep on cry-ing?

Lise *(speaks)*
I tried it
It doesn't work
A pretty girl crying
It doesn't work
But this works
This they believe

(Mother *fakes loud orgasmic cries. The* Jury, *as* Soldiers, *surround* Mother. Lise's Brown Shirt *leaves* Lise *and is drawn to* Mother. Lise *watches as* Mother *smiles dazzlingly at the* Soldiers *and falls back in their arms.)*

Lise *(speaks over music)*
These were
The hoodlums
They had blunt pistols
And short brutal knives
They cut into the paintings on the walls
And from them I
Learned my
Lessons

(Lise *dances with the* Mirror *in a child's mad denial of catastrophe.)*

Lise (sings)
Yesterday we were rich
And today we are poor
Yesterday we were rich
And today we are poor

(As the music ends, Mother *gets to her feet, and adjusts her clothing and smooths her coiffure.* Jury *marches upstage and stands at attention.)*

In Scene 3, Marshall, *who is black, introduces himself. In the Next Witness: Marshall,* He *sardonically presents his concept of the conventional role* He *is expected to play in this trial as* He *has in* Lise's *life. (*He *addresses the* Jury *as "Menschen," a German locution.)*

Lise's Mother *takes the witness stand in Scene 4. In the "Prosecutor's March," accompanied by* Marching Men *(the* Jury*),* She *describes the family's flight from Germany to America (after her husband has been ransomed from a prison camp).* Lise's Father *is shot dead (as* He *works as a counterman in a small luncheonette) and the* Mother *attempts to exert stricter control over her daughter's life, since* Lise *has met* Marshall *and has initiated a friendship with* Him *("The Stockboy's Blues").*

In the "Your Face Motet" (music insert), the Mother *is joined by two* Members of the Jury, *who castigate* Lise *for her sensual appearance and behavior.* Lise *runs away from their disapproval and finds* Harry. He *seems familiar. (In fact,* Harry *is played by the same actor who plays the* Father.*)*

MOTET from APPLE PIE

Words by Myrna Lamb, Music by Nicholas Meyers

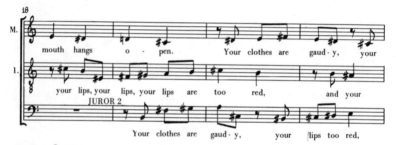

lips are red, —— mouth o - pen. Your clothes are

mouth, your— mouth hangs o - pen. Your clothes are

2. your mouth hangs o - pen. Your clothes are

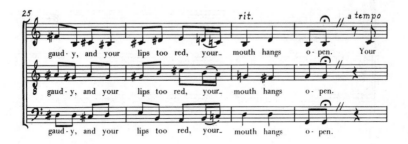

rit.   *a tempo*

gaud - y, and your lips too red, your— mouth hangs o - pen. Your

gaud - y, and your lips too red, your— mouth hangs o - pen.

gaud - y, and your lips too red, your— mouth hangs o - pen.

face, your face, too much some - how. Your peas - ant

Your face, your

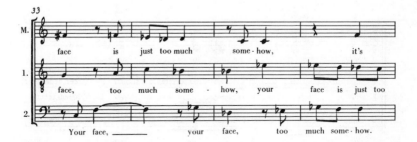

M.   face is just too much some - how, it's

1.   face, too much some - how, your face is just too

2.   Your face, —— your face, too much some - how.

just too much some - how. Pa - tri - cian fac - es

much some - how, your peas - ant face, your face. ——

Your peas - ant face, too much, your face. ——

Spotlight upstage reveals **Harry,** *stepping from behind ropes.* He *wears a stylized version of a forties business suit.* He *carries a straw hat and a sample case.* Lise *is downstage, watching* Him.

Harry
Your Honor? Gentlemen of the Jury. My name is Harry. I'm Harry in Lise's trial. Well, what can I say? Lise wanted me to be important, a captain of industry, a banker, a politician. Actually, I'm an intellectual. Books. I read and think about writing books. Between books, I'm a salesman. Salesman. Backbone of the American economy, you know. *(Pause)* And you may also know to what and where the backbone leads. *(Pause)* My feet hurt, too. They just march from closed door to closed door. But I never blamed Lise for that.

Lise (sings)
What do I feel about
This so disturbing kind of man
His image brings to mind
People who died in the prison camp

I don't cry now
What use is it
Did I see it
Did I dream it
Did I

They look alike
Seen through barbed wire
Like little old men

Like sad old men
Without complaint
Their ears so huge
Noses prominent
On their small silent heads

Lise (speaks over music)
But it doesn't have to be that way
He might be a different kind of man
Charming, intelligent, creative
Someone with great promise
Even my mother might approve

(Mother *enters on this last thought.*)

Mother (to audience)
Why did she think I would approve? Her choice was predictable. And regrettable.

(Mother *exits.*)

Lise *and* Harry *present a vaudeville version of their meeting and the subsequent problems of their relationship in the "Mating Dance."* Lise *turns from* Harry *to* Marshall. *In the "Love Theme," Lise and Marshall (both older now) make an attempt to love and trust one another. They are momentarily happy. Lise, pregnant with Marshall's child, has a grotesque experience when a Doctor demands her sexual submission as a price for his illegal services in Witness: The Doctor.*

Horrified by Lise's behavior, the Mother intercedes. In Witness: The Right Man, Lise is offered a "suitable wedding prospect," but the Groom walks out. Marshall returns to find Lise in her wedding gown, and furious at her betrayal, He threatens to kill Lise. Lise taunts Him, translating the gun in his hands into sexual image as She invites him to "kill" Her (Gun Scene).

Lise subsequently marries Harry, who is less than "suitable," but a most compelling figure in Lise's life.

SCENE 13   Witness: Harry and Harry's Rag

The lights go up on Harry, *who twirls a cane and prepares to present His side of the situation.*

Harry
Your Honor. Gentlemen of the Jury. I could have had any job I wanted. I just didn't want *any* job. When Lise and I were married, and she seemed unhappy, I thought it was the job I had. Kept me on the road. And I thought it wasn't such a good idea, being on the road and leaving her home, alone . . . and unhappy.

(Music starts.)

Harry (sings)
My name is Harry Joseph
I preserve the status quo
I do believe it can prevail

My right to try and fail

I speak the lingo gracefully
It comes like rain to my dry tongue
Approached the top
Just as I say
A few shop terms along the way

But out of town
Was where I failed
The road was closed for me

Harry (speaks)
The constant traveling became an impediment to marital felicity.

(Two prosperous-looking Gentlemen of the Jury *dance on as* Bosses.)

First Boss (sings)
What's with this guy
Can't he trust his wife?

Second Boss (sings)
He always comes back a few days early

First Boss (sings)
Checkin' up
We'll give him a hand

Second Boss (sings)
You mean cut out the travel?

First Boss (sings)
I mean cut out the need
The job
In short

Second Boss
Indeed!

First Boss (sings)
Is yours!

Second Boss (sings)
Is mine?

First Boss (sings)
Is yours
By the way

Second Boss (sings)
What you say?

First Boss (sings)
I hope you trust your wife

Second Boss (sings)
I trust my wife

First Boss (sings)
But Oh you kid!

Second Boss (speaks)
So fire the bum!

First Boss (speaks)
I already did!

Harry (sings)
I did my work and did it well
What hell to drop your job this way
They gave me six months severance pay

But I kept losing my résumé

(Bosses Three *and* Four *have now joined the first* Two.)

Bosses Ensemble (Sing)
It seemed the sum of his whole life
Was one lump sum
So fresh
So green
So he ate it up
Like lettuce vinegar and oil

This verdant crop
This spoil supreme

(Bosses *dance*.)

Boss One
But like a dream it faded

Boss Two
All the green grew jaded

Harry (speaks)
I was broke.

Bosses One and Two (speak)
Look for another job!

Boss Three (sings)
It's not exactly you're not young enough

Boss Four (sings)
Forty's tough

(The rest of the scene is completely sung.)

Boss Three
Boy
Even though we know you've
Got the stuff

Boss Four
But in business it's our policy

Boss Three
Invest

Boss Four
In the best

Bosses Three and Four
Screw the rest!

Boss Three
Not that you're old, my boy
It's just a passing stage . . .

Boss Four
Turning page . . .

Boss Three
Awkward age . . .

Boss Four
Between your up-and-coming . . .

Boss Three
And your golden years

Boss Four
Calm your fears

Harry
It kind of twists your guts up
Deep inside
If truth be told
To hear you're overqualified
Too old
Too good
And just too old
I hope you guys don't mind
I have to plead
I'm here to try
To fill your need
Revamp
Retrench
Retrain
Or die

Bosses Ensemble
Mister Harry Joseph
We would like to spare you pain

Bosses Two and Four
Our training program's really up to date

Bosses One and Three
Minorities
Some women

Bosses Two and Four
And the youngest vets

Bosses Ensemble
Let's face it, Harry
You're too late

Bosses One and Three
However if you don't mind just stepping
Down a peg

Bosses Two and Four
There's a place . . .

Bosses One and Three
At the bottom . . .

Bosses Two and Four
Not much pay

Bosses One and Three
If that's the pace you want

Bosses Two and Four
It's saving face you want

Bosses One and Three
Well then, it's done . . .

Bosses Two and Four
It's decided and . . .

Bosses Ensemble
You'll be okay!

Harry
I'm taking what you offer me
It's all I want
So all you had to do was ask
I'm glad to take the lesser task
To satisfy
You want the truth
I swear it's true
Now would I lie to you?

Well anyway
That's how it is
I try . . . .
And fail

(The Bosses *dance off, drawing out revolvers as* They *go.* They *shoot* Harry. *He freezes.)*

Harry's persistent failure drives Lise *to look for* Marshall *once more.* Marshall *has gone into politics, and* Lise *helps him with his career. In the "Freedom Anthem," they mouth all the platitudes of a political campaign, while the* Electorate *(or* Jury) *sings and waves banners.*

Harry trails Lise *and* Marshall *as they dance at a political rally. The* Mother *sings "Yesterday Is Over" in her new role as* Chanteuse. *There is a confrontation among* Lise, Marshall, *and* Harry. Harry *hasn't a chance.* Lise *believes that now* Marshall *has become "suitable" and she has earned a "successful life" with him.* Marshall *replies.*

SCENE 18 Witness: Marshall's reply

Mother (speaks)
There is no way of avoiding it. It will be just as I have said.

Lise (speaks)
Here I am, Marshall. We can have anything we want now.

Marshall (speaks over music)
Oh yeah
It's in
It's hip
The new *thing*
A handsome black man on a nice high platform too
No denyin' it
Ol' Marshall is *pretty* up there
But the point is Baby
He won't go there with *you*

Marshall (sings)
Settle down now Honey
Get it straight

We're gonna get it down now Honey
Honey you were up there big as life
You always had a hustle goin' for ya'
Sellin' that rancid brand of Apple Pie
That rancid brand goes back to the store
No greasy upper crust
No poison green dream apples
No more

You had no right
To come into my life with your sickness
Into my life
In your guise of a pure little victim

Gotta tell you that I'm full of hate
You see this hate is cold now, Baby
And it fills my guts up so you're through
There's nothin' here—there's nothin' workin' for ya'
So shove that rancid brand of Apple Pie
'Cause both of you go back to the store
No greasy upper crust
No poison green dream apples
No more

You had no right
To come into my life with your sickness
Into my life
In your guise of a pure little victim
You've done it right
I've become what you wanted to make me
I've done all right
I've done all right
I've done all right
Right!

Marshall (speaks)
So grind away, Bitch in heat
This black cat abdicates
I will not be your hamburger meat
You and me, we will settle up an old score
I'm proclaiming your Apple Pie goes back to the store
'Cause I don't buy that any more
Under that efficient coat of paint
You display the taint of voracious bitch appetite
Devouring men in your lust for their power over you

So you're the wrong shade Baby
And that ain't all
But it's enough

(He *exits.*)

SCENE 19   Survival Songs

This scene is entirely sung with an echo effect on music and words. The echo is the past. Lights dim. Jury *and* Mother *appear.* They *are carrying* Harry's *prison suit and cap.*

Lise	Jury and Mother
	Ich lieb das marshieren
I know	Ich bin da nicht allein
There's no way	Ich kann mich verlierne
Of changing things	Zerbrechen das verdammte Schwein
In the bound'ries	Ich heil das schonen Vaterland
Of my mind	Land voll Gnaden
It's by men	Weil dies Land hat mich geboren
That we're defined	Mich und die Kameraden
	Ich lieb das marshieren
	Ich bin da night allein
I live inside a prison	Ich kann mich verlieren
The prison guard	Zerbrechen das
My mother	Verdammte Schwein
She doesn't own	Ich heil
The prison	Das schonen Vaterland
But she upholds	Land voll
All its rulings	Gnaden
No self-indulgence	Weil dies Land hat mich geboren
No self-defeat for her	Mich und die
Right is Might!	Right is Might!

(While Mother *sings reprise of scene 10,* She *clothes* Lise *in prison camp garb and hands* Lise *a Luger.)*

Mother
Lise dear
I meant to tell you
How well you look
How bright you are

You can make
A great success
I guarantee
You'll go far

A little something
With the hair
A little something
With the teeth
A little something
With the nose
Achieving beauty
You'll be reaching
Perfection

Lise dear
You must refuse
Sensuality
Defer to me

You must work
To consecrate your very life
To the search for
The *Right Man*

(Jury *and* Mother *exit.*)

Lise (Lise *is in her prison dress and cap, and* Her *face is made up to
look maddened with pain and destruction.* Her *skin is chalk white,
dead looking, with great black circles under the eyes.* She *should
look frightening, as though* She *has returned from horror and death.*)
We survive
Remember
By our wits
By our ability
To suffer grief and degradation
We're basically not human
Don't you see
Subhuman
They say
But just not human
We survive
The constant threat of death
The sight of mothers
And of sisters killed in front of us
It shakes us
Don't you see
But later on we handle
All the bodies
In a familiar way
For they are family

We know the hiding places
In the hair of the head
Other places
I'm too delicate to mention
A few gold fillings in the teeth
Overlooked
Some good gold rings
A diamond or two
Several banks
A few magnificent Cartels
Some Protocols
From a really strong Zion trend
Today the Camp
Tomorrow the World
The World
Tomorrow
The World

(Marshall, Harry, Mother, *and* Jury *appear. Drumbeat in music be-*
comes heartbeat, also an echo from the past. The heartbeat becomes
louder and louder and faster and faster. All look at Lise. *There is a*
long, threatening moment. Then Lise *hands the gun to* Harry, *who is*
wearing the World War I officer's dress uniform of Lise's Father. Harry
points gun at Marshall, *at* Mother, *at* Jury, *then at* Lise.)

Lise
What are you doing?
WHAT ARE YOU DOING?

Harry (removes his spiked helmet)
... Which reminds me of this guy ...

(Harry *shoots himself. There is a red stain across the slide of his face*
on projection screen.)

Mother
It was inevitable.

Lise, Mother, and Jury (sing)
He survives

Lise
You tell me
By his wits
By his ability
To overcome his imperfections
If Harry's not surviving

Lise, Mother, and Jury
Who's to blame

Lise
Can I be
Can I
Am I your

Lise, Mother, and Jury
Villain
He survives

Lise
You tell me

Lise, Mother, and Jury
And succeeds

Lise
Although you know the world he values

Lise, Mother, and Jury
Turns away from him

Lise
But tell me who's to blame
Are you the ones who violate his courage
And soil his very name

Lise, Mother, and Jury
And so are you to blame?

What difference does it make when fables
Conquer the truth
Lies can choke us
But the truth is worse to swallow
You see I don't want to be here
On the side that will lose
I want to win
I want to survive

Lise (alone)
Someone is at fault
The victim has himself to blame
I must become myself the one who's
Strong and alive
I must survive
Above all

Lise, Mother and Jury
Survive
Survive
Above all
Survive

Lise (spoken alone)
I will survive!

The trial breaks into an orgy of degradation, despite Lise's *cry of survival. In the Final Judgment,* Lise *is tied and spread-eagled by the vengeful* Jury. *All of the* Characters *of her remembered past tell* Lise *that* She *is not "fit to live."*

(Music reaches a crescendo. Then there is silence.)

Mother
Gentlemen of the Jury, have we reached a verdict?

First Juror
Guilty!

Second Juror
Guilty!

Third Juror
Guilty!

Fourth Juror
Guilty!

Marshall
Guilty!

Harry
Guilty!

(A little, masked Judge *steps from behind the ropes. There is a long drum roll. The* Judge's *hands and arms emerge from beneath the black robe. The* Judge *is holding a gun.* Lise, *whose arms are stretched above her head since her wrists are still manacled on suspended ropes, is turned to face the audience and held by the* Jury. *The* Judge, *upstage of and behind* Lise *on the rake, slowly raises the gun to point it directly upward and then slowly lowers the gun to aim it directly at the back of* Lise's *head. A slide on the projection screen shows* Lise's *face. There is a gunshot. The manacled* Lise *slumps. The slide shows a bloodstain across the face. The music becomes a wild distorted version of* Lise's *Childhood Waltz, as the* Judge *dances with the* Jury *and the* Mother. *The* Judge *turns for a moment in the dance, and when he turns again toward the audience, he has removed his robe, wig, and mask to reveal himself as the* Mirror. *There is a pause. Then the band begins "Yesterday Is Over." The* Mother, Jury, Marshall, Harry, *and the* Mirror *sing "Yesterday Is Over" and slowly walk upstage to exit behind the projection screen.)*

Mother, Jury, Harry, Marshall, Mirror
Yesterday is over
And now there's just today
Yesterday is over
Our dreams are far away

When we were young
We could dance to romance
In time unending
A time depending
On a love from above
A turtledove

Yesterdays are over
They never come again
The future tense
Running hence
Had a sense of old
"We-knew-them-when"

(Music and voices fade. Band begins Lise's *theme.* Lise's *"body" moves in a macabre gallows dance. We see the* Mirror *mask on her face. She sings one last little echoing line.)*

Lise
I'm Lise
Little Lise of Nuremberg. . . . La—La-la-la-la-la *La-la*

*(*Lise *is abruptly still. One last sting from the band. Silence.)*

The End

Adrienne Kennedy

Funnyhouse of a Negro   A PLAY IN ONE ACT

CHARACTERS

Negro-Sarah	
Duchess of Hapsburg	*One of herselves*
Queen Victoria Regina	*One of herselves*
Jesus	*One of herselves*
Patrice Lumumba	*One of herselves*
Sarah's Landlady	*Funnyhouse Lady*
Raymond	*Funnyhouse Man*
The Mother	

Author's Note

Funnyhouse of a Negro is perhaps clearest and most explicit when the
play is placed in the girl Sarah's room. The center of the stage works well
as her room, allowing the rest of the stage as the place for herselves. Her
room should have a bed, a writing table and a mirror. Near her bed
is the statue of Queen Victoria; other objects might be her photographs
and her books. When she is placed in her room with her belongings, then
the director is free to let the rest of the play happen around her.

BEGINNING

Before the closed Curtain a Woman *dressed in a white nightgown
walks across the Stage carrying before her a bald head. She moves as
one in a trance and is mumbling something inaudible to herself. Her
hair is wild, straight and black and falls to her waist. As she moves,
she gives the effect of one in a dream. She crosses the Stage from
Right to Left. Before she has barely vanished, the* CURTAIN *opens. It is
a white satin Curtain of a cheap material and a ghastly white, a material that brings to mind the interior of a cheap casket, parts of it are
frayed and look as if it has been gnawed by rats.*

THE SCENE

Two Women *are sitting in what appears to be a Queen's chamber. It
is set in the middle of the Stage in a strong white* LIGHT, *while the rest
of the Stage is in unnatural* BLACKNESS. *The quality of the white light
is unreal and ugly. The Queen's chamber consists of a dark monu-
mental bed resembling an ebony tomb, a low, dark chandelier with
candles, and wine-colored walls. Flying about are great black* RAVENS.
Queen Victoria *is standing before her bed holding a small mirror in
her hand. On the white pillow of her bed is a dark, indistinguishable
object. The Duchess of Hapsburg is standing at the foot of the bed.
Her back is to us as is the* Queen's. *Throughout the entire scene, they
do not move. Both Women are dressed in royal gowns of white, a
white similar to the white of the Curtain, the material cheap satin.
Their headpieces are white and of a net that falls over their faces.
From beneath both their headpieces springs a headful of wild kinky*

hair. *Although in this scene we do not see their faces, I will describe them now. They look exactly alike and will wear masks or be made up to appear a whitish yellow. It is an alabaster face, the skin drawn tightly over the high cheekbones, great dark eyes that seem gouged out of the head, a high forehead, a full red mouth and a head of frizzy hair. If the characters do not wear a mask then the face must be highly powdered and possess a hard expressionless quality and a stillness as in the face of death. We hear* KNOCKING.

Victoria. (*Listening to the knocking.*) It is my father. He is arriving again for the night. (*The* Duchess *makes no reply.*) He comes through the jungle to find me. He never tires of his journey.

Duchess. How dare he enter the castle, he who is the darkest of them all, the darkest one? My mother looked like a white woman, hair as straight as any white woman's. And at least I am yellow, but he is black, the blackest one of them all. I hoped he was dead. Yet he still comes through the jungle to find me.

(*The* KNOCKING *is louder.*)

Victoria. He never tires of the journey, does he, Duchess? (*Looking at herself in the mirror.*)

Duchess. How dare he enter the castle of Queen Victoria Regina, Monarch of England? It is because of him that my mother died. The wild black beast put his hands on her. She died.

Victoria. Why does he keep returning? He keeps returning forever, coming back ever and keeps coming back forever. He is my father.

Duchess. He is a black Negro.

Victoria. He is my father. I am tied to the black Negro. He came when I was a child in the south, before I was born he haunted my conception, diseased my birth.

Duchess. Killed my mother.

Victoria. My mother was the light. She was the lightest one. She looked like a white woman.

Duchess. We are tied to him unless, of course, he should die.

Victoria. But he is dead.

Duchess. And he keeps returning.

(*The* KNOCKING *is louder;* BLACKOUT. *The* LIGHTS *go out in the Chamber. Onto the Stage from the Left comes the* Figure *in the white nightgown carrying the bald head. This time we hear her speak.*)

Mother. Black man, black man, I never should have let a black man put his hands on me. The wild black beast raped me and now my skull is shining. (*She disappears to the Right.*)

(*Now the* LIGHT *is focused on a single white square wall that is to the Left of the Stage, that is suspended and stands alone, of about five feet in dimension and width. It stands with the narrow part facing the audience. A* Character *steps through. She is a faceless, dark character*

*with a hangman's rope about her neck and red blood on the part that
would be her face. She is the* Negro. *The most noticeable aspect of
her looks is her wild kinky hair. It is a ragged head with a patch of
hair missing from the crown which the* Negro *carries in her hand. She
is dressed in black. She steps slowly through the wall, stands still
before it and begins her monologue:*)

Negro. Part of the time I live with Raymond, part of the time with
God, Maxmilliam and Albert Saxe Coburg. I live in my room. It is
a small room on the top floor of a brownstone in the West Nineties in
New York, a room filled with my dark old volumes, a narrow bed
and on the wall old photographs of castles and monarchs of England.
It is also Victoria's chamber. Queen Victoria Regina's. Partly because
it is consumed by a gigantic plaster statue of Queen Victoria who is
my idol and partly for other reasons; three steps that I contrived out
of boards lead to the statue which I have placed opposite the door as I
enter the room. It is a sitting figure, a replica of one in London, and
a thing of astonishing whiteness. I found it in a dusty shop on Morn-
ingside Heights. Raymond says it is a thing of terror, possessing the
quality of nightmares, suggesting large and probable deaths. And of
course he is right. When I am the Duchess of Hapsburg I sit opposite Victoria in my headpiece and we talk. The other time I wear
the dress of a student, dark clothes and dark stockings. Victoria always wants me to tell her of whiteness. She wants me to tell her of
a royal world where everything and everyone is white and there are
no unfortunate black ones. For as we of royal blood know, black
is evil and has been from the beginning. Even before my mother's
hair started to fall out. Before she was raped by a wild black beast.
Black was evil.

As for myself I long to become even a more pallid Negro than I am
now; pallid like Negroes on the covers of American Negro magazines;
soulless, educated and irreligious. I want to possess no moral value,
particularly value as to my being. I want not to be. I ask nothing
except anonymity. I am an English major, as my mother was when
she went to school in Atlanta. My father majored in Social Work. I
am graduated from a city college and have occasional work in libraries,
but mostly spend my days preoccupied with the placement and geometric position of words on paper. I write poetry filling white page
after white page with imitations of Edith Sitwell. It is my dream to
live in rooms with European antiques and my Queen Victoria, photographs of Roman ruins, walls of books, a piano, oriental carpets and
to eat my meals on a white glass table. I will visit my friends' apartments which will contain books, photographs of Roman ruins, pianos
and oriental carpets. My friends will be white.

I need them as an embankment to keep me from reflecting too much
upon the fact that I am a Negro. For, like all educated Negroes—out
of life and death essential—I find it necessary to maintain a stark
fortress against recognition of myself. My white friends, like myself,
will be shrewd, intellectual and anxious for death. Anyone's death.
I will mistrust them, as I do myself, waver in their opinion of me, as
I waver in the opinion of myself. But if I had not wavered in my

opinion of myself, then my hair would never have fallen out. And if my hair hadn't fallen out, I wouldn't have bludgeoned my father's head with an ebony mask.

In appearance I am good-looking in a boring way; no glaring Negroid features, medium nose, medium mouth and pale yellow skin. My one defect is that I have a head of frizzy hair, unmistakably Negro kinky hair; and it is indistinguishable. I would like to lie and say I love Raymond. But I do not. He is a poet and is Jewish. He is very interested in Negroes.

(The Negro stands by the wall and throughout her following speech, the following characters come through the wall, disappearing off into varying directions in the darkened night of the Stage: Duchess, Queen Victoria, Jesus, Patrice Lumumba. Jesus is a hunchback, yellow-skinned dwarf, dressed in white rags and sandals. Patrice Lumumba is a black man. His head appears to be split in two with blood and tissue in eyes. He carries an ebony mask.)

Sarah's (Negro) Second Speech. The rooms are my rooms; a Hapsburg chamber, a chamber in a Victorian castle, the hotel where I killed my father, the jungle. These are the places myselves exist in. I know no places. That is, I cannot believe in places. To believe in places is to know hope and to know the emotion of hope is to know beauty. It links us across a horizon and connects us to the world. I find there are no places, only my funnyhouse. Streets are rooms, cities are rooms, eternal rooms. I try to create a space for myselves in cities, New York, the midwest, a southern town, but it becomes a lie. I try to give myselves a logical relationship but that too is a lie. For relationships was one of my last religions. I clung loyally to the lie of relationships, again and again seeking to establish a connection between my characters. Jesus is Victoria's son. Mother loved my father before her hair fell out. A loving relationship exists between myself and Queen Victoria, a love between myself and Jesus but they are lies.

(Then to the Right front of the Stage comes the WHITE LIGHT. It goes to a suspended stairway. At the foot of it, stands the Landlady. She is a tall, thin, white woman dressed in a black and red hat and appears to be talking to someone in a suggested open doorway in a corridor of a rooming house. She laughs like a mad character in a funnyhouse throughout her speech.)

Landlady. (Who is looking up the stairway.) Ever since her father hung himself in a Harlem hotel when Patrice Lumumba was murdered she hides herself in her room. Each night she repeats: He keeps returning. How dare he enter the castle walls, he who is the darkest of them all, the darkest one? My mother looked like a white woman, hair as straight as any white woman's. And I am yellow but he, he is black, the blackest one of them all. I hoped he was dead. Yet he still comes through the jungle.

I tell her: Sarah, honey, the man hung himself. It's not your blame. But, no, she stares at me: No, Mrs. Conrad, he did not hang himself, that is only the way they understand it, they do, but the truth is that I bludgeoned his head with an ebony skull that he carries about with him. Wherever he goes, he carries black masks and heads.

She's suffering so till her hair has fallen out. But then she did always hide herself in that room with the walls of books and her statue. I always did know she thought she was somebody else, a Queen or something, somebody else.

Blackout

SCENE   Funnyman's Place

The next scene is enacted with the Duchess *and* Raymond. *Raymond's place is suggested as being above the Negro's room and is etched in with a prop of blinds and a bed. Behind the blinds are mirrors and when the blinds are opened and closed by Raymond this is revealed. Raymond turns out to be the funnyman of the funnyhouse. He is tall, white and ghostly thin and dressed in a black shirt and black trousers in attire suggesting an artist. Throughout his dialogue he laughs. The* Duchess *is partially disrobed and it is implied from their attitudes of physical intimacy—he is standing and she is sitting before him clinging to his leg. During the scene Raymond keeps opening and closing the blinds.*

Duchess. (Carrying a red paper bag.) My father is arriving and what am I to do?

(Raymond *walks about the place opening the blinds and laughing.*)

Funnyman. He is arriving from Africa, is he not?

Duchess. Yes, yes, he is arriving from Africa.

Funnyman. I always knew your father was African.

Duchess. He is an African who lives in the jungle. He is an African who has always lived in the jungle. Yes, he is a nigger who is an African who is a missionary teacher and is now dedicating his life to the erection of a Christian mission in the middle of the jungle. He is a black man.

Funnyman. He is a black man who shot himself when they murdered Patrice Lumumba.

Duchess. (Goes on wildly.) Yes, my father is a black man who went to Africa years ago as a missionary teacher, got mixed up in politics, was revealed and is now devoting his foolish life to the erection of a Christian mission in the middle of jungle in one of those newly freed countries. Hide me. *(Clinging to his knees.)* Hide me here so the nigger will not find me.

Funnyman. (Laughing.) Your father is in the jungle dedicating his life to the erection of a Christian mission.

Duchess. Hide me here so the jungle will not find me. Hide me.

Funnyman. Isn't it cruel of you?

Duchess. Hide me from the jungle.

Funnyman. Isn't it cruel?

Duchess. No, no.

Funnyman. Isn't it cruel of you?

Duchess. No. *(She screams and opens her red paper bag and draws from it her fallen hair. It is a great mass of dark wild. She holds it up to him. He appears not to understand. He stares at it.)* It is my hair. *(He continues to stare at her.)* When I awakened this morning it had fallen out, not all of it but a mass from the crown of my head that lay on the center of my pillow. I arose and in the greyish winter morning light of my room I stood staring at my hair, dazed by my sleeplessness, still shaken by nightmares of my mother. Was it true, yes, it was my hair. In the mirror I saw that, although my hair remained on both sides, clearly on the crown and at my temples my scalp was bare. *(She removes her black crown and shows him the top of her head.)*

Funnyman. (Staring at her.) Why would your hair fall out? Is it because you are cruel? How could a black father haunt you so?

Duchess. He haunted my very conception. He was a wild black beast who raped my mother.

Funnyman. He is a black Negro. *(Laughing.)*

Duchess. Ever since I can remember he's been in a nigger pose of agony. He is the wilderness. He speaks niggerly groveling about wanting to touch me with his black hand.

Funnyman. How tormented and cruel you are.

Duchess. (As if not comprehending.) Yes, yes, the man's dark, very dark-skinned. He is the darkest, my father is the darkest, my mother is the lightest. I am in between. But my father is the darkest. My father is a nigger who drives me to misery. Any time spent with him evolves itself into suffering. He is a black man and the wilderness.

Funnyman. How tormented and cruel you are.

Duchess. He is a nigger.

Funnyman. And your mother, where is she?

Duchess. She is in the asylum. In the asylum bald. Her father was a white man. And she is in the asylum.

(He takes her in his arms. She responds wildly.)

Blackout

KNOCKING *is heard; it continues, then somewhere near the Center of the Stage a Figure appears in the darkness, a large dark faceless Man carrying a mask in his hand.*

Man. It begins with the disaster of my hair. I awaken. My hair has fallen out, not all of it, but a mass from the crown of my head that lies on the center of my white pillow. I arise and in the greyish winter morning light of my room I stand staring at my hair, dazed by sleeplessness, still shaken by nightmares of my mother. Is it true? Yes.

It is my hair. In the mirror I see that although my hair remains on both sides, clearly on the crown and at my temples my scalp is bare. And in the sleep I had been visited by my bald crazy mother who comes to me crying, calling me to her bedside. She lies on the bed watching the strands of her own hair fall out. Her hair fell out after she married and she spent her days lying on the bed watching the strands fall from her scalp, covering the bedspread until she was bald and admitted to the hospital. Black man, black man, my mother says, I never should have let a black man put his hands on me. She comes to me, her bald skull shining. Black diseases, Sarah, she says. Black diseases. I run. She follows me, her bald skull shining. That is the beginning.

Blackout

SCENE   Queen's Chamber

Her hair is in a small pile on the bed and in a small pile on the floor, several other small piles of hair are scattered about her and her white gown is covered with fallen out hair. Queen Victoria *acts out the following scene: She awakens (in pantomime) and discovers her hair has fallen. It is on her pillow. She arises and stands at the side of the bed with her back toward us, staring at hair. The* Duchess *enters the room, comes around, standing behind* Victoria, *and they stare at the hair.* Victoria *picks up a mirror. The* Duchess *then picks up a mirror and looks at her own hair. She opens the red paper bag that she is carrying and takes out her hair, attempting to place it back on her head (for unlike* Victoria, *she does not wear her headpiece now). The* LIGHTS *remain on. The unidentified* Man *returns out of the darkness and speaks. He carries the mask.*

Man. *(Patrice Lumumba.)* I am a nigger of two generations. I am Patrice Lumumba. I am a nigger of two generations. I am the black shadow that haunted my mother's conception. I belong to the generation born at the turn of the century and the generation born before the depression. At present I reside in New York City in a brownstone in the West Nineties. I am an English major at a city college. My nigger father majored in social work, so did my mother. I am a student and have occasional work in libraries. But mostly I spend my vile days preoccupied with the placement and geometric position of words on paper. I write poetry filling white page after white page with imitations of Sitwell. It is my vile dream to live in rooms with European antiques and my statue of Queen Victoria, photographs of Roman ruins, walls of books, a piano and oriental carpets and to eat my meals on a white glass table. It is also my nigger dream for my friends to eat their meals on white glass tables and to live in rooms with European antiques, photographs of Roman ruins, pianos and oriental carpets. My friends will be white. I need them as an embankment to keep me from reflecting too much upon the fact that I am Patrice Lumumba who haunted my mother's conception. They are necessary for me to maintain recognition against myself. My white friends, like myself, will be shrewd intellectuals and anxious for death. Anyone's death. I will despise them as I do myself. For if

I did not despite myself then my hair would not have fallen and if my hair had not fallen then I would not have bludgeoned my father's face with the ebony mask.

(The LIGHT *remains on him. Before him a* BALD HEAD *is dropped on a wire,* Someone *screams. Another wall is dropped, larger than the first one was. This one is near the front of the Stage facing thus. Throughout the following monologue, the* Characters: Duchess, Victoria, Jesus *go back and forth. As they go in their backs are to us but the* Negro *faces us, speaking:)*

I always dreamed of a day when my mother would smile at me. My father . . . his mother wanted him to be Christ. From the beginning in the lamp of their dark room she said—I want you to be Jesus, to walk in Genesis and save the race. You must return to Africa, find revelation in the midst of golden savannas, nim and white frankopenny trees, white stallions roaming under a blue sky, you must walk with a white dove and heal the race, heal the misery, take us off the cross. She stared at him anguished in the kerosene light . . . At dawn he watched her rise, kill a hen for him to eat at breakfast, then go to work down at the big house till dusk, till she died.

His father told him the race was no damn good. He hated his father and adored his mother. His mother didn't want him to marry my mother and sent a dead chicken to the wedding. I DON'T want you marrying that child, she wrote, she's not good enough for you, I want you to go to Africa. When they first married they lived in New York. Then they went to Africa where my mother fell out of love with my father. She didn't want him to save the black race and spent her days combing her hair. She would not let him touch her in their wedding bed and called him black. He is black of skin with dark eyes and a great dark square brow. Then in Africa he started to drink and came home drunk one night and raped my mother. The child from the union is me. I clung to my mother. Long after she went to the asylum I wove long dreams of her beauty, her straight hair and fair skin and grey eyes, so identical to mine. How it anguished him. I turned from him, nailing him on the cross, he said, dragging him through grass and nailing him on a cross until he bled. He pleaded with me to help him find Genesis, search for Genesis in the midst of golden savannas, nim and white frankopenny trees and white stallions roaming under a blue sky, help him search for the white doves, he wanted the black man to make a pure statement, he wanted the black man to rise from colonialism. But I sat in the room with my mother, sat by her bedside and helped her comb her straight black hair and wove long dreams of her beauty. She had long since begun to curse the place and spoke of herself trapped in blackness. She preferred the company of night owls. Only at night did she rise, walking in the garden among the trees with the owls. When I spoke to her she saw I was a black man's child and she preferred speaking to owls. Nights my father came from his school in the village struggling to embrace me. But I fled and hid under my mother's bed while she screamed of remorse. Her hair was falling badly and after a while we had to return to this country.

He tried to hang himself once. After my mother went to the asylum he had hallucinations, his mother threw a dead chicken at him, his father laughed and said the race was no damn good, my mother appeared in her nightgown screaming she had trapped herself in blackness. No white doves flew. He had left Africa and was again in New York. He lived in Harlem and no white doves flew. Sarah, Sarah, he would say to me, the soldiers are coming and a cross they are placing high on a tree and are dragging me through the grass and nailing me upon the cross. My blood is gushing. I wanted to live in Genesis in the midst of golden savannas, nim and white frankopenny trees and white stallions roaming under a blue sky. I wanted to walk with a white dove. I wanted to be a Christian. Now I am Judas. I betrayed my mother. I sent your mother to the asylum. I created a yellow child who hates me. And he tried to hang himself in a Harlem hotel.

Blackout

(*A* BALD HEAD *is dropped on a string. We hear* LAUGHING.)

SCENE   Duchess's Place

The next scene is done in the Duchess of Hapsburg's place which is a chandeliered ballroom with SNOW *falling, a black and white marble floor, a bench decorated with white flowers, all of this can be made of obviously fake materials as they would be in a funnyhouse. The* Duchess *is wearing a white dress and as in the previous scene a white headpiece with her kinky hair springing out from under it. In the scene are the* Duchess *and* Jesus. Jesus *enters the room, which is at first dark, then suddenly* BRILLIANT, *he starts to cry out at the* Duchess, *who is seated on a bench under the chandelier, and pulls his hair from the red paper bag holding it up for the* Duchess *to see.*

Jesus. My hair. (*The Duchess does not speak,* Jesus *again screams.*) My hair. (*Holding the hair up, waiting for a reaction from the* Duchess.)

Duchess. (*As if oblivious.*) I have something I must show you. (*She goes quickly to shutters and darkens the room, returning standing before* Jesus. *She then slowly removes her headpiece and from under it takes a mass of her hair.*) When I awakened I found it fallen out, not all of it but a mass that lay on my white pillow. I could see, although my hair hung down at the sides, clearly on my white scalp it was missing.

(*Her baldness is identical to* Jesus's.)

Blackout

The LIGHTS *come back up. They are* Both *sitting on the bench examining each other's hair, running it through their fingers, then slowly the* Duchess *disappears behind the shutters and returns with a long red comb. She sits on the bench next to* Jesus *and starts to comb her remaining hair over her baldness. (This is done slowly.)* Jesus *then takes the comb and proceeds to do the same to the* Duchess *of Hapsburg's hair. After they finish they place the* Duchess's *headpiece back on and we can see the strands of their hair falling to the floor.* Jesus *then lies down across the bench while the* Duchess *walks back and forth, the* KNOCKING *does not cease. They speak in unison as the* Duchess *walks about and* Jesus *lies on the bench in the fallen snow, staring at the ceiling.*

Duchess *and* Jesus. *(Their hair is falling more now, they are both hideous.)* My father isn't going to let us alone. (KNOCKING.) Our father isn't going to let us alone, our father is the darkest of us all, my mother was the fairest, I am in between, but my father is the darkest of them all. He is a black man. Our father is the darkest of them all. He is a black man. My father is a dead man.

(Then they suddenly look up at each other and scream, the LIGHTS *go to their heads and we see that they are totally bald. There is a* KNOCK-ING. LIGHTS *go to the stairs and the* Landlady.*)*

Landlady. He wrote to her saying he loved her and asked her forgiveness. He begged her to take him off the cross, *(He had dreamed she would.)* stop them from tormenting him, the one with the chicken and his cursing father. Her mother's hair fell out, the race's hair fell out because he left Africa, he said. He had tried to save them. She must embrace him. He said his existence depended on her embrace. He wrote her from Africa where he is creating his Christian center in the jungle and that is why he came here. I know that he wanted her to return there with him and not desert the race. He came to see her once before he tried to hang himself, appearing in the corridor of my apartment. I had let him in. I found him sitting on a bench in the hallway. He put out his hand to her, tried to take her in his arms, crying out—Forgiveness, Sarah, is it that you never will forgive me for being black? Sarah, I know you were a child of torment. But forgiveness. That was before his breakdown. Then, he wrote her and repeated that his mother hoped he would be Christ but he failed. He had married her mother because he could not resist the light. Yet, his mother from the beginning in the kerosene lamp of their dark rooms in Georgia said: I want you to be Jesus, to walk in Genesis and save the race, return to Africa, find revelation in the black. He went away.

But Easter morning, she got to feeling badly and went into Harlem to see him; the streets were filled with vendors selling lilacs. He had checked out of that hotel. When she arrived back at my brownstone he was here, dressed badly, rather drunk, I had let him in again. He sat on a bench in the dark hallway, put out his hand to her, trying to take her in his arms, crying out—forgiveness, Sarah, forgiveness for my being black, Sarah. I know you are a child of torment. I know on dark winter afternoons you sit alone weaving stories of your mother's beauty. But Sarah, answer me, don't turn away, Sarah. Forgive my blackness. She would not answer. He put out his hand to her. She ran past him on the stairs, left him there with his hand out to me, repeating his past, saying his mother hoped he would be Christ. From the beginning in the kerosene lamp of their dark rooms she said: "Wally, I want you to be Jesus, to walk in Genesis and save the race. You must return to Africa, Wally, find revelation in the midst of golden savannas, nim and white frankopenny trees and white stallions roaming under a blue sky. Wally, you must find the white dove and heal the pain of the race, heal the misery of the black man, Wally, take us off the cross, Wally." In the kerosene light she stared at me anguished from her old Negro face—but she ran past him leaving him. And now he is dead, she says, now he is dead. He left Africa and now Patrice Lumumba is dead.

(*The next scene is enacted back in the* Duchess of Hapsburg's *place.* Jesus *is still in the* Duchess's *chamber, apparently he has fallen asleep and as we see him he awakens with the* Duchess *by his side, and sits here as in a trance. He rises terrified and speaks.*)

Jesus. Through my apocalypses and my raging sermons I have tried so to escape him, through God Almighty I have tried to escape being black. (*He then appears to rouse himself from his thoughts and calls:*) Duchess, Duchess. (*He looks about for her, there is no answer. He gets up slowly, walks back into the darkness and there we see that she is hanging on the chandelier, her bald head suddenly drops to the floor and she falls upon* Jesus. *He screams.*) I am going to Africa and kill this black man named Patrice Lumumba. Why? Because all my life I believed my Holy Father to be God, but now I know that my father is a black man. I have no fear for whatever I do, I will do in the name of God, I will do in the name of Albert Saxe Coburg, in the name of Victoria, Queen Victoria Regina, the monarch of England, I will.

Blackout

SCENE   In the Jungle, RED SUN, FLYING THINGS, Wild Black Grass

The effect of the jungle is that it, unlike the other Scenes, is over the entire Stage. In time this is the longest Scene in the play and is played the slowest, as the slow, almost standstill stages of a dream. By lighting the desired effect would be—suddenly the jungle has overgrown the chambers and all the other places with a violence and a dark brightness, a grim yellowness.

Jesus *is the first to appear in the center of the jungle darkness. Unlike in previous scenes, he has a nimbus above his head. As they each successively appear, they all too have nimbuses atop their heads in a manner to suggest that they are saviours.*

Jesus. I always believed my father to be God.

(*Suddenly they all appear in various parts of the jungle.* Patrice Lumumba, *the* Duchess, Victoria, *wandering about speaking at once. Their speeches are mixed and repeated by one another:*)

All. He never tires of the journey, he who is the darkest one, the darkest one of them all. My mother looked like a white woman, hair as straight as any white woman's. I am yellow but he is black, the darkest one of us all. How I hoped he was dead, yet he never tires of the journey. It was because of him that my mother died because she let a black man put his hands on her. Why does he keep returning? He keeps returning forever, keeps returning and returning and he is my father. He is a black Negro. They told me my Father was God but my father is black. He is my father. I am tied to a black Negro. He returned when I lived in the south back in the twenties, when I was a child, he returned. Before I was born at the turn of the century, he haunted my conception, diseased my birth . . . killed my mother. He killed the light. My mother was the lightest one. I am bound to him unless, of course, he should die.

But he is dead.

And he keeps returning. Then he is not dead.

Then he is not dead.

Yet, he is dead, but dead he comes knocking at my door.

(This is repeated several times, finally reaching a loud pitch and then All rushing about the grass. They stop and stand perfectly still. All speaking tensely at various times in a chant.)

I see him. The black ugly thing is sitting in his hallway, surrounded by his ebony masks, surrounded by the blackness of himself. My mother comes into the room. He is there with his hand out to me, groveling, saying—Forgiveness, Sarah, is it that you will never forgive me for being black.

Forgiveness, Sarah, I know you are a nigger of torment.

Why? Christ would not rape anyone.

You will never forgive me for being black.

Wild beast. Why did you rape my mother? Black beast, Christ would not rape anyone.

He is in grief from that black anguished face of his. Then at once the room will grow bright and my mother will come toward me smiling while I stand before his face and bludgeon him with an ebony head.

Forgiveness, Sarah, I know you are a nigger of torment.

(Silence. Then they suddenly begin to laugh and shout as though they are in victory. They continue for some minutes running about laughing and shouting.)

Blackout

Another WALL *drops. There is a white plaster statue of Queen Victoria which represents the Negro's room in the brownstone, the room appears near the staircase highly lit and small. The main prop is the statue but a bed could be suggested. The figure of Victoria is a sitting figure, one of astonishing repulsive whiteness, suggested by dusty volumes of books and old yellowed walls.*

The Negro Sarah *is standing perfectly still, we hear the* KNOCKING, *the* LIGHTS *come on quickly, her* Father's *black figure with bludgeoned hands rushes upon her, the* LIGHT GOES BLACK *and we see her hanging in the room.*

LIGHTS *come on the laughing* Landlady. *And at the same time remain on the hanging figure of the* Negro.

Landlady. The poor bitch has hung herself. (*Funnyman Raymond appears from his room at the commotion.*) The poor bitch has hung herself.

Raymond. (*Observing her hanging figure.*) She was a funny little liar.

Landlady. (*Informing him.*) Her father hung himself in a Harlem hotel when Patrice Lumumba died.

Raymond. Her father never hung himself in a Harlem hotel when Patrice Lumumba was murdered. I know the man. He is a doctor, married to a white whore. He lives in the city in rooms with European antiques, photographs of Roman ruins, walls of books and oriental carpets. Her father is a nigger who eats his meals on a white glass table.

End

Sylvia Plath

Poppies in October

Even the sun-clouds this morning cannot manage such skirts.
Nor the woman in the ambulance
Whose red heart blooms through her coat so astoundingly——

A gift, a love gift
Utterly unasked for
By a sky

Palely and flamily
Igniting its carbon monoxides, by eyes
Dulled to a halt under bowlers.

O my God, what am I
That these late mouths should cry open
In a forest of frost, in a dawn of cornflowers.

Morning Song

Love set you going like a fat gold watch.
The midwife slapped your footsoles, and your bald cry
Took its place among the elements.

Our voices echo, magnifying your arrival. New statue.
In a drafty museum, your nakedness
Shadows our safety. We stand round blankly as walls.

I'm no more your mother
Than the cloud that distils a mirror to reflect its own slow
Effacement at the wind's hand.

All night your moth-breath
Flickers among the flat pink roses. I wake to listen:
A far sea moves in my ear.

One cry, and I stumble from bed, cow-heavy and floral
In my Victorian nightgown.
Your mouth opens clean as a cat's. The window square

Whitens and swallows its dull stars. And now you try
Your handful of notes;
The clear vowels rise like balloons.

Kindness

Kindness glides about my house.
Dame Kindness, she is so nice!
The blue and red jewels of her rings smoke
In the windows, the mirrors
Are filling with smiles.

What is so real as the cry of a child?
A rabbit's cry may be wilder
But it has no soul.
Sugar can cure everything, so Kindness says.
Sugar is a necessary fluid,

Its crystals a little poultice.
O kindness, kindness
Sweetly picking up pieces!
My Japanese silks, desperate butterflies,
May be pinned any minute, anaesthetized.

And here you come, with a cup of tea
Wreathed in steam.
The blood jet is poetry,
There is no stopping it.
You hand me two children, two roses.

Lady Lazarus

I have done it again.
One year in every ten
I manage it——

A sort of walking miracle, my skin
Bright as a Nazi lampshade,
My right foot

A paperweight,
My face a featureless, fine
Jew linen.

Peel off the napkin
O my enemy.
Do I terrify?——

The nose, the eye pits, the full set of teeth?
The sour breath
Will vanish in a day.

Soon, soon the flesh
The grave cave ate will be
At home on me

And I a smiling woman.
I am only thirty.
And like the cat I have nine times to die.

This is Number Three.
What a trash
To annihilate each decade.

What a million filaments.
The peanut-crunching crowd
Shoves in to see

Them unwrap me hand and foot——
The big strip tease.
Gentleman, ladies,

These are my hands,
My knees.
I may be skin and bone,

Nevertheless, I am the same, identical woman.
The first time it happened I was ten.
It was an accident.

The second time I meant
To last it out and not come back at all.
I rocked shut

As a seashell.
They had to call and call
And pick the worms off me like sticky pearls.

Dying
Is an art, like everything else.
I do it exceptionally well.

I do it so it feels like hell.
I do it so it feels real.
I guess you could say I've a call.

It's easy enough to do it in a cell.
It's easy enough to do it and stay put.
It's the theatrical

Comeback in broad day
To the same place, the same face, the same brute
Amused shout:

"A miracle!"
That knocks me out.
There is a charge

For the eyeing of my scars, there is a charge
For the hearing of my heart——
It really goes.

And there is a charge, a very large charge,
For a word or a touch
Or a bit of blood

Or a piece of my hair or my clothes.
So, so, Herr Doktor.
So, Herr Enemy.

I am your opus,
I am your valuable,
The pure gold baby

That melts to a shriek.
I turn and burn.
Do not think I underestimate your great concern.

Ash, ash—
You poke and stir.
Flesh, bone, there is nothing there——

A cake of soap,
A wedding ring,
A gold filling.

Herr God, Herr Lucifer,
Beware
Beware.

Out of the ash
I rise with my red hair
And I eat men like air.

Joan Didion

from *Play It As It Lays*

"You drive," the man had said. "We'll pick up my car after."

He was wearing white duck pants and a white sport shirt and he had a moon face and a eunuch's soft body. The hand resting on his knee was pale and freckled and boneless and ever since he got in the car he had been humming *I Get a Kick Out of You.*

"You familiar with this area, Maria?"

The question seemed obscurely freighted. "No," Maria said finally.

"Nice homes here. Nice for kids." The voice was bland, ingratiating, the voice on the telephone. "Let me ask you one question, all right?"

Maria nodded, and tightened her grip on the steering wheel.

"Get pretty good mileage on this? Or no?"

"Pretty good," she heard herself saying after only the slightest pause. "Not too bad."

"You may have noticed, I drive a Cadillac. Eldorado. Eats gas but I like it, like the feel of it."

Maria said nothing. That, then, had actually been the question. She had not misunderstood.

"If I decided to get rid of the Cad," he said, "I might pick myself up a little Camaro. Maybe that sounds like a step down, a Cad to a Camaro, but I've got my eye on this particular Camaro, exact model of the pace car in the Indianapolis 500."

"You think you'll buy a Camaro," Maria said in the neutral tone of a therapist.

"Get the right price, I just might. I got a friend, he can write me a sweet deal if it's on the floor much longer. They almost had a buyer last week but lucky for me—here, Maria, right here, pull into this driveway."

Maria turned off the ignition and looked at the man in the white duck pants with an intense and grateful interest. In the past few minutes he had significantly altered her perception of reality: she saw now that she was not a woman on her way to have an abortion. She was a woman parking a Corvette outside a tract house while a man in white pants talked about buying a Camaro. There was no more to it than that. "Lucky for you what?"

"Lucky for me, the guy's credit didn't hold up."

. . .

The floor of the bedroom where it happened was covered with newspapers. She remembered reading somewhere that newspapers were antiseptic, it had to do with the chemicals in the ink, to deliver a baby in a farmhouse you covered the floor with newspapers. There was something else to be done with newspapers, something unexpected, some emergency trick: quilts could be made with newspapers. In time of disaster you could baste newspapers to both sides of a cotton blanket and end up with a warm quilt. She knew a lot of things about disaster. She could manage. Carter could never manage but she could. She could not think where she had learned all these tricks. Probably in her mother's *American Red Cross Handbook*, gray with a red cross on the cover. There, that was a good thing to think about, at any rate not a bad thing if she kept her father out of it. If she could concentrate for even one minute on a picture of herself as a ten-year-old sitting on the front steps of the house in Silver Wells reading the gray book with the red cross on the cover (splints, shock, rattlesnake bite, rattlesnake bite was why her mother made her read it) with the heat shimmering off the corrugated tin roof of the shed across the road (her father was not in this picture, keep him out of it, say he had gone into Vegas with Benny Austin), if she could concentrate for one more minute on that shed, on whether this minute twenty years later the heat still shimmered off its roof, those were two minutes during which she was not entirely party to what was happening in this bedroom in Encino.

Two minutes in Silver Wells, two minutes here, two minutes there, it was going to be over in this bedroom in Encino, it could not last forever. The walls of the bedroom were cream-colored, yellow, a wallpaper with a modest pattern. Whoever had chosen that wallpaper would have liked maple furniture, a maple bedroom set, a white chenille bedspread and a white Princess telephone, all gone now but she could see it as it must have been, could see even the woman who had picked the wallpaper, she would be a purchaser of Audubon prints and scented douches, a hoarder of secret sexual grievances, a wife. Two minutes in Silver Wells, two minutes on the wallpaper, it could not last forever. The table was a doctor's table but not fitted with stirrups: instead there were two hardbacked chairs with pillows tied over the backs. "Tell me if it's too cold," the doctor said. The doctor was tall and haggard and wore a rubber apron. "Tell me now because I won't be able to touch the air conditioner once I start."

She said that it was not too cold.

"No, it's too cold. You don't weigh enough, it's too cold."

He adjusted the dial but the sound remained level. She closed her eyes and tried to concentrate on the sound. Carter did not like air conditioners but there had been one somewhere. She had slept in a room with an air conditioner, the question was where, never mind the question, that question led nowhere. "This is just induced menstruation," she could hear the doctor saying. "Nothing to have any emotional difficulties about, better not to think about it at all, quite often the pain is worse when we think about it, don't like anesthetics, anesthetics are where we run into trouble, just a little local on the cervix, there, relax, Maria, I said *relax*."

No moment more or less important than any other moment, all the same: the pain as the doctor scraped signified nothing beyond itself, no more constituted the pattern of her life than did the movie on television in the living room of this house in Encino. The man in the white duck pants was sitting out there watching the movie and she was lying in here not watching the movie, and that was all there was to that. Why the volume on the set was turned up so high seemed another question better left unasked. "Hear that scraping, Maria?" the doctor said. "That should be the sound of music to you . . . don't scream, Maria, there are people next door, almost done, almost over, better to get it all now than do it again a month from now . . . I said don't make any noise, Maria, now I'll tell you what's going to happen, you'll bleed a day or so, not heavily, just spotting, and then a month, six weeks from now you'll have a normal period, not this month, this month you just had it, it's in that pail."

He went into the bathroom then (later she would try to fix in her mind the exact circumstances of his leaving the bedroom, would try to remember if he took the pail with him, later that would seem important to her) and by the time he came back the contractions had stopped. He gave her one envelope of tetracycline capsules and another of ergot tablets and by six o'clock of that hot October afternoon she was out of the bedroom in Encino and back in the car with the man in the white duck pants. The late sun seemed warm and benevolent on her skin and everything she saw looked beautiful, the summer pulse of life itself made manifest. As she backed out of the driveway she smiled radiantly at her companion.

"You missed a pretty fair movie," he said. "Paula Raymond." He reached into his pocket for what seemed to be a cigarette holder. "Ever since I gave up smoking I carry these by the dozen, they look like regular holders but all you get is air."

Maria stared at his outstretched hand.

"*Take* it. I noticed you're still smoking. You'll thank me some day."

"Thank you."

"I'm a regular missionary." The man in the white duck pants resettled his soft bulk and gazed out the car window. "Gee, Paula Raymond was a pretty girl," he said then. "Funny she never became a star."

Diane Johnson

from The Shadow Knows

Oh well, I don't suppose I need to go on about all our quarrels, our
estrangement. In most ways I suppose they are usual and predictable.
A Famous Inspector could chart by heart the stages of a disintegrating
marriage—I suppose he would be a great student of human nature.
It makes me uncomfortable to find that the biggest drama of my life
should turn out to be like others, so alike it is not even interesting to
look back on it. With what feelings of singularity you lend yourself
to each thrilling act of girlhood, marriage, to the growing troupe of
exquisite babies with their tender fingers, like the beautiful mother
in a diaper ad you are, and then it begins to seep away, the picture
is torn off the billboard and torn into little bits and these bits washed
down a drain, a whirling vortex of disappearing candlelight suppers,
vanished pet names, caresses down the drain. All gone. Shorn wet
bodies shiver slightly in the chill of the real sour air, their garments
of deception gone. The air smells of madness, and ill nature. I avert
my eyes from the sight of the engripping despair of my former bridegroom, who is congealing without knowing it. Embarrassment is what
I felt, is what I feel.

The situation can be looked at from Gavin's point of view, too. He
told me a dream he had: there is Gavin, his mind streaming tears, in
a room filled with female figures, with masks over their faces, their
hands folded in their laps, bellies swollen, their forms quivering alternately bright or blurry through his tears; the room is filled under his
feet with objects, treacherous wheeled things, plastic cars that crunch
sharply under his feet, toy dogs uttering anguished shrieks, something
slippery—baby oil—that nearly brings him down, and, his vision im-
peded by tears of both self-pity and rage, he must make his way
across this alien and dangerous floor amid the rocking fertile female
creatures who ignore him. Their unintelligible hum seems mocking.
He thinks he will stride through the room bravely anyway to get to
the refrigerator, but when he does there's nothing in it but bits of
disgusting things he sees they are saving for him to step in.

He may hate these females, he may fear them, but what decides him
to kill them? That's what I don't understand. From the newspapers
I have figured out that most murders happen one of two ways; with
the first kind, people are arguing, growing angry and angrier and
angrier until their hatred is intolerable and someone reaches for something and puts an end to it, bang.

The other kind of murder is premeditated, brooded upon, done for
revenge or gain. The first kind is commoner, but estranged husbands,

I have counted up, do both kinds. They lurk, they brood. Here's
one in the paper tonight:

FATHER KILLS ESTRANGED WIFE,
CHILDREN OUTSIDE CHURCH

MINNEAPOLIS. A father of five waiting outside St. Anthony's Catholic
Church in bitter winter weather shot his estranged wife and four
young children as they came out of the eleven o'clock service while
horrified bystanders and priest . . .

When Andrew and I became lovers and after Gavin and I were separated, I used to think that Gavin would come and shoot Andrew and
me. I expected him to but he didn't, and the worry gradually went
away until now. I know this is a foolish worry, considering that Gavin
is a sane lawyer and Osella is literally mad. I know—but how do
I know?

Whoever it is, I don't like waiting for him these evenings. With the
settling dark the danger seems more immediate, and I remember things
and hear things. I asked Ev not to watch the TV because I am afraid
we wouldn't hear over its noise the noise of the stealthy hand fumbling our latches. Our murderer, to my mind, has supernatural powers. Walls will dissolve away, locks melt with the force of his malice.
His malice can murder through walls. Our ears strain for footsteps
outside, his hesitant scuffling, a murderer walking up and down unseen
outside, finding chinks in the wall where he will put his fingers and
push it in. A ratlike rustling chills us; we don't know if it's a person
or not out there. It's just dark, we have had supper. I am writing
this and Ev is reading a *True Confession* story, "I Need a Man Every
Day." I think it's funny she should seek vicarious thrills when real
ones threaten. "It ain't half thrillin enough," she says, "to take my
mind off that poor cat with his eyes bulgin out." I am afraid to go
to the window, and ought to be writing my essay on long "A." Will
time forevermore drag silently and slowly like this, mind like a metro-
nome ticking off the details of our persecution?

This afternoon after lunch when Ivan and India went down for naps,
I took Polly and Petey with me to Bess's. I couldn't bear staying home,
is all. We went along to the car, which was parked in the usual place
in the open garage. On the windshield was another foul mess, apparently vomit. My own stomach lurched precariously but this was, after
all, the second time for this; you get inured. If this sort of thing is
all, I can bear it, I thought.

"Braaaagh, blaaagh," Polly and Petey said, excited with this second
deviation from perfect peace occurring in their day. They were happy
that we had to go to the car wash; I was glad, at least, that the gas
tank was almost empty. If you fill up with gas at the car wash, your
wash only costs 49¢ instead of $1.50. I am developing a core of calm
resource and thrift, I told myself.

The men at the car wash looked impassive and unjudging as they
washed the windshield, as though they were used to all sorts of human

frailties splattered across the windshields of the world and it was their business to clean them, not to inquire.

But I was afraid, this new thing made me more afraid. Of course. I saw the world as through that windshield, through a film of someone's hate smearing everything over. But it was good to be reminded that our danger is real, the threats are real; I must be serious and serene, must protect, must prevail.

Sometimes I scare myself with this idea: you are alone with someone you love and trust, whom you have always known, whom you were a child with, maybe, and have seen each other cry, and are known to one another's mothers. Now you are grown and it is a cloudless day, as blue as the eyes of your friend. The two of you are away in the country, I imagine lying under a pasture tree surrounded by all the innumerable pleasures of exquisite days—fragrance, the grass to lie on, blue flies singing, your picnic lunch in a basket and the friend smiles over you at this moment of perfect repose, of perfect rapport; leans toward you smiling, and then his hands are around your neck, crushing your neck, but even when you are dying still you cannot see anything in the blue eyes that you had never seen before; they are the last thing you see, illimitably familiar and strange.

"I know who it is," Bess said when we were safely at her house and had told her about it all. "It's the checker you insulted at the market."

I *had* insulted a checker at the market. I suppose I ought to note that incident. Had gone to the market—this was a couple of weeks ago, just before Christmas—and I was worrying about not having heard from Andrew, so it must have been at least that long ago, before the letter. Anyway, had bought a whole week's worth of groceries, feeling surly and detached, and depressed also about the approach of Christmas. I'd assembled an enormous grotesque cartload of food and was waiting in a huge line, numbly shuffling along, listening to idiot conversations on every hand and viewing moronic assemblages of disgusting TV dinners in other people's carts (I am trying to reproduce my frame of mind then); finally got to the check stand, piled up my provisions on the conveyor belt, had written out my check except for the amount of purchase, and was standing patiently. Impatiently. But the checker, a lively handsome brown Mexican girl, kept not checking me out. Someone came and asked for change. Someone came and asked to buy a pack of cigarettes. She rang up the cigarettes and used the last of the cash-register tape. Had to change the roll. Another checker had to come help her. Then another checker asked the price of something and they began a conversation about it. At this, something inside me, some spring of impatience and frustration, sprang, and I tore the check in half; "Forget it," I said, and stalked away leaving the torn check and all the groceries heaped up in front of her, thinking even as I did so what a dumb thing that was to do, now I have to go to another market and go through the whole stupid thing over again, what was the point of a stupid gesture like that, and so on, so that I hardly noticed until I almost bumped into her that this girl, in a livid fury, me having evidently violated more deeply than I knew some Latinate code of civility, had flung herself from behind her counter into my path with her hands outstretched toward me in claws, hissed something I didn't properly hear and then pulled back, turned away with the other checker screaming warning. The other customers stood all around in a silence of embarrassment or disapproval, naturally angry at me for the extra delay while she cleared away my pile of groceries, no wonder. And as I slunk out I noticed the two torn halves of my check in her apron pocket.

"Yes, Inspector, we knew the deceased, a well-known troublemaker in the neighborhood stores."

"Of course that's it," Bess said, laughing. "It's her way of saying you make me sick."

For Bess the perils of the world are nothing, speaking of their power to terrify and kill, compared to the perils you encounter in the dark abysses of your mind, strange powers there which drive you straight into the arms of murderers or under the wheels of buses. I've never been able to guess the sinister powers Bess has met in her own mind, through being psychoanalyzed, but she claims to have met them all right; she talks of them with the genial candor of the psychoanalyzed, but I've never been impressed. She was molested by a baby-sitter or something, is all. It seems to me her real problem, Lynnie, is tangible and external.

Bess is Bess Harvill, that is, wife of Joe Harvill, senior partner in Briggs, Harvill & Mason, and she has been a true friend to me when it might have been expected she would henceforward after our divorce have attended only to Gavvy, junior member of the firm, and in the interest of her long acquaintance with Cookie Mason deplore the adulterous currents which threaten to rend the flawless harmony of Briggs, Harvill & Mason, or to deplore it in behalf of good wives everywhere, or just to keep generally to the safest social sailing, but instead she has been a good helpful true friend to me. So of course to me it seems that however riddled her heart is with dark secrets, and however riddled *mine* is—for she tells me, doubtless correctly, that I'm not aware of a hundredth of them—anyhow I am very lucky in having this friendship.

Bess is impervious to fear because her heart is pure; her strength is as the strength of ten. My impure heart is what renders me so craven, so craven I am almost enjoying the fearfulness of the past few days. Is that true? Well it's exhilarating, and to the extent that it's a reflex of my own feelings of guilt (for I'm not so unsophisticated in these matters as Bess and maybe the Famous Inspector may think), it is a worthy state—even noble, like the fear felt by freedom fighters in countries run by cruel generals. I feel I have done right to sin against the Law. I am fearful yet resolute.

This state of mind, fearful yet resolute, has gone on a long time, and I know the exact moment it began, luring me to crime, if you can put such an immodest name to my pursuits. Entering into fear and liberty is exhilarating and elating as it must be to fly in an open plane, but also the thin air makes you giddy and liable to error.

My error was to think you can do as you please. My life is not a good argument for this view but my heart believes it. Maybe my life is ashes but I still believe it.

I believe sometimes things are shown you by symbols and predictions. Standing before a picture in a museum, you are suddenly overtaken by tears, or you have cut yourself and a bloody gash lies across your palm. When I was still married to Gavin, at the end, I lost my wedding ring; I had grown thin. It slipped off my finger and sank into the sand of the play yard and could not be found.

On this day, early morning, I looked out into the leafy tree that screened the window of my dressing room and someone seemed to look back at me. I thought at first it was a person, a person with a black corsair eye which glared at me, a beaked face, hooked like the nose of a dream lover glaring reproachfully at my pale life, but, also, recognizing me as someone greedy and desiring.

But it was not a person, it was a bird, and this was more shocking yet, chilling—an immense bird of yellow and green. A parrot, in fact. I was soothed for an instant, a parrot escaped, a poor baffled creature I could look in the paper for the owner. But this reasoning thought did not still the racing of my blood, nor could I wrest my imprisoned stare from his staring eye. He knew me. Then he flew away, on immense wings, like a hawk. Unclipped wings.

When I told Osella, she was not surprised. "Imagine, a parrot, wild, flying free in North America," I was saying, and she looked at me with an expression full of signification and said, "Oh, it's you, is it? I been wonderin. I might have knowed. Well, then, I expect you did see a parrot, you sure did."

All that day and all the next my head was full of parroty phrases of wifely love and obedience and motherly concern but my voice developed an odd croak as I said them. With my keen parroty eye for spotting little running rodents far beneath me, I saw the creatures of my household newly. Poor Gavin had grown so thin. How could those attenuated little arms embrace me? That other one was so fat; perhaps she was consuming him? Why doesn't she keep her kitchen cleaner? I spied into drawers like a contemptuous stranger.

The day after that I stopped parroting affectionate phrases. I glared with lidless eyes. To Gavin it must have seemed that his wife had left, and he told me later that it was about this time that he started going by himself to "Adult" movies, embarrassedly, furtively, not himself knowing why. He would call and say he was working late; then he would stop at such a movie, blushingly shove his three dollars at the ticket girl and duck in, and there be filled almost immediately with shame and dash shamefully out.

Me, I felt myself to have grown bright green wings, and to have grown them to some purpose, so I flew home one afternoon about three weeks later with one of my professors, as I had been wanting to. A mild owlish bachelor accustomed to seductions, set up for them with an apartment in the Heights, fancy, with soft sofas. There I allowed myself to be undressed, explored, me watching him all the time at his explorations, with my beady bright eye studying his responses as attentively as I might hang upon his opinion of my seminar papers. How pleased I was that I could make him pant and quiver, that I had, evidently, my share of female power beyond that which had been conferred upon me legally by the rite of marriage. And I had an appetite, or the beginning of an appetite, after that long time in a cage. It was terrific. I loved it. And there began my life of crime.

My life of crime had nothing to do with falling in love with Andrew; that came later. Falling in love with Andrew reformed me, or has ruined me forever. Well, they say no one is so earnest, so convinced, so fanatical in his rectitude as the sinner reformed. I have the reform view of True Love now. Now I can't imagine the embraces of another man; Andrew has got my body and my imagination both. I am in a smaller cage than ever.

Well, thinking about it, I suppose that calling myself a criminal and a hawk is a bit grandiose for what was after all ordinary adultery. Bess would laugh, and a Famous Inspector, too, if he had a sense of humor, which on the whole I think he hasn't but takes a traditional view of such things. But it's funny that seeing a parrot should have set me off. You never know what will set someone off. I beleaguered my friends with talk of omens.

"Death," they usually said. "Birds presage death." But my presentment then was not of death.

My life lit up like a Christmas tree. I had gotten the idea that I had the solution to it, to getting through life with Gavvy and the children: I would have lovers, discreetly; by lovers be put into a kindly frame of mind to be good to Gavin and the children, made more cheerful. I had been freed, I thought, by that parrot sight, by it somehow enabled to see that although everybody could not expect in this world to have a perfect marriage, a resourceful adult could adjust, could come to terms with life. Lovers would just be one of the terms of mine. I *know* what a detective would think about this. But I am obliged to tell it. I would have lovers at least until I had satisfied a deep, deep feeling I had, I think it was of curiosity; it was the same hotting up of the blood I felt when I went to the library, though of course more intense, something seeming to pump the blood around in my veins noisily when I even thought about the warm future peopled with strong-hearted, witty lovers and covert lunches. I thought no nonsense about love, but about charm, affection, long furtive afternoons of lovemaking, except Thursday afternoons when Osella was off; then I would stay home and tell enchanting stories to my children. All this would have to be enough. Most people, after all, did not have so much—did they?

I still don't know how Osella knew. She dropped dark, smirking hints into his drink, along with his ice cubes, in whispers in the kitchen, or whenever it was she told him.

Maybe she could smell sex. Sometimes when I came in she would look at me so long and keenly that I would look away, and she would expand her huge chest with a deep breath and exhale and sigh and turn and shuffle off, her shoes, where she had trod over the backs, flopping against her bare pink heels.

I don't know whether Osella has a need for or a horror of sex. Perhaps something horrible had happened to her. Maybe something with Mr. Spinner. She made up fears about sex. For instance she would say, "You better watch Petey, you don't want him doin nothin to his little sisters. I knows about kids," or, if the children rolled and scuffled, "Don't you let him get up top a her that way," this when they were about five and seven.

Maybe she had been raped by her brothers. But I could never think that Osella's feelings about sex could be personal, except for her clearly quite personal interest in Mr. Spinner's tool. Because of her giant body you could not imagine her having so much awareness of its needs. "Imagine fucking Osella," Gavvy said once, and we squirmed with horror. But now—I wonder. Perhaps she felt a greater, a huge need, the whole of her feeling, as I do, the smooth swelling, the pulsing throat, the need for a man's hand stroking my belly, his lips there, a man hard inside me.

But I would conceal from a police inspector my need for a man. It wouldn't dispose him to look any farther for our murderer. An adulteress in her blood, by her nature, must seem worse than an adulteress from principle or circumstance. A wanton woman is her own murderer, having first slain womanliness, delicacy, virtue, isn't that so?

Maybe Osella knew, and maybe Osella tried to warn me, but I didn't catch on. I remember one afternoon I came home from my adventuring and Osella sitting at the kitchen table rolled her eyes around on me, eyes wearing an expression of groggy fury I had come to see there more and more often, not recognizing it, though, for madness.

"I sees things," she said.

"What've you seen today, Osie?" asked I gaily; I felt happy.

"I seen Mr. Spinner in the woods once," she said. "I wasn't but seventeen or so. Me and John Henry been marrit a couple a years but I dint tell John Henry. I had done gone back there to get some crab apples, I believe. This was summertime. Mr. Spinner he a very high-suited man, spent lots of money on them fine clothes he wore. That man was a fine preacher, too. When I heard him practicin these speeches—he give them at the college for they commencin activities —I always like to shouted myself. He had a gift.

"Miz Spinner she cried to him nights. I heard them once in a while. But she never had nothin to cry about I could see, as they was rich, and that man never lif a hand to her, and he was good to they kids. A dignified man, bein a college president.

"So I went back woods to get me some crab apples, and I come up on a glade and there I seen Mr. Spinner with one of the girls from the school, red-headed, looked like she didn't have no eyebrows or eyelashes. I seen her close up once after that. Nekkid, both of them was.

This girl was layin on her back with her knees stickin up and Mr. Spinner was kissin her knees.

"That did seem passin strange, now dint it, kissin knees? Just lovin up them skinny knees. I stop back in the bushes and just watched in amaze, only one thing ever did make me feel more strange since then." A long sly glance at me.

"Oh, Osella, how embarrassing, did they see you?" I asked.

"Nobody sees Osella if she don want to be seen," she said, smirking as if she had been invisible watching me naked that afternoon.

Well, among these innuendoes, grimaces, distant silences, we all—Gavin, Osella and I—lived along like this awhile. But like canaries in a mine we sickened on the sour air of our household, and one after another we began to show the symptoms of the toxic poison, Gavin next. It was about a week after this that Gavin came up to bed one night and said, "I've decided to get myself fixed."

I was reading in bed and looked up surprised, not knowing what he meant, or thinking he meant fixed, healed.

"God knows we've got enough kids and I never want any more." Then I understood but I just stared. I suppose I should have been pleased, since it was I who had to wear the diaphragm or else swallow pills, which made me queasy, or have the babies and care for them. But it sounded like a terrible idea.

"What if I died, or we get divorced and you married someone else?" I said.

Suddenly he was screaming. "Why do you say that? What a horrible thing to say!" he screamed. He was white. Then he became controlled: I wouldn't want any in any case; it's a simple operation, it doesn't affect the libido; social responsibility, sensible.

"I know," I said, "they do it to you in underdeveloped nations in the train depot."

"You have to sign this paper," he said, handing me a paper, spreading it out on the book on my lap, and putting a pen in my hand. "To avoid subsequent litigation."

My head hung.

"I can't think of any objection you could possibly have," he said.

"I'm signing, but I don't like it. It seems like something we should discuss. We should have long discussion . . ." But I signed, because I was frightened. I thought he had figured out my real objection, which was what if I got pregnant, then I couldn't tell him it was his.

This recollection lends a certain congruous irony to my present situation, I think. Actually, about Gavvy, I do not know if the operation was ever performed.

Like canaries in a mine, in the sour air of our household we continued to sicken, next Osella. On a Monday morning she said to me just as I was leaving to take Polly and Petey to school, "You and me has to talk serious about my burden."

"Your burden?" Why were people saying these bewildering things to me?

"It's gettin too much. Two years I borne it. I has to let it drop, if you don't cooperate. If I can't bear up I'll have to leave, and then you know what would happen, or maybe you don't know, the children would all die before they was twenty-one."

"Run out to the car," I said to the children, who were looking, naturally, rather alarmed.

"What do you mean talking that way in front of them, Osella?" I said.

"I'm tellin you I can no longer bear mah burden," she said more loudly, and I noticed that her eyes were that way again, drugged and narrow. "Two years I borne it now."

"I know things are difficult around here," I said. "You can see that. Gavin and I—strains—we should give you more money, but—Big Raider?—strains—" I don't know what I said, exactly.

"You want me to spell it out?" she said. "You think I don't know what's wrong?"

Now my heart absolutely stopped with crafty attention. How could she really know? Did she? Why was she saying all this right now on a busy morning? What *was* wrong, when it came to that? Were things not getting better?

"Spell it out," I said with unconcern like a princess. I imagined she would accuse me of deceiving Gavvy and then I would deny it and sweep out insultedly.

"Right, all right then. I knows you is witchin," she said. "You think I don't know about your witchin? All the strength I have is holdin you back. Oh, for a while I didn't know as it was you or Gavvy, which one. But I knowed it was someone, someone here witchin. I could feel the evil upstairs and now I ain't goin upstairs any more. Mah strength is gone."

"Oh, for God's sake, we'll talk about it later," I snarled and rushed out exasperated; what new stupid thing was life going to bring now? Witching was I?

In fact some pictures in our bathroom were witch pictures, little drawings on bark used for witchcraft in Mexico. I think I had told her that. So I put it right out of my mind for then, witching indeed, and I went to my class and then to the library until time to pick Petey and Polly up again, refusing to employ my mind even one minute on this new nutty thing of Osella's any sooner than I had to. That's how I was in those days, more force and resolve, and not, like now, maundering and irresolute.

So I was so blank-minded when we came home and up the steps and saw a litter of charred wood and paper burning and smoldering on the kitchen doorstep that I couldn't even think what it might be.

Closer up, we could see it was of course the pictures—you could make out bits of burnt paper and broken glass and the charred frame—but also there was a slightly charred doll dressed in a scrap of cloth from a dress I had sewed myself. This doll had mostly escaped the flames, so I saw what was what.

There was Polly's doll Mabel, dressed in my dress, her legs burned off, finishing in melted stumps, and a paring knife stuck through her belly. I picked up Mabel, mostly to hide her from Polly, so Polly wouldn't see her, and put her in my book bag.

Angrily I stamped in and called for Osella. She was coming down from upstairs, I listened impatient for her fat slow steps. Then she lurched strangely into the kitchen, madness streaming off her like oil, madness showing in the swaying gait, in the white rolling and smoldering of her eyes, so that I could only think in a sick sudden panic of the burned bodies of Ivan and India; Osella had gone mad. Where were they? And I began to scream and scream for them, backing sweating away from Osella, Ivan, Ivan, India, India. Then I could hear them upstairs squeaking "Mommy's home" serenely.

"I smelt something burnin and it was them devil pictures," Osella said, her voice sounding normal and calm in spite of her deranged aspect. I stopped backing away in that craven fashion and stood forward to deal with this. "Go outside," I told Petey and Polly, but they didn't; they lingered behind me. I was shivering.

"I done smelt something and I knowed to expect trouble so I went up there and right before my eyes they done burst into flames. I had knowed they was ready, but I didn't think they was ready yet. I don't read that close."

"Osella, you burned them." Maybe she was drunk. She looked drunk. Ivan and India were clumping on the stairs and Osella was blocking my way to them. Her huge body took almost the whole space between the counter and the kitchen table.

Osella looked at me. "*You* burnt them," she said. I saw that she believed this. It was then I really understood that Osella was raving mad. I had never seen anyone raving mad before; there is no mistaking it when you look close. What did you do? And *then* I saw that in her hand beneath her apron she was carrying the bread knife. She had had it upstairs with her; she hadn't picked it up since she came into the kitchen. What had she been going to do with it? Maybe slaughter Ivan and India, and I felt faint.

"Osella," I said, so scared but walking around the table within her reach, slowly inching around to get to Ivan and India, "I forgot we have to go visit Mrs. Harvill. I promised to take the kids over there. We're late. I'll go up and get India and Ivan." Around the table safely, Osella swaying, hand still on bread knife but not lunging toward me. Ivan and India dragging junk down the stairs; I grabbed them up by the arms, one little kid on each side, them screaming with outrage, scuttled down the hall with them, through the living room, and put them out the front door: you stay out here.

Back in the kitchen, Osella had stood unmoving this whole time at the kitchen table, her one hand outspread on it, leaning on it supporting herself, in the other hand the bread knife and in the eyes that look, that helpless drugged crazy look.

"Petey and Polly, go out to the car," I said to them in that reserve fierce voice that children do obey; they opened the kitchen door and backed out like timid little visitors, and I backed out the stair passage again, watching Osella, until I could get out the front door. India and Ivan, disconsolate tots, brightened to see me, and they giggled excitedly.

"Osella made a big fire. It went whoom up to the ceiling," Ivan said.

"Walk with Mommy," I said, picking up India. Petey and Polly were already scuttling down the garden steps toward the car. Osella had come as far after us as the open kitchen door and now began to emit loud terrible howls.

"I done saved them babies!" she screamed. "Them pictures was killin them. I tried to keep you off." Now her voice became an exhausted whisper: "Mah strength is gone, mah strength is gone. I done told Gavvy he haf to hep hisself now. I done tried. Gavvy he so blind. Well, Gavvy a blind man that's gonna see light. I been carryin this weight, but mah strength is gone."

In her hand the knife. Slowly walking toward us. Scurrying, stumbling, down the steps to the street we went, and I threw the kids in the car and got in and locked the doors around us. It wouldn't start. I suppose I flooded it. Osella put her face against the windshield, glaring in at us through the window as if we were fish, the children laughing but scared, patting the glass her nose pressed against, or she was the fish, her mouth going and going, bubbles of mad rage coming out which we could hardly hear but only could see her opening and closing mouth.

"We will not look at her," I told the children. "We will pretend we cannot see or hear her. Then if she goes away we will open the car doors and jump out and run to Lynnie's house."

In the end that's what we did. After about ten minutes Osella seemed to tire of us, or to become confused and to forget what it was she wanted of us, and she wandered off back up the steps and stood at the top looking down on us. There was a chance she meant to trick us into coming out, fancied herself swooping down like a revengeful witch, but we could outrun her; she couldn't do stairs fast. At the agreed moment children and I burst from the car and began to run away. At the top of the steps I saw Osella lurch but whether in pursuit I don't know. We just ran.

It is strange to be fleeing for your life along your own block with no one noticing much. We slowed to a walk, walked as fast as we could, me carrying India. Did we wear harried excited faces? We passed people walking their dogs, and at the sight of them I would get a big confessional lump in the throat wanting to tell them that although we looked normal too, hurrying along the street, it was really that the maid had gone crazy and was trying to kill us with a bread knife. But then I would turn my eyes away and sidle past them, ashamed to be a person someone wants to kill. Maybe you think the stranger will turn against you, too. Each new person that we passed increased our terror.

I can imagine running down a long street, and someone gone berserk, a knifer or a rapist, is chasing you; you are too frightened to scream but all your power is concentrated in your heart, pushing you along in a frenzy. But you are getting tired; you are running more slowly, and his steps are closer behind you. Then, thank God, from an open doorway a figure steps out with a face of calm mercy and beckons you to shelter and safety. This happened to someone, I read about it in the papers: a figure steps out with mercy and you rush to him, fling yourself into his haven. Then as you look at him the warm flood of relief is checked with a gasp, a cry, for he is laughing at you with mocking malicious eyes. Together your assailant and your rescuer press you into the doorway, laughing, with the points of their knives against your belly. In my imagination they both look like the Famous Inspector, who in turn looks like my lover Andrew Mason. Funny.

But anyway then, swiftly as they always do, madness and terror passed over like cloud shadows and we were at Bess's sane house, and I rather relished saying with great aplomb, "Osella has gone crazy, I'm afraid; there's something strange about her eyes and she's burnt me in effigy." The children were laughing; Bess, too. After fright comes such elation. We thought we could hear the sound of dim shrieks from the direction of our house.

"But from here it sounds much the same as when she's singing," Bess said. "Maybe she's just singing." And other noises on the still afternoon air. It was just possible she was smashing things up. Something would have to be done. I called Gavin, who surprised me by saying he would come home. You never knew with Gavin; he had not come home when Polly broke her leg.

Bess minded the children. I know she minds my children for me more than I mind Lynnie, but she likes to, because they provide normal company for Lynnie.

Gavvy and I went back to our house, hesitating outside, hearing from within not shrieks but a lot of heavy thumping, and things being dragged around. "You stay here, I'll go in alone," Gavvy said, which made me laugh, it was so like a line from a movie. Indeed the whole thing was. Self-consciously we addressed ourselves to the unreal actuality that our maid had gone crazy. Gavin went in and came out almost immediately carrying the kitchen knives. "You're right, she's had some kind of break," he said. "She's packing her clothes but we should try to get her to a hospital. You go back to Bess's and call an ambulance."

But it was too late. Osella put all her clothes into a taxi and was driven off, the black taxi driver ignoring Gavvy's remonstrances, protectively driving her off. The ambulance came and went away again empty. This was the first time I completely understood that you may live with someone peacefully enough for a long time—years, maybe decades—and then one day they can look at you with eyes of blazing hate and go away in a taxi never to be seen again.

In the night when Gavvy was asleep, deep breathing and he always seemed so sweet and at peace then, I crept downstairs to the kitchen where I had left my book bag and took Mabel out. Twisted melted stump legs, knife in her belly, a dress made out of my dress. I looked at Mabel's dress, neatly sewn. Little sleeves, it had, even, and a snap to fasten it at Mabel's neck and a rent in front over the belly where the knife had savagely gone through.

I have never seen Osella again. For me it is as if she had died and her disembodied voice comes back from the spirit world along the telephone wire carrying whispered words of hatred. Sometimes she calls every day, sometimes not for a week or so. Where can she have hidden herself, in her hugeness, her madness, but in some demonic place to sit beside John Henry's malign corpse plotting things? I mean, I can't understand how she could be, say, in an apartment at Stockton and Twelfth and singing in her church choir on Sundays. What is she doing for money? How does she avoid being carted away by the first person who really looks in her soft deranged eyes?

She did come back once, when I wasn't home, and talked to Ev through the kitchen door. That was before we moved to this unit; I've never seen her around here. "Hello," she said to her black sister, smiling; "I come to see if mah babies wouldn't like to go for a walk with they ole mammy Osella. I been walkin by." Ivan and India crowded to the door with noisy shrieks of joy to see her, but Ev saw Polly's scared eyes, I guess, for Polly remembered, and Ev said, "No, they can't come out today, N. expectin them to stay in."

"Lord, woman, jus down the street, Osella's goin buy 'em some ice cream. Let 'em come out in the yard here."

"Ice cream! Ice cream!"

"No," Ev said, "you get along from here," in her polite voice, and shut the door.

"Nigger slut!" Osella shrieked, and then, they said, she stood quietly outside the door for maybe fifteen minutes, holding her big plastic pocketbook, and then waddled away down the steps.

I don't know if Gavin has ever seen her again. He tried to find her at first. When she began her phone calls with "things to tell," he would try to talk her into meeting him somewhere so he could catch her and get her to a doctor. "Yes, I want to hear these things you have to tell," he would say to her on the phone; "why don't you meet me?" But she was too cagey for that.

Instead she told her "things" over the phone, lies so excessive I stopped worrying whether Gavvy would believe them. She was working for a movie star. She was soon to be married to the famous Big Raider. She was being kept in a house with seventeen rooms and a swimming pool until her marriage. She had been offered a singing career, and, endlessly whispering it, "Miss N. just a whore, you know, you ought to see what she do; I seen her in the woods, with a man between her knees," and Gavvy would listen endlessly, rocking patiently to the monotonous sibilance, telephone held loosely as if he wasn't listening at all, making faces to communicate his boredom.

"Maybe she'll say something that'll give a clue to where she is," he explained, but she never did, but just called and ranted and Gavvy listened.

And shortly, oh, in not too many days at all, while we were dressing to go out, Gavin said, "There are marks on your neck." I looked in the mirror. There were; so what. I picked up my hairbrush.

Calmly he asked, "Who are you having an affair with?"

The scene is very clear. I watched it in my mirror: my eyes flying open in innocent astonishment. Various denials springing to my lips while Gavvy stares over my shoulder into the mirror, into my mirrored face, and fixes my gaze with his own knowing and deep eyes which seem to contain both the blood-and-bone knowledge of the cuckold and the practiced, courtroom knowingness of the Assistant District Attorney. I mentally review my case and my chances.

"Don't be silly," I say, and go on brushing my hair.

Gavin traces with his finger a scratch on my back I cannot see but can feel the soreness of, and I shrink, not from pain but from his touch. He senses the nature of my revulsion and smirks unpleasantly at this confirmation of his guess.

Then I attack him: "Ask Osella, she knows what I do, I tell her everything. She'll be happy to tell you everything she knows." I turn to walk away. Gavin opens his mouth, steps back; I essay an amused sarcastic laugh at the whole silly discussion.

"Osella is crazy, but what she says is true, all the same," Gavin said. "She knows things intuitively, and I intuitively know she's right. I realized when she started talking about it over the phone. She used to hint and I didn't pay any attention. Now that she raves, I somehow know she's right." And I intuitively knew that he knew that she knew, so there we were.

Then there followed a long silence or else one of those split seconds which expand in recollection because of the number and complexity of the many thoughts and considerations the mind reviews, perhaps simultaneously—truths, possible lies, consequences, probabilities. I saw images of Gavin's anger superimposed upon his presently calm face, I felt a certain leaping of excited blood, as before a battle—all this and more, however long it took, us swaying there, and finally I said, "Well, if you know already, why ask?" and turned indifferently away.

Now Gavin stepped around in front of me and I saw that this did not end the matter; this was no friendly chat. His face seemed to be dissolving in ripples, as if someone had dropped a rock in the middle of it; his eyes swam. I caught a glimpse of a sort of seaweed of demons behind them. It occurred to me crazily that I had gotten the curse of seeing into people's brains through their eyes, but then the glimpse closed over. I couldn't understand his face at all. I had no sense of personal danger.

"Oh, my darling," Gavvy said in a mumbling way, as if his teeth had dislodged. He breathed deeply and put a hand on each of my shoulders as if we were going to have a man-to-man talk. I was just in my slip, I think, because my shoulders were bare.

"We've had a lot of trouble," he said, "too many kids, all those years of my law school, neither of us is an easy person to live with. I suspect most couples face this moment some time or other."

A courtroomy quality had crept into his voice. My vigilance relaxed, was replaced by a distinct cold feeling at the base of my spine which climbed it like mercury and diffused into my shoulder blades. I did not understand this sensation but attended to it minutely, distracting from what Gavin was saying, but he was giving a peroration about our marriage, its trials and difficulties, about commitment and understanding, about unity and our children, about trying, about the sanctity of the home, about his great love for me and for our children. Gavin a veritable marital Clarence Darrow. Mutual forgiveness. No one is ever blameless. He for example was not blameless. And he knows he had not been as helpful, as supportive as he might have been. I, on the other hand, must know that I have not been all the things— enumerated—all the things I should have been. Gentle, urgent voice speaking searchingly into my face, hands gripping my shoulders, his pretty blond curls rumpled, face all earnest dimples. Blue shirt.

"I won't press you about it, and I promise I won't bring it up again. Just give me your word you'll break off this affair, and that will be that. We'll start over. Sometimes, I think, these shocks can be healthy, can bring everyone to a sense of what he has at stake, to reexamine the relationship, or to galvanize the situation. That was probably your motive at some level—did you ever think of that? To bring about a confrontation. And I *am* shocked, in the best sense. I really have come to my senses about a lot that's been happening between us; how destructive Osella has been, for example. I see what we have to do. We can do it. Tell the person—I won't ask who it is—that it's over. Break it off. The important thing is *us*. I've really awakened. It's worked, it's no longer needed. But you can understand that I would have to know the affair is over. You can understand that. I won't pry, won't ever ask, just tell me when you've broken off and together we . . ." So good in court, it is said of Gavvy, so earnest, boyish and convincing.

"No," replied an inner witch insolently in my voice.

"No?"

"No, I won't break off. No, that is, I won't stop doing whatever I'm doing if I've been doing anything, which I by no means admit. I will do what I want. Stop bothering me, and stop telling me what to do. I will do what I want," or other words like this spoken with a thrilled and rising abandon.

"Of course, if you've found somebody who really matters to you, that makes it more serious," Gavin said, preserving his judicious tone, "but I doubt, when you consider carefully, that the reality situation . . ."

It was that I had identified the chill in my backbone: I had understood it was my deep dislike for Gavvy. I don't like you, I don't even like you, over and over in my head like going over railroad tracks with all the excitement of wild dashing. And then the inner devil or brattish child began to scream in my voice, quite insanely, I suppose, "I *will* do what I want, I *will* do what I want!"

At this, dearly beloved—I can hear the mellifluous tones of some Famous Inspector instructing his flock—here, my children, here in this corpse you see the embodied or rather, unhappily, the disembodied perils of erotic self-indulgence and willfulness. Of these the principal sin is willfulness. A person cannot do just what he wants.

But I think I only meant, I will do what I want now because that is more honest than to do as I ought. Trash, Osella always spoke of, and it is trashy to live with someone you dislike and pretend to like him and pretend to love him and talk to him and feed him, when all the time you love someone else.

Then Gavin ran mad, his face a field of throbbing knots. I thought, well, here is the second, maybe the third person to run mad here recently, counting this outburst of mine, but I had myself subsided and watched blankly as he raved and went through my dresser drawers "looking for evidence," he said, and packed his own clothes and piled his thousands of books into the car ("What's Daddy doing, what's he doing?" "Moving his books") in a kind of efficient frenzy, and I floated dim-wittedly about on the driveway, confounded by my sense that although something important was happening here, I was not adequately grasping it or coping with it. The children were infected by the excitement of it but not, I hope, by the deep poison of hate and finality that had seeped into the air. They did not seem to sense it, and I'm glad of that.

"You were very stupid," Gavin said, following me back into the kitchen. "I made you a generous offer, to forget your infidelity. I can use this against you, you know. I can take the children, I probably will. How will you live? No judge on earth would—you made a mistake—I was very generous . . ."

I don't suppose I said anything back. I was beginning to be scared that he wouldn't go after all, but he did, drove away in his car, and when I went into the kitchen with the children, there was no Gavvy, just as there was no Osella. They had left. Was I a sinking ship? There was, I remember, a feeling of deep deep peace.

The deep deep peace, the balmy, lidless solitude of the deserted. How I hate it now and how I loved it then, not needing to speak to anyone or answer them, or answer to them. Cold reality of course set in, but not then. Then I locked the doors and windows ceremoniously, with my little train of children went around the house locking everything;

this was a female house now; and then had a serious talk with Petey and Polly about Daddy and Mommy. "Now you can get his pillow," Polly said. Then we made fudge.

An odd thing is that Gavvy in a way disappeared as entirely as Osella; I have never really seen him again either. Oh, we had to meet at the lawyer's, and I can see his outline in his car sometimes as he waits outside for the children, but he will never look at me, and so I can't really see him.

Joanna Russ

When It Changed

Katy drives like a maniac; we must have been doing over 120 kilometers per hour on those turns. She's good, though, extremely good, and I've seen her take the whole car apart and put it together again in a day. My birthplace on Whileaway was largely given to farm machinery and I refuse to wrestle with a five-gear shift at unholy speeds, not having been brought up to it, but even on those turns in the middle of the night, on a country road as bad as only our district can make them, Katy's driving didn't scare me. The funny thing about my wife, though: she will not handle guns. She has even gone hiking in the forests above the forty-eighth parallel without firearms, for days at a time. And that *does* scare me.

Katy and I have three children between us, one of hers and two of mine. Yuriko, my eldest, was asleep in the back seat, dreaming twelve-year-old dreams of love and war: running away to sea, hunting in the North, dreams of strangely beautiful people in strangely beautiful places, all the wonderful guff you think up when you're turning twelve and the glands start going. Some day soon, like all of them, she will disappear for weeks on end to come back grimy and proud, having knifed her first cougar or shot her first bear, dragging some abominably dangerous dead beastie behind her, which I will never forgive for what it might have done to my daughter. Yuriko says Katy's driving puts her to sleep.

For someone who has fought three duels, I am afraid of far, far too much. I'm getting old. I told this to my wife.

"You're thirty-four," she said. Laconic to the point of silence, that one. She flipped the lights on, on the dash—three kilometers to go and the road getting worse all the time. Far out in the country. Electric-green trees rushed into our headlights and around the car. I reached down next to me where we bolt the carrier panel to the door and eased my rifle into my lap. Yuriko stirred in the back. My height but Katy's eyes, Katy's face. The car engine is so quiet, Katy says, that you can hear breathing in the back seat. Yuki had been alone in the car when the message came, enthusiastically decoding her dot-dashes (silly to mount a wide-frequency transceiver near an I. C. engine, but most of Whileaway is on steam). She had thrown herself out of the car, my gangly and gaudy offspring, shouting at the top of her lungs, so of course she had had to come along. We've been intellectually prepared for this ever since the Colony was founded, ever since it was abandoned, but this is different. This is awful.

"Men!" Yuki had screamed, leaping over the car door. "They've come back! Real Earth men!"

We met them in the kitchen of the farmhouse near the place where they had landed; the windows were open, the night air very mild. We had passed all sorts of transportation when we parked outside—steam tractors, trucks, an I. C. flatbed, even a bicycle. Lydia, the district biologist, had come out of her Northern taciturnity long enough to take blood and urine samples and was sitting in a corner of the kitchen shaking her head in astonishment over the results; she even forced herself (very big, very fair, very shy, always painfully blushing) to dig up the old language manuals—though I can talk the old tongues in my sleep. And do. Lydia is uneasy with us; we're Southerners and too flamboyant. I counted twenty people in that kitchen, all the brains of North Continent. Phyllis Spet, I think, had come in by glider. Yuki was the only child there.

Then I saw the four of them.

They are bigger than we are. They are bigger and broader. Two were taller than I, and I am extremely tall, one meter eighty centimeters in my bare feet. They are obviously of our species but *off*, indescribably off, and as my eyes could not and still cannot quite comprehend the lines of those alien bodies, I could not, then, bring myself to touch them, though the one who spoke Russian—what voices they have—wanted to "shake hands," a custom from the past, I imagine. I can only say they were apes with human faces. He seemed to mean well, but I found myself shuddering back almost the length of the kitchen—and then I laughed apologetically—and then to set a good example (*interstellar amity*, I thought) did "shake hands" finally. A hard, hard hand. They are heavy as draft horses. Blurred, deep voices. Yuriko had sneaked in between the adults and was gazing at *the men* with her mouth open.

He turned *his* head—those words have not been in our language for six hundred years—and said, in bad Russian:

"Who's that?"

"My daughter," I said, and added (with that irrational attention to good manners we sometimes employ in moments of insanity), "My daughter, Yuriko Janetson. We use the patronymic. You would say matronymic."

He laughed, involuntarily. Yuki exclaimed. "I thought they would be *good-looking!*" greatly disappointed at this reception of herself. Phyllis Helgason Spet, whom someday I shall kill, gave me across the room a cold, level venomous look, as if to say: *Watch what you say. You know what I can do.* It's true that I have little formal status, but Madam President will get herself in serious trouble with both me and her own staff if she continues to consider industrial espionage good clean fun. Wars and rumors of wars, as it says in one of our ancestors' books. I translated Yuki's words into *the man's* dog-Russian, once our *lingua franca*, and *the man* laughed again.

"Where are all your people?" he said conversationally.

I translated again and watched the faces around the room; Lydia embarrassed (as usual), Spet narrowing her eyes with some damned scheme, Katy very pale.

"This is Whileaway," I said.

He continued to look unenlightened.

"Whileaway," I said. "Do you remember? Do you have records? There was a plague on Whileaway."

He looked moderately interested. Heads turned in the back of the room, and I caught a glimpse of the local professions-parliament delegate; by morning every town meeting, every district caucus, would be in full session.

"Plague?" he said. "That's most unfortunate."

"Yes," I said. "Most unfortunate. We lost half our population in one generation."

He looked properly impressed.

"Whileaway was lucky," I said. "We had a big initial gene pool, we had been chosen for extreme intelligence, we had a high technology and a large remaining population in which every adult was two-or-three experts in one. The soil is good. The climate is blessedly easy. There are thirty millions of us now. Things are beginning to snowball in industry—do you understand?—give us seventy years and we'll have more than one real city, more than a few industrial centers, full-time professions, full-time radio operators, full-time machinists, give us seventy years and not everyone will have to spend three-quarters of a lifetime on the farm." And I tried to explain how hard it is when artists can practice full-time only in old age, when there are so few, so very few who can be free, like Katy and myself. I tried also to outline our government, the two houses, the one by professions and the geographic one; I told him the district caucuses handled problems too big for the individual towns. And that population control was not a political issue, not yet, though give us time and it would be. This was a delicate point in our history; give us time. There was no need to sacrifice the quality of life for an insane rush into industrialization. Let us go our own pace. Give us time.

"Where are all the people?" said that monomaniac.

I realized then that he did not mean people, he meant *men,* and he was giving the word the meaning it had not had on Whileaway for six centuries.

"They died," I said. "Thirty generations ago."

I thought we had poleaxed him. He caught his breath. He made as if to get out of the chair he was sitting in; he put his hand to his chest; he looked around at us with the strangest blend of awe and sentimental tenderness. Then he said, solemnly and earnestly:

"A great tragedy."

I waited, not quite understanding.

"Yes," he said, catching his breath again with that queer smile, that adult-to-child smile that tells you something is being hidden and will be presently produced with cries of encouragement and joy, "a great tragedy. But it's over." And again he looked around at all of us with the strangest deference. As if we were invalids.

"You've adapted amazingly," he said.

"To what?" I said. He looked embarrassed. He looked inane. Finally he said, "Where I come from, the women don't dress so plainly."

"Like you?" I said. "Like a bride?" for the men were wearing silver from head to foot. I had never seen anything so gaudy. He made as if to answer and then apparently thought better of it; he laughed at me again. With an odd exhilaration—as if we were something childish and something wonderful, as if he were doing us an enormous favor —he took one shaky breath and said, "Well, we're here."

I looked at Spet, Spet looked at Lydia, Lydia looked at Amalia, who is the head of the local town meeting, Amalia looked at I don't know whom. My throat was raw. I cannot stand local beer, which the farmers swill as if their stomachs had iridium linings but I took it anyway, from Amalia (it was her bicycle we had seen outside as we parked), and swallowed it all. This was going to take a long time. I said, "Yes, here you are," and smiled (feeling like a fool), and wondered seriously if male-Earth-people's minds worked so very differently from female-Earth-people's minds, but that couldn't be so or the race would have died out long ago. The radio network had got the news around planet by now and we had another Russian speaker, flown in from Varna; I decided to cut out when *the man* passed around pictures of his wife, who looked like the priestess of some arcane cult. He proposed to question Yuki, so I barreled her into a back room in spite of her furious protests, and went out on the front porch. As I left, Lydia was explaining the difference between parthenogenesis (which is so easy that anyone can practice it) and what we do, which is the merging of ova. That is why Katy's baby looks like me. Lydia went on to the Ansky Process and Katy Ansky, our one full-polymath genius and the great-great-I don't know how many times great-grandmother of my own Katharina.

A dot-dash transmitter in one of the outbuildings chattered faintly to itself: operators flirting and passing jokes down the line.

There was a man on the porch. The other tall man. I watched him for a few minutes—I can move very quietly when I want to—and when I allowed him to see me, he stopped talking into the little machine hung around his neck. Then he said calmly, in excellent Russian, "Did you know that sexual equality has been reestablished on Earth?"

"You're the real one," I said, "aren't you? The other one's for show." It was a great relief to get things cleared up. He nodded affably.

"As a people, we are not very bright," he said. "There's been too much genetic damage in the last few centuries. Radiation. Drugs. We can use Whileaway's genes, Janet." Strangers do not call strangers by the first name.

"You can have cells enough to drown in," I said. "Breed your own."

He smiled. "That's not the way we want to do it." Behind him I saw Katy come into the square of light that was the screened-in door. He went on, low and urbane, not mocking me, I think, but with the self-confidence of someone who has always had money and strength to spare, who doesn't know what it is to be second-class or provincial. Which is very odd, because the day before, I would have said that was an exact description of me.

"I'm talking to you, Janet," he said, "because I suspect you have more popular influence than anyone else here. You know as well as I do that parthenogenetic culture has all sorts of inherent defects, and we do not—if we can help it—mean to use you for anything of the sort. Pardon me; I should not have said 'use.' But surely you can see that this kind of society is unnatural."

"Humanity is unnatural," said Katy. She had my rifle under her left arm. The top of that silky head does not quite come up to my collarbone, but she is as tough as steel; he began to move, again with that queer smiling deference (which his fellow had showed to me but he had not), and the gun slid into Katy's grip as if she had shot with it all her life.

"I agree," said the man. "Humanity is unnatural. I should know. I have metal in my teeth and metal pins here." He touched his shoulder. "Seals are harem animals," he added, "and so are men; apes are promiscuous and so are men; doves are monogamous and so are men; there are even celibate men and homosexual men. There are homosexual cows, I believe. But Whileaway is still missing something." He gave a dry chuckle. I will give him the credit of believing that it had something to do with nerves.

"I miss nothing," said Katy, "except that life isn't endless."

"You are—?" said the man, nodding from me to her.

"Wives," said Katy. "We're married." Again the dry chuckle.

"A good economic arrangement," he said, "for working and taking care of the children. And as good an arrangement as any for randomizing heredity, if your reproduction is made to follow the same pattern. But think, Katharina Michaelason, if there isn't something better that you might secure for your daughters. I believe in instincts, even in Man, and I can't think that the two of you—a machinist, are you? and I gather you are some sort of chief of police—don't feel somehow what even you must miss. You know it intellectually, of course. There is only half a species here. Men must come back to Whileaway."

Katy said nothing.

"I should think, Katharina Michaelason," said the man gently "that you, of all people, would benefit most from such a change," and he walked past Katy's rifle into the square of light coming from the door. I think it was then that he noticed my scar, which really does not show unless the light is from the side: a fine line that runs from temple to chin. Most people don't even know about it.

"Where did you get that?" he said, and I answered with an involuntary grin. "In my last duel." We stood there bristling at each other for several seconds (this is absurd but true) until he went inside and shut the screen door behind him. Katy said in a brittle voice, "You damned fool, don't you know when we've been insulted?" and swung up the rifle to shoot him through the screen, but I got to her before she could fire and knocked the rifle out of aim; it burned a hole through the porch floor. Katy was shaking. She kept whispering over and over, "That's why I never touched it, because I knew I'd kill someone. I knew I'd kill someone." The first man—the one I'd spoken with first—was still talking inside the house, something about the grand movement to recolonize and rediscover all that Earth had lost. He stressed the advantages to Whileaway: trade, exchange of ideas, education. He, too, said that sexual equality had been reestablished on Earth.

Katy was right, of course; we should have burned them down where they stood. Men are coming to Whileaway. When one culture has the big guns and the other has none, there is a certain predictability about the outcome. Maybe men would have come eventually in any case, I like to think that a hundred years from now my great-grand-children could have stood them off or fought them to a standstill, but even that's no odds; I will remember all my life those four people I first met who were muscled like bulls and who made me—if only for a moment—feel small. A neurotic reaction, Katy says. I remember everything that happened that night; I remember Yuki's excitement in the car, I remember Katy's sobbing when we got home as if her heart would break, I remember her lovemaking, a little peremptory as always, but wonderfully soothing and comforting. I remember prowling restlessly around the house after Katy fell asleep with one bare arm flung into a patch of light from the hall. The muscles of her forearms are like metal bars from all that driving and testing of her machines. Sometimes I dream about Katy's arms. I remember wandering into the nursery and picking up my wife's baby, dozing for a while with the poignant, amazing warmth of an infant in my lap, and finally returning to the kitchen to find Yuriko fixing herself a late snack. My daughter eats like a Great Dane.

"Yuki," I said, "do you think you could fall in love with a man?" and she whooped derisively. "With a ten-foot toad!" said my tactful child.

But men are coming to Whileaway. Lately I sit up nights and worry about the men who will come to this planet, about my two daughters and Betta Katharinason, about what will happen to Katy, to me, to my life. Our ancestors' journals are one long cry of pain and I suppose I ought to be glad now, but one can't throw away six centuries, or even (as I have lately discovered) thirty-four years. Sometimes I laugh at the question those four men hedged about all evening and never quite dared to ask, looking at the lot of us, hicks in overalls, farmers in canvas pants and plain shirts: *Which of you plays the role of the man?* As if we had to produce a carbon copy of their mistakes! I doubt very much that sexual equality has been reestablished on Earth. I do not like to think of myself mocked, of Katy deferred to as if she were weak, of Yuki made to feel unimportant or silly, of my other children cheated of their full humanity or turned into strangers. And I'm afraid that my own achievements will dwindle from what they were—or what I thought they were—to the not-very-interesting curiosa of the human race, the oddities you read about in the back of the book, things to laugh at sometimes because they are so exotic, quaint but not impressive, charming but not useful. I find this more painful than I can say. You will agree that for a woman who has fought three duels, all of them kills, indulging in such fears is ludicrous. But what's around the corner now is a duel so big that I don't think I have the guts for it; in Faust's words: *Verweile doch, du bist so schoen!* Keep it as it is. Don't change.

Sometimes at night I remember the original name of this planet, changed by the first generation of our ancestors, those curious women for whom, I suppose, the real name was too painful a reminder after the men died. I find it amusing, in a grim way, to see it all so completely turned around. This, too, shall pass. All good things must come to an end.

Take my life but don't take away the meaning of my life.

For-A-While.

Diane Wakoski

No More Soft Talk

Don't ask a geologist about rocks.
Ask me.

That man,
he said.

What can you do with him?
About him?
He's a rock.

No, not a rock,
I said.
　　Well,
a very brittle rock, then.
One that crumbles easily, then.
Is crushed to dust, finally.

Me,
I said.
I am the rock.
The hard rock.
You can't break me.

I am trying to think how a woman
can be a rock,
when all she wants is to be soft,
to melt to the lines
her man draws for her.

But talking about rocks
intelligently
must be
talking about different kinds
of rock.

What happens to the brain
in shock? Is it
like an explosion
of flowers and blood,
staining the inside
of the skull?

I went to my house,
to see my man,
found the door locked,
and something I didn't plan
on—a closed bedroom door
(my bed),

another woman's handbag on the couch.
Is someone in the bedroom?

Yes, yes,
a bed full of snakes all bearing new young,
a bed full of slashed wrists,
a bed of carbines and rifles with no ammunition,
a bed of my teeth in another woman's fingers.

Then the answer to rocks,
as I sit here and talk.

The image of an explosion:
a volcanic mountain
on a deserted Pacific island.
What comes up,
like gall in my throat,
a river of abandoned tonsils that can no longer cry,
a sea of gold wedding rings and smashed glasses,
the lava, the crushed and melted rock
comes pouring out now,
down this mountain you've never seen,
from this face that believed in you,
rocks that have turned soft,
but now are bubbling out of the lips of a mountain,
into the ocean, raising the temperature
to 120 degrees.
If your ship were here
it would melt all the caulking.

This lava,
hot and soft,
will cool someday,
and turn back into the various stones.
None of it is
my rock.
My rock doesn't crumble.

My rock is the mountain.
Love me
if you can.
I will not make it easy for you
any more.

To An Autocrat

Today you told me
you kicked the first lady
you lived with
out
because she washed her underwear,
blue silky things,
and hung them in the bathroom to dry.

A few days ago
you told me
another girl got kicked out
for mentioning
grandchildren.

These anecdotes
about taboos
begin to extend from telephone calls
to toothbrushing
and leave me trembling
as I suppose you think a lady should
afraid to make any independent move.
There is no doubt
you possess this house
and everything in it.
You can move me out or in
at will;
have done so to prove your power.
My only weapon
is logic
which salts you like a withering garden snail.
                                                Because
it is you
who give me lectures
about the hang-ups of marriage,
and of people wanting to possess each other.
Save your stories for men,
I ought to tell you,
because any woman who buys them
is a guerilla fighter who believes you've been master
of your house too long.
When you move all us silly ones
with our dripping underwear out
and install this one liberated lady with her fine panties
and spider-web bras,
her short icy slips,
and satin garters that draw your eyes up her legs
like filings following a magnet,
and you never see a vestige of how she launders them,
and she follows all your rules
and makes no demands,
while we poor offenders are always needing things

and trying to live our own lives too,
then,
sir,
I tremble for you
for real.
Will she cut your throat one night as you sleep
or take off your balls?
Will she steal you blind
and leave with your stockbroker
or debilitate you with your own weaknesses
and jump in to mastery after
she's spoiled you for anything but drink and talk?
She is your fate,
anyway,
if you don't realize
that living together
is what makes us human and decent.
We give in to others' needs, their rights,
making a fair division of privileges
and chores.
Our dog finds a long beam of sunshine
coming in an afternoon window
and she stretches her doberman body
to fit it.
          She follows the sunshine around the house
from morning to late afternoon,
stretching or curling into the patterns it makes
on the floor.
She is not perfect,
but she fits
the hours of the day.
                    She understands
living /
          loving what you have,
making
the fit.

W. Rings On Her Fingers & Bells On Her Toes
She Shall Have Music Wherever She Goes

where the mushrooms grow
large and bulbous
landing mysteriously on the grass
wetly fallen from the sky in the morning
as if they are parachutes.
fingers inside the
head and stem,
just as
there are arms reaching out
from the trees

the dark green soot in the woods
with just a circle of sky
above
surrounded,
the magnificent leaves falling
out of my life;
if it were autumn
there would be
no need for adjectives,

      that place where I
      get headaches,
      forget how the gold leaves
      buckle my eye with the sunshine,
      and the red ones match any
      blood that should come out of my lip,

there is a place where night is darker
than I've ever seen dark before;
where the mushroom ghosts
come and lead me with their beautiful
fingers, where the spirals
stand out of my brain
like electric sparks
saying why do you feel this way
lead to the dark spot of forest—
but it's not nearly so lightless
as that room where I'm sleeping—
the ghosts with beautiful fingers
tell me how to get there in my bare feet.
my hair winds around my ears
the leaves like honey crush into my ear
as I lie down on the forest floor.
the ghosts growing out of the ground
have cool memories of your cheek,
things I cannot stand to think of any more,
knowing they are false.

he told me of his girl
who had three holes drilled in her
ear
lobe,
to wear three studs, of
descending,
ascending
sizes—
but I had one hole
pierced into each ear,
threaded with gold
and waited
for those rings
to replace
the ones in my throat

words
I hadn't meant to speak
coming out of my mouth
in the middle of the night,
in the dark
he told me of the girl
with dark hair,
large breasts and small waist
who reminded him of his mother
who he thought was 17 and so
beautiful with gypsy ankles
in her name and veils around her
words
but the room was darker
at night
than my forest

it is true
there is love that
is decided upon
and love that spreads like a stain
of ink in absorbent cloth
there is love
that makes sense of your life
and love that makes you senseless
about life

what do we do with our lives
when there is more shadow than light?
the mushrooms can only grow
where it's cool
damp, and somewhat
dark
they are filled with the fingers
of old lovers,
husbands,
wives,
people weighted down with rings /

my ears
just prickling with ghosts' fingers
the white lies
on the grass
of a dark

is it beautiful?

past.

Joyce Carol Oates

The Dead

Useful in acute and chronic depression, where accompanied by anxiety, insomnia, agitation; psychoneurotic states manifested by tension, apprehension, fatigue. . . . They were small yellow capsules, very expensive. She took them along with other capsules, green-and-aqua, that did not cost quite so much but were weaker. *Caution against hazardous occupations requiring complete mental alertness.* What did that mean, "complete mental alertness?" Since the decline of her marriage, a few years ago, Ilena thought it wisest to avoid complete mental alertness. That was an overrated American virtue.

For the relief of anxiety and the relief of the apprehension of anxiety: small pink pills. *Advise against ingestion of alcohol.* But she was in the habit of drinking anyway, always before meeting strangers and often before meeting friends, sometimes on perfectly ordinary, lonely days when she expected to meet no one at all. She was fascinated by the possibility that some of these drugs could cause paradoxical reactions—fatigue and intense rage, increase and decrease in libido. She liked paradox. She wondered how the paradoxical reactions could take place in the same body, at the same time. Or did they alternate days? *For the relief of chronic insomnia:* small harmless white barbiturates. In the morning, hurrying out somewhere, she took a handful of mood-elevating pills, swallowed with some hot water right from the faucet, or coffee, to bring about a curious hollow-headed sensation, exactly as if her head were a kind of drum. Elevation! She felt the very air breathed into her lungs suffused with a peculiar dazzling joy, worth every risk.

Adverse reactions were possible: *confusion, ataxia, skin eruptions, edema, nausea, constipation, blood dyscrasias, jaundice, hepatic dysfunction, hallucinations, tremor, slurred speech, hyperexcitement. . . .* But anything was possible, after all!

A young internist said to her, "These tests show that you are normal," and her heart had fallen, her stomach had sunk, her very intestines yearned downward, stricken with gravity. Normal? Could that be? She had stared at him, unbelieving. "The symptoms you mention—the insomnia, for instance—have no organic basis that we can determine," he said.

Then why the trembling hands, why the glitter to the eyes, why, why the static in the head? She felt that she had been cheated. This was not worth sixty dollars, news like this. As soon as she left the doctor's office she went to a water fountain in the corridor and took a few capsules of whatever was in her coat pocket, loose in the pocket along with tiny pieces of lint and something that looked like the flaky

skins of peanuts, though she did not remember having put peanuts
in any of her pockets. She swallowed one, two, three green-and-aqua
tranquillizers, and a fairly large white pill that she didn't recognize,
found in the bottom of her purse with a few stray hairs and paper
clips. This helped a little. "So I'm normal!" she said.

She had been living at that time in Buffalo, New York, teaching part-
time at the university. Buffalo was a compromise between going to
California, as her ex-husband begged, and going to New York, where
she was probably headed. Her brain burned dryly, urging her both
westward and eastward, so she spent a year in this dismal Midwestern city in upstate New York, all blighted elms and dingy skies
and angry politicians. The city was in a turmoil of excitement; daily
and nightly the city police prowled the university campus in search
of troublesome students, and the troublesome students hid in the
bushes along buildings, eager to plant their homemade time bombs
and run; so the campus was not safe for ordinary students or ordinary
people at all. Even the "normal," like Ilena, long wearied of political
activism, were in danger.

She taught twice a week and the rest of the time avoided the university. She drove a 1965 Mercedes an uncle had willed her, an uncle
rakish and remote and selfish, like Ilena herself, who had taken a kind
of proud pity on her because of her failed marriage and her guilty
listlessness about family ties. The uncle, a judge, had died in St. Louis;
she had to fly there to get the car. The trip back had taken her nearly
a week, she had felt so unaccountably lazy and sullen. But, once back
in Buffalo, driving her stodgy silver car, its conservative shape protecting her heavily, she felt safe from the noxious street fumes and
the darting, excitable eyes of the police and the local Buffalo taxpayers
—in spite of her own untidy hair and clothes.

The mood-elevating pills elevated her several feet off the ground and
made her stammer rapidly into the near, dim faces of her students,
speaking faster and faster in the hope that the class period would
end sooner. But the tranquilizers dragged her down, massaged her
girlish heart to a dreamy condition, fingered the nerve ends lovingly,
soothingly, wanted only to assure her that all was well. In her inherited car she alternately drove too fast, made nervous by the speedier
pills, or too slowly, causing warlike sounds from the rear, the honking
of other drivers in American cars.

In the last two years Ilena had been moving around constantly: packing up the same clothes and items and unpacking them again, always
eager, ready to be surprised, flying from one coast to the other to
speak at universities or organizations interested in "literature," hope-
ful and adventurous as she was met at various windy airports by
strangers. Newly divorced, she had felt virginal again, years younger,
truly childlike and American. Beginning again. Always beginning.
She had written two quiet novels, each politely received and selling
under one thousand copies, and then she had written a novel based
on an anecdote overheard by her at the University of Michigan, in
a girls' rest room in the library, about a suicide club and the "system-
atic deaths of our most valuable natural resource, our children"—

as one national reviewer of the novel said gravely. It was her weakest novel, but it was widely acclaimed and landed her on the cover of a famous magazine, since her *Death Dance* had also coincided with a sudden public interest in the achievement of women in "male-dominated fields." Six magazines came out with cover stories on the women's liberation movement inside a three-month period; Ilena's photograph had been exceptionally good. She found herself famous, and fame made her mouth ironic and dry with a sleeplessness that was worse than ever, in spite of her being "normal."

The pills came and went in cycles—the yellow capsules favored for a while, then dropped for the small pink pills, tranquillizers big enough to nearly knock her out taken with some gin and lemon, late at night. These concoctions were sacred to her, always kept secret. Her eyes grew large with the prospect of all those "adverse reactions" that were threatened but somehow never arrived. She was lucky, she thought. Maybe nothing adverse would ever happen to her. She had been twenty-six years old at the start of the breakup of her marriage; it was then that most of the pills began, though she had always had a problem with insomnia. The only time she had truly passed out, her brain gone absolutely black, was the winter day—very late in the afternoon—when she had been in her office at a university in Detroit, with a man whom she had loved at that time, and a key had been thrust in the lock and the door opened—Ilena had screamed, "No! Go away!" It had been only a cleaning lady, frightened off without seeing anything, or so the man had assured Ilena. But she had fainted. Her skin had gone wet and cold; it had taken the terrified man half an hour to bring her back to normal again. "Ilena, I love you, don't die," he had begged. Finally she was calm enough to return to her own home, an apartment she shared with her husband in the northwestern corner of the city; she went home, fixed herself some gin and bitter lemon, and stood in the kitchen drinking it while her husband yelled questions at her. "Where were you? Why were you gone so long?" She had not answered him. The drink was mixed up in her memory with the intense relief of having escaped some humiliating danger, and the intense terror of the new, immediate danger of her husband's rage. Why was this man yelling at her? Whom had she married, that he could yell at her so viciously? The drinking of that gin was a celebration of her evil.

That was back in 1967; their marriage had ended with the school year; her husband spent three weeks in a hospital half a block from his mother's house in Oswego, New York, and Ilena had not gone to see him, not once, being hard of heart, like stone, and terrified of seeing him again. She feared his mother, too. The marriage had been dwindling all during the Detroit years—1965–1967—and they both left the city shortly before the riot, which seemed to Ilena, in her usual poetic, hyperbolic, pill-sweetened state, a cataclysmic flowering of their own hatred. She had thought herself good enough at hating, but her husband was much better. "Die. Why don't you die. *Die*," he had whispered hypnotically to her once, as she lay in bed weeping very early one morning, before dawn, too weary to continue their battle. Off and on she had spoken sentimentally about having children, but Bryan was wise enough to dismiss that scornfully—"You don't bring children into the world to fix up a rotten marriage," he said. She had not known it was rotten, exactly. She knew that he was jealous of her. A mutual friend, a psychiatrist, had told her gently that her having published two novels—unknown as they were, and financial failures—was "unmanning" to Bryan, who wanted to write but couldn't. Was that her fault? What could she do? "You could fail at something yourself," she was advised.

In the end she had fallen in love with another man. She had set out to love someone in order to punish her husband, to revenge herself upon him; but the revenge was forgotten, she had really fallen in love in spite of all her troubles . . . in love with a man who turned out to be a disappointment himself, but another kind of disappointment.

Adverse reactions: *confusion, ataxia, skin eruptions, edema, nausea, constipation, blood dyscrasias, jaundice, hepatic dysfunction, hallucinations.* . . . Her eyes filmed over with brief ghostly uninspired hallucinations now and then, but she believed this had nothing to do with the barbiturates she took to sleep, or the amphetamines she took to speed herself up. It was love that wore her out. Love, and the air of Detroit, the gently wafting smoke from the manly smokestacks of factories. Love and smoke. The precise agitation of love in her body, what her lover and her husband did to her body; and the imprecise haze of the air, of her vision, filmed-over and hypnotised. She recalled having loved her husband very much at one time. Before their marriage in 1964. His name was Bryan Donohue, and as his wife she had been *Ilena Donohue*, legally; but a kind of maiden cunning had told her to publish her novels as *Ilena Williams*, chaste Ilena, the name musical with *l*'s. Her books were by that Ilena, while her nights of sleeplessness beside a sleeping, twitching, perspiring man were spent by the other Ilena. At that time she was not famous yet and not quite so nervous. A little insomnia, that wasn't so bad. Many people had insomnia. She feared sleep because she often dreamed of the assassination of Kennedy, which was run and rerun in her brain like old newsreels. Years after that November day she was still fresh with sorrow for him, scornful of her own sentimentality but unable to control it. How she had wept! Maybe she had been in love with Kennedy, a little. . . . So, sleeping brought him back to her not as a man: as a corpse. Therefore she feared sleep. She could lie awake beside a breathing, troubled corpse of her own, her partner in this puzzling marriage, and she rehearsed her final speech to him so many times that it became jaded and corny to her, out of date as a monologue in an Ibsen play.

"There is another man, of course," he had said flatly.

"No. No one."

"Yes, another man."

"No."

"Another man, I know, but I'm not interested. Don't tell me his name."

"There is no other man."

"Obviously there is. Probably a professor at that third-rate school of yours."

"No."

Of course, when she was in the company of the *other man*, it was Bryan who became "the other" to him and Ilena—remote and masculine and dangerous, powerful as a nightmare figure, with every right to embrace Ilena in the domestic quiet of their apartment. He had every right to make love to her, and Gordon did not. They were adulterers, Ilena and Gordon. They lost weight with their guilt, which was finely wrought in them as music, precious and subtle and prized, talked over endlessly. Ilena could see Gordon's love for her in his face. She loved that face, she loved to stroke it, stare at it, trying to imagine it as the face of a man married to another woman. . . . He was not so handsome as her own husband, perhaps. She didn't know. She only knew, bewildered and stunned, that his face was the center of the universe for her, and she could no more talk herself out of this whimsy than she could talk herself out of her sorrow for Kennedy.

Her husband, Bryan Donohue: tall, abrupt, self-centered, amusing, an instructor in radiology at Wayne Medical School, with an interest in jazz and a desire to write articles on science, science and sociology, jazz, jazz and sociology, anything. He was very verbal and he talked excellently, expertly. Ilena had always been proud of him in the presence of other people. He had a sharp, dissatisfied face, with very dark eyes. He dressed well and criticized Ilena when she let herself go, too rushed to bother with her appearance. In those days, disappointed by the low salary and the bad schedule she received as an instructor at a small university in Detroit, Ilena had arrived for early classes—she was given eight-o'clock classes every semester—with her hair barely combed, loose down to her shoulders, snarled and bestial from a night of insomnia, her stockings marred with snags or long disfiguring runs, her face glossy with the dry-mouthed euphoria of tranquillizers, so that, pious and sour, she led her classes in the prescribed ritual prayer—this was a Catholic university, and Ilena had been brought up as a Catholic—and felt freed, once the prayer was finished, of all restraint.

Bad as the eight-o'clock classes were, the late-afternoon classes (4:30–6:00) were worse: the ashes of the day, tired undergraduates who needed this course to fill out their schedules, high-school teachers—mainly nuns and "brothers"—who needed a few more credits for their Master's degrees, students who worked, tired unexplained strangers with rings around their eyes of fatigue and boredom and the degradation of many semesters as "special students." When she was fortunate enough to have one or two good students in these classes, Ilena charged around in excitement, wound up by the pills taken at noon with black coffee, eager to draw them out into a dialogue with her. They talked back and forth. They argued. The other students sat docile and perplexed, waiting for the class to end, glancing from Ilena to one of her articulate boys, back to Ilena again, taking notes only when Ilena seemed to be saying something important. What was so exciting about Conrad's *Heart of Darkness*, they wondered, that Mrs. Donohue could get this worked up?

Her copper-colored hair fell in a jumble about her face, and her skin sometimes took a radiant coppery beauty from the late afternoon sun as it sheered mistily through the campus trees, or from the excitement of a rare, good class, or from the thought of her love for Gordon, who would be waiting to see her after class. One of the boys in this late-afternoon class—Emmett Norlan—already wore his hair frizzy and long, though this was 1966 and a few years ahead of the style, and he himself was only a sophomore, a small precocious irritable argumentative boy with glasses. He was always charging up to Ilena after class, demanding that she explain herself—"You use words like 'emotions,' you bully us with your *emotions!*" he cried. "When I ask you a question in class, you distort it! You try to make everyone laugh at me! It's a womanly trick, a *female* trick, not worthy of you!" Emmett took everything seriously, as seriously as Ilena; he was always hanging around her office, in the doorway, refusing to come in and sit down because he was "in a hurry" and yet reluctant to go away, and Ilena could sense by a certain sullen alteration of his jaw that her lover was coming down the hall to her office. . . .

"See you," Emmett would say sourly, backing away.

Gordon was a professor of sociology, a decade or more older than Ilena, gentle and paternal; no match for her cunning. After a particularly ugly quarrel with her husband, one fall day, Ilena had looked upon this man and decided that he must become her lover. At the time she had not even known his name. *A lover. She would have a lover.* He was as tall as her own husband, with a married, uncomfortable look about his mouth—tense apologetic smiles, creases at the corners of his lips, bluish-purple veins on his forehead. A handsome man, but somehow a little gray. His complexion was both boyish and gray. He did not dress with the self-conscious care of her husband Bryan; his clothes were tweedy, not very new or very clean, baggy at the knees, smelling of tobacco and unaired closets. Ilena, determined to fall in love with him, had walked by his home near the university—an ordinary brick two-story house with white shutters. Her heart pounded with jealousy. She imagined his domestic life: a wife, four children, a Ford with a dented rear fender, a lawn that was balding, a street that was going bad—one handsome old Tudor home had already been converted into apartments for students, the sign of inevitable disaster. Meeting him, talking shyly with him, loving him at her finger tips was to be one of the gravest events in her life, for, pill-sweetened as she was, she had not seriously believed he might return her interest. He was Catholic. He was supposed to be happily married.

When it was over between them and she was teaching, for two quick, furtive semesters at the University of Buffalo, where most classes were canceled because of rioting and police harassment, Ilena thought back to her Detroit days and wondered how she had survived, even with the help of drugs and gin: the central nervous system could not take such abuse, not for long. She had written a novel out of her misery, her excitement, her guilt, typing ten or fifteen pages an evening until her head throbbed with pain that not even pills could ease. At times, lost in the story she was creating, she had felt an eerie longing to remain there permanently, to simply give up and go mad. *Adverse reactions: confusion, hallucinations, hyperexcitement. . . .* But she had not gone mad. She had kept on typing, working, and when she was finished it was possible to pick up, in her fingers, the essence of that shattering year: one slim book.

Death Dance. *The story of America's alienated youth . . . shocking revelations . . . suicide . . . drugs . . . waste . . . horror . . .* $5.98.

It had been at the top of the *New York Times* best-seller list for fifteen weeks.

Gordon had said to her, often, "I don't want to hurt you, Ilena. I'm afraid of ruining your life." She had assured him that her life was not that delicate. "I could go away if Bryan found out, alone. I could live alone," she had said lightly, airily, knowing by his grimness that he would not let her—surely he would not let her go? Gordon thought more about her husband than Ilena did, the "husband" he had met only once, at a large university reception, but with whom he now shared a woman. Two men, strangers, shared her body. Ilena wandered in a perpetual sodden daze, thinking of the . . . the madness of loving two men . . . the freakishness of it, which she could never really comprehend, could not assess, because everything in her recoiled from it: this could not be happening to her. Yet the fact of it was in her body, carried about in her body. She could not isolate it, could not comprehend it. Gazing at the girl students, at the nuns, she found herself thinking enviously that their lives were unsoiled and honest and open to any possibility, while hers had become fouled, complicated, criminal, snagged, somehow completed without her assent. She felt that she was going crazy.

Her teaching was either sluggish and uninspired, or hysterical. She was always wound up and ready to let go with a small speech on any subject—Vietnam, the oppression of blacks, religious hypocrisy, the censorship haggling over the student newspaper, any subject minor or massive—and while her few aggressive students appreciated this, the rest of her students were baffled and unenlightened. She sat in her darkened office, late in the afternoon, whispering to Gordon about her classes: "They aren't going well. I'm afraid. I'm not any good as a teacher. My hands shake when I come into the classroom. . . . The sophomores are forced to take this course and they hate me, I know they hate me. . . ." Gordon stroked her hands, kissed her face, her uplifted face, and told her that he heard nothing but good reports about her teaching. He himself was a comfortable, moderately popular professor; he had been teaching for fifteen years. "You have some very enthusiastic students," he said. "Don't doubt yourself, Ilena, please; if you hear negative things it might be from other teachers who are jealous. . . ." Ilena pressed herself gratefully into this good man's embrace, hearing the echo of her mother's words of years ago, when Ilena would come home hurt from school for some minor girlish reason: "Don't mind them, they're just *jealous*."

A world of jealous people, like her husband: therefore hateful, therefore dangerous. Out to destroy her. Therefore the pills, tiny round pills and large button-sized pills, and the multicolored capsules.

There were few places she and Gordon could meet. Sometimes they walked around the campus, sometimes they met for lunch downtown, but most of the time they simply sat in her office and talked. She told him everything about her life, reviewing all the snarls and joys she had reviewed, years before, with Bryan, noticing that she emphasized the same events and even used the same words to describe them. She told him everything, but she never mentioned the drugs. He would disapprove. Maybe he would be disgusted. Like many Catholic men of his social class, and of his generation, he would be frightened by weakness in women, though by his own admission he drank too much. If he commented on her dazed appearance, if he worried over her fatigue—"Does your husband do this to you? Put you in this state?" —she pretended not to understand. "What, do I look so awful? So ugly?" she would tease. That way she diverted his concern, she bullied him into loving her, because he was a man to whom female beauty was important—his own wife had been a beauty queen many years ago, at a teachers' college in Ohio. "No, you're beautiful. You're beautiful," he would whisper.

They teased each other to a state of anguish on those dark winter afternoons, never really safe in Ilena's office—she shared the office with a nun, who had an early teaching schedule but who might conceivably turn up at any time, and there was always the possibility of the cleaning lady or the janitor unlocking the door with a master key —nightmarish possibility! Gordon kissed her face, her body, she clasped her hands around him and gave herself up to him musically, dreamily, like a rose of rot with only a short while left to bloom, carrying the rot neatly hidden, deeply hidden. She loved him so that her mind went blank even of the euphoria of drugs or the stimulation of a good, exciting day of teaching; she felt herself falling back into a blankness like a white flawless wall, pure material, pure essence, a mysterious essence that was fleshly and spiritual at once. Over and over they declared their love for each other, they promised it, vowed it, repeated it in each other's grave accents, echoing and unconsciously imitating each other, Ilena carrying home to her apartment her lover's gentleness, his paternal listening manner. Maybe Bryan sensed Gordon's presence, his influence on her, long before the breakup. Maybe he could discern, with his scientist's keen heatless eye, the shadow of another personality, powerful and beloved, on the other side of his wife's consciousness.

Ilena vowed to Gordon, "I love you, only you," and she made him believe that she and Bryan no longer slept in the same bed. This was not true: she was so fearful of Bryan, of his guessing her secret, that she imitated with her husband the affection she gave to Gordon, in that way giving herself to two men, uniting them in her body. *Two men. Uniting them in her body.* Her body could not take all this. Her body threatened to break down. She hid from Bryan, spending an hour or more in the bathtub, gazing down through her lashes at her bluish bruised body, wondering how long this phase of her life could last—the taunting of her sanity, the use of her rather delicate body by two normal men. *This is how a woman becomes prehistoric,* she thought. *Prehistoric. Before all personalized, civilized history. Men make love to her and she is reduced to protoplasm.*

She recalled her girlhood and her fear of men, her fear of someday having to marry—for all her female relatives urged marriage, marriage! —and now it seemed to her puzzling that the physical side of her life should be so trivial. It was not important, finally. She could have taken on any number of lovers, it was like shaking hands at a party, moving idly and absent-mindedly from one man to another; nothing serious about it at all. Why had she feared it so? And that was why the landscape of Detroit took on to her such neutral bleakness, its sidewalks and store windows and streets and trees, its spotted skies, its old people, its children—all unformed, unpersonalized, unhistoric. Everyone is protoplasm, she thought, easing together and easing apart. Some touch and remain stuck together; others touch and part. . . . But, though she told herself this, she sometimes felt her head weighed down with a terrible depression and she knew she would have to die, would have to kill her consciousness. She could not live with two men.

She could not live with one man.

Heated, hysterical, she allowed Gordon to make love to her in that office. The two of them lay exhausted and stunned on the cold floor— unbelieving lovers. Had this really happened? She felt the back of her mind dissolve. Now she was committed to him, she had been degraded, if anyone still believed in degradation; now something would happen, something must happen. She would divorce Bryan; he would divorce his wife. They must leave Detroit. They must marry. They must change their lives.

Nothing happened.

She sprang back to her feet, assisted by this man who seemed to love her so helplessly, her face framed by his large hands, her hair smoothed, corrected by his hands. She felt only a terrible chilly happiness, an elation that made no sense. And so she would put on her coat and run across the snowy, windswept campus to teach a class in freshman composition, her skin rosy, radiant, her body soiled and reeking beneath her clothes, everything secret and very lovely. Delirious and articulate, she lived out the winter. She thought, eying her students: *If they only knew.* . . . It was all very high, very nervous and close to hysteria; Gordon loved her, undressed her and dressed her, retreated to his home where he undressed and bathed his smallest children, and she carried his human heat with her everywhere on the coldest days, edgy from the pills of that noon and slightly hungover from the barbiturates of the night before, feeling that she was living her female life close to the limits, at the most extreme boundaries of health and reason. Her love for him burned inward, secretly, and she was dismayed to see how very soiled her clothes were, sometimes as if mocking her. Was this love, was it a stain like any other? But her love for him burned outward, making her more confident of herself, so that she did not hesitate to argue with her colleagues. She took part in a feeble anti-Vietnam demonstration on campus, which was jeered at by most of the students who bothered to watch, and which seemed to embarrass Gordon, who was not "political." She did not hesitate to argue with hard-to-manage students during class, sensing herself unladylike and impudent and reckless in their middle-class Catholic eyes, a *woman* who dared to say such things!—"I believe in birth control, obviously, and in death control. Suicide must be recognized as a natural human right." This, at a Catholic school; she had thought herself daring in those days.

Emmett Norlan and his friends, scrawny, intense kids who were probably taking drugs themselves, at least smoking marijuana, clustered around Ilena and tried to draw her into their circle. They complained that they could not talk to the other professors. They complained about the "religious chauvinism" of the university, though Ilena asked them what they expected—it was a Catholic school, wasn't it? "Most professors here are just closed circuits, they don't create anything, they don't communicate anything," Emmett declared contemptuously. He was no taller than Ilena herself, and she was a petite woman. He wore sloppy, soiled clothes, and even on freezing days he tried to go without a heavy coat; his perpetual grimy fatigue jacket became so familiar to Ilena that she was to think of him, sharply and nostalgically, whenever she saw such a jacket in the years to come. The boy's face was surprisingly handsome, in spite of all the frizzy hair and beard and the constant squinting and grimacing; but it was small and boyish. He had to fight that boyishness by being tough. His glasses were heavy, black-rimmed, and made marks on either side of his nose—he often snatched them off and rubbed the bridge of his nose, squinting nearsightedly at Ilena, never faltering in his argument. Finally Ilena would say, "Emmett, I have to go home. Can't we talk about this some other time?"—wondering anxiously if Gordon had already left school. She was always backing away from even the students she liked, always edging away from her fellow teachers; she was always in a hurry, literally running from her office to a classroom or to the library, her head ducked against the wind and her eyes narrowed so that she need not see the faces of anyone she knew. In that university she was friendly with only a few people, among them the head of her department, a middle-aged priest with a degree from Harvard. He was neat, graying, gentlemanly, but a little corrupt in his academic standards: the Harvard years had been eclipsed long ago by the stern daily realities of Detroit.

The end for Ilena at this school came suddenly, in Father Hoffman's office.

Flushed with excitement, having spent an hour with Gordon in which they embraced and exchanged confidences—about his wife's sourness, her husband's iciness—Ilena had rushed to a committee that was to examine a Master's degree candidate in English. She had never sat on one of these committees before. The candidate was a monk, Brother Ronald, a pale, rather obese, pleasant man in his thirties. His lips were more womanish than Ilena's. The examination began with a question by a professor named O'Brien: "Please give us a brief outline of English literature." Brother Ronald began slowly, speaking in a gentle, faltering voice—this question was always asked by this particular professor, so the candidate had memorized an answer, perfectly —and O'Brien worked at lighting his pipe, nodding vaguely from time to time. Brother Ronald came to a kind of conclusion some fifteen minutes later, with the "twentieth century," mentioning the names of Joyce, Lawrence, and T. S. Eliot. "Very good," said O'Brien. The second examiner, Mr. Honig, asked nervously: "Will you describe tragedy and give us an example, please?" Brother Ronald frowned. After a moment he said, "There is *Hamlet* . . . and *Macbeth*. . . ." He seemed to panic then. He could think of nothing more to say. Honig, himself an obese good-natured little man of about fifty, with a Master's degree from a local university and no publications, smiled encouragingly at Brother Ronald; but Brother Ronald could only stammer, "Tragedy has a plot . . . a climax and a conclusion. . . . It has a moment of revelation . . . and comic relief. . . ." After several minutes of painful silence, during which the only sounds were of O'Brien's sucking at his pipe, Brother Ronald smiled shakily and said that he did not know any more about tragedy.

Now it was Ilena's turn. She was astonished. She kept glancing at O'Brien and Honig, trying to catch their eyes, but they did not appear to notice. Was it possible that this candidate was considered good enough for an advanced degree, was it possible that anyone would allow him to teach English anywhere? She could not believe it. She said, sitting up very straight, "Brother Ronald, please define the term 'Gothicism' for us." Silence. Brother Ronald stared at his hands. He tried to smile. "Then could you define the term 'heroic couplet' for us," Ilena said. Her heart pounded combatively. The monk gazed at her, sorrowful and soft, his eyes watery; he shook his head *no*, he didn't know. "Have you read any of Shakespeare's sonnets?" Ilena asked. Brother Ronald nodded gravely, *yes*. "Could you discuss one of them?" Ilena asked. Again, silence. Brother Ronald appeared to be thinking. Finally he said, "I guess I don't remember any of them. . . ." "Could you tell us what a sonnet is, then?" Ilena asked. "A short poem," said Brother Ronald uncertainly. "Could you give us an example of any sonnet?" said Ilena. He stared at his hands, which were now clasped together. They were pudgy and very clean. After a while Ilena saw that he could not think of a sonnet, so she said sharply, having become quite nervous herself, "Could you talk to us about any poem at all? One of your favorite poems?" He sat in silence for several seconds. Finally Ilena said, "Could you give us the *title* of a poem?"

A miserable half minute. But the examination was nearly over: Ilena saw the monk glance at his wrist watch.

"I've been teaching math at St. Rose's for the last five years . . ." Brother Ronald said softly. "It wasn't really my idea to get a Master's degree in English . . . my order sent me out. . . ."

"Don't you know any poems at all? Not even any titles?" Ilena asked.

"Of course he does. We studied Browning last year, didn't we, Brother Ronald?" O'Brien said. "You remember. You received a B in the course. I was quite satisfied with your work. Couldn't you tell us the title of a work of Browning's?"

Brother Ronald stared at his hands and smiled nervously.

"*That's my last duchess up there on the wall. . . .*" O'Brien said coaxingly.

Brother Ronald was breathing deeply. After a few seconds he said, in a voice so soft they could almost not hear it, "*My last duchess? . . .*"

"Yes, that is a poem," Ilena said.

"Now it's my turn to ask another question," O'Brien said briskly. He asked the monk a very long, conversational question about the place of literature in education—did it have a place? How would he teach a class of high-school sophomores a Shakespearean play, for instance?

The examination ended before Brother Ronald was able to answer.

They dismissed him. O'Brien, who was the chairman of the examining committee, said without glancing at Ilena, "We will give him a B."

"Yes, a B seems about right," the other professor said quickly.

Ilena, whose head was ringing with outrage and shame, put her hand down flat on the table. "No," she said.

"What do you mean, no?"

"I won't pass him."

They stared at her. O'Brien said irritably, "Then I'll give him an A, to balance out your C."

"But I'm not giving him a C. I'm not giving him anything. How can he receive any other grade than F? I won't sign that paper. I can't sign it," Ilena said.

"I'll give him an A also," the other professor said doubtfully. "Then . . . then maybe he could still pass . . . if we averaged it out. . . ."

"But I won't sign the paper at all," Ilena said.

"You have to sign it."

"I won't sign it."

"It is one of your duties as a member of this examining board to give a grade and to sign your name."

"I won't sign it," Ilena said. She got shakily to her feet and walked out. In the corridor, ghostly and terrified, Brother Ronald hovered. Ilena passed by him in silence.

But the next morning she was summoned to Father Hoffman's office.

The story got out that she had been fired, but really she had had enough sense to resign—to write a quick resignation note on Father Hoffman's memo pad. They did not part friends. The following year, when her best-selling novel was published, Father Hoffman sent her a letter of congratulations on university stationery, charmingly worded: "I wish only the very best for you. We were wrong to lose you. Pity us." By then she had moved out of Detroit, her husband was in San Diego, she was living in a flat in Buffalo, near Delaware Avenue, afraid of being recognized when she went out to the drugstore or the supermarket. *Death Dance* had become a selection of the Book-of-the-Month Club; it had been sold for $150,000 to a movie producer famous for his plodding, "socially significant" films, and for the first time in her life Ilena was sleepless because of money—rabid jangling thoughts about money. She was ashamed of having done so well financially. She was terrified of her ability to survive all this noise, this publicity, this national good fortune. For, truly, *Death Dance* was not her best novel: a hectic narrative about college students and their preoccupation with sex and drugs and death, in a prose she had tried to make "poetic." Her more abrasive colleagues at the University of Buffalo cautioned her against believing the praise that was being heaped upon her, that she would destroy her small but unique talent if she took all this seriously, etc. Even her new lover, a critic, separated from his wife and several children, a fifty-year-old ex-child prodigy, warned her against success: "They want to make you believe you're a genius, so they can draw back and laugh at you. First they hypnotize you, then they destroy you. Believe nothing."

The flow of barbiturates and amphetamines gave her eyes a certain wild sheen, her copper hair a frantic wasteful curl, made her voice go shrill at the many Buffalo parties. She wondered if she did not have the talent, after all, for being a spectacle. Someone to stare at. The magazine cover had flattered her wonderfully: taken by a Greenwich Village photographer as dreamily hungover as Ilena herself, the two of them moving about in slow motion in his studio, adjusting her hair, her lips, her eyelashes, the tip of her chin, adjusting the light, altering the light, bringing out a fantastic ethereal glow in her eyes and cheeks and forehead that Ilena had never seen in herself. The cover had been in full color and Ilena had looked really beautiful, a pre-Raphaelite virgin. Below her photograph was a caption in high alarmed black letters: ARE AMERICAN WOMEN AVENGING CENTURIES OF OPPRESSION?

Revenge!

Death Dance was nominated for a National Book Award, but lost out to a long, tedious, naturalistic novel; someone at Buffalo who knew the judges told Ilena that this was just because the female member of the committee had been jealous of her. Ilena, whose head seemed to be swimming all the time now, and who did not dare to drive around in her Mercedes for fear of having an accident, accepted all opinions, listened desperately to everyone, pressed herself against her lover, and wept at the thought of her disintegrating brain.

This lover wanted to marry her, as soon as his divorce was final; his name was Lyle Myer. He was the author of twelve books of criticism and a columnist for a weekly left-wing magazine; a New Yorker, he had never lived outside New York until coming to Buffalo, which terrified him. He was afraid of being beaten up by the police. Hesitant, sweet, and as easily moved to sentimental tears as Ilena herself, he was always telephoning her or dropping in at her flat. Because he was, or had been, an alcoholic, Ilena felt it was safe to tell him about the pills she took. He seemed pleased by this confidence, this admission of her weakness, as if it bound her more hopelessly to him—just as his teen-aged daughter, whose snapshot Ilena had seen, was bound to be a perpetual daughter to him because of her acne and rounded shoulders, unable to escape his love. "Drugs are suicidal, yes, but if they forestall the actual act of suicide they are obviously beneficial," he told her.

With him, she felt nothing except a clumsy domestic affection: no physical love at all.

She was so tired most of the time that she did not even pretend to feel anything. With Gordon, in those hurried steep moments back in Detroit, the two of them always fearful of being discovered, her body had been keyed up to hysteria and love had made her delirious; with Bryan, near the end of their marriage, she had sometimes felt a tinge of love, a nagging doubtful rush that she often let fade away again, but with Lyle her body was dead, worn out, it could not respond to his most tender caresses. She felt how intellectualized she had become, her entire body passive and observant and cynical.

"Oh, I have to get my head straight. I have to get my head straight," Ilena wept.

Lyle undressed her gently, lovingly. She felt panic, seeing in his eyes that compassionate look that had meant Gordon was thinking of his children: how she had flinched from that look!

The end had come with Gordon just as abruptly as it had come with Father Hoffman, and only a week later. They had met by accident out on the street one day, Gordon with his wife and the two smallest children, Ilena in a trench coat, bareheaded, a leather purse with a frayed strap slung over her shoulder. "Hello, Ilena," Gordon said guiltily. He was really frightened. His wife, still a handsome woman, though looking older than her thirty-seven years, smiled stiffly at Ilena and let her gaze travel down to Ilena's watermarked boots. "How are you, Ilena?" Gordon said. His eyes grabbed at her, blue and intimidated. His wife, tugging at one of the little boys, turned a sour, ironic smile upon Ilena and said, "Are you one of my husband's students?" Ilena guessed that this was meant to insult Gordon, to make him feel old. But she explained politely that she was an instructor in the English Department, "but I'm leaving after this semester," and she noticed covertly that Gordon was not insulted, not irritated by his wife's nastiness, but only watchful, cautious, his smile strained with the fear that Ilena would give him away.

"In fact, I'm leaving in a few weeks," Ilena said.

His wife nodded stiffly, not bothering to show much regret. Gordon smiled nervously, apologetically. With relief, Ilena thought. He was smiling with relief because now he would be rid of her.

And so that had ended.

They met several times after this, but Ilena was now in a constant state of excitement or drowsiness; she was working out the beginning chapters of *Death Dance*—now living alone in the apartment, since her husband had moved out to a hotel. Her life was a confusion of days and nights, sleepless nights, headachey days, classes she taught in a dream and classes she failed to meet; she spent long periods in the bathtub while the hot water turned tepid and finally cold, her mind racing. She thought of her marriage and its failure. Marriage was the deepest, most mysterious, most profound exploration open to man: she had always believed that, and she believed it now. Because she had failed did not change that belief. This plunging into another's soul, this pressure of bodies together, so brutally intimate, was the closest one could come to a sacred adventure; she still believed that. But she had failed. So she forced herself to think of her work. She thought of the novel she was writing—about a "suicide club" that had apparently existed in Ann Arbor, Michigan—projecting her confusion and her misery into the heads of those late-adolescent girls, trying not to think of her own personal misery, the way love had soured in her life. Her husband. Gordon. Well, yes, men failed at being men; but maybe she had failed at being a woman. She had been unfaithful to two men at the same time. She deserved whatever she got.

Still, she found it difficult to resist swallowing a handful of sleeping pills.... Why not? Why not empty the whole container? There were moments when she looked at herself in the bathroom mirror and raised one eyebrow flirtatiously. *How about it? ... Why not die? ...* Only the empty apartment awaited her.

But she kept living because the novel obsessed her. She had to write it. She had to solve its problems, had to finish it, send it away from her completed. And, anyway, if she had taken sleeping pills and did not wake up, Gordon or Bryan would probably discover her before she had time to die. They often telephoned, and would have been alarmed if she hadn't answered. Gordon called her every evening, usually from a drugstore, always guiltily, so that she began to take pity on his cowardice. Did he fear her committing suicide and leaving a note that would drag him in? Or did he really love her? ... Ilena kept assuring him that she was all right, that she would be packing soon, yes, yes, she would always remember him with affection; no, she would probably not write to him, it would be better not to write. They talked quickly, sadly. Already the frantic hours of love-making in that office had become history, outlandish and improbable. Sometimes Ilena thought, *My God, I really love this man,* but her voice kept on with the usual conversation—what she had done that day, what he had done, what the state of her relationship with Bryan was, what his children were doing, the plans his wife had for that summer.

So it had ended, feebly; she had not even seen him the last week she was in Detroit.

Bryan called her too, impulsively. Sometimes to argue, sometimes to check plans, dates. He knew about the pills she took, though not about their quantity, and if she failed to answer the telephone for long he would have come over at once. Ilena would have been revived, wakened by a stomach pump, an ultimate masculine attack upon her body, sucking out her insides in great gasping shuddering gulps. . . . So she took only a double dose of sleeping pills before bed, along with the gin, and most of the time she slept soundly enough, without dreams. The wonderful thing about pills was that dreams were not possible. No dreams. The death of dreams. What could be more lovely than a dreamless sleep? . . .

In late April, Bryan had a collapse of some kind and was admitted to a local clinic; then he flew to his mother's, in Oswego. Ilena learned from a mutual friend at Wayne Medical School that Gordon had had a general nervous collapse, aggravated by a sudden malfunctioning of the liver brought on by malnutrition—he had been starving himself, evidently, to punish Ilena. But she worked on her novel, incorporating this latest catastrophe into the plot; she finished it in January of 1968, in Buffalo, where she was teaching a writing seminar; it was published in early 1969, and changed her life.

Lyle Myer pretended jealousy of her—all this acclaim, all this fuss! He insisted that she agree to marry him. He never mentioned, seemed deliberately to overlook, the embarrassing fact that she could love him only tepidly, that her mind was always elsewhere in their dry, fateful struggles, strung out with drugs or the memory of some other man, someone she half remembered, or the letters she had to answer from her agent and a dozen other people, so many people inviting her to give talks, to accept awards, to teach at their universities, to be interviewed by them, begging and demanding her time, her intense interest, like a hundred lovers tugging and pulling at her body, engaging it in a kind of love-making to which she could make only the feeblest of responses, her face locked now in a perpetual feminine smile. . . . With so much publicity and money, she felt an obligation to be feminine and gracious to everyone; when she was interviewed she spoke enthusiastically of the place of art in life, the place of beauty in this modern technological culture—she seemed to stress, on one national late-night television show, the tragedy of small trees stripped bare by vandals in city parks as much as the tragedy of the country's current foreign policy in Vietnam. At least it turned out that way. It was no wonder people could not take her seriously: one of the other writers at Buffalo, himself famous though more *avant-garde* than Ilena, shrugged her off as that girl who was always "licking her lips to make them glisten."

She did not sign on for another year at Buffalo, partly because of the political strife there and partly because she was restless, agitated, ready to move on. She sold the Mercedes and gave to the Salvation Army the furniture and other possessions Bryan had so cavalierly—indifferently—given her, and took an apartment in New York. She began writing stories that were to appear in fashion magazines, Ilena's slick, graceful prose an easy complement to the dreamlike faces and bodies of models whose photographs appeared in those same magazines, everything muted and slightly distorted as if by a drunken lens, the "very poetry of hallucination"—as one reviewer had said of *Death Dance*. Lyle flew down to see her nearly every weekend; on other weekends he was with his "separated" family. She loved him, yes, and she agreed to marry him, though she felt no hurry—in fact, she felt no real interest in men at all, her body shrinking when it was touched even accidentally, not out of fear but out of a kind of chaste boredom. So much, she had had so much of men, so much loving, so much mauling, so much passion. . . .

What, she was only twenty-nine years old?

She noted, with a small pang of vanity, how surprised audiences were when she rose to speak. *Ilena Williams looks so young!* They could not see the fine vibrations of her knees and hands, already viciously toned down by Librium. They could not see the colorless glop she vomited up in motel bathrooms, or in rest rooms down the hall from the auditorium in which she was speaking—she was always "speaking," invited out all over the country for fees ranging from $500 to a colossal $2000, speaking on "current trends in literature" or "current mores in America" or answering questions about her "writing habits" or reading sections from her latest work, a series of short stories in honor of certain dead writers with whom she felt a kinship. "I don't exist as an individual but only as a completion of a tradition, the end of something, not the best part of it but only the end," she explained, wondering if she was telling the truth or if this was all nonsense, "and I want to honor the dead by reimagining their works, by reimagining their obsessions . . . in a way marrying them, joining them as a woman joins a man . . . spiritually and erotically. . . ." She spoke so softly, so hesitantly, that audiences often could not hear her. Whereupon an energetic young man sitting in the first row, or onstage with her, would spring to his feet and adjust the microphone. "Is that better? Can you all hear now?" he would ask. Ilena saw the faces in the audience waver and blur and fade away, sheer protoplasm, and panic began in her stomach—what if she should vomit right in front of everyone? on this tidy little lectern propped up on dictionaries for her benefit? But she kept on talking. Sometimes she talked about the future of the short story, sometimes about the future of civilization—she heard the familiar, dead, deadened word *Vietnam* uttered often in her own voice, a word that had once meant something; she heard her voice echoing from the farthest corners of the auditorium as if from the corners of all those heads, her own head hollow as a drum, occasionally seeing herself at a distance—a woman with long but rather listless copper-red hair, thin cheeks, eyes that looked unnaturally enlarged. *Adverse reactions: confusion, edema, nausea, constipation, jaundice, hallucinations. . . .* Did that qualify as a legitimate hallucination, seeing herself from a distance, hearing herself from a distance? Did that qualify as a sign of madness?

During the fall and winter of 1969 and the spring of 1970 she traveled everywhere, giving talks, being met at airports by interested strangers, driven to neat disinfected motel rooms. She had time to write only a few stories, which had to be edited with care before they could be published. Her blood pounded barbarously, while her voice went on and on in that gentle precise way, her body withdrawing from any man's touch, demure with a dread that could not show through her clothes. She had been losing weight gradually for three years, and now she had the angular, light-boned, but very intense look of a precocious child. People wanted to protect her. Women mothered her, men were always taking her arm, helping her through doorways; the editor of a famous men's magazine took her to lunch and warned her of Lyle Myer's habit of marrying young, artistic women and then ruining them—after all, he had been married three times already, and the pattern was established. Wasn't it? When people were most gentle with her, Ilena thought of the tough days when she'd run across that wind-tortured campus in Detroit, her coat flapping about her, her body still dazzled by Gordon's love, damp and sweaty from him, and she had dared run into the classroom, five minutes late, had dared to take off her coat and begin the lesson. . . . The radiators in that old building had knocked as if they might explode; like colossal arteries, like her thudding arteries, overwhelmed with life.

In the fall of 1970 she was invited back to Detroit to give a talk before the local Phi Beta Kappa chapter; she accepted, and a few days later she received a letter from the new dean of the School of Arts—new since she had left—of her old university, inviting her to a reception in her honor, as their "most esteemed ex-staff member." It was all very diplomatic, very charming. She had escaped them, they had gotten rid of her, and now they could all meet together for a few hours. . . . Father Hoffman sent a note to her also, underscoring the dean's invitation, hoping that she was well and as attractive as ever. So she accepted.

Father Hoffman and another priest came to pick her up at the Sheraton Cadillac Hotel; she was startled to see that Father Hoffman had let his hair grow a little long, that he had noble, graying sideburns, and that the young priest with him was even shaggier. After the first awkward seconds—Father Hoffman forgot and called her "Mrs. Donohue"—they got along very well. Ilena was optimistic about the evening; her stomach seemed settled. As soon as they arrived at the dean's home she saw that Gordon was not there; she felt immensely relieved, though she had known he would not come, would not want to see her again . . . she felt immensely relieved and accepted a drink at once from Father Hoffman, who was behaving in an exceptionally gallant manner. "Ilena is looking better than ever," he said as people crowded around her, some of them with copies of her novel to sign, "better even than all her photographs. . . . But we don't want to tire her out, you know. We don't want to exhaust her." He kept refreshing her drink, like a lover or a husband. In the old days everyone at this place had ignored Ilena's novels, even the fact of her being a "writer," but now they were all smiles and congratulations—even the wives of her ex-colleagues, sturdy, dowdy women who had never seemed to like her. Ilena was too shaky to make any sarcastic observations about this to Father Hoffman, who might have appreciated them. He did say, "Times have changed, eh, Ilena?" and winked at her roguishly. "For one thing, you're not quite as excitable as you used to be. You were a very *young* woman around here." She could sense, beneath his gallantry, a barely disguised contempt for her—for all women—and this knowledge made her go cold. She mumbled something about fighting off the flu. Time to take a "cold tablet." She fished in her purse and came out with a large yellow capsule, a tranquillizer, and swallowed it down with a mouthful of Scotch.

Father Hoffman and Dr. O'Brien and a new, young assistant professor —a poet whose first book would be published next spring—talked to Ilena in a kind of chorus, telling her about all the changes in the university. It was much more "community-oriented" now. Its buildings—its "physical plant"—were to be open to the neighborhood on certain evenings and on Saturdays. The young poet, whose blond hair was very long and who wore a suede outfit and a black silk turtleneck shirt, kept interrupting the older men with brief explosions of mirth. "Christ, all this is a decade out of date—integration and all that crap—the NAACP and good old Martin Luther King and all that crap—the blacks don't want it and I agree with them one hundred percent! King is dead and so is Civil Rights—just another white middle-class week-night activity the blacks saw through long ago! I agree with them one hundred percent!" He seemed to be trying to make an impression on Ilena, not quite looking at her, but leaning toward her with his knees slightly bent, as if to exaggerate his youth. Ilena sipped at her drink, trying to hide the panic that was beginning. Yes, the NAACP was dead, all that was dead, but she didn't want to think about it—after all, it had been at a civil-rights rally that she and Bryan had met, years ago in Madison, Wisconsin. . . . "I haven't gotten around to reading your novel yet," the poet said, bringing his gaze sideways to Ilena.

Ilena excused herself and searched for a bathroom.

The dean's wife took her upstairs, kindly. Left alone, she waited to be sick, then lost interest in being sick; she had only to get through a few more hours of this and she would be safe. And Gordon wasn't there. She looked at herself in the mirror and should have been pleased to see that she looked so pretty—not beautiful tonight but pretty, delicate—she had worked hard enough at it, spending an hour in the hotel bathroom steaming her face and patting astringent on it, hoping for the best. She dreaded the cracks in her brain somehow working their way out to her skin. What then, what then? . . . But beauty did no good for anyone; it conferred no blessing upon the beautiful woman. Nervously, Ilena opened the medicine cabinet and peered at the array of things inside. She was interested mainly in prescription containers. Here were some small green pills prescribed for the dean's wife, for "tension." Tension, good! She took two of the pills. On another shelf there were some yellow capsules, perhaps the same as her own, though slightly smaller; she checked, yes, hers were 5 mg. and these were only 2. So she didn't bother with them. But she did discover an interesting white pill for "muscular tension," Dean Sprigg's prescription; she took one of these.

She descended the stairs, her hand firm on the bannister.

Before she could return safely to Father Hoffman, she was waylaid by someone's wife—the apple-cheeked Mrs. Honig, a very short woman with white hair who looked older than her husband, who looked, in fact, like Mrs. Santa Claus, motherly and dwarfed; Mrs. Honig asked her to sign a copy of *Death Dance*. "We all think it's so wonderful, just so wonderful for you," she said. Another woman joined them. Ilena had met her once, years before, but she could not remember her name. Mr. Honig hurried over. The conversation seemed to be about the tragedy of America—"All these young people dying in a senseless war," Mrs. Honig said, shaking her white hair; Mr. Honig agreed mournfully. "Vietnam is a shameful tragedy," he said. The dean's wife came by with a tray of cheese and crackers; everyone took something, even Ilena, though she doubted her ability to eat. She doubted everything. It seemed to her that Mrs. Honig and these other people were talking about Vietnam, and about drugs and death—could this be true?—or was it another hallucination? "Why, you know, a young man was killed here last spring, he took part in a demonstration against the Cambodian business," Mrs. Honig said vaguely; "they say a policeman clubbed him to death. . . ." "No, Ida, he had a concussion and died afterward," Mr. Honig said. He wiped his mouth of cracker crumbs and stared sadly at Ilena. "I think you knew him . . . Emmett Norlan?"

Emmett Norlan?

"You mean—Emmett is dead? He died? He died?" Ilena asked shrilly.

The blond poet came over to join their group. He had known Emmett, yes, a brilliant young man, a martyr to the Cause—yes, yes—he knew everything. While Ilena stared into space he told them all about Emmett. *He* had been an intimate friend of Emmett's.

Ilena happened to be staring toward the front of the hall, and she saw Gordon enter. The dean's wife was showing him in. Flakes of snow had settled upon the shoulders of his gray coat. Ilena started, seeing him so suddenly. She had forgotten all about him. She stared across the room in dismay, wondering at his appearance—he wore his hair longer, his sideburns were long and a little curly, he even had a small wiry brown beard—But he did not look youthful, he looked weary and drawn.

Now began half an hour of Ilena's awareness of him and his awareness of her. They had lived through events like this in the past, at other parties, meeting in other groups at the university; a dangerous, nervous sensation about their playing this game, not wanting to rush together. Ilena accepted a drink from a forty-year-old who looked zestful and adolescent, a priest who did not wear his Roman collar but, instead, a black nylon sweater and a medallion on a leather strap; Ilena's brain whirled at such surprises. What had happened? In the past there had been three categories: men, women, and priests. She had known how to conduct herself discreetly around these priests, who were masculine but undangerous; now she wasn't so sure. She kept thinking of Emmett dead. Had Emmett really been killed by the police? Little Emmett? She kept thinking of Gordon, aware of him circling her at a distance of some yards. She kept thinking of these people talking so casually of Vietnam, of drugs, of the death of little Emmett Norlan—these people—the very words they used turning flat and banal and safe in their mouths. "The waste of youth in this country is a tragedy," the priest with the sweater and the medallion said, shaking his head sadly.

Ilena eased away from them to stare at a Chagall lithograph, "Summer Night." Two lovers embraced, in repose; yet a nightmarish dream blossomed out of their heads, an intricate maze of dark depthless foliage, a lighted window, faces ghastly-white and perhaps a little grotesque. . . . Staring at these lovers, she sensed Gordon approaching her. She turned to him, wanting to be casual. But she was shaking. Gordon stared at her and she saw that old helplessness in his eyes— what, did he still love her? Wasn't she free of him yet? She began talking swiftly, nervously. "Tell me about Emmett. Tell me what happened." Gordon, who seemed heavier than she recalled, whose tired face disappointed her sharply, spoke as always in his gentle, rather paternal voice; she tried to listen. She tried to listen but she kept recalling that office, the two of them lying on the floor together, helpless in an embrace, so hasty, so reckless, grinding their bodies together in anguish. . . . They had been so close, so intimate, that their blood had flowed freely in each other's veins; on the coldest days they had gone about blood-warmed, love-warmed. Tears filled Ilena's eyes. Gordon was saying, "The story was that he died of a concussion, but actually he died of liver failure. Once he got in the hospital he just disintegrated . . . he had hepatitis . . . he'd been taking heroin. . . . It was a hell of a thing, Ilena. . . ."

She pressed her fingers hard against her eyes.

"Don't cry, please," Gordon said, stricken.

A pause of several seconds: the two of them in a kind of equilibrium, two lovers.

"Would you like me to drive you back to your hotel?" Gordon said.

She went at once to get her coat. Backing away, always backing away . . . she stammered a few words to Father Hoffman, to the dean and his wife, words of gratitude, confusion. Good-by to Detroit! *Good-by, good-by.* She shook hands. She finished her drink. Gordon helped her on with her coat—a stylish black coat with a black mink collar, nothing like the clothes she had worn in the old days. Out on the walk, in the soft falling snow, Gordon said nervously: "I know you're going to be married. Lyle Myer. I know all about it. I'm very happy. I'm happy for you. You're looking very well."

Ilena closed her eyes, waiting for her mind to straighten itself out. Yes, she was normal; she had gone to an internist in Buffalo and had been declared normal. *You are too young to be experiencing menopause,* the doctor had said thoughtfully; *the cessation of menstrual periods must be related to the Pill or to an emotional condition.* She thought it better not to tell Gordon all that. "Thank you," she said simply.

"I'm sorry they told you about Emmett," Gordon said. "There was no reason to tell you. He liked you so much, Ilena; he hung around my office after you left and all but confessed he was in love with you . . . he kept asking if you wrote to me and I said no, but he didn't believe me . . . he was always asking about you. . . ."

"When did he die?"

"Last spring. His liver gave out. Evidently it was just shot. Someone said his skin was bright yellow."

"He was taking heroin? . . ."

"God, yes. He was a wreck. The poor kid just disintegrated, it was a hell of a shame. . . ."

He drove her back downtown. They were suddenly very comfortable together, sadly comfortable. Ilena had been in this car only two or three times in the past. "Where is your wife?" she asked shyly. She watched him as he answered—his wife was visiting her mother in Ohio, she'd taken the children—no, things were no better between them—always the same, always the same—Ilena thought in dismay that he was trivialized by these words: men were trivialized by love and by their need for women.

"I've missed you so much . . ." Gordon said suddenly.

They walked through the tufts of falling snow, to the hotel. A gigantic hotel, all lights and people. Ilena felt brazen and anonymous here. Gordon kept glancing at her, as if unable to believe in her. He was nervous, eager, a little drunk; an uncertain adolescent smile hovered about his face. "I love you, I still love you," he whispered. In the elevator he embraced her. Ilena did not resist. She felt her body warming to him as toward an old friend, a brother. She did love him. Tears of love stung her eyes. If only she could get her head straight, if only she could think of what she was supposed to think of . . . someone she was supposed to remember. . . . In the overheated room they embraced gently. Gently. Ilena did not want to start this love again, it was a mistake, but she caught sight of Gordon's stricken face and could not resist. She began to cry. Gordon clutched her around the hips, kneeling before her. He pressed his hot face against her.

"Ilena, I'm so sorry . . ." he said.

She thought of planets: sun-warmed planets revolving around a molten star. Revolving around a glob of light. And the planets rotated on their own private axes. But now the planets were accelerating their speed, they wobbled on their axes and the strain of their movement threatened to tear them apart. She began to sob. Ugly, gasping, painful sobs. . . . "Don't cry, please, I'm so sorry," Gordon said. They lay down together. The room was hot, too hot. They had not bothered to put on a light. Only the light from the window, a dull glazed wintry light; Ilena allowed him to kiss her, to undress her, to move his hands wildly about her body as she wept. What should she be thinking of? Whom should she remember? When she was with Lyle she thought back to Gordon . . . now, with Gordon, she thought back to someone else, someone else, half-remembered, indistinct, perhaps dead. . . . He began to make love to her. He was eager, breathing as sharply and as painfully as Ilena herself. She clasped her arms around him. That firm hard back she remembered. Or did she remember? . . . Her mind wandered and she thought suddenly of Bryan, her husband. He was her ex-husband now. She thought of their meeting at that civil-rights rally, introduced by mutual friends, she thought of the little tavern they had gone to, on State Street in Madison, she thought of the first meal she'd made for Bryan and that other couple . . . proud of herself as a cook, baking them an Italian dish with shrimp and crabmeat and mushrooms . . . yes, she had been proud of her cooking, she had loved to cook for years. For years. She had loved Bryan. But suddenly she was not thinking of him; her mind gave way to a sharper thought and she saw Emmett's face: his scorn, his disapproval.

She stifled a scream.

Gordon slid from her, frightened. "Did I hurt you? Ilena?"

She began to weep uncontrollably. Their bodies, so warm, now shivered and seemed to sting each other. Their hairs seemed to catch at each other painfully.

"Did I hurt you? . . . " he whispered.

She remembered the afternoon she had fainted. Passed out cold. And then she had came to her senses and she had cried, like this, hiding her face from her lover because crying made it ugly, so swollen. . . . Gordon tried to comfort her. But the bed was crowded with people. A din of people. A mob. Lovers were kissing her on every inch of her body and trying to suck up her tepid blood, prodding, poking, inspecting her like that doctor in Buffalo—up on the table, naked beneath an oversized white robe, her feet in the stirrups, being examined with a cold sharp metal device and then with the doctor's fingers in his slick rubber gloves—checking her ovaries, so casually—*You are too young for menopause,* he had said. Was it the pills, then? The birth-control pills? *This kind of sterility is not necessarily unrelated to the Pill,* the doctor had conceded, and his subtlety of language had enchanted Ilena. . . .

"Don't cry," Gordon begged.

She had frightened him off and he would not make love to her. He only clutched at her, embraced her. She felt that he was heavier, yes, than she remembered. Heavier. Older. But she could not concentrate on him: she kept seeing Emmett's face. His frizzy hair, his big glasses, his continual whine. Far inside her, too deep for any man to reach and stir into sensation, a dull, dim lust began for Emmett, hardly more than a faint throbbing. Emmett, who was dead. She wanted to hold him, now, instead of this man—Emmett in her arms, his irritation calmed, his glasses off and set on the night table beside the bed, everything silent, silent. Gordon was whispering to her. *Love. Love.* She did not remember that short scratchy beard. But she was lying in bed with an anxious, perspiring, bearded man, evidently someone she knew. They were so close that their blood might flow easily back and forth between their bodies, sluggish and warm and loving.

She recalled her husband's face: a look of surprise, shock. She had betrayed him. His face blended with the face of her student, who was dead, and Gordon's face, pressed so close to her in the dark that she could not see it. The bed was crammed with people. Their identities flowed sluggishly, haltingly, from vein to vein. One by one they were all becoming each other. Becoming protoplasm. They were prototoplasm that had the sticky pale formlessness of semen. They were all turning into each other, into protoplasm. . . . Ilena was conscious of something fading in her, in the pit of her belly. Fading. Dying. *The central sexual organ is the brain,* she had read, and now her brain was drawing away, fading, dissolving.

"Do you want me to leave?" Gordon asked.

She did not answer. Against the hotel window: soft, shapeless clumps of snow. She must remember something, she must remember someone . . . there was an important truth she must understand. . . . But she could not get it into focus. Her brain seemed to swoon backward in an elation of fatigue, and she heard beyond this man's hoarse, strained breathing the gentle breathing of the snow, falling shapelessly upon them all.

"Do you want me to leave?" Gordon asked.

She could not speak.

Margaret Atwood

At First I Was Given Centuries

At first I was given centuries
to wait in caves, in leather
tents, knowing you would never come back

Then it speeded up: only
several years between
the day you jangled off
into the mountains, and the day (it was
spring again) I rose from the embroidery
frame at the messenger's entrance.

That happened twice, or was it
more; and there was once, not so
long ago, you failed,
and came back in a wheelchair
with a moustache and a sunburn
and were insufferable.

Time before last though, I remember
I had a good eight months between
running alongside the train, skirts hitched, handing
you violets in at the window
and opening the letter; I watched
your snapshot fade for twenty years.

And last time (I drove to the airport
still dressed in my factory
overalls, the wrench
I had forgotten sticking out of the back
pocket; there you were,
zippered and helmeted, it was zero
hour, you said Be
Brave) it was at least three weeks before
I got the telegram and could start regretting.

But recently, the bad evenings
there are only seconds
between the warning on the radio and the
explosion; my hands
don't reach you

and on quieter nights
you jump up from
your chair without even touching your dinner
and I can scarcely kiss you goodbye
before you run out into the street and they shoot

You Refuse To Own

You refuse to own
yourself, you permit
others to do it for you:

you become slowly more public,
in a year there will be nothing left
of you but a megaphone

or you will descend through the roof
with the spurious authority of a
government official,
blue as a policeman, grey as a used angel,
having long forgotten the difference
between an annunciation and a parking ticket

or you will be slipped under
the door, your skin furred with cancelled
airmail stamps, your kiss no longer literature
but fine print, a set of instructions.

If you deny these uniforms
and choose to repossess
yourself, your future

will be less dignified, more painful, death will be sooner,
(it is no longer possible
to be both human and alive) : lying piled with
the others, your face and body
covered so thickly with scars
only the eyes show through.

We hear nothing these days
from the ones in power

Why talk when you are a shoulder
or a vault

Why talk when you are
helmeted with numbers

Fists have many forms;
a fist knows what it can do

without the nuisance of speaking:
it grabs and smashes.

From those inside or under
words gush like toothpaste.

Language, the fist
proclaims by squeezing
is for the weak only.

Against Still Life

Orange in the middle of a table:

It isn't enough
to walk around it
at a distance, saying
it's an orange:
nothing to do
with us, nothing
else: leave it alone

I want to pick it up
in my hand
I want to peel the
skin off; I want
more to be said to me
than just Orange:
want to be told
everything it has to say

And you, sitting across
the table, at a distance, with
your smiles contained, and like the orange
in the sun: silent:

Your silence
isn't enough for me
now, no matter with what
contentment you fold
your hands together; I want
anything you can say
in the sunlight:

stories of your various
childhoods, aimless journeyings,
your loves; your articulate
skeleton; your posturings; your lies.

These orange silences
(sunlight and hidden smile)
make me want to
wrench you into saying;
now I'd crack your skull
like a walnut, split it like a pumpkin
to make you talk, or get
a look inside

But quietly:
if I take the orange
with care enough and hold it
gently

I may find
an egg
a sun

an orange moon
perhaps a skull; center
of all energy
resting in my hand

can change it to
whatever I desire
it to be

and you, man, orange afternoon
lover, wherever
you sit across from me
(tables, trains, buses)

if I watch
quietly enough
and long enough

at last, you will say
(maybe without speaking)
(there are mountains
inside your skull
garden and chaos, ocean
and hurricane; certain
corners of rooms, portraits
of great-grandmothers, curtains
of a particular shade;
your deserts; your private
dinosaurs; the first
woman)

all I need to know:
tell me
everything
just as it was
from the beginning.

More and More

More and more frequently the edges
of me dissolve and I become
a wish to assimilate the world, including
you, if possible through the skin
like a cool plant's tricks with oxygen
and live by a harmless green burning.

I would not consume
you, or ever
finish, you would still be there
surrounding me, complete
as the air.

Unfortunately I don't have leaves.
Instead I have eyes

and teeth and other non-green
things which rule out osmosis.

So be careful, I mean it,
I give you a fair warning:

This kind of hunger draws
everything into its own
space; nor can we
talk it all over, have a calm
rational discussion.

There is no reason for this, only
a starved dog's logic about bones.

Erica Jong

Pandora's Box or My Two Mothers

FROM FEAR OF FLYING

Of course it all began with my mother. My mother: Judith Stoloff White, also known as Jude. Not obscure. But hard to get down on paper. My love for her and my hate for her are so bafflingly intertwined that I can hardly *see* her. I never know who is who. She is me and I am she and we are all together. The umbilical cord which connects us has never been cut so it has sickened and rotted and turned black. The very intensity of our need has made us denounce each other. We want to eat each other up. We want to strangle each other with love. We want to run screaming from each other in panic before either of these things can happen.

When I think of my mother I envy Alexander Portnoy. If only I had a *real* Jewish mother—easily pigeonholed and filed away—a real literary porperty. (I am always envying writers their relatives: Nabokov and Lowell and Tucci with their closets full of elegant aristocratic skeletons, Roth and Bellow and Friedman with their pop parents, sticky as Passover wine, greasy as matzoh-ball soup.)

My mother smelled of *Joy* or *Diorissimo,* and she didn't cook much. When I try to distill down to basics what she taught me about life, I am left with this:

1.   Above all, never be *ordinary.*
2.   The world is a predatory place: Eat faster!

"Ordinary" was the worst insult she could find for anything. I remember her taking me shopping and the look of disdain with which she would freeze the salesladies in Saks when they suggested that some dress or pair of shoes was "very popular—we've sold fifty already this week." That was all she needed to hear.

"No," she would say, "we're not interested in that. Haven't you got something a little more unusual?" And then the saleslady would bring out all the weird colors no one else would buy—stuff which would have gone on sale but for my mother. And later she and I would have an enormous fight because I yearned to be ordinary as fiercely as my mother yearned to be unusual.

"I can't *stand* that hairdo" (she said when I went to the hairdresser with Pia and came back with a pageboy straight out of *Seventeen* Magazine), "it's so terribly *ordinary.*" Not ugly. Not unbecoming. But *ordinary.* Ordinariness was a plague you had to ward off in every possible way. You warded it off by redecorating frequently. Actually my mother thought that all the interior decorators (as well as clothes designers and accessory designers) in America were organized in an espionage ring to learn her most recent decorating or dressmaking ideas and suddenly popularize them. And it was true that she had an uncanny sense of coming fashions (or did I only imagine this, conned as I was by her charisma?). She did the house in antique gold just before antique gold became the most popular color for drapes and rugs and upholstery. Then she screamed that everyone had "stolen" her ideas. She installed Spanish porcelain tiles in the foyer before it caught on "with the *yentas* on Central Park West"—from whose company she carefully excluded herself. She brought white fur rugs home from Greece before they were imported by all the stores. She discovered wrought-iron flowered chandeliers for the bathroom in advance of all the "fairy decorators"—as she contemptuously called them.

She had antique brass headboards and window shades that matched the wallpaper and pink and red towels in the bathrooms when pink and red was still considered an avant-garde combination. Her fear of ordinariness came out most strongly in her clothes. After the four of us got older, she and my father traveled a lot for business, and she picked up odd accessories everywhere. She wore Chinese silk pajamas to the theater, Balinese toe-rings on her sandaled feet, and tiny jade Buddhas mounted as dangling earrings. She carried an oiled rice-paper parasol in the rain and had toreador pants made out of Japanese fingernail tapestries. At one point in my adolescence it dawned on me that she would rather look weird and ugly than common and pretty. And she often succeeded. She was a tall, rail-thin woman with high cheekbones and long red hair, and her strange get-ups and extreme make-up sometimes gave her a Charles Adamsy look. Naturally, I longed for a bleached-blond, milk-coated Mama who played bridge, or at least for a dumpy brunette PTA Mom in harlequin glasses and Red Cross shoes.

"Couldn't you please wear something *else?*" I pleaded when she was dressing for Parents' Day in tapestried toreador pants and a Pucci pink silk sweater and a Mexican serape. (My memory must be exaggerating—but you get the general idea.) I was in seventh grade, and at the height of my passion for ordinariness.

"What's wrong with what I'm wearing?"

What wasn't wrong with it! I shrank back into her walk-in closet, looking in vain for something ordinary. (An apron! A housedress! An angora sweater set! Something befitting a mother in a Betty Crocker ad, a Mother with a capital M.) The closet reeked of *Joy* and mothballs. There were cut velvet capes and feather boas and suede slacks and Aztec cotton caftans and Japanese silk kimonos and Irish tweed knickers, but absolutely nothing like an angora sweater set.

"It's just that I wish you'd wear something more plain," I said sheepishly, "something people won't stare at."

She glowered at me and drew herself up to her full height of five feet ten inches.

"Are you ashamed of your own mother? Because if you are, Isadora, I feel sorry for you. I really do. There is nothing good about being *ordinary.* People don't respect you for it. In the last analysis, people *run after* people who are different, who have confidence in their *own* taste, who don't run with the herd. You'll find out. There is nothing gained by giving in to the pressures of group vulgarity. . . ." And we left for school in a cab trailing whiffs of *Joy,* and with Mexican fringes flapping, figuratively, in the wind.

When I think of all the energy, all the misplaced artistic aggression which my mother channeled into her passion for odd clothes and new decorating schemes, I wish she had been a successful artist instead. Three generations of frustrated artists: my grandfather fucking models and cursing Picasso and stubbornly painting in the style of Rembrandt, my mother giving up poetry and painting for arty clothes and compulsive reupholstering, my sister Randy taking up pregnancy as if it were a new art form she had invented (and Lalah and Chloe following after her like disciples).

There is nothing fiercer than a failed artist. The energy remains, but, having no outlet, it implodes in a great black fart of rage which smokes up all the inner windows of the soul. Horrible as successful artists often are, there is nothing crueler or more vain than a failed artist. My grandfather, as I've said, used to paint over my mother's canvases instead of going out to buy new canvas. She switched to poetry for a while, to escape him, but then met my father who was a song writer and stole her images to use in lyrics. Artists are horrible. "Never, never get involved with a man who wants to be an artist," my mother used to say, who knew.

Another interesting sidelight is that both my mother and my grandfather have a way of dismissing the efforts of anybody who seems to be having a good time working at something or having a moderate success at it. There is, for example, a middling-to-good novelist (whose name I won't mention) who happens to be a friend of my parents. He has written four novels, none of them distinguished in style, none of them best sellers, and none prize-winners, but nevertheless, he seems fairly pleased with himself and he seems to be enjoying the status of resident sage at cocktail parties and writer-in-residence at some junior college in New Jersey whose name escapes me. Maybe he actually likes writing. Some strange people do.

"I don't know how he keeps grinding them out," my mother will say, "he's such an *ordinary* writer. He's not stupid, he's nobody's fool. . . ." (My mother never calls people "intelligent"; "not stupid" is as far as she will commit herself.) ". . . But his books are so *ordinary* . . . and none of them has really even made money yet. . . ."

And there's the rub! Because while my mother *claims* to respect originality above all, what she really respects is money and prizes. Moreover, there is the implication in all her remarks about other artists that there is scarcely any point in their persevering just for the piddling rewards they get. Now if her novelist-friend had won a Pulitzer or an NBA—or sold a book to the movies—that would be something. Of course, she would put that down, too. But the respect would be written all over her face. On the other hand, the humble *doing* of the

thing means nothing to her; the inner discoveries, the pleasure of the
work. Nothing. With an attitude like that, no wonder she turned
to upholstery.

Re: her interest in predation. She started out, I think, with the normal
Provincetown–Art Students League communism of her day, but gradually, as affluence and arteriosclerosis overtook her (together, as is often
the case), she converted to her own brand of religion composed of
two parts Robert Ardrey and one part Konrad Lorenz.

I don't think either Ardrey or Lorenz intended what she extracted in
their names: a sort of neo-Hobbesianism in which it is proven that
life is nasty, mean, brutish, and short; the desire for status and money
and power is universal; territoriality is instinctual; and selfishness,
therefore, is the cardinal law of life. ("Don't twist what I'm saying,
Isadora; even what people call *al*truism is selfishness by another
name.")

How all this clogged up every avenue of creative and rebellious expression for me is clear:

1. I couldn't be a hippy because my mother already dressed like a
   hippy (while believing in territoriality and the universality of
   war).
2. I couldn't rebel against Judaism because I hadn't any to rebel
   against.
3. I couldn't rail at my Jewish mother because the problem was
   deeper than Jewishness or mothers.
4. I couldn't be an artist on pain of being painted over.
5. I couldn't be a poet on pain of being crossed out.
6. I couldn't be anything else because that was *ordinary.*
7. I couldn't be a communist because my mother had been there.
8. I couldn't be a rebel (or, at very least, a pariah) by marrying Ben-
   nett because my mother would think that was "at any rate, *not*
   ordinary."

What possibilities remained open to me? In what cramped corner
could I act out what I so presumptuously called my life? I felt rather
like those children of pot-smoking parents who become raging squares.
I could perhaps, take off across Europe with Adrian Goodlove, and
never come home to New York at all.

And yet . . . I also have another mother. She is tall and thin, but her
cheeks are softer than willow tips, and when I nuzzle into her fur
coat on the ride home, I feel that no harm can come to me ever. She
teaches me the names of flowers. She hugs and kisses me after some
bully in the playground (a psychiatrist's son) grabs my new English
tricycle and rolls it down a hill into the playground fence. She sits
up nights with me listening to the compositions I have written for
school and she thinks I am the greatest writer in history even though
I am only eight. She laughs at my jokes as if I were Milton Berle and
Groucho Marx and Irwin Corey rolled into one. She takes me and
Randy and Lalah and Chloe ice-skating on Central Park Lake with
ten of our friends, and while all the other mothers sit home and play

bridge and send maids to call for their children, she laces up all our skates (with freezing fingers) and then puts on her own skates and glides around the lake with us, pointing out danger spots (thin ice), teaching us figure eights, and laughing and talking and glowing pink with the cold. I am so proud of her!

Randy and I boast to our friends that our mother (with her long flowing hair and huge brown eyes) is so young that she never has to wear make-up. She's no old fuddy-duddy like the other mothers. She wears turtlenecks and ski pants just like us. She wears her long hair in a velvet ribbon just like us. And we don't even call her Mother because she's so much fun. She isn't like anyone else.

On my birthday (March 26, Aries, the Rites of Spring), I awaken to find my room transformed into a bower. Around my bed are vases of daffodils, irises, anemones. On the floor are heaps of presents, wrapped in the most fanciful tissue papers and festooned with paper flowers. There are Easter eggs, hand painted by my mother to look like Fabergé eggs. There are boxes of chocolates and jelly eggs ("for a sweet year," she says, hugging me), and there is always a giant birthday card, painted in water colors and showing me in all my glory: the most beautiful little girl in the world, long blond hair, blue eyes, and masses of flowers in my arms. My mother flatters me, idealizes me—or is that how she really sees me? I am pleased and I am puzzled. I am really the most beautiful girl in the world to her, aren't I? Or aren't I? Then what about my sisters? And what about the way she screams at me loud enough to make the roof fall in?

My other mother never screams, and I owe everything I am to her. At thirteen I follow her through all the art museums of Europe, and through her eyes I see Turner's storms and Tiepolo's skies and Monet's haystacks and Rodin's monument to Balzac and Botticelli's *Primavera* and da Vinci's *Madonna of the Rocks*. At fourteen I get the *Collected Poems of Edna St. Vincent Millay* for my birthday, at fifteen e.e. cummings, at sixteen William Butler Yeats, at seventeen Emily Dickinson, and at eighteen my mother and I are no longer on speaking terms. She introduces me to Shaw, to Colette, to Orwell, to Simone de Beauvoir. She furiously debates Marxism with me at the dinner table. She gives me ballet lessons and piano lessons and weekly tickets to the New York Philharmonic (where I am bored and spend much time in the ladies' room applying Revlon's *Powder Pink* Lustrous Lipstick to my thirteen-year-old lips).

I go to the Art Students League every Saturday and my mother painstakingly criticizes my drawings. She shepherds my career as if it were her own: I must learn cast and figure drawing in charcoal first, then still lifes in pastels, then finally oil painting. When I apply for the High School of Music and Art, my mother worries over my portfolio with me, takes me to the exam, and reassures me, as I worriedly recapitulate each part of it to her. When I decide I want to be a doctor as well as an artist, she starts buying me books on biology. When I start writing poetry, she listens to each poem and praises it as if I were Yeats. All my adolescent maunderings are beautiful to her. All my drawings, greeting cards, cartoons, posters, oil paintings presage future greatness to her. Surely *no* girl could have a more devoted mother, a mother more interested in her becoming a whole person, in becoming, if she wished, an artist. Then why am I so furious with her? And why does she make me feel that I am nothing but a blurred carbon copy of her? That I have never had a single thought of my own? That I have no freedom, no independence, no identity at all?

Perhaps sex accounted for my fury. Perhaps sex was the real Pandora's box. My mother believed in free love, in dancing naked in the Bois de Boulogne, in dancing in the Greek Isles, in performing the Rites of Spring. Yet of course, she did *not*, or why did she say that boys wouldn't respect me unless I "played hard to get"? That boys wouldn't chase me if I "wore my heart on my sleeve," that boys wouldn't call me if I "made myself cheap"?

Sex. I was terrified of the tremendous power it had over me. The energy, the excitement, the power to make me feel totally crazy! What about that? How do you make that jibe with "playing hard to get"?

I never had the courage to ask my mother directly. I sensed, despite her bohemian talk, that she disapproved of sex, that it was basically unmentionable. So I turned to D. H. Lawrence, and to *Love Without Fear*, and to *Coming of Age in Samoa*. Margaret Mead wasn't much help. What did I have in common with all those savages? (Plenty, of course, but at the time I didn't realize it.) Eustace Chesser, M.D., was good on all the fascinating details ("How to Manage the Sex Act," penetration, foreplay, afterglow), but he didn't seem to have much to say about *my* moral dilemmas: how "far" to go? inside the bra or outside? when to swallow, if ever. It was all so complicated. And it seemed so much more complicated for *women*. Basically, I think, I was furious with my mother for not teaching me how to be a woman, for not teaching me how to make peace between the raging hunger in my cunt and the hunger in my head.

So I learned about women from men. I saw them through the eyes of male writers. Of course, I didn't think of them as *male* writers. I thought of them as *writers*, as authorities, as gods who knew and were to be trusted completely.

Naturally I trusted everything they said, even when it implied my own inferiority. I learned what an orgasm was from D. H. Lawrence, disguised as Lady Chatterley. I learned from him that all women worship "the Phallos"—as he so quaintly spelled it. I learned from Shaw that women never can be artists; I learned from Dostoyevsky that they have no religious feeling; I learned from Swift and Pope that they have too *much* religious feeling (and therefore can never be quite rational); I learned from Faulkner that they are earth mothers and at one with the moon and the tides and the crops; I learned from Freud that they have deficient superegos and are ever "incomplete" because they lack the one thing in this world worth having: a penis.

But what did all this have to do with me—who went to school and got better marks than the boys and painted and wrote and spent Saturdays doing still lifes at the Art Students League and my weekday afternoons editing the high-school paper (Features Editor; the Editor-in-Chief had never been a girl—though it also never occurred to us then to question it)? What did the moon and the tides and earth-mothering and the worship of the Lawrentian "phallos" have to do with me or with my life?

I met my first "phallos" at thirteen years and ten months on my parents' avocado-green silk living-room couch, in the shade of an avocado-green avocado tree, grown by my avocado green-thumbed mother from an avocado pit. The "phallos" belonged to Steve Applebaum, a junior and art major when I was a freshman and art major, and it had a most memorable abstract design of blue veins on its Kandinsky-purple underside. In retrospect, it was a remarkable specimen; circumcised, of course, and huge (what is huge when you have no frame of reference?), and with an impressive life of its own. As soon as it began to make its drumlinlike presence known under the tight zipper of Steve's chinos (we were necking and "petting-below-the-waist" as one said then), he would slowly unzip (so as not to snag it?) and with one hand (the other was under my skirt and up my cunt) extract the huge purple thing from between the layers of his shorts, his blue Brooks-Brothers shirttails, and his cold, glittering, metal-zippered fly. Then I would dip one hand into the vase of roses my flower-loving mother always kept on the coffee table, and with a right hand moistened with water and the slime from their stems, I would proceed with my rhythmic jerking off of Steve. How exactly did I do it? Three fingers? Or the whole palm? I suppose I must have been rough at first (though later I became an expert). He would throw his head back in ecstasy (but controlled ecstasy: my father was watching TV in the dining room) and would come into his Brooks-Brothers shirttails or into a handkerchief quickly produced for the purpose. The technique I have forgotten, but the feeling remains. Partly, it was reciprocity (tit for tat, or clit for tat), but it was also power over him—one that painting or writing couldn't approach. And then I was coming too—maybe not like Lady Chatterley, but it was something.

Toward the end of our idyll, Steve (who was then seventeen and I fourteen) wanted me to take "it" in my mouth.

"Do people really do that?"

"Sure," he said with as much nonchalance as he could muster. He went to my parents' bookshelf in search of Van de Velde (carefully hidden behind *Art Treasures of the Renaissance*). But it was too much for me. I couldn't even pronounce it. And would it make me pregnant? Or maybe my refusal had something to do with the continuing social education which my mother was instilling in me along with Art History. Steve lived in the Bronx. I lived in a duplex on Central Park West. If I was going to worship a "phallos" it was not going to be a Bronx phallos. Perhaps one from Sutton Place?

Ultimately, I said goodbye to Steve and took up masturbation, fasting, and poetry. I kept telling myself that masturbation at least kept me pure.

Steve continued to woo me with bottles of Chanel No. 5, Frank
Sinatra records, and beautifully lettered quotations from the poems
of Yeats. He called me whenever he got drunk and on every one of
my birthdays for the next five years. (Was it just jerking him off
which inspired such loyalty?)

But meanwhile I repented for my self-indulgence by undergoing a sort
of religious conversion which included starvation (I denied myself
even water), studying *Siddhartha,* and losing twenty pounds (and with
them, my periods). I also got a Joblike rash of boils and was sent
to my first dermatologist—a German lady refugee who said, mem-
orably, "Za skeen is za meeroar of za zoul" and who referred me to
the first of my many psychiatrists, a short doctor whose name was
Schrift.

Dr. Schrift (the very same Dr. Schrift who had flown to Vienna with
us) was a follower of Wilhelm Stekel and he tucked his shoelaces
under the tongues of his shoes. (I am not sure whether or not this
was part of the Stekelian method.) His apartment building on Madison Avenue had very dark and narrow halls whose walls were covered
with gold, seashell-spotted wallpaper, such as you might find in the
bathroom of an old house in Larchmont. Waiting for the elevator, I
used to stare at the wallpaper and wonder if the landlord had gotten
a good deal on a bathroom wallpaper close-out. Why else paper a
lobby with gold seashells and tiny pink fishes?

Dr. Schrift had two Utrillo prints and one Braque. (It was my first
shrink, so I didn't realize these were the standard APA-approved
prints.) He also had a Danish-modern desk (also APA-approved), and
a brownish Foamland couch with a compulsive little plastic cover at
the foot and a hard wedge-shaped pillow, covered with a paper napkin, at the head.

He insisted that the horse I was dreaming about was my father. I was
fourteen and starving myself to death in penance for having finger-
fucked on my parents' avocado-green silk couch. He insisted that
the coffin I was dreaming about was my mother. What could be the
reason my periods had stopped? A mystery.

"Because I don't want to be a woman. Because it's too confusing.
Because Shaw says you can't be a woman and an artist. Having babies
uses you up, he says. And I want to be an artist. That's all I've
ever wanted."

Because I wouldn't have known how to say it then, but Steve's finger
in my cunt felt good. At the same time, I knew that soft, mushy feeling to be the enemy. If I yielded to that feeling, it would be goodbye
to all the other things I wanted. "You have to choose," I told myself
sternly at fourteen. Get thee to a nunnery. So, like all good nuns,
I masturbated. "I am keeping myself free of the power of men," I
thought, sticking two fingers deep inside each night.

Dr. Schrift didn't understand. "Ackzept being a vohman," he hissed
from behind the couch. But at fourteen all I could see were the dis-
advantages of being a woman. I longed to have orgasms like Lady

Chatterley's. Why didn't the moon turn pale and tidal waves sweep over the surface of the earth? Where was my gamekeeper? All I could see was the swindle of being a woman.

I would roam through the Metropolitan Museum of Art looking for one woman artist to show me the way: Mary Cassatt? Berthe Morisot? Why was it that so many women artists who had renounced having children could then paint nothing but mothers and children? It was hopeless. If you were female and talented, life was a trap no matter which way you turned. Either you drowned in domesticity (and had Walter Mittyish fantasies of escape) or you longed for domesticity in all your art. You could never escape your femaleness. You had conflict written in your very blood.

Neither my good mother nor my bad mother could help me out of this dilemma. My bad mother told me she would have been a famous artist but for me, and my good mother adored me, and wouldn't have given me up for the world. What I learned from her I learned by example, not exhortation. And the lesson was clear: being a woman meant being harried, frustrated, and always angry. It meant being split into two irreconcilable halves.

"Maybe you'll do better than me," my good mother said. "Maybe you'll do both, darling. But as for me, I never could."

Nikki Giovanni

Woman Poem

you see, my whole life
is tied up
to unhappiness
its father cooking breakfast
and me getting fat as a hog
or having no food
at all and father proving
his incompetence
again
i wish i knew how it would feel
to be free

its having a job
they won't let you work
or no work at all
castrating me
(yes it happens to women too)

its a sex object if you're pretty
and no love
or love and no sex if you're fat
get back fat black woman be a mother
grandmother strong thing but not woman
gameswoman romantic woman love needer
man seeker dick eater sweat getter
fuck needing love seeking woman

its a hole in your shoe
and buying lil sis a dress
and her saying you shouldn't
when you know
all too well—that you shouldn't

but smiles are only something we give
to properly dressed social workers
not each other
only smiles of i know
your game sister
which isn't really
a smile

joy is finding a pregnant roach
and squashing it
not finding someone to hold
let go get off get back don't turn
me on you black dog

how dare you care
about me
you ain't got no good sense
cause i ain't shit you must be lower
than that to care

its a filthy house
with yesterday's watermelon
and monday's tears
cause true ladies don't
know how to clean

its intellectual devastation
of everybody
to avoid emotional commitment
"yeah honey i would've married
him but he didn't have no degree"

its knock-kneed mini skirted
wig wearing died blond mamma's scar
born dead my scorn your whore
rough heeled broken nailed powdered
face me
whose whole life is tied
up to unhappiness
cause its the only
for real thing
i
know

Revolutionary Dreams

i used to dream militant
dreams of taking
over america to show
these white folks how it should be
done
i used to dream radical dreams
of blowing everyone away with my perceptive powers
of correct analysis
i even used to think i'd be the one
to stop the riot and negotiate the peace
then i awoke and dug
that if i dreamed natural
dreams of being a natural
woman doing what a woman
does when she's natural
i would have a revolution

Alice Walker

Everyday Use

I will wait for her in the yard that Maggie and I made so clean and wavy yesterday afternoon. A yard like this is more comfortable than most people know. It is not just a yard. It is like an extended living room. When the hard clay is swept clean as a floor and the fine sand around the edges lined with tiny, irregular grooves, anyone can come and sit and look up into the elm tree and wait for the breezes that never come inside the house.

Maggie will be nervous until after her sister goes: she will stand hopelessly in corners, homely and ashamed of the burn scars down her arms and legs, eying her sister with a mixture of envy and awe. She thinks her sister has held life always in the palm of one hand, that "no" is a word the world never learned to say to her.

You've no doubt seen those TV shows where the child who has "made it" is confronted, as a surprise, by her own mother and father, tottering in weakly from backstage. (A pleasant surprise, of course: What would they do if parent and child came on the show only to curse out and insult each other?) On TV mother and child embrace and smile into each other's faces. Sometimes the mother and father weep, the child wraps them in her arms and leans across the table to tell how she would not have made it without their help. I have seen these programs.

Sometimes I dream a dream in which Dee and I are suddenly brought together on a TV program of this sort. Out of a dark and soft-seated limousine I am ushered into a bright room filled with many people. There I meet a smiling, gray, sporty man like Johnny Carson who shakes my hand and tells me what a fine girl I have. Then we are on the stage and Dee is embracing me with tears in her eyes. She pins on my dress a large orchid, even though she has told me once that she thinks orchids are tacky flowers.

In real life I am a large, big-boned woman with rough, man-working hands. In the winter I wear flannel nightgowns to bed and overalls during the day. I can kill and clean a hog as mercilessly as a man. My fat keeps me hot in zero weather. I can work outside all day, breaking ice to get water for washing; I can eat pork liver cooked over the open fire minutes after it comes steaming from the hog. One winter I knocked a bull calf straight in the brain between the eyes with a sledge hammer and had the meat hung up to chill before nightfall. But of course all this does not show on television. I am the way my daughter would want me to be: a hundred pounds lighter, my skin like an uncooked barley pancake. My hair glistens in the hot bright lights. Johnny Carson has much to do to keep up with my quick and witty tongue.

But that is a mistake. I know even before I wake up. Who ever knew a Johnson with a quick tongue? Who can even imagine me looking a strange white man in the eye? It seems to me I have talked to them always with one foot raised in flight, with my head turned in whichever way is farthest from them. Dee, though. She would always look anyone in the eye. Hesitation was no part of her nature.

"How do I look, Mama?" Maggie says, showing just enough of her thin body enveloped in pink skirt and red blouse for me to know she's there, almost hidden by the door.

"Come out into the yard," I say.

Have you ever seen a lame animal, perhaps a dog run over by some careless person rich enough to own a car, sidle up to someone who is ignorant enough to be kind to him? That is the way my Maggie walks. She has been like this, chin on chest, eyes on ground, feet in shuffle, ever since the fire that burned the other house to the ground.

Dee is lighter than Maggie, with nicer hair and a fuller figure. She's a woman now, though sometimes I forget. How long ago was it that the other house burned? Ten, twelve years? Sometimes I can still hear the flames and feel Maggie's arms sticking to me, her hair smoking and her dress falling off her in little black papery flakes. Her eyes seemed stretched open, blazed open by the flames reflected in them. And Dee. I see her standing off under the sweet gum tree she used to dig gum out of; a look of concentration on her face as she watched the last dingy gray board of the house fall in toward the red-hot brick chimney. Why don't you do a dance around the ashes? I'd wanted to ask her. She had hated the house that much.

I used to think she hated Maggie, too. But that was before we raised the money, the church and me, to send her to Augusta to school. She used to read to us without pity; forcing words, lies, other folks' habits, whole lives upon us two, sitting trapped and ignorant underneath her voice. She washed us in a river of make-believe, burned us with a lot of knowledge we didn't necessarily need to know. Pressed us to her with the serious way she read, to shove us away at just the moment, like dimwits, we seemed about to understand.

Dee wanted nice things. A yellow organdy dress to wear to her graduation from high school; black pumps to match a green suit she'd made from an old suit somebody gave me. She was determined to stare down any disaster in her efforts. Her eyelids would not flicker for minutes at a time. Often I fought off the temptation to shake her. At sixteen she had a style of her own: and knew what style was.

I never had an education myself. After second grade the school was closed down. Don't ask me why: in 1927 colored asked fewer questions than they do now. Sometimes Maggie reads to me. She stumbles along good-naturedly but can't see well. She knows she is not bright.

Like good looks and money, quickness passed her by. She will marry John Thomas (who has mossy teeth in an earnest face) and then I'll be free to sit here and I guess just sing church songs to myself. Although I never was a good singer. Never could carry a tune. I was always better at a man's job. I used to love to milk till I was hooked in the side in '49. Cows are soothing and slow and don't bother you, unless you try to milk them the wrong way.

I have deliberately turned my back on the house. It is three rooms, just like the one that burned, except the roof is tin; they don't make shingle roofs any more. There are no real windows, just some holes cut in the sides, like the portholes in a ship, but not round and not square, with rawhide holding the shutters up on the outside. This house is in a pasture, too, like the other one. No doubt when Dee sees it she will want to tear it down. She wrote me once that no matter where we "choose" to live, she will manage to come see us. But she will never bring her friends. Maggie and I thought about this and Maggie asked me, "Mama, when did Dee ever *have* any friends?"

She had a few. Furtive boys in pink shirts hanging about on washday after school. Nervous girls who never laughed. Impressed with her they worshiped the well-turned phrase, the cute shape, the scalding humor that erupted like bubbles in lye. She read to them.

When she was courting Jimmy T she didn't have much time to pay to us, but turned all her faultfinding power on him. He *flew* to marry a cheap city girl from a family of ignorant flashy people. She hardly had time to recompose herself.

When she comes I will meet—but there they are!

Maggie attempts to make a dash for the house, in her shuffling way, but I stay her with my hand. "Come back here," I say. And she stops and tries to dig a well in the sand with her toe.

It is hard to see them clearly through the strong sun. But even the first glimpse of leg out of the car tells me it is Dee. Her feet were always neat-looking, as if God himself had shaped them with a certain style. From the other side of the car comes a short, stocky man. Hair is all over his head a foot long and hanging from his chin like a kinky mule tail. I hear Maggie suck in her breath. "Uhnnnh," is what it sounds like. Like when you see the wriggling end of a snake just in front of your foot on the road. "Uhnnnh."

Dee next. A dress down to the ground, in this hot weather. A dress so loud it hurts my eyes. There are yellows and oranges enough to throw back the light of the sun. I feel my whole face warming from the heat waves it throws out. Earrings gold, too, and hanging down to her shoulders. Bracelets dangling and making noises when she moves her arm up to shake the folds of the dress out of her armpits. The dress is loose and flows, and as she walks closer, I like it. I hear Maggie go "Uhnnnh" again. It is her sister's hair. It stands straight up like the wool on a sheep. It is black as night and around the edges are two long pigtails that rope about like small lizards disappearing behind her ears.

"Wa-su-zo-Tean-o!" she says, coming on in that gliding way the dress makes her move. The short stocky fellow with the hair to his navel is all grinning and he follows up with "Asalamalakim, my mother and sister!" He moves to hug Maggie but she falls back, right up against the back of my chair. I feel her trembling there and when I look up I see the perspiration falling off her chin.

"Don't get up," says Dee. Since I am stout it takes something of a push. You can see me trying to move a second or two before I make it. She turns, showing white heels through her sandals, and goes back to the car. Out she peeks next with a Polaroid. She stoops down quickly and lines up picture after picture of me sitting there in front of the house with Maggie cowering behind me. She never takes a shot without making sure the house is included. When a cow comes nibbling around the edge of the yard she snaps it and me and Maggie *and* the house. Then she puts the Polaroid in the back seat of the car, and comes up and kisses me on the forehead.

Meanwhile Asalamalakim is going through motions with Maggie's hand. Maggie's hand is as limp as a fish, and probably as cold, despite the sweat, and she keeps trying to pull it back. It looks like Asalamalakim wants to shake hands but wants to do it fancy. Or maybe he don't know how people shake hands. Anyhow, he soon gives up on Maggie.

"Well," I say. "Dee."

"No, Mama," she says. "Not 'Dee,' Wangero Leewanika Kemanjo!"

"What happened to 'Dee'?" I wanted to know.

"She's dead," Wangero said. "I couldn't bear it any longer, being named after the people who oppress me."

"You know as well as me you was named after your aunt Dicie," I said. Dicie is my sister. She named Dee. We called her "Big Dee" after Dee was born.

"But who was *she* named after?" asked Wangero.

"I guess after Grandma Dee," I said.

"And who was she named after?" asked Wangero.

"Her mother," I said, and saw Wangero was getting tired. "That's about as far back as I can trace it," I said. Though, in fact, I probably could have carried it back beyond the Civil War through the branches.

"Well," said Asalamalakim, "there you are."

"Uhnnnh," I heard Maggie say.

"There I was not," I said, "before 'Dicie' cropped up in our family, so why should I try to trace it that far back?"

He just stood there grinning, looking down on me like somebody inspecting a Model A car. Every once in a while he and Wangero sent eye signals over my head.

"How do you pronounce this name?" I asked.

"You don't have to call me by it if you don't want to," said Wangero.

"Why shouldn't I?" I asked. "If that's what you want us to call you, we'll call you."

"I know it might sound awkward at first," said Wangero.

"I'll get used to it," I said. "Ream it out again."

Well, soon we got the name out of the way. Asalamalakim had a name twice as long and three times as hard. After I tripped over it two or three times he told me to just call him Hakim-a-barber. I wanted to ask him was he a barber, but I didn't really think he was, so I didn't ask.

"You must belong to those beef-cattle people down the road," I said. They said "Asalamalakim" when they met you, too, but they didn't shake hands. Always too busy: feeding the cattle, fixing the fences, putting up salt-lick shelters, throwing down hay. When the white folks poisoned some of the herd the men stayed up all night with rifles in their hands. I walked a mile and a half just to see the sight.

Hakim-a-barber said, "I accept some of their doctrines, but farming and raising cattle is not my style." (They didn't tell me, and I didn't ask, whether Wangero (Dee) had really gone and married him.)

We sat down to eat and right away he said he didn't eat collards and pork was unclean. Wangero, though, went on through the chitlins and corn bread, the greens and everything else. She talked a blue streak over the sweet potatoes. Everything delighted her. Even the fact that we still used the benches her daddy made for the table when we couldn't afford to buy chairs.

"Oh, Mama!" she cried. Then turned to Hakim-a-barber. "I never knew how lovely these benches are. You can feel the rump prints," she said, running her hands underneath her and along the bench. Then she gave a sigh and her hand closed over Grandma Dee's butter dish. "That's it!" she said. "I knew there was something I wanted to ask you if I could have." She jumped up from the table and went over in the corner where the churn stood, the milk in it clabber by now. She looked at the churn and looked at it.

"This churn top is what I need," she said. "Didn't Uncle Buddy whittle it out of a tree you all used to have?"

"Yes," I said.

"Uh huh," she said happily. "And I want the dasher, too."

"Uncle Buddy whittle that, too?" asked the barber.

Dee (Wangero) looked up at me.

"Aunt Dee's first husband whittled the dash," said Maggie so low you almost couldn't hear her. "His name was Henry, but they called him Stash."

"Maggie's brain is like an elephant's," Wangero said, laughing. "I can use the churn top as a centerpiece for the alcove table," she said, sliding a plate over the churn, "and I'll think of something artistic to do with the dasher."

When she finished wrapping the dasher the handle stuck out. I took it for a moment in my hands. You didn't even have to look close to see where hands pushing the dasher up and down to make butter had left a kind of sink in the wood. In fact, there were a lot of small sinks; you could see where thumbs and fingers had sunk into the wood. It was beautiful light yellow wood, from a tree that grew in the yard where Big Dee and Stash had lived.

After dinner Dee (Wangero) went to the trunk at the foot of my bed and started rifling through it. Maggie hung back in the kitchen over the dishpan. Out came Wangero with two quilts. They had been pieced by Grandma Dee and then Big Dee and me had hung them on the quilt frames on the front porch and quilted them. One was in the Lone Star pattern. The other was Walk Around the Mountain. In both of them were scraps of dresses Grandma Dee had worn fifty and more years ago. Bits and pieces of Grandpa Jarrell's Paisley shirts. And one teeny faded blue piece, about the size of a penny matchbox, that was from Great Grandpa Ezra's uniform that he wore in the Civil War.

"Mama," Wangero said sweet as a bird. "Can I have these old quilts?"

I heard something fall in the kitchen, and a minute later the kitchen door slammed.

"Why don't you take one or two of the others?" I asked. "These old things was just done by me and Big Dee from some tops your grandma pieced before she died."

"No," said Wangero. "I don't want those. They are stitched around the borders by machine."

"That'll make them last better," I said.

"That's not the point," said Wangero. "These are all pieces of dresses Grandma used to wear. She did all this stitching by hand. Imagine!" She held the quilts securely in her arms, stroking them.

"Some of the pieces, like those lavender ones, come from old clothes her mother handed down to her," I said, moving up to touch the quilts. Dee (Wangero) moved back just enough so that I couldn't reach the quilts. They already belonged to her.

"Imagine!" she breathed again, clutching them closely to her bosom.

"The truth is," I said, "I promised to give them quilts to Maggie, for when she marries John Thomas."

She gasped like a bee had stung her.

"Maggie can't appreciate these quilts!" she said. "She'd probably be backward enough to put them to everyday use."

"I reckon she would," I said. "God knows I been saving 'em for long enough with nobody using 'em. I hope she will!" I didn't want to bring up how I had offered Dee (Wangero) a quilt when she went away to college. Then she had told me they were old-fashioned, out of style.

"But they're *priceless!*" she was saying now, furiously; for she has a temper. "Maggie would put them on the bed and in five years they'd be in rags. Less than that!"

"She can always make some more," I said. "Maggie knows how to quilt."

Dee (Wangero) looked at me with hatred. "You just will not understand. The point is these quilts, *these* quilts!"

"Well," I said, stumped. "What would *you* do with them?"

"Hang them," she said. As if that was the only thing you *could* do with quilts.

Maggie by now was standing in the door. I could almost hear the sound her feet made as they scraped over each other.

"She can have them, Mama," she said, like somebody used to never winning anything, or having anything reserved for her. "I can 'member Grandma Dee without the quilts."

I looked at her hard. She had filled her bottom lip with checkerberry snuff and it gave her face a kind of dopey, hangdog look. It was Grandma Dee and Big Dee who taught her how to quilt herself. She stood there with her scarred hands hidden in the folds of her skirt. She looked at her sister with something like fear but she wasn't mad at her. This was Maggie's portion. This was the way she knew God to work.

When I looked at her like that something hit me in the top of my head and ran down to the soles of my feet. Just like when I'm in church and the spirit of God touches me and I get happy and shout. I did something I never had done before: hugged Maggie to me, then dragged her on into the room, snatched the quilts out of Miss Wangero's hands and dumped them into Maggie's lap. Maggie just sat there on my bed with her mouth open.

"Take one or two of the others," I said to Dee.

But she turned without a word and went out to Hakim-a-barber.

"You just don't understand," she said, as Maggie and I came out to the car.

"What don't I understand?" I wanted to know.

"Your heritage," she said. And then she turned to Maggie, kissed her, and said, "You ought to try to make something of yourself, too, Maggie. It's really a new day for us. But from the way you and Mama still live you'd never know it."

She put on some sunglasses that hid everything above the tip of her nose and her chin.

Maggie smiled; maybe at the sunglasses. But a real smile, not scared. After we watched the car dust settle I asked Maggie to bring me a dip of snuff. And then the two of us sat there just enjoying, until it was time to go in the house and go to bed.

Marie-Elise

Definition

I envy you
    your steady silence
    inside your calm world
       of introspective
          indifference.
I envy you;
I,
    (who was raised on clichés
    and harsh arguments)
  wean myself now
    from our wordless affair
    with the satiety of one
    who has taken
    more than her share
  while you
    hold your appetite
    firmly
    behind a vacant stare.
Alone
  I pacify my pain
            quietly
  chewing these thoughts slowly
  remembering not to swallow
    until each tasteless phrase
    is stretched smooth;
    each gnash and grit
      dissolving,
      drooling helplessly
        onto page
            after page,
                after page.

Diapering This Poem

Diapering this poem,
    I listen to my hands
        folding fatigue,
           creasing silence.
I never smile while self-exiled:
    following a blind muse
    like a whining child.
I am only skilled
    at stealing rhyme
    from mother goose and father time.
Here:
    This poem is clean
           and dry.
    Would you like to hold it
    till it starts to cry?

Gemini

Gemini
    a poem for two voices

Call me names
           listening to you
Listening to you,
           the irises easily lose track.
I can stand firmly.
           trapped in liquid,
I disconnect myself
           floating,
From pain
       they disconnect themselves
And you hear
       from conversation,
With blurred vision.
           and hear you with blurred vision.

Don't ask me
       why can't emotions
To give you my heart.
           be like movement?
It's not available
       flowing through moments,
For abuse
      falling back into gravity
Or repair.
      to be forgotten
The edges are worn
        by the body . . .

And shredded,
             not like these motions
But well memorized.
                 we make

Thumb through it.
             when we meet:
I may lend it
             remembering,
For a limited time,
             gesturing
So you can study
             to avoid touching,
With care.
             not wanting
I'll be ready
             to start once again
When you return it
             from the beginning.
To start once again
             listening to you,
From the beginning.
             i disconnect myself . . .
Without it, I'd be lost
             trapped in liquid,
In some romantic
             floating
Plot
      in some romantic plot.
Of anti-climax.

prose/poem
Written after overhearing a conversation
on a Greyhound Bus
Just outside of Oxnard, California

"I'll tell you something," he said
his voice creased and wrinkled
as a used paper bag
"A woman is like the moon:
elusive and dreamlike,
winking through them clouds full 'a promise.
But when you wake up
on top of her
you discover she's cold and barren
'an has warts on her ass."

He leaned back and let the wine rinse
any further philosophy

past the hemp in his throat
while his audience of one
farted in agreement.
No one spoke; and the moon
the moon stared boldly
through the flat gray window
corpulent and round as a fertile womb.
Clouds passed over her like tired eyelids
while the wine clawed the walls
of its glass prison
as it passed from hand to hand.

Touching a Friend

I would never calm
those wild hairs
(that swim in the moist sky
above your gaze)
with harshness
of hands.

These approaching fingers
are merely wings
unwrinkling.

Suggestions for Further Reading

This bibliography has been divided into six parts: Journals, Autobiographies, and Letters; Novels; Short Stories; Poetry; Drama; and Essays and Criticism.

I. JOURNALS, AUTOBIOGRAPHIES, LETTERS

Albertson, Chris. *Bessie.* New York: Stein & Day, 1972.

Anderson, Margaret. *The Fiery Mountain.* New York: Horizon Press, 1969.

———. *My Thirty Years' War.* Westport, Conn.: Greenwood Press, 1970.

Angelou, Maya. *I Know Why the Caged Bird Sings.* New York: Random House, 1970.

———. *Gather Together in My Name.* New York: Bantam, 1975.

Calisher, Hortense. *Herself.* New York: Dell, 1974.

Chisholm, Shirley. *Unbought and Unbossed.* New York: Avon, 1971.

Devlin, Bernadette. *The Price of My Soul.* New York: Random House, 1970.

Duncan, Isadora. *My Life.* New York: Boni & Liveright, 1927.

Frank, Anne. *The Diary of a Young Girl.* New York: Washington Square Press, 1972.

Gilman, Charlotte Perkins. *The Living Charlotte Perkins Gilman.* New York: Arno Press, 1972.

Hellman, Lillian. *Unfinished Woman.* Boston: Little, Brown, 1969.

———. *Pentimento.* New York: New American Library, 1974.

Hinz, Evelyn J. *A Woman Speaks: The Lectures and Interviews of Anaïs Nin.* Chicago: Swallow Press, 1976.

Knef, Hildegard. *The Gift Horse.* New York: McGraw-Hill, 1971.

Lessing, Doris. *Particularly Cats.* New York: Simon & Schuster, 1967.

Lindbergh, Anne Morrow. *Gift From the Sea.* New York: Random House, 1955.

———. *Bring Me a Unicorn.* New York: New American Library, 1974.

———. *Hour of Gold, Hour of Lead.* New York: New American Library, 1974.

Luhan, Mabel Dodge. *Intimate Memories: Background.* New York: Kraus Reprint, 1933.

McCarthy, Mary. *Memories of a Catholic Girlhood.* New York: Harcourt Brace Jovanovich, 1957.

MacDonald, Betty. *The Egg and I.* Philadelphia: J. B. Lippincott, 1963.

Mansfield, Katherine. *Journal.* New York: Alfred A. Knopf, 1946.

Mead, Margaret. *Coming of Age in Samoa.* New York: William Morrow, 1971.

———. *Blackberry Winter.* New York: William Morrow, 1972.

Milford, Nancy. *Zelda.* New York: Avon, 1974.

Moffat, Mary, and Painter, Charlotte, eds., *Revelations: Diaries of Women.* New York: Random House (Vintage), 1975.

Nin, Anaïs. *The Diary of Anaïs Nin.* Vols. 1–4. New York: Harcourt Brace Jovanovich, 1972.

Stein, Gertrude. *The Autobiography of Alice B. Toklas.* New York: Harcourt Brace Jovanovich, 1933.

Tillich, Hannah. *From Time to Time*. New York: Stein & Day, 1973.
Woolf, Virginia. *A Writer's Diary*. New York: Harcourt Brace Jovanovich, 1973.

II. NOVELS

Adler, Renata. *Speedboat*. New York: Random House, 1976.
Arnow, Harriet. *The Dollmaker*. New York: Macmillan, 1967.
Ashton-Warner, Sylvia. *Spinster*. New York: Simon & Schuster, 1971.
———. *Teacher*. New York: Simon & Schuster, 1971.
Atwood, Margaret. *Edible Woman*. Toronto: McClelland & Stewart, 1969.
———. *Surfacing*. New York: Simon & Schuster, 1973.
———. *Lady Oracle*. New York: Simon & Schuster, 1975.
Bambara, Toni Cade. *Gorilla My Love*. New York: Random House, 1972.
Barnes, Djuna. *Nightwood*. New York: New Directions, 1946.
Bawden, Nina. *A Woman of My Age*. New York: Lancer, 1967.
Beattie, Ann. *Chilly Scenes of Winter*. New York: Doubleday, 1976.
Birstein, Ann. *Summer Situations*. New York: Avon, 1973.
Brown, Rita Mae. *Rubyfruit Jungle*. Plainfield, Vt.: Daughters, 1973.
Buck, Pearl. *The Good Earth*. New York: Washington Square Press, 1937.
Byatt, A. S. *The Game*. New York: Charles Scribner's Sons, 1967.
Cather, Willa. *My Antonia*. Boston: Houghton Mifflin, 1961.
Compton-Burnett, Ivy. *Dolores*. Edinburgh: Blackwood, 1961.
Didion, Joan. *Play It As It Lays*. New York: Farrar, Straus & Giroux, 1970.
Dinesen, Isak. *Shadows on the Grass*. New York: Random House, 1961.
———. *Out of Africa*. New York: Random House, 1972.
Drabble, Margaret. *Jerusalem the Golden*. New York: Belmont Tower Books, 1973.
Fitzgerald, Zelda. *Save Me the Waltz*. Carbondale, Ill.: Southern Illinois University Press, 1967.
Frame, Janet. *Intensive Care*. New York: George Braziller, 1970.
Glasgow, Ellen. *Vein of Iron*. New York: Harcourt Brace Jovanovich, 1935.
———. *The Woman Within*. New York: Harcourt Brace Jovanovich, 1954.
———. *Barren Ground*. New York: Hill & Wang, 1957.
Godden, Rumer. *Doll's House*. New York: Viking Press, 1970.
Gould, Lois. *Final Analysis*. New York: Random House, 1974.
Gray, Francine du Plessix. *Lovers and Tyrants*. New York: Simon & Schuster, 1976.
Green, Hannah (Joanne Greenberg). *I Never Promised You a Rose Garden*. New York: Holt, Rinehart & Winston, 1964.
Hall, Radclyffe. *The Well of Loneliness*. Maplewood, N.J.: Hammond, 1944.
Hill, Carol. *Let's Fall in Love*. New York: Random House, 1974.
Hochman, Sandra. *Walking Papers*. New York: Viking Press, 1971.
Johnson, Diane. *Burning*. New York: Harcourt Brace Jovanovich, 1971.
———. *The Shadow Knows*. New York: Alfred A. Knopf, 1974.
Jong, Erica. *Fear of Flying*. New York: Holt, Rinehart & Winston, 1973.

Kaufman, Sue. *The Diary of a Mad Housewife.* New York: Random House, 1967.

LeGuin, Ursula. *The Dispossessed.* New York: Harper & Row, 1974.

———. *The Left Hand of Darkness.* New York: Ace Books, 1974.

Lessing, Doris. *The Four-Gated City.* New York: Alfred A. Knopf, 1969.

———. *The Golden Notebook.* New York: Bantam, 1973.

———. *The Grass Is Singing.* New York: Popular Library, 1973.

———. *The Memoirs of a Survivor.* New York: Alfred A. Knopf, 1975.

Lurie, Alison, *War Between the Tates.* New York: Random House, 1974.

McCarthy, Mary. *The Group.* New York: New American Library, 1972.

McCullers, Carson. *The Member of the Wedding.* New York: Bantam, 1969.

———. *The Heart Is a Lonely Hunter.* New York: Bantam, 1970.

Martinerie, Andree. *A Life's Full Summer.* New York: Harcourt Brace Jovanovich, 1972.

Mitchell, Margaret. *Gone With the Wind.* New York: Macmillan, 1936.

Murdoch, Iris. *A Severed Head.* New York: Viking Press, 1963.

Newman, Frances. *The Hard-Boiled Virgin.* New York: Boni & Liveright, 1926.

Nin, Anaïs. *Children of the Albatross.* Chicago: Swallow Press, 1959.

———. *Ladders to Fire.* Chicago: Swallow Press, 1959.

———. *A Spy in the House of Love.* New York: Bantam, 1974.

Oates, Joyce Carol. *Them.* New York: Vanguard, 1969.

———. *Do with Me What You Will.* New York: Vanguard, 1973.

Olsen, Tillie. *Yonnondio: From the Thirties.* New York: Dell, 1975.

Ozick, Cynthia. *Trust.* New York: New American Library, 1966.

Petry, Ann. *The Street.* New York: Pyramid Publications, 1974.

Plath, Sylvia. *The Bell Jar.* New York: Harper & Row, 1971.

Porter, Katherine Anne. *Ship of Fools.* Boston: Little, Brown, 1962.

Rhys, Jean. *After Leaving Mr. Mackenzie.* New York: Harper & Row, 1931.

Richardson, Dorothy. *Pilgrimage.* New York: Alfred A. Knopf, 1967.

Schaeffer, Susan Fromberg. *Falling.* New York: Macmillan, 1973.

Shulman, Alix Kates. *Memoirs of an Ex-Prom Queen.* New York: Alfred A. Knopf, 1972.

Smedley, Agnes. *Daughter of Earth.* Old Westbury, N.Y.: Feminist Press, 1973.

Spark, Muriel. *The Prime of Miss Jean Brodie.* Philadelphia: J. B. Lippincott, 1962.

Stead, Christina. *The Man Who Loved Children.* New York: Avon, 1966.

Stein, Gertrude. *Three Lives.* London: Pushkin Press, 1945.

———. *Ida.* New York: Random House, 1972.

Undset, Sigrid. *Kristin Lavransdatter.* New York: Alfred A. Knopf, 1923.

Weingarten, Violet. *A Loving Wife.* New York: Alfred A. Knopf, 1969.

Weldon, Fay. *Female Friends.* New York: St. Martin's Press, 1974.

Welty, Eudora. *Delta Wedding.* New York: Harcourt Brace Jovanovich, 1946.

———. *Losing Battles.* New York: Random House, 1970.

West, Rebecca. *The Fountain Overflows.* New York: Avon, 1974.

Wharton, Edith. *The Age of Innocence*. New York: New American Library, 1962.
———. *Descent of Man and Other Stories*. New York: Books for Libraries, 1904.
———. *Ethan Frome*. New York: Watts, 1965.
———. *The House of Mirth*. New York: New American Library, 1964.
Woolf, Virginia. *Mrs. Dalloway*. New York: Harcourt Brace Jovanovich, 1949.
———. *To the Lighthouse*. New York: Harcourt Brace Jovanovich, 1949.
———. *Jacob's Room and the Waves*. New York: Harcourt Brace Jovanovich, 1960.

III. SHORT STORIES

Beattie, Ann. *Distortions*. New York: Doubleday, 1976.
Bowen, Elizabeth. *Ann Lee's and Other Stories*. New York: Books for Libraries, 1926.
Chopin, Kate. *The Awakening*. New York: G. P. Putnam's Sons, 1964.
Colette, Sidonie. *Break of the Day and The Blue Lantern*. New York: Noonday Press, 1966.
Freeman, Mary Wilkins. *Best Stories of Mary E. Wilkins*. St. Clair Shores, Mich.: Scholarly Press, 1971.
Gaskell, Elizabeth. *Wives and Daughters*. New York: E. P. Dutton, 1972.
Gilman, Charlotte Perkins. *The Yellow Wallpaper*. Old Westbury, N.Y.: Feminist Press, 1973.
Lessing, Doris. *A Man and Two Women*. New York: Simon & Schuster, 1963.
———. *African Stories*. New York: Simon & Schuster, 1965.
McCarthy, Mary. *Cast a Cold Eye*. New York: New American Library, 1972.
McCullers, Carson. *The Mortgaged Heart*. New York: Bantam, 1972.
Mansfield, Katherine. *The Short Stories of Katherine Mansfield*. New York: Alfred A. Knopf, 1937.
Nin, Anaïs. *Under a Glass Bell and Other Stories*. Chicago: Swallow Press, 1968.
Oates, Joyce Carol. *By the North Gate*. New York: Vanguard, 1963.
———. *Marriages and Infidelities*. New York: Vanguard, 1972.
O'Connor, Flannery. *Everything That Rises Must Converge*. New York: Farrar, Straus & Giroux, 1965.
———. *A Good Man Is Hard to Find*. New York: Doubleday, 1970.
Olsen, Tillie. *Tell Me a Riddle*. New York: Dell, 1971.
Paley, Grace. *Little Disturbances of Man*. New York: New American Library, 1973.
Porter, Katherine Anne. *The Leaning Tower*. New York: New American Library, 1970.
Slesinger, Tess. *Time: The Present*. New York: Simon & Schuster, 1935.
———. *On Being Told That Her Second Husband Has Taken His First Lover*. New York: Quadrangle, 1974.
Spark, Muriel. *Collected Short Stories*. New York: Alfred A. Knopf, 1968.
Stafford, Jean. *Collected Stories*. New York: Farrar, Straus & Giroux, 1969.

Walker, Alice. *In Love and Trouble: Stories of Black Women.* New York: Harcourt Brace Jovanovich, 1974.
Welty, Eudora. *Selected Short Stories of Eudora Welty.* New York: Modern Library, 1954.

IV. POETRY

Akhmatova, Anna. *Poem Without a Hero.* Ardis, 1973.
Angelou, Maya. *Just Give Me a Drink of Cool Water: 'Fore I Die.* New York: Random House, 1971.
———. *Oh Pray My Wings Are Gonna Fit Me Well.* New York: Random House, 1975.
Atwood, Margaret. *Power Politics.* Toronto: Anansi, 1971.
———. *You Are Happy.* New York: Harper & Row, 1974.
Bishop, Elizabeth. *The Complete Poems.* New York: Farrar, Straus & Giroux, 1970.
Brooks, Gwendolyn. *Selected Poems.* New York: Harper & Row, 1971.
———. *The World of Gwendolyn Brooks.* New York: Harper & Row, 1971.
Danielle, Babette. *Coming of Age.* Bloomington, Ind.: Indiana University Press, 1963.
Doolittle, Hilda. *Trilogy.* New York: New Directions, 1973.
Evans, Mari. *I Am a Black Woman.* New York: William Morrow, 1970.
Giovanni, Nikki. *Gemini.* Indianapolis: Bobbs-Merrill, 1972.
Guest, Barbara. *Moscow Mansions: Poems.* New York: Viking Press, 1973.
Jong, Erica. *Fruits and Vegetables.* New York: Holt, Rinehart & Winston, 1971.
———. *Half-Lives.* New York: Holt, Rinehart & Winston, 1973.
Kaufman, Shirley. *The Floor Keeps Turning.* Pittsburgh: University of Pittsburgh Press, 1970.
Kizer, Carolyn. *Knock upon Silence.* Seattle: University of Washington Press, 1968.
Lessing, Doris. *Fourteen Poems.* New York: Scorpion Press, 1959.
Levertov, Denise. *The Jacob's Ladder.* New York: New Directions, 1961.
———. *O Taste and See.* New York: New Directions, 1964.
———. *The Sorrow Dance.* New York: New Directions, 1967.
———. *Relearning the Alphabet.* New York: New Directions, 1970.
Lorde, Audre. *Cables to Rage.* Detroit, Mich.: Broadside, 1970.
Lowell, Amy. *Can Grande's Castle.* St. Clair Shores, Mich.: Scholarly, 1918.
MacDonald, Cynthia. *Amputations.* New York: George Braziller, 1972.
Miles, Josephine. *Poems, 1930–1960.* Bloomington, Ind.: Indiana University Press, 1960.
Mistral, Gabriela. *Crickets & Frogs.* New York: Atheneum, 1972.
Moore, Marianne. *Collected Poems.* New York: Macmillan, 1951.
Plath, Sylvia. *The Colossus.* New York: Alfred A. Knopf, 1962.
———. *Ariel.* New York: Harper & Row, 1968.
Rich, Adrienne. *A Change of World.* New York: AMS Press, 1951.
———. *Snapshots of a Daughter-in-Law.* New York: W. W. Norton, 1967.
———. *Diving into the Wreck.* New York: W. W. Norton, 1973.

———. *Poems, Selected and New, 1950–1974.* New York: W. W. Norton, 1975.

Rukeyser, Muriel. *One Life.* New York: Simon & Schuster, 1957.

———. *Mazes.* New York: Simon & Schuster, 1970.

———. *Speed of Darkness.* New York: Random House, 1971.

———. *Breaking Open.* New York: Random House, 1973.

Sarton, May. *Plant Dreaming Deep.* New York: W. W. Norton, 1968.

———. *As We Are Now.* New York: W. W. Norton, 1973.

———. *Journal of a Solitude.* New York: W. W. Norton, 1973.

Sexton, Anne. *Live or Die.* Boston: Houghton Mifflin, 1966.

———. *Transformations.* Boston: Houghton Mifflin, 1972.

———. *The Awful Rowing Toward God.* Boston: Houghton Mifflin, 1975.

Spark, Muriel. *Collected Poems.* New York: Alfred A. Knopf, 1968.

Wakoski, Diane. *Coins and Coffins.* New York: Hawk's Well Press, 1962.

———. *The Motorcycle Betrayal Poems.* New York: Simon & Schuster, 1971.

V. DRAMA

Childress, Alice. *A Hero Ain't Nothin' but a Sandwich.* New York: Avon, 1973.

———. *The Wedding Band.* New York: Samuel French, 1973.

Delaney, Shelagh. *A Taste of Honey: A Play.* New York: Grove Press, 1959.

Hansberry, Lorraine. *Raisin in the Sun.* New York: Random House, 1969.

Hellman, Lillian. *Collected Plays.* Boston: Little, Brown, 1972.

Howard, Sidney. *The Silver Cord: A Comedy in Three Acts.* New York: Samuel French, 1928.

Jellicoe, Ann. *The Giveaway: A Comedy.* London: Faber & Faber, 1970.

Kennedy, Adrienne. *Funnyhouse of a Negro.* New York: Samuel French, 1969.

Lamb, Myrna. *Mod Donna.* New York: Pathfinder, 1971.

Luce, Clare Booth. *The Women.* New York: Random House, 1937.

Sullivan, Victoria, and Hatch, James. *Plays By and About Women.* New York: Vintage Books, 1974.

Terry, Megan. *The Gloaming, Oh My Darling Viet Rock and Other Plays.* New York: Simon & Schuster, 1967.

Warner, Sylvia Townsend. *Mr. Fortune's Maggot.* New York: Viking Press, 1927.

VI. ESSAYS AND CRITICISMS

Bogan, Louise. *Achievement in American Poetry.* Chicago: Henry Regnery, 1950.

Calder, Jenni. *Women and Marriages in Victorian Fiction.* London: Thames & Hudson, 1976.

Chesler, Phyllis. *Women and Madness.* New York: Doubleday, 1972.

Cornillon, Susan K. *Images of Women in Fiction: Feminist Perspectives.* Bowling Green, Ohio: Bowling Green University Popular Press, 1972.

Deegan, Dorothy. *The Stereotype of the Single Woman in American Novels.* New York: Octagon Books, 1969.

Ferguson, Mary Anne. *Images of Women in Literature.* Boston: Houghton Mifflin, 1973.

Fryer, Judith J. *The Faces of Eve: Women in the Nineteenth Century American Novel.* New York: Oxford University Press, 1976.

Heilbrun, Carolyn G. *Toward a Recognition of Androgyny.* New York: Alfred A. Knopf, 1973.

Millett, Kate. *Sexual Politics.* New York: Doubleday, 1970.

Moers, Ellen. *Literary Women.* New York: Doubleday, 1976.

Oates, Joyce Carol. *New Heavens, New Earth.* New York: Vanguard, 1974.

O'Connor, Flannery. *Mystery and Manners.* New York: Farrar, Straus & Giroux, 1970.

Rogers, Katharine M. *The Troublesome Helpmate: A History of Misogyny in Literature.* Seattle: University of Washington Press, 1968.

Showalter, Elaine. *Women's Liberation and Literature.* New York: Harcourt Brace Jovanovich, 1971.

Spacks, Patricia Meyer. *The Female Imagination.* New York: Avon, 1972.

Stein, Gertrude. *Writings and Lectures 1909–1945.* Baltimore: Penguin, 1971.

Woolf, Virginia. *A Room of One's Own.* New York: Harcourt Brace Jovanovich, 1929.

———. *Three Guineas.* New York: Harcourt Brace Jovanovich, 1963.